20 PRACTICE SETS *for*

SSC CHSL

(10+2) Exam

with 3 Online Tests

- **Corporate Office :** 45, 2nd Floor, Maharishi Dayanand Marg, Corner Market, Malviya Nagar, New Delhi-110017

  Tel. : 011-49842349 / 49842350

Typeset by Disha DTP Team

Get free access to Online Test(s)?

INSTRUCTIONS

1. You can access your test on any Window based Desktop, android tablets or ipads and mobile phones absolutely free.
2. Visit the link below or scan the QR code:

   3 Mock Tests - SSC CHSL Exam

   http://bit.ly/sschsl
3. Click on **"Attempt Free Mock Tests"**, a Registration window pops up, enter all the details in the form & click "Sign UP".
4. User is now logged in the account & all the Mock Tests appears in the grid. User can attempt the Free Mock Test(s) by clicking the **"Start"** button.
5. Contact us at support@mylearninggraph.com for any support.

For further information about the books from DISHA,

Log on to **www.dishapublication.com** or email to **info@dishapublication.com**

CONTENTS

PRACTICE SETS

3 PRACTICE SETS ONLINE

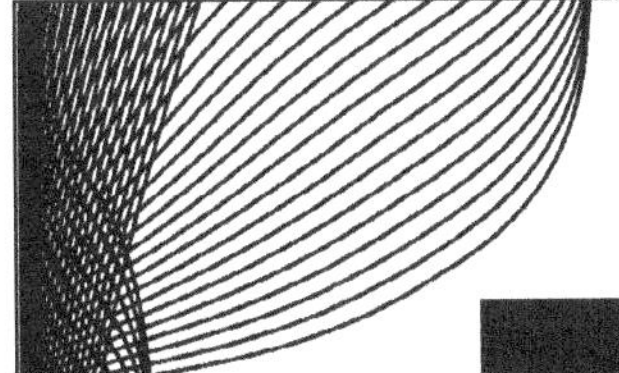

SSC CHSL

Solved Paper- 2017

Time : 1 hr. **Held on : 17-03-2018** **Max. Marks : 100**

English Language

Directions (Qs. 1-2): In the following question, some part of the sentence may have errors. Find out which part of the sentence has an error and select the appropriate option. If a sentence is free from error; select 'No error;

1. He cooked the (a) / dinner and (b)/than put the radio on (c) / No error (d)
2. Proteins are providers of energy in an emergency (a) / and are primarily used as building blocking (b) / for growth and repair of many body tissues: (c) / No error (d)
3. In the following question, the sentence given with blank to be filled in with an appropriate word. Select the correct alternative out of the four and indicate it by selecting the appropriate option.
   Anita _____ her work by the time he came.
   (a) had done (b) has done
   (c) is done (d) would done
4. In the following question, the sentence given with blank to be filled in with an appropriate word. Select the correct alternative out of the four and indicate it by selecting the appropriate option.
   He won't pay the rent _____ how many times his landlord
   berates him.
   (a) seeing as (b) however
   (c) although (d) no matter
5. In the following question, out of the given four alternatives, select the one which best expresses the meaning of the given word.
   Hackneyed
   (a) Tired (b) Fresh
   (c) Uncommon (d) New
6. In the following question, out of the given four alternatives select the one which is best expresses the in meaning of the given word.
   Accede
   (a) Admit (b) Submit
   (c) Grown (d) Consent
7. In the following question, out of the given four alternatives, select the one which is opposite in meaning of the given word.
   Inundate
   (a) Engulf (b) Immerse
   (c) Overrun (d) Underwhelm
8. In the following question, out of the given four alternatives, select the one which is opposite in meaning of the given word.
   Wholesome
   (a) Impure (b) Healthy
   (c) Pure (d) Safe
9. Rearrange the parts of the sentence in correct order.
   The invention of the turbine by
   P : The begining of jet transport
   Q : Ohain in Germany in 1939 signalled
   R : Frank whittle in England and Hans von
   (a) QRP (b) RQP
   (c) PQR (d) RPQ
10. A sentence has been given in Active/Passive voice. Out of the four given alternatives, select the one which best expresses the same sentence in Passive/Active voice.
    One can achieve reward by hard work.
    (a) Reward could be achieved by hard work.
    (b) Reward is needed for hard work.
    (c) Reward is achieved by hard work.
    (d) Reward can be achieved by hard work.
11. A sentence has been given in Direct /Indirect speech. Out of the four given alternatives, select the one which best expresses the same sentence in Indirect /Direct Speech.
    She said. 'Let us wait the seat'
    (a) She proposed that they should wait for the seat.

(b) She proposed that they could wait for the seat.
(c) She proposed to wait for the seat.
(d) She proposed let us wait for seat.

12. In the following question, a word has been written in four different ways out of which only one is correctly spelt. Select the correctly spelt word.
(a) Acquaintance (b) Acuainatance
(c) Acquaintence (d) Akquaintance

Directions (Qs. 13-17): In the following passage, some of the words have been left out. Read the passage carefully and select the correct answer for the given blank out of the four alternatives.

The_**13**_conversation-starter cultivated by years of ostentatious_**14**_ society is a simple 'how do you do'? followed by a polite shaking of hands and an optional comment on the weather. But aside _**15**_ the mental trauma this ritual causes to those unfortunate souls who suffer from clammy hands, it also doesn't provide much incentive to go on. Fascinating as the weather can be from time _**16**_ time, one can speak only so much about the _**17**_ of the sun and express sympathy towards the depressions the Bay of Bengal faces.

13. (a) basic (b) base
(c) basically (d) basics
14. (a) Humanity (b) Humanly
(c) Humanely (d) Human
15. (a) form (b) from
(c) of (d) for
16. (a) to (b) at
(c) so (d) is
17. (a) brightness (b) bright
(c) brightly (d) brighter

18. In the following question, out of the four alternatives. select the alternative which best expresses the meaning of the idiom/phrase.
Back to the drawing board
(a) A creative person will always find a solution to any problem.
(b) An artist will express his feelings by drawing.
(c) It is better to work on a fanciful idea bound to fail than have no ideas at all.
(d) Used to indicate that an idea has been unsuccessful and that a new one must be devised.

19. In the following question, out of the four alternatives, select the alternative which best expresses the meaning of the idiom/phrase.
In cahoots with
(a) A marriage made in heaven.
(b) A group of criminals.
(c) With lot of determination.
(d) In an alliance or partnership with.

20. In the following question, out of the four alternatives, select the alternative which is the best substitute of the words /sentence
Acutely distressing
(a) Palatable (b) Harrowing
(c) Gratifying (d) Suave

21. In the following question, out of the four alternatives, select the alternative which is the best substitute of the words sentence.
Revel in and make the most of something pleasing
(a) Abhor (b) Bask
(c) Fret (d) Edgy

22. In the following question, out of the four alternatives, select the alternative which will improve the bracketed part of the sentence. In case no improvement is needed, select 'no improvement'.
This stove (had) a flat kerosene tank at the bottom.
(a) have
(b) has
(c) has had
(d) no improvement

23. In the following question, out of the four alternatives, select the alternative which will improve the bracketed part of the sentence. In case no improvement is needed, select 'no improvement'
By the running water and electricity (had arrive), making the well and the lamp post redundant.
(a) had arriving (b) had arrived
(c) arriving (d) no improvement

24. The question below consists of a set of labelled sentences. Out of the four options given, select the most logical order of the sentences to form a coherent paragraph.
A-laver enabled you
A-controlled the burner flame
B-to raise or lower the wicks
C-and this is how you
(a) BAC (b) ACB
(c) BCA (d) ABC

25. In the following question, four words are given out of which one word is correctly spelt. Select the correctly spelt word.
(a) megalomaniac (b) megalomeniac
(c) megallomaniac (d) megallomeniac

General Intelligence & Reasoning

26. In the following question, select the related word pair from the given alternatives.
Shout : Speak : : ? : ?
(a) Petrol : Fuel (b) Rage : Anger
(c) Drown : Water (d) Famous : People

27. In the following question, select the related number from the given alternatives.
46 : 48 : : 61 : ?
(a) 67 (b) 71
(c) 65 (d) 63

28. In the following question, select the related letter/ letters from the given alternatives.
VOT : SLQ : : HRX : ?
(a) EMS (b) KOC
(c) EOU (d) RVH

29. In the following question, select the odd word pair from the given alternatives.
(a) Car-Road (b) Water-Ship
(c) Track-Train (d) Sky-Aeroplane

30. In the following question, four number pairs are given. The number on left side of (–) is related to the number of the right side of (–) with some logic/Rule/Relation. Three are similar on basis of same Logic/Rule/Relation. Select the odd one out from the given alternatives.
(a) 12-24 (b) 14-28
(c) 44-88 (d) 33-88

31. In the following question, select the odd letter/ letters from the given alternatives.
(a) LFZ (b) PJC
(c) SMG (d) XRL

32. Arrange the given words in the sequence in which they occur in the dictionary.
1. Lighten 2. Liftoff
3. Lemonade 4. Leisure
5. Ladies
(a) 32451 (b) 21345
(c) 13245 (d) 54321

33. In the following question, select the missing number from the given series.
23, 24, 26, 27, 29, ?
(a) 31 (b) 30
(c) 33 (d) 32

34. A series is given with one term missing. Select the correct alternative from the given ones that will complete the series.
PCM, REO, TGQ ,VIS, ?
(a) XKU (b) WLV
(c) XLV (d) WKU

35. The ratio of the present ages of Reena and her husband is 4 : 5. 8 years from now, ages of her husband and her son will be in the ratio 24 : 9. If the present age of Reena is 32 years, then what will be her son's present age (in years)?
(a) 12 (b) 15
(c) 10 (d) 8

36. From the given alternatives, select the word which **CANNOT** be formed using the letters of the given word.
Preparation
(a) Paper (b) Ration
(c) part (d) people

37. In a certain code language, **"PROP"** is writen as **"67"** and **"RATE"** is written as **"46"** How is **"MOCK"** written in that code language?
(a) 41 (b) 40
(c) 42 (d) 44

38. In a certain code language '–' represents '×', '÷' represents '+' represennts '÷' and '×' represents '–' Find out the answer to following question.
$35 - 12 + 10 \times 50 \div 14 = ?$
(a) 31 (b) 6
(c) 27 (d) 15

39. The following equation is incorrect. Which two signs should be interchanged to correct the equation?
$16 \div 4 \times 8 - 10 + 14 = 12$
(a) × and – (b) ÷ and ×
(c) ÷ and – (d) – and +

40. If 19! 3 = 32, 13!4 = 18 and 12!2 = 20, then find the value of 17!3 = ?
(a) 16 (b) 28
(c) 4 (d) 8

41. Which of the following terms follows the trend of the given list?
xzyxyxyxy, xyzxyxyxy, xyxzyxyxy, xyxyzxyxy, xyxyxzyxy ____
(a) zxyxyxyxy (b) xzyxyxyxy
(c) xyzxyxyxy (d) xyxyxyzxy

42. Two navy ships start from the same port. Ship A travels 23 km West, then turns to its left and travels 19 km. Ship B travels 19 km West, then turns North and travels 5 km, then turns to its left and travels 4 km. Where is ship A with respect to ship B?
(a) 14 km South (b) 24 km North
(c) 24 km South (d) 14 km North

43. In the question two statements are given, followed by two conclusions. I and II. You have to consider the statements to be true even if it seems to be at variance from commonly known facts. You have to decide which of the given conclusions, if any follows from the given statements.
Statement I: All scissors are knives
Statement II: Some blades are scissors
Conclusion I: Some knives are blades
Conclusion II : All blades are knives
(a) Only conclusion I follows
(b) Only conclusion II follows
(c) Both conclusions I and II follow
(d) Neither conclusion I nor conclusion II follows

44. In the following figure, rectangle represents Cinematographers, circle represents Lyricists triangle represents Trekkers and square represents Joggers. Which set of letters represents Trekkers who are not Joggers?

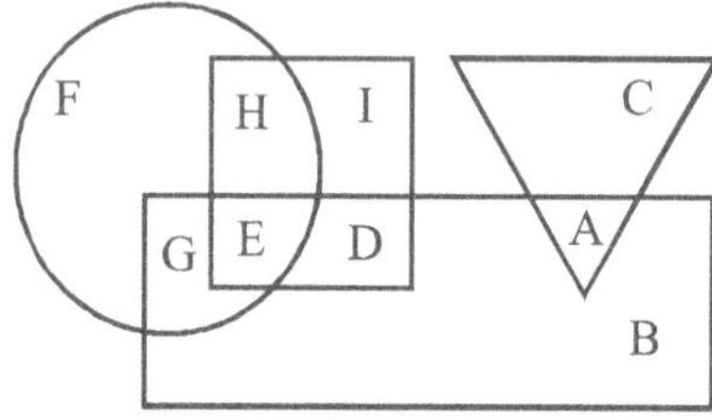

(a) Id (b) Ad
(c) CI (d) AC

45. A series is given with one term missing. Select the correct alternative from the given ones that will complete the series
HOT, GMQ, FKN, EIK, ?
(a) CHI (b) CGH
(c) DGH (D) DHI

46. In the following question, select the missing number from the given series.
93, 100, 107, 114, ?, 128
(a) 120 (b) 121
(c) 123 (d) 122

47. In the following question, four groups of three numbers are given. In each group the second and third number are related to the first number by a Logic/ Rule/ Relation. Three are similar on basis of same Logic\Rule\Relation. Select the odd one out from the given alternatives,
(a) (10, 20, 30) (b) (12, 22, 32)
(c) (27, 37, 47) (d) (19, 29, 49)

48. If a mirror is placed on the line MN, then which of the answer figures is the right image of the given figure?

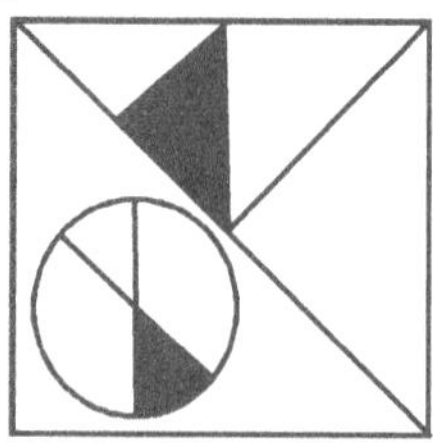

M N

(a)

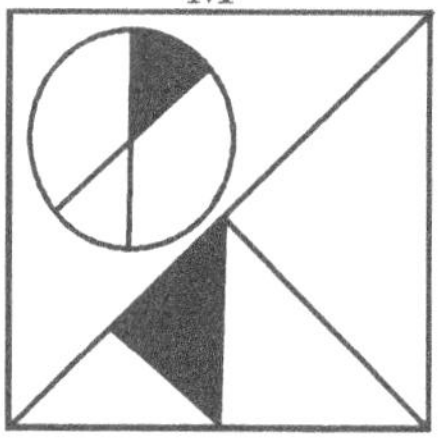

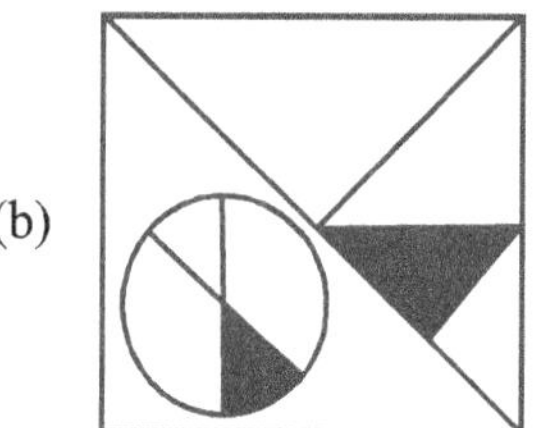

(b)

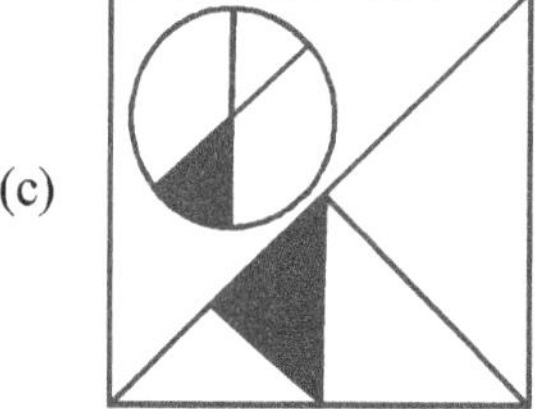

(c)

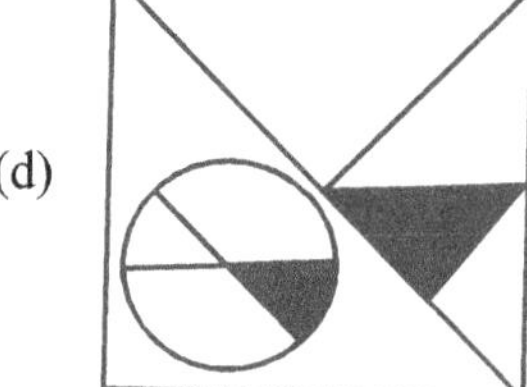

(d)

49. Which of the following cube in the answer figure cannot be made based on the unfolded cube in the question figure?

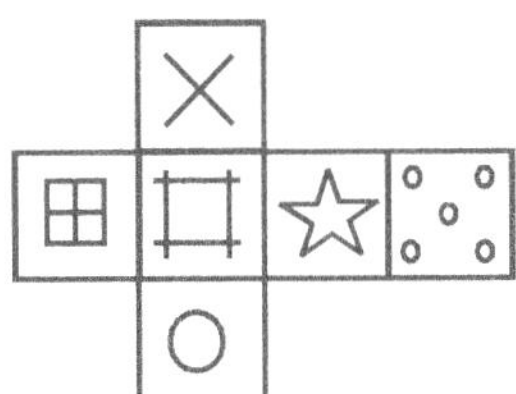

(a) 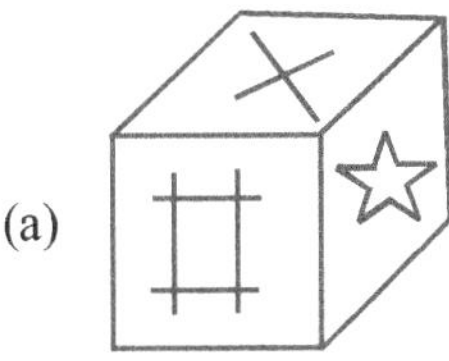

(b) 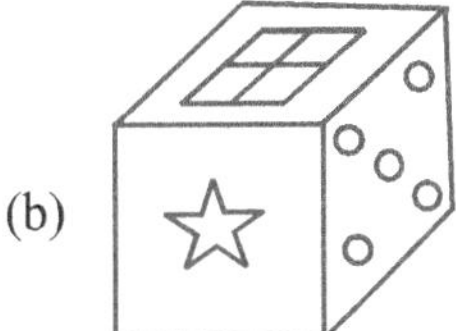

(c) 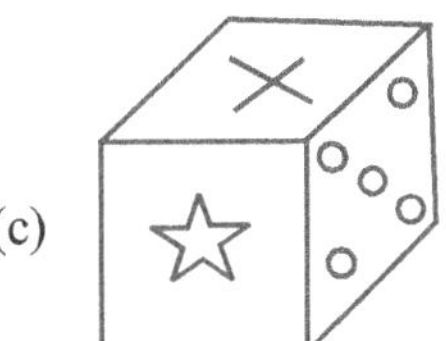

(d) 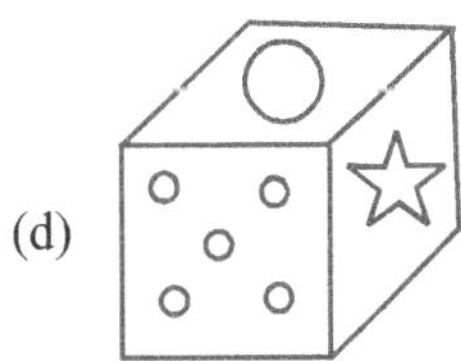

50. A word is represented by only one set of numbers as given, in any one of the alternatives. The sets of numbers given in the alternatives are represented by two Classes of alphabets as shown in the given two matrices. The columns and rows of Matrix-I are numbered from 0 to 4 and that of Matrix-II are numbered from 5 to 9. A letter from these matrices can be represented first by its is row and next by its column, for example 'D' can be represented by 31, 43 etc and 'W' can be represented by 76,57 etc. Similarly, you have to identify the set for the word 'SKIP',

Matrix-I					
	0	1	2	3	4
0	A	B	F	D	B
1	K	H	C	K	G
2	H	C	I	C	I
3	M	D	J	F	F
4	A	K	J	D	J

Matrix-II					
	5	6	7	8	9
5	U	P	W	R	Y
6	O	P	O	U	Z
7	O	W	Y	R	X
8	S	V	N	Z	T
9	N	N	X	Z	Q

(a) 41, 97, 23, 65 (b) 44, 86, 11, 56
(c) 21, 98, 31, 86 (d) 85, 13, 24, 56

Quantitative Aptitude

51. In a company 2/3 of the workers are girls, 1/2 of the girls are married and 1/3 of the married girls live in hostel. If 3/4 of the boys are married and 2/3 of married boys live in hostel. Calculate the part of workers who don't live in hostel.
(a) 11/18 (b) 15/18
(c) 17/18 (d) 13/18

52. If a number 657423547X46 is divisible by 11, then find the value of X.
(a) 7 (b) 9
(c) 8 (d) 6

53. Determine the value of $\frac{x-y}{x+2y}$ when $\frac{2x+y}{x-4y}=3$
(a) 3/5 (b) 7/10
(c) 4/5 (d) 9/10

54. For what value of 'y' $x^2+\frac{1}{12}x+y^2$ is a perfect square?
(a) 1/24 (b) 1/12
(c) 1/6 (d) 1/3

55. Which of the following statement is CORRECT about the tangents?
(a) The tangents drawn at the end of diameter of a circle are parallel to each other.

(b) The line segment which joins the point of contact of two parallel tangents to the circle is the diameter of the circle.
(c) Tangents drawn from the external points subtends equal angle at the center.
(d) All option are correct.

56. Which of the following option is CORRECT for SAS similarity criterion for the triangle ABC and DEF?

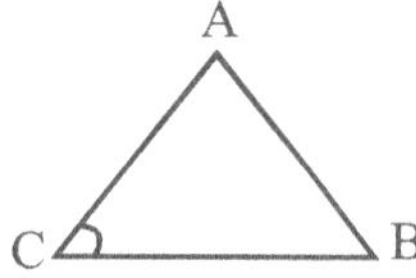

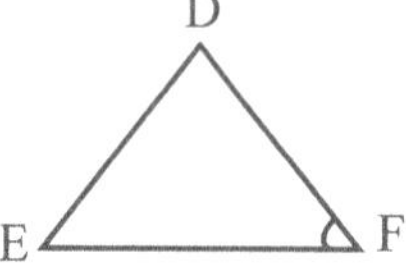

(a) $\angle A = \angle D$ and $\frac{AB}{DE} = \frac{AC}{DF}$
(b) $\angle B = \angle E$ and $\frac{AB}{DE} = \frac{BC}{EF}$
(c) $\angle C = \angle F$ and $\frac{AC}{DF} = \frac{BC}{EF}$
(d) All option are correct

57. If price of the table is increased by 25%, then a person can buy 25 table less for ₹ 25000. What is the original price (in ₹) of the table?
(a) 225 (b) 250
(c) 200 (d) 167

58. A sum of ₹ 125 is divided among u, v and w in such a way that u gets ₹ 10 more than v and v gets ₹ 5 more than w. What is the ratio of their shares?
(a) 12 : 10 : 9 (b) 10 : 8 : 7
(c) 13 : 10 : 7 (d) 5 : 4 : 3

59. In an alloy, lead and tin are in the ratio of 2 : 3. In the second alloy, the ratio of same elements is 3 : 4. If equal quantities of these two alloy are mixed to form a new alloy, then what will be the ratio of these two elements in the new alloy?
(a) 1 : 3 (b) 29 : 41
(c) 25 : 37 (d) 31 : 43

60 Average age of 6 boys is 14 years. Average age of 11 girls is 12 years. What is the average age (in years) of all boys and girls?
(a) 12.7 (b) 14.6
(c) 19.3 (d) 8.5

61. Simple interest on a sum for 10 years is equal to 5% of the principal. In how many years interest will be equal to the principal?
(a) 100 (b) 150
(c) 200 (d) 250

62. The ratio of selling price to the cost price is 21 : 16. What is the profit percentage?
(a) 35.75 (b) 21.75
(c) 27.75 (d) 31.25

63. Dinesh purchases 10 dozens of apples at the rate of ₹ 180 per dozen. He sold each one of them at the rate of ₹ 19.5. What is the profit (in percentage) of Dinesh?
(a) 30 (b) 15
(c) 18 (d) 25

64. If $x = 4 + \sqrt{15}$, then what is the value of $[x^2 + (1/x^2)]$?
(a) 62 (b) 64
(c) 34 (d) 36

65. Some masons promised to do a work in 10 days but 8 of them were absent and remaining did the work in 18 days. What was the original number of masons?
(a) 10 (b) 21
(c) 15 (d) 18

66. A boat goes 8 km upstream and 12 km downstream in 7 hours. It goes 9 km upstream and 18 km downstream in 9 hours. What is the speed (in km/h) of the boat in still water?
(a) 5 (b) 4
(c) 2 (d) 3

Directions (Qs. 67-70): The pie chart shows the results of an online survey which asked people about their favourite movie. Study the diagram and answer the following questions.

Name of People

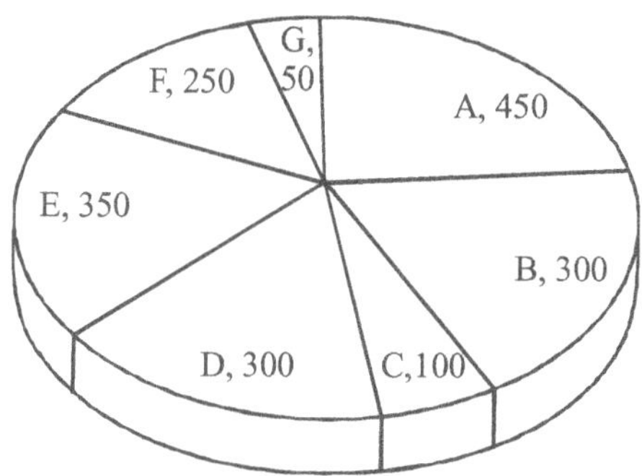

67. Which movie is the favourite of most people surveyed?
(a) F (b) D
(c) A (d) E

68. What is the total numbers of people who have responded to the survey?
(a) 1800 (b) 2100
(c) 2400 (d) 2000

69. The measure of the central angle of the sector representing number of people whose favourite movie is C is ______ degrees.
(a) 15 (b) 20
(c) 30 (d) 10

70. Respondents who say their favourite movie is D and those who say their favourite movie is B constitute what percent of the total respondents?
(a) 30 (b) 33.33
(c) 40 (d) 25

71. The perimeter and the length of one of the diagonals of a rhombus is 26 cm and 5 cm respectively. Find the length of Its other diagonal (in cm).
(a) 6 (b) 12
(c) 24 (d) 18

72. If the area of a semi-circle is 1925 cm^2, then find its radius (in cm).
(a) 70 (b) 31
(c) 62 (d) 35

73. The total surface area of a cube is 253.5 cm^2. Find its side (in cm).
(a) 7.5 (b) 5.5
(c) 6.5 (d) 8.5

74. ΔDEF is right angled at E. If $m\angle F = 30°$, then find the valuc of (sinD 1/(c)).
(a) $-1/2\sqrt{3}$ (b) $\left(3\sqrt{3}-2\right)/6$
(c) $\left(\sqrt{2}-\sqrt{3}\right)/\sqrt{6}$ (d) $\left(2\sqrt{2}-1\right)/\sqrt{2}$

75. ΔDEF is right angled at E. If cosec D = 25/24, then what is the value of cos F ?
(a) 25/7 (b) 24/7
(c) 24/25 (d) 7/24

General Awareness

76. Generally unemployment in a developing country takes place because of _____
(a) lack of complementary factors of production
(b) seasonal factors
(c) lack of effective demand
(d) switch over from one job to another

77. The Ex-officio Secretary of NDC is _____
(a) Vice-Chairman of Planning Commission
(b) General Secretary of Lok Sabha
(c) Secretary of Finance Ministry
(d) Secretary of Planning Commission

78. Who of the following founded the Vikramashila University?
(a) Devapala I
(b) Dharmpala
(c) Gopala
(d) Devapala II

79. Which Governor General of India used to write poetry with the name of "Owen Meredith"?
(a) Lord Dalhousie (b) Lord Ripon
(c) Lord Lytton (d) Lord Canning

80 Which of the following pairs is **NOT** correctly matched?
(a) Etna : Italy
(b) Fujiyama : Japan
(c) Popa : Myanmar
(d) Krakatau : Malaysia

81. The highest mountain peak of Chhotanagpur Plateau is _____
(a) Dhoopgarh
(b) Pachmarhi
(c) Parasnath
(d) Mahabaleshwar

82. Begum Akhtar is associated to which art form?
(a) Dance (b) Painting
(c) Music (d) Folk Art

83. Which of the following countries has built the world's biggest air purifier, a 328 feet high tower, to combat air pollution?
(a) Germany (b) India
(c) Australia (d) China

84. Who among the following writers won the 2017 Sahitya Academy Award for Hindi literature?
(a) Niranjan Mishra
(b) Ramesh Kuntal Megh
(c) Uday Narayana Singh
(d) Shrikant Deshmukh

85. Which is the largest City of Nepal?
(a) Hetauda (b) Pokhara
(c) Biratnagar (d) Kathmandu

86. Elements having same atomic numbers but different mass number are called _____
(a) isotones (b) Isotopes
(c) isotopes (d) isobar

87. Washing soda is used _____
    I. for removing permanent hardness of water
    II. for disinfecting drinking water
    III. as a cleaning agent for domestic purpose
    (a) Only I and II (b) Only I and III
    (c) Only II and III (d) All I, II and III

88. What are the minimum qualifications of a person to become a member of Lok Sabha?
    I. Must be a citizen of India.
    II. Must not be less than 25 years of age.
    III. Must hold an office of profit under Union Government.
    (a) Only I and II (b) Only II
    (c) Both I and III (d) I, II and III

89. The India Parliament should meet at least _____
    (a) Once a year
    (b) Twice a year
    (c) Thrice a year
    (d) Four times in a year

90. Which is the longest part of alimentary canal?
    (a) Oesophagus (b) Small intestine
    (c) Large intestine (d) Buccul cavity

91. Organs having different structure and components but perform similar functions are called _____
    (a) Analogous organs
    (b) Homologous organs
    (c) Heterogeneous organs
    (d) Homogenous organs

92. In August 2017, Environment Ministry of India launched 'Gai Yatra' to protect _____
    (a) Tigers (b) Elephants
    (c) Lions (d) Rhino

93. Which country has made the world's largest amphibious aircraft named AG600?
    (a) United States of America
    (b) Russia
    (c) China
    (d) Saudi Arabia

94. In August 2017, which of the following launched world's first future contracts in 'diamonds'?
    (a) Indian Commodity Exchange (ICEX)
    (b) Multi Commodity Exchange (MCEX)
    (c) National Association of Securities Dealers Automated Quotations (NASDAQ)
    (d) None of these

95. On 3 January 2018, Lok Sabha passed Ancient Monuments and Archaeological Sites and Remains (Amendment) Bill, 2017. The Bill seeks to permit construction in 'Prohibited areas' for _____
    (a) Private Purposes
    (b) Public Purposes
    (c) Both public and private Purposes
    (d) None of these

96. What is the resistance (in Ω) of an electrical component if a current of 0.2. A passes through it on application of 8 V of potential difference across it?
    (a) 40 (b) 1.6
    (c) 80 (d) 3.2

97. The value of acceleration due to gravity (g)_____
    (a) is greater at the poles than at the equator
    (b) is lesser at the poles than at the equator
    (c) is greater at the North pole than at the South pole
    (d) is greater at the South pole than at the North pole

98. Seismic waves are recorded by an instrument called the _____
    (a) seismograph (b) odograph
    (c) isograph (d) lithograph

99. Which of the statements given below are **correct**?
    (a) In 2017, Dani Pedrosa raced in MotoGP for Yamaha.
    (b) Alexander Zverev won the Tennis 2017 Miami Open Men's Singles.
    (c) Viktor Axelsen won the Badminton 2017 BWF Super Series Finals Men's Singles.
    (a) Only B
    (b) Only C
    (c) Both A and C
    (d) None of these

100. Computer networks constituting the internet are connected by telephones, underwater cables and_____
    (a) e-mail
    (b) e-books
    (c) Public telephone booths
    (d) Satellites

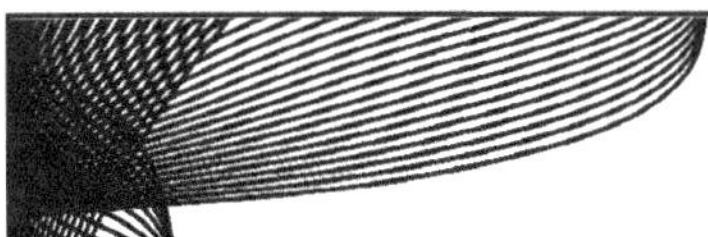

Hints & Explanations

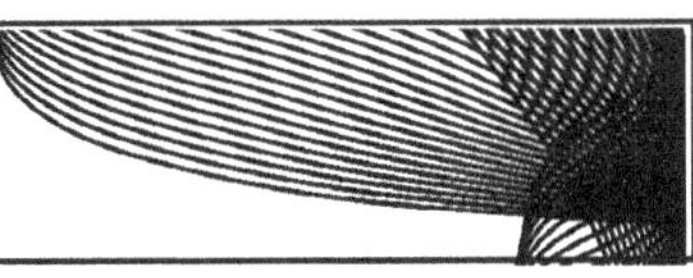

1. (c) Replace 'than' with 'then'.
2. (b) Replace 'blocking' with 'blocks'.
3. (a) Past perfect tense is required to fill the blank.
4. (d) 'no matter' is the correct word to fill the blank meaningfully.
5. (a) Hackneyed means overused, worn out, overworked so, 'tired' will be its correct synonym.
6. (d) Accede means agree to a demand, request, or treaty so, 'consent' will be its correct synonym.
7. (d) Inundate means overwhelm (someone) with things or people to be dealt with therefore, 'underwhelm' will be its correct antonym.
8. (a) Wholesome means healthy good, beneficial etc. therefore, 'impure' will be its correct antonym.
9. (b) 10. (d) 11. (a) 12. (a) 13. (a)
14. (d) 15. (b) 16. (a) 17. (a) 18. (d)
19. (d) 20. (b) 21. (b) 22. (d)
23. (b) Past perfect tense is required to make the sentence grammatically correct.
24. (c) 25. (a)
26. (b) When we speak very loudly, it is a shout. Similarly, when anger is expressed uncontrollably, it is a rage.
27. (d) 46 + 2 = 48, Similarly, 61 + 2 = 63.
28. (c) 4S,

V O T
–3↓ –3↓ –3↓
S L Q

H R X
Similarly, –3↓ –3↓ –3↓
E O U

29. (a) Except this option, in other three options first is used as a mode by the second.
30. (d) Except 33 – 88, in other three options right side is twice the left side.
31. (b) L F Z, P J C, S M G, X R L

–6 –6   –6 –7   –6 –6   –6 –6

32. (d) The dictionary sequence of the given word is : Ladies, Leisure, Lemonade, Lift off, Lighten.
33. (b)

23 → 24 → 26 → 27 → 29 → 30
+1 +2 +1 +2 +1

Thus, 30 is the next number.

34. (a)

P C M   R E O   T G Q   V I S   X K U
+2 +2 +2 +2

35. (c) $\frac{\text{Reena (R)}}{\text{Her husband(H)}} = \frac{4}{5}$

$\Rightarrow \frac{32}{H} = \frac{4}{5}$ ($\because$ Reena's present age is 32)

$\Rightarrow$ H = 40 years.

After 8 years,

$\frac{H+8}{\text{Her son (S)}+8} = \frac{24}{9}$

$\Rightarrow \frac{40+8}{S+8} = \frac{24}{9} \Rightarrow \frac{48}{S+8} = \frac{24}{9}$

$\Rightarrow$ S = 10

Thus, present age of Reena's son is 10 years.

36. (d) Alphabet 'l' is absent in the word 'Preparation'. Thus, 'people' can't be formed.
37. (d) The pattern followed in coding is sum of the place value of the alphabets + 2. Therefore, MOCK = 13 + 15 + 3 + 11 = 42 + 2 = 44.
38. (b) 35 × 12 ÷ 10 – 50 + 14
= 35 × 1.2 – 50 + 14
= 42 – 50 + 14 = 56 – 50 = 6
39. (b) 16 ÷ 4 × 8 – 10 + 14 = 12
16 × 4 ÷ 8 – 10 + 14 = 12 {After interchanging ÷ and x} 8 – 10 + 14 = 12
12 = 12
40. (b) 19 ! 3 = (19 – 3) × 2 = 32
13 ! 4 = (13 – 4) × 2 = 18
12 ! 2 = (12 – 2) × 2 = 20
17 ! 3 = (17 – 3) × 2 = 28

41. (d) 'z' is moving one place to the right in the given sequence. Thus, next term will be xyxyxyzxy.

42. (c)

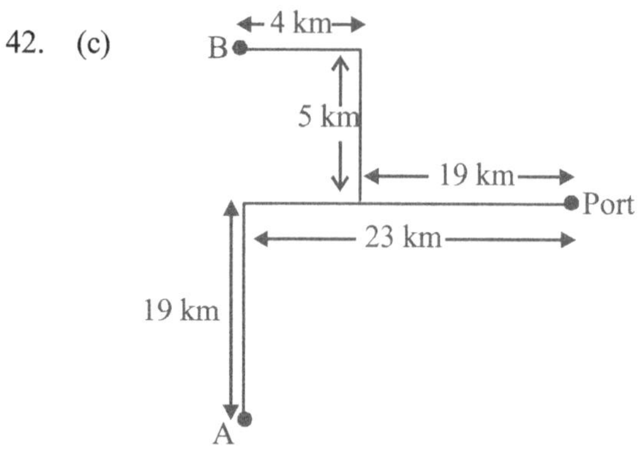

Thus, ship A is 24 km south of ship B.

43. (a)

BLADES SCISSORS KNIVES

Conclusions :
I. True
II. False

44. (d) Trekkers who are not joggers is represented by the triangle. Hence, AC is the required set of letters.

45. (c)

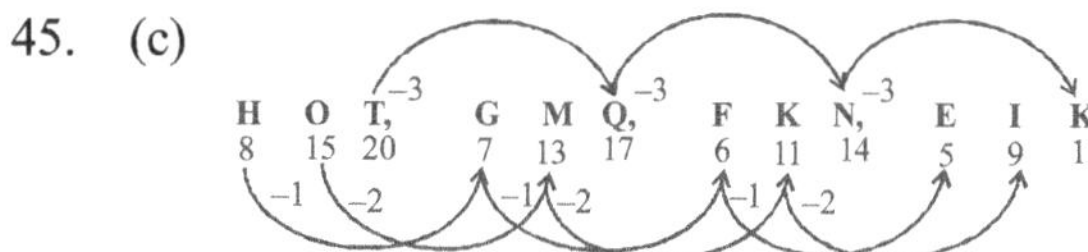

So, the next term will be DGH as per the above sequence.

46. (b) 93, 100, 107, 114, 121, 128 (each +7)

Hence, 121 is the missing term.

47. (d) Second and third terms are 10 and 20 respectively more than the first term. However, (19, 29, 49) doesn't follow this rule.

48. (a) 49. (b) 50. (d)

51. (d) Number of married girls live in hostel.

$= \frac{2}{3} \times \frac{1}{2} \times \frac{1}{3} = \frac{1}{9}$ of total number of girls.

Number of girls not live in hostel

$= \frac{2}{3} - \frac{1}{9} = \frac{5}{9}$ of total number of girls.

Number of married boys live in hostel

$= \frac{1}{3} \times \frac{3}{4} \times \frac{2}{3} = \frac{1}{6}$ of total number of boys

Number of boys not live in hostel

$= \frac{1}{3} - \frac{1}{6} = \frac{1}{6}$ of total number of boys

∴ Part of workers who don't live in hostel

$= \frac{1}{6} + \frac{5}{9} = \frac{13}{18}$.

52. (b) As the given number is divisible by 11. So the difference of sum of its digit at even and odd places must be completely divisible by 11.

In the given number 657423547 × 46

$(4 + 7 + 5 + 2 + 7 + 6) - (6 + x + 4 + 3 + 4 + 5)$

$= 31 - (22 + x) = 9 - x$

∴ For x = 9; the given number will be compleetly divisible by 11.

53. (c) $\frac{2x+4}{x-4y} = 3 \Rightarrow \frac{2\frac{x}{y}+1}{\frac{x}{y}-4} = 3$

Let $\frac{x}{y} = k$

then, $\frac{2k+1}{k-4} = 3$

K = 13

Now, $\frac{x-y}{x+2y} = \frac{\frac{x}{y}-1}{\frac{x}{y}+2} = \frac{k-1}{k+2}$

$= \frac{13-1}{13+2} = \frac{12}{15} = \frac{4}{5}$

54. (a) From, $(x + y)^2 = x^2 + 2xy + y^2$

Here, $x^2 + 2xy + y^2 = x^2 + \frac{x}{12} + y^2$

On equating the co–efficient, we have

$2xy = \frac{x}{12} \Rightarrow y = \frac{1}{24}$

55. (d)

56. (d) Here ΔABC and ΔDEF are similar then,

$\frac{AC}{DF} = \frac{AB}{DE}$ and $\angle A = \angle D$ {from S.A.S.}

$\frac{AC}{DF} = \frac{BC}{EF}$ and $\angle C = \angle F$ {from S.A.S.}

and $\frac{AB}{DE} = \frac{BC}{EF}$ and $\angle B = \angle E$ {from S.A.S.}

57. (c) Let original price of each table is ₹ x.
When price increases by 25%

then, new price = $\left(1+\frac{25}{100}\right)x = 1.25x$

From question,

$\frac{25000}{x} - \frac{25000}{1.25x} = 25$

$x = \frac{0.25 \times 1000}{1.25} = 200$

Hence, original price of each table = ₹ 200

58. (b) Let we get ₹x, then v gets ₹ (x + 5)
and u gets ₹ (x + 15)
From question, x + x + 5 + x + 15 = 125
3x = 105 ⇒ x = 35
so, w gets ₹35, v gets ₹ 40 and u gets ₹ 50
Hence, ratio of shares of u : v : w
= 50 : 40 : 35 = 10 : 8 : 7

59. (b) In alloy 1, Tead : Tin = 2x : 3x
In alloy 2, Lead : T in = 3y : 4y
When equal qunatities of two alloys mix,
then, (2x + 3x) = (3y + 4y)

$5x = 7y \Rightarrow x = \frac{7}{5}y$

In the mixture, ratio of Lead: Tin
= (2x + 3y) : (3x + 4y)

$= \left(2\times\frac{7y}{5}+3y\right):\left(3\times\frac{7}{5}y+4y\right)$

$= \frac{29}{5}y : \frac{41}{5}y$

Lead : Tin = 29 : 41

60. (a) Average age of all (boys & girls)

$= \frac{6\times14+11\times12}{6+11}$

$= \frac{84+132}{17} = 12.7$ years.

61. (c) From, S.I. = $\frac{prt}{100}$

$\frac{p*5}{100} = \frac{p.r.10}{100} \Rightarrow r = \frac{1}{2}$

Now, when S.I. = P

then, $t = \frac{p\times100}{p\times\frac{1}{2}} = 200$ years.

62. (d) Profit percent = $\frac{(21-16)}{16}\times100 = 31.25\%$

63. (a) 10 dozens apples = 120 apples
Cost price of 10 dozens of apples
= 180 × 10 = ₹ 1800
selling price of 120 apples
= 19.5 × 120 = ₹ 2340

Profit percent = $\frac{(2340-1800)}{1800}\times100 = 30\%$

64. (a) $x = 4+\sqrt{15}$

then, $\frac{1}{x} = \frac{1}{4+\sqrt{15}}$

$= \frac{4-\sqrt{15}}{(4+\sqrt{15})(4-\sqrt{15})} = 4-\sqrt{15}$

Now, $x^2+\frac{1}{x^2} = \left(x+\frac{1}{x}\right)^2 - 2$

$= (4 + 4)^2 - 2 = 62$

65. (d) Let the original number of masons was x.
from question,
work done by 1 mason = 10x = 18 (x – 8)
8x = 18 × 8

$\therefore\ x = \frac{18\times8}{8} = 18$

66. (d) Let the upstream and downstream speed of the boat is A and B km/hr.
then, from question.

$\frac{8}{A}+\frac{12}{B} = 7$ ...(i)

and $\frac{9}{A}+\frac{18}{B} = 7$ ...(ii)

from (i) and (ii), we get
A = 2 and B = 4
So, speed of the boat in still water

$= \frac{A+B}{2} = \frac{2+4}{2} = 3$ km/h

67. (c) The movie which is most favourite of people surveyed is A.

68. (a) Total number of people who have responded to the survey
$= 300 + 100 + 300 + 350 + 250 + 50 + 450$
$= 1800$

69. (b) Central angle made by C
$= \frac{100}{1800} \times 360° = 20°$

70. (b) Total number of people whose favourite movies is D and B = 300 + 300 = 600
Percent of total respondents $= \frac{600}{1800} \times 100$
= 33.33X

71. (b) Let ABCD is a rhombus then, side

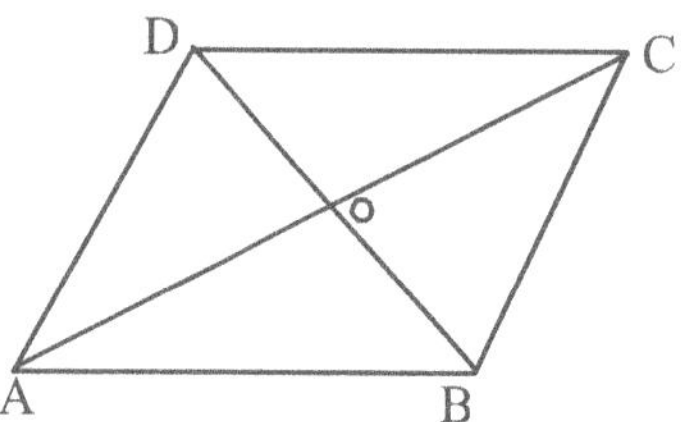

$AB = AC = CD \ AD = \frac{26}{4} = \frac{13}{2}$ cm

Diagonal BD = 5 cm $\Rightarrow OB = \frac{5}{2}$ cm

In ΔA OB, $AO = \sqrt{(AB)^2 - (BO)^2}$

$= \sqrt{\left(\frac{13}{2}\right)^2 - \left(\frac{5}{2}\right)^2}$

$= \frac{12}{2}$ cm
Diagonal AC = 12 cm.

72. (d) Area of semicircle of radius (r) $= \frac{\pi r^2}{2}$

$\frac{\pi r^2}{2} = 1925$

$r^2 = \frac{1925 \times 2}{\pi}$

$r = \sqrt{\frac{1925 \times 2 \times 7}{22}}$

r = 35 cm.

73. (c) total surface area of a cube of side (s) $= 6 \times s^2$
then, $6s^2 = 253.5$

$S = \sqrt{\frac{253.5}{6}}$

S = 6.5 cm.

74. (b) In ΔDEF, $\angle(D + E + F) = 180°$
$\angle D = 180° - 90° - 30°$
$\angle D = 60°$

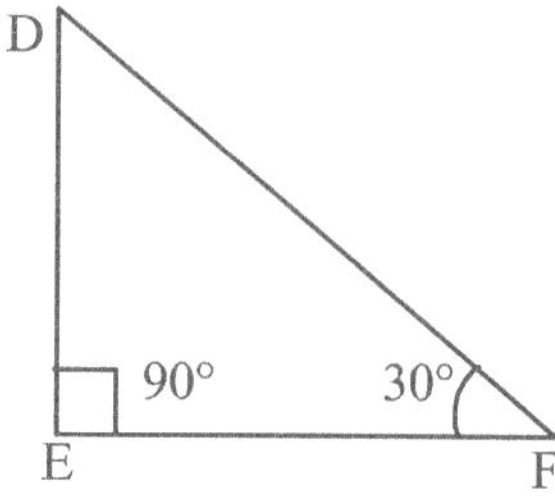

$\sin D = \sin 60° = \frac{\sqrt{3}}{2}$

$\sin D - \frac{1}{3} = \frac{\sqrt{3}}{2} - \frac{1}{3}$

$= \frac{3\sqrt{3} - 2}{6}$

75. (c) $\text{cosec } D = \frac{25}{24} \Rightarrow \sin D = \frac{24}{25}$

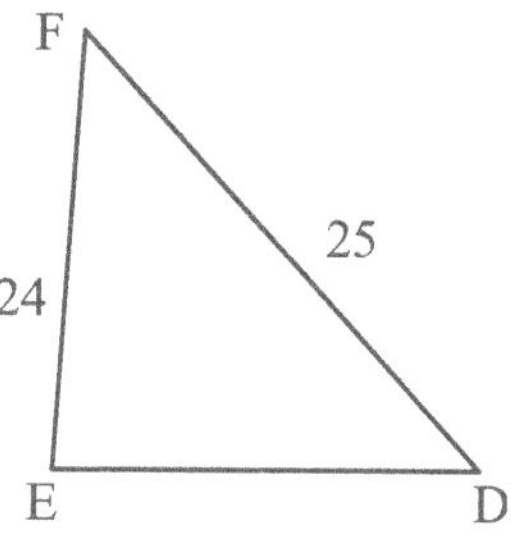

∴ In ΔDEF
EF = 24 cm
DF = 25 cm

then, $\cos F = \frac{EF}{FD} = \frac{24}{25}$

76.	(a)	77.	(d)	78.	(b)	79.	(c)	80.	(d)
81.	(c)	82.	(c)	83.	(d)	84.	(b)	85.	(d)
86.	(c)	87.	(b)	88.	(c)	89.	(b)	90.	(b)
91.	(a)	92.	(b)	93.	(c)	94.	(a)	95.	(b)
96.	(a)	97.	(a)	98.	(a)	99.	(b)	100.	(d)

SSC

Combined Higher Secondary Level Exam-2016

Time : 1 hr. **Held on : 8.02.2017** **Max. Marks : 100**

General Intelligence & Reasoning

DIRECTIONS (Qs. 1-4): *Choose the related word/ letters number from the given alternatives.*

1. Horse : Neigh : : Elephant : ?
(a) Quack (b) Trumpet
(c) Mew (d) Grunt

2. GH : 78 : : ? : 1819
(a) HG (b) LM
(c) RS (d) IJ

3. CAR : RAC : : TYRE : ?
(a) RUBBER (b) ERTY
(c) ERYT (d) STEEL

4. 12 : 60 : : 28 : ?
(a) 160 (b) 150
(c) 145 (d) 140

DIRECTIONS (Qs. 5-8): *Choose the odd word/letters number/number pair from the given alternatives.*

5. (a) Sirius (b) Proximacentauri
(c) Deimos (d) Alpha centauri

6. (a) PON (b) SRQ
(c) XYZ (d) VUT

7. (a) 1919 (b) 5656
(c) 6761 (d) 7760

8. (a) 2890 (b) 3375
(c) 1728 (d) 1331

DIRECTIONS (Qs. 9-12): *A series is given with one term missing. Choose the correct alternative from the given ones that will complete the series.*

9. Double, Triple, Quadruple, ?
(a) Quintuple (b) Nonuple
(c) Sextuple (d) Octuple

10. AC, EG, ?, MO
(a) IK (b) IJ
(c) IL (d) IM

11. ?, WX, AB, FG
(a) TU (b) XW
(c) PQ (d) UV

12. 30, 60, 360, 3600, ?
(a) 48500 (b) 50500
(c) 50400 (d) 40800

13. In the following question, two statements are given each followed by two conclusions I and II. You have to consider the statements to be true even if they seem to be at variance from commonly known facts. You have to decide which of the given conclusions, if any, follows from the given statements.

Statements :
I. Women generally prefer window shopping.
II. Males generally are not fond of window shopping and they feel that it is sheer waste of time.

Conclusions :
I. Shopping behavior is different for males and females.
II. If males go for window shopping, they don't utilize much time is selecting a product.

(a) Only conclusion II follows
(b) Conclusion I and II both follow
(c) Neither I nor II follow
(d) Only conclusion I follows

14. Five boys A, B, C, D and E are standing in a line. A is taller than E but shorter than D. B is shorter than E and C is the tallest. Who is in the middle?
(a) A (b) C
(c) D (d) E

15. Arrange the given words in the sequence in which they occur in the dictionary.
(i) Treadmill
(ii) Treason
(iii) Treacherous
(iv) Tread
(a) (ii), (iii), (iv), (i)
(b) (iii), (iv), (ii), (i)
(c) (iii), (iv), (i), (ii)
(d) (i), (ii), (iii), (iv)

16. In a certain code language, "RIVER" is written as "12351" and "RED" is written as "156". How is "DRIVER" written in that code language?
(a) 612311 (b) 612531
(c) 621351 (d) 612351

17. In the following question, select the missing number from the given series.

49	169	484
81	144	625
16	25	?

(a) 37 (b) 47
(c) 48 (d) 25

18. If "+" means "minus", "×" means "divided by", " ÷ " means "plus" and "–" means "multiplied by", then
$126 \times 14 + 7 - 3 \div 2 = ?$
(a) –10 (b) –12
(c) –17 (d) –41

19. In the following question, which one set of letters when sequentially placed at the gaps in the given letter series shall complete it?
d _ ba_c_a_cb_
(a) cdbda (b) cdbad
(c) bdacd (d) abdca

20. Neeraj is facing north, then he turns 45 degree right and goes 25 m, then turns in south – east direction to move 25 m and from there 25 m to east. In which direction/place is he from his original place?
(a) North
(b) East
(c) West
(d) South

21. A word is represented by only one set of numbers as given in any one of the alternatives. The sets of numbers given in the alternatives are represented by two classes of alphabets as shown in the given two matrices. The columns and rows of Matrix – I are numbered from 0 to 4 and that of Matrix – II are numbered from 5 to 9. A letter from these matrices can be represented first by its row and next by its column, for example, 'E' can be represented by 02, 11, etc. and 'G' can be represented by 65, 56 etc. Similarly, you have to identify the set for the word 'EAGER;'.

Matrix – I

	0	1	2	3	4
0	S	T	E	D	B
1	A	E	O	F	A
2	E	T	P	A	N
3	D	G	A	S	M
4	G	A	Q	W	I

Matrix – II

	5	6	7	8	9
5	F	G	M	R	C
6	G	N	R	K	L
7	A	R	Y	J	F
8	R	B	W	G	Y
9	S	V	Q	H	T

(a) 02, 10, 65, 11, 68
(b) 02, 10, 65, 87, 85
(c) 02, 10, 65, 11, 85
(d) 02, 10, 65, 59, 85

22. Introducing a boy Ankit said, "He is the son of daughter of my grandfather's son". How is that boy related to Ankit?
(a) Cousin (b) Brother
(c) Father – in – law (d) Nephew

23. If a mirror is placed on the line MN, then which of the answer figure is the right image of the given figure?

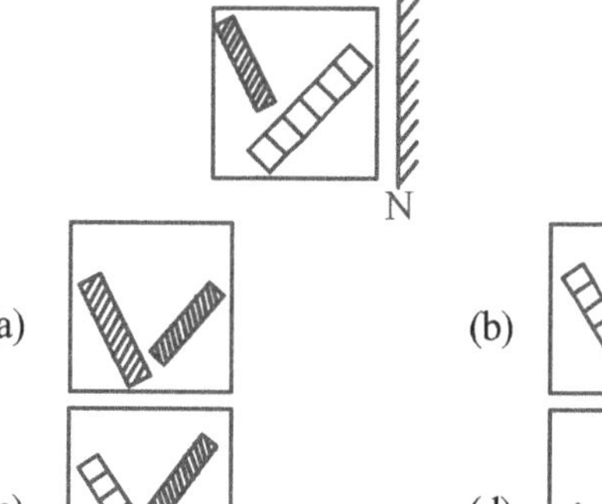

24. Identify the diagram that best represents the relationship among the given classes.
Earth, Saturn, Planet, Star

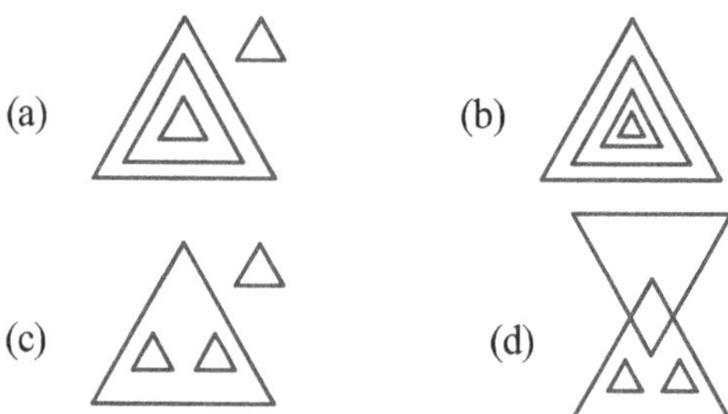

25. A piece of paper is folded and punched own below in the question figures. From the given answer figures, indicates how it will appear when opened.

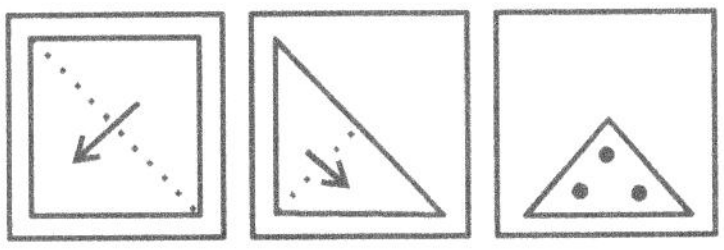

(a) 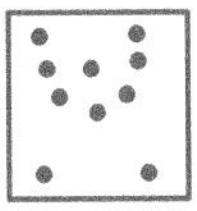 (b)

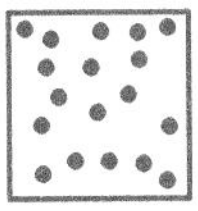

(c) 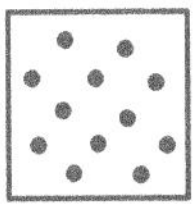 (d)

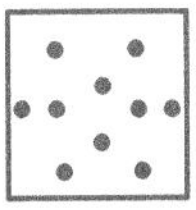

General Awareness

26. Which drug is used as an Anti–Anxiety drug?
(a) Warfarin (b) Diazepam
(c) Latanoprost (d) Hydralazine

27. *Ficus benghalensis* is the scientific name of ________.
(a) Banyan (b) Pineapple
(c) Babul (d) Tulsi

28. *Equus burchellii* is the scientific name of __________.
(a) Horse (b) Zebra
(c) Buffalo (d) Ass

29. Atomic number of which of the following elements is greater than that of Copper?
(a) Iron (b) Chromium
(c) Zinc (d) Manganese

30. Vacuum Tubes were used by __________ Generation of Computers.
(a) First (b) Second
(c) Third (d) Fourth

31. Ghumura is a folk dance of ________.
(a) Odisha (b) Andhra Pradesh
(c) Jammu & Kashmir (d) Maharashtra

32. 7 workers work in a printing press. Each gets paid ₹ 450 per day. The 8th worker demands ₹ 500 per day. If this worker is hired then all other workers must be paid ₹ 500. The marginal resource (labour) cost of the 8th worker is ______.
(a) ₹ 50 (b) ₹ 850
(c) ₹ 400 (d) ₹ 100

33. An increase of 1% per annum in the rate of growth of the money supply will increase inflation in the long run by ________.
(a) Zero percent
(b) One percent
(c) 0.5 percent
(d) More than one percent

34. Which of the following is false with reference to a photo-voltaic cell?
(a) It is another name as solar cell
(b) It can be used as infra-red detectors
(c) It can store light energy in the form of electrical energy
(d) It converts electric energy into light energy

35. Methane an air pollutant is produced ________.
(a) by action of ultraviolet light on nitrogenous compounds.
(b) as a by-product of manufacturing ammoniacal fertilizers
(c) by burning of coal in insufficient air
(d) by digestion of food by animals

36. In the National Flag of India, Ashoka Chakra is a __________ spoked wheel.
(a) 8 (b) 12
(c) 16 (d) 24

37. The longest day of the year in the Northern Hemisphere occur on __________.
(a) 20th May (b) 21st June
(c) 20th July (d) 21st August

38. Chandragupta Maurya was an ardent follower of ________.
(a) Sikhism (b) Jainism
(c) Buddhism (d) Jewism

39. The First Battle of Panipat in 1526 was fought between the Lodi Empire and __________.
(a) Babur (b) Humayun
(c) Akbar (d) Aurangzeb

40. Who Invented Ceiling fan?
(a) Loyd Groff Copeman
(b) Bartolomeo Cristofori
(c) Leonardo da Vinci
(d) Philip Diehl

41. Rate of work done is __________ .
(a) Energy (b) Power
(c) Momentum (d) Impulse

42. What is the unit of the physical quantity, "Young's modulus"?
(a) newton (b) erg
(c) joule (d) pascal

43. Pradhan Mantri Mudra Yojana was announced under the leadership of __________.
(a) Jawaharlal Nehru (b) Indira Gandhi
(c) Narendra Modi (d) Manmohan Singh

44. The number of parliamentary seats (Lok Sabha) of Punjab is __________.
(a) 2 (b) 13
(c) 20 (d) 25

45. Who has the record of highest number of Gold Medals in the history of Olympics?
(a) Usain Bolt (b) Michael Phelps
(c) Larisa Latynina (d) Ian Thorpe

46. Who is the author of "Gently Falls : The Bakula"?
(a) Amitav Ghosh (b) Mitali Meelan
(c) Ravinder Singh (d) Sudha Murty

47. Which fort is also known as the Golden Fort?
(a) Chittorgarh (b) Kumbhalgarh
(c) Ranthambore (d) Jaisalmer

48. Highest Civilian Honour received by Shabana Azmi is __________.
(a) Padma Shri (b) Padma Bhushan
(c) Padma Vibhushan (d) Bharat Ratna

49. Which of the following is false?
(a) Hydrogen atom is roughly a third of the mass of tritium
(b) Deuterium is called heavy hydrogen
(c) Deuterium atom has 1 neutron
(d) Protium is the rarest isotope of hydrogen

50. Which Indian lake is renowned as the Lagoon lake of India?
(a) Kanjia Lake (b) Agra Lake
(c) Mansar Lake (d) Chilika Lake

Quantitative Aptitude

51. What is the LCM (least common multiple) of 57 and 93?
(a) 1767 (b) 1567
(c) 1576 (d) 1919

52. If sec $-\frac{5\pi}{4}$ = x, then value of x is
(a) $-11\sqrt{3}$ (b) $-\sqrt{2}$
(c) -1 (d) $\sqrt{3}$

53. Marked price of an item is Rs 500. On purchase of 2 items discount is 8%, on purchase of 3 items discount is 16%. Radha buys 5 items, what is the effective discount?
(a) 20.4 percent (b) 23.25 percent
(c) 12.8 percent (d) 35 percent

54. If tan (A/2) = x, then the value of x is
(a) sin A/(1 – cosA)
(b) sin A/(1 + cosA)
(c) [sin A/(1 + cosA)]
(d) [sin A/(1 – cosA)]

55. If 2sec A – (1 + sinA)/cos A = x, then the value of x is
(a) cosec A/(1 + sin A)
(b) cos A/(1 + sin A)
(c) cos A(1 + sin A)
(d) cosec A(1 + sin A)

56. The mean of marks secured by 60 students in division A of class X is 64, 40 students of division B is 60 and that of 60 students of division C is 58. Find the mean of marks of the students of three divisions of Class X.
(a) 60.05 (b) 59.35
(c) 62.15 (d) 60.75

57. The difference between simple and compound interests compounded annually on a certain sum of money for 2 years at 5% per annum is Rs. 45. The sum is
(a) ₹36000 (b) ₹72000
(c) ₹18000 (d) ₹54000

58. The price of an article is cut by 33%, to restore to its original value, the new price must be increased by
(a) 33 percent (b) 49.25 percent
(c) 24.81 percent (d) 41.25 percent

59. The third proportional of two numbers 9 and 24 is
(a) 39 (b) 48
(c) 72 (d) 64

60. The total surface area of a hemisphere is 166.32 sq cm, find its radius?
(a) 4.2 cm (b) 8.4 cm
(c) 1.4 cm (d) 2.1 cm

61. ΔABC is similar to ΔDEF. Length of AB is 18 cm and length of the corresponding side DE is 10 cm. What is the ratio of Perimeter of ΔABC. Perimeter of ΔDEF?
(a) 5 : 9 (b) 9 : 5
(c) 81 : 25 (d) 25 : 81

62. Two cars travel from city A to city B at a speed of 36 km/hr and 48 km/hr respectively. If one car takes 3 hours lesser time than the other car for the journey, then the distance between City A and City B is
(a) 518 km (b) 432 km
(c) 648 km (d) 346 km

63. A shopkeeper by selling 13 Titan watches, earns a profit equal to the selling price of 3 Titan watches. His profit percentage is
(a) 30 percent (b) 23 percent
(c) 46 percent (d) 16 percent

64. The line passing through (–2, 5) and (6,b) is perpendicular to the line 20x + 5y = 3. Find b?
(a) –7 (b) 4
(c) 7 (d) –4

65. Find the sum of interior angles of a dodecagon?
(a) 1620° (b) 1800°
(c) 1440° (d) 1260°

66. A does 80% of a work in 20 days. He then calls in B and they together finish the remaining work in 4 days. How long B alone would take to do the whole work?
(a) 12.5 days (b) 100 days
(c) 22.5 days (d) 35 days

67. The area of a circle is 616 sq cm, find its circumference?
(a) 44 cm (b) 88 cm
(c) 22 cm (d) 176 cm

68. If $3x - 8(2 - x) = -19$, then the value of x is
(a) –3/11 (b) –33/11
(c) –3/5 (d) –33/5

69. If $x - y = 6$ and $xy = 40$, then find $x^2 + y^2$?
(a) 116 (b) 80
(c) 89 (d) 146

70. Product of digits of a 2–digit number is 27. If we add 54 to the number, the new number obtained is a number formed by interchange of the digits. Find the number.
(a) 39 (b) 93
(c) 63 (d) 36

71. If $2x - 3(2x - 2) > x - 1 < 2 + 2x$, then x can take which of the following values?
(a) 2 (b) –2
(c) 4 (d) –4

DIRECTIONS (Q. 72): *Refer the below data table and answer following Question.*

	Number of employees	Annual salary (in lakhs)	Bonus as percent of annual salary
Manager	3	30	30%
Executive	8	16	20%
Trainee	4	2	20%

72. What is the average bonus (in rupees)?
(a) 5419995 (b) 160000
(c) 361333 (d) 126000

73. Refer the below data table and answer the following Questions:-

	2011	2012	2013	2014	2015
Company A	3000	5000	4000	5000	5000
Company B	1000	1000	1000	2000	2000
Company C	4000	2000	2000	2000	3000

For which of the following pairs of years the total exports from the three Companies together are equal?
(a) 2011 & 2012 (b) 2013 & 2015
(c) 2011 & 2014 (d) 2014 & 2015

DIRECTIONS (Qs. 74-75): *Refer the below data table and answer the following Question.*

Year	Profit or (–Loss) in Rs Crore
2011	–10
2012	5
2013	10
2014	–15
2015	–5

74. What was the total Profit or Loss of the company in last 5 years?
(a) Profit of ₹ 15 crores
(b) Loss of ₹ 5 crores
(c) Loss of ₹ 15 crores
(d) Profit of ₹ 25 crores

75. Refer the below data table and answer following Question.

India's exports in 2015	Value in million US$
Jewellery	675
Software	500
Cotton	525
Steel	575
Electronics	725

Jewellery was what percent of total exports?
(a) 25 percent (b) 27.5 percent
(c) 22.5 percent (d) 20 percent

English Language

76. Select the word with the correct spelling.
(a) brooches (b) linoleam
(c) limekilne (d) cherubick

77. In the following question, out of the four alternatives, select the alternative which best expresses the meaning of the idiom/phrase: An outline representing or bounding the shape or form of something.
(a) tracery (b) contour
(c) doodle (d) pattern

78. In the following question, some part of the sentence may have errors. Find out which part of the sentence has an error and select the appropriate option. If a sentence is free from error, select 'No Error'.
Soon as he (A)/saw the policeman, (B)/he ran away, (C)/No error (D).
(a) A (b) B
(c) C (d) D

79. Rearrange the parts of the sentence in correct order.
We are told that its
P - Public Distribution System
Q - Creating a functional
R - Sole purpose is the noble goal of
(a) QRP (b) RQP
(c) PRQ (d) PQR

80. Select the word with the correct spelling.
(a) lammented (b) scabbard
(c) ordenance (d) synaptick

81. In the following question, a sentence has been given in Direct/Indirect speech. Out of the four alternatives suggested, select the one, which best express the same sentence in Indirect/Direct speech.
Gokul said to Sumit, "Why did not you attend the meeting yesterday?"
(a) Gokul asked Sumit why he did not attend the meeting the day before.
(b) Gokul asked Sumit why he had not attended that meeting yesterday.
(c) Gokul asked Sumit why he had not attended the meeting the day before.
(d) Gokul asked Sumit why he did not attend that meeting yesterday.

82. In the following question, out of the four alternatives, select the alternative which best expresses the meaning of the idiom/phrase.
to lose one's head
(a) to lose respect within your community
(b) to become complacent and gradually worsen your performance
(c) to become confused or overly emotional about someone or something
(d) to lose sense or start behaving like a lunatic

83. In the following question, out of the four alternative, select the alternative which is the best substitute of the phrase.
A person famous and respected within a particular sphere.
(a) eminent (b) obscure
(c) despotic (d) imperative

84. In the following question, a sentence has been given in Active/Passive voice. Out of four alternatives suggested, select the one, which best expresses the same sentence in Passive/Active voice.
We shall invite Suresh.
(a) Suresh would be invited by us.
(b) Suresh would have been invited by us.
(c) Suresh will be invited by us.
(d) Suresh will have been invited by us.

85. Select the antonym of
amenable
(a) responsive (b) pliable
(c) docile (d) unsusceptible

86. Select the synonym of
to subsume
(a) to bate (b) to obviate
(c) to preclude (d) to incorporate

87. Improve the bracketed part of the sentence
I perfer black coffee (over) cappuccino.
(a) rather than (b) to
(c) instead of (d) no improvement

88. In the following question, some part of the sentence may have errors. Find out which part of the sentence has an error and select the appropriate option. If a sentence is free from error, select "No Error".
'You must not (A)/look down into (B)/ parents' advice. (C)/ No error(D)
(a) A (b) B
(c) C (d) D

89. Improve the bracketed part of the sentence.
The priest agreed (to answer on) questions on theology.
(a) to answer (b) for answering
(c) to answer for (d) no improvement

90. Select the synonym of
to lash
(a) to endear (b) to fondle
(c) to chastise (d) to snuggle

91. In the following question, the sentence given with blank to be filled in with an appropriate word. Select the correct alternative out of the four and indicate it by selecting the appropriate option.
Arun's financial ____________ has helped him earn a fortune on the stock market.

(a) dexterity (b) readiness
(c) expertise (d) knack

92. In the following question, sentence given with blank is to be filled in with an appropriate word. Select the correct alternative out of the four and indicate it by selecting the appropriate option.
Fuel suppliers will __________ the national oil shortage by raising prices to increase their bottom lines.
(a) use (b) misuse
(c) ventuse (d) exploit

93. Select the antonym of
to muster
(a) to convocate (b) to rally
(c) to estrange (d) to aggregate

94. In the following question, out of the four alternatives, select the alternative which best expresses the meaning of the idiom/phrase.
head over heels
(a) to think with instead of heart
(b) to run away from an unpleasant situation
(c) to take a nasty fall
(d) to be madly in love

95. Rearrange the parts of the sentence in correct order.
So, increasingly,
P-paying to provide revenues
Q-for the Central government
R-the poor have been
(a) RPQ (b) RQP
(c) PQR (d) QPR

DIRECTIONS (Qs. 96-100): *In the following passage, some of the words have been left out. Read the passage carefully and select the correct answer for the given blank out of the four alternatives.*

The scenario ________ dramatically today. We have the ________ of powerfull Internet monopolies that are much bigger ________ the telcos. Not surprisingly, these companies now see the ________ of monopoly. They would like to combine with telcos to create monopolies for their platforms, ensuring that they control the future of the Internet and freeze their competition ________.

96. (a) change (b) had changed
(c) has changed (d) changing

97. (a) emerging (b) emerge
(c) emergence (d) emergency

98. (a) then (b) than
(c) to (d) of

99. (a) virtues (b) respectability
(c) trust (d) innocence

100. (a) off (b) about
(c) in (d) out

ANSWER KEY									
1	(b)	21	(c)	41	(b)	61	(b)	81	(c)
2	(c)	22	(d)	42	(d)	62	(b)	82	(d)
3	(c)	23	(c)	43	(c)	63	(a)	83	(a)
4	(d)	24	(c)	44	(b)	64	(c)	84	(c)
5	(c)	25	(c)	45	(b)	65	(b)	85	(d)
6	(c)	26	(b)	46	(d)	66	(b)	86	(d)
7	(b)	27	(a)	47	(d)	67	(b)	87	(b)
8	(a)	28	(b)	48	(b)	68	(a)	88	(b)
9	(a)	29	(c)	49	(d)	69	(a)	89	(a)
10	(a)	30	(a)	50	(d)	70	(a)	90	(c)
11	(a)	31	(a)	51	(a)	71	(b)	91	(c)
12	(c)	32	(b)	52	(b)	72	(c)	92	(d)
13	(d)	33	(b)	53	(c)	73	(a)	93	(c)
14	(a)	34	(d)	54	(b)	74	(c)	94	(d)
15	(c)	35	(d)	55	(b)	75	(c)	95	(a)
16	(d)	36	(d)	56	(d)	76	(a)	96	(c)
17	(b)	37	(b)	57	(c)	77	(b)	97	(c)
18	(a)	38	(b)	58	(b)	78	(a)	98	(b)
19	(a)	39	(a)	59	(d)	79	(b)	99	(a)
20	(b)	40	(d)	60	(a)	80	(b)	100	(d)

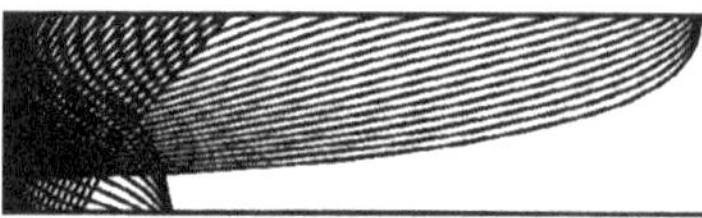

Hints & Explanations

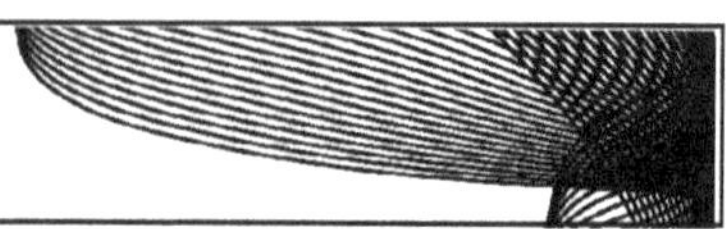

1. (b) Sound of horse is neigh.
Similarly,
Sound of elephant is trumpet.

2. (c) According to alphabetical order :

G H → 7 8 (↓ ↓); Similarly, R S → 18 19 (↓ ↓)

3. (c) $\overleftarrow{\frac{CAR}{RAC}}$ Reverse Order
Similarly,
$\overleftarrow{\frac{TYRE}{ERYT}}$ Revers Order

4. (d) $12 \times 5 = 60$
$28 \times 5 = 140$.

5. (c) Except Deimos (It is a satellite), All others are Star systems.

6. (c) Except, XYZ, All others are opposite alphabetical sequence.

7. (b) $1919 \Rightarrow 1+9+1+9=20$
$5656 \Rightarrow 5+6+5+6=22$
$6761 \Rightarrow 6+7+6+1=20$
$7760 \Rightarrow 7+7+6+0=20$
Except 5656, Sum of all digit of number is equal to 20.

8. (a) Except 2890, All are cube of a number.
$(15)^3=3375, (12)^3=1728, (11)^3=1331$.

9. (a) The next term is quintuple because quintuple means five times.

10. (a) The common difference between first and second letter is one letter according to alphabetical sequence.
So, answer will be IK.

11. (a) $\boxed{TU} \xrightarrow{+2} WX \xrightarrow{+3} AB \xrightarrow{+4} FG$

12. (c) 30 60 360 3600 $\boxed{50400}$
×2, ×6, ×10, ×14
+4, +4, +4

13. (d) According to statement
Only conclusion - I follows.

14. (a) C > D > A > E > B
So, A is in the middle.

15. (c) According to dictionary order,
Treacherous → Tread → Treadmill → Treason.
(1) (2) (3) (4)

16. (d) As,

R I V E R → 1 2 3 5 1 (↓ ↓ ↓ ↓ ↓); R E D → 1 5 6 (↓ ↓ ↓)

Similarly,

D R I V E R → 6 1 2 3 5 1 (↓ ↓ ↓ ↓ ↓ ↓)

17. (b) $\sqrt{49}=7$ $\sqrt{169}=13$ $\sqrt{484}=22$
$\sqrt{81}=\frac{+9}{16}$ $\sqrt{144}=\frac{+12}{25}$ $\sqrt{625}=\frac{+25}{47}$
So, Answer is 47.

18. (a) If,

+ = –	× = ÷
÷ = +	– = ×

then,
$126 \div 14 - 7 \times 3 + 2 = -10$

19. (a) d<u>c</u>ba / <u>d</u>c<u>b</u>a / <u>d</u>cb<u>a</u>
So, answer is cdbda.

20. (b)

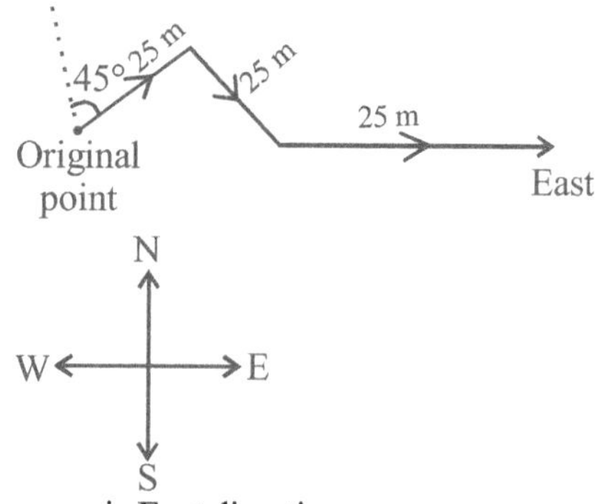

So, answer is East direction.

21. (c)

E A G E R → 02 10 65 11 85 (↓ ↓ ↓ ↓ ↓)

22. (d) Nephew.

24. (c)

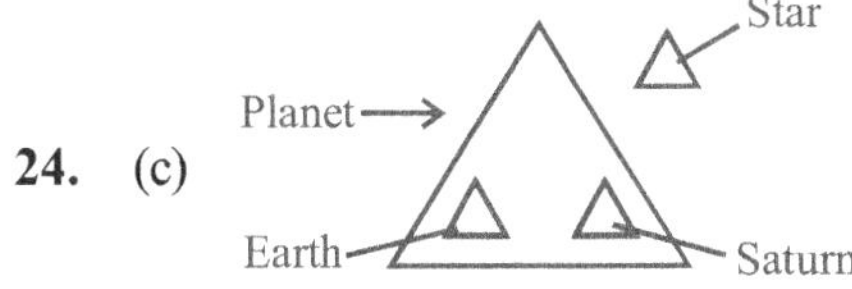

25. (c) Required answer =

51. (a) LCM of 57 and 93,

3	57, 93
	19, 31

$\Rightarrow$ $3 \times 19 \times 31 = 1767$.
So, Required answer is 1767.

52. (b) $\sec\left(-\frac{5\pi}{4}\right) = x$

$\therefore$ $\sec\left(\frac{-5 \times 180°}{4}\right) = \sec(-225°)$

$= -\sec(180° + 45°)$

$= -\sec 45° = -\sqrt{2}$

$\therefore$ $x = -\sqrt{2}$

53. (c) Marked price of each item = 500
No. of items = 5
$\therefore$ Total marked price = $500 \times 5 = 2500$
Total discount

$$= 2 \times 500 \times \frac{8}{100} + 3 \times 500 \times \frac{16}{100} = 320$$

$\therefore$ Effective discount $= \frac{320}{2500} \times 100$

$= 12.8\%$

54. (b) $\because$ $\tan\left(\frac{A}{2}\right) = \frac{\sin A}{(1 + \cos A)}$

$\therefore$ $x = \frac{\sin A}{(1 + \cos A)}$

55. (b) $2\sec A - \frac{(1 + \sin A)}{\cos A} = x$

then,

$$\frac{2}{\cos A} - \frac{(1 + \sin A)}{\cos A} = \frac{2 - 1 - \sin A}{\cos A}$$

$$= \frac{1 - \sin A}{\cos A} \times \frac{(1 + \sin A)}{(1 + \sin A)} = \frac{1 - \sin^2 A}{\cos A(1 + \sin A)}$$

$$= \frac{\cos^2 A}{\cos A(1 + \sin A)} = \frac{\cos A}{1 + \sin A}$$

56. (d) Mean of marks of the students

$$= \frac{(60 \times 64 + 40 \times 60 + 60 \times 58)}{160}$$

$$= \frac{9720}{160} = 60.75$$

57. (c) Here,
P = ?
R = 5%
T = 2 years
Difference = 45

$\because$ Difference between S.I. and C.I. $= \frac{PR^2}{(100)^2}$

$$45 = \frac{P \times (5)^2}{(100)^2}$$

$\therefore$ $P = \frac{45 \times 100 \times 100}{25} = 18000$

58. (b) Let the price of the article = ₹ 100
New Price = 100 − 33 = 67
Therefore the new price must be increased by

$$\frac{(100 - 67) \times 100}{67} = \frac{3300}{67} = 49.25\%$$

59. (d) Here, a = 9, b = 24 and c = ?
So,

$$\frac{9}{24} = \frac{24}{c}$$

$\therefore$ $c = \frac{24 \times 24}{9} = 64$

60. (a) Here,
Total surface area of hemisphere = 166.32 sq cm.
r = ?

$\because$ $3\pi r^2 = 166.32$

$$3 \times \frac{22}{7} \times r^2 = 166.32$$

$\therefore$ $r^2 = \frac{166.32 \times 7}{3 \times 22} = 17.64$

$\therefore$ r = 4.2 cm.

61. (b) $\because$ $\Delta ABC \sim \Delta DEF$
Since,

$$\frac{\text{Perimeter of } \Delta ABC}{\text{Perimeter of } \Delta DEF} = \frac{AB}{DE} = \frac{18}{10} = \frac{9}{5}$$

$\therefore$ Ratio of perimeter = 9 : 5

62. (b) According to question,
Speed of cars = 36 km/hr and 48 km/hr
So,
$36 \times t = 48(t-3)$
$36t = 48t - 48 \times 3$
$12t = 48 \times 3$
$\therefore$ $t = \frac{48 \times 3}{12} = 12$ hours
$\therefore$ Distance = $12 \times 36 = 432$ km.

63. (a) Let selling price of each watches = ₹ 1
$\therefore$ Selling price of 13 watches = 13
$\because$ Profit = 3 × selling pric of watches
$= 3 \times 1 = 3$.
$\therefore$ Cost price of 13 wateres = (13 – 3) = 10
$\therefore$ Profit percentage $= \frac{3}{10} \times 100 = 30\%$

64. (c) Here,
$20x + 5y = 3$
$\Rightarrow 5y = -20x + 3$
$\therefore y = -4x + \frac{3}{5}$
Slope of 20x + 5y = 3 Þ –4
We know, product of slopes = –1 for perpendicular lines
Hence, the slope of the line which passes through (–2, 5) and (6, b) $= \frac{b-5}{6-(-2)}$
Now,
$$\frac{b-5}{6+2} = \frac{1}{4}$$
$\Rightarrow$ $b - 5 = 2$
$\therefore$ $b = 5 + 2 = 7$

65. (b) n = 12
$\therefore$ Sum of interior angle of dodecagon
$= 180(n-2)$
$= 180(12-2)$
$= 180 \times 10$
$= 1800°$.

66. (b) Work done by A in 20 days $= \frac{80}{100} = \frac{4}{5}$

Work done by A in 1 day $= \frac{4}{5 \times 20} = \frac{1}{25}$ ...(i)

Work done by A and B in 4 days $= \frac{20}{100} = \frac{1}{5}$

(Because remaining 20% is done in 4 days by A and B).
$\therefore$ Work done by A and B in 1 day
$= \frac{1}{5 \times 4} = \frac{1}{20}$ ...(ii)
$\therefore$ Work done by B in 1 day $= \frac{1}{20} - \frac{1}{25} = \frac{1}{100}$
$\therefore$ B can complete the work in 100 days.

67. (b) Area of circle = 616 sqcm.
$\pi r^2 = 616$
$\frac{22}{7} \times r^2 = 616$
$r^2 = \frac{616 \times 7}{22} = 196$ cm
$\therefore$ r = 14 cm
$\therefore$ Circumference of circle = $2\pi r$
$= 2 \times \frac{22}{7} \times 14 = 88$ cm.

68. (a) $3x - 8(2-x) = -19$
$3x - 16 + 8x = -19$
$11x = -3$
$\therefore$ $x = \frac{-3}{11}$

69. (a) Here,
$x - y = 6$, $xy = 40$, $x^2 + y^2 = ?$
$(x-y)^2 = (6)^2$
$x^2 + y^2 - 2.x.y = 36$
$\therefore$ $x^2 + y^2 = 36 + 2xy$
$\Rightarrow$ $36 + 2 \times 40$
$= 116$

70. (a) Let digit at ten's place be x and digit at unit's place be y.
$\therefore$ The number = 10x + y
When digit are interchanged, the new number
= 10y + x
According to question,
Product of digits = 27 i.e., xy = 27 ...(i)
Also,
$10x + y + 54 = 10y + x$

$9x-9y=-54$
$x-y=-6$
$\therefore\ x=y-6$ ...(ii)
From (i) and (ii),
$y(y-6)=27$
$y^2-6y-27=0$
$y^2-9y+3y-27=0$
$(y-9)(y+3)=0$
$\therefore\ y=9$ or $y-3$
$\therefore\ x=3$
When x = 3, and y = 9
$\therefore$ Required number = $10x+y$
$=10\times3+9$
$\Rightarrow\ 30+9=39.$

71. (b) Here,
$2x-3(2x-2)>x-1<2+2x$
$2x-6x+6>x-1$
$\Rightarrow\ 2x-6x-x>-7$
$\Rightarrow\ -5x>-7$
$x<7/5$ ...(i)
$(x-1)<(2+2x)$
$x-1<2+2x$
$-3<x$ ...(ii)
From (i) and (ii),
$x=-2.$

72. (c) $\because$ Number of employees = (3 + 8 + 4) = 15
$\therefore$ Total bonus of all employees

$$=\left(\frac{3\times30\times30}{100}+\frac{8\times16\times20}{100}+\frac{4\times2\times20}{100}\right)$$

$=27+25.6+1.6$ lakhs
-54.2 lakhs.
$\therefore$ Average bonus

$$=\frac{5420000}{15}=361333.33\approx361333$$

73. (a) Total exports from the three companies together in 2011
= (3000 + 1000 + 4000) = 8000
Total exports from the three companies together in 2012
= (5000 +1000 + 2000) = 8000
Total export from the three companies together in 2013
= (4000 + 1000 + 2000) = 7000.
Total export from three companies together in 2014
= (5000 + 2000 + 2000) = 9000
Total export from the three companies together in 2015
= (5000 + 2000 + 3000) = 10000.
So, Total export from the three companies together in 2011 and 2012 are equal.

74. (c) Loss of ₹ 15 crores in last 5 years.

75. (c) Export of Jewellery in 2015 = 675
Total exports in 2015 = (675 + 500 + 525 + 575 + 725) = 3000
$\therefore$ Required percentage

$$=\frac{675\times100}{3000}=22.5\%$$

77. (b) An outline representing or bounding the shape or form of something is called 'contour'.
Other options are incorrect. Tracery means a pattern of lines and curves in stone on the top part of some church window. Doodle refers to lines and shapes drawn in a haphazard manner. Pattern refers to the regular way in which something happens or is done.

78. (a) There is incorrect use of idiom 'as soon as' in this part. The sentence should begin with "As soon as he ...".

79. (b) The sentence begins with 'we are told that its' use of 'its' here indicates that the following fragment should contain something which relates to 'its'.
So option 'R' suitably fits here followed by fragments 'Q' and 'P' respectively.

80. (b) 'Scabbard' is the only correctly spelt word which means a cover for a sword.
Correct spellings of other words are as follows:
Lammented → Lamented
Ordenance → Ordinance
Synaptick → Synaptic

81. (c) Since the given sentence is in past tense, it will be changed to past perfect tense in indirect speech; Gokul asked Sumit why he had not attended the meeting the day before.

82. (d) 'To lose one's head' means to lose sense and/or start behaving like a lunatic.

83. (a) A person famous and respected within a particular sphere is known as 'eminent'. Other options are incorrect. 'Obsense' means someone/something not well known, 'despotic' refers to dictatorial and 'imperative' means very important and needs immediate attention.

84. (c) The correct sentence in passive voice is: Suresh will be invited by us.

85. (d) 'Amenable' means 'easy to control' or some one who can be easily influenced. Options (a), (b) and (c) are synonyms of the word, hence are incorrect. Option (d) means opposite of the word 'amenable', hence it is the right answer.

86. (d) 'Subsume' means to include something in a particular group. The word 'incorporate' also has similar meaning. So option (d) is the correct answer.

87. (b) 'I prefer black coffee to cappuccino' is the correct usage of preposition 'to' here. So option (b) is the correct answer.

88. (b) In part of 'B' of the sentence there is incorrect use of the phrase. The correct phrase should be 'look down on' which means to undervalue or disregard something.

89. (a) The bracketed part, 'to answer on', is incorrect usage. The correct usage is 'to answer'. So, option (a) is the right answer.

90. (c) To lash means to hit something with great force. The word 'chastise' refers to punishing somebody physically. It is a synonym of the word 'lash'. So option (c) is the right answer.

91. (c) 'Expertise' refers to expert knowledge or skill in a particular subject or activity. 'Financial expertise' is the correct usage in the given context. So option (c) is the correct answer.

92. (d) 'Exploit' means to treat someone unfairly to get benefit for yourself. In the given context, it is the most appropriate usage of the word. So, option (d) is the correct answer.

93. (c) 'To muster' means to gather or aggregate things whereas 'to estrange' means to isolate or alienate. It is an antonym of the given word. So option (c) is the right answer.

94. (d) To fall 'head over heels in love' with someone means you love the person very much. So, option (d) is the correct answer.

95. (a) 'R' should be the first sentence fragment as it contains a subject 'the poor'. Next fragment should be 'p' as it tells what the subject does. 'Q' should be last fragment as it contains 'object' of the sentence. So sequence 'RPQ' is the righ answer.

96. (c) Since the sentence refers to something that has happened in present tense. So the its verb form should be in present perfect tense. Only option (c) is in the appropriate tense. So, it is the right answer.

97. (c) The 'of' after the blank indicates that there should be a noun in the blank. In the given context 'emergence of powerful internet monopolies' makes the most sense. So (c) is the correct answer.

98. (b) There is comparative form 'bigger' before the blank. It should be followed by 'than' to make the sentence correct. So, option (b) is the correct answer.

99. (a) In the given context, 'Virtues of monopoly' is the correct usage. So, option (a) is the right answer.

100. (d) The phrase 'freeze out' means to prevent someone from taking part in something. In the given context its use is appropriate. So, option (d) is the right answer.

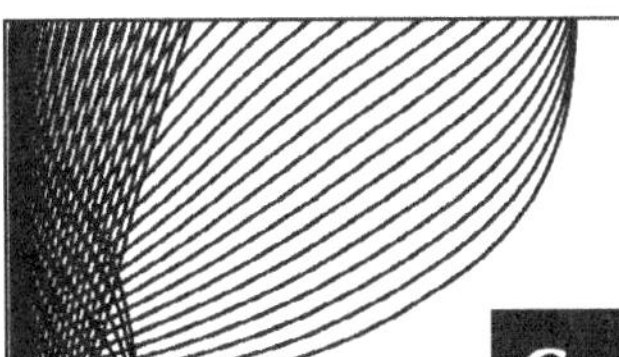

SSC

Combined Higher Secondary Level Exam-2015

Time : 2 Hours | **Held on : 06-12-2015** | **Max. Marks : 200**

PART I : GENERAL INTELLIGENCE

1. From the given alternative words, select the word which cannot be formed using the letters of the given word.
HARBINGER
(a) GARBAGE (b) RANGER
(c) BARRING (d) GARNER

2. From the given alternative words, select the word which be formed using the letters of the given word.
ENDEARMENT
(a) TEMPER (b) MEANS
(c) TENDER (d) TENT

3. If BOY is represented as 42, then GIRL is represented as :
(a) 46 (b) 48
(c) 40 (d) 43

DIRECTIONS (Qs. 4-12) : *Select the related word/ letters/ number from the given alternatives.*

4. 6 : 42 :: 5 : ?
(a) 40 (b) 30
(c) 35 (d) 45

5. Hockey : India :: Baseball :?
(a) USA (b) Russia
(c) Australia (d) China

6. Ant : Fly : Bee :: Hamster : Squirrel : ?
(a) Rodent (b) Mouse
(c) Cat (d) Spider

7. 144 : 13 : : 49 : ?
(a) 8 (b) 10
(c) 11 (d) 9

8. ABDE : GHJK :: MNPQ : ?
(a) RTUW (b) STVX
(c) CEFH (d) RSUV

9. ACE : GIK : : MOQ : ?
(a) SUW (b) VXZ
(c) RTU (d) STU

10. GNIDAER : READING :: NOITULOS :?
(a) Solunoit (b) Nailosut
(c) Pollution (d) Solution

11. Brick : Wall : : Cell :?
(a) Chlorophyll (b) Organs
(c) DNA (d) Tissue

12. 21 : 3 :: 574 : ?
(a) 23 (b) 82
(c) 113 (d) 97

DIRECTIONS (Qs. 13-21): *Find the odd word/letters/ number pair from the given alternatives.*

13. (a) GLOVES (b) SWEATER
(c) SHAWL (d)
UMBRELLA

14. (a) PORTRAIT (b) DRAW
(c) PAINT (d) SKETCH

15. (a) HAND (b) NOSE
(c) MOUTH (d) EYES

16. (a) 6 : 22 (b) 8 : 25
(c) 13 : 40 (d) 15 : 46

17. (a) 21 (b) 81
(c) 71 (d) 51

18. (a) HNOP (b) VUTS
(c) RQPO (d) HGFE

19. (a) D卍ST (b) Q37Q
(c) N⌉_⌈OP (d) KZM⌉┼⌈

20. (a) 100 (b) 125
(c) 343 (d) 216

21. (a) VXB (b) PSV
(c) DGJ (d) FIL

DIRECTIONS (Qs. 22-25): *A series is given, with one/two term missing. Choose the correct alternatives from the given ones that will complete the series.*

22. 6, 2, 9, 4, 12, –, –

(a) 6, 15 (b) 4, 13
(c) 8, 24 (d) 13, 15

23. A D H M S ?

(a) T (b) W
(c) X (d) Z

24. –1, 0, 3, 8, 15, ?

(a) 23 (b) 26
(c) 24 (d) 25

25. ACEZXVGIKTRP ?

(a) M (b) N
(c) O (d) L

DIRECTIONS (Qs. 26-28): *Select the missing number from the given responses.*

26.

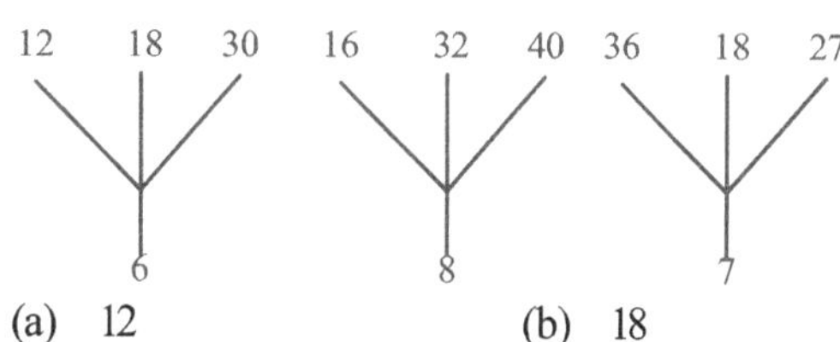

(a) 12 (b) 18
(c) 6 (d) 9

27.

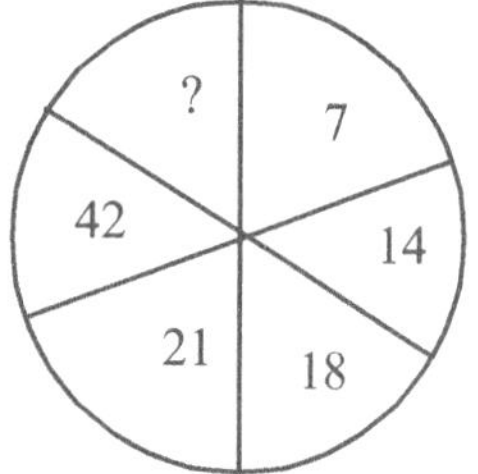

(a) 58 (b) 45
(c) 54 (d) 42

28.

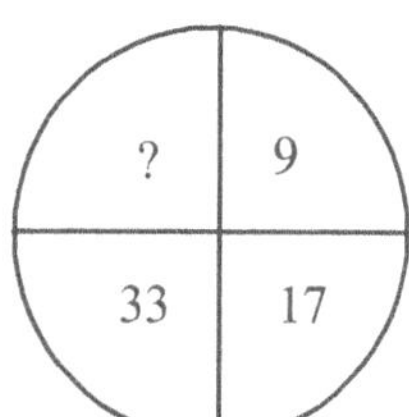

(a) 60 (b) 65
(c) 68 (d) 55

29. In a line, Naresh is 17th from the left & 22nd from the right. How many students are there in the line ?

(a) 40 (b) 38
(c) 39 (d) 37

30. Some equations have been solved on the basis of certain system. Find the correct answer for the unsolved equations on that basis ?

If $72 \times 19 = 23$, $13 \times 48 = 35$ and $16 \times 43 = 18$ then $39 \times 22 = ?$

(a) 27 (b) 51
(c) 31 (d) 21

31. Which one set of letters when sequentially placed at the gaps in the given letter series shall complete it ?

ab_cba_bcc_aabccb_ _ bccba

(a) abbac (b) cccab
(c) cabaa (d) abcab

32. From the given answer figures, select the one in which the question figure is hidden/ embedded.

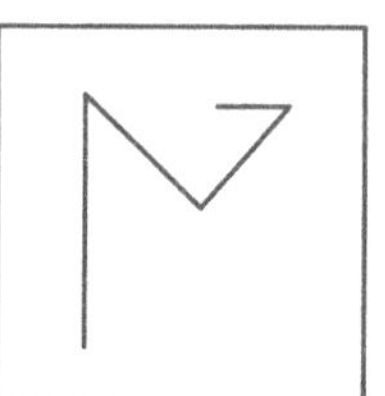

(a) 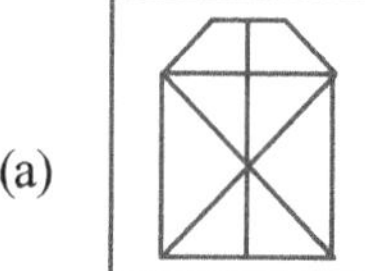

(b) 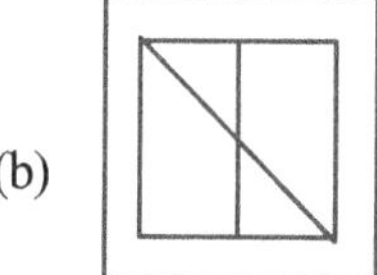

(c) 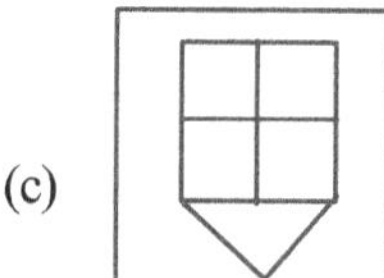

(d) 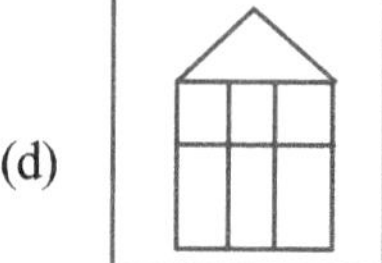

33. If LISTEN is coded as 593417 then SILENT is code as :
(a) 591734 (b) 391754
(c) 591743 (d) 395174

34. What is the best way to order the progression in Hardware ?
1. Silicon chips 2. Transistors
3. Vacuum tube 4. Integrated circuits.
(a) 3, 4, 1, 2 (b) 4, 2, 3, 1
(c) 4, 1, 3, 2 (d) 3, 2, 4, 1

35. Of the 5 towns A, B, C, D and E situated close to each other. A is to the west of B,C is to the south of A, E is to the north of B and D is to the east of E. Then C is in which direction with respect to D?
(a) South–West (b) North–West
(c) North–East (d) South–East

36. Karthik travelled 3 km east, then took a right and travelled 4 kms. How far is he from starting point ?
(a) 12 kms (b) 3 kms
(c) 7 kms (d) 5 kms

37. Find the number of triangles in the following figure :

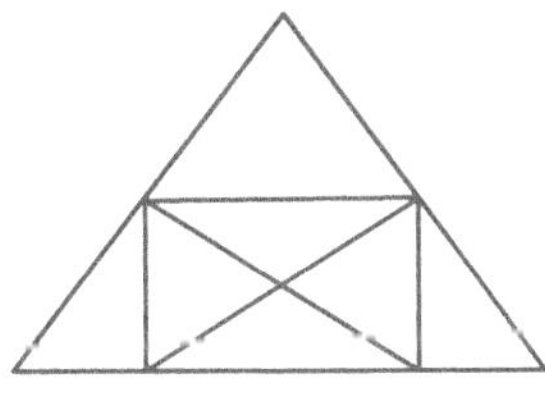

(a) 8 (b) 14
(c) 10 (d) 12

38. Find out the set of numbers amongst the four sets of numbers given in the alternative which is most like the set given in the question. (12, 24, 144)
(a) (15, 45, 90) (b) (10, 25, 100)
(c) (14, 28, 112) (d) (13, 26, 169)

DIRECTIONS (Qs. 39 & 40): *One/ two statement are given, each followed by two conclusion/ assumption, I and II. You have to consider the statement to be true even if they seem to be at variance from commonly known facts. You have to decide which of the given conclusion/ assumptions, if any, follows from the given statements.*

39. **Statement**
Continuous training is essential for all employees to increase their productivity
Assumptions
I. Training is an essential component for productivity.
II. Profitability & productivity are supplementary to each other.
(a) Only assumption II is implicit
(b) Neither assumption I nor II are implicit.
(c) Both assumption I and II are implicit
(d) Assumption I is implicit.

40. **Statement**
Travelling by metro in Delhi is more convenient and economical.
Assumptions
I. Other modes of transport are not available.
II. Metro services are reasonably good.
(a) Only assumption I is implicit
(b) Neither I nor II are implicit.
(c) Both I and II are implicit
(d) Only assumption II is implicit.

41. In a class of 45, Neha's rank is 15th from first, what is her rank from the last ?
(a) 30 (b) 32
(c) 33 (d) 31

42. If + means ÷, ÷ means ×, and × means +, then following will be :
$64 + 8 \times 32 \div 4$
(a) 128
(b) 160
(c) 136
(d) 144

43. A word is represented by only one set of numbers as given in any one of the alternatives. The sets of numbers given in the alternatives are represented by two classes of alphabets as in two matrices given below. The columns and rows of Matrix I are numbered from 0 to 4 and that of Matrix II are numbered from 5 to 9. A letter from these matrices can be represented first by its row and next by its column, e.g. 'A' can be represented by 03, 14 etc, and 'L' can be represented by 56, 65 etc. Similarly, you have to identify the set for the word 'BRIDE'.

MATRIX – I

	0	1	2	3	4
0	E	S	P	A	R
1	R	E	S	P	A
2	A	R	E	S	P
3	P	A	R	E	S
4	S	P	A	R	E

MATRIX–II

	5	6	7	8	9
5	B	U	I	L	D
6	U	I	L	D	B
7	I	L	D	B	U
8	L	D	B	U	I
9	D	B	U	I	L

(a) 96, 03, 75, 67, 22
(b) 55, 57, 21, 22, 86
(c) 96, 03, 75, 85, 22
(d) 55, 21, 57, 86, 22

DIRECTIONS (Qs. 44-45): *Arrange the following words as per order in the dictionary.*

44. 1. Voracious 2. Voucher
3. Vortex 4. Voluntary
(a) 2, 4, 1, 3 (b) 4, 1, 3, 2
(c) 1, 4, 2, 3 (d) 3, 1, 4, 2

45. 1. Absolute 2. Abrasive
3. Absorption 4. Abundance
5. Abiogenesis
(a) 2, 5, 1, 3,, 4 (b) 3, 4, 5, 2, 1
(c) 5, 2, 3, 1, 4 (d) 5, 2, 1, 3, 4

46. Which answer figure will complete the pattern in the question figure ?

(a) 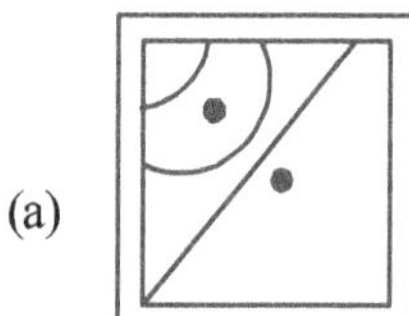

(b) 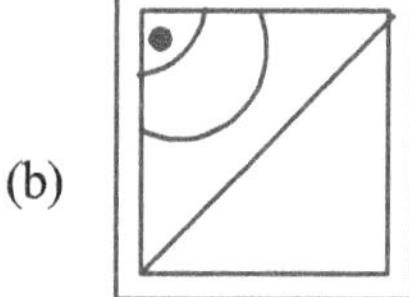

(c) 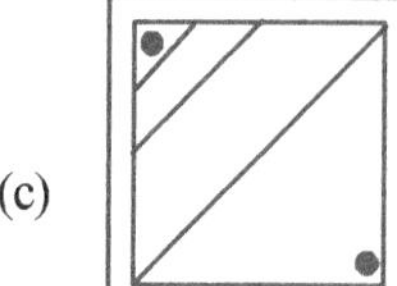

(d) 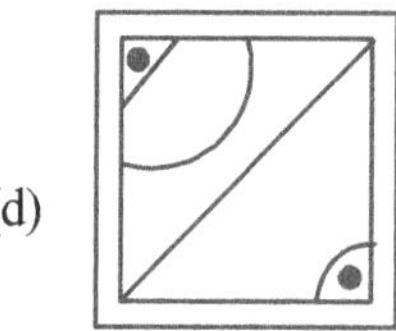

47. Identify the diagram that best represents the relationship among classes given below :
Athletes, Sprinters, Marathon runner

(a) 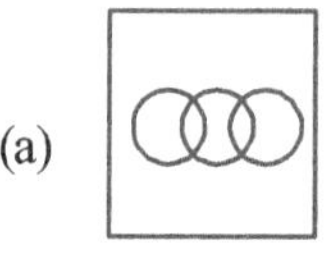
(b) 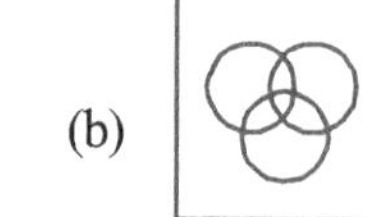
(c) 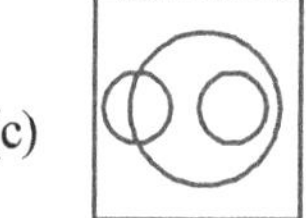
(d) 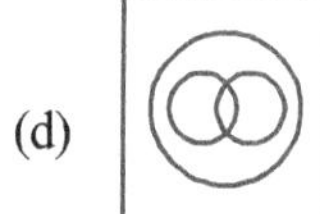

48. A piece of paper is folded and punched as shown below in the question figures. From the given answer figures, indicate how it will appear when opened.

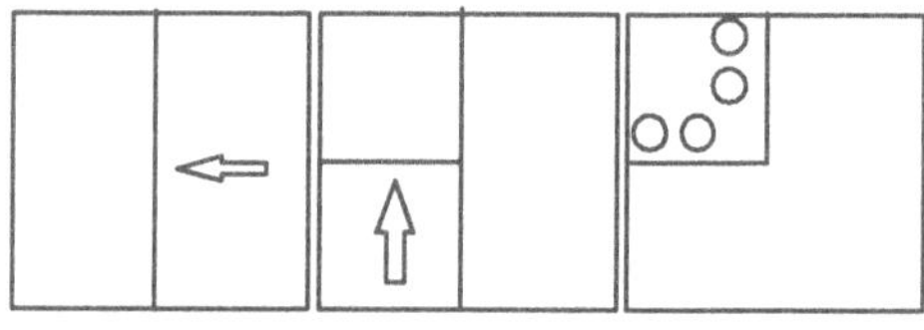

(a) 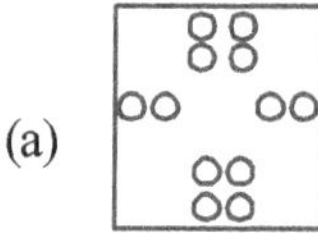
(b) 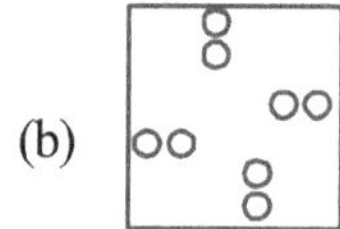
(c) 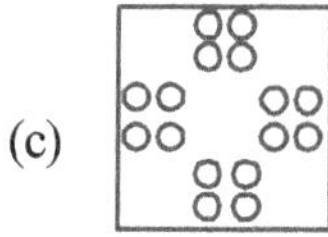
(d) 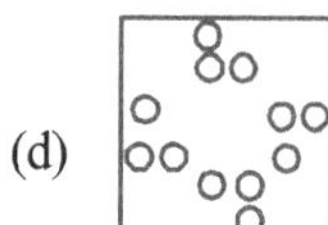

49. Which one of the following is water image of "COMMISSION"?
(a) NOISSIMMOƆ
(b) COMMI ƧƧIOИ
(c) CO MMIƧƧIOИ
(d) NOISSIMMOƆ

50. Find the wrong number in the given series ?
15, 28, 30, 39, 48
(a) 28 (b) 15
(c) 30 (d) 39

PART II : ENGLISH LANGUAGE

DIRECTIONS (Qs. 51-54): *Out of the four alternatives, choose the one which can be substituted for the given words/sentences and indicate it by blackening the appropriate circle in the Answer Sheet.*

51. Submission to all that happens as inevitable.
(a) Fatalism (b) Pragmatism
(c) Pessimism (d) Superstition

52. A person who is easily deceived or tricked.
(a) Trickster (b) Trouble
(c) Tangible (d) Gullible

53. Lasting for a very short time.
(a) Friable (b) Ephemeral
(c) Metronomic (d) Eternal

54. Rules governing socially acceptable behaviour.
(a) Etiquette (b) Politeness
(c) Formality (d) Behaviour

DIRECTIONS (Qs. 55-56) : *A sentence has been given in Direct/Indirect. Out of the four alternatives suggested, select the one which best expresses the same sentence in Indirect/Direct and mark your answer in the Answer sheet.*

55. I said to him, "Do you definitely need the suit next week?"
(a) I asked him if he definitely needed the suit the following week.
(b) I asked him if he needed the suit the next week.
(c) I asked him if he definitely need the suit the following week.
(d) I asked him if definitely he needed he suit the next week.

56. Meera's mother told her not to forget to buy the milk.
(a) Meera's mother reminded her, "Don't forget to buy the milk".
(b) Meera's mother said to her, "Your must buy the milk".
(c) Meera was told by her mother "Buy the milk."
(d) Meera's mother said "Remember to buy the milk."

DIRECTIONS (Qs. 57-66) : *In the following passage some of the words have been left out. Read the passage carefully and choose the correct answer to each question out of the four alternative and fill in the blanks.*

Although we can __I__ the __II__ bodies of our solar system __III__ a telescope, it is only __IV__ who can __V__ the depth of outer space. It is reported that they have seen __VI__ galaxies, stars taking __VII__ and __VIII__, and 'black holes'. They say that the deeper they look __IX__ the universe, the more they know __X__ the universe originated.

57. (a) (I) reach (b) (I) observe
(c) (I) look (d) (I) find

58. (a) (II) heaver (b) (II) heavy
(c) (II) heavier (d) (II) heavenly

59. (a) (III) by (b) (III) through
(c) (III) with (d) (III) at

60. (a) (IV) astronomers (b) (IV) astronomy
(c) (IV) Stunned (d (IV) astrologers

61. (a) (V) viewed (b) (V) views
(c) (V) overview (d) (V) view

62. (a) (VI) shine (b) (VI) stunning
(c) (VI) stunned (d) (VI) stun

63. (a) (VII) born (b) (VII) borne
(c) (VII) birth (d) (VII) berth

64. (a) (VIII) die (b) (VIII) died
(c) (VIII) dyeing (d) (VIII) dying

65. (a) (IX) into (b) (IX) at
(c) (IX) through (d) (IX) on

66. (a) (X) why (b) (X) where
(c) (X) how (d) (X) what

DIRECTIONS (Qs. 67-70): *Four alternatives are given for the Idiom/Phrase underlined. Choose the alternative which best expresses the meaning of the Idiom/Phrase and mark it in the Answer Sheet.*

67. <u>A Sacred Cow</u>
(a) a person never to be criticised
(b) a saintly person
(c) a very religious person
(d) a helpful person

68. <u>To shun evil company</u>
(a) To kick out evil company
(b) To give up evil company
(c) To put off evil company
(d) To let loose evil company

69. He has made a dog's breakfast of these accounts.
(a) A total mess
(b) A breakfast for the dogs..
(c) An accurate summary
(d) A breakbast being served by the dogs

70. You will be reminded of the seamy side of life if you visit the slum tenements.
(a) the softer aspects
(b) the impleasant aspects
(c) the pleasanter aspects
(d) the gentler aspects

DIRECTIONS (Qs. 71-74) : *Sentences are given with blanks to be filled in with an appropriate word(s). Four alternatives are suggested for each question. Choose the correct alternative out of the four and indicate it by blackening the appropriate circle in the Answer Sheet.*

71. This house ________ ten rooms
(a) consisted with (b) consist of
(c) consists of (d) consists by

72. Have you even _____ the wolf cry ?
(a) heard (b) heard of
(c) hear out (d) hear

73. Afreen _______ that the weather was very pleasant that day ?
(a) suggested (b) argued
(c) announced (d) remarked

74. Mrs. Hall was prepared to excuse the scientist's strange habits and _______ temper.
(a) irritate (b) irate
(c) irritable (d) irritation

DIRECTIONS (Qs. 75-78): *Choose the word opposite in meaning to the given word and mark it in the Answer Sheet.*

75. Illicit
(a) legal (b) correct
(c) approved (d) noble

76. Demand
(a) supply (b) claim
(c) request (d) petition

77. Descent
(a) discern (b) ascent
(c) dissent (d) assent

78. Notorious
(a) prominent (b) infamous
(c) honourable (d) reputed

DIRECTIONS (Qs. 79-82): *Four words are given in each question, out of which only one word is correctly spelt. Find the correctly spelt word and mark your answer in the Answer sheet.*

79. (a) prediliction (b) predilection
(c) predalection (d) pridilection

80. (a) accumulate (b) acummulate
(c) accumullate (d) secummulate

81. (a) restaurent (b) restuarant
(c) resturent (d) restaurant

82. (a) manoeuvre (b) manouvre
(c) manuvere (d) manouevr

DIRECTIONS (Qs. 83-86): *A sentence/ a part of the sentence is underlined. Below are given alternatives to the underlined part which may improve the sentence. Choose the correct alternative. In case no improvement is needed choose "No improvement".*

83. Rani has completed her graduation from a reputed university last year.
(a) completed
(b) No Improvement
(c) was completed
(d) had been compelted

84. The terrorist as well as his accomplices was killed in the encounter.
(a) was being killed
(b) were killed
(c) No improvement
(d) have been killed

85. The Councillor behaves as if he is the Chief Minister.
(a) has been (b) were
(c) No improvement (d) was

86. Inspite of age he is my senior.
(a) He is my senior, in keeping with his age.
(b) He is my senior in regard of his age.
(c) No improvement
(d) In respect of age, he is my senior.

DIRECTIONS (Qs. 87-90): *The 1st and the last part of the sentence are numbered 1 and 6. The rest of the sentence is split is into four parts and named P, Q, R & S. These four parts are not given in their proper order. Read the sentence and find out which of the four combinations is correct. Then find the correct answer and indicate it in the Answer Sheet.*

87. 1. Everyone
P. the case calmly
Q. acknowledges
R. who knows you
S. when he considers
6. that you have been wronged.
(a) PSQR (b) QRSP
(c) SRPQ (d) RQSP

88. 1. It is those good works
P. that lead to peak performance
Q. which we do with passion
R. our understanding of our purpose
S. and which come to reflect
6. in this life.
(a) PRQS (b) QPSR
(c) QSRP (d) SRQP

89. 1. I am a self confessed technophobe.
P. I believe that computer is responsible for the dying of the art of conversation.
Q. I have come to hate technology and the way it dominates every aspect of life.
R. For many, it has become the most important object both in home and at the workplace.
S. One of the worst offenders is the computer.
6. Small wonder then, that I have managed to keep this ubiquitous machine out of my home.
(a) PQRS (b) QSRP
(c) RPSQ (d) SRPQ

90. 1. Moisturisers for the face
P. as oily ones may block
Q. in greater concentration on the face
R. the oil glands found
S. should be chosen carefully.
6. and cause pimple/acne to break out.
(a) SRPQ (b) SQPR
(c) SPRQ (d) SPQR

DIRECTIONS (Qs. 91-94): *Some parts of the sentences have errors and some are correct. Find out which part of a sentence has an error and blacken the circle corresponding to the appropriate correct option. If a sentence is free from error, blacken the circle corresponding to "No error" option in the Answer Sheet.*

91. Scientist now hope that cloning can successfully be conducted in human beings in the near future.
(a) human beings in the near future.
(b) can successfully be conducted in
(c) Scientists now hope that cloning
(d) No Error

92. When one takes great risks they must be prepared for great losses.
(a) When one takes great risks
(b) No Error
(c) they must be prepared
(d) for great losses.

93. What delicious flavour these mangoes have!
(a) have!
(b) What delicious
(c) flavour these mangoes
(d) No Error

94. They had to put of the garden party because of the heavy rain.
(a) because of the heavy rain
(b) No Error
(c) They had to
(d) put of the garden party

DIRECTIONS (Qs. 95-98): *Out of the four alternatives, choose the one which best expresses the meaning of the given word and mark it in the Answer Sheet.*

95. Vocation
(a) virtue (b) holiday
(c) break up (d) occupation

96. Limpid
(a) ruffled (b) crippled
(c) lopsided (d) clear

97. Merge
(a) blend (b) meet
(c) mixture (d) contact

98. Gourmet
(a) fussy (b) constant
(c) gastronome (d) praise

DIRECTIONS (Qs. 99 & 100): *A sentence has been given in Active/ Passive Voice. Out of the four alternatives suggested, select the one which best expresses the same sentence in Passive/Active Voice and mark your answer in the Answer Sheet.*

99. Please close the door.
(a) Please be the door closed by you
(b) Let the door be closed by you.
(c) You please close the door.
(d) You close the door yourself.

100. We must take care of our parents.
(a) Our parents will be taken care of by us.
(b) Our parents are taken care of by us.
(c) Our parents must be cared for by us.
(d) Our parents had been taken care of by us.

PART III : QUANTITATIVE APTITUDE

101. In ΔABC, $\angle B = 60°$, and $\angle C = 40°$; AD and AE are respectively the bisector of $\angle A$ and perpendicular on BC. The measure of $\angle EAD$ is :
(a) 9° (b) 11°
(c) 12° (d) 10°

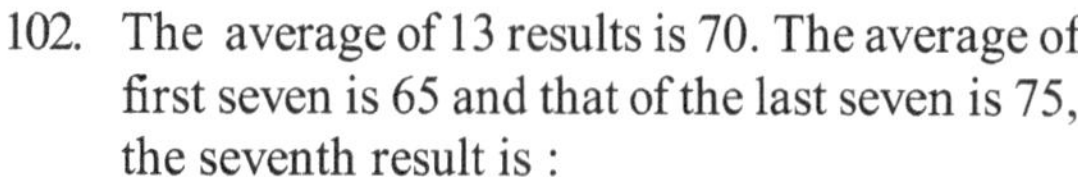

102. The average of 13 results is 70. The average of first seven is 65 and that of the last seven is 75, the seventh result is :
(a) 70 (b) 70.5
(c) 68 (d) 67

103. A contractor was engaged to construct a road in 16 days. After working for 12 days with 20 labours it was found that only 5/8th of the road had been constructed. To complete the work in stipulated time the number of extra labours required is :
(a) 12 (b) 10
(c) 18 (d) 16

104. If $p = -0.12$, $q = -0.01$ & $r = -0.015$, then the correct relationship among the three is :
(a) $q > p > r$ (b) $p > q > r$
(c) $p > r > q$ (d) $p < r < q$

DIRECTIONS (Qs. 105-108): *The Expenditure of a family in a month is represented by a Pie–chart. Read it and answer thee questions.*

105. The ratio of the amount spent on food and clothes ?
(a) 2 : 5 (b) 4 : 1
(c) 4 : 5 (d) 5 : 1

106. The % money spent on food compared to house rent is by?
(a) 12.5% (b) None of the options
(c) 25% (d) 50%

107. The total money spent on clothes and miscellaneous items are :
(a) None of the options (b) ₹3600
(c) ₹900 (d) ₹2000

108. If the total amount spent is ₹ 7,200. Find the amount spent on food ?
(a) ₹3000 (b) ₹4500
(c) ₹6000 (d) ₹1500

109. If $a = \dfrac{\sqrt{3}-\sqrt{2}}{\sqrt{3}+\sqrt{2}}$ and $b = \dfrac{\sqrt{3}+\sqrt{2}}{\sqrt{3}-\sqrt{2}}$, then the value of $\dfrac{a^2}{b}+\dfrac{b^2}{a}$ is :
(a) 970 (b) 930
(c) 1030 (d) 1025

DIRECTIONS (Qs. 110-114): *Study the following bar graph and answer the questions.*

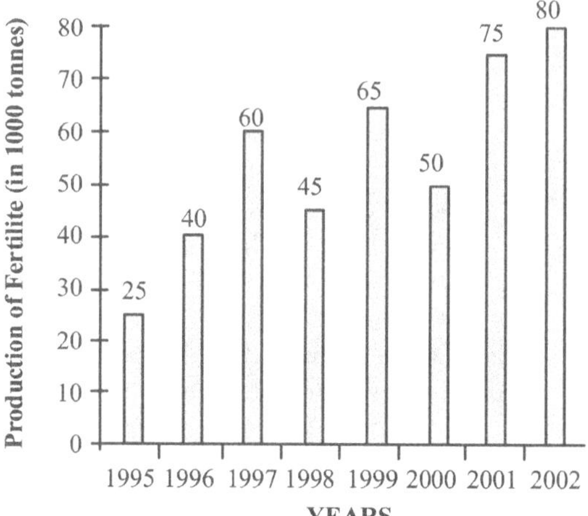

110. The number of years, the production of fertilizers was more than average production of the given years is :
(a) 2 (b) 1
(c) 3 (d) 4

111. The percentage increase in production of fertilizers in 2002 compared to that in 1995 is :
(a) 200% (b) 180%
(c) 220% (d) 240%

112. The percentage decline in the production of fetilizers from 1997 to 1998 is :
(a) 27.5% (b) 25%
(c) 26% (d) 23%

113. The average production of 1996 and 1997 is exactly equal to the average production of the years ?
(a) 2000 and 2001
(b) 1999 and 2000
(c) 1995 and 2001
(d) 1995 and 1999

114. The percentage increase in production as compared to previous year is maximum in year :
(a) 1999 (b) 1996
(c) 1997 (d) 2002

115. If for non–zero x, $x^2 - 4x - 1 - 0$ the value of $x^2 - \dfrac{1}{x^2}$ is :
(a) 10 (b) 4
(c) 12 (d) 18

116. The length of two parallel sides of a trapezium are 15 cm and 20 cm. If its area is 175 sq. cm, then its height is :
(a) 10 cm (b) 15 cm
(c) 25 cm (d) 20 cm

117. A hemispherical bowl has internal radius of 6 cm. The internal surface area would be : (take π =3.14)
(a) 400 cm^2 (b) 289.75 cm^2
(c) 225 cm^2 (d) 226.08 cm^2

118. A train 150 m long passes a km stone in 30 seconds and another train of the same length travelling in opposite direction in 10 seconds. The speed of the second train is :
(a) 125 km/hr (b) 25 km/hr
(c) 90 km/hr (d) 75 km/hr

119. If water is freezed to become ice, its volume is increased by 10%, then if the ice is melted to water again, its volume will be decreased by :
(a) 8% (b) $9\frac{1}{2}\%$
(c) 9% (d) $9\frac{1}{11}\%$

120. The simplified value of following is :
$$\left(\frac{3}{15}a^5b^5c^3 \times \frac{5}{9}ab^5c^4\right) \div \frac{10}{27}a^2bc^3$$
(a) $\frac{9}{10}a^2bc^4$ (b) $\frac{1}{10}a^4b^4c^{10}$
(c) $\frac{3}{10}a^4b^{10}c^4$ (d) $\frac{3}{10}ab^4c^3$

121. A number of boys raised ₹ 12,544 for a famine fund, each boy has given as many rupees as there were boys. The number of boys was:
(a) 122 (b) 132
(c) 112 (d) 102

122. The value of x in the equation
$$\tan^2\frac{\pi}{4} - \cos^2\frac{\pi}{3} - x\sin\frac{\pi}{4}\cos\frac{\pi}{4}\tan\frac{\pi}{3} \text{ is :}$$
(a) $\frac{\sqrt{3}}{2}$ (b) $\frac{3\sqrt{3}}{4}$
(c) $\frac{2}{\sqrt{3}}$ (d) $\frac{1}{\sqrt{3}}$

123. ABCD is a square. Draw a triangle QBC on side BC considering BC as base and draw a triangle PAC on AC as its base such that $\Delta QBC \sim \Delta PAC$.
Then $\frac{\text{Area of } \Delta QBC}{\text{Area of } \Delta PAC}$ is equal to:
(a) $\frac{2}{1}$ (b) $\frac{1}{3}$
(c) $\frac{1}{2}$ (d) $\frac{2}{3}$

124. The current ages of Sonali and Monali are in the ratio 5 : 3. Five years from now, their ages will be in the ratio 10 : 7. Then, Monali's current age is:
(a) 9 years (b) 15 years
(c) 3 years (d) 5 years

125. The compound interest on ₹12000 for 9 months at 20% per annum, interest being compounded quarterly is :
(a) ₹1750 (b) ₹1891.50
(c) ₹2136.40 (d) ₹2089.70

126. Value of the expression :
$$\frac{1+2\sin 60°\cos 60°}{\sin 60° + \cos 60°} + \frac{1-2\sin 60°\cos 60°}{\sin 60° - \cos 60°}$$
(a) 0 (b) 2
(c) $\sqrt{3}$ (d) $2\sqrt{3}$

127. If $\frac{\sin\theta + \cos\theta}{\sin\theta - \cos\theta} = 3$ then the value of $\sin^2\theta$ is :
(a) $\frac{4}{5}$ (b) $\frac{2}{5}$
(c) $\frac{1}{5}$ (d) $\frac{3}{5}$

128. If $\sin 2\theta = \frac{\sqrt{3}}{2}$ then the value of $\sin 3\theta$ is equal to :
(take $(0° \le \theta \le 90°)$)
(a) 0 (b) $\frac{\sqrt{3}}{2}$
(c) 1 (d) $\frac{1}{2}$

129. The volume of the largest right circular cone that can be cut out of a cube of edge 7 cm? $\left(\text{use } \Pi = \frac{22}{7}\right)$
(a) 13.6 cm^3 (b) 121 cm^3
(c) 147.68 cm^3 (d) 89.8 cm^3

130. Two positive whole numbers are such that the sum of the first and twice the second number is 8 and their difference is 2. The numbers are :

(a) 7,5 (b) 6,4
(c) 3,5 (d) 4,2

131. The speed of a car is 54 km/hr. What is its speed in m/sec?
(a) 150 m/sec (b) 19.44 m/sec
(c) 194.4 m/sec (d) 15 m/sec

132. The income of a company increases 20% per annum. If its income is ₹ 26,64,000 in the year 2012, then its income in the year 2010 was :
(a) ₹28,20,000 (b) ₹28,55,,000
(c) ₹18,50,000 (d) ₹21,20,000

133. The distance between centres of two circles of radii 3 cm and 8 cm is 13 cm. If the points of contact of a direct common tangent to the circles are P and Q, then the length of the lien segment PQ is :
(a) 11.9 cm (b) 11.5 cm
(c) 12 cm (d) 11.58 cm

134. A shopkeeper marks his goods 20% higher than the cost price and allows a discount of 5%. The percentage of his profit is :
(a) 14% (b) 15%
(c) 10% (d) 20%

135. In ΔABC, $AB = BC = K$, $AC = \sqrt{2}K$, then ΔABC is a :
(a) Isosceles triangle
(b) Right angled triangle
(c) Equilateral triangle
(d) Right isosceles triangle

136. The smallest five digit number which is divisible by 12, 18 and 21 is :
(a) 50321 (b) 10224
(c) 30256 (d) 10080

137. By selling an article for ₹450. I lose 20%. For what amount, should I sell it to gain 20%?
(a) ₹490 (b) ₹470
(c) ₹562.50 (d) ₹675

138. In an exam the sum of the scores of A and B is 120, that of B and C is 130 and that of C and A is 140. Then the score of C is :
(a) 65 (b) 60
(c) 70 (d) 75

139. If $\alpha + \beta = 90°$ then the expression

$\frac{\tan\alpha}{\tan\beta} + \sin^2\alpha - \sin^2\beta$ is equal to :
(a) $\sec^2\beta$ (b) $\tan^2\beta$
(c) $\sec^2\alpha$ (d) $\tan^2\alpha$

140. Two circles of radii 5 cm and 3 cm touch externally, then the ratio in which the direct common tangent to the circles divides externally the line joining the centres of the circles is :
(a) 2.5 : 1.5 (b) 1.5 : 2.5
(c) 3 : 5 (d) 5 : 3

141. A fruit seller buys oranges at the rate of ₹ 10 per dozen and sells at the rate of ₹12 per dozen. His gain percent is :
(a) 15% (b) 20%
(c) $8\frac{1}{3}\%$ (d) 12%

142. The outer circumference of a circular race–track is 528 metre. The track is everywhere 14 metre wide. Cost of levelling the track at the rate of ₹ 10 per sq. metre is :
(a) ₹77660 (b) ₹76760
(c) ₹66760 (d) ₹67760

143. If $1^3 + 2^3 + ... + 10^3 - 3025$, then the value of $2^3 + 4^3 + ... + 20^3$ is :
(a) 5060 (b) 12100
(c) 24200 (d) 7590

144. The surface area of a sphere is 616 cm^2. The volume of the sphere would be :
(a) 2100 cm^2 (b) 2500 cm^2
(c) $1437\frac{1}{3}$ cm^2 (d) $1225\frac{3}{5}$ cm^2

145. A vessel contains 60 litres of milk. 12 litres of milk taken out from it and replaced by water. Then again from mixture, 12 litres are again taken out and replaced by water. The ratio of milk and water in the resultant mixture is :
(a) 16 : 10 (b) 9 : 5
(c) 15 : 10 (d) 16 : 9

146. If $(2a - 1)^2 + (4b - 3)^2 + (4c + 5)^2 = 0$ then the value of $\frac{a^3 + b^3 + c^3 - 3abc}{a^2 + b^2 + c^2}$ is:
(a) $1\frac{3}{8}$ (b) $3\frac{3}{8}$
(c) $2\frac{3}{8}$ (d) 0

147. A house was sold for ₹ y by giving a discount of x%, then the list price was :
(a) $\frac{100y}{100 - x}$ (b) $\frac{100x}{100 - y}$
(c) $\frac{100y}{1 - x}$ (d) $\frac{100y}{1 - \frac{x}{100}}$

148. If $a+\frac{1}{b}-1$ and $b+\frac{1}{c}-1$ then $c+\frac{1}{a}$ is equal to
(a) 0 (b) 1
(c) 2 (d) $\frac{1}{2}$

149. If 20 women can lay a road of length 100m in 10 days. 10 women can lay the same road of length 50 m in :
(a) 20 days (b) 10 days
(c) 5 days (d) 15 days

150. $83\frac{1}{3}\%$ of ₹90 is equal to 60% of ?
(a) ₹124 (b) ₹125
(c) ₹123 (d) ₹122

PART IV : GENERAL AWARENESS

151. Whose army did Alexander, the Greek ruler confront on the banks of the river Jhelum ?
(a) Ambi
(b) Chandragupta Maurya
(c) Porus
(d) Dhanananda

152. The most suitable soil for the production of cotton is ?
(a) Black lava soil (b) Loamy soil
(c) Well drained soil (d) Alluvial soil

153. The largest producer of Lignite in India is:
(a) Kerala (b) Rajasthan
(c) Tamil Nadu (d) Gujarat

154. When was RTI Act enacted in India ?
(a) 15th August 2005
(b) 15th March 2005
(c) 15th June 2005
(d) 15th July 2005

155. The famous activist Medha Patakar is associated with which movement ?
(a) Narmada Bachao Andolan
(b) Save the Tiger
(c) Preserve the wet lands
(d) Beti Padao Andolan

156. Lender of the Last Resort is :
(a) IDBI (b) NABARD
(c) SBI (d) RBI

157. Sex–ratio is calculated as :
(a) No of females per 1,000 males in a Country
(b) No of males per 1,000 females in a Country
(c) No. of children per 1,000 people in a Country.
(d) No of people per 1,000 children in a Country.

158. Who has been named ICC World Cup 2015 Ambassador?
(a) Sanath Teran Jayasuriya
(b) Allan Robeet Border
(c) Sir Issac Vivian Alexander Richards
(d) Sachin Tendulkar

159. Soldering of two metals is possible because of the property of :
(a) Osmosis
(b) Viscosity
(c) Surface tension
(d) Cohesion

160. Stalactites & Stalagmites form due to the precipitation of :
(a) $CaCl_2$ (b) $MgCO_3$
(c) $MgCl_2$ (d) $CaCO_3$

161. Which of the following is a form of sexual reproduction :
(a) Fission
(b) Fragmentation
(c) Budding
(d) Harmaphroditism

162. Who among the following is not a Bharatanatyam dancer ?
(a) Sitara Devi
(b) Leela Samson
(c) Geeta Ramachandran
(d) Sonal Mansingh

163. The 73rd Constitutional amendment act is related to ?
(a) Panchayat Raj
(b) Foreign Exchange
(c) Finance Commission
(d) RBI

164. Ryder Cup is a famous tournament of :
(a) Badminton (b) Golf
(c) Cricket (d) Lawn Tennis

165. Kanha National Park is located in :
(a) Tamil Nadu
(b) Bihar
(c) Andhra Pradesh
(d) Madhya Pradesh

166. Who wrote 'Discovery of India'?
   (a) Mahatma Gandhi
   (b) Jawahar Lal Nehru
   (c) Bal Gangadhar Tilak
   (d) APJ Abdul Kalam

167. Who is the first woman IPS officer in India ?
   (a) Sarojini Naidu
   (b) Kiran Bedi
   (c) Bachendri Pal
   (d) Indira Gandhi

168. Perfectly inelastic demand is equal to :
   (a) One
   (b) Zero
   (c) Infinite
   (d) Greater than one

169. In which region of electromagnetic spectrum does the Lyman series of hydrogen atom lie ?
   (a) x–ray (b) Ultraviolet
   (c) Visible (d) Infrared

170. Which of the following is the right expansion of ILO?
   (a) International Labour Organization
   (b) Indian Legal Orientation
   (c) Internatioanl Law and Order
   (d) Inter–State Lawful Ordinance

171. Which state of India has made rain water harvesting compulsory for all houses ?
   (a) Tamil Nadu (b) Punjab
   (c) Haryana (d) Maharashtra

172. An electrochemcial cell which is used as a source of direct electrical current at constant voltage under standard conditions is called a :
   (a) Power transistor
   (b) Battery
   (c) Generator
   (d) Uninterrupted power supply (UPS)

173. In 2010 a newspaper published its 70,000th issue. Which was the newspaper ?
   (a) The Oxford Gazette
   (b) The Washington Post
   (c) The Times of London
   (d) The Hindustan Times

174. Impeachment Proceedings against the President for Violation of the Constitution can be initiated in :
   (a) The Supreme Court
   (b) The Rajya Sabha
   (c) Either House of Parliament
   (d) The Lok Sabha

175. Who built the "Purana Quilla"?
   (a) Babar (b) Shershah
   (c) Aurangzeb (d) Akbar

176. The opening ceremony of the ICC Cricket World Cup 2015 was held on 12 February 2015 in which cities of New Zealand and Australia ?
   (a) Christchurch and Melbourne
   (b) Hemilton and Perth
   (c) Napier and Adelaide
   (d) Wellington and Sydney

177. A light wave is incident over a plane surface with velocity X. After reflection the velocity becomes :
   (a) x (b) 2x
   (c) $\frac{x}{4}$ (d) $\frac{x}{2}$

178. The five key indicators of global climate change of our planet are :
   (a) Sea–level, Rising temperatures, Rainfall, Nitrogen and Actic Sea ice
   (b) None of the options
   (c) Arctic sea ice, carbon dioxide, Global temperature, Sea level and land ice.
   (d) Antartic sea ice, Oxygen, Rainfall, Drought and Sea level

179. In operating system, Round Robin Scheduling means:
   (a) A kind of scheduling
   (b) A process allocation policy
   (c) A memory allocation policy
   (d) Repetition policy

180. The area reserved for the welfare of wild life is called
   (a) Sanctuary
   (b) Botanical garden
   (c) Forest
   (d) National pak

181. Where did Chandragupta maurya spent his last days ?
   (a) Thaneshwar
   (b) Kanchi
   (c) Patliputra
   (d) Shravanabelagola

182. Project tiger programme was launched in :
(a) 1994 (b) 1973
(c) 1975 (d) 1971

183. The National Green Tribunal deals with cases relating to ?
(a) Criminal offenses
(b) Issues relating to protection and conservation of historical monuments.
(c) Civil cases
(d) Environmental protection and conservation of forests.

184. Who was the First Speaker of the Lok Sabha ?
(a) K.S. Hegde
(b) Hukum Singh
(c) Ganesh Vasudev
(d) Neelam Sanjeeva Reddy

185. FORTRAN is called :
(a) Floppy Translator
(b) Formula Translator
(c) File Translator
(d) Format Translator

186. Which Indian newspaper has the largest readership ?
(a) The Malayala Manorama
(b) Indian Express
(c) The Hindu
(d) The Dainik Jagran

187. The gas dissolved in water that makes it basic is ?
(a) ammonia
(b) hydrogen
(c) sulphur dioxide
(d) carbon dioxide

188. The biggest oil spill in world history took place in the ?
(a) Persian Gulf
(b) Caspian Sea
(c) Mediterrarean Sea
(d) South China sea

189. Among the foollowing which country has the highest life expectancy ?
(a) USA (b) Switzerland
(c) Japan (d) Denmark

190. Yellow complexion, Medium stature, Oblique eye with an epicanthic fold is the characteristic feature of :
(a) Australoids (b) Negroid
(c) Mengoloid (d) Cancosoid

191. Chromosome designation of Turner syndrome is :
(a) 44A + XO (b) 44A + XXY
(c) 44A + XXX (d) 44A + XYY

192. The redness in atmosphere at Sunrise and Sunset is due to:
(a) Dispersion of light
(b) Scattering of light
(c) Refraction of light
(d) Reflection of light

193. Which day is celebrated as International Yoga Day ?
(a) April 23 (b) September 21
(c) July 21 (d) June 21

194. December 1 is celebrated as :
(a) Indian Navy Day (b) UNICEF Day
(c) Children's Day (d) World AIDS Day

195. Distant objects are visible as a little out of focus in this condition :
(a) hypermetropia (b) presbiopia
(c) astigmatism (d) myopia

196. Maximum oxygen is available from :
(a) Green forests (b) Deserts
(c) Grass lands (d) Phytoplanktons

197. Which one of the following tribes practices pastoral nomadism ?
(a) Boro (b) Masai
(c) Pygmies (d) Eskimo

198. Who was the first Secretary General of UNO?
(a) Kurt Waldheim
(b) Dag Hammarskjold
(c) Trygve Lie
(d) U–Thant

199. Who is the author of 'Indica'?
(a) Fa–Hien
(b) Hiuen Tsang
(c) Megasthanes
(d) Seleucus

200. In a reaction of the type $A + B \rightarrow C + D$ one could ensure it to be a first order reaction by :
(a) Increasing the concentration of a reactant
(b) Adding a catalyst
(c) Increasing the temperature
(d) Increasing the concentration of a product

1. (a) Word GARBAGE cannot be formed as requires two As.
2. (c) ENDREARMENT,
   Word TENDER can be formed
3. (a) BOY $= 2 + 15 + 25 = 42$
   GIRL $= 7 + 9 + 18 + 12 = 46$
   (Alphabets have been coded as per their position in English alphabet)
4. (c) $6 \times 7 = 42$
   $5 \times 7 = 35$
   So, $6 : 42 :: 5 : 35$
5. (a) Hockey is national game of India in the same way baseball is national game of USA.
6. (b) Ant, fly and bee are insects while hamster, squirrel are rodents. Mouse is also a rodent.
7. (a) $(12)^2 : (12+1)$
   Similarly $(7)^2 : (7+1) = 8$
8. (b)
   $A \xrightarrow{+1} B \xrightarrow{+2} D \xrightarrow{+1} E$
   $G \xrightarrow{+1} H \xrightarrow{+2} J \xrightarrow{+1} K$
   $M \xrightarrow{+1} N \xrightarrow{+2} P \xrightarrow{+1} Q$
   $S \xrightarrow{+1} T \xrightarrow{+2} V \xrightarrow{+1} X$
9. (a) $A \xrightarrow{+2} C \xrightarrow{+2} E$
   $G \xrightarrow{+2} I \xrightarrow{+2} K$
   $M \xrightarrow{+2} O \xrightarrow{+2} Q$
   $\boxed{S} \xrightarrow{+2} \boxed{U} \xrightarrow{+2} \boxed{W}$
   So SUW is the correct answer
10. (d) Arranging in reverse order

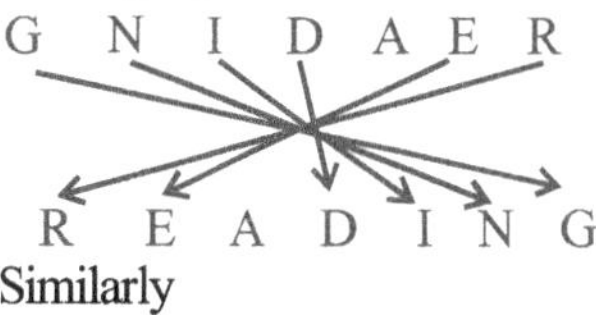

Similarly

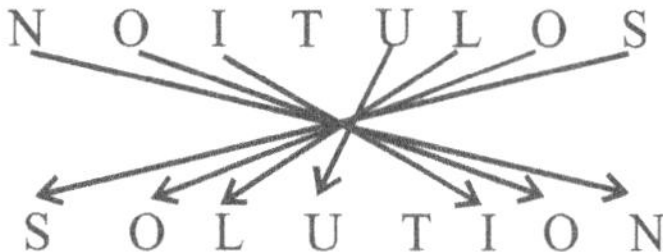

11. (d) Brick is a single unit of wall in the same way cell is single unit of tissue.
12. (b) $21 : 3 \Rightarrow 7 : 1$
    $574 : 82 \Rightarrow 7 : 1$
13. (d) Gloves, Sweater, shawl are worn in winter season while umbrella is used in rainy season.
14. (a) We used to draw, sketch or paint a portrait.
15. (a) Nose, Eyes and mouth are in upper portion of body while hands are in lower portion.
16. (a) $8 \times 3 + 1 = 25$ So $8 : 25$
    $13 \times 3 + 1 = 40$ So $13 : 40$
    $15 \times 3 + 1 = 46$ So $15 : 46$
    But $6 \times 3 + 1 = 19 \neq 22$
    So $6 : 22$ is odd
17. (c) 21, 81 and 51 are composite number while 71 is prime number.
18. (a) RQPO, VUTS and HGFE are set of 4 consecutive letters in reverse order but HNOP is not.
19. (b) D卍ST, N⌐⌙OP, KZM卐 all are combination of 3 letters and symbol while Q37Q is not.
20. (a) 125, 343, 216 are cubes while 100 is not.
21. (a) $P \xrightarrow{+3} S \xrightarrow{+3} V$
    $D \xrightarrow{+3} G \xrightarrow{+3} J$
    $F \xrightarrow{+3} I \xrightarrow{+3} L$
    But VXB does not follow this pattern.
22. (a)

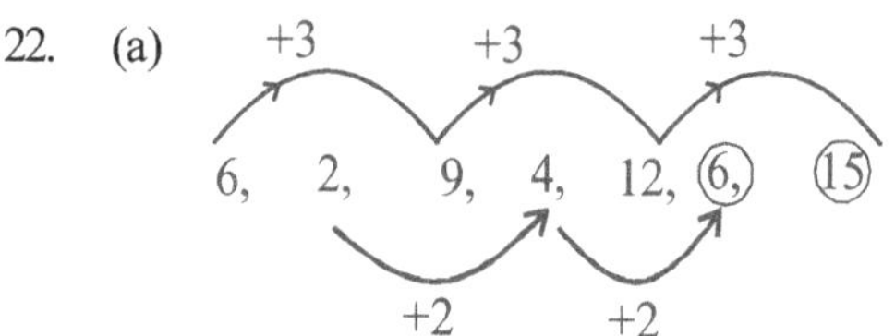

So, missing terms in the series are 6, 15.

23. (d) $A \xrightarrow{+3} D \xrightarrow{+4} H \xrightarrow{+5}$
    $M \xrightarrow{+6} S \xrightarrow{+7} Z$
24. (c) $-1 \xrightarrow{+1} 0 \xrightarrow{+3} 3 \xrightarrow{+5}$
    $8 \xrightarrow{+7} 15 \xrightarrow{+9} 24$

25. (a)

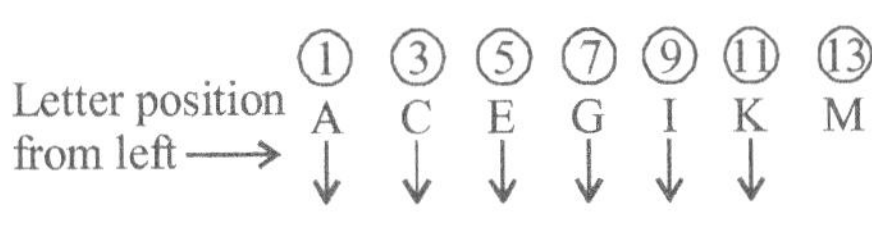

26. (d)

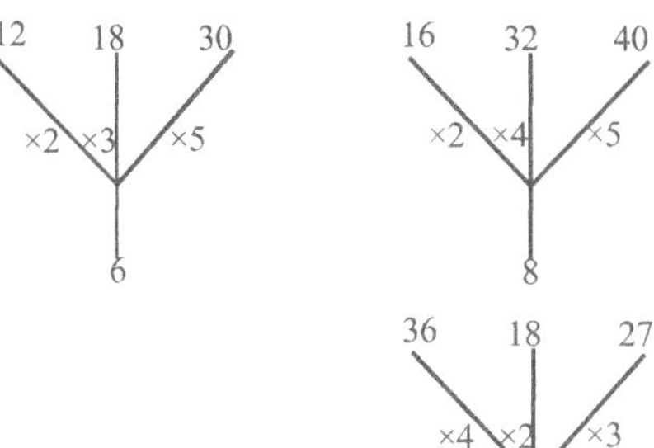

27. (c)

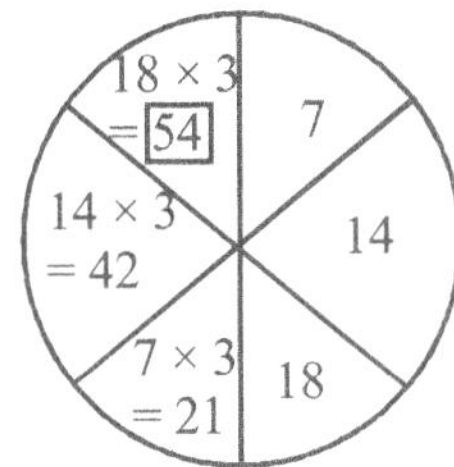

28. (b)

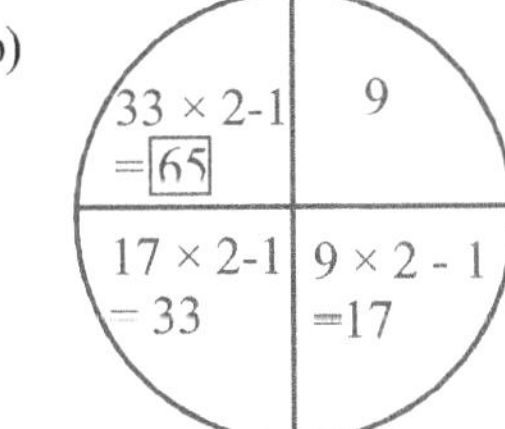

29. (b) Naresh is 17th from left and 22nd from the right.
So, total number of students in the line = 17 + 22 – 1 = 38

30. (c) $72 \times 19 = 23 \Rightarrow (7 \times 2 + 1 \times 9 = 23)$
$13 \times 48 = 35 \Rightarrow (1 \times 3 + 4 \times 8 = 35)$
$16 \times 43 = 18 \Rightarrow (1 \times 6 + 4 \times 3 = 18)$
So, $39 \times 22 = ? \Rightarrow (3 \times 9 + 2 \times 2 = 31)$

31. (c) The series is
a b c c b a a b c c b a a b c c b a a b c c b a
So, missing set of letters is c a b a a.

32. (a) The figure is embedded in

33. (d) L I S T E N
↓ ↓ ↓ ↓ ↓ ↓
5 9 3 4 1 7
So, code for word SILENT is 395174.

34. (d) Order of progresseon in hardware is Vacuum tube → Transistor → Integrated circuits → Silicon Chips.

35. (a)

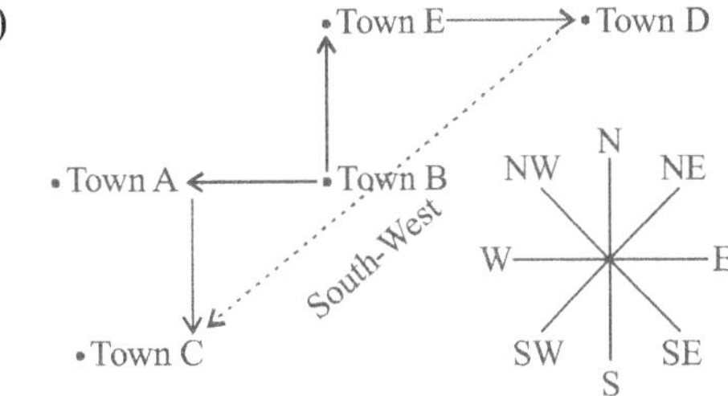

So, C is in south-west of D.

36. (d)

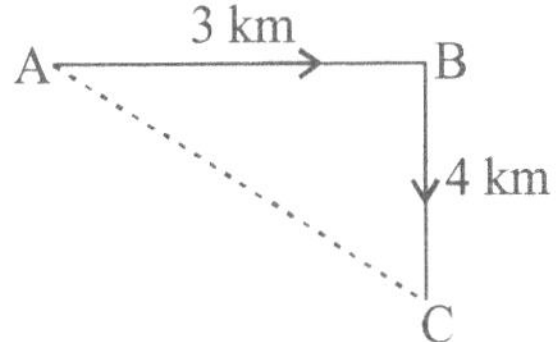

In Δ ABC

$$AC = \sqrt{(AB)^2 + (BC)^2}$$

$$AC = \sqrt{(3)^2 + (4)^2} = \sqrt{9+16} = 5 \text{ kms.}$$

37. (b)

38. (d) $12 \xrightarrow{\times 2} 24 \xrightarrow{\times 12} 144$
$13 \xrightarrow{\times 2} 26 \xrightarrow{\times 13} 169$
So, (13, 26, 169) follows the same pattern.

39. (d) Continuous training is essential for all employees to increase productivity so we can assume that for good productivity training is necessary to avoid losses due to unskilled person but statement does not imply profitability and productivity are supplementary to each other. It depends upon other factors also.

40. (d) Travelling by metro in Delhi is more convenient and economical. So we can assume that metro services are reasonably good. So assumption II is implicit.

41. (d) Total number of students in the class = 45.
Neha's rank from first = 15th

So number of students from the last $= 45 - (1 + 14) = 30$
So, Neha's rank from the last is 31st.

42. (c) Writing the expression with actual sign
$64 \div 8 + 32 \times 4 = 8 + 128 = 136$

43. (d) If we read Matrix I & II carefully, alphabets in the word BRIDE can be found in this pattern.

B	R	I	D	E
55	21	57	86	22

44. (b) The words can be arranged in following order in dictionary :
Voluntary ⟶ Voracious ⟶ Vortex ⟶ Voucher
(4) (1) (3) (2)
So, correct order is 4,1,3,2

45. (d) Abiogenesis ⟶ Abrasive ⟶ Absolute ⟶ Absorption ⟶ Abundance
(5) (2) (1) (3) (4)
So, correct order is 5,2,1,3,4

46. (b) Dot is only in first circle so figure (b) will complete the picture in the question figure.

47. (d) Sprinters and Marathon runner both are athletes. Some sprinters can be marathon runners also.

48. (c)
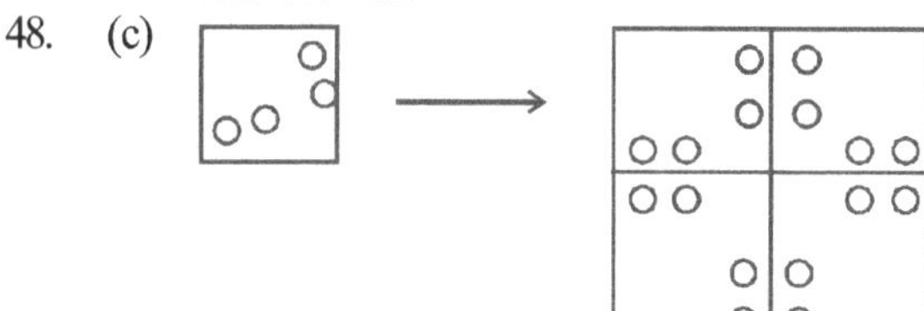

49. (c) Water image of
C O M M I S S I O N
↓ ↓ ↓ ↓ ↓ ↓ ↓ ↓ ↓ ↓
C O W W I Ƨ Ƨ I O И

50. (c)

51. (a) Fatalism means acceptance of the belief that all events are predetermined and inevitable.

52. (d) Gullible means someone who can be easily deceived or duped

53. (b) Ephemeral means lasting for a very short time.

54. (a) Etiquette means the code of polite behaviour in society or among members of a particular group.

55. (a) 56. (a)

57. (b) Since 'observe' means to watch something carefully.

58. (d) Since 'heavenly' means belonging to the heavens or sky.

59. (c)

60. (a) Since 'astronomers' are the experts who study the stars and planets using scientific equipments such as telescopes.

61. (d) 62. (b) 63. (c) 64. (d) 65. (a)

66. (c)

67. (a) 'A sacred cow' means a person held to be above criticism.

68. (b)

69. (a) A dog's breakfast means a complete mess.

70. (b) 'The seamy side of life' means the most unpleasant or roughest aspect of life.

71. (c) 72. (a)

73. (d) Here 'remarked' refers to giving your opinion about something or stating a fact.

74. (c) Since 'irritable' means showing a tendency to be easily annoyed.

75. (a) Illicit means something which is forbidden by law. Whereas Legal means relating to the law. Therefore, legal is the antonym of a Illicit.

76. (a) 'Demand' means a strong need for something. Whereas 'Supply' means to make something needed available to someone. Therefore 'supply' is the correct antonym of 'demand'.

77. (b) 'Descent' means an act of moving downwards. Whereas 'ascent' means the act of climbing or moving upwards. Therefore, 'ascent' is the antonym of 'descent'.

78. (c) 'Notorious' means someone known for some bad quality. 'Honourable' means someone honest and fair, or deserving praise and respect. Therefore, 'Honourable' is the antonym of 'notorious'.

79. (b) 80. (a) 81. (d) 82. (a)

83. (a) We will use 'completed' as it is simple past which is used to express the idea that an action started and finished at a specific time in the past.

84. (c)

85. (b) We will replace 'is' with 'were' because in an unreal conditional sentence where the events are contrary to the facts, the we use 'if' clauses with 'were' even if the pronoun is singular.

86. (d)

87. (d) The correct combination is RQSP.

88. (b) The correct combination is QPSR.
89. (b) The correct combination is QSRP.
90. (c) The correct combination is SPRQ.
91. (b) 92. (c) 93. (d) 94. (d)
95. (d) 'Vocation' means the work in which a person is employed or occupation. Therefore, occupation is the synonym of vocation.
96. (d) 'Limpid' means perfectly clear. Therefore, clear is the correct synonym of Limpid.
97. (a) 'Merge' means to blend or combine to form a single entity. Therefore, blend is the correct synonym of Merge.
98. (c) 'Gourmet' means a connoisseur of good food. Whereas Gastronome means a lover of good food. Therefore, 'Gastronome' is the synonym of 'Gourmet'.
99. (b) 100. (c)
101. (d)

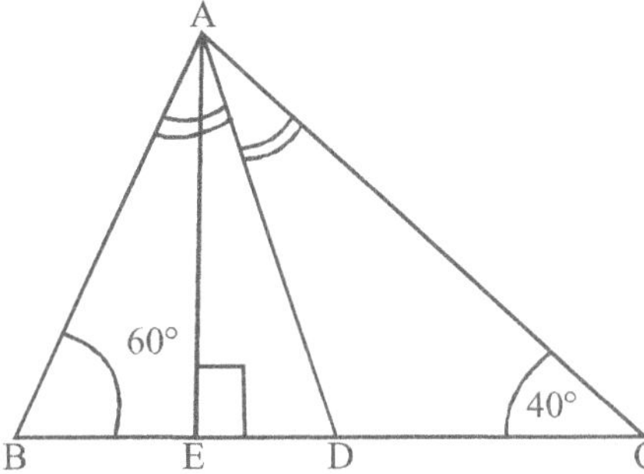

In ΔABC
$\angle A = 180° - (60° + 40°) = 80°$
$\angle BAD = \angle DAC = 40°$ (AD is bisector of $\angle A$)
In $\angle AEC$
$\angle EAC = 180° - (90° + 40°) = 50°$
So, $\angle EAD = \angle EAC - \angle DAC$
$= 50° - 40°$
$\angle EAD = 10°$

102. (a) Sum of 13 results $= 13 \times 70 = 910$
Sum of 7 results $= 7 \times 65 = 455$
Sum of last 7 results $= 7 \times 75 = 525$
So, 7th result $(455 + 525) - 910 = 70$

103. (d)

Days	No.of Labourers
12	20
4	?

Work done
$5/8$
$1 - \frac{5}{8} = \frac{3}{8}$
$m_1 D_1 . w_2 = m_2 D_2 W_1$

$20 \times 12 \times \frac{3}{8} = M_2 \times 4 \times \frac{5}{8}$

$\Rightarrow M_2 = \frac{20 \times 12 \times 3 \times 8}{4 \times 5 \times 8} = 36$

Hence, $36 - 20 = 16$ more men needed to complete the remaining work in 4 days.

104. (d) $p = -0.12;\quad q = -0.01;\ r = -0.015$
So, $p < r ; p < q$
$= p < r < q$

105. (d) Ratio of amount spend on food and clothes $= 150 : 30 = 5 : 1$

106. (b) % money spent on food compared to house rent

$= \frac{150}{120} \times 100 = 125\%$

107. (a) Money spent on clothes and miscellaneous items cannot be determined as total money is not given.

108. (a) Amount spent on food $= \frac{150}{360} \times 7200 =$ ₹3000

109. (a) $a = \frac{\sqrt{3}-\sqrt{2}}{\sqrt{3}+\sqrt{2}} \times \frac{\sqrt{3}-\sqrt{2}}{\sqrt{3}-\sqrt{2}}$

$= \frac{\left(\sqrt{3}-\sqrt{2}\right)^2}{3-2} = \frac{3+2-2\sqrt{6}}{1} = 5-2\sqrt{6}.$

$b = \frac{\sqrt{3}+\sqrt{2}}{\sqrt{3}-\sqrt{2}} \times \frac{\sqrt{3}+\sqrt{2}}{\sqrt{3}+\sqrt{2}}$

$= \frac{\left(\sqrt{3}+\sqrt{2}\right)^2}{3-2} = 5+2\sqrt{6}$

So, $\frac{a^2}{b} + \frac{b^2}{a} = \frac{\left(5-2\sqrt{6}\right)^2}{5+2\sqrt{6}} + \frac{\left(5+2\sqrt{6}\right)^2}{5-2\sqrt{6}}$

$= \frac{\left(5-2\sqrt{6}\right)^3 + \left(5+2\sqrt{6}\right)^3}{(5)^2 - \left(2\sqrt{6}\right)^2}$

$= \frac{(5)^3 - \left(2\sqrt{6}\right)^3 - 3(5)\left(2\sqrt{6}\right)\left(5-2\sqrt{6}\right) + (5)^3 + \left(2\sqrt{6}\right)^3 + 3(5)\left(2\sqrt{6}\right)\left(5+2\sqrt{6}\right)}{25-24}$

$= \frac{125 - 48\sqrt{6} - 150\sqrt{6} + 60(6) + 125 + 48\sqrt{6} + 150\sqrt{6} + 60(6)}{1}$

$=125+125+360+360$
$=250+720$
$=970$

110. (d) Average production of the given years

$$=\frac{25+40+60+45+65+50+75+80}{8}$$

$$=\frac{440}{8}=55$$

So, during 1997, 1999, 2001 and 2002 production was more than average production.

111. (d) % increase in production in 2002 compared to that of 1995 $=\frac{80}{25}\times100-100=320-100$

$=220\%$

112. (b) % age decline in production from 1997 to 1998 is

$$\frac{60-45}{60}\times100=\frac{15}{60}\times100=25\%$$

113. (c) Average production of 1996 and 1997 =

$$\frac{40+60}{2}=50$$

Average production of years 1995 and 2001

$$=\frac{25+25}{2}=50$$

So average production of 1996 and 1997 is equal to average production of 1995 and 2001.

114. (b) Percentage increase in production as compared to previous year is maximum in

$$1996=\frac{40-25}{25}\times100=60\%$$

115. (d) $x^2-4x-1=0$ can be written as $x^2-4x+4-1=4$

So $(x-4)^2-1=4$

$x-2=\sqrt{4+1}$

$x=\sqrt{5}+2$

So, $x^2+\frac{1}{x^2}=\left(2+\sqrt{5}\right)^2+\frac{1}{\left(2+\sqrt{5}\right)^2}$

$$=4+5+4\sqrt{5}+\frac{1}{4+5+4\sqrt{5}}$$

$$=9+4\sqrt{5}+\frac{1}{9+4\sqrt{5}}$$

$$=\frac{\left(9+4\sqrt{5}\right)^2+1}{9+4\sqrt{5}}$$

$$=\frac{81+16(5)+72\sqrt{5}+1}{9+4\sqrt{5}}$$

$$=\frac{162+72\sqrt{5}}{9+4\sqrt{5}}$$

$$=\frac{162+72\sqrt{5}}{9+4\sqrt{5}}\times\frac{9-4\sqrt{5}}{9-4\sqrt{5}}$$

$$=\frac{\left(162+72\sqrt{5}\right)\left(9-4\sqrt{5}\right)}{1}$$

$=$

$(162)(9)-(162)(4)\left(\sqrt{5}\right)+72(9)\sqrt{5}-72(4)$

$=1458-648\sqrt{5}+648\sqrt{5}-1440$
$=1458-1440=18.$

116. (a) Area of trapezium
=

$$\frac{\text{Sum of length of parallel sides}}{2}\times\text{Height (H)}$$

$$175=\frac{15+20}{2}\times H$$

$$H=\frac{175+2}{35}=10\text{cm.}$$

117. (d) Internal Radius of hemisphere = 60
Internal surface area $=2\pi r^2$
$=2\times3.14\times(6)^2$
$=226.08\text{ cm}^2.$

118. (c) Speed of first train $=\frac{150}{30}=5$m/sec

Let the speed of second train be x m/sec
Relative speed = (5 + x) m/sec

$\therefore\frac{300}{5+x}=10$
$50+10x=300$

$$x=\frac{300-50}{10}=25\text{m/sec}$$

$= 25 \times \frac{18}{5} = 90\text{km/h}$

119. (d) Let initial volume = 100

$\text{Volume after increase} = 100 \times \frac{110}{100} = 110$

$\text{So, decrease} = \frac{110-100}{110} \times 100$

$= \frac{10}{110} \times 100 = 9\frac{1}{11}\%$

120. (c) $\left(\frac{3}{15} a^5 b^6 c^3 \times \frac{5}{9} a b^5 c^4\right) \div \frac{10}{27} a^2 b c^3$

$= \frac{1}{9} a^6 b^{11} c^7 \div \frac{10}{27} a^2 b c^3$

$= \frac{1}{9} a^6 b^{11} c^7 \times \frac{27}{10} a^{-2} b^{-1} c^{-3}$

$= \frac{3}{10} a^{6-2} b^{11-1} c^{7-3} = \frac{3}{10} a^4 b^{10} c^4$

121. (c) Contribution of each boy = Number of boys
Total contribution raised = ₹ 12544

So, number of boys = $\sqrt{12544} = 112$

122. (a) $\tan^2\frac{\pi}{4} - \cos^2\frac{\pi}{3} = x \sin\frac{\pi}{4}\cos\frac{\pi}{4}\tan\frac{\pi}{3}$

$\tan\frac{\pi}{4} = 1; \quad \cos\frac{\pi}{3} = \frac{1}{2}; \quad \cos\frac{\pi}{4} = \frac{1}{\sqrt{2}};$

$\sin\frac{\pi}{4} = \frac{1}{\sqrt{2}}; \ \tan\frac{\pi}{3} = \sqrt{3}$

$\text{So, } (1)^2 - \left(\frac{1}{2}\right)^2 = x\left(\frac{1}{\sqrt{2}}\right)\left(\frac{1}{\sqrt{2}}\right)\left(\sqrt{3}\right)$

$\Rightarrow \frac{3}{4} = \frac{\sqrt{3}x}{2}$

$x = \frac{3 \times 2}{\sqrt{3} \times 4} = \frac{\sqrt{3}}{2}$

123. (c)

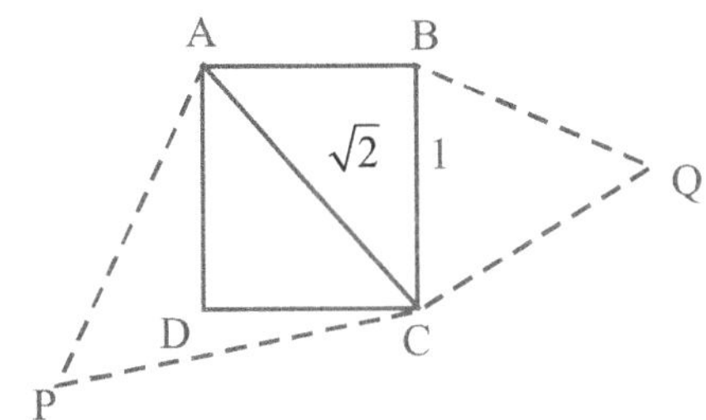

ABCD is a square.

$\Delta QBC \sim \Delta PAC$
(Given)

$\therefore \frac{\text{Area } \Delta QBC}{\text{Area } \Delta PAC} = \frac{BC^2}{AC^2}$

If BC = 1 then AC = $\sqrt{2}$

$\therefore \text{Required ratio} = \frac{BC^2}{AC^2} = \frac{1}{2}$

124. (a) Ratio of present ages of Sonali and Monali = 5 : 3
After 5 years ratio of ages of both girls = 10:7
Let actual present ages are 5x and 3x years.

$= \frac{5x+5}{3x+5} = \frac{10}{7} = 35x + 35 = 30x + 50$

$5x = 15$

$x = 3$

So, Monali age = 3 × 3 = 9 years

125. (b) P = ₹ 12000;
R = 20% per annum = 5% per quarter

T = 9 months = 3 quarters

$\text{So, } A = 12000\left(1 + \frac{5}{10}\right)^3$

$= 12000 \times 1.05 \times 1.05 \times 1.05$

= ₹ 13891.1

So, CI = 13891.10 – 12000 = ₹ 1891.10

126. (c) $\frac{1 + 2\sin 60^\circ \cos 60^\circ}{\sin 60^\circ + \cos 60^\circ} + \frac{1 - 2\sin 60^\circ \cos 60^\circ}{\sin 60^\circ - \cos 60^\circ}$

$= \frac{1 + 2\left(\frac{\sqrt{3}}{2}\right)\left(\frac{1}{2}\right)}{\frac{\sqrt{3}}{2} + \frac{1}{2}} + \frac{1 - 2\left(\frac{\sqrt{3}}{2}\right)\left(\frac{1}{2}\right)}{\frac{\sqrt{3}}{2} - \frac{1}{2}}$

$= \frac{1 + \frac{\sqrt{3}}{2}}{\frac{\sqrt{3}+1}{2}} + \frac{1 - \frac{\sqrt{3}}{2}}{\frac{\sqrt{3}-1}{2}}$

$\left[\because \sin 60^\circ = \frac{\sqrt{3}}{2}, \ \cos 60^\circ = \frac{1}{2}\right]$

$= \frac{2+\sqrt{3}}{\sqrt{3}+1} + \frac{2-\sqrt{3}}{\sqrt{3}-1}$

$= \frac{2+\sqrt{3}}{\sqrt{3}+1} \times \frac{\sqrt{3}-1}{\sqrt{3}-1} + \frac{2-\sqrt{3}}{\sqrt{3}-1} \times \frac{\sqrt{3}+1}{\sqrt{3}+1}$

$= \frac{2\sqrt{3}+3-2-\sqrt{3}}{3-1} + \frac{2\sqrt{3}-3-\sqrt{3}+2}{3-1}$

$= \frac{1+\sqrt{3}}{2} + \frac{\sqrt{3}-1}{2} = \frac{2\sqrt{3}}{2} = \sqrt{3}$

127. (a) $\frac{\sin\theta+\cos\theta}{\sin\theta-\cos\theta} = 3$

By componendo and dividendo

$\frac{2\sin\theta}{2\cos\theta} = \frac{4}{2} = 2$

So, $\tan\theta = 2$

$\sin^2\theta = (1-\cos^2\theta) = \left(1-\frac{1}{\sec^2\theta}\right)$

$= \frac{\sec^2\theta-1}{\sec^2\theta}$

$= \frac{\tan^2\theta}{1+\tan^2\theta} = \frac{(2)^2}{1+(2)^2}$

$= \frac{4}{5}$

128. (c) $\sin 2\theta = \frac{\sqrt{3}}{2} = \sin 60°$

$\Rightarrow 2\theta = 60°$,

$\theta = 30°$

$\sin 3\theta = \sin 3\,(30°) = 90°$

$= \sin 90° = 1$

129. (d) Volume of cube $= a^3 = (7)^3 = 343\ cm^3$

Volume of right circular cone $= \frac{1}{3}\pi r^2 h$

Radius of cone = 3.5cm

Height of cone = 7cm

So, Volume of cone $= \frac{1}{3} \times \frac{22}{7} \times 3.5 \times 3.5 \times 7$

$= 89.8cm^3$.

130. (d) Let the two numbers are x and y

So, $x + 2y = 8$ ...(i)

$x - y = 2$ ...(ii)

Solving both equations

$x = 4;\ y = 2$

So, numbers are 4,2

131. (d) Speed of car in m/sec $= 54 \times \frac{5}{18} = 15$m/sec

132. (c) Income in 2012 = ₹26, 64,000

Every year % of increase in income = 20%

So, income of company in 2012 = 26,64,000

$\times \frac{100}{120} \times \frac{100}{120}$

= ₹18,50,000

133. (c)

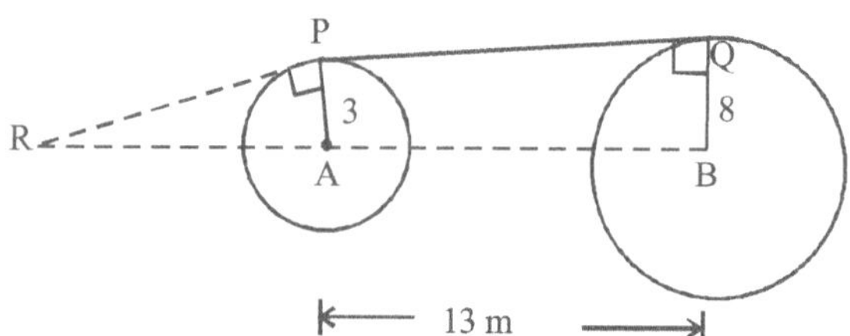

$\Delta PRA \sim \Delta QRB$ (By AAA axiom)

$= \frac{PR}{QR} = \frac{RA}{RB} = \frac{AP}{BQ}$

$= \frac{PR}{PR+PQ} = \frac{RA}{RA+RB} = \frac{3}{8}$

$= \frac{PR}{PR+PQ} = \frac{RA}{RA+13} = \frac{3}{8}$ ...(i)

From (i) $RA = \frac{39}{5}$ cm

In right angled ΔAPR

$PR^2 = AR^2 - AP^2 = \left(\frac{39}{5}\right)^2 - (3)^2 = \frac{1296}{25}$

$= PR = \frac{36}{5}$

From (i) $\frac{\frac{36}{5}}{\frac{36}{5}+PQ} = \frac{3}{8}$

$= 3\left(\frac{36}{5}+PQ\right) = \frac{36}{5} \times 8$

$= \frac{36}{5} + PQ = \frac{8\times12}{5}$

$PQ = \frac{96}{5} - \frac{36}{5} = \frac{60}{5} = 12$cm

134. (a) Let CP of goods = ₹ 100

So, MP = $100 \times \frac{120}{100}$ = ₹ 120

SP after allowing 5% discount = $120 \times \frac{95}{100}$

= ₹ 114

So, profit = 114 – 100 = 14%

135. (d) In ΔABC

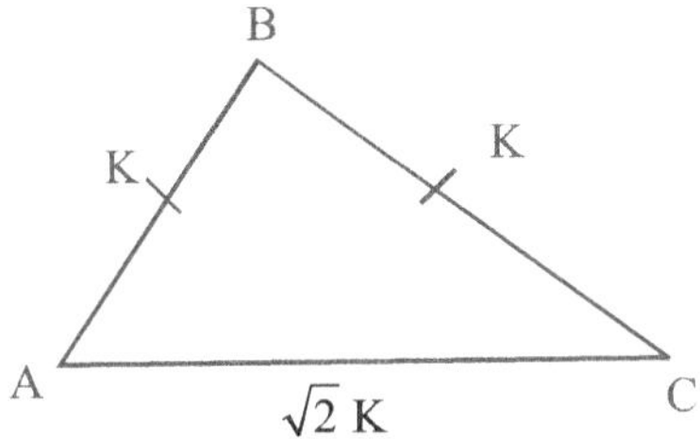

$AC = \sqrt{2}K$

$AC^2 = 2K^2$

$AC^2 = AB^2 + BC^2$

So ΔABC is right angled triangle

So, in ΔABC

$$\frac{AB}{AC} = \frac{K}{\sqrt{2}K} = \frac{1}{\sqrt{2}}$$

So $\cos\theta = \frac{1}{\sqrt{2}}$

$\theta = 45°$

So, ABC, $\angle B = 90°$; $\angle C = 45°$; $\angle A = 45°$

So, ABC is right isoscles triangle.

136. (d) Lowest 5 digit number = 10,000

The number which is divisible by 12, 18 and 21 is LCM of 12, 18, 12 which is 252.

$\frac{10000}{252}$ gives 172 as remainder

So, 252 – 172 = 80

10,000 + 80 = 10080

If 10080 when divided by 12, 18 and 21 gives 0 as remainder

So, 10080 is the least 5–digit number.

137. (d) SP = ₹ 450

Loss = 20%

$\therefore$ CP = $450 \times \frac{100}{100 - \text{loss}} = 450 \times \frac{100}{80}$

= ₹ 562.50

SP for getting 20% gain = $562.50 \times \frac{120}{100}$

= ₹ 675.

138. (d) $A + B = 120$ ...(i)

$B + C = 130$ ...(ii)

$C + A = 140$ ...(iii)

Adding all three equations

$2A + 2B + 2C = 390$

$A + B + C = 195$

But, $A + B = 120$

So, $C = 195 - 120 = 75$

139. (c) $\alpha + \beta = 90° \Rightarrow \beta = 90° - \alpha$

$$= \frac{\tan\alpha}{\tan\beta} + \sin^2\alpha + \sin^2\beta$$

$$= \frac{\tan(90° - \beta)}{\tan\beta(90° - \alpha)} + \sin^2(90 - \beta) + \sin^2\beta$$

$$= \frac{\tan\alpha}{\cot\alpha} + \cos^2\beta + \sin^2\beta$$

$$= \tan^2\alpha + 1$$

$$= \sec^2\alpha$$

140. (d) Using property of direct common tangent

Required ratio = Ratio of radii = 5 : 3

141. (b) CP = $\frac{10}{12}$ = ₹ 0.833

SP = $\frac{12}{10}$ = ₹ 1

So, Gain% = $\frac{1 - 0.833}{0.833} \times 100$

$= \frac{0.167}{0.833} \times 100 = 20\%.$

142. (d)

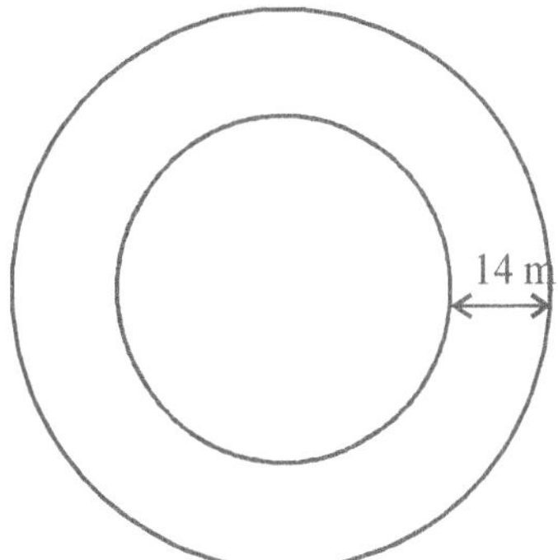

Outer circumference = 528m

$\therefore$ Outer radius = $\frac{528 \times 7}{2 \times 22}$ = 84m

$\therefore$ Inner radius = 84 – 14 = 70m

Outer area of circular race – track

$= \frac{22}{7} \times 84 \times 84$

$= 22176 m^2$

Inner area of circular race – track

$= \frac{22}{7} \times 70 \times 70$

$= 15400 m^2$.

So area of track = 22176 – 15400 = 6776m^2

Cost of levelling the circular track = 6776 × 10 = ₹ 67760

143. (c) $2^3 + 4^3 + 6^3 + \text{-------} + 20^3$

$= 2^3 (1^3 + 2^3 + 3^3 + \text{------} + 10^3)$

$= 2^3 \times \left(\frac{(n)(n+1)}{2}\right)^2 8 \times \left(\frac{10 \times 11}{2}\right)^2$

$= 8 \times 3025 = 24200$

144. (c) Surface area of sphere = 616cm^2

$4\pi r2 = 616 \; r = \sqrt{\frac{616 \times 7}{4 \times 22}} = 7cm$

So, volume of sphere $= \frac{4}{3} \pi (7)^3$

$= \frac{4}{3} \times \frac{22}{7} \times 7 \times 7 \times 7$

$= 1437 \frac{1}{3} cm^3$

145. (d) 12ℓ of milk taken out of 60ℓ milk So 20% water is added to milk

Milk = 48ℓ; Water = 12ℓ

Now, again 20% water is added to this mixture

$\underset{(\text{milk})}{48} \xrightarrow[-9.6]{20\%} \underset{(\text{milk})}{38.4} \text{ and } \underset{(\text{water})}{21.6}$

So, ratio of milk and water = 38.4 : 21.6

= 16 : 9

146. (d) $(2a - 1)^2 + (4b - 3)^2 + (4c + 5)^2 = 0$

$= 2a - 1 = 0; \quad 4b - 3 = 0;$

$a = \frac{1}{2}; \quad b = \frac{3}{4};$

$4c + 5 = 0$

$c = \frac{-5}{4}$

$a^3 + b^3 + c^3 - 3abc = (a + b + c)(a^2 + b^2 + c^2 - ab - bc - ca)$

But $a + b + c = 0$

So, $a^3 + b^3 + c^3 - 3abc = 0$

So, $\frac{a^3 + b^3 + c^3 - 3abc}{a^3 + b^3 + c^3} = 0$

147. (a) Let list price = ₹ z

So, Sale price (y) $= \frac{z(100 - x)}{100}$

$= z = \frac{100y}{100 - x}$

148. (b) $a + \frac{1}{b} = 1$ and $b + \frac{1}{c} = 1$

$b = 1 - \frac{1}{c}$

So, $a + \frac{1}{1 - \frac{1}{c}} = 1$

$\Rightarrow a + \frac{c}{c - 1} = 1$

$\Rightarrow a = 1 - \frac{c}{c - 1}$

$\Rightarrow a = \frac{c - 1 - c}{c - 1} = -\frac{1}{c - 1}$

So, $c + \frac{1}{a} = c + \left(\frac{1}{1/c - 1}\right)$

$= c - (c - 1)$

$= c - c + 1$

$= 1$

149. (b) Required number of days $= \frac{10 \times 20 \times 50}{10 \times 100}$

= 10 days

150. (b) $\frac{250}{3}\%$ of 90

$= 90 \times \frac{250}{300}$

60% of $x = \frac{60}{100} x$

So, $90 \times \frac{250}{300} = \frac{60}{100} x$

$x = \frac{90 \times 250 \times 100}{300 \times 60}$

$x = \frac{3 \times 125}{3 \times 2} = 125$

151. (c) Porus fought Alexander the Great in the Battle of the Hydaspes (also known as Jhelum) in 326 BC and is believed to be defeated.
152. (a) Black soil or Black Lava Soil is considered most suitable for sowing cotton crops.
153. (c) Neyveli lignite field in Tamil Nadu is the largest lignite coal mine in India.
154. (c) Right to Information Act (RTI) was enacted on 15th June 2005 and came fully into force on 12th October 2005.
155. (a) Indian Social activist Medha Patkar is the founder member of Narmada Bachao Andolan.
156. (d) As a Banker to Banks, the Reserve Bank of India acts as the "lender of the last resort".
157. (a) Sex ratio is used to describe the number of females per 1000 males in country. In the Population Census of 2011 it was revealed that the population ratio in India 2011 is 940 females per 1000 of males.
158. (d) Sachin Tendulkar was named as the ICC Cricket World Cup 2015 Ambassador.
159. (d)
160. (d) Stalactites and Stalagmites are formed due to the precipitation of Calcium carbonate ($CaCO_3$).
161. (d) Hermaphroditism is a form of sexual reproduction in which an organism can self-fertilize or mate with another individual of the same species.
162. (b) Leela Samson is a Bharatanatyam dancer, choreographer instructor and writer from India.
163. (a) 73rd Constitutional amendment act is related to provide 3-tier system of Panchayati Raj for all states having population of over 20 lakh.
164. (b) Ryder Cup is a biennial men's gold competition between teams from Europe and the United States.
165. (d) Kanha Tiger Reserve, also called "Kanha National Park" is one of the tiger reserve of India and the largest national Park of Madhya Pradesh.
166. (b) The Discovery of India was written by India's first Prime Minister Jawaharlal Nehru during his imprisoment in 1942-46 at Ahmednagar fort in Maharashtra.
167. (b) Kiran Bedi was the first woman IPS officer in India. Bedi joined the Indian Police Service (IPS) in 1972.
168. (b) When the price elasticity of demand for a good is perfectly inelastic i.e. $E_d = 0$.
169. (b) Lyman series of hydrogen atom spectral lines in the Ultraviolet.
170. (a) ILO stands for International Labour Organisation which is a United Nations agency dealing with Labour issues.
171. (a) In Tamil Nadu, rain water harvesting was made compulsory for every building to avoid ground water depletion.
172. (b) An electric battery is a devices consisting of two or more electrochemical cells that convert stored chemical energy into electrical energy.
173. (c) The Times of London in 2010 Published its 70,000th issue.
174. (c) Impeachment of the president for violation of consititution of India may start in either of the two houses of the Parliament.
175. (b) Purana Qila was built by the Afghan king Sher Shah Suri.
176. (a) The opening ceremonies of ICC Cricket World Cup 2015 was held on 12th February 2015 in Christchurch, New Zealand and Melbourne, Australia.
177. (b)

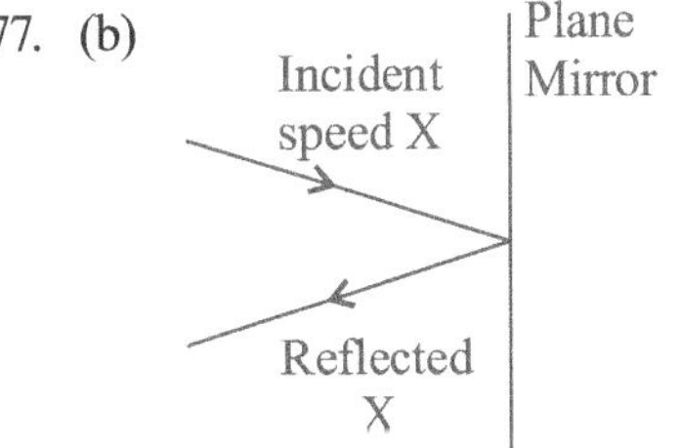

Therefore, relative speed= x + x = 2x
178. (c) NASA has developed a series of interactive a maps and graphs to describe the global climte and how it change over time. The focus of 5 key climate indications include Arctic sea ice, carbon dioxide concentration, Global surface temperature, Sea level and land ice.
179. (b)
180. (d) The area reserved for the welfare of wildlife is called National Park.
181. (d) Chandragupta Maurya is said to have lived as an ascetic at Shravanabelagola for several years before starving himself to death, as per Jain Practice of Sallekhana.
182. (b) Project Tiger was launched in 1973 by the Government of India during Prime Minister Indira Gandhi's tenure.

183. (d) The National Green Tribunal deals with cases relating to environmental protection and conservation of forests and other natural resources.
184. (c) Ganesh Vasudev Mavalankar was the first speaker of Lok Sabha.
185. (b) FORTRAN is derived from Formula Translator.
186. (d) According to the figures compiled by Media Research Users Council (MRUC) in the Indian Readership Survey (IRS) 2014, the Indian newspaper with the largest readership is the Dainik Jagran.
187. (a)
188. (a) Kuwait Spill in Persian Gulf, Kuwait of 19th January 1991 was the biggest oil spill in world history.
189. (c) Japan has the highest life expectancy among the countries across the world.
190. (c)
191. (a) Turner Syndrome, represented by 44A + XO. This occur in females in which one of the X-chromosome is missing.
192. (b) Scattering of light causes redness in atmosphere at Sunrise and Sunset.
193. (d) International Yoga day is celebrated annually on June 21.
194. (d) World AIDS Day is observed on 1st December, to raise awareness of the AIDS pandemic caused by the spread of HIV infection.
195. (d) Myopia also known as short sightedness is a condition of the eye where one looking at a distant object seems a little out of focus.
196. (d) In the process of photosynthesis, phytoplankton release oxygen into the water. Half of the world's oxygen is produced from phytoplankton photosynthesis. The other half is produced via photosynthesis on land by trees, shrubs, grasses and other plants.
197. (c) Pygmies follow practices of pastoral nomadism.
198. (c) Trygve Lie was the first secretary General of UNO.
199. (c) Megasthenes gave an account of India in his book 'Indica'.
200. (a)

PRACTICE SET- 1

GENERAL INTELLIGENCE & REASONING

DIRECTIONS (Qs. 1-3): *In questions, select the related word/letters/number from given alternatives.*

1. Crime : Court : : Disease : ?
   (a) Doctor (b) Medicine
   (c) Hospital (d) Treatment
2. ADGJ : BEHK : : DGJM : ?
   (a) KPUB (b) GJMP
   (c) KNQT (d) PSVY
3. 7 : 56 : : 5 : ?
   (a) 25 (b) 26
   (c) 30 (d) 35

DIRECTIONS (Qs. 4-5): *In questions, find the odd word/letters/number pair from the given alternatives.*

4. (a) Cabbage (b) Carrot
   (c) Potato (d) Beetroot
5. (a) GFI (b) VUX
   (c) POR (d) LKM

DIRECTIONS (Qs. 6-7): *In questions, a series is given, with one term missing. Choose the correct alternative from the given ones that will complete the series.*

6. CGJ, KOR, TXA, __?__.
   (a) ACE (b) JDP
   (c) FJM (d) UWY
7. B-1, D-2, F-4, H-8, J-16, __?__.
   (a) K-64 (b) L-32
   (c) M-32 (d) L-64

DIRECTIONS (Qs. 8-9): *In question, find the missing number from the given responses.*

8. If A = 1, B = 2 and N = 14, then BEADING = ?
   (a) 2154 (14) 97
   (b) 2514 (14) 79
   (c) 25149 (14) 7
   (d) 2154(14)79
9. Arrange the letters to form a word and suggest what is it.
   NGDEALN
   (a) State (b) Country
   (c) River (d) Ocean

DIRECTION (Q. 10): *In question, which one set of letters when sequentially placed at the gaps in the given letter series shall complete it ?*

10. a _ n _ b _ _ n c b _ _ n c b
    (a) b c a b a b (b) b a c b a b
    (c) a b c b c b (d) a b b c c a
11. In a class of 45 students, a boy is ranked 20th. When two boys joined, his rank was dropped by one. What is his new rank from the end ?
    (a) 25th (b) 26th
    (c) 27th (d) 28th
12. Introducing a girl, Ram said to his son-in-law. "Her brother is the only son of my brother-in-law." Who is the girl of Ram?
    (a) Sister-in-law (b) Niece
    (c) Daughter (d) Sister
13. If an electric train runs in the direction from North to South with a speed of 150 km/hr covering 2000 km, then in which direction will the smoke of its engine go ?
    (a) N→S (b) S→N
    (c) E→W (d) No direction
14. Which figure represents the relation among Computer, Internet and Information Communication Technology?

(a) 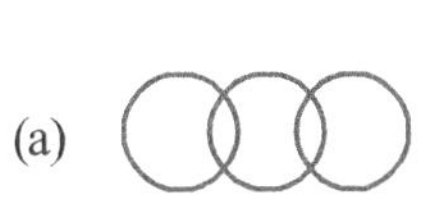 (b) 

(c)  (d) 

15. Choose the correct alternative.

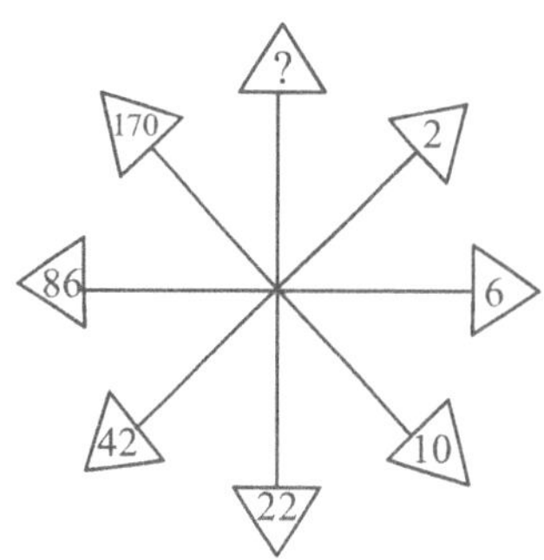

(a) 422 (b) 374
(c) 256 (d) 342

16. Murthy drove from town A to town B. In the first hour, he travelled $\frac{1}{4}$ of the journey. In the next one hour, he travelled $\frac{1}{2}$ of the journey. In the last 30 minutes, he travelled 80 km. Find the distance of the whole journey.

(a) 240km (b) 300km
(c) 320km (d) 360km

17. Find the answer of the following:

$7+3=421$
$11+7=477$
$9+5=445$
$6+2=?$

(a) 444 (b) 412
(c) 475 (d) 487

18. A, B, C, D and E are five boys sitting in a circle facing the centre. C is sitting immediately to the left of E. A is sitting between D and E. Then, who is sitting between B and A?

(a) C (b) E
(c) D (d) None of these

DIRECTION (Q. 19): *In question, one statement is given, followed by three conclusions, I, II, and III. You have to consider the statements to be true, even if they seem to be at variance from commonly known facts. You are to decide which of the given Conclusions can definitely be drawn from the given statement(s). Indicate your answer.*

19. Statements:

1. SAGE is a reputed publisher of both journals and books.
2. All publishing of SAGE is highly qualitative.

Conclusions:

I. SAGE publishes qualitative articles.
II. SAGE did not publish lowest quality articles.
III. SAGE enriches its publications by high scrutinization.

(a) Only conclusion III
(b) All conclusions .
(c) Only conclusions I and II
(d) Only conclusions II and III

20. If a mirror is placed on the line MN, then which of the answer figures is the correct image of the question figure?

Question figure:

Answer figures :

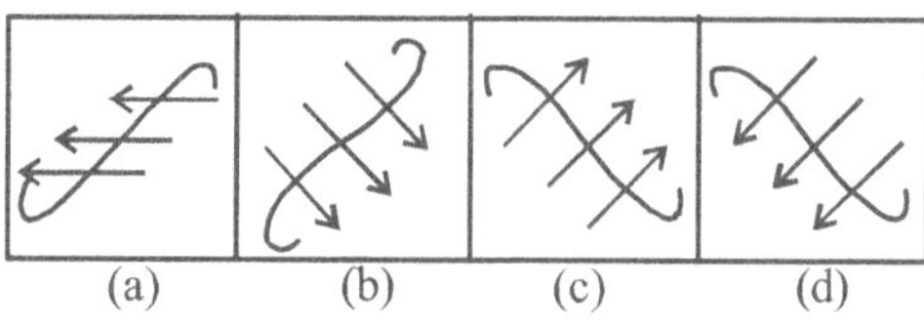

21. Identify the answer figure from which the pieces given in question figure have been cut.

Question figure :

Answer figures:

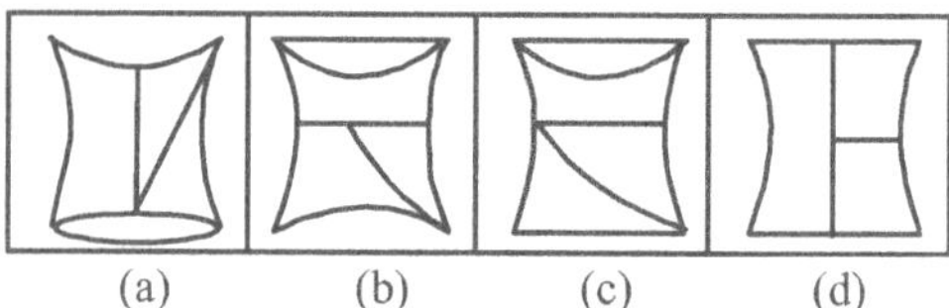

DIRECTION (Q. 22) : *In question, which answer figure will complete the pattern in the question figure?*

22. Question figure:

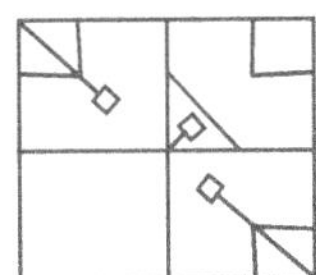

Answer Figures :

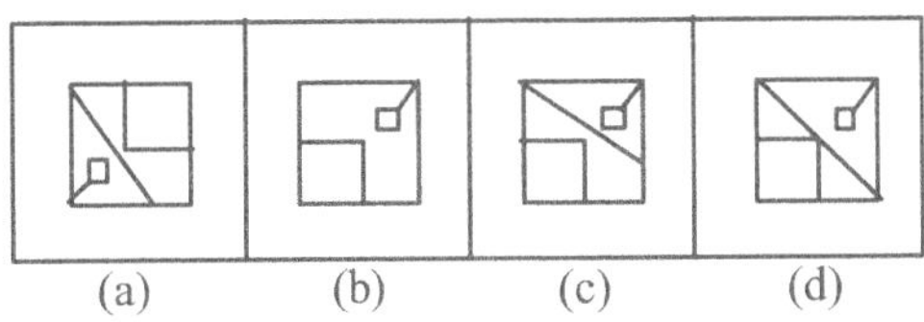

23. Which of the answer figures is not made up only by the components of the question figure ?

Question figure:

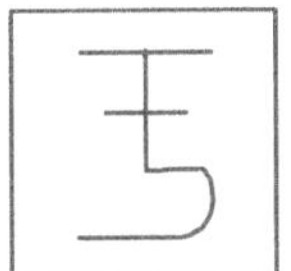

Answer figures:

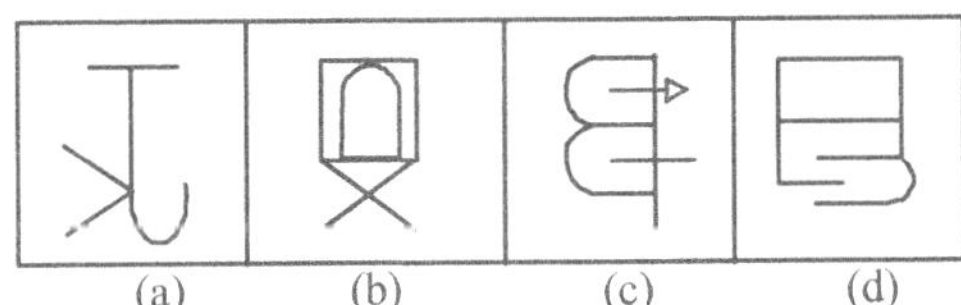

24. A piece of paper is folded and cut as shown below in the question figures. From the given answer figures. indicate how it will appear when opened.

Question figure:

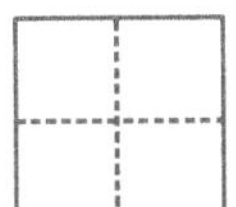

Answer Figures :

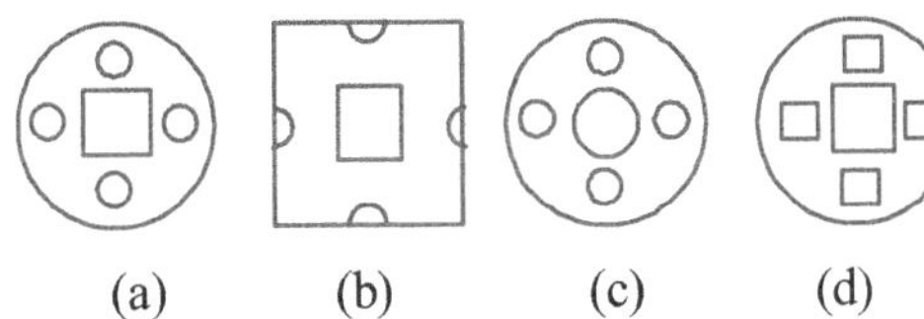

25. A word is represented by one set of numbers as given in any one of the alternatives. The sets of numbers given in the alternatives are represented by two classes of alphabets as in two matrices given below. The columns and rows of Matrix I are numbered from 0 to 4 and that of Matrix II are numbered from 5 to 9. A letter from these matrices can be represented first by its row and next by its column e.g., 'A' can be represented by 40, 01, 13, 32, and 'N' can be represented by 56, 68, 89 etc. Similarly, you have to identify the set for the word given below :

SIX-KIDS

Matrix-I

	0	1	2	3	4
4	A	F	K	P	U
3	F	K	A	U	P
2	P	U	F	K	A
1	K	P	U	A	F
0	U	A	P	F	K

Matrix-II

	5	6	7	8	9
9	D	I	N	S	X
8	X	S	I	D	N
7	N	X	S	I	D
6	S	D	X	N	I
5	I	N	D	X	S

(a) 86, 87, 99 – 40, 41, 86, 64
(b) 98, 96, 85 – 42, 78, 88, 77
(c) 77, 69, 76 – 22, 95, 28, 31
(d) 65, 55, 67 – 05, 25, 91, 40

QUANTITATIVE APTITUDE

26. The value of $\left(\frac{-1}{216}\right)^{-\frac{2}{3}}$ is :

(a) $\frac{1}{36}$ (b) $-\frac{1}{36}$
(c) -36 (d) 36

27. The ussnit's digit in the product $7^{35} \times 3^{71} \times 11^{55}$ is :
(a) 1 (b) 3
(c) 7 (d) 9

28. When the price of a radio was reduced by 20%, its sale increased by 80%. What was the net effect on the sale?
(a) 44% increase (b) 44% decrease
(c) 66% increase (d) 75% increase

29. How much water must be added to 48 ml of alcohol to make a solution that contains 25% alcohol ?
(a) 24 ml (b) 72 ml
(c) 144 ml (d) 196 ml

30. Ravi's salary is 150% of Amit's salary. Amit's salary is 80% of Ram's salary. What is the ratio of Ram's salary to Ravi's salary?
(a) 1 to 2 (b) 2 to 3
(c) 5 to 6 (d) 6 to 5

31. A sum of money invested at compound interest amounts in 3 years to ₹ 2,400 and in 4 years to ₹ 2,520. The interest rate per annum is :
(a) 6% (b) 5%
(c) 10% (d) 12%

32. A man borrows ₹ 6000 at 10% compound rate of interest. He pays back ₹ 2000 at the end of each year to clear his debt. The amount that he should pay to clear all his dues at the end of third year is
(a) ₹ 6000 (b) ₹ 3366
(c) ₹ 3060 (d) ₹ 3066

33. At what percentage above the cost price must an article be marked so as to gain 33% after allowing the customer a discount of 5%?
(a) 48% (b) 43%
(c) 40% (d) 38%

34. The batting average of 40 innings of a cricket player is 50 runs. His highest score exceeds his lowest score by 172 runs. If these two innings are excluded, the average of the remaining 38 innings is 48. His highest score was :
(a) 172 (b) 173
(c) 174 (d) 176

35. The lengths of three sides of a triangle are known. In which of the cases given below, it is impossible to get a triangle?
(a) 15 cm, 12 cm, 10 cm
(b) 3.6 cm, 4.3 cm, 5.7 cm
(c) 17 cm, 12 cm, 6 cm
(d) 2.3 cm 4.4 cm, 6.8 cm

36. The perimeters of two similar triangles ABC and PQR are 36 cm, and 24 cm, respectively. If PQ = 10 cm, then the length of AB is :
(a) 16 cm (b) 12 cm
(c) 14 cm (d) 15 cm

37. Two isosceles triangles have equal vertical angles and their areas are in the ratio 9 : 16. The ratio of their corresponding heights is :
(a) 3 : 4 (b) 4 : 3
(c) 2 : 1 (d) 1 : 2

38. If in the following figure, PA = 8 cm, PD = 4 cm, CD = 3 cm, then AB is equal to :

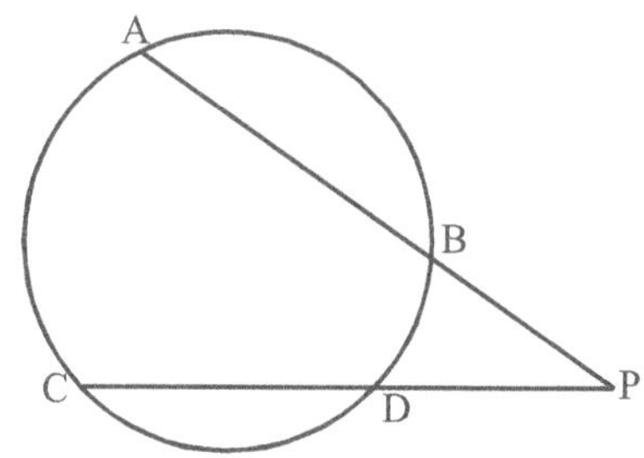

(a) 3.0 cm (b) 3.5 cm
(c) 4.0 cm (d) 4.5 cm

39. In a triangle ABC, $\angle A = x$, $\angle B = y$ and $\angle C = y + 20$. If $4x - y = 10$, then the triangle is :
(a) Right-angled (b) Obtuse-angled
(c) Equilateral (d) None of these

40. Which one of the following is a factor of $x^3 - 19x + 30$?
(a) $x-2$ (b) $x+2$
(c) $x-1$ (d) $x+1$

41. If $2x^2 - 7xy + 3y^2 = 0$, then the value of x : y is :
(a) 3 : 2 (b) 2 : 3
(c) 3 : 1 or 1 : 2 (d) 5 : 6

42. If $27 \times (81)^{2n+3} - 3^m = 0$, then what is m equal to?
(a) $2n+5$ (b) $5n+6$
(c) $8n+3$ (d) $8n+15$

43. If the L.C.M and H.C.F. of two numbers are 2400 and 16, one number is 480; find the second number.
(a) 40 (b) 80
(c) 60 (d) 50

44. The average age of 80 boys in a class is 15. The average age of a group of 15 boys in the class is 16 and the average age of another 25 boys in the class is 14. What is the average age of the remaining boys in the class ?
(a) 15.25 (b) 14
(c) 14.75
(d) Cannot be determined

45. 40% of 265 + 35% of 180 = 50% of?
(a) 338 (b) 84.5
(c) 253.5 (d) 169

DIRECTIONS (Qs. 46 to 48): *The following table, gives the annual production (in thousands) of 5 products of a famous toy company. Study the table and then answer the questions that follow :*

Year	Ludo	Scrabble	Chess	Monopoly	Carrom
1992	200	150	78	90	65
1993	150	180	100	105	70
1994	180	175	92	110	85
1995	195	160	120	125	75
1996	220	185	130	135	80

46. What is the approximate percentage increase in the production of Monopoly form 1993 to 1995?
(a) 10 (b) 20
(c) 5 (d) 25

47. For which toy category there has been a continuous increase in the production over the years?
(a) Ludo (b) Chess
(c) Monopoly (d) Carrom

48. What is the percentage drop in the production of Ludo from 1992 to 1994 ?
(a) 30 (b) 50
(c) 20 (d) 10

49. A circle road runs around a circular garden. If the difference between the circumference of the outer circle and the inner circle is 44 m, the width of the road is
(a) 4m (b) 7m
(c) 3.5m (d) 7.5m

50. The perimeter of a square whose area is equal to that of a circle with perimeter $2\pi x$ is :
(a) $2\pi x$ (b) $\sqrt{\pi}x$
(c) $4x\sqrt{\pi}$ (d) $4\pi\sqrt{x}$

ENGLISH LANGUAGE

DIRECTIONS (Qs. 51-52): *Fill in the blanks with the appropriate word* or *group of words from the options given below.*

51. Although I was _________ of his plans, I encouraged him, because there was no one else who was willing to help.
(a) sceptical (b) remorseful
(c) fearful (d) excited

52. You have no business to _________ pain on a weak and poor person.
(a) inflict (b) put
(c) direct (d) force

DIRECTIONS (Qs. 53-54): *Select the word or group of words that is most similar in meaning to the words in capital letters.*

53. REPAST
(a) Past (b) Fond memories
(c) Peacefulness (d) Meal

54. ABEYANCE
(a) Temporary suspension
(b) Abstinence
(c) Hatred
(d) Memory

DIRECTIONS (Qs. 55-56): *Select the word or group of words that is most* ***opposite*** *in meaning to the words in capital letters.*

55. Exonerate
(a) Reject (b) Contract
(c) Accuse (d) Admit

56. Exodus
(a) Home-coming (b) Influx
(c) Restoration (d) Return

DIRECTIONS (Qs. 57-58): *Look at the underlined part of each sentence. Below each sentence, three possible situations for the underlined part are given. If one of them (a), (b) or (c) is better than the underlined part, indicate your response on the Answer against the corresponding letter (a), (b) or (c). If none of these substitutions improves the sentence, indicate (d) as your Answer. Thus a "No Improvement" response will be signified by the letter (d).*

57. More than one person <u>was killed</u> in the accident.
(a) were killed (b) are killed
(c) have been killed (d) No improvement

58. Not a word <u>they spoke</u> to the unfortunate about victims of the earthquake.
(a) did they speak (b) they will speak
(c) they had spoken (d) No improvement

DIRECTIONS (Qs. 59-60): *In this section, you are required to spot errors in sentences. Each sentence is divided into three parts. Read each sentence to find out whether there is an error in any of the parts. No sentence has more than one error. Some of the sentences do not have any error. When you find an error in a sentence, the letter indicated under that part of the sentence is the answer and therefore the same may be marked on the separate Answer Sheet. If there is no error in any part.*

59. He went to England to work as a doctor (a) / but returned (b) / as he could not endure the weather there. (c) / No error (d)

60. She inquired whether (a) anyone (b) seen (c) her baby. No error (d)

DIRECTIONS (Qs. 61-62): *In questions given below out of four alternatives. Choose the one which can be substitued for the given word/sentence.*

61. Words inscribed on tomb
(a) Epitome (b) Epistle
(c) Epilogue (d) Epitaph

62. One who eats everything
(a) Omnivorous (b) Omniscient
(c) Irrestible (d) Insolvent

DIRECTIONS (Qs. 63-64): *Find the correctly spelt word.*

63. (a) Pessenger (b) Passenger
(c) Pasanger (d) Pesanger

64. (a) Benefitted (b) Benifited
(c) Benefited (d) Benefeted

DIRECTIONS (Qs. 65-69): *Select the most appropriate word from the options against each number:*

Life is an **(65)** series of challenges and opportunities to be seized. You have to plan for exercising the right career choices and **(66)** the right opportunities. Planned **(67)** rather than a hasty decision is **(68)** as far as your career is concerned. You need to **(69)** what occupational groups, qualifications and type of organizations are suitable for you.

65. (a) enticing (b) exciting
(c) encharming (d) enhancing

66. (a) catching (b) offsetting
(c) grabbing (d) conceiving

67. (a) delay (b) hindrance
(c) application (d) execution

68. (a) desirable (b) deciphered
(c) inevitable (d) acceptable

69. (a) check (b) classify
(c) divide (d) analyse

DIRECTIONS (Qs. 70-71): *In the following questions four alternatives are given for the idiom/phrase italicised and underlined in the sentence.*

70. Companies producing goods <u>*play to the gallery*</u> to boost their sales.
(a) Advertise
(b) cater to the public taste
(c) attempt to appeal to popular taste
(d) depend upon the public for approval

71. Since he knew what would happen, he should be left to <u>*stew in his own juice*</u>.
(a) Make a stew
(b) Boil
(c) Suffer in his own juice
(d) Suffer for his own act

DIRECTION (Q. 72): *In each of the following questions, a sentence has been given in Direct/Indirect Speech. Out of the four alternatives suggested select the one which best expresses the same sentence in Indirect/Direct Speech*

72. Rajesh said, "I bought a car yesterday."
(a) Rajesh said that I have bought a car the previous day.
(b) Rajesh told that he had bought a car yesterday.
(c) Rajesh said that he had bought a car the previous day.
(d) Rajesh said that he bought a car the previous day.

Direction (Qs. 73-75): *In the following questions, the 1st sentences of the passage are numbered 1 and the rest of the passage is split into four parts and named P, Q, R and S. These four pasts are not given in their proper order. Read the sentence and find out which of the combinations is correct. Then find the correct answer*

73. When
P. the mother bird came home
Q. the storm had subsided
R. cried
S. and on not finding her young ones. piteously
(a) QSPR (b) PSRQ
(c) PRSQ (d) QPSR

74. The guide said that
P. nowhere in the world
Q. a fairer building
R. you will find
S. than the Taj Mahal
(a) RQPS (b) PRQS
(c) PSQR (d) RQSP

75. The students knew that
P. to control
Q. in the college administration
R. our new principal
S. took a number of strong measures unruly students
(a) RSPQ (b) RSQP
(c) PQRS (d) QRPS

GENERAL AWARENESS

76. Which of the following symbiotic associations forms a lichen?
(a) An algae and a fungus
(b) An algae and a bryophyte
(c) A bacterium and a fungus
(d) A bacterium and a gymnosperm

77. Which Amendment Act is referred as mini constitution?
(a) 7th Constitutional Amendment Act, 1956
(b) 24th Constitutional Amendment Act, 1971
(c) 42nd Constitutional Amendment Act, 1976
(d) 44th Consitutional Amendment Act, 1978

78. Arihant is a
(a) Multi barrel rocket launcher
(b) Airborne Early Warning and Control System
(c) Unmarmed Combat Aerial Vehicle
(d) Nuclear-powered ballistic missile submarine

79. Denatured alcohol
(a) is a form of alcohol
(b) is unfit for drinking as it contains poisonous substances
(c) contains coloured impurities
(d) is sweet to taste

80. The city of Prayag was named Allahabad - the city of Allah by
(a) Aurangzeb
(b) Akbar
(c) Shahjahan
(d) Bahadur Shah Zafar

81. Chromosomes are made up of
(a) DNA (b) Protein
(c) DNA and Protein (d) RNA

82. While the computer executes a program, the program is held in
(a) RAM (b) ROM
(c) Hard Disk (d) Floppy Disk

83. Presidential form of government consists of the following?
(a) Popular election of the President
(b) No overlap in membership between the executive and the legislature
(c) Fixed term of office
(d) All of the above

84. Which of the following places of Sikh religious heritage is not in India?
(a) Nankana Sahib (b) Nanded
(c) Paonta Sahib (d) Keshgarh Sahib

85. The total population divided by available arable land area is referred to as
(a) Population density
(b) Nutritional density
(c) Agricultural density
(d) Industrial density

86. In human body, vitamin A is stored in the –
(a) liver (b) skin
(c) lung (d) kidney

87. Ondometer is a –
(a) Measuring instrument for distance covered by motor wheels
(b) Measuring instrument for frequency of electromagnetic waves
(c) Device for measuring sound intensity
(d) Measuring instrument for electric power

88. Which acid is used in rubber, textile, leather and electroplating industries ?
(a) Ethanoic acid (b) Methanoic acid
(c) Malanic acid (d) Butairic acid

89. The book, "A China Passage' was written by
(a) MJ Akbar
(b) Jagmohan
(c) Anees Jung
(d) John Kenneth Galbraith

90. Which city will host the 2022 Common Wealth Games?
(a) Gold Coast, Australia
(b) Durban, South Africa
(c) Lusaka, Zambia
(d) Nairobi, Kenya

91. Natural radioactivity was discovered by
(a) Marie Curie
(b) Earnest Rutherford
(c) Henry Bacquerel
(d) Enrico Fermi

92. Mahatma Gandhi left South Africa to return to India in
(a) 1911 (b) 1915
(c) 1917 (d) 1919

93. The Battle of Plassey was fought in
(a) 1757 (b) 1782
(c) 1748 (d) 1764

94. The Indian space programme began in
(a) 1961 (b) 1962
(c) 1965 (d) 1969

95. The language of discourses of Gautama Buddha was
(a) Bhojpuri (b) Magadhi
(c) Pali (d) Sanskrit

96. The World Braille Day (WBD) is observed on which date?
(a) January 3 (b) January 5
(c) January 2 (d) January 4

97. Who led the Indian delegation at the 6th RCEP Inter-sessional Ministerial Meeting (IMM)?
(a) Ajit Doval (b) Suresh Prabhu
(c) Sushma Swaraj (d) CR Chaudhary

98. India's first agri and food business online learning platform has launched in which city?
(a) Kochi (b) Agartala
(c) Warangal (d) Nagpur

99. Which of the following is the official mascot of 2018 Men's Hockey World Cup?
(a) Olly (b) Zabivaka
(c) Gauchito (d) Rhino

100. Which country to host four nation summit on Syria crisis?
(a) Turkey (b) Russia
(c) Israel (d) Iran

Hints & Explanations

1. (c) "Court" is the place where the judge gives his decision on crime. Similarly, Hospital is the place where the doctor diagnoses the disease of the patient.

2. (b) As,

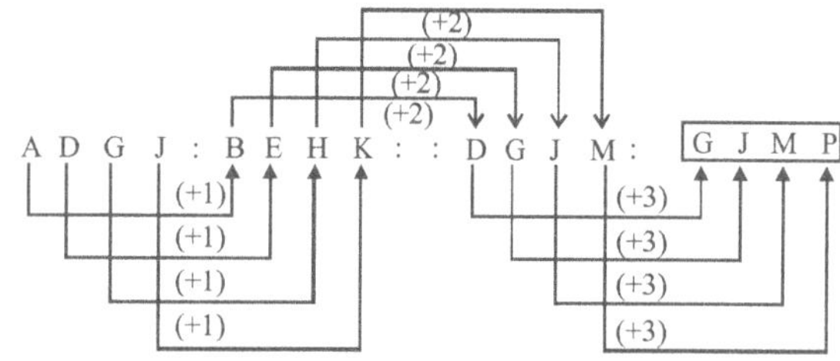

So, GJMP is the correct answer.

3. (c) As,

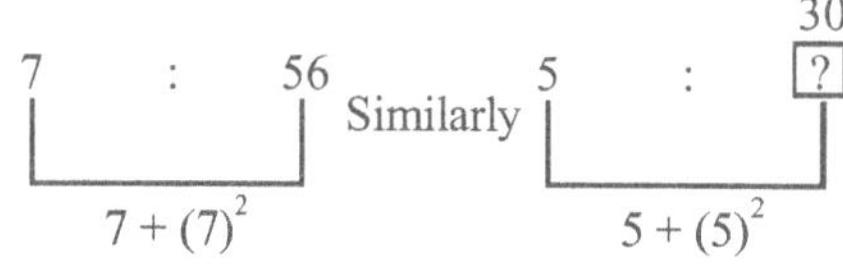

4. (a) All others, except (a) are root vegetables.

5. (d) As,

$G \xrightarrow{(-1)} F \xrightarrow{(+3)} I$

$V \xrightarrow{(-1)} U \xrightarrow{(+3)} X$

$P \xrightarrow{(-1)} O \xrightarrow{(+3)} R$

But, $L \xrightarrow{(-1)} K \xrightarrow{(+2)} M$

So, LKM is odd word

6. (c) The pattern of the series is as follows:

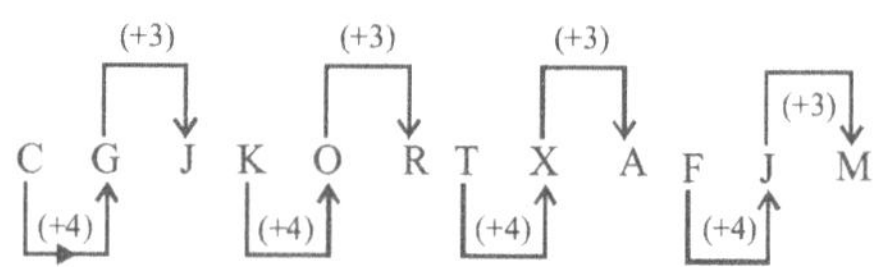

7. (b) The pattern of the series is as follows:

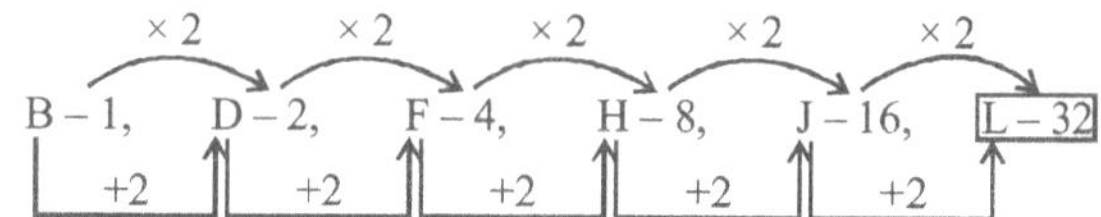

8. (c) It is based on position of English alphabet.

B	E	A	D	I	N	G
↓	↓	↓	↓	↓	↓	↓
2	5	1	4	9	(14)	7

9. (b) After arranging the letters, we get word 'ENGLAND' which is the name of the country.

10. (a) a **b** n **c** b / **a b** n c b / **a b** n c b

11. (c) After 2 boys joined, total strength of class $= 45 + 2 = 47$
As, rank was dropped by one from 20th rank, new rank is 21st.
Rank of the boy from the beginning $= 21$
No. of students below his rank $= 47 - 21 \Rightarrow 26$
Rank from the end $= (47 - 21) + 1 \Rightarrow 27$.

12. (b)

Brother-in-law
(Ram)Husband (+) ⟺ sister (−) ⟷ Brother(+)
Niece
Girl (−) ⟷ Brother (+)

Hence, girl is the niece of Ram.

13. (d) An electric train does not emit smoke.
Therefore, no smoke will be going in any of the direction.

14. (b)

Information-Communication Technology
Computer
Internet

15. (d)

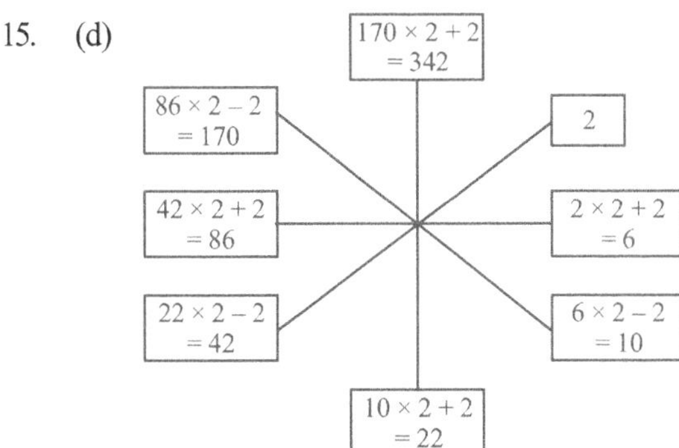

16. (c) Let total Journey $= x$ km.

Ist hour, he travelled $= \frac{x}{4}$ km.

Next hour, he travelled $= \frac{x}{2}$ km.

$$\text{Total distance travelled} = \left(\frac{x}{4} + \frac{x}{2}\right)\text{km}$$

$$= \frac{3x}{4}\text{km}$$

$$\text{Remaining distance} = \left(x - \frac{3x}{4}\right)\text{km}$$

$$= \frac{x}{4}\text{km}$$

It is given that, last
last 30 min, he travelled $= 80$ km

$$\Rightarrow \frac{x}{4} = 80$$

$$x = 320 \text{ km.}$$

17. (b) As, $7 + 3 = 421 = (7 - 3)(7 \times 3)$
$11 + 7 = 477 = (11 - 7)(11 \times 7)$
$9 + 5 = 445 = (9 - 5)(9 \times 5)$
$6 + 2 = (6 - 2)(6 \times 2) = 412$

18. (c)

Right
D A
B E
C
Left

19. (b) Conclusions :

I. (✓)
II. (✓)
III. (✓)
All follow given statements.

20.	(d)	21.	(c)	22.	(c)
23.	(c)	24.	(a)	25.	(b)

26. (d) $\left(\frac{-1}{216}\right)^{-\frac{2}{3}} = \left(\frac{-1}{6^3}\right)^{-\frac{2}{3}}$

$$= \left(-\frac{1}{6}\right)^2 = (-6)^2 = 36$$

27. (a) Unit's digit in $(7^4) = 1$. Therefore, unit's digit in $(7^4)^8$ i.e. 7^{32} will be 1. Hence, unit's digit in

$(7)^{35} = 1 \times 7 \times 7 \times 7 = 3$

Again, unit's digit in $(3)^4 = 1$
Therefore, unit's digit in the expansion of

$(3^4)^{17} = (3)^{68} = 1$

$\Rightarrow$ Unit's digit in the expansion of

$(3^{71}) = 1 \times 3 \times 3 \times 3 = 7$

and unit's digit in the expanison of

$(11^{35}) = 1$

Hence, unit's digit in the expansion of

$7^{35} \times 3^{71} \times 11^{55} = 3 \times 7 \times 1 = 1$

28. (a) Let the original price be x and sale be of y units.

Then, the revenue collected initially = x × y

Now, new price = 0.8x, new sale = 1.8 y

Then, new revenue collected = 1.44xy

$\% \text{ increase in revenue} = \frac{0.44xy}{xy} \times 100 = 44\%$

Shortcut Method

$\text{Net effect} = -20 + 80 + \frac{(-20 \times 80)}{100}$

$= 60 - 16 = 44\%$

29. (c) Let quantity of water to be added be x ml.

Then, $(x + 48) \times \frac{25}{100} = 48$ or x = 144 ml.

30. (c) Let the salary of Ram be ₹ 100.

Then, salary of Amit = ₹ 80

and salary of Ravi = 150% of 80 = ₹ 120

Ratio of Ram's salary to Ravi's salary

= 100 : 120 = 5 : 6

31. (b) Let the rate of interest be r%.

Therefore, $\frac{2520}{2400} = \frac{\left(1 + \frac{r}{100}\right)^4}{\left(1 + \frac{r}{100}\right)^3}$

$\Rightarrow 1 + \frac{r}{100} = \frac{21}{20}$ or r = 5%

32. (b) Amount = 6000

Rate = 10%

$\text{First year interest} = \frac{6000 \times 10 \times 1}{100} = ₹\ 600$

At the end of first year amount

= 6000 + 600 – 2000 = 4600

At the end of second year

$\text{Interest} = \frac{4600 \times 10 \times 1}{100} = 460$

At the second year amount

= 4600 + 460 – 2000 = 3060

At the end of third year

$\text{Interest} = \frac{3060 \times 10 \times 1}{100} = 306$

Amount at the end of third year

= 3060 + 306 = ₹ 3366

Amount refund in third year = ₹ 3366

33. (c) Let the cost price be ₹ 100.

Gain of 33% = ₹ 33

$\Rightarrow$ SP = ₹ 133

Let the marked price be ₹ x. The SP of ₹ 133 has been arrived after giving a discount of 5% on marked price.

i.e. x × 0.95 = ₹ 133

$\Rightarrow x = \frac{133}{0.95} = ₹.140$

Required increase = ₹ 140 – ₹ 100 = ₹ 40

Hence required percentage = 40%.

34. (c) Total score of 40 innings = 40 × 50 = 2000

Total score of 38 innings = 38 × 48 = 1824

Let the highest score be x and the lowest score be y.

Sum of the highest and the lowest score

= x + y = 2000 – 1824

$\Rightarrow$ x + y = 176 ...(i)

and by question, x – y = 172 ...(ii)

Solving (i) and (ii), we get x = 174

35. (d) To construct a triangle, it is necessary that the sum of any two sides is greater than the third side. Checking with options, we find that it is not possible for the measurements given in (d) as 2.3 + 4.4 < 6.8.

36. (d)

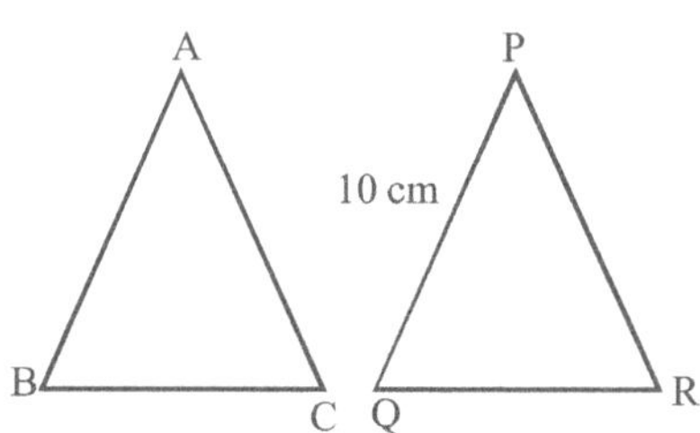

ΔABC and ΔPQR are similar.

$$\frac{AB}{PQ}=\frac{\text{Perimeter of } \Delta ABC}{\text{Perimeter of } \Delta PQR} \Rightarrow \frac{AB}{PQ}=\frac{36}{24}$$

or $AB=\frac{36}{24}\times 10=15$

37. (a) For the two similar triangles, we have

$$\frac{h_1^2}{h_2^2}=\frac{\text{Area of 1st } \Delta}{\text{Area of IInd } \Delta}=\frac{9}{16}$$

$\Rightarrow h_1 : h_2 = 3 : 4$

38. (d) We know that
PC × PD = PA × PB

$\Rightarrow \quad PB=\frac{28}{8}=3.5\,cm$

Therefore, AB = AP – BP = 8 – 3.5 = 4.5 cm

39. (a) We have, $x+y+(y+20)=180$
or $x+2y=160$ ...(i)
and $4x-y=10$ ...(ii)
From (i) and (ii), $y=70, x=20$
Angles of the triangles are 20°, 70°, 90°.
Hence the triangle is a right angled.

40. (a) If $f(x)=0$ at $x=0$, then $(x-0)$ is a factor of $f(x)$.
Checking with the options, we find that

$f(2)=(2)^3-19\times(2)+30=0$

Therefore, $x-2$ is a factor of $x^3-19x+30$

41. (c) $2x^2-7xy+3y^2=0$

$2\left(\frac{x}{y}\right)^2-7\left(\frac{x}{y}\right)+3=0$ (Dividing by y^2)

$$\frac{x}{y}=\frac{-b\pm\sqrt{b^2-4ac}}{2a}$$

$$=\frac{7\pm\sqrt{49-24}}{2\times 2}=\frac{7\pm 5}{4}=3,\frac{1}{2}$$

$\Rightarrow \frac{x}{y}=\frac{3}{1}$ or $\frac{x}{y}=\frac{1}{2}$

42. (d) Given, $27\times(81)^{2n+3}-3^m=0$

$\Rightarrow 3^3\times(3)^{8n+12}=3^m$

$\Rightarrow 3^{8n+15}=3^m \Rightarrow m=8n+15$

(on comparing)

43. (b) ∵ Product of numbers = (LCM × HCF)
⇒ 480 × second number = 2400 × 16
⇒ second number = 80

44. (a) Average age of the remaining boys

$$=\frac{(80\times15)-(15\times16+25\times14)}{40}$$

$$=\frac{1200-590}{40}=15.25$$

45. (a) 40% of 265 + 35% of 180 = 50% of ?
$\Rightarrow 265\times0.4+180\times0.35=?\times0.5$

$\Rightarrow 106+63=?\times0.5 \Rightarrow ?=\frac{169}{0.5}=338$

46. (b) Percentage increase in the production of

monopoly $=\frac{(125-105)}{105}\times100=\frac{20}{105}\times100$

$=19.05\% \approx 20\%$

47. (c) Production of monopoly has shown continuous increase over the years.

48. (d) % drop $=\frac{200-180}{200}\times100=10\%$

49. (b) Let R be the radius of circular road

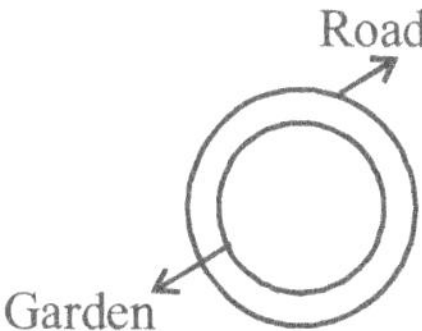

i.e., R = radius of outer circle.
Let r be the radius of inner circle(garden).
circumference of the road = 2 π R
circumference of the garden = 2πr
Given : 2 π R – 2 π r = 44 m
⇒ 2π (R – r) = 44 ⇒ R – r = 7m
Hence, the width of the road = R – r = 7m

50. (c) Area of the circle = $\pi(x)^2$ where radius of circle = x
Let side of the square be y.

Then, $y^2=\pi(x)^2 \Rightarrow y=x\sqrt{\pi}$

Perimeter of the square is $=4y=4x\sqrt{\pi}$

51. (a) The word 'sceptical' means suspicious or doubtful.

52. (a) The word 'inflict' means burden someone with or impose.

53. (d) 'Repast' means 'meal'.
54. (a) 'Abeyance' means 'not being used for a period of time'.
55. (c) Exonerate means pronounce not guilty of criminal charges, its opposite is accuse.
56. (b) Exodus means mass departure; it opposite is influx
57. (a) More than one person were killed in the accident.
58. (a) Not a word did they speak to the unfortunate victims of the earthquake.
59. (d)
60. (c) She inquired whether anyone had seen her baby.
61. (d) 62 (a)
63. (b) 64. (c)
65. (b) Exciting means creating or arousing excitement. Ex: After coming back from Switzerland, she gave an exciting account of her trip.
66. (c) Grab means get hold of or seize quickly and easily. Ex: She grabbed the opportunity that came her way.
67. (d) Execution means the act of performing; of doing something successfully; Ex: He executed the plan successfully.
68. (a) Desirable means worth having, seeking or achieving; Ex: a desirable job.
69. (a) Check means be careful or certain to do something; make certain of something; Ex: Check the door if it is closed.
70. (c) 71. (d) 72. (d) 73. (d) 74. (b)
75. (b) 76. (a) 77. (c)
78. (d) Arihant is a Nuclear powered ballistic missile submarine.
79. (b)
80. (b) Emperor Akbar named Prayag as Allahabad - City of God- also called Allahabad in 1575 AD. The city of Allahabad is situated at the confluence of three rivers - Ganga, Yamuna and the invisible Saraswati. Every 12th year when the waters are felt to be especially purifying, Allahabad holds a much greater festival called Kumbh Mela. Built by Emperor Akbar in 1583 AD, the Allahbad fort stands on the banks of the river Yamuna near the confluence site i.e SANGAM.
81. (c) 82. (a) 83. (d) 84. (a)
85. (a)
86. (a) In human body, vitamin A is stored in the **liver**.
87. (b) Ondometer is a **measuring instrument for frequency of electromagnetic waves.**
88. (b) **Methanoic acid** is a colorless, pungent smelling liquid with a boiling point 373.5 K. Due to the presence of aldehyde-like hydrogen, it is powerful reducing agent.It reduces Tollen's reagent and Fehling's solution.

    It is used in **rubber, textile, dyeing, leather** and **electroplating industries**.
89. (d) The book "A China Passage" was written by John Kenneth Galbraith in which he wrote about his visit to China between September 4th to September 23rd 1972.
90. (b) Durban, South Africa will be the host of 2022 commonwealth game.
91. (a) Natural Radio activity was discovered by Henry Becquerel in 1895.
92. (c) Mahatma Gandhi returned to India from South Africa permanently in 1917.
93. (a) The Battle of Plassey, 23 June 1757, was a decisive British East India Company victory over the Nawab of Bengal and his French allies, establishing Company rule in South Asia which expanded over much of the Indies for the next 190 years. The battle took place at Palashi, Bengal, on the river banks of the Bhagirathi River, about 150 km north of Calcutta, near Murshidabad, then capital of undivided Bengal. The belligerents were Siraj-ud-daulah, the last independent Nawab of Bengal, and the British East India Company.
94. (b) Indian Space programme began in 1962.
95. (c) 96. (d) 97. (d) 98. (c)
99. (a) 100. (a)

PRACTICE SET- 2

GENERAL INTELLIGENCE & REASONING

DIRECTIONS (Qs. 1-3) : *In questions, select the related word/letters/number from given alternatives.*

1. Uttarakhand : Dehradun : : Mizoram : ?
(a) Aizawl (b) Kohima
(c) Shillong (d) Darjeeling

2. YQXP : JBIA : : OVNU : ?
(a) FAGZ (b) HRIS
(c) DKCJ (d) DNEO

3. 1 : 1 : : 10 : ?
(a) 12 (b) 110 (c) 210 (d) 1000

4. The following numbers fall in a group. Which one does not belong to the group?
53, 63, 83, 73
(a) 53 (b) 63
(c) 83 (d) 73

5. Which one is the same as Mumbai, Kolkata and Cochin?
(a) Delhi (b) Kanpur
(c) Chennai (d) Sholapur

DIRECTION (Qs. 6-7): *In question, a series is given, with one term missing. Choose the correct alternative from the given ones that will complete the series.*

6. CEG, JLN, QSU, __?__.
(a) QOS (b) TVY
(c) HJL (d) UVW

7. 285, 253, 221, 189, ?
(a) 150 (b) 182
(c) 157 (d) 156

8. In a certain code language PRESENTATION is written as ENESTAITPRON. How would INTELLIGENCE be written in that code language ?
(a) TETGLLTNENCE
(b) LLKKTGTEEBTB
(c) LLENLLTNTETG
(d) LLTEIGENINCE

9. A word is given in capital letters. It is followed by four words. Out of these four words, three can not be formed from the letters of the word in capital letters. Point out the word which cannot be formed.
SUPERINTENDENT
(a) DENTIST (b) PERTINENT
(c) TEENER (d) RETENTION

DIRECTION (Q.10): *Which one set of letters when sequentially placed at the gaps in the given letter series shall complete it ?*

10. ba _ ba _ _ bbaaa _ bbb _ _ aa
(a) baabab (b) babbaa
(c) baaaab (d) bababa

11. Rakesh ranks 15th from the top and 45th from the bottom in a class. How many students are there in the class?
(a) 64 (b) 59
(c) 54 (d) None of these

12. Moni is daughter of Sheela. Sheela is the wife of my wife's brother. How is Moni related to my wife ?
(a) Cousin (b) Niece
(c) Sister (d) Sister-in-law

13. Ram moves from a point X to 20 metres towards North. Then he moves 40 metres towards West. Then he moves 20 metres North. Then he moves 40 metres towards East and then 10 metres towards right and he reaches to a point Y. Find the distance and direction of Y from X ?
(a) 30 metres, North (b) 30 metres, South
(c) 40 metres, North (d) 40 metres, South

14. Which figure represents the relation among Currency, Rupee and Dollar ?
(a) 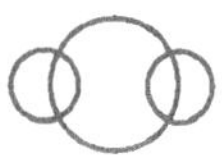 (b) 
(c)  (d)

DIRECTIONS (Qs. 15-16): *In questions, find the missing number from the given responses.*

15.

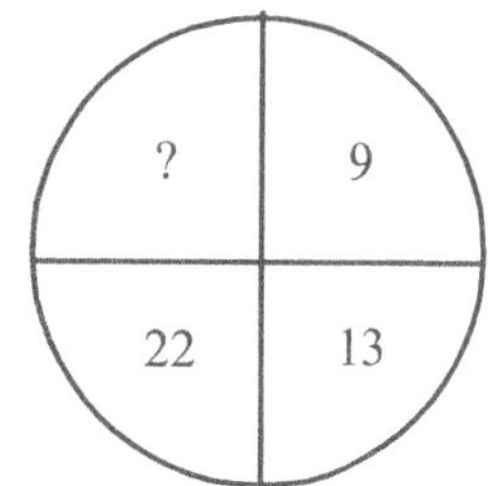

(a) 40 (b) 38
(c) 39 (d) 44

16.

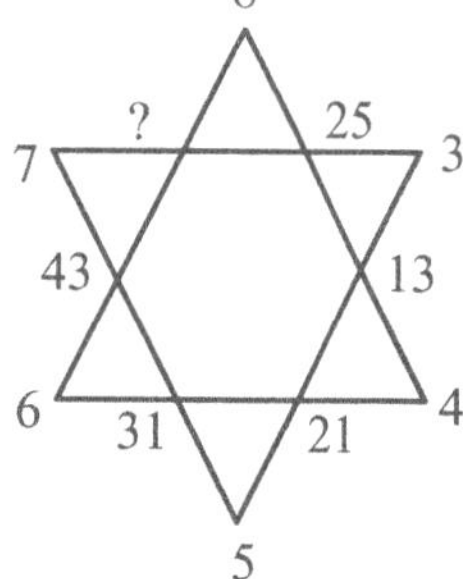

(a) 56 (b) 57
(c) 58 (d) 59

17. Nitin's age was equal to square of some number last year and the following year it would be cube of a number. If again Nitin's age has to be equal to the cube of some number, then for how long he will have to wait?

(a) 10 years (b) 38 years
(c) 39 years (d) 64 years

18. Six persons are sitting in a circle. A is facing B, B is to the right of E and left of C. C is to the left of D. F is to the right of A. Now D exchanges his seat with F and E with B. Who will be sitting to the left of D ?

(a) D (b) E
(c) A (d) B

19. From the given alternatives select the word which **cannot** be formed using the letters of the given word.

QUINTESSENCE

(a) Essence (b) Entice
(c) Sequin (d) Question

DIRECTION (Q. 20): *In question, which answer figure will complete the pattern in the question figure?*

20. Question figure :

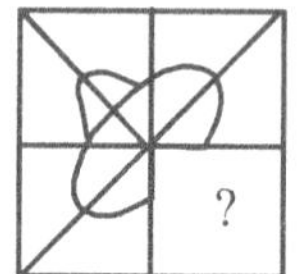

Answer Figures :

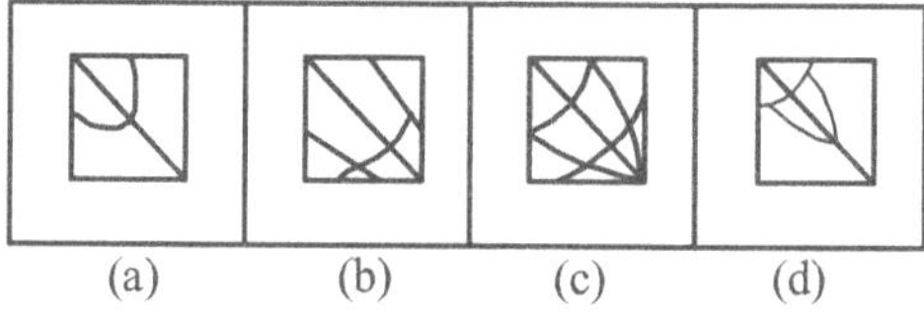

21. Four different positions of dice are as shown below. What number is opposite to face 3 ?

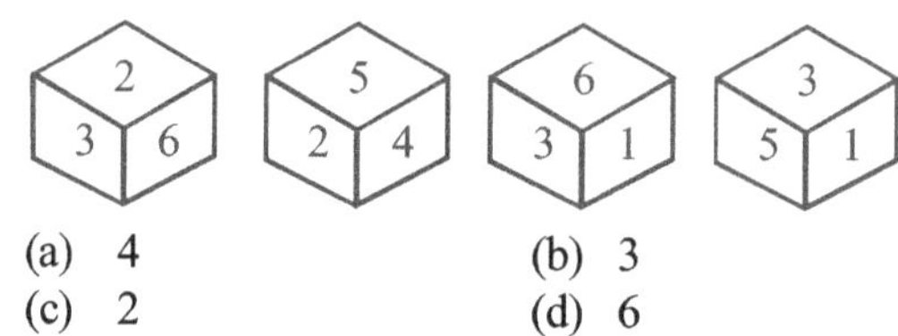

(a) 4 (b) 3
(c) 2 (d) 6

DIRECTIONS (Qs. 22-23): *In each of the following questions, which answer figure will complete the question figure?*

22. Question Figure:

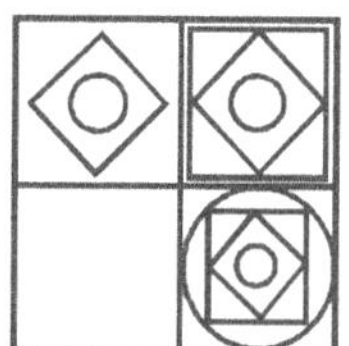

Answer Figures:

(a) 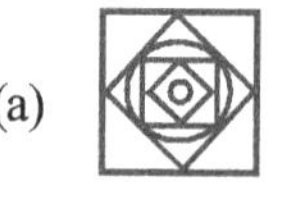

(b) 

(c) 

(d) 

23. Question Figure :

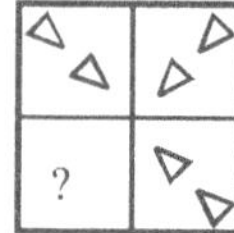

Answer Figures:

(a) 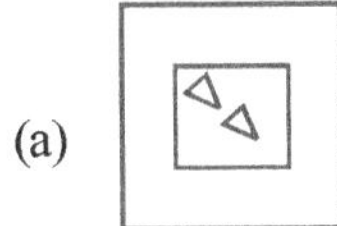 (b) 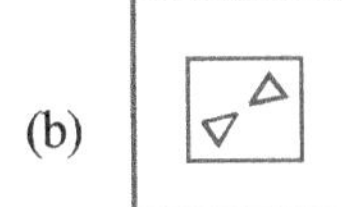

(c)  (d)

DIRECTION (Q. 24): *In the following questions, select the answer figure in which the question figure is hidden/embedded.*

24. Questlon Figure:

Answer Flgures :

(a) 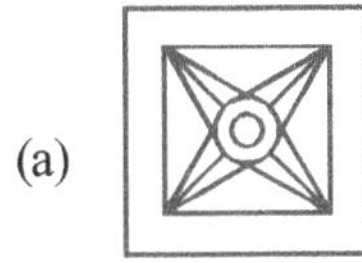 (b) 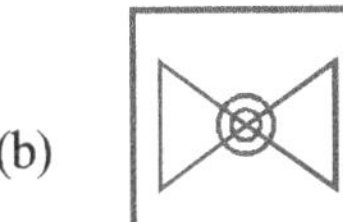

(c) 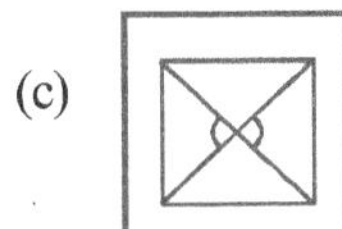 (d) 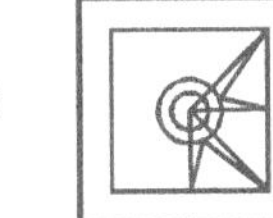

25. A word is represented by only one set of numbers as given in anyone of the alternatives. The sets of numbers given in the alternatives are represented by two classes of alphabets as in the two matrices given below. The columns and rows of matrix I are numbered from 0 to 4 and that of matrix II numbered from 5 to 9. A letter from these matrices can be represented first by its row and next by its column e.g., 'C' can be represented by 00, 12, 23, etc. and 'M' can be represented by 56, 67, 77, etc. Similarly, you have to identify the set for the given word - GOD.

Matrix-I

	0	1	2	3	4
0	C	D	E	F	G
1	G	D	C	G	E
2	E	F	G	C	D
3	G	C	F	D	E
4	D	C	F	G	E

Matrix-II

	5	6	7	8	9
5	L	M	N	O	P
6	O	L	M	N	P
7	L	O	M	P	N
8	N	O	P	M	L
9	P	L	M	N	O

(a) 10, 11, 65 (b) 95, 79, 12
(c) 30, 65, 40 (d) 00, 10, 75

QUANTITATIVE APTITUDE

26. Which is the smallest of the following numbers ?

(a) $\sqrt{7}$ (b) $\frac{1}{\sqrt{7}}$

(c) $\frac{\sqrt{7}}{7}$ (d) $\frac{1}{7}$

27. If $x^{1/3} + y^{1/3} = z^{1/3}$, then $(x + y - z)^3 + 27xyz$ is equal to?

(a) 3 (b) 0
(c) 1 (d) 2

28. A bag contains Rs 216 in the form of one rupee, 50 paise and 25 paise coins in the ratio of 2 : 3 : 4. The number of 50 paise coins is :

(a) 96 (b) 144
(c) 114 (d) 141

29. In a mixture of 45 litres, the ratio of milk and water is 4 : 1. How much water must be added to make the mixture ratio 3 : 2 ?

(a) 72 litres (b) 24 litres
(c) 15 litres (d) 1.5 litres

30. A started a business with ₹ 4500 and another person B joined after some period with ₹ 3000. Determine this period after B joined the business if the profit at the end of the year is divided in the ratio 2 : 1

(a) After 3 months (b) After 4 months
(c) After 6 months (d) After $2\frac{1}{2}$ months

31. A cistern has two taps (which fill it in 12 min and 15 min, respectively) and an exhaust tap. When all three taps are opened together, it takes 20 min to fill the empty cistern. How long will the exhaust tap take to empty it ?

(a) 20 min (b) 16 min
(c) 12 min (d) 10 min

32. 12 men complete a work in 18 days. Six days after they had started working, 4 men joined them. How many days will all of them take to complete the remaining work ?
(a) 10 days (b) 12 days
(c) 15 days (d) 9 days

33. A motor boat whose speed is 15 km/h in still water goes 30 km downstream and comes back in four and a half hours. The speed of the stream is :
(a) 46 km/h (b) 6 km/h
(c) 7 km/h (d) 5 km/h

34. 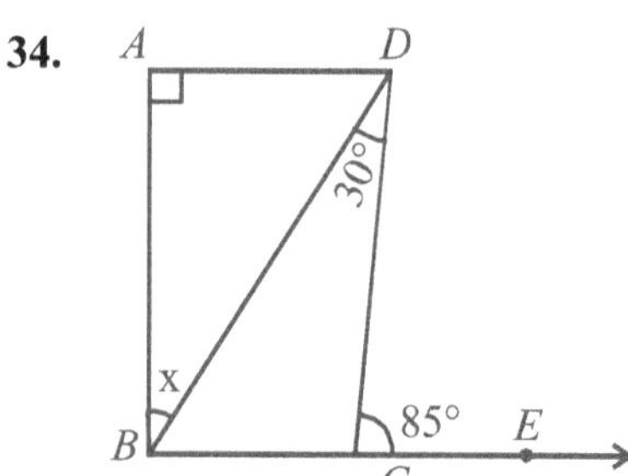

If $AD \parallel BE$, $\angle DCE = 85°$ and $\angle BDC = 30°$, then what is the value of x?
(a) 30° (b) 35°
(c) 45° (d) 55°

35. The L.C.M. of two number is 630 and their H.C.F. is 9. If the sum of numbers is 153, their difference is
(a) 17 (b) 23
(c) 27 (d) 33

36. What is the number of points in the plane of a ΔABC which are at equal distance from the vertices of the triangle?
(a) 0 (b) 1
(c) 2 (d) 3

37. Find the compound interest on Rs 25625 for 12 months at 16% per annum, compounded quarterly.
(a) 29977.62 (b) 4352.62
(c) 4100 (d) 29725

38. If a dividend of ` 57,834 is to be divided among Meena, Urmila and Vaishali in the proportion of 3:2:1, find Urmila's share.
(a) ₹19,281 (b) ₹17,350
(c) ₹23,133 (d) ₹19,278

39. A certain number of men can do a work in 60 days. If there were 8 men more it could be finished in 10 days less. How many men are there ?
(a) 75 men (b) 40 men
(c) 48 men (d) 45 men

40. For what value of k, will the expression $3x^3 - kx^2 + 4x + 16$ be divisible by $\left(x - \frac{k}{2}\right)$?
(a) 4 (b) –4
(c) 2 (d) 0

41. *a, b, c* and *d* are four consecutive numbers. If the sum of *a* and *d* is 103, what is the product of *b* and *c* ?
(a) 2652 (b) 2562
(c) 2970 (d) 2550

42. If the HCF of $x^3 + mx^2 - x + 2m$ and $x^2 + mx - 2$ is a linear polynomial, then what is the value of m?
(a) 1 (b) 2
(c) 3 (d) 4

43. If mean of y and $\frac{1}{y}$ is M, then what is the mean of y^3 and $\frac{1}{y^3}$?
(a) $\frac{M(M^2 - 3)}{3}$ (b) M^3
(c) $M^3 - 3$ (d) $M(4M^2 - 3)$

44. A cyclist covers a distance of 750 m in 2 min 30 sec. What is the speed in km/h of the cyclist ?
(a) 18 km/h (b) 15 km/h
(c) 20 km/h (d) None of these

45. The average age of a man and his son is 16 years. The ratio of their ages is 15 : 1 respectively. What is the son's age?
(a) 30 years (b) 32 years
(c) 2 years (d) 4 years

46. The equation of a line parallel to the line $3x - 4y + 5 = 0$ and passing through the point $(2, -3)$ is
(a) $2x - 3y = 7$ (b) $3x + 4y = 9$
(c) $4x + 3y = 8$ (d) $3x - 4y = 18$

DIRECTIONS (Qs. 47-48): *The adjacent histogram shows the average pocket money received by 60 students for a span of one month. Study the diagram and answer the question.*

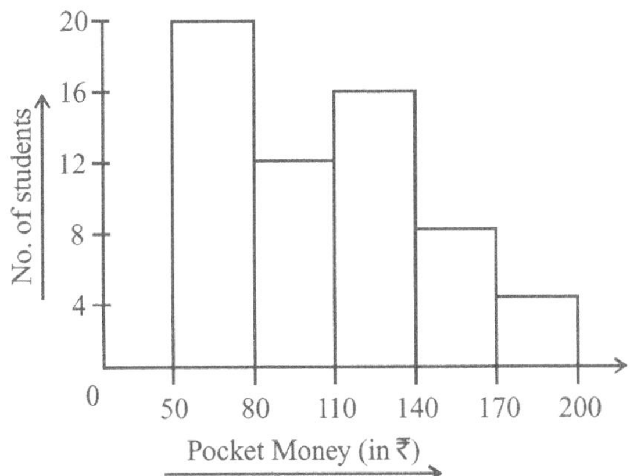

47. Maximum number of students received pocket money between
(a) 50 – 80 (b) 140–170
(c) 80 – 110 (d) 110 – 140

48. The number of students who received pocket money upto ₹ 140 is
(a) 20 (b) 32
(c) 48 (d) 56

49. Semi-circular lawns are attached to all the edges of a rectangular field measuring 42 m × 35m. The area of the total field is :
(a) 3818.5 m^2 (b) 8318 m^2
(c) 5813 m^2 (d) 1358 m^2

50. A steel wire has been bent in the form of a square of area 121 cm^2. If the same wire is bent in the form of a circle, then the area of the circle will be :
(a) 130 cm^2 (b) 136 cm^2
(c) 145 cm^2 (d) None of these

ENGLISH LANGUAGE

DIRECTIONS (Qs. 51-52): *In the following questions four alternatives are given for the idiom/phrase italicised and underlined in the sentence.*

51. The project did not appear to *hold out* bright prospects.
(a) Highlight (b) show
(c) Offer (d) promise

52. I am afraid he is *burning the candle* at both ends and ruining his life.
(a) wasting his money
(b) becoming overgenerous
(c) overtaxing his energies
(d) losing his objectives

DIRECTIONS (Qs. 53-54): *In questions given below out of four alternatives. Choose the one which can be substitued for the given word/sentence.*

53. The custom or practice of having more than one husband at same time
(a) Polygyny (b) Polyphony
(c) Polyandry (d) Polychromy

54. Tending to move away from the centre or axis
(a) Centrifugal (b) Centripetal
(c) Axiomatic (d) Awry

DIRECTIONS (Qs. 55-56): *In this section, you are required to spot errors in sentences. Each sentence is divided into three parts. Read each sentence to find out whether there is an error in any of the parts. No sentence has more than one error. Some of the sentences do not have any error. When you find an error in a sentence, the letter indicated under that part of the sentence is the answer and therefore the same may be marked on the separate Answer Sheet. If there is no error in any part, mark (d) as the answer.*

55. These are (a) his (b) conclusion remarks. (c) No error (d)

56. The shopkeeper offered either to exchange (a) the goods (b) or refund the money. (c) No error (d)

DIRECTIONS (Qs. 57-59): *Look at the underlined part of each sentence. Below each sentence, three possible situations for the underlined part are given. If one of them (a), (b) or (c) is better than the underlined part, indicate your response on the Answer Sheet against the corresponding letter (a), (b) or (c). If none of these substitutions improves the sentence, indicate (d) as your response on the Answer Sheet. Thus a "No Improvement" response will be signified by the letter (d).*

57. I am used to hard work.
(a) work hard (b) work hardly
(c) hard working (d) No improvement

58. Twenty kilometres are not a great distance in these days of fast moving vehicles.
(a) is not a great distance
(b) is no distance
(c) aren't a great distance
(d) No improvement

59. They were working as usually.
(a) usual (b) as usual
(c) usually (d) No improvement

DIRECTIONS (Qs. 60-61): *Pick out the nearest correct meaning or synonym of the words given below:*

60. RECUPERATE
(a) recapture (b) delight
(c) recover (d) overcome

61. ALMS
(a) blessings (b) charity
(c) prayers (d) worship

DIRECTIONS (Qs. 62-63): *Pick out the opposite meaning or antonym of the words given below:*

62. INDICT
(a) condemn (b) reprimand
(c) acquit (d) allege

63. VACILLATE
(a) amplify (b) stimulate
(c) consistent (d) eradicate

DIRECTIONS (Qs. 64-66): *Choose the correct spelling of the given word.*

64. (a) Efflorascence (b) Efflorescence
(c) Eflloreseence (d) Eflorescence

65. (a) Aliennate (b) Allienate
(c) Alienate (d) Alienatte

66. (a) Gragarious (b) Gragerious
(c) Gregarious (d) Grigareous

DIRECTIONS (Qs. 67-68): *In the following questions, sentences are given with blanks to be filled with appropriate word(s). Choose the correct alternative form the given options and indicate it.*

67. It is not fair to cast .... on honest and innocent persons.
(a) aspiration (b) aspersions
(c) inspiration (d) adulation

68. No country can .... to practice a constant, rigid foreign policy in view of the world power dynamics.
(a) obliviate (b) anticipate
(c) afford (d) envisage

DIRECTION (Q. 69): *In these questions, the sentences have been given in Active / Passive Voice. From the given alternatives, choose the one which best expresses the given sentence in Passive / Active Voice.*

69. The Principal has granted him a scholarship.
(a) A scholarship has granted to him by the Principal.
(b) He has been granted a scholarship by the Principal.
(c) He has granted a scholarship by the Principal.
(d) A scholarship was granted to him by the Principal.

DIRECTIONS (Qs. 70-71): *In the following questions, the 1st and last sentences of the passage are numbered 1 & 6 and the rest of the passage is split into four parts and named P, Q, R and S. These four parts are not given in their proper order. Read the sentence and find out which of the four combinations is correct. Then find the correct answer*

70. 1. Kapil
P. left in an aeroplane
Q. after reading
R. had decided.
S. to build his own boat nine years earlier
6. a sailing magazine.
(a) PRQS (b) RSQP
(c) RQPS (d) PSRQ

71. 1. When
P. it becomes an honour
Q. in recognition of their great performance
R. illustrious personalities
S. win an award
6. of a lifetime
(a) RPQS (b) PQRS
(c) QRSP (d) RSQP

DIRECTIONS (Qs. 72-75): *In the following passages, some of the words have been left out. First read the passage over and try to understand what it is about. Then fill in the blanks with the help of the alternatives given. Mark your answer in the Answer-Sheet.*

Several commentators have remarked that Finance Minister Arun Jaitley's budget for 2017-18 lacks much **72**. But everything has to be viewed in **73**. This year's Budget was presented at a time when there are several **74** clouds hanging over the economy. We are still reeling **75** the effects of demonetisation, which must have earned a prominent place in the record books as one of the biggest policy induced disasters of all time.

72. (a) Confidence (b) Fizz
(c) work (d) effort

73. (a) place (b) perspective
(c) distance (d) mirror

74. (a) white (b) storm
(c) clean (d) black

75. (a) to (b) off
(c) of (d) from

GENERAL AWARENESS

76. Which Article of the Indian Constitution guarantees rights to arrested persons ?
(a) Article 22 (b) Article 35
(c) Article 20 (d) Article 42

77. Cryogenic is a science deals with
(a) High Temperatures (b) Low Pressure
(c) High Pressure (d) Low Temperature

78. .... is an active factor of production
(a) Product (b) Labour
(c) Wages (d) Price

79. When total utility becomes maximum, then marginal utility will be
(a) Maximum
(b) Minimum
(c) Either maximum or minimum
(d) Zero

80. Wood Spirit is which of the following ?
(a) Ethyl Alcohol (b) Propanol
(c) Methyl Alcohol (d) Butanol

81. Study of crop production is ....
(a) Entology (b) Ecology
(c) Botany (d) Agronomy

82. Tattvabodhini Sabha was founded by ...... In 1839
(a) Swami Vivekanand
(b) Keshav Chandra Sen
(c) Dabendranath Tagore
(d) Swami Sahajanamd

83. After the revolt of 1857, British pursued the policy of..............
(a) Divide and Policies
(b) Rules and Regulation
(c) Divide and Rule
(d) Unity and Poliy

84. Prithvi-I missile was inducted into the ....in 1994
(a) Indian Army (b) Indian Air Force
(c) Indian Navy (d) All of these

85. ....is issued by the court in case of illegal detention of a person
(a) Quo Warranto (b) Habeas Corpus
(c) Mandamus (d) Certiorari

86. At the time of Emergency, the Indian State become unitary from ....
(a) Semi Federal (b) Federal
(c) Unitary (d) Quasi-federal

87. Bos Taurus is a scientific name of...................
(a) Buffalo (b) Horse
(c) Cow (d) Cat

88. .... is the Kuchipudi dancer
(a) Anupama Mohan (b) Bimbavati Devi
(c) Arush Mudgal (d) Swapnasundari

89. Which of the following is not a chief organ of the United Nations Organisations?
(a) International Labour Organisation
(b) Security Council
(c) International Court of Justice
(d) General Assembly

90. Who was the Viceroy when the Simon Commission visited India?
(a) Lord Chelmsford (b) Lord Reading
(c) Lord Irwin (d) Lord Wellington

91. Animals active at night are called
(a) Diurnal (b) Nocturnal
(c) Parasites (d) Nacto-diurnal

92. Lines joining places of equal temperature are called
(a) Isotherms (b) Isohyets
(c) Isomers (d) Isobars

93. Natural radioactivity was discovered by
(a) Marie Curie
(b) Earnest Rutherford
(c) Henry Bacquerel
(d) Enrico Fermi

94. How many days moon takes to revolve around the earth?
(a) $26\frac{1}{3}$ (b) $27\frac{1}{3}$
(c) $28\frac{2}{3}$ (d) $29\frac{1}{2}$

95. In which atmospheric layer are the communication satellites located?
(a) Stratosphere (b) Ionosphere
(c) Troposphere (d) Mesosphere

96. The book, 'Born Again on the Mountain' is authored by
(a) Pooja Rani (b) Arunima Sinha
(c) Bachendri Pal (d) Urbashi Lal
(d) Rafael Nadal

97. Which state has recently celebrated the Kati Bihu festival 2018?
(a) Meghalaya (b) Assam
(c) West Bengal (d) Jharkhand

98. The scientists of which space agency have found superflares flares from the Young Red Dwarf Stars imperiling planets?
(a) ISRO (b) JAXA
(c) NASA (d) Roscosmos

99. Who has won the Wildlife Photographer Of The Year 2018?
(a) Thomas D Mangelsen
(b) Michael Nichols
(c) Marsel van Oosten
(d) Pal Hermansen

100. Which country is host to the Interfaith Alliance Forum 2018?
(a) Iran (b) Israel
(c) India (d) UAE

Hints & Explanations

1. (a) Dehradun is capital of Uttarakhand. Similarly, Aizawl is capital of Mizoram.

2. (c)

(−1) (−1)
Y Q X P : J B I A
(−1) (−1)

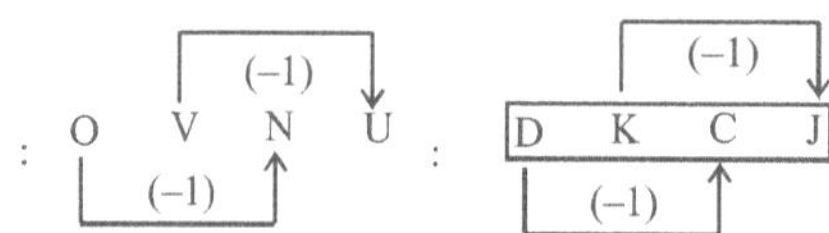

3. (d) As, $(1)^3$: 1
Similarly,
$(10)^3 : 1000$

4. (b) Here, only 63 is not belonging to group because it is divisible by 3.

5. (c) Mumbai, Kolkata and Cochin all are coastal city. Similarly, Chennai is also a coastal city.

6. (c)

$C \xrightarrow{+2} E \xrightarrow{+2} G \quad J \xrightarrow{+2} L \xrightarrow{+2} N \quad Q \xrightarrow{+2} S \xrightarrow{+2} U$

Similarly, $H \xrightarrow{+2} J \xrightarrow{+2} L$

7. (c) 285 253 221 189 **157**
−32 −32 −32 −32

8. (d)

PR	ES	EN	TA	TI	ON	→	EN	ES	TA	IT	PR	ON
1	2	3	4	5	6		3	2	4	5	1	6

Similarly,

IN	TE	LL	IG	EN	CE	→	**LL**	**TE**	**IG**	**EN**	**IN**	**CE**
1	2	3	4	5	6		**3**	**2**	**4**	**5**	**1**	**6**

9. (d) RETENTION

10. (b) ba/ b ba a / b bbaaa/ b bbb a a aa

11. (b) Clearly, no. of students in the class = 14+1 +44 ⇒ 59.

12. (b)

13. (c)

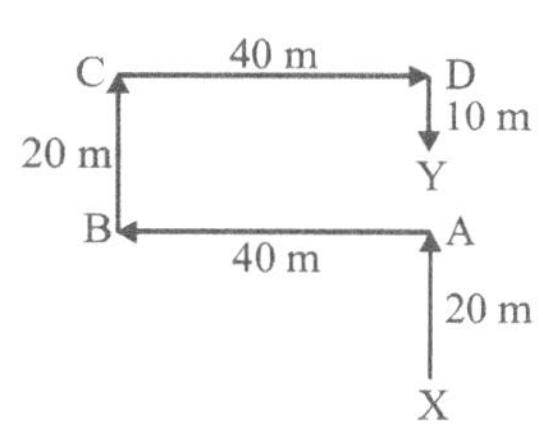

Required distance = XY = AX + AY
= 20 + 10
= 30 m, North

14. (b)

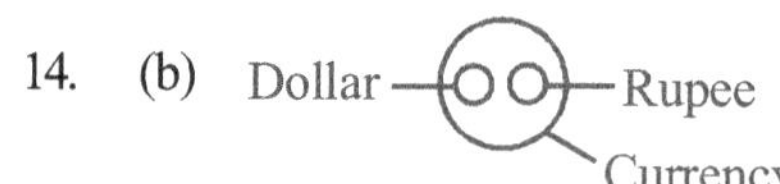

15. (b)

$22 + 4^2 = 38$ | 9
$13 + 3^2 = 22$ | $9 + 2^2 = 13$

16. (b)

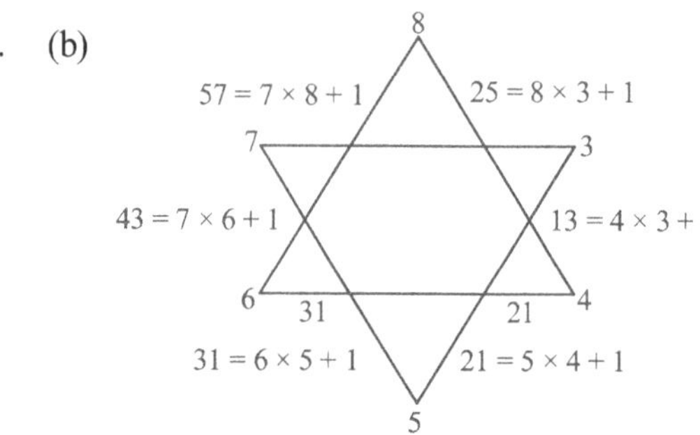

17. (b) Clearly, we have to first find two numbers whose difference is 2 and of which the smaller one is a perfect square and the bigger one a perfect cube.

Such numbers are 25 and 27.

Thus, Nitin is now 26 years old. Since the next perfect cube after 27 is 64,

So required time period = (64 – 26) years = 38 years.

18. (c)

(E) B, E (B), F (D), A, (F) D, C

Now, A is to the left of D.

19. (d) There is no 'O' letter in the keyword.
20. (d)
21. (a) The numbers 1, 2, 5 and 6 are on the adjacent faces of the number 3. So, the number 4 lies opposite 3.
22. (a) 23. (c) 24. (a)
25. (c) G $\Rightarrow$ 04, 10, 22, 30, 43
O $\Rightarrow$ 58, 65, 76, 86, 99
D $\Rightarrow$ 01, 11, 24, 33, 40

Option	G	O	D
(a)	10	~~11~~	~~65~~
(b)	~~95~~	~~79~~	~~12~~
(c)	30	65	40
(d)	~~00~~	~~10~~	~~75~~

26. (d) Clearly, $\frac{1}{7} < \frac{1}{\sqrt{7}} = \frac{\sqrt{7}}{7} < \sqrt{7}$

$\Rightarrow \frac{1}{7}$ is the smallest number.

27. (b) The given equation = $x^{1/3} + y^{1/3} = z^{1/3}$ cubing both sides
$(x^{1/3} + y^{1/3})^3 = z$
$\Rightarrow x + y + 3\,(x^{2/3})\,(y^{1/3}) + 3(x^{1/3})\,(y^{2/3}) = z$
$\Rightarrow x + y + 3[(x^{2/3})\,(y^{1/3}) + (x^{1/3})\,(y^{2/3})] = z$
$\Rightarrow x + y + 3\,(x^{1/3})\,(y^{1/3})\,(x^{1/3} + y^{1/3}) = z$
putting $x^{1/3} + y^{1/3} = z^{1/3}$
$\Rightarrow x + y + 3\,(x^{1/3})\,(y^{1/3})\,(z^{1/3}) = z$
$\Rightarrow x + y - z = -3\,(x^{1/3})\,(y^{1/3})\,(z^{1/3})$
$\Rightarrow (x + y - z)^3 = -3\,(x^{1/3})\,(y^{1/3})\,(z^{1/3})$
$\Rightarrow (x + y - z)^3 = -27xyz$ (cubing both sides)
$\Rightarrow (x + y - z)^3 = +27xyz = 0$

28. (b) Let the no. of one rupee, 50 paise and 25 paise coins be 2x, 3x and 4x respectively.
According to question,

$$₹\left(2x + \frac{3x}{2} + \frac{4x}{4}\right) = \text{Rs. } 216$$

$$\Rightarrow \frac{8x + 6x + 4x}{4} = 216$$

$\therefore$ x = 48
$\therefore$ Number of 50 paise coins = 48 × 3 = 144

29. (c) Quantity of milk = $45 \times \frac{4}{5} = 36$ litres

Quantity of water = $45 \times \frac{1}{5} = 9$ litres

Let x litres of water be added to make the ratio 3 : 2

Then, $\frac{36}{9 + x} = \frac{3}{2}$

$\Rightarrow 72 = 27 + 3x \Rightarrow x = 15$ litres

30. (a) Let B joined after x months.
Then, 4500 × 12 : 3000 (12 – x) = 2 : 1
Ratio of their investments

$$= \frac{4500 \times 12}{3000(12 - x)} = \frac{2}{1}$$

$\Rightarrow x = 3$

31. (d) Let the exhaust tap empties the tank in x minutes.

Then, $\frac{1}{12} + \frac{1}{15} - \frac{1}{x} = \frac{1}{20}$ or

$\frac{1}{x} = \frac{1}{12} + \frac{1}{15} - \frac{1}{20}$

or $\frac{1}{x} = \frac{5 + 4 - 3}{60} = \frac{6}{60} = \frac{1}{10}$ or x = 10 min

32. (d) In 1 day, work done by 12 men = $\frac{1}{18}$

In 6 days, work done by 12 men = $\frac{6}{18} = \frac{1}{3}$

Remaining work = $\frac{2}{3}$

Now, $m_1 \times d_1 \times w_2 = m_2 \times d_2 \times w_1$

or $12 \times 18 \times \frac{2}{3} = 16 \times d_2 \times 1$

or $d_2 = \frac{4 \times 18 \times 2}{16} = 9$ days

33. (d) Let the speed of the stream be x km/h.
Then, upstream speed = (15 – x) km/h.
and downstream speed = (15 + x) km/h.

Now, $\frac{30}{(15+x)}+\frac{30}{(15-x)}=4.5$

Solving these equations, we get x = 5 km/h.

34. (b) $AD \parallel BE$

$\therefore \quad \angle ADC = \angle DCE$ (alternate angles)

$\Rightarrow \angle ADB + 30^\circ = 85^\circ$

$\Rightarrow \quad \angle ADB = 55^\circ$

and $\quad \angle BAD = 90^\circ$ (given)

Now, in ΔABD,

$\angle ABD + \angle ADB + \angle BAD = 180^\circ$

$\Rightarrow \quad x + 55^\circ + 90^\circ = 180^\circ$

$\Rightarrow \quad x = 180^\circ - 145^\circ = 35^\circ$

35. (c) Let numbers be x and y.

$\because$ Product of two numbers = their (LCM × HCF)

$\Rightarrow xy = 630 \times 9$

Also, $x + y = 153$ (given)

since $x - y = = \sqrt{(x+y)^2 - 4xy}$

$\Rightarrow x - y = \sqrt{(153)^2 - 4(630 \times 9)}$

$= \sqrt{23409 - 22680} = \sqrt{729} = 27$

36. (b) Number of points is one, because circumcentre is the only point in the plane of a triangle, which is equidistant from the vertices of the triangle.

$OA = OB = OC = r$

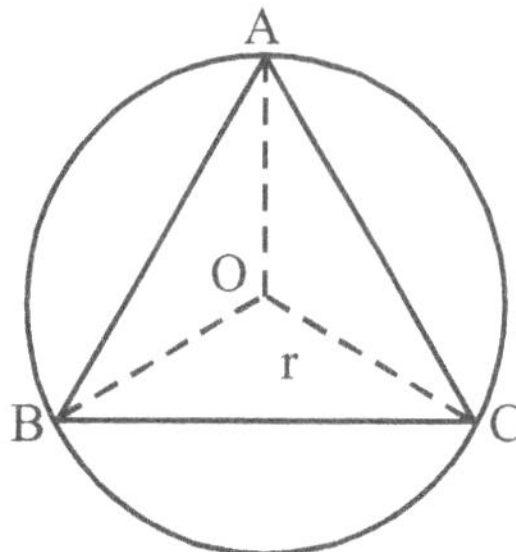

37. (b) Principal (P) = Rs 25625

Rate (r) = 16% $= \frac{16}{4}\% = 4\%$

Time = 12 months = 4 quarters

$A = 25625\left(1+\frac{4}{100}\right)^4 = 25625\left(\frac{26}{25}\right)^4$

$25625 \times \frac{26}{25} \times \frac{26}{25} \times \frac{26}{25} \times \frac{26}{25} =$ ₹ 29977.62

C.I. = A – P = 29977.62 – 25625 = ₹4352.62

38. (d) Share of Urmila in dividend = $\left(\frac{2}{6} \times 57834\right)$

= ₹ 19278

39. (b) We have :

x men to the work in 60 days and (x + 8) men do th work in

(60 – 10 =) 50 days.

Then by "basic formula", $60x = 50(x + 8)$

$\therefore x = \frac{50 \times 8}{10} = 40$ men.

40. (b) The expression $3x^3 - kx^2 + 4x + 16$ is divisible by $x - \frac{k}{2}$.

Then, $x = \frac{k}{2}$ satisfy the equation

$\Rightarrow 3\left(\frac{k}{2}\right)^3 - k\left(\frac{k}{2}\right)^2 + 4\left(\frac{k}{2}\right) + 16 = 0$

$\Rightarrow \frac{3k^3 - 2k^3 + 16k + 128}{8} = 0$

$\Rightarrow k^3 + 16k + 128 = 0$

$\Rightarrow (k + 4)(k^2 - 4k + 32) = 0$

$\Rightarrow k + 4 = 0$

$\Rightarrow k = -4$

41. (a) Here d = a + 3

a + a + 3 = 103

2a = 100

a = 50

So, numbers are 50, 51, 52 and 53

$\therefore b \times c = 51 \times 52 = 2652$

42. (a) Let $f_1(x) = x^3 + mx^2 - x + 2m$

and $f_2(x) = x^2 + mx - 2$

Let $m = 1$

$\therefore \quad f_1(x) = x^3 + x^2 - x + 2$

and $f_2(x) = x^2 + x - 2 = (x + 2)(x - 1)$

When $x = 1$,

$f(1) = 1 + 1 - 1 + 2 \neq 0$

When $x = -2$,

$f(-2) = (-2)^3 + (-2)^2 - (-2) + 2 = 0$

Required value of m is 1.

43. (d) Mean of y and $\frac{1}{y} = M$

$$\Rightarrow \frac{y+\frac{1}{y}}{2} = M \Rightarrow y + \frac{1}{y} = 2M \quad ...(i)$$

Now, mean of y^3 and $\frac{1}{y^3}$ is

$$\frac{y^3+\frac{1}{y^3}}{2} = \frac{\left(y+\frac{1}{y}\right)^3 - 3\left(y+\frac{1}{y}\right)}{2}$$

$$\Rightarrow \frac{y^3+\frac{1}{y^3}}{2} = \frac{(2M)^3 - 6M}{2}$$

$$= \frac{(2M)\left[(2M)^2 - 3\right]}{2} = M(4M^2 - 3)$$

44. (a) Speed $= \left(\frac{750}{150}\right)$ m/sec $= 5$ m/sec

$$= \left(5 \times \frac{18}{5}\right) \text{km/hr} = 18 \text{ km/hr}.$$

45. (c) Let the age of father and son be 15x years and x years respectively.

Now, according to the question, $\frac{15x + x}{2} = 16$

or, $x = \frac{16 \times 2}{16} = 2$ years

Hence age of the son = 2 years

46. (d) The required line is parallel to $3x - 4y + 5 = 0$

or $y = \frac{3}{4}x + \frac{5}{4}$ $\Rightarrow$ Their slopes are equal

$\therefore\ m = \frac{3}{4}$

Also, it passes through $(2, -3)$. so $y = mx + c$

$$\Rightarrow -3 = \frac{3}{4} \times 2 + c \Rightarrow c = -\frac{9}{2}$$

$\therefore$ The required equation is

$$y = \frac{3}{4}.x - \frac{9}{2}$$

or $3x - 4y = 18$

47. (a)
48. (c) $20 + 12 + 16 = 48$
49. (a) Area of the field = Area of rectangle + Area of circle with diameter 35 m + Area of circle with diameter 42 m.

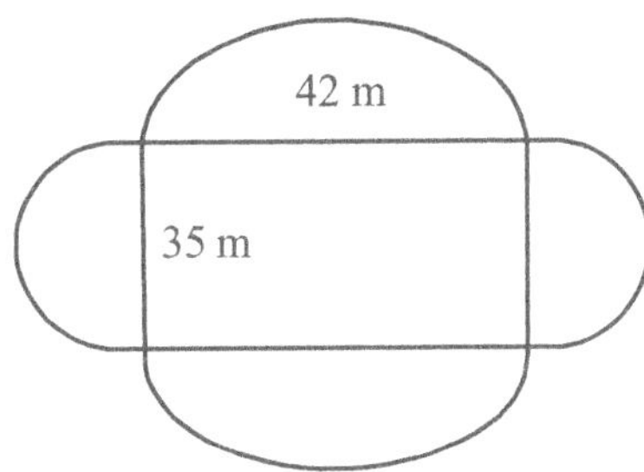

$$= 42 \times 35 + 2 \times \frac{1}{2} \times \frac{22}{7} \times (21)^2 + 2 \times \frac{1}{2} \times \frac{22}{7} \times (17.5)^2$$

$$= 1470 + 1386 + 962.5 = 3818.5 \text{ m}^2$$

50. (d) Perimeter of the square = circumference of the circle

We have, $4 \times 11 = 2\pi r \Rightarrow r = \frac{4 \times 11}{2 \times \pi}$

Area of the circle $= \pi r^2$

$$= \pi \times \left(\frac{4 \times 11}{2 \times \pi}\right)^2 = 49\pi$$

$$= 154 \text{ cm}^2$$

51. (c) 52. (c) 53. (c) 54. (a)
55. (c) 56. (a)
57. (a) work hard is correct choice.
58. (a) Twenty kilometres is not a great distance in these days of fast moving vehicles.
59. (b) they are working as usual.
60. (c) Once I fall ill, it takes me long to recuperate. That is, I take a long time to recover my health or strength after I have been ill.
61. (b) When a cyclone affects an area, the people are deprived of their belongings. You then give them money, clothes, food etc. Such gifts to the poor and needy are called alms. Since they are given out of charity (kindness and tolerance), these gifts are also known as charity.

62. (c) Indict means to charge someone with a crime or something wrong. Accuse also means the same, acquit means to free of charge.
63. (d) Vacillate means to move from one place to another and consistent means to stay the same, eradicate means to remove.
64. (b) 65. (c)
66. (c) 'Gregarious' is the correctly spelt word which means fond of company or sociable.
67. (b) 68. (b)
69. (b) The transformation follows the simple rules related to the transformation of an Assertive Sentence.
70. (b) 71. (d) 72. (b) 73 (b)
74. (b) 75. (d)
76. (a) Article 22 proceeds to guarantee certain fundamental rights to every arrested person.
77. (d) Cryogenics is the study of the production and behaviour of materials at very low temperatures.
78. (b) Some of the important factors of production are: (i) Land (ii) Labour (iii) Capital (iv) Enterprnuer. Land is a passive factor whereas labour is an active factor of production
79. (d) When total utility is maximum at the 5th unit, marginal utility is zero
80. (c) Wood spirit is a poisonous colorless liquid used as a solvent and fuel; ingestion may cause blindness or death. Called also methyl or wood alcohol.
81. (d) Agronomy is the science and technology of producing and using plants for food, fuel, fiber, and land reclamation
82. (c) The Tattwabodhinl Sabha ("Truth Propagating/Searching Society") was a group started in Calcutta on 6 October 1839 as a splinter group of the Brahmo Samaj, reformers of Hinduism and Indian Society. The founding member was Debendranath Tagore
83. (c) After the revolt, the British pursued the policy of divide and rule, towards the general populace.
84. (a) Prithvi (Sanskrit: prthvi "Earth") is a tactical surface-to-surface short-range ballistic missile .This class of Prithvi missile was inducted into the Indian Army in 1994
85. (b) Habeas corpus ("You may have the body") is a recourse in law whereby a person can report an unlawful detention or imprisonment before a court, usually through a prison official
86. (d) Professor K.C. Wheare, who regards the American constitution as the model of a true federation has described the Indian constitution as 'quasi federal', that is 'a unitary state with subsidiary federal features rather than a federal state with subsidiary unitary features
87. (c) Cows are raised in many different countries around the world, mainly for the cowsnatural resources such as milk, meat
88. (a) Anupama Mohan is one of the best-known disciples of Kuchipudi.
89. (a)
90. (c) Lord Irwin was the viceroy of India when Simon Commission visited India.
91. (b) Animals active at night are called Nocturnal.
92. (a) Isotherm is a line on the map connecting points having the same temperature at a given time.
93. (c) Henry Becquerel is associated with the discovery of Radioactivity.
94. (b) The Moon taken $27\frac{1}{3}$ days to revolve around the earth.
95. (b)
96. (b) Arunima Sinha wrote the book "Born again on the mountain", which was launched by PM Narendra Modi in 2014.
97. (b) 98. (c) 99 (c) 100 (d)

PRACTICE SET- 3

GENERAL INTELLIGENCE & REASONING

DIRECTIONS (Qs. 1-3): *In questions, select the related word/letters/number from given alternatives.*

1. ACE : FHJ : : OQS : ?
   (a) TVX (b) UWY
   (c) PRT (d) RTU
2. Saint : Meditation : : Scientist : ?
   (a) Research (b) Knowledge
   (c) Spiritual (d) Rational
3. 18 : 5 :: 12 : ?
   (a) 4 (b) 10
   (c) 3 (d) 6

DIRECTIONS (Qs. 4 - 5): *In questions, find the odd word/letters/number pair from the given alternatives.*

4. (a) Kolkata (b) Vishakhapatnam
   (c) Bengaluru (d) Haldia
5. (a) HGFE (b) PONM
   (c) DCBA (d) MSTU

DIRECTIONS (Qs. 6-7): *In questions below, a series is given with one term missing. Choose the correct alternative from the given ones that will complete the series.*

6. FAG, GAF, HAI, IAH, _______
   (a) JAK (b) HAK
   (c) JAI (d) HAL
7. 3, 6, 9, 15, 24, 39, 63, ?
   (a) 100 (b) 87
   (c) 102 (d) 99
8. If A = 1, AGE = 13, then CAR = ?
   (a) 19 (b) 20
   (c) 21 (d) 22
9. Arrange the following words as per order in the dictionary :
   1. Emplane 2. Empower
   3. Embrace 4. Elocution
   5. Equable
   (a) 5, 1, 3, 2, 4 (b) 4, 2, 1, 3, 5
   (c) 4, 3, 1, 2, 5 (d) 4, 5, 2, 3, 1

DIRECTION (Q. 10): *In question below, which one set of letters when sequentialy placed at the gaps in the given letter series shall complete it?*

10. LU_TUPLUBTU_LUBT_P_UBTUP
    (a) LBPU (b) BPUL
    (c) PBUL (d) BUPL
11. Govind is 48 years old. He is twice as old as his son Prem is now. How old was Prem seven years before?
    (a) 16 (b) 17
    (c) 13 (d) 18
12. Pointing to a man, a lady said "His mother is the only daughter of my mother". How is the lady related to the man?
    (a) Mother (b) Daughter
    (c) Sister (d) Aunt
13. After walking 10 m, Shankar turned left and covered a distance of 6 m, then turned right and covered a distance of 20 m. In the end, he was moving towards the south. From which direction did Shankar start his journey?
    (a) West (b) North
    (c) South (d) East
14. If '–' stands for '+', '+' stands for '×', '×' stands for '–' then which one of the following is not correct ?
    (a) $22 + 7 - 3 \times 9 = 148$
    (b) $33 \times 5 - 10 + 20 = 228$
    (c) $7 + 28 - 3 \times 52 = 127$
    (d) $44 - 9 + 6 \times 11 = 87$
15. Find the missing number.?

	11			22			121	
3	28	4	5	57	3	6	?	5
	5			20			25	

    (a) 176 (b) 115
    (c) 157 (d) 131
16. Find the missing number.?

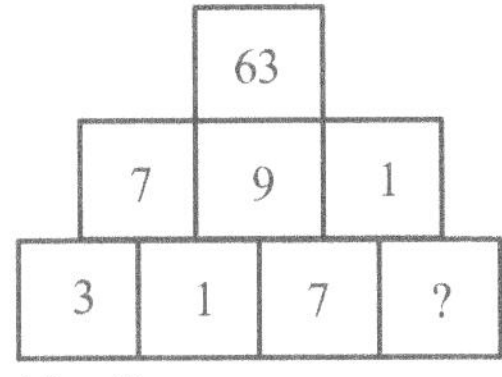

    (a) 3 (b) 9
    (c) 5 (d) 2

17. Five policemen are standing in a row facing south. Shekhar is to the immediate right of Dhanush. Bala is between Basha and Dhanush. David is at the extreme right end of the row. Who is standing in the middle of the row?

(a) Bala (b) Basha
(c) Shekhar (d) Dhanush

DIRECTION (Q. 18): *In the following question, one statement is given followed by two conclusions I and II. You have to consider the statements to be true even if they seem to be at variance from commonly known facts. You have to decide which of the given conclusions, if any follow from the given statements.*

18. **Statement :** Songs always have singers to sing them.

Conclusions:

I. Singers make a song.
II. There is no un-sung song.

(a) Only conclusion II follows
(b) Both conclusions I and II follow
(c) Neither conclusion I nor II follows
(d) Only conclusion I follows

19. Which of the following states the relationship between Sociology, Psychology and Humanities ?

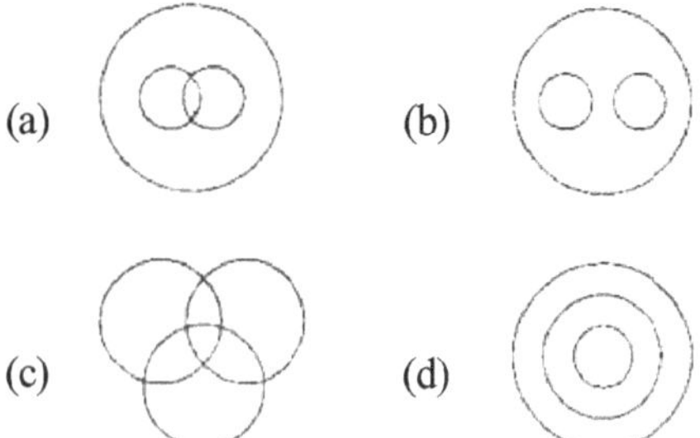

20. Select the related figure from the given alternatives.

Question figures

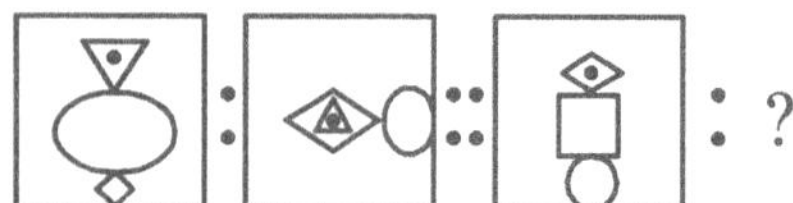

Answer figures

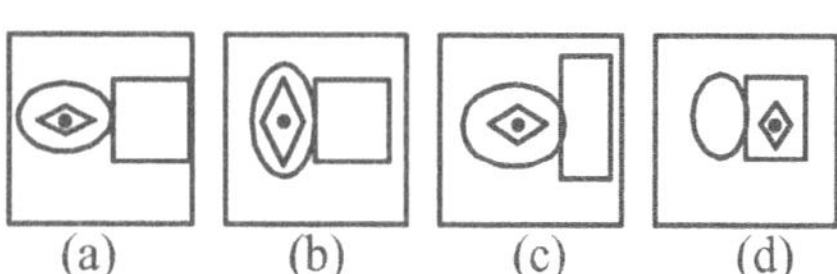

21. From the given alternatives select the word which can be formed using the letters given in the word.

ULTRANATIONALISM

(a) ULTRAMONTANE
(b) ULTRAMODERN
(c) ULTRAIST
(d) ULULATE

22. In the following question, select the answer figure in which the question figure is hidden / embedded.

Question Figure:

Answer Figures:

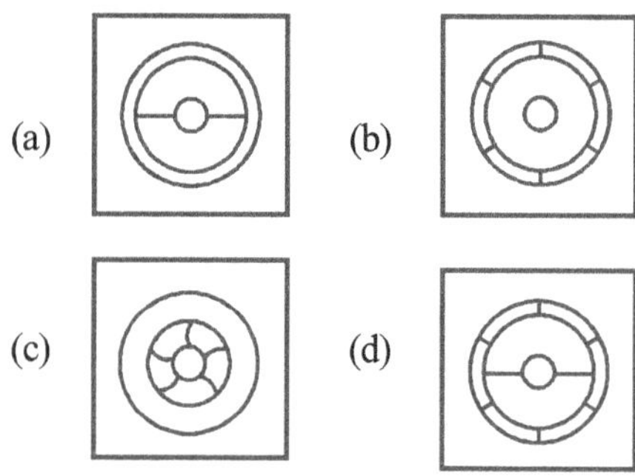

DIRECTIONS (Qs. 23-24): *In each of the following questions, a piece of paper is folded and cut as shown below in the question figures. From the given answer figures, indicate how It will appear when opened?*

23. **Question Figures:**

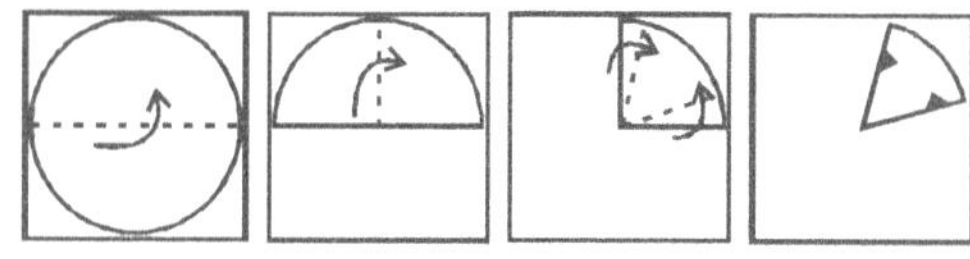

Answer Figures:

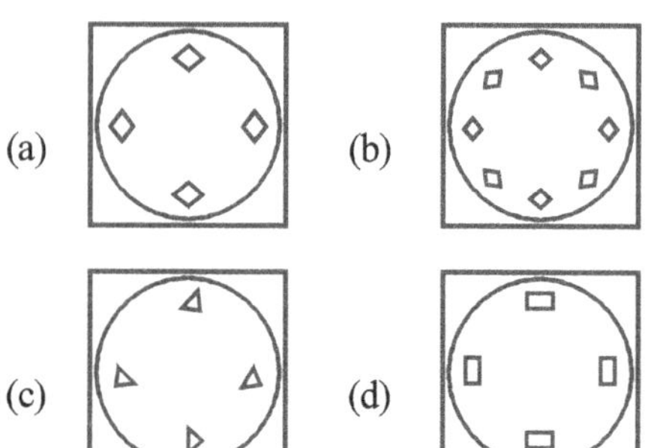

24. **Question Figures:**

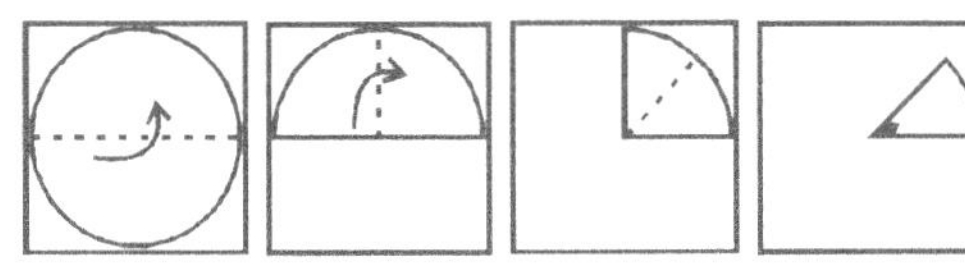

Answer Figures:

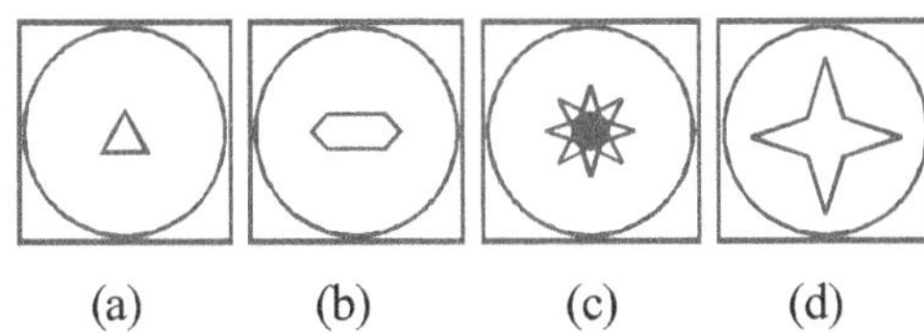

(a) (b) (c) (d)

25. A word is represented by only one set of numbers as given in anyone of the alternatives. The sets of numbers given in the alternatives are represented by two classes of alphabets as in two matrices given below. The columns and rows of matrix I are numbered from 0 to 4 and that of matrix II numbered from 5 to 9. A letter from these matrices can be represented first by its row and next by its column e.g .. 'B' can be represented by 01, 10, 22, etc. and 'F' can be represented by 55, 76,86, etc. Similarly, you have to identify the set for the given word - CAGE.

Matrix-I

	0	1	2	3	4
0	A	B	C	D	E
1	B	C	D	E	A
2	C	D	B	A	E
3	D	C	B	E	A
4	E	B	A	C	D

Matrix-II

	5	6	7	8	9
5	F	G	H	I	J
6	G	F	I	J	H
7	I	F	G	J	H
8	H	F	G	I	J
9	J	F	G	J	I

(a) 95, 82, 31, 14
(b) 20, 00, 65, 40
(c) 14, 20, 41, 86
(d) 00, 21, 41, 95

QUANTITATIVE APTITUDE

26. What is the value of $2+\sqrt{2}+\frac{1}{2+\sqrt{2}}-\frac{1}{2-\sqrt{2}}$?

(a) 2 (b) $2-\sqrt{2}$
(c) $4+\sqrt{2}$ (d) $2\sqrt{2}$

27. What is the value of $1.\overline{34}+4.1\overline{2}$?

(a) $\frac{133}{90}$ (b) $\frac{371}{90}$
(c) $5\frac{219}{990}$ (d) $5\frac{461}{990}$

28. A sum of money is divided among A, B, C and D in the ratio 3 : 5 : 8 : 9 respectively. If the share of D is ₹ 1,872 more than the share of A, then what is the total amount of money of B & C together?

(a) ₹ 4,156 (b) ₹ 4,165
(c) ₹ 4,056 (d) ₹ 4,068

29. What approximate compound interest can be obtained on an amount of ₹3,980 after 2 years at 8 p.c.p.a. ?

(a) 650 (b) 680
(c) 600 (d) 662

30. A man walks at the speed of 5 km/hr and runs at the speed of 10 km/hr. How much time will the man require to cover the distance of 28 km, if he covers half (first 14 km) of his journey walking and half of his journey running ?

(a) 8.4 hrs (b) 6 hrs
(c) 5 hrs (d) 4.2 hrs

31. In a 30 litres mixture of water and milk, 50% is milk. How much pure milk need to be added to this mixture to make mixture 30% water?

(a) 10 litres (b) 18 litres
(c) 15 litres (d) 20 litres

32. A bag contains 5 green and 7 red balls. Two balls are drawn. The probability that one is green and the other is red is

(a) $\frac{5}{132}$ (b) $\frac{7}{132}$
(c) $\frac{35}{66}$ (d) $\frac{31}{66}$

33. By selling 8 dozen pencils, a shopkeeper gains the selling price of 1 dozen pencils. What is the gain?

(a) $12\frac{1}{2}\%$ (b) $13\frac{1}{7}\%$
(c) $14\frac{2}{7}\%$ (d) $87\frac{1}{2}\%$

34. Two houses are collinear with the base of a tower and are at distance 3 m and 12 m from the base of the tower. The angles of elevation from these two houses of the top of the tower are complementary. What is the height of the tower?

(a) 4m (b) 6m
(c) 7.5m (d) 36m

35.

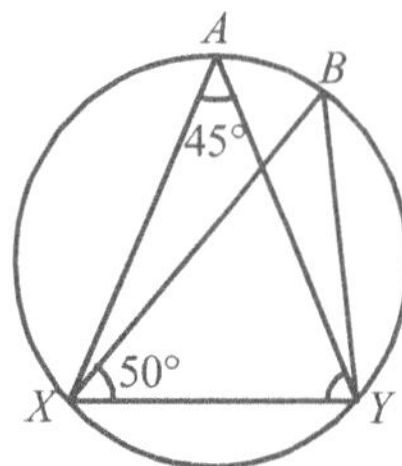

In the figure given above, what is $\angle BYX$ equal to?

(a) 85° (b) 50°
(c) 45° (d) 90°

36. The value of k for which the lines $2x + ky + 7 = 0$ and $27x - 18y + 25 = 0$ are perpendicular to each other, is

(a) $k = -1$ (b) $k = 2$
(c) $k = 3$ (d) $k = -2$

37. The sum of the three consecutive numbers in G.P. is 21 and the sum of their squares is 189. The product of the numbers is

(a) 72 (b) 216
(c) 108 (d) 144

38. If $x + \frac{1}{y} = 1$ and $y + \frac{1}{z} = 1$, what is the value of xyz?

(a) 1 (b) −1
(c) 0 (d) $\frac{1}{2}$

39. The length of a line segment *AB* is 2 unit. It is divided into two parts at the point *C* such that $AC^2 = AB \times CB$. What is the length of *CB*?

(a) $3+\sqrt{2}$ units (b) $3-\sqrt{5}$ units
(c) $2-\sqrt{5}$ units (d) $\sqrt{3}$ units

40. If $\frac{37}{13} = 2 + \cfrac{1}{x + \cfrac{1}{y + \cfrac{1}{z}}}$

where *x, y, z* are natural numbers, then what is *z* equal to?

(a) 1
(b) 2
(c) 3
(d) Cannot be determined due to insufficient data

41. What is $27 \times 1.\bar{2} \times 5.526\bar{2} \times 0.\bar{6}$ equal to?

(a) $121.\overline{57}$ (b) $121.\overline{75}$
(c) $121.7\bar{5}$ (d) None of these

42. What should come in place of the question mark (?) in the following questions?

$8^{9.4} \times 4^{12.8} \times 64^{8.1} = 16^{?}$

(a) 41.8 (b) 16.2
(c) 18.4 (d) 25.6

43. An aeroplane flies along the four sides of a square at the speeds of 200, 400, 600 and 800 km/h. Find the average speed of the plane around the field.

(a) 384 km/h (b) 370 km/h
(c) 368 km/h (d) None of these

44. A, B and C can do a work in 6, 8 and 12 days respectively. Doing that work together they get an amount of Rs. 1350. What is the share of B in that amount?

(a) ₹450 (b) ₹168.75
(c) ₹337.50 (d) ₹718.75

45. A and B started a business by investing ₹35,000 and ₹ 20,000 respectively. B left the business after 5 months and C joined the business with a sum of ₹ 15,000. The profit earned at the end of the year is ₹ 84,125. What is B's share of profit?

(a) ₹14133
(b) ₹15,000
(c) ₹13,460
(d) Cannot be determined

DIRECTIONS (Qs. 46 - 48): *Study the following table carefully in answer the questions that follow :*

Number of Executives recruited by Six different organisations over the years

Organisation	P	Q	R	S	T	U
2004	458	512	418	502	476	492
2005	522	536	472	500	482	523
2006	480	495	464	508	488	518
2007	506	505	428	444	490	534
2008	427	485	422	512	510	498
2009	492	488	444	499	512	510

46. What is the total number of Executives recruited by all the organisations together in the year 2006?
(a) 2927 (b) 3042
(c) 2864 (d) 2953

47. What is the ratio of the total number of Executives recruited by organisation U in the years 2007 and 2009 together to the total number of Executives recruited by organisation P in the same years?
(a) 436 : 517 (b) 499 : 522
(c) 517 : 436 (d) 522 : 499

48. What is the average number of Executives recruited by organisation S over all the years together? (rounded off to the nearest integer)
(a) 494 (b) 482
(c) 514 (d) 506

49. A hollow cylindrical iron pipe of length 1.4 m has base radius 2.5 cm and thickness of the metal is 1 cm. What is the volume of the iron used in the pipe?
(a) 2640 cu cm (b) 2604 cu cm
(c) 2460 cu cm (d) None of these

50. A solid metallic cube of edge 4 cm is melted and recast into solid cubes of edge 1 cm. If x is the surface area of the melted cube and y is the total surface area of all the cubes recast, then what is $x : y$?
(a) 2 : 1 (b) 1 : 2
(c) 1 : 4 (d) 4 : 1

ENGLISH LANGUAGE

DIRECTIONS (Qs. 51-52): *Each of the question in this section has a sentence with a blank space and four words given after the sentence. Select whichever word you consider most appropriate for the blank space and indicate your choice on the Answer Sheet.*

51. An accomplice is a partner in ________.
(a) business (b) crime
(c) construction (d) gambling

52. A person who pretends to be what he is not is called an________.
(a) imbiber (b) impresario
(c) imitator (d) imposter

DIRECTIONS (Qs. 53-54): *Select the word or group of words that is most* ***similar*** *in meaning to the words in capital letters.*

53. IMPETUS
(a) Courage (b) Impatience
(c) Arrogance (d) Driving energy

54. PHILANDERER
(a) Time waster (b) Spendthrift
(c) Male flirt (d) Wanderer

DIRECTIONS (Qs. 55-56) : *Select the word or group of words that is most* ***opposite*** *in meaning to the words in capital letters.*

55. PROCRASTINATE
(a) To be prompt (b) To adjudicate
(c) To teach (d) To help others

56. PROCLIVITY
(a) Speed (b) Weakness
(c) Disgust (d) Disinclination

DIRECTIONS (Qs. 57-58) : *Look at the underlined part of each sentence. Below each sentence, three possible substitutions for the underlined part are given. If one of them (i.e.,) (a), (b) or (c) is better than the underlined part, indicate your response on the Answer Sheet against the corresponding letter (a), (b) or (c). If none of the substitutions improves the sentence, indicate (d) as your response on the Answer Sheet. Thus, 'No improvement' response will be signified by the letter (d).*

57. If I <u>were</u> you, I would do it at once.
(a) was (b) am
(c) would be (d) No improvement

58. They set a strong guard, lest anyone <u>could</u> escape.
(a) would (b) might
(c) should (d) No improvement

DIRECTIONS (Qs. 59-60): *Each question in this section has a sentence with three underlined parts labelled (a), (b) and (c). Read each sentence to find out whether there is any error in any underlined part and indicate your response in the Answer Sheet against the corresponding letter i.e., (a) or (b) or (c). If you find no error, your response should be indicated as (d).*

59. <u>My detailed statement</u> (a) <u>is respectively</u> (b) <u>submitted.</u> (c) <u>No error.</u> (d)

60. <u>I am waiting</u> (a) <u>for my friend</u> (b) <u>since this morning.</u> (c) <u>No error.</u> (d)

DIRECTIONS (Qs. 61-62) : *In the following questions four alternatives are given for the idiom/phrase italicised and underlined in the sentence. Choose the alternative which best expresses the meaning of idiom/phrase.*

61. Sobhraj could be easily arrested because the police were *tipped off in a advance*.
(a) Toppled over
(b) Bribed
(c) Given advance information
(d) Threatened

62. I met him after a long time, but he gave me *the cold shoulder*.
(a) scolded me (b) insulted me
(c) abused me (d) ignored me

DIRECTIONS (Qs. 63-65) : *In the following questions, a word has been spelt in four different ways, one of which is correct. Choose the correctly spelt word.*

63. (a) Dysentary (b) Dysantery
(c) Dysentry (d) Dysentery

64. (a) Rejevanation (b) Rejuvenation
(c) Rejvenation (d) Rejuenation

65. (a) accomodate (b) acommodate
(c) accommodate (d) accommodat

DIRECTIONS (Qs. 66-70): *Select the most appropriate word from the options against each number :*

One fine morning a **(66)** man knocked at the doors of the home for the aged run by nuns. He told the nun in charge that as he was **(67)** to Delhi, he wanted to leave his servant-maid to the **(68)** of the nuns. He assured the nun of sending some money every month **(69)** she was an orphan. The nun **(70)** her saying that she had got an excellen master.

66. (a) gentle (b) bad
(c) nice (d) good

67. (a) moved (b) shifted
(c) changed (d) transferred

68. (a) care (b) home
(c) custody (d) protection

69. (a) because (b) and
(c) though (d) if

70. (a) loved (b) praised
(c) consoled (d) condoled

DIRECTION (Q. 71): *In these questions, the sentences have been given in Active / Passive Voice. From the given alternatives, choose the one which best expresses the given sentence in Passive / Active Voice.*

71. I saw him leaving the house.
(a) Leaving the house he was seen by me.
(b) He was seen leaving the house by me.
(c) He had been seen leaving the house.
(d) He was seen to be leaving the house.

DIRECTIONS (Qs. 72-73): *In each of the following questions, out of the four alternatives, choose the one which can be substituted for the given words/sentence.*

72. A person interested in collecting, studying and selling of old things
(a) Antiquarian (b) Junk-dealer
(c) Crank (d) Archealogist

73. Policeman riding on motorcycles as guards to a VIP
(a) Outriders (b) Servants
(c) Commandos (d) Attendants

DIRECTIONS (Qs. 74-75): *In the following questions, the 1st and the last parts of the sentence are numbered 1 and 6. The rest of the sentence is split into four parts and named P, Q, R and S. These four parts are not given in their proper order. Read the sentence and find out which of the four combinations is correct. Then find the correct answer.*

74. Can any one
P. falsehood triumph
Q. and let
R. for a long time
S. suppress truth
permanently?
(a) RQSP (b) QPRS
(c) SRQP (d) PRQS

75. And then word
P. came from inside
Q. meet the released civilians
R. that after all
S. the press could
but fleetingly.
(a) RSQP (b) SRPQ
(c) PRSQ (d) RPQS

GENERAL AWARENESS

76. Which one of the following is not a computer language?
(a) Cobol (b) Visual Basic
(c) HTML (d) Netscape

77. Who among the following was the first Governor General of India?
(a) Lord Amherst
(b) Lord William Bentinck
(c) Sir Charles Metcalfe
(d) Robert Clive

78. Which one of the following is not a constituent of biogas?
(a) Methane (b) Carbon dioxide
(c) Hydrogen (d) Nitrogen dioxide

79. In which one of the following sessions was the Indian National Congress split into moderates and extremists?
(a) Nagpur (b) Allahabad
(c) Surat (d) Calcutta

80. Bar is a unit of which one of the following?
(a) Force (b) Energy
(c) Pressure (d) Frequency

81. Which of the following metals are present in haemoglobin and chlorophyll, respectively?
(a) Fe and Mg (b) Fe and Zn
(c) Mg and Zn (d) Zn and Mg

82. A mother of blood group O has a group O child. What could be the blood group of father of the child?
(a) Only O (b) A or B or O
(c) A or B (d) Only AB

83. Who among the following was the founder of the Muslim League?
(a) Muhammad Ali Jinnah
(b) Shaukat Ali
(c) Nawab Salimullah
(d) Aga Khan

84. Which one among the following is not a source of tax revenue for the Central Government in India ?
(a) Income tax (b) Customs duuties
(c) Service tax (d) Motor Vehicle tax

85. Which one of the following causes the chikungunia disease?
(a) Bacteria (b) Helminthic worm
(c) Protozoan (d) Virus

86. Which one of the following vitamins helps in clotting of blood?
(a) Vitamin-A (b) Vitamin-B_6
(c) Vitamin-D (d) Vitamin-K

87. The 'Thomas Cup is associated with
(a) Table Tennis (b) Lawn Tennis
(c) Badminton (d) Billiards

88. What is the purpose of adding baking soda to dough?
(a) To generate moisture
(b) To give a good flavour
(c) To give good colour
(d) To generate carbon dioxide

89. The Dandi March of Gandhi-is an example of
(a) Non-Coopefation (b) Direct Action
(c) Boycott (d) Civil Disobedience

90. Which one of the following inscriptions relate to the Chalukya king, Pulakesin II ?
(a) Nasik (b) Maski
(c) Hathigumpha (d) Aihole

91. Yeast is an important source of
(a) protein (b) vitamin B
(c) invertase (d) vitamin C

92. The longest river of peninsular India is
(a) Godavari (b) Krishna
(c) Kaveri (d) Narmada

93. Which one of the following National Park/ Sanctuary is not in Rajasthan ?
(a) Sariska National Park
(b) Sambar Wildlife Sanctuary
(c) Rajaji National Park
(d) Rhanthambore National Park

94. 'Pehli Udaan' is a name given to
(a) Launching of Air Asia in India
(b) SBI's Savings Account Scheme for children
(c) Proposed Bullet Train in India
(d) Satellite sent to Mars

95. Which one of the following is not a line of demarcation between two countries ?
(a) Durand Line (b) Mac Mahon Line
(c) Plimsoll Line (d) Maginot Line

96. Who has been appointed as the new chairman of the Union Public Service Commission (UPSC)?
(a) S R Hashim (b) Deepak Gupta
(c) Alka Sirohi (d) David Syiemlieh

97. Which of the following cities is the venue of the 4th Edition Of Global Partners' Forum?
(a) Kochi (b) Chennai
(c) Kolkata (d) New Delhi

98. Who is the head of IRDA panel to study feasibility of paying claims in installments?
(a) Suresh Mathur (b) Injeti Srinivas
(c) Vinod Paul (d) Rakes

99. The 2018 Vishwa Shanti Ahimsa Sammelan (VSAS) has started in which state?
(a) West Bengal (b) Maharashtra
(c) Gujarat (d) Uttar Pradesh

100. Which US-based Dalit writer has won the 2018 Shakti Bhatt First Book Prize?
(a) Deepak Unnikrishnan
(b) Aanchal Malhotra
(c) Sujatha Gidla
(d) San

Hints & Explanations

1. (c) A C E
+5↓ +5↓ +5↓
F H J

Similarly, O Q S
+5↓ +5↓ +5↓
T V X

2. (a) As, a saint practices meditation. Similarly, a scientist does research.
3. (c) 18/3 – 1 = 5
12/3 – 1 = 3
4. (c)
5. (d) $H \xrightarrow{(-1)} G \xrightarrow{(-1)} F \xrightarrow{(-1)} E$
$P \xrightarrow{(-1)} O \xrightarrow{(-1)} N \xrightarrow{(-1)} M$
$D \xrightarrow{(-1)} C \xrightarrow{(-1)} B \xrightarrow{(-1)} A$
$M \xrightarrow{(+6)} S \xrightarrow{(+1)} T \xrightarrow{(+1)} U$
M S T U is odd word
6. (a) $F \xrightarrow{+1} G \xrightarrow{+1} H \xrightarrow{+1} I \xrightarrow{+1} J$
$A \xrightarrow{+0} A \xrightarrow{+0} A \xrightarrow{+0} A \xrightarrow{+0} A$
$G \xrightarrow{-1} F \xrightarrow{+3} I \xrightarrow{-1} H \xrightarrow{+3} K$
7. (c) 3 + 3 = 6
6 + 3 = 9
9 + 6 = 15
15 + 9 = 24
24 + 15 = 39
39 + 24 = 63
63 + 39 = 102
8. (d) As, A + G + E = 1 + 7 + 5 = 13
Similarly, C + A + R = 3 + 1 + 18 = 22
9. (c) As per dictionary

4 Elocution → 3 Embrace → 1 Emplane → 2 Empower → 5 Equable.

10. (b) Words LUB and TUP are in consecutive order.
LUB/TUP/LUB/TUP/LUB/TUP/LUB/TUP

11. (b) Govind's age = 48 years
According to question
Prem's age = 48/2 = 24 years
Prem's age seven years before = 24 – 7
= 17 years.
12. (a) Mother ↓(–) Mother = Lady ↓(–) Man (+)

His (man) mother is the only daughter of my (lady) mother.

13. (b) 10 m, 6 m, 20 m, Left, Right

From the diagram, it is clear that Shankar started his journey from North to South.
14. (c) By options–
(a) 22 × 7 + 3 – 9 = 148
154 + 3 – 9
157 – 9 = 148 (Correct)
(b) 33 – 5 + 10 × 20 = 228
33 – 5 + 200
200 + 33 – 5
233 – 5 = 228 (Correct)
(c) 7 × 28 + 3 – 52 = 127
196 + 3 – 52
199 – 52 = 147 (Incorrect)
(d) 44 + 9 × 6 – 11 = 87
44 + 54 – 11
98 – 11 = 87 (Correct)
15. (a)

	11			22			121	
3	11 + 5 + 4 × 3 = 16 + 12 = 28	4	5	22 + 20 + 5 × 3 = 42 + 15 = 57	3	6	121 + 25 + 6 × 5 = 146 + 30 = 176	5
	5			20			25	

16. (a)

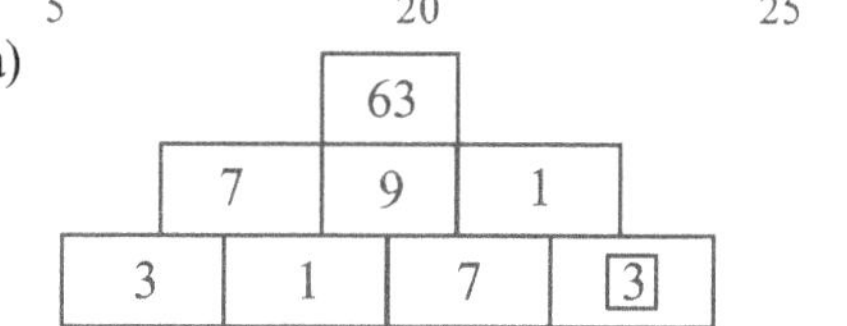

$\Rightarrow 63$

$\Rightarrow 7\times1\times9=63$

$\Rightarrow 3\times1\times7\times\boxed{3}=63$

17. (d) Standing arrangement : (facing south)

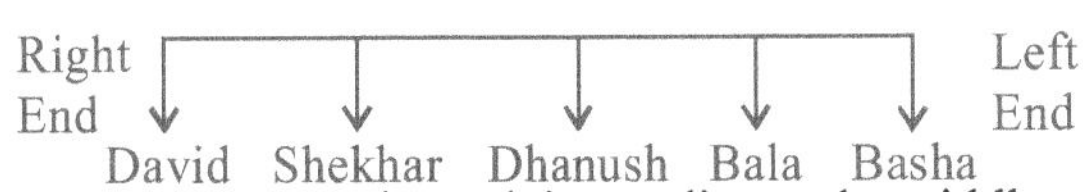

Hence, Dhanush is standing at the middle of the row.

18. (d) Any written piece is recognised as song when it is sung by a singer. Therefore, only Conclusion I follows.

19. (a)

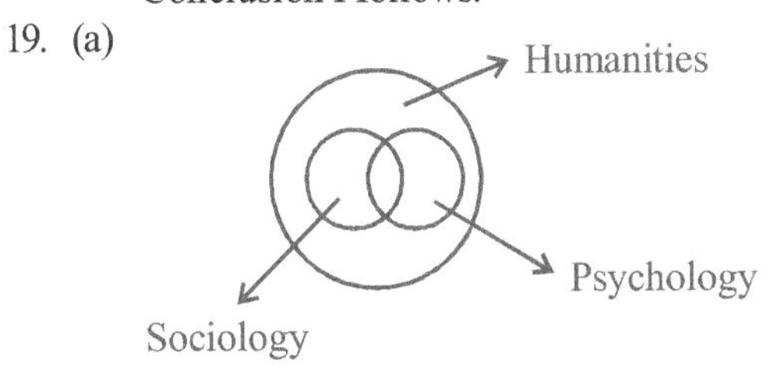

20. (a) The middle element adjacents to the right side line after rotating 90° anticlock wise. The bottom element goes up on the top and becomes enlarge.
The top element becomes the inner figure of bottom element.

21. (c) By options–
(a) can not be formed as there is no 'E' in the given word.
(b) can not be formed as there is no 'D' in the given word.
(d) can not be formed as there is no 'E' and only 'U' in the given word.
So, option (c) can be formed.

22. (d) 23. (b) 24. (c)

25. (b) $C\Rightarrow 02, 11, 20, 31, 43$
$A\Rightarrow 00, 14, 23, 34, 42$
$G\Rightarrow 56, 65, 77, 87, 97$
$E\Rightarrow 04, 13, 24, 33, 40$

Option	C	A	G	E
(a)	95	82	31	14
(b)	20	00	65	40
(c)	14	20	41	86
(d)	00	21	41	95

26. (a) $2+\sqrt{2}+\frac{1}{2+\sqrt{2}}-\frac{1}{2-\sqrt{2}}$

$=2+\sqrt{2}+\frac{2-\sqrt{2}-2-\sqrt{2}}{4-2}$

$=2+\sqrt{2}+\frac{(-2\sqrt{2})}{2}=2+\sqrt{2}-\sqrt{2}=2$

27. (d) $\because 1.\overline{34}=\frac{134-1}{99}=\frac{133}{99}$

and $4.1\overline{2}=\frac{412-41}{90}=\frac{371}{90}$

$\therefore\ 1.\overline{34}+4.1\overline{2}=\frac{133}{99}+\frac{371}{90}=\frac{1330+4081}{990}$

$=\frac{5411}{990}=5\frac{461}{990}$

28. (c) Share of $B+C=\frac{1872}{9-3}\times(5+8)=₹\ 4056$

29. (d) Equivalent % interest for compound rate of interest of 8% for 2 years

$=8+8+\frac{8\times8}{100}=16.64\%$

So, interest = 16.64% of 3980 ≈ 662

30. (d) Total time required $=\frac{14}{5}+\frac{14}{10}$

$=\frac{28+14}{10}=4.2$ hrs

31. (d) 30 litres mixture contains 15 litres of water. When milk added to this, quentity of water will same in sance (*i.e.* 15 l).
Let $x\ell$ of pure milk to be added, then 30% of $(30+x)=15$
solve, $x=20$

32. (c) There are $5+7=12$ balls in the bag and out of these two balls can be drawn in $^{12}C_2$ ways. There are 5 green balls, therefore, one green ball can be drawn in $^5C_1$ ways; similarly, one red ball can be drawn in $^7C_1$ ways so that the number of ways in which we can draw one green ball and the other red is $^5C_1\times{}^7C_1$.
Hence, P (one green and the other red)

$=\frac{^5C_1\times{}^7C_1}{^{12}C_2}=\frac{5}{1}\times\frac{7}{1}\times\frac{1\times2}{12\times11}=\frac{35}{66}$

33. (c) Let the cost price = ₹ x
Profit = ₹ x
Cost price of 8 dozen pencil = ₹ 7x

Gain per cent $=\frac{x}{7x}\times100$

$=\frac{100}{7}=14\frac{2}{7}\%$

34. (b) Let the height of the tower be h m and $\angle CBD = \theta$ then $\angle DAC = 90^\circ - \theta$
(Because both angles are complementary)

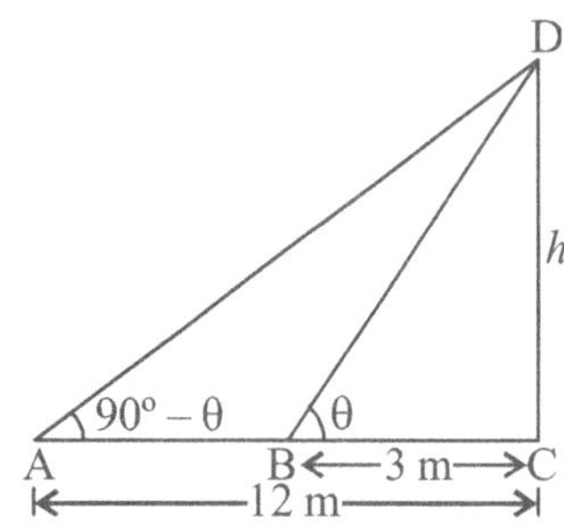

$\therefore$ In ΔBCD,

$\tan\theta = \frac{CD}{BC} \Rightarrow \tan\theta = \frac{h}{3}$

Now, in ΔACD

$\tan(90^\circ - \theta) = \frac{CD}{AC} \Rightarrow \cot\theta = \frac{h}{12}$

$\frac{1}{\tan\theta} = \frac{h}{12}$

$h\tan\theta = 12$

Put the value of $\tan\theta$

$h \times \frac{h}{3} = 12$

$h^2 = 36 \quad \therefore h = 6$

Then, height of tower = 6 m.

35. (a) We know that, the triangle of same segment of a circle makes an equal angles.

$\therefore \angle XBY = \angle XAY = 45^\circ$

In ΔBXY, $\angle BXY + \angle XBY + \angle BYX = 180^\circ$

$\Rightarrow 50^\circ + 45^\circ + \angle BYX = 180^\circ$ $(\because \angle BXY = 50^\circ)$

$\Rightarrow \angle BYX = 180^\circ - 95^\circ = 85^\circ$

36. (c) $2x + ky + 7 = 0 \Rightarrow ky = -2x - 7 \Rightarrow y = \frac{-2}{k}x - \frac{7}{k}$

$27x + 18y + 25 = 0 \Rightarrow 18y = 27x + 25$

$\Rightarrow y = \frac{3}{2}x + \frac{25}{18}$

$\therefore \frac{-2}{k} \times \frac{3}{2} = 1 \Rightarrow k = 3$

37. (b) Let the three nmumbers in G.P. be a, ar, ar^2.

Given $a + ar + ar^2 = 21 \Rightarrow a(1 + r + r^2) = 21$ ...(i)

Also, $a^2 + a^2r^2 + a^2r^4 = 189 \Rightarrow a^2(1 + r^2 + r^4) = 189$. ..(ii)

So,

$$\frac{a^2(1+r^2+r^4)}{\left[a(1+r+r^2)\right]^2} = \frac{189}{(21)^2} = \frac{189}{441} = \frac{3}{7}$$

or, $\frac{1+2r^2+r^4-r^2}{(1+r+r^2)^2} = \frac{3}{7}$

or, $\frac{(1+r^2)^2-r^2}{(1+r+r^2)^2} = \frac{3}{7}$

or, $\frac{(1+r^2+r)(1+r^2-r)}{(1+r+r^2)} = \frac{3}{7}$

or, $\frac{1+r^2-r}{1+r+r^2} = \frac{3}{7}$

or, $7(1 + r^2 - r) = 3(1 + r + r^2)$

or, $4r^2 - 10r + 4 = 0$

or, $2r^2 - 5r + 2 = 0$

or, $2r^2 - 4r - r + 2 = 0$

or, $2r(r-2) - (r-2) = 0$

or, $(r-2)(2r-1) = 0$

or, $r = 2, \frac{1}{2}$

From equation (i)

$a = \frac{21}{1+r+r^2}$

$\therefore$ For $r = 2$, $a = \frac{21}{1+2+4}$ and for $r = \frac{1}{2}$, $a = 12$

Hence, the three numbers are 3, 6, 12 or 12, 6, 3

Their product $= 3 \times 6 \times 12 = 216$

38. (b) Given that, $x + \frac{1}{y} = 1$

$\Rightarrow xy + 1 = y$ ...(i)

and $y + \frac{1}{z} = 1 \Rightarrow 1 - \frac{1}{z} = y$

$\Rightarrow \frac{z-1}{z} =$ ...(ii)

From eq. (ii),

$y = \frac{z-1}{z}$

Comparing eqn. (i) with (ii)

$xy + 1 = \frac{z-1}{z}$

$\Rightarrow xyz + z = z - 1$

$\Rightarrow xyz = -1$

39. (b) Given, $AC^2 = AB \times CB$

$\Rightarrow x^2 = 2 \times (2 - x)$

$\Rightarrow x^2 = 4 - 2x$

A——x——C——(2 − x)——B
⟵ 2 ⟶

$\Rightarrow \quad x^2+2x-4=0$

$\Rightarrow \quad x=\dfrac{-2\pm\sqrt{4+16}}{2\times 1}$

$\Rightarrow \quad x=-1\pm\sqrt{5}$

Now, $BC=(3\pm\sqrt{5})=3\pm\sqrt{5}$

40. (b) $\dfrac{37}{13}=2+\cfrac{1}{x+\cfrac{1}{y+\cfrac{1}{z}}}$

$\Rightarrow \quad \dfrac{37}{13}$ can be expressed as

$=2+\cfrac{1}{1+\cfrac{2}{11}}=2+\cfrac{1}{1+\cfrac{1}{5+\cfrac{1}{2}}}$

Now, this is compared by

$2+\cfrac{1}{x+\cfrac{1}{y+\cfrac{1}{z}}}=2+\cfrac{1}{1+\cfrac{1}{5+\cfrac{1}{2}}}$

$\therefore z=2$

41. (d) $27\times 1.\bar{2}\times 5.526\bar{2}\times 0.\bar{6}$

$=27\times 1\dfrac{2}{9}\times 5\dfrac{4736}{9000}\times\dfrac{6}{9}$

$=27\times\dfrac{11}{9}\times\dfrac{49736}{9000}\times\dfrac{6}{9}$

$=\dfrac{11\times 49736\times 2}{9000}=\dfrac{1094192}{9000}=121.577$

42. (d) $8^{9.4}\times 4^{12.8}\times 64^{8.1}=16^{?}$

$8^{2\times 4.7}\times 4^{12.8}\times 64^{8.1}=16^{?}$

$64^{4.7}\times 4^{12.8}\times 64^{8.1}=16^{?}$

$64^{4.7+8.1}\times 4^{12.8}=16^{?}$

$(64\times 4)^{12.8}=16^{?}$

$(256)^{12.8}=16^{?}$

$16^{2\times 12.8}=16^{?}$

$16^{25.6}=16^{?}$

$?=25.6$

43. (a) Let each side of the square be x km and let the average speed of the plane around the field be y km/h. Then,

$\dfrac{x}{200}+\dfrac{x}{400}+\dfrac{x}{600}+\dfrac{x}{800}=\dfrac{4x}{y}$

$\Rightarrow \dfrac{25x}{2400}=\dfrac{4x}{y}\Rightarrow y=\left(\dfrac{2400\times 4}{25}\right)=384.$

$\therefore$ Average speed = 384 km/h.

44. (a) A's one day's work $=\dfrac{1}{6}$

B's one day's work $=\dfrac{1}{8}$

C's one day's work $=\dfrac{1}{12}$

A's share : B's share : C's share

$=\dfrac{1}{6}:\dfrac{1}{8}:\dfrac{1}{12}$

Multiplying each ratio by the L.C.M. of their denominators, the ratios become 4 : 3 : 2

$\therefore$ B's share $=\dfrac{1350\times 3}{9}=$ Rs.450

45. (c) Ratio of equivalent capitals of A, B and C for 1 month

$=35000\times 12:20000\times 5:15000\times 7$

$=35\times 12:20\times 5:15\times 7=84:20:21$

Sum of the ratios $=84+20+21=125$

$\therefore$ B's share = ₹$\left(\dfrac{20}{125}\times 84125\right)$ = ₹13460

46. (d) Total executives recruited were 2953.

47. (d) Required ratio equals 1044 : 998 = 522 : 499

48. (a) Required average number of executives = sum of no. of all executives

$=\dfrac{2965}{6}\approx 494$

49. (a) $\therefore$ Volume of pipe, $V=\pi\left(r_1^2-r_2^2\right)\times h$

$=\dfrac{22}{7}[(3.5)^2-(2.5)^2]\times 140$

$=\dfrac{22}{7}(12.25-6.25)\times 140$

$=22\times 6\times 20=2640$ cu cm

50. (c) Volume of solid cube $=(4)^3=64\text{ cm}^3$

Volume of recast cube $=(1)^3=1\text{ cm}^3$

$\therefore$ Total surface area of cube : Total surface area of recast cube

$=x:y$

$\Rightarrow \quad x:y=6(4)^2:6(1)^2\times 64=1:4$

51. (b) An accomplice is a partner in crime. Thus option (b) is the answer.
52. (d) Imbiber means one who absorbs something. Impresario means a person who organizes concert and plays. Imitator is the one who copies another person. Imposter is the pretender, so correct answer is option (d).
53. (d) 'Impetus' means 'something that encourages a process or activity.'
54. (c) 'Philanderer' means 'a man who has sexual relations with different women.'
55. (a) 'Procrastinate' means to delay or linger in a decision. 'Prompt' means done without delay.
56. (d) 'Proclivity' means a natural tendency (or inclination) to do something.
57. (d) If I were you, I would do it at once.
58. (c) They set a strong guard, lest anyone should escape.
59. (b) My detailed statement is respectfully submitted.
60. (a) I have been waiting for my friend since morning.
61. (a) The underlined portion should be deleted.
62. (d) and indulging in other sports.
63. (b) I was told
64. (c) 65. (d) 66. (a) 67. (d) 68. (c)
69. (a) 70. (c)
71. (b) He was seen leaving the house by me.
72. (a) 73. (a) 74. (c) 75. (b)
76. (d) Netscape is an Internet browser that was popular during the early 1990's.
77. (a)
78. (d) Nitrogen dioxide (NO_2) is not a component of biogas.
79. (c) The 23rd Session (1907) of the Congress was held at Surat.In the session, there was an open clash between the Moderates and the Extremists and ultimately it led to a split in the Congress.
80. (c) 1 Bar = 10^5 Pa. Both bar and Pa are the unit of pressure.
81. (a) Fe and Mg metals are present in haemoglobin and chlorophyll respectively.
82. (b) The blood group of father of the child could be A or B or O.
83. (c) The All India Muslim League, a political organization was founded in 1906 by Aga Khan under the Nawab of Dhaka Salimullah. Its main purpose was to safeguard the political rights of Muslims in India.
84. (d) Motor Vehicle tax is not a source of tax revenue for the central government in India.
85. (d) Chikungunia is caused by chikenguniya virus which is an insect borne virus of genus *Alphavirus*. Symptoms show high fever, maculopapular rash, headache, etc.
86. (d) Vitamin-K adds in blood clotting. Vitamin-K acts as an essential cofactor for factor-II, VII, IX, X and also for proteins Z, C and S.
87. (c) Thomas Cup is associated with Badminton.
88. (d) Baking soda has sodium bicarbonate as the chief constituent. It decomposes on heating giving carbon dioxide. This causes dough, cakes, biscuits etc. to expand and become light.
89. (d) The Dandi March of Gandhi was an important part of the Indian Independence Movement.It was a direct action campaign of tax resistance and non-violent protest against British saltmonopoly and triggered the wider Civil Disobedience Movement.
90. (d) Aihole inscription is found at Aihole in Karnataka state India, was written by the Ravikriti,court poet of Chalukya king,Pulakeshin II who reigned from 610 to 642 CE.The poetic verses of Ravikirti,in praise of the king, can be read in the Meguti temple,dated 634CE.
91. (b) Yeast is an important source of vitamin B. Yeasts is eukaryotic microorganisms classified in the kingdom Fungi, with 1,500 species (estimated to be 1% of all fungal species). Yeasts are unicellular, although some species with yeast forms may become multicellular through the formation of strings of connected budding cells known as pseudohyphae, or false hyphae, as seen in most molds.
92. (a) Godavari is the longest river of peninsular India. From its source to the Eastern Ghats, the Godavari River flows through gentle, somewhat monotonous terrain, along the way receiving the Darna, Purna, Manjra, Pranhita, and Indravati rivers. Upon entering the Eastern Ghats region, however, the river flows between steep and precipitous banks, its width contracting until it flows through a deep cleft only 600 feet (180 metres) wide, known as the Gorge.
93. (c) 94. (b)
95. (c) Plimsol line is not a line of demarcation between two countries.
96. (d) 97. (d) 98. (a) 99. (b) 100. (c)

PRACTICE SET- 4

GENERAL INTELLIGENCE & REASONING

DIRECTIONS (Qs. 1-2): *In questions, select the related word/letters/number from given alternatives.*

1. ACE : BDF : : GIK : ?37
   (a) HJL (b) AXP
   (c) CFG (d) GFC
2. hive : bee :: eyrie : ?
   (a) Pigeon (b) Sparrow
   (c) Parrot (d) Eagle

DIRECTIONS (Qs. 3-4): *In questions, find the odd word/ letters/number pair from the given alternatives.*

3. (a) vwqp (b) yxmn
   (c) gfkl (d) cbrs
4. (a) (324,18) (b) (441,72)
   (c) (117,81) (d) (186,14)
5. Which one of the given responses would be a meaningful order of the following words?
   1. Sowing 2. Tilling
   3. Reaping 4. Weeding
   (a) 3, 1, 2, 4 (b) 2, 1, 4, 3
   (c) 1, 2, 4, 3 (d) 1, 3, 2, 4

DIRECTIONS (Qs. 6-7): *In questions below, a series is given with one term missing. Choose the correct alternative from the given ones that will complete the series.*

6. –1, 0, ?, 8, 15, 24
   (a) 4 (b) 3
   (c) 2 (d) 1
7. 24, 35, 20, 31, 16, 27, __, __
   (a) 9, 9 (b) 5, 30
   (c) 8, 25 (d) 12, 23
8. In a language FIFTY is written as CACTY, CAR as POL, TAR as TOL, how can TARIFF be written in that language?
   (a) TOEFEL (b) TOEFDD
   (c) TOLADD (d) TOLACC
9. Which one set of letters when sequentially placed at the gaps in the given letter series shall complete it?
   rtx _ sx _ z _ txy _ _ yz
   (a) y y r x s (b) y y s x r
   (c) y y r s x (d) y y x r s
10. A is in the east of B which is in the North of C. If D is in the South of C., then in which direction of A, is D.
    (a) North – West (b) South
    (c) East (d) South–West
11. Rearrange the given jumbled letters to make a meaningful word.
    Given letters : riytaraplamen
    (a) Lamination (b) Realignment
    (c) Parliamentary (d) Replacement
12. Introducing a boy, a girl said, "He is the son of the daughter of the father of my uncle." How is the boy related to the girl?
    (a) Brother (b) Nephew
    (c) Uncle (d) Son-in-law
13. In the following figure, the boys who are cricketer and sober are indicated by which number?

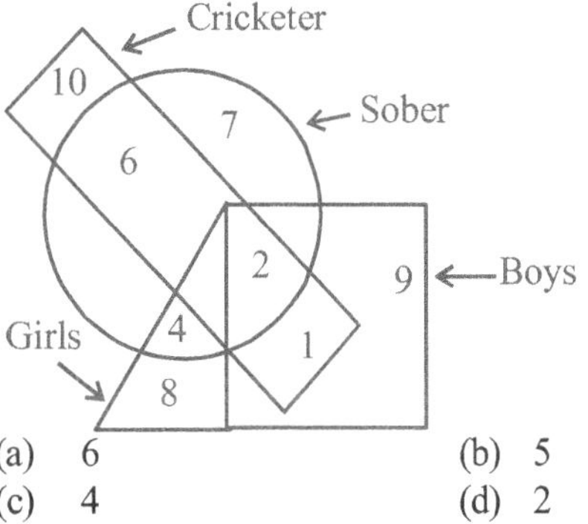

    (a) 6 (b) 5
    (c) 4 (d) 2
14. Some equations are solved on the basis of a certain system. Find the correct answer for the unsolved equation on that basis.
    5 * 6 = 35, 8 * 4 = 28, 6 * 8 = ?
    (a) 46 (b) 34
    (c) 23 (d) 38

DIRECTIONS (Qs. 15-16): *In each of the following questions, select the missing number from the given responses.*

15.

6, 24, 60, 120, 210, ?

(a) 330 (b) 336
(c) 428 (d) 420

16.

12	15	16
03	04	05
04	06	04
40	66	?

(a) 104 (b) 320
(c) 25 (d) 84

17. Six girls are standing in such a way that they form a circle, facing the centre. Subbu is to the left of Pappu, Revathi is between Subbu and Nisha, Aruna is between Pappu and Keertana. Who is to the left of Pappu?

(a) Keertana (b) Nisha
(c) Aruna (d) Subbu

DIRECTION (Q. 18): *In the following question, two statements are given followed by four conclusions I, II, III and IV. You have to consider the statements to be true even if they seem to be at variance from commonly known facts. You have to decide which of the given conclusions, if any follow from the given statements.*

18. Statements:

I. Some cats are dogs.
II. No dog is a toy.

Conclusions:

I. Some dogs are cats.
II. Some toys are cats.
III. Some cats are not toys.
IV. All toys are cats.

(a) Only Conclusions I and either II or III.
(b) Only Conclusions II and III follow
(c) Only Conclusions I and II follow
(d) Only Conclusion I follows

19. Arrange the following words according to the dictionary:

1. Matter 2. Motive
3. Mockery 4. Manage
5. Movies

(a) 4, 1, 2, 5, 3 (b) 4, 2, 3, 5, 1
(c) 3, 2, 1, 4, 5 (d) 4, 1, 3, 2, 5

DIRECTION (Q. 20): *In Question which one of the following diagrams represents the correct relationship among :*

20. Lion, Fox and Carnivorous

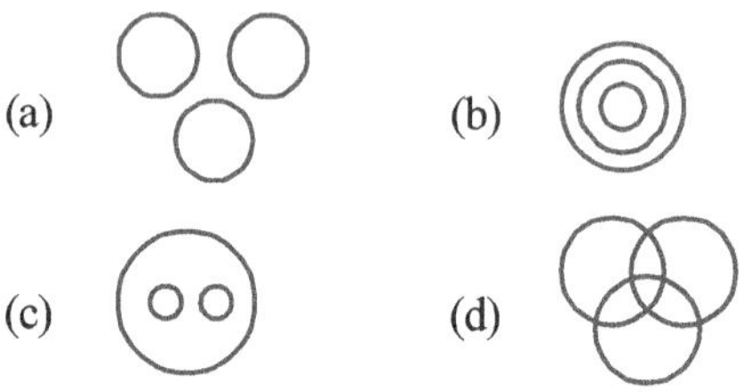

DIRECTIONS (Qs. 21-22): *In each of the following questions, if a mirror is placed on the line AB, then which of the answer figures is the right image of the given figure?*

21. Question Figure:

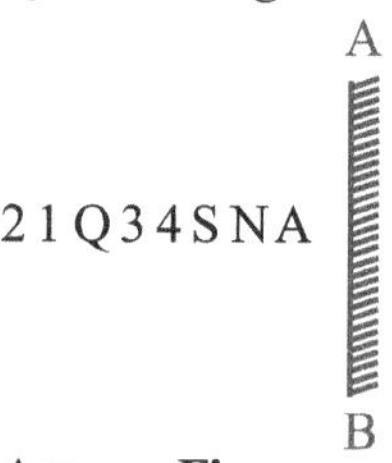

Answer Figures:

(a) ΑИƧ4ƐϘ1Ƨ (b) ΑИƧ4ƐϘ1Ƨ
(c) Ƨ1ϘƐ4ƧИΑ (d) ANS4ƐQ12

22. Question Figure:

Answer Figures:

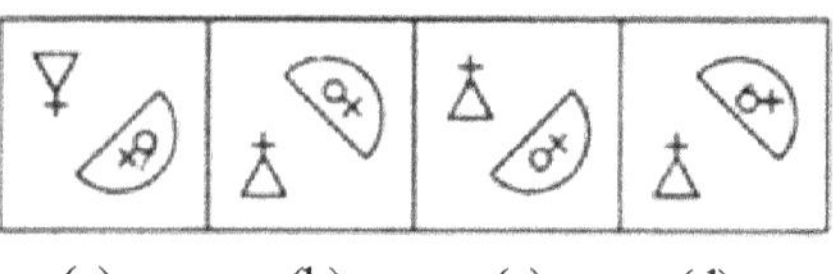

(a) (b) (c) (d)

23. How many triangles are there in the following square?

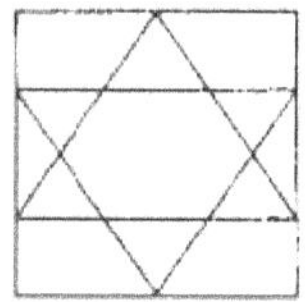

(a) 7 (b) 12
(c) 6 (d) 9

24. Find out the alternative figure which contains figure (X) as its part.

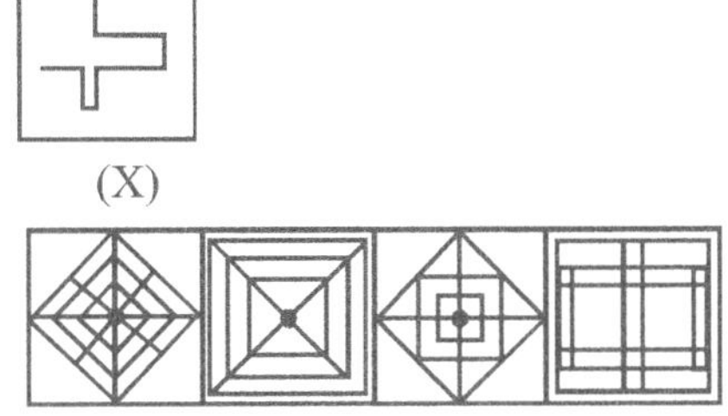

DIRECTION (Q. 25): *A word is represented by only one set of numbers as given in any one of the alternatives. The sets of numbers given in the alternatives are represented by two classes of alphabets as in two matrices given below. The columns and rows of Matrix I are numbered from 0 to 4 and that of Matrix II are numbered from 5 to 9. A letter from these matrices can be represented first by its row and next by its column e.g., 'E' can be represented by 01, 13 etc., and 'L' can be represented by 56, 77 etc. Similarly, you have to identify the set for the word given in each question.*

25. **Matrix I**

	0	1	2	3	4
0	Z	M	G	R	C
1	J	L	D	B	G
2	M	B	C	M	H
3	R	L	N	G	I
4	B	D	M	R	J

Matrix II

	5	6	7	8	9
5	X	K	T	E	S
6	Q	A	U	X	P
7	U	V	O	W	E
8	T	Y	A	F	U
9	O	O	E	V	A

LANE

(a) 11, 66, 33, 96 (b) 31, 87, 32, 97
(c) 31, 66, 33, 97 (d) 11, 67, 32, 97

QUANTITATIVE APTITUDE

26. What is the value of

$\sqrt{7.84}+\sqrt{0.0784}+\sqrt{0.000784}+\sqrt{0.00000784}$?

(a) 3.08 (b) 3.108
(c) 3.1008 (d) 3.1108

27. A three-digit number is divisible by 11 and has its digit in the unit's place equal to 1. The number is 297 more than the number obtained by reversing the digits. What is the number?

(a) 121 (b) 231
(c) 561 (d) 451

28. What is 40% of 50% of $\frac{3}{4}$ of 3200?

(a) 480 (b) 560
(c) 420 (d) 600

29. A bag contains 5 white and 7 black balls and a man draws 4 balls at random. The odds against these being all black is:

(a) 7 : 92 (b) 92 : 7
(c) 92 : 99 (d) 99 : 92

30. A trader marked a watch 40% above the cost price and then gave a discount of 10%. He made a net profit of ₹ 468 after paying a tax of 10% on the gross profit. What is the cost price of the watch?

(a) ₹ 1200 (b) ₹ 1800
(c) ₹ 2000 (d) ₹ 2340

31. 42 men take 25 days to dig a pond. If the pond would have to be dug in 14 days, then what is the number of men to be employed?

(a) 67 (b) 75
(c) 81 (d) 84

32. If the diameter of a wire is decreased by 10%, by how much per cent (approximately) will the length be increased to keep the volume constant?

(a) 5% (b) 17%
(c) 20% (d) 23%

33. From a series of 50 observations, an observation with value 45 is dropped but the mean remains the same. What was the mean of 50 observations?

(a) 50 (b) 49
(c) 45 (d) 40

34. Mr. Duggal invested ₹20,000 with rate of interest @ 20 pcpa. The interest was compounded half-yearly for the first one year and in the next year it was compounded yearly. What will be the total interest earned at the end of two years?

(a) ₹ 8,800 (b) ₹ 9,040
(c) ₹ 8,040 (d) ₹ 9,800

35. The average age of the family of five members is 24. If the present age of youngest member is 8 years then what was the average age of the family at the time of the birth of the youngest member?
(a) 20 years (b) 16 years
(c) 12 years (d) 18 years

36. Product of two co-prime numbers is 117. Their L.C.M. should be:
(a) 1
(b) 117
(c) equal to their H.C.F.
(d) cannot be calculated

37. A candidate appearing for an examination has to secure 35% marks to pass. But he secured only 40 marks and failed by 30 marks. What would be the maximum marks of test?
(a) 280 (b) 180
(c) 200 (d) 150

38. By selling a table for Rs 330, a trader gains 10%. Find the cost price of the table.
(a) 300 (b) 363
(c) 297 (d) 270

39. A ladder of 17 ft length reaches a window which is 15 ft above the ground on one side of the street. Keeping its foot at the same point the ladder is turned to the other side of the street and now it reaches a window 8 ft high. What is the width of the street?
(a) 23 ft (b) 15 ft
(c) 25 ft (d) 30 ft

40. The difference between compound interest and simple interest on a certain amount of money at 5% per annum for 2 years is ₹ 15. Find the sum :
(a) ₹ 4500 (b) ₹ 7500
(c) ₹ 5000 (d) ₹ 6000

41. If $x+\left(\frac{1}{x}\right)=p$, then what is $x^6+\left(\frac{1}{x^6}\right)$ equal to?
(a) p^6+6p (b) p^6-6p
(c) $p^6+6p^4+9p^2+2$ (d) $p^6-6p^4+9p^2-2$

42. If $(x+y+z=0)$, then what is $(x+y)(y+z)(z+x)$ equal to?
(a) $-xyz$ (b) $x^2+y^2+z^3$
(c) $x^3+y^3+z^3+3xyz$ (d) xyz

43. 40 men can cut 60 trees is 8 hrs. If 8 men leaves the job how many trees will be cut in 12 hours ?
(a) 72 (b) 60
(c) 48 (d) 36

44. A monkey ascends a greased pole 12 metres high. He ascends 2 metres in first minute and slips down 1 metre in the alternate minute. In which minute, he reaches the top ?
(a) 21st (b) 22nd
(c) 23rd (d) 24th

45. The average age of a lady and her daughter is 28.5. The ratio of their ages is 14 : 5 respectively. What is the daughters age?
(a) 12 years
(b) 15 years
(c) 18 years
(d) Cannot be determined

DIRECTIONS (Qs. 46-48): *Study the following Pie-chart carefully and answer the questions given below.*

Survey conducted on 10500 people to find out various Professionals in the town and percentage of Female Professionals amongst them

Various Professionals = 10500

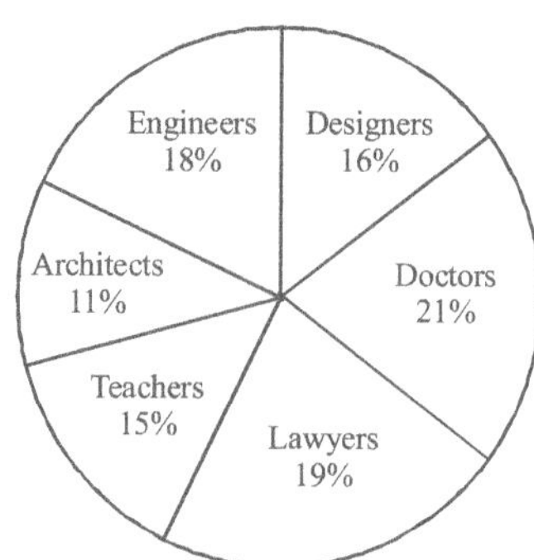

Percentage of Female Professionals

Profession	Percentage
Doctors	20%
Engineers	60%
Architects	40%
Teachers	80%
Lawyers	40%
Designers	35%

46. What is the difference between the total number of male and female professionals in the town ?
(a) 1284 (b) 1134
(c) 1054 (d) 1164

47. Female Doctors are what per cent of the female Teachers in the town?
(a) 42 (b) 28
(c) 15 (d) 35

48. What is the ratio of the number of male Architects to the number of male Teachers in the town ?
(a) 11 : 5 (b) 3 : 2
(c) 5 : 11 (d) 2 : 3

49. The ratio of the length and the breadth of a rectangle is 4 : 3 and the area of the rectangle is 1728 sq cm. What is the ratio of the breadth and the area of the rectangle ?
(a) 1 : 38 (b) 1 : 24
(c) 1 : 42 (d) 1 : 48

50. A person has four iron bars whose lengths are 24 m, 36 m, 48 m and 72 m respectively. This person wants to cut pieces of same length from each of four bars. What is the least number of total pieces if he is to cut without any wastage?
(a) 10 (b) 15
(c) 20 (d) 25

ENGLISH LANGUAGE

DIRECTIONS (Qs. 51-55): *Select the most appropriate word from the options against each number :*

Auctions are public __(51)__ of goods, conducted by an __(52)__ auctioneer. He encourages buyers to __(53)__ higher prices and finally names the __(54)__ bidder as the buyer of the goods. This is called 'knocking down' the goods, for when the bidding ends the auctioneer __(55)__ a small hammer on a table in front of him.

51. (a) sale (b) marketing
(c) promotion (d) viewing

52. (a) authoritative (b) allowed
(c) authentic (d) approved

53. (a) bid (b) buy
(c) get (d) bargain

54. (a) smartest (b) highest
(c) biggest (d) strongest

55. (a) bangs (b) thrashes
(c) smashes (d) hits

DIRECTIONS (Qs. 56-58): *In the following questions four alternatives are given for the idiom/phrase italicised and underlined in the sentence. Choose the alternative which best expresses the meaning of idiom/phrase.*

56. He *passed himself off* as a noble man.
(a) Was regarded as
(b) Pretended to be
(c) Was thought to be
(d) Was looked upon

57. This matter has been *hanging fire* for the last many months and must therefore be decided one way or the other.
(a) going on slowly (b) hotly debated
(c) stuck up (d) ignored

58. In the armed forces, it is considered a great privilege to *die in harness*.
(a) die on a horse back
(b) die in the battlefield
(c) die while still working
(d) die with honour

DIRECTIONS (Qs. 59-60): *In questions given below out of four alternatives, choose the one which can be substituted for the given word/sentence.*

59. That which cannot be corrected
(a) Unintelligible (b) Indelible
(c) Illegible (d) Incorrigible

60. The study of ancient societies
(a) Anthropology (b) Archaeology
(c) History (d) Ethnology

DIRECTIONS (Qs. 61-62): *Look at the underlined part of each sentence. Below each sentence, three possible substitutions for the underlined part are given. If one of them (i.e.,) (a), (b) or (c) is better than the underlined part, indicate your response on the Answer Sheet against the corresponding letter (a), (b) or (c). If none of the substitutions improves the sentence, indicate (d) as your response on the Answer Sheet. Thus, 'No improvement' response will be signified by the letter (d).*

61. We need honest workers, not people of redoubtable integrity.
(a) doubting (b) doubtful
(c) doubtless (d) No improvement

62. By the time he arrived, everybody had gone home.
(a) when he arrived
(b) at which he arrived
(c) by which he arrived
(d) No improvement

DIRECTIONS (Qs. 63-64): *Each of the following items is followed by four words* or *group of words. Fill in the blanks with the appropriate word* or *group of words.*

63. The prisoner showed no ________ for his crimes.
(a) hatred (b) obstinacy
(c) remorse (d) anger

64. It is inconceivable that in many schools children are subjected to physical ________ in the name of discipline.
(a) violation (b) exercise
(c) violence (d) security

DIRECTIONS (Qs. 65-66): *Each question below consists of a word in capital letters followed by four words or group of words. Select the word or group of words that is most similar in meaning to the words in capital letters.*

65. GLEAN
(a) To groom (b) To gather bit by bit
(c) To discover (d) To polish

66. TACTILE
(a) Considerate
(b) Strong
(c) Sharp
(d) Pertaining to the organs of touch

DIRECTIONS (Qs. 67-68): *Each questions below consists of a word in capital letters followed by four words or group of words. Select the word or group of words that is most* **opposite** *in meaning to the words in capital letters.*

67. DEFERENTIAL
(a) Discount (b) Disrespectful
(c) Preconception (d) Acute

68. FELICITOUS
(a) Unfriendly (b) Uneasy
(c) Unheard of (d) Inappropriate

DIRECTIONS (Qs. 69-70): *Find the correctly spelt words.*

69. (a) Excessive (b) Exccessive
(c) Exxcesive (d) Excesive

70. (a) Indipensable (b) Indipenseble
(c) Indispansible (d) Indispensable

DIRECTIONS (Qs. 71-72): *In this section, you are required to spot errors in sentences. Each sentence is divided into three parts. Read each sentence to find out whether there is an error in any of the parts. No sentence has more than one error. Some of the sentences do not have any error. When you find an error in a sentence, the letter indicated under that part of the sentence is the answer and therefore the same may be marked on the separate Answer Sheet. If there is no error in any part, mark (d) as the answer.*

71. They sit (a) at the window (b) and watch the traffic (c) No error (d)

72. I started early (a) for the station lest I (b) should miss the train (c) No error (d)

DIRECTIONS (Qs. 73–74): *The questions below consist of a set of labelled sentences. These sentences, when properly sequenced form a coherent paragraph. Select the most logical order of sentences from among the options.*

73. The man
P. and no one passing him in the street
Q. was singularly inconspicuous
R. who was called Alfred Nobel
S. would have given him
another look.
(a) RQPS (b) QPSR
(c) PSQR (d) SPRQ

74. In paleopathology
P. would be to obtain
Q. the fundamental objective
R. background information
S. as much
on the skeleton as possible.
(a) PRQS (b) RPSQ
(c) QPSR (d) SRQP

DIRECTION (Q. 75): *In the following questions, a sentence has been given in Direct/Indirect form. Out of the four alternatives suggested, select the one which best expresses the same sentence in Indirect/ Direct form.*

75. Socrates said, "Virtue is its own reward.".
(a) Socrates said that virtue had its own rewards.

(b) Socrates says that virtue is its own reward.
(c) Socrates said that virtue is its own reward.
(d) Socrates said that virtue was its own reward.

GENERAL AWARENESS

76. Which one of the following is a programme that converts high level language to machine language?
(a) Linker (b) Assembler
(c) Interpreter (d) Compiler

77. Which one of the following glands produces the growth hormone (somatotrophin)?
(a) Adrenal (b) Pancreas
(c) Pituitary (d) Thyroid

78. Who among the following was not a member of the Constituent Assembly?
(a) Sardar Vallabhbhai Patel
(b) Acharya JB Kriplani
(c) Lok Nayak Jayprakash
(d) K M Munshi

79. Laser is a device to produce
(a) a beam of white light
(b) coherent light
(c) microwaves
(d) X-rays

80. In the human body, Cowper's glands form a part of which one of the following system?
(a) Digestive system
(b) Endocrine system
(c) Reproductive system
(d) Nervous system

81. Mist is a result of which one of the following
(a) Condensation (b) Evaporation
(c) Sublimation (d) Saturation

82. 'Dyarchy' was first introduced in India under
(a) Morley-Minto reforms
(b) Montford reforms
(c) Simon Commision plan
(d) Government of India Act, 1935

83. Fiscal Policy in India is formulated by
(a) the Reserve Bank of India
(b) the Planning Commission
(c) the Finance Ministry
(d) the Securities and Exchange Board of India

84. Malaria in the human body is caused by which one of the following organisms?
(a) Bacteria (b) Virus
(c) Mosquito (d) Protozoan

85. The focal length of convex lens is
(a) the same for all colours
(b) shorter for blue light than for red
(c) shorter for red light than for blue
(d) maximum for yellow light

86. The Indian Research Station 'Himadri' is located at
(a) Siachen (b) Darjeeling
(c) Arctic Region (d) Antarctica

87. The programme of 'Operation Flood' was concentrated on
(a) increasing irrigation facilities.
(b) flood control.
(c) increasing the milk production.
(d) increase the flood grains production.

88. Article 324 of the Indian Constitution deals with the
(a) imposition of President's Rule in States.
(b) appointment of Finance Commission.
(c) powers and functions of the Chief Election Commissioner.
(d) functions of the Union Public Service Commission.

89. The founder of the Lodi Dynasty was
(a) Bahlul Lodi
(b) Sikandar Shah Lodi
(c) Jalal Khan Lodi
(d) Ibrahim Lodi

90. The Fundamental Rights can be suspended by the
(a) Governor (b) President
(c) Law Minister (d) Prime Minister

91. Which one of the following is a warm ocean current ?
(a) Gulf Stream (b) Kurile
(c) Canary (d) Labrador

92. Who was the first posthumous recipient of Bharat Ratna?
(a) M.G. Ramachandran
(b) B.R. Ambedkar
(c) K. Kamraj
(d) Lal Bahadur Shastri

93. Which day is observed as "International Day of Non-Violence"
(a) 1 st May (b) 2 nd October
(c) 24 th October (d) 30 th January

94. Amuktamalyada is the work of :
(a) Krishnadeva Raya
(b) Vachcharaj
(c) Kharavela
(d) Allasani Peddana

95. Yakshagana is a folk dance-drama of:
(a) Maharashtra (b) Karnataka
(c) Gujarat (d) W. Bengal

96. Kaziranga National Park is famous for
(a) One-horned Rhinos
(b) Tigers
(c) Swamp Dears (Barasingha)
(d) Elephants

97. The 27th IAEA Fusion Energy Conference (FEC 2018) has started in which city?
(a) Lucknow (b) Gandhi Nagar
(c) Jaipur (d) New Delhi

98. Who is the author of the book "Nehru and Bose: Parallel Lives"?
(a) Arpita Ghosh
(b) Abhijit Mukherjee
(c) Rudrangshu Mukherjee
(d) Sudip Bandyopa

99. Which Union Minister of India will be honoured with the 2018 Carnot Prize of Kleinman Center for Energy Policy?
(a) D V Sadananda Gowda
(b) Nitin Gadkari
(c) Piyush Goyal
(d) Arun Jaitley

100. The first-ever joint maritime exercise will be conducted between ASEAN and which country?
(a) Brazil (b) China
(c) Japan (d) Russia

Hints & Explanations

1. (a) As,

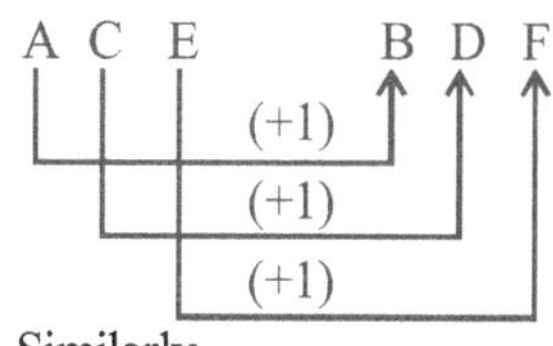

Similarly

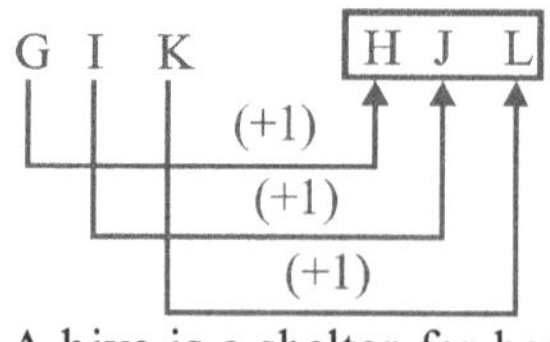

2. (d) A hive is a shelter for bees. Whereas, A eyrie is a large nest of an eagle.

3. (a) $v \xrightarrow{(+1)} w$ $p \xrightarrow{(+1)} q$
$y \xrightarrow{(-1)} x$ $m \xrightarrow{(+1)} n$
$g \xrightarrow{(-1)} f$ $k \xrightarrow{(+1)} \ell$
$c \xrightarrow{(-1)} b$ $r \xrightarrow{(+1)} s$

4. (a) Except (a), all others are not divisible by 2nd term.

5. (b) Meaning full words

1 2 3 4
Tilling → Sowing → Weeding → Reaping.

6. (b) –1 0 ③ 8 15 24
+1 +3 +5 +7 +9

7. (d) There are two numbers series:

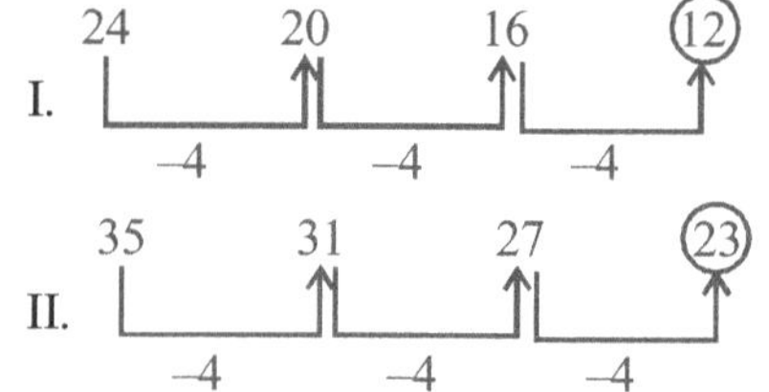

8. (d)

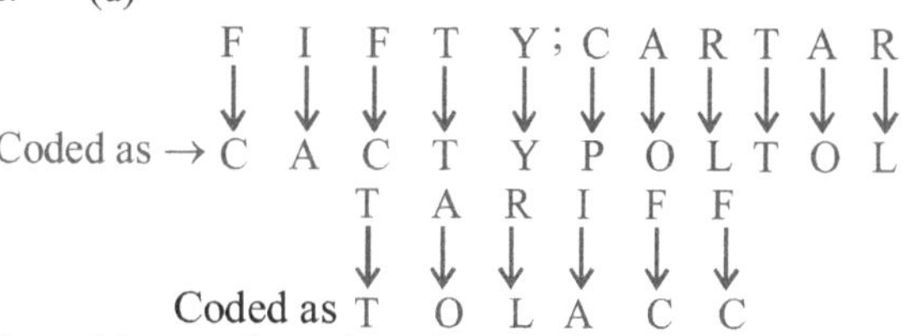

9. (c) rtxy/ sxyz/ rtxy/ sxyz.

10. (d) B → A, C → B, C → D, A → D

It is clearly shown that, D is in south west of A.

11. (c) Parliamentary
12. (a) The father of the boy's uncle → the grandfather of the boy and daughter of the grandfather → sister of father.
13. (d)

Regions Persons ↓	1	2	4	6	7	8	9	10
Boys □	✓	✓	×	×	×	×	✓	×
Girls △	×	×	✓	×	×	✓	×	×
Sober ○	×	✓	✓	✓	✓	×	×	×
Cricketer ▭	✓	✓	×	✓	×	×	×	✓

Region 2 presents the boys who are cricketer and sober.

14. (a) 5 * 6/2 → 3 5
8 * 4/2 → 2 8
6 * 8/2 → 4 6

15. (b) $1 \times 2 \times 3 = 6$
$2 \times 3 \times 4 = 24$
$3 \times 4 \times 5 = 60$
$4 \times 5 \times 6 = 120$
$5 \times 6 \times 7 = 210$
$6 \times 7 \times 8 = 336$

16. (d) First Column
$12 \times 3 + 4 = 40$
Second Column
$15 \times 4 + 6 = 66$
Third Column
$16 \times 5 + 4 = \boxed{84}$

17. (d)

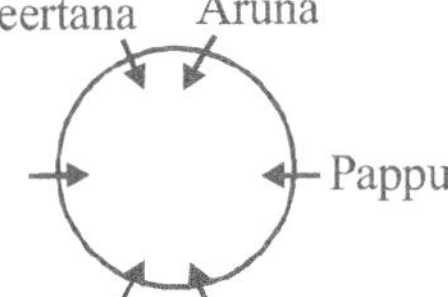

18. (a) Cats Dogs Toy
OR
Toy Cats Dogs

Conclusion I : True
II : Complementary Pair
III : Complementary Pair
IV : False

So, only conclusion I and either II or III.

19. (d) Arrangement of words according to dictionary:

4. Manage

1. Matter
↓
3. Mockery
↓
2. Motive
↓
5. Movies

20. (c)

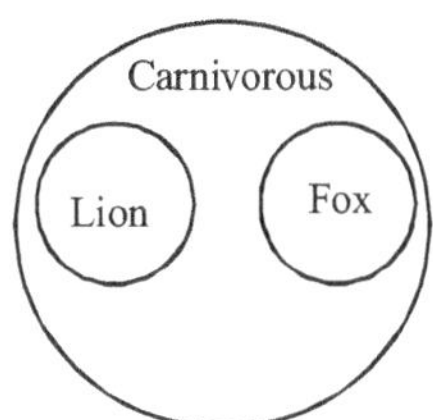

21. (b) AИƧꟻƐϘIƧ
22. (b)
23. (b) There are 12 triangles in the given square.

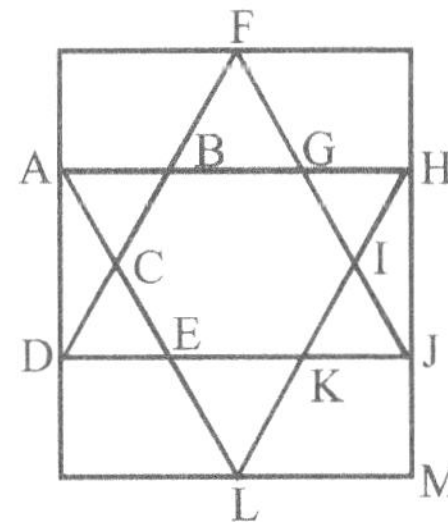

Δ ABC, Δ ACD, Δ ABD, Δ AFD
Δ FGB, Δ HIG, Δ HJI, Δ IJK
Δ HJK, Δ HML, Δ EKL, Δ CED

24. (d)

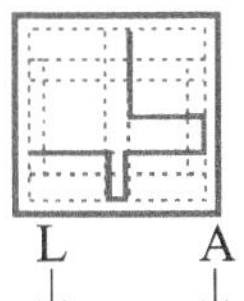

25. (b) L → 31, A → 87, N → 32, E → 97

26. (d)

$$\sqrt{7.84} + \sqrt{0.0784} + \sqrt{0.000784} + \sqrt{0.00000784}$$

$$= \sqrt{\frac{784}{100}} + \sqrt{\frac{784}{10000}} + \sqrt{\frac{784}{1000000}} + \sqrt{\frac{784}{100000000}}$$

$$= \frac{28}{10} + \frac{28}{100} + \frac{28}{1000} + \frac{28}{10000}$$

$$= 2.8 + 0.28 + 0.028 + 0.0028 = 3.1108$$

27. (d) On taking option (d).
The reverse digit of 451 is 154.
Now, 154 + 297 = 451 is equal to the original number.

28. (a) 40% of 50% of $\frac{3}{4}$ of 3200

$$= \frac{4}{10} \times \frac{5}{10} \times \frac{3}{4} \times 3200 = 4 \times 5 \times 3 \times 8 = 480$$

29. (b) There are 7 + 5 = 12 balls in the bag and the number of ways in which 4 balls can be drawn is $^{12}C_4$ and the number of ways of drawing 4 black balls (out of seven) is $^7C_4$.
Hence, P (4 black balls)

$$= \frac{^7C_4}{^{12}C_4} = \frac{7.6.5.4}{1.2.3.4} \times \frac{1.2.3.4}{12.11.10.9} = \frac{7}{99}$$

Thus the odds against the event 'all black balls' are

$$(1 - \frac{7}{99}) : \frac{7}{99} \text{ i.e., } \frac{92}{99} : \frac{7}{99} \text{ or } 92 : 7$$

30. (c) Let the cost price of the watch = ₹x
After 40% marked price and 10% discount

$$= x \times \frac{90}{100} \times \frac{140}{100} = \frac{126x}{100}$$

$$\text{Profit} = \frac{126x}{100} - x = \frac{26x}{100}$$

According to question,
Pay 10% tax on profit

$$= \frac{26x}{100} \times \frac{90}{100} = 468$$

$$x = \frac{468 \times 100 \times 100}{26 \times 90} = ₹2000$$

31. (b) Let the number of men be n

Men **Days**

42 ↓ 25 ↑
n 14

$$\therefore \quad \frac{n}{42} = \frac{25}{14} \Rightarrow n = 75$$

32. (d) Volume of wire = $\pi r^2 h$

$$\text{New radius of the wire} = \frac{r \times 90}{100} = \frac{9r}{10}$$

Let new length of the wire be L.
∴ Volume of new wire

$$= \pi \left(\frac{9r}{10}\right)^2 \times L = \frac{81}{100} \pi r^2 L$$

According to question,

$$\pi r^2 h = \frac{81}{100} \pi r^2 L \Rightarrow L = \frac{100}{81} h$$

$$\text{Increase in length} = \frac{100}{81} h - h = \frac{19}{81} h$$

$$\text{Percent increase} = \frac{19/81h}{h} \times 100\% = 23.46\%$$

$$= 23\% \text{ (approx)}$$

33. (c) Let the observation mean = x
∴ Sum of 50 observations = 50x
According to question,

$$\therefore \quad \frac{50x - 45}{49} = x$$

$\Rightarrow$ 50x − 45 = 49x
∴ x = 45

34. (b) Interest earned in 1st half of a year

$$= 20{,}000 \times \frac{1}{2} \times \frac{20}{100} = 2000$$

Similarly, During second half, interest earned = 2200
During second year, interest earned = 4840 (Note : Interest is calculated as compound)
Total interest earned at the end of two years = 2000 + 220 + 4840 = ₹9040.

35. (b) Total age of the family of five members = 24 × 5 = 120
Total age of the family of five members before 8 years
= 120 − 5 × 8 = 120 − 40 = 80

$$\text{So, required average age} = \frac{80}{5} = 16 \text{ yr.}$$

36. (b) H.C.F of co-prime numbers is 1.

37. (c) Suppose maximum marks = x

$$\text{then } x \times \frac{35}{100} = 40 + 30 \Rightarrow x \times \frac{35}{100} = 70$$

$$\Rightarrow x = \frac{70 \times 100}{35} = 200 \text{ marks}$$

38. (a) S.P. = Rs 330, Gain = 10%

$$\therefore \quad C.P. = \left(\frac{100}{100 + \text{Gain }\%}\right) \times S.P.$$

$$= \text{Rs } \frac{100}{100 + 10} \times 330$$

$$= \frac{100}{110} \times 330 = \text{Rs } 300.$$

39. (a)

E, D, 8 ft, 17 ft, 17 ft, 15 ft, A, D, C

In ΔABE,

$BE^2 = AE^2 + AB^2 \Rightarrow AB^2 = 17^2 - 8^2$

or $AB^2 = 289 - 64 = 225 \Rightarrow AB$

$AB = 15$ ft

In ΔBCD,

$BD^2 = BC^2 + CD^2 \Rightarrow BC^2 = 17^2 - 15^2$

$= 289 - 225 = 64$

$\Rightarrow BC = 8$ ft

$\therefore$ Width of the street $= AB + BC = 15 + 8 = 23$ ft

40. (d) $D = \left(\frac{R}{100}\right)^2 \times P$

$P = D \times \left(\frac{100}{R}\right)^2 = \frac{1500 \times 10000}{25} = ₹6000$

41. (d) Given, $x + \frac{1}{x} = p$

$\Rightarrow \left(x + \frac{1}{x}\right)^2 = p^2$

$\Rightarrow x^2 + \frac{1}{x^2} + 2 = p^2$

$\Rightarrow x^2 + \frac{1}{x^2} = p^2 - 2$ ... (i)

$\Rightarrow \left(x^2 + \frac{1}{x^2}\right)^3 = (p^2 - 2)^3$

$\Rightarrow x^6 + \frac{1}{x^6} + 3\left(x^2 + \frac{1}{x^2}\right) = p^6 - 8 - 6p^2 (p^2 - 2)$

$\Rightarrow x^6 + \frac{1}{x^6} + 3(p^2 - 2) = p^6 - 8 - 6p^4 + 12p^2$

[from equation (i)]

$\Rightarrow x^6 + \frac{1}{x^6} = p^6 - 6p^4 + 9p^2 - 2$

42. (a) Given, $x + y + z = 0$

$\therefore$ $(x + y)(y + z)(z + x) = (-z)(-x)(-y) = -xyz$

43. (a) $M_1 = 40, D_1 = 8$ (As days and hrs both denote time)

$W_1 = 60$ (cutting of trees is taken as work)

$M_2 = 40 - 8 = 32, D_2 = 12, W_2 = ?$

Putting the values in the formula

$M_1 D_1 W_2 = M_2 D_2 W_1$

We have, $40 \times 8 \times W_2 = 32 \times 12 \times 60$

or, $W_2 = \frac{32 \times 12 \times 60}{40 \times 8} = 72$ trees.

44. (a) In 2 minutes, he ascends = 1 metre

$\therefore$ 10 metres, he ascends in 20 minutes.

$\therefore$ He reaches the top in 21st minute.

45. (b) Average age = 28.5

$\therefore$ Total age $= 28.5 \times 2 = 57$

$\therefore$ Daughter's age $= \frac{5}{19} \times 57 = 15$ years

46. (b) % of female professionals =

$= [20\% \text{ of } 21\% + 60\% \text{ of } 18\% + 40\% \text{ of } 11\% + 80\% \text{ of } 15\% + 40\% \text{ of } 19\% + 35\% \text{ of } 16\%]$

$= \frac{1}{100}[420 + 1080 + 440 + 1200 + 760 + 560]\%$

$= \frac{4460}{100}\% = 44.6\%$

$\therefore$ % of male professionals

$= 100\% - 44.6\% = 55.4\%$

$\therefore$ Required difference

$= (55.4 - 44.6)\%$ of 10500

$= 10.8\%$ of 10500

$= 10.8 \times 105 = 1134$

47. (d) Required %

$= \frac{20\% \text{ of } 21}{89\% \text{ of } 15} \times 100\% \approx \frac{20 \times 21}{80 \times 15} \times 100\%$

$\frac{420}{12} \approx 35\%$

48. (a) Required ratio $= \frac{60 \times 11}{20 \times 15} = 11 : 5$

49. (d) $(4x)(3x) = 1728$

$\Rightarrow x^2 = 144 \therefore x = 12$

$\Rightarrow$ length = 48; breadth = 36

$\therefore$ Required ratio $= \frac{36}{36 \times 48} = 1 : 48$

50. (b) $24 = 12 \times 2$,

$36 = 12 \times 3$,

$48 = 12 \times 4$,

and $72 = 12 \times 6$

$\therefore$ HCF (24, 36, 48, 72) = 12

Total pieces = 2 + 3 + 4 + 6 = 15

51. (a) 52. (d) 53. (a) 54. (b) 55. (a)
56. (b) 57. (a) 58. (c) 59. (d) 60. (b)

61. (b) We need honest workers, not people of doubtful integrity.

Redoubtable (adj.) (Of a person): causing fear and respect

Doubtful : Uncertain, undecided and contingent, often use to admitting of doubt.

62. (d) By the time he arrived, everybody had gone home.

63. (c) Remorse is an emotion/action/feeling after the crime is done. Hatred is for the other people who saw/hear/ gone through crime but certainly not for the prisoner. Crime is done in anger and a cause. Obstinacy is stubbornness. Only emotion that suits the context is Remorse.

64. (c) If it would have been 'security' then it would have been 'provided' in the statement not 'subjected'. Exercise does

not fit. Violation (to breech) is also out of place. Use of 'physical' in statement indicates 'violence'. It fits best in the blank.

65. (b) 'Glean' means 'to gather ears of corn left'.
66. (d) 'Tactile' means 'connecting wiht your sense of touch'.
67. (b) 'Deferential' means behaviour that shows respect.
68. (d) 'Felicitous' means very suitable or giving a good result.
69. (a) 70. (d)
71. (b) They sit by the window and watch the traffic.
72. (d) I started early for the station lest I should miss the train.
73. (a) 74. (c) 75. (d)
76. (d) A compiler is a special programme that processes statements written in a particular programming language and turns them into machine language or "code" that a computer's processor uses.
77. (c) Somatotrophin is produced by the anterior pituitary. It is a peptide hormone that induces growth, cell reproduction and regeneration.
78. (c) The Constitution of India was drafted by the constituent assembly and it was set up under the cabinet Mission plan on 16 May 1946. The members of the constituent assembly were elected by the Provincial assemblies by method of single transferable vote system of proportional representations. Members of the committee: Sardar Vallabhbhai Patel, K. M. Munshi,Acharya J.B kriplani . Lok Nayak Jai Prakash was not the member of the constituent assembly.
79. (b) A laser is a device that emits coherent light through a process called stimulated emission.
80. (c) Cowper's gland is related to reproductive system. Cowper's gland is the bulbourethal gland found in human males. They are found in pair and secrete viscous secretion called pre ejaculate that helps in coitus.
81. (a) Mist is a thin fog resulting from condensation in the air near to the earth's surface.
82. (a) Dyarchy was a system of double government introduced by British India.
83. (c) The Department of Economic Affairs (DEA) under Ministry of Finance is the nodal agency of the Union Government to formulate and monitor country's economic policies and programmes having a bearing on domestic and international aspects of economic management.
84. (d) Malaria is a mosquito borne disease of humans and other animals caused by Plasmodium protozoan. Severe disease is largely caused by Plasmodium falciparum whereas mild forms are due to *P vivax*, *P oval* and *P malariae*.
85. (b) The focal length of a convex lens is shorter for blue light than for red.
86. (c) Himadri Station is India's first Arctic research station located at Spitsbergen, Svalbard, Norway. It was inaugurated on the 1st of July, 2008 by the Minister of Earth Sciences.
87. (c) Operation Flood in India, a project of the National Dairy Development Board (NDDB) was the world's biggest dairy development program which made India, a milk-deficient nation, the largest milk producer in the world, surpassing the USA in 1998, with about 17 percent of global output in 2010-11, which in 30 years doubled the milk available per person, and which made dairy farming India's largest self-sustainable rural employment generator. All this was achieved not merely by mass production, but by production by the masses.
88. (c) powers and functions of the chief Election Commissioner
89. (a) Bahlul Khan Lodi was the founder of Lodi dynasty of the Delhi Sultanate in India upon the abdication of the last claimant from the previous Sayyid rule.
90. (b) The Fundamental Rights can be suspended during the Emergency under Article 359 of the Constitution by the President of India.
91. (a) Gulf Stream is a warm ocean current. It flows along the North America and drifts towards western Europe, thus raising the temperature of western coast considerably.
92. (d) Lal Bahadur Shastri was the first posthumous recipient of Bharat Ratna in 1966. Lal Bahadur Shastri was the third Prime Minister of the Republic of India and a leader of the Indian National Congress party. Shastri joined the Indian independence movement in the 1920s.
93. (b) 94. (a) 95. (b)
96. (a) Kaziranga National Park is a national park in the Golaghat and Nagaon districts of the state of Assam, India. A World Heritage Site, the park hosts two-thirds of the world's great one-horned rhinoceroses.
97. (b) 98. (c) 99. (c) 100. (b)

PRACTICE SET- 5

GENERAL INTELLIGENCE & REASONING

DIRECTIONS (Qs. 1-2) : *In questions below, select the related word/letters/number from the given alternatives.*

1. 9 : 24 :: ? : 6
(a) 3 (b) 2
(c) 1 (d) 5

2. STAR : SBUT :: WARD : ?
(a) XBAW (b) ESBX
(c) FAME (d) DRAW

DIRECTIONS (Qs. 3-4) : *In questions find the odd word/letters//numbers pair from the given alternatives:*

3. (a) (25,49) (b) (121, 169)
(c) (7, 169) (d) (9,25)

4. (a) HEAT (b) MEAT
(c) MEET (d) BEAT

DIRECTIONS (Qs. 5 - 6): *A series is given, with one term missing. Choose the correct alternative from the given ones that will complete the series.*

5. BDFH, IKMO, PRTV, _
(a) WYAC (b) WXYA
(c) WXYZ (d) WYZA

6. 2, 65, 7, 59, 12, 53, _, _
(a) 15, 42 (b) 17, 45
(c) 17, 47 (d) 18, 48

7. How Many triangles are there in the given figure ?

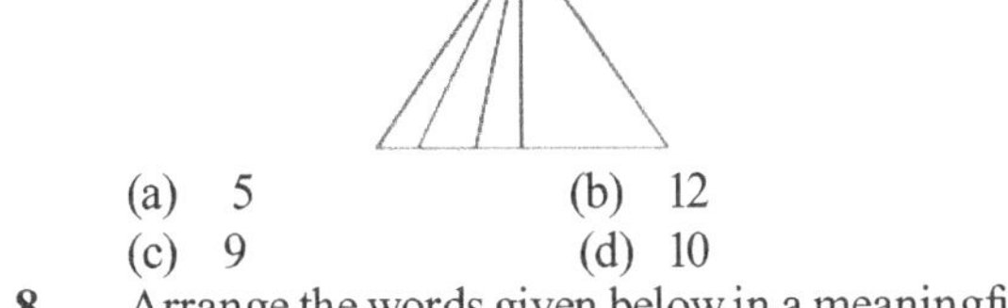

(a) 5 (b) 12
(c) 9 (d) 10

8. Arrange the words given below in a meaningful sequence.
1. Elephant 2. Cat
3. Mosquito 4. Tiger
5. Whale
(a) 5, 3, 1, 2, 4 (b) 3, 2, 4, 1, 5
(c) 1, 3, 5, 4, 2 (d) 2, 5, 1, 4, 3

9. If GOODNESS is coded as HNPCODTR, how can GREATNESS be written in that code?
(a) HQFZSMFRT (b) HQFZUFRTM
(c) HQFZUODTR (d) HQFZUMFRT

10. From the given alternatives select the word which cannot be formed using the letters of the given word.
LEGALIZATION
(a) ALERT (b) ALEGATION
(c) GALLANT (d) NATAL

11. Which one set of letters when sequentially placed at the gaps in the given letter series shall complete it?
B_CCABB_CABBC_AB_CCA
(a) BCBC (b) BCCB
(c) BBCC (d) BBBC

12. Seema walks 30 m North. Then she turns right and walks 30 m then she turns right and walks 55 m. Then she turns left and walks 20 m. Then she again turns left and walks 25 m. How many metres away is she from her Original position?
(a) 45 m (b) 50 m
(c) 66 m (d) 55 m

13. A family consisted of a man, his wife, his three sons, their wives and three children in each son's family. How many members are there in the family ?
(a) 12 (b) 13
(c) 15 (d) 17

14. If the 5th date of a month is Tuesday, what date will be 3 days after the 3rd Friday in the month?
(a) 17 (b) 22
(c) 19 (d) 18

15. Which of the following states the relationship between Manager, Labour Union and Worker?
(a) (b)
(c) (d)

16. 12 year old Rahul is three times as old as his brother Paras. How old will Rahul be when be is twice as old as Paras?
(a) 14 years (b) 20 years
(c) 16 years (d) 18 years

DIRECTIONS (Qs. 17-18) : *In each of the following questions, select the missing number from the given responses.*

17. 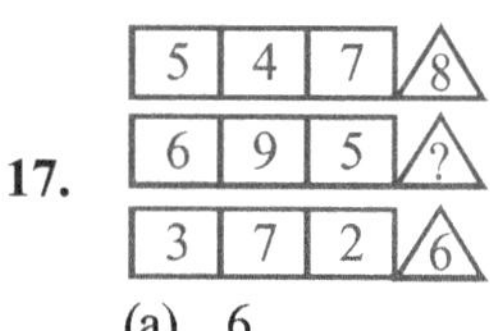

(a) 6 (b) 4
(c) 10 (d) 8

18. 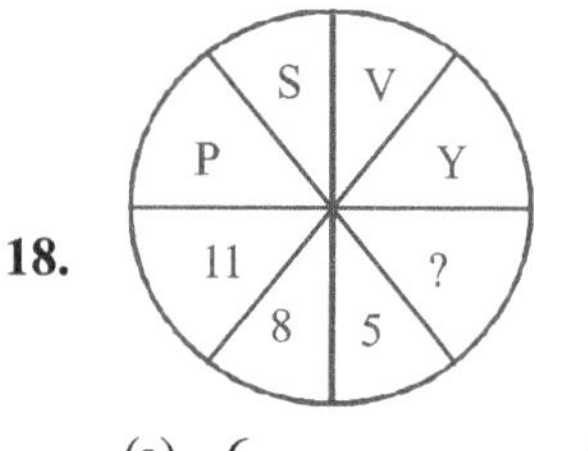

(a) 6 (b) 7
(c) 3 (d) 2

DIRECTION (Q.19) : *In question below, some statements are given followed by three conclusions respectively. You have to consider the statements to be true even if they seem to be at variance from commonly known facts. You have to decide which of the given conclusions if any, follow from the given statements.*

19. **Statement :** Pictures can tell a story. All story books have pictures. Some story books have words.
Conclusions: I. Pictures can tell a story better than words can.
II. The stories in story books are very simple.
III. Some story books have both words and pictures.
(a) Only conclusion I follows
(b) Only conclusion II follows
(c) Only conclusion III follows
(d) Both conclusions I and II follow

20. There are five houses P, Q, R, S and T. P is right of Q and T is left of R and right of P. Q is right of S. Which house is in the middle ?
(a) P (b) Q
(c) T (d) R

DIRECTION (Q. 21): *In question below, which answer figure will complete the pattern in the question figure ?*

21. **Question figure :**

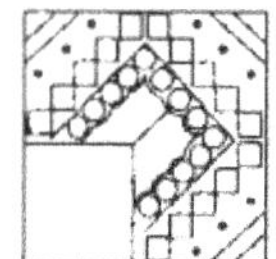

Answer figures :

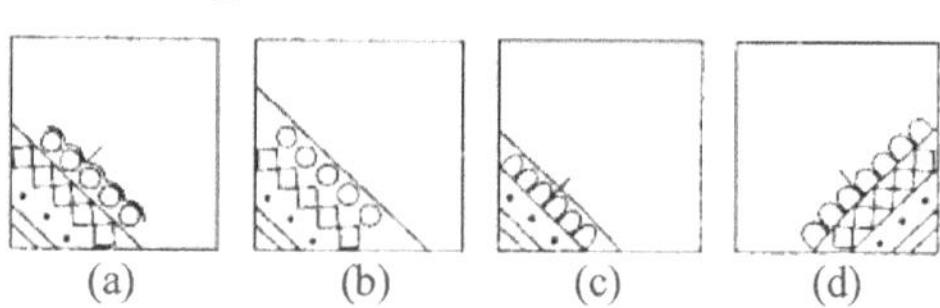

22. A Circular sheet of paper is folded in particular manner, punched once and then unfolded. Find Out the manner in which the paper was folded and punched from amongst the answer figures.
Question figure :

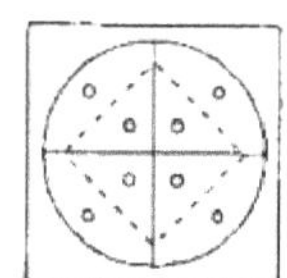

Answer figures:

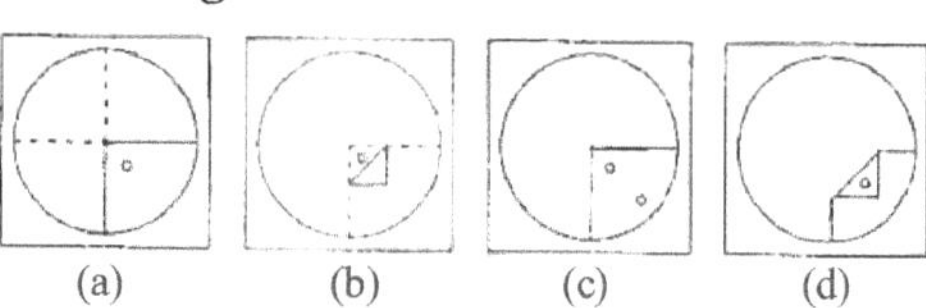

23. Select a suitable figure from the four alternatives that would complete the figure matrix.
Question figure:

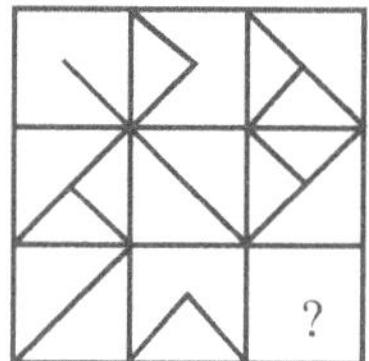

Answer figures:

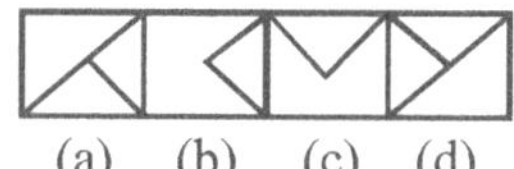

24. Which is the correct image if the picture is held in front of a mirror?
Question figure:

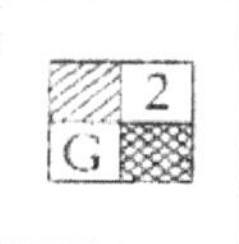

Answer figures:

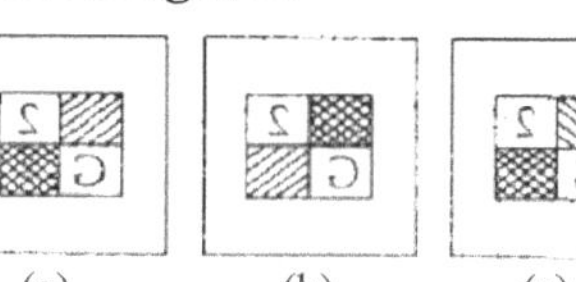

DIRECTION (Q. 25) : *A word is represented by only one set of numbers as given in any one of the alternatives. The sets of numbers given in the alternatives are represented by two classes of alphabets as in two matrices given below. The columns and rows of Matrix I are numbered from 0 to 4 and that of Matrix II are numbered from 5 to 9. A letter from these matrices can be represented first by its row and next by its column e.g., 'E' can be represented by 01, 13 etc., and 'L' can be represented by 56, 77 etc. Similarly, you have to identify the set for the word given in each question.*

25. **Matrix I**

	0	1	2	3	4
0	A	E	M	N	P
1	N	P	A	E	M
2	E	M	N	P	A
3	P	A	E	M	N
4	M	N	P	A	E

Matrix II

	5	6	7	8	9
5	I	L	R	S	T
6	R	S	T	I	L
7	T	I	L	R	S
8	L	R	S	T	I
9	S	T	I	L	R

AIRS
(a) 12, 76, 99, 78 (b) 43, 55, 86, 95
(c) 00, 68, 78, 88 (d) 24, 69, 56, 78

QUANTITATIVE APTITUDE

26. $\frac{1}{\sqrt{9}-\sqrt{8}}-\frac{1}{\sqrt{8}-\sqrt{7}}+\frac{1}{\sqrt{7}-\sqrt{6}}-\frac{1}{\sqrt{6}-\sqrt{5}}+\frac{1}{\sqrt{5}-\sqrt{4}}$ equal to

(a) 0 (b) 1
(c) 5 (d) $\frac{1}{3}$

27. What is the sum of the digits of the least number which when divided by 52, leaves 33 as remainder, when divided by 78 leaves 59 and when divided by 117, leaves 98 as remainder ?
(a) 17 (b) 18
(c) 19 (d) 21

28. If 1 is subtracted from the numerator of a fraction it becomes (1/3) and if 5 is added to the denominator the fraction becomes (1/4). Which fraction shall result, if 1 is subtracted from the numerator and 5 is added to the denominator ?
(a) $\frac{5}{12}$ (b) $\frac{7}{23}$
(c) $\frac{1}{8}$ (d) $\frac{2}{3}$

29. 38L of milk was poured into a tub and the tub was found to be 5% empty. To completely fill the tub, what amount of additional milk must be poured?
(a) 1 *L* (b) 2 *L*
(c) 3 *L* (d) 4 *L*

30. Prakash, Sunil and Anil started a business jointly investing ₹11 lakhs, ₹ 16.5 lakhs and ₹ 8.25 lakhs respectively. The profit earned by them in the business at the end of three years was ₹ 19.5 lakhs. What will be the 50% of Anil's share in the profit?
(a) ₹4.5 lakhs (b) ₹2.25 lakhs
(c) ₹2.5 lakhs (d) ₹3.75 lakhs

31. A ball is dropped from a height 64 m above the ground and every time it hits the ground it rises to a height equal to half of the previous. What is the height attained after it hits the ground for the 16th time?
(a) 2^{-12} m (b) 2^{-11} m
(c) 2^{-10} m (d) 2^{-9} m

32. If ₹ 8400 is divided among *A*, *B* and *C* in the ratio $\frac{1}{5}:\frac{1}{6}:\frac{1}{10}$, what is the share of *A*?
(a) ₹ 3200 (b) ₹ 3400
(c) ₹ 3600 (d) ₹ 3800

33. There are 45 male and 15 female employees in an office. If the mean salary of the 60 employees is ₹ 4800 and the mean salary of the male employees is ₹ 5000, then the mean salary of the female employees is
(a) ₹ 4200 (b) ₹ 4500
(c) ₹ 5600 (d) ₹ 6000

34. A train started from a station with a certain number of passengers. At the first halt, $\frac{1}{3}$rd of its passengers got down and 120 passengers got in. At the second halt, half of the passengers got down and 100 persons got in. Then, the train left for its destination with 240 passengers. How many passengers were there in the train when it started?
(a) 540 (b) 480
(c) 360 (d) 240

35. The radius of a circle is 13 cm and xy is a chord which is at a distance of 12 cm from the centre. The length of the chord is

(a) 12 cm (b) 10 cm
(c) 20 cm (d) 15 cm

36. In the given figure, measure of ∠ABC is

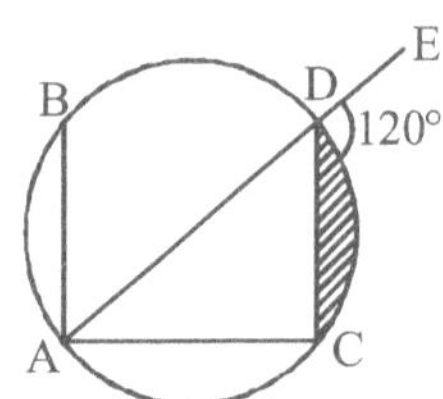

(a) 20° (b) 40°
(c) 60° (d) 80°

37. *ABC* is an equilateral triangle inscribed in a circle. *D* is any point on the arc *BC*. What is ∠*ADB* equal to?

(a) 90° (b) 60°
(c) 45° (d) None of these

38. The angle made by the line $x + \sqrt{3}y - 6 = 0$ with positive direction of x-axis is

(a) 120° (b) 150°
(c) 30° (d) 60°

39. A round balloon of unit radius subtends an angle of 90° at the eye of an observer standing at a point, say A. What is the distance of the centre of the balloon from the point A?

(a) $1/\sqrt{2}$ (b) $\sqrt{2}$
(c) 2 (d) 1/2

40. What is one of the value of x in the equation

$$\sqrt{\frac{x}{1-x}} + \sqrt{\frac{1-x}{x}} = \frac{13}{6}?$$

(a) $\frac{5}{13}$ (b) $\frac{7}{13}$
(c) $\frac{9}{13}$ (d) $\frac{11}{3}$

41. If pqr = 1, what is the value of the expression

$$\frac{1}{1+p+q^{-1}} + \frac{1}{1+q+r^{-1}} + \frac{1}{1+r+p^{-1}}?$$

(a) 1 (b) –1
(c) 0 (d) 1/3

42. What should be subtracted from $27x^3 - 9x^2 - 6x - 5$ to make it exactly divisible by $(3x - 1)$?

(a) –5 (b) –7
(c) 5 (d) 7

43. $(a + b + c)^2 - (a - b - c)^2 = ?$

(a) 4a(b + c) (b) 2a(b + c)
(c) 3a(b + c) (d) 4a(b – c)

44. A man is walking at a speed of 10 km per hour. After every kilometre, he takes rest for 5 minutes. How much time will he take to cover a distance of 5 kilometres?

(a) 48 min. (b) 50 min.
(c) 45 min. (d) 55 min.

45. The angle of elevation of the top of an unfinished pillar at a point 150 m from its base is 30°. If the angle of elevation at the same point is to be 45°, then the pillar has to be raised to a height of how many metres?

(a) 59.4m (b) 61.4m
(c) 62.4m (d) 63.4m

DIRECTIONS (Qs. 46-48): *Study the following table carefully in answer the questions that follow :*

Number of Executives recruited by Six different organisations over the years

Organisation	P	Q	R	S	T	U
2004	458	512	418	502	476	492
2005	522	536	472	500	482	523
2006	480	495	464	508	488	518
2007	506	505	428	444	490	534
2008	427	485	422	512	510	498
2009	492	488	444	499	512	510

46. What is the per cent increase in the number of Executives recruited by organisation R in 2005 from the previous year? (rounded off to two digits after decimal)

(a) 18.67 (b) 12.92
(c) 16.48 (d) 13.21

47. The number of Executives recruited by organisation T in the year 2008 forms approximately what percent of the total number of Executives recruited by all the organisations together in that year?

(a) 11 (b) 31
(c) 18 (d) 26

48. If the area of a circle, inscribed in an equilateral triangle is 4π cm², then what is the area of the triangle?

(a) $12\sqrt{3}$ cm² (b) $9\sqrt{3}$ cm²
(c) $8\sqrt{3}$ cm² (d) 18 cm²

49. The HCF of $X^4 - 1$ and $X^4 - 2X^3 - 2X^2 - 2X - 3$ is

(a) $(x^2+1)(x-1)$ (b) (x^2+1)
(c) $(x^2+1)(x+1)$ (d) $(x+1)$

50. A cone is inscribed in a hemisphere such that their bases are common. If C is the volume of the cone and H that of the hemisphere, then what is the value of C : H?

(a) 1 : 2 (b) 2 : 3
(c) 3 : 4 (d) 4 : 5

ENGLISH LANGUAGE

DIRECTIONS (Qs. 51-52): *Fill in the blanks with the appropriate word or group of words.*

51. Happiness consists in being ____what we have?
    (a) contented to (b) contented with
    (c) contented for (d) contented in
52. His rude behaviour is a _____ his organization.
    (a) disgrace for (b) disgrace on
    (c) disgrace upon (d) disgrace to

DIRECTIONS (Qs. 53-54): *Look at the underlined part of each sentence. Below each sentence, three possible situations for the underlined part are given. If one of them (a), (b) or (c) is better than the underlined part, indicate your response on the Answer Sheet against the corresponding letter (a), (b) or (c). If none of the substitutions improves the sentence, indicate (d) as your response on the Answer Sheet. Thus, "No improvement" response will be signified by the letter (d).*

53. Those are your new shoes, aren't they ?
    (a) isn't it ? (b) is it so ?
    (c) are they ? (d) No improvement
54. He told to us everything he knew.
    (a) us everything he knew
    (b) us everything he is knowing
    (c) us everything he was knowing
    (d) No improvement

DIRECTIONS (Qs. 55-57): *In this section, you are required to spot errors in sentences. Each sentence is divided into three parts. Read each sentence to find out whether there is an error in any of the parts. No sentence has more than one error. Some of the sentences do not have any error. When you find an error in a sentence, the letter indicated under that part of the sentence is the answer and therefore the same may be marked on the separate Answer Sheet. If there is no error in any part, response will be signified by the letter (d).*

55. I wanted to see (a) whethey they (b) had actually read the notes. (c) No error (d)
56. They made him treasurer considered (a) because they (b) him to be honest and efficient (c) No error (d)
57. Having finished the paper early (a) he had came out of the hall (b) almost an hour before the bell rang. (c) No error (d)

DIRECTIONS (Qs. 58-59): *In questions given below out of four alternatives choose the one which can be substituted for the given word/sentence.*

58. A place where bees are kept in called
    (a) An apiary (b) A mole
    (c) A hive (d) A sanctury
59. A religious discourse
    (a) Preach (b) Stanza
    (c) Sanctorum (d) Sermon

DIRECTIONS (Qs. 60-61) : *Each questions below consists of a word in capital letters followed by four words or group of words. Select the word or group of words that is most similar in meaning to the words in capital letters.*

60. PALPABLE
    (a) Trembling (b) Weak
    (c) Obvious (d) Foolish
61. USURP
    (a) To climb upon
    (b) to yield
    (c) To seize power or position illegally
    (d) To demand unlawfully high interest on a loan

DIRECTIONS (Qs. 62 - 64): *Which word or words explains the meaning of the following idioms :*

62. To turn over a new leaf
    (a) To change completely one's course of action
    (b) To shift attention to new problems
    (c) To cover up one's faults by wearing new marks
    (d) To change the old habits and adopt new ones
63. To wrangle over an ass's shadow
    (a) To act in a foolish way
    (b) To quarrel over trifles
    (c) To waste time on petty things
    (d) To do something funny
64. All Agog
    (a) Everybody (b) All ready
    (c) Restless (d) Almighty

DIRECTIONS (Qs. 65-66) : *Each questions below consists of a word in capital letters followed by four words or group of words. Select the word or group of words that is most opposite in meaning to the words in capital letters.*

65. OUTLANDISH
(a) Modern (b) Moderate
(c) Disrespectful (d) Coward

66. ABSOLVE
(a) To remember someone fondly
(b) To imitate someone
(c) To pretend
(d) To declare someone guilty

DIRECTIONS (Qs. 67 - 68): *Find the correctly spelt world*

67. (a) Forefiet (b) Forefeit
(c) Forfeit (d) Forfiet

68. (a) Comemorate (b) Commemmorate
(c) Momemmorate (d) Commemorate

DIRECTIONS (Qs. 69 - 72): *Select the most appropriate word from the options against each number :*

Experienced climber Aron Ralston set out on a __69__ hiking adventure, which proved to be a __70__ event. Despite it being a common safety practice amongst climbers to inform others when undertaking unaccompanied hiking trips, Aron had not __71__ anyone of his plans. During his climbing adventure Aron's right arm became pinned against the canyon wall by a 360 kg boulder. Aron was unable to free himself, and after six days of being __72__ he made the decision to break the bones in his forearm and then amputate his arm below the elbow. Once free he made his way down a cliff and walked 8 km to seek assistance. Aron survived.

69. Which of these fits gap 94?
(a) authorised (b) alerted
(c) signalled (d) cautioned

70. Which of these fits gap 92?
(a) supervised (b) solo
(c) team (d) shared

71. Which of these fits gap 95?
(a) suppressed (b) captive
(c) trapped (d) entangled

72. Which of these fits gap 93?
(a) beath-taking (b) fail-safe
(c) stimulating (d) life-changing

DIRECTIONS (Qs. 73-75): *In the following questions, the 1st and the last sentences of the passage are numbered 1 and 6. The rest of the passage is split into four parts and named P, Q, R and S. These four parts are not given in their proper order. Read the sentence and find out which of the four combinations is correct. Then find the correct answer.*

73. 1. Generally speaking,
P. for me by those who have invited me or
Q. follow programmes that have been worked out
R. who offer themselves as guides and usually in such cases
S. the journeys that I undertake for the purpose of publicity
6. I find the thing I have to do wearisome.
(a) RPQS (b) SQPR
(c) QRPS (d) PRSQ

74. 1. Jeff is a very good dancer,
P. who always tries new dance steps
Q. while the rest of the class struggles
R. which are demonstrated,
S. and masters them quickly
6. to learn them.
(a) RPQS (b) SQPR
(c) QRPS (d) PRSQ

DIRECTION (Q. 75): *In the following questions, a sentence has been given in Direct/Indirect. Out of the four alternatives suggested, select the one which best expresses the same sentence in Indirect/Direct and mark.*

75. He said to the interviewer, "Could you please repeat the question?"
(a) He requested the interviewer if he could please repeat the question
(b) He requested the interviewer to please repeat the question.
(c) He requested the interviewer to repeat the question.
(d) He requested the interviewer if he could repeat the question.

GENERAL AWARENESS

76. When had Muslim league passed the resolution "Divide and Quit" movement ?
(a) 1945 (b) 1943
(c) 1944 (d) None of these

77. 88th amendement of the Indian Constitution is related to –
(a) The demarcation of new boundaries between states
(b) The Constitution of the National Judicial Commission
(c) Empowering the Centre to levy and appropriate Service tax
(d) Readjustment of electroal constituencies on the basis of the population census 2001

78. A boat will submerge when it displaces water equal to its own –
(a) volume (b) weight
(c) surface area (d) density

79. Which organ of Human body is affected by Alzheimer disease ?
(a) Brain (b) Bone Marrow
(c) Lung (d) Intestine

80. What is the chemical name of vitamin E ?
(a) Calciferol (b) Tocopherol
(c) Riboflavin (d) Phylloquinone

81. According to the Constitution of India, the Right to Property is a –
(a) Fundamental Right (b) Directive Principle
(c) Legal Right (d) Social Right

82. Babar declared himself as an emperor first at –
(a) Samarqand (b) Farghana
(c) Kabul (d) Panipat

83. How many times has financial emergency been declared in India, so far?
(a) Five times (b) Four times
(c) Once (d) Never

84. Who is the author of "The Unseen Indira Gandhi"?
(a) K.P. Mathur
(b) Bilal Siddique
(c) Anurag Mathur
(d) N.R. Narayana Murthy

85. The mirror used in search light is –
(a) Concave Mirror (b) Convex Mirror
(c) Plane Mirror (d) None of these

86. A hybrid computer is the one having the combined properties of
(a) Super and micro computers
(b) Mini and micro computers
(c) Analog and digital computers
(d) Super and mini computers

87. How many members can be nominated to both the Houses of the Parliament by the President ?
(a) 14 (b) 16
(c) 10 (d) 12

88. Presidential form of government consists of the following :
(a) Popular election of the President
(b) No overlap in membership between the executive and the legislature
(c) Fixed term of office
(d) All of the above

89. Moraines are formed in
(a) Monsoon region (b) River deltas
(c) Arid regions (d) Glacial regions

90. Longest cell in human body is:
(a) Blood cell (b) Bone cell
(c) Nerve cell (d) Muscle cell

91. Which of the following is known as 'Seven Pagodas'?
(a) Mahabalipuram temple
(b) Karle caves
(c) Chaityas
(d) Elephanta caves

92. The study of lake is called
(a) Topology (b) Hydrology
(c) Limnology (d) Potomology

93. Which countries are separated by the McMahon line?
(a) India and Bangladesh
(b) India and Pakistan
(c) China and Tibet
(d) India and China

94. The 'Chipko Movement' is related to
(a) Wildlife preservation
(b) Scientific agriculture
(c) Forest conservation
(d) Deforestation

95. Who amongst the following in the author of the book 'A Bend in the River?
(a) Chetan Bhagat (b) VS Naipaul
(c) Kiran Desai (d) Anita Desai

96. The book "The Secret Chord" has been authored by whom?
(a) Alice Hoffman (b) Geraldine Brooks
(c) T D Ramakrishnan (d) Tishani Doshi

97. Which of the following national parties will form new government in Bhutan?
(a) Druk Phuensum Tshogpa
(b) People's Democratic Party
(c) Bhutan Kuen-Nyam Party
(d) Druk Nyamrup Tshogpa

98. Which of the following space agencies have successfully launched an unmanned Bepi Colombo spacecraft to Mercury?
(a) European Space Agency and JAXA
(b) ISRO and NASA
(c) JAXA and NASA
(d) ISRO and European Space Agency

99. Which country to host four nation summit on Syria crisis?
(a) Turkey (b) Russia
(c) Israel (d) Iran

100. Which state has recently celebrated the Kati Bihu festival 2018?
(a) Meghalaya (b) Assam
(c) West Bengal (d) Jharkhand

Hints & Explanations

1. (a) As, $9 \times 3 - 3 = 24$
   $3 \times 3 - 3 = 6$

2. (b) S T A R —Reverse→ R A T S (+1, +1, +1, +1) → S B U T

   Similarly,

   W A R D —Reverse→ D R A W (+1, +1, +1, +1) → E S B X

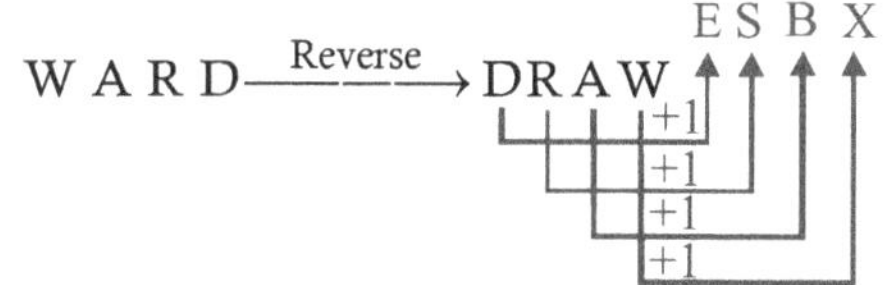

3. (c) Except in the number pair (7, 169) in all other number pairs both the numbers are perfect squares.
   $(25, 49) \Rightarrow [(5)^2, (7)^2]$
   $(121, 169) \Rightarrow [(11)^2, (13)^2]$
   $(9, 25) \Rightarrow [(3)^2, (5)^2]$

4. (c) In the word MEET, the second and the third letters are the same.

5. (a)

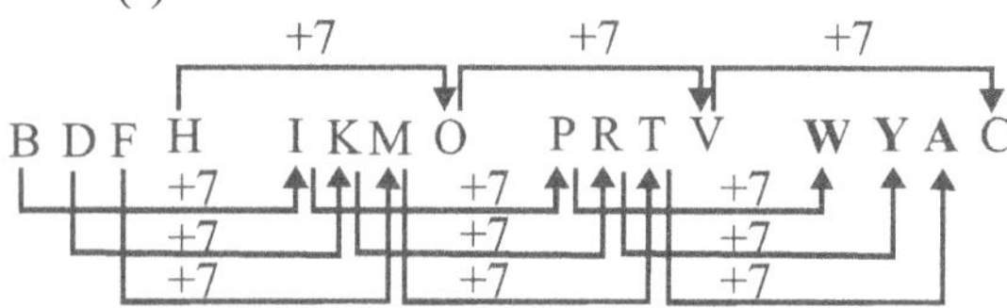

6. (c)

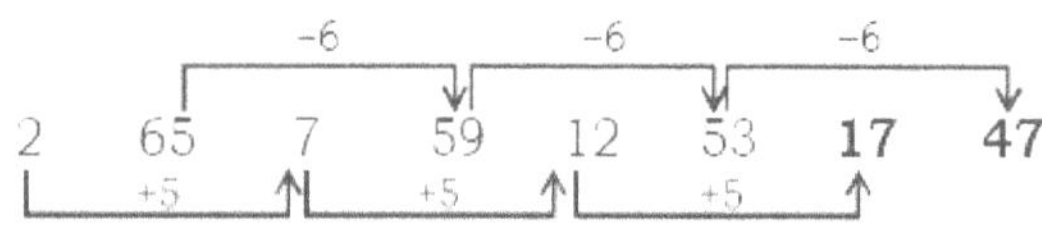

7. (d)

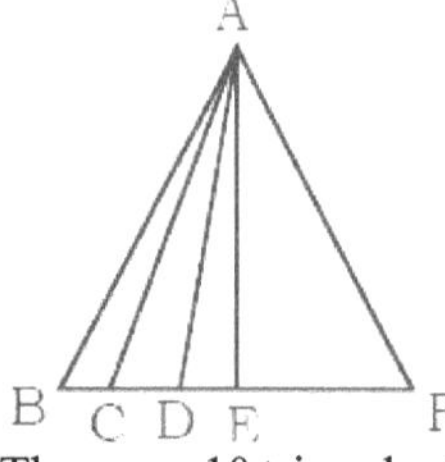

   There are 10 triangles in the given figure – ABC, ABD, ABE, ABF, ACD, ACE, ACF, ADE, ADF, and AEF

8. (b) The correct order is:

   3 2 4 1 5
   Mosquito → Cat → Tiger → Elephant Whale

9. (d) G O O D N E S S
   +1 −1 +1 −1 +1 −1 +1 −1
   H N P C O D T R

   Similarly,

   G R E A T N E S S
   +1 −1 +1 −1 +1 −1 +1 −1 +1
   H Q F Z U M F R T

10. (a) ALERT can not be formed as there is no 'R' in the word LEGALIZATION. Hence, (a) is the correct choice.

11. (b) The sequence BBCCA is repeated
    BBCCA/BBC CA/BBCCA/BBCCA

12. (b) 30 m, 30 m, 55 m, 25 m, 20 m, Starting Point

    North, West, East, South

    Required distance = 30m + 20 m = 50 m

13. (d) A man + his wife = 1 + 1 = 2
    His three sons + their wives = 3 + 3 = 6
    Three children in each one's family = $3 \times 3 = 9$
    Total members = 2 + 6 + 9 = 17

14. (d) 5th date of a month is Tuesday
    Friday will be on = 5 + 3
    = 8th of a month
    1st Friday is on 1st of a month
    2nd Friday is on 8th of a month
    3rd Friday will be on 15th of a month
    3 days after 15th = 15 + 3 = 18

15. (a)

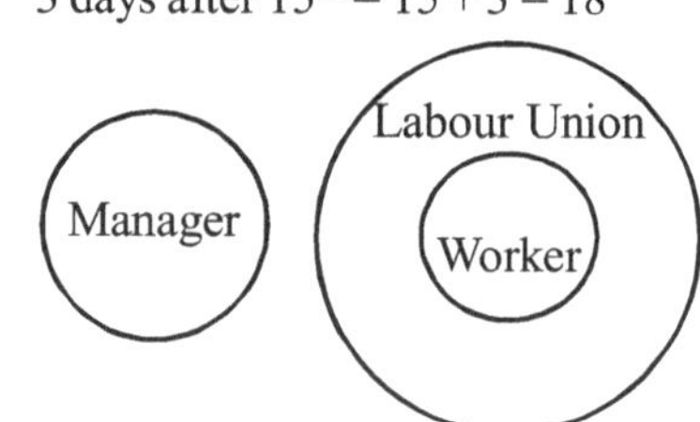

16. (c) Rahul's present age = 12 yrs,
Paras " " = 4 yrs
Let Rahul be twice as old as Paras after x yrs from now.
Then, $12 + x = 2\,(4 + x)$
$= 12 + x = 8 + 2x \Rightarrow x = 4$
Hence, Rahul's required age $= 12 + x \Rightarrow 16$ yrs

17. (c) As, $(5 + 4 + 7)/2 = 8$
$(3 + 7 + 2)/2 = 6$
Similarly,
$(6 + 9 + 5)/2 = 10.$

18. (d) Putting the position of the letters in reverse order
P = 11, S = 8, V = 5 and Y = 2.

19. (c)

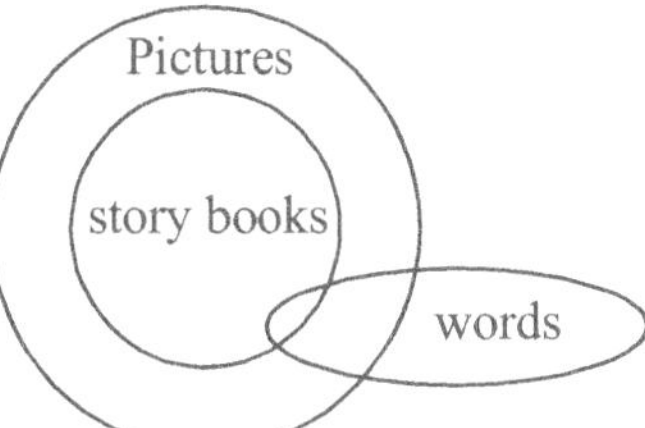

Conclusions : (a) False
(b) False
(c) True
(d) False

20. (a) S Q P T R

21. (a) 22. (c)

23. (b) The third figure in each row comprises of parts which are not common to the first two figures.

24. (c)

25. (b) A → 43, I → 55, R → 86, S → 95

26. (c) $\frac{1}{\sqrt{9}-\sqrt{8}} - \frac{1}{\sqrt{8}-\sqrt{7}} + \frac{1}{\sqrt{7}-\sqrt{6}} - \frac{1}{\sqrt{6}-\sqrt{5}} + \frac{1}{\sqrt{5}-\sqrt{4}}$ (on rationalisation)

$= \left(\sqrt{9}+\sqrt{8}\right) - \left(\sqrt{8}+\sqrt{7}\right) + \left(\sqrt{7}+\sqrt{6}\right) - \left(\sqrt{6}+\sqrt{5}\right) + \left(\sqrt{5}+\sqrt{4}\right)$

$= \sqrt{9} + \sqrt{4} = 3 + 2 = 5$

27. (a) Here, $52 - 33 = 78 - 59 = 117 - 98 = 19$
Now, $52 = 13 \times 2 \times 2$
$78 = 13 \times 2 \times 3$
$117 = 13 \times 3 \times 3$
$\therefore$ LCM $= 13 \times 2 \times 2 \times 3 \times 3 = 468$
$\therefore$ Required number $= 468 - 19 = 449$
Hence, the sum of digits is 17.

28. (c) Let the numerator and denominator of a fraction are x and y, respectively,
According to question,

$\frac{x-1}{y} = \frac{1}{3} \Rightarrow 3x - 3 = y \Rightarrow 3x - y = 3$ ...(i)

and $\frac{x}{y+5} = \frac{1}{4} \Rightarrow 4x - y = 5$ ...(ii)

On solving eqs. (i) and (ii), we get
$x = 2$ and $y = 3$
$\therefore$ Required fraction
$= \frac{x-1}{y+5} = \frac{2-1}{3+5} = \frac{1}{8}$

29. (b) Let tub capacity x L.

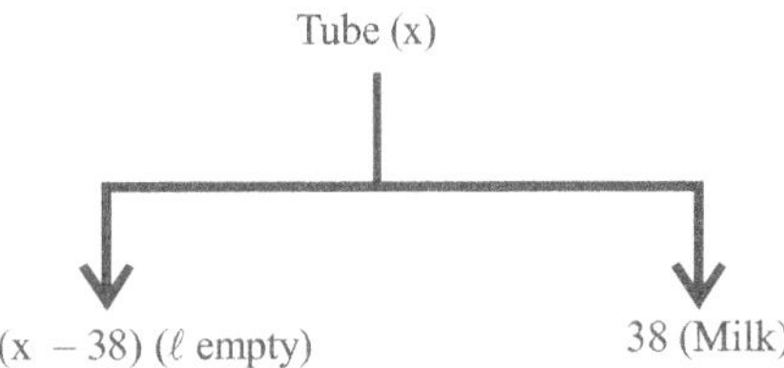

Now, $x \times \frac{95}{100} = 38$
x = 40 L,
Additional milk = 40 L – 38 L = 2L.

30. (b) Profit will be shared in the ratio of
$11 \times 3 : 16.5 \times 3 : 8.25 \times 3$
$= 11 : 16.5 : 8.25$
$= 44 : 66 : 33$
Anil's share in the profit
$= \frac{33}{143} \times 19.5 = 14.5$ lakh
50% of Anil's share = 2.25 lakh

31. (c) After 1st hit ball height will be $= \frac{1}{2}(64)$
After 2nd hit ball height will be
$= \left(\frac{1}{2}\right)^2 (64)$
....
....
....
After 16th hit ball height will be
$= \left(\frac{1}{2}\right)^{16} (64) = \frac{1}{2^{16}}\left(2^6\right) = 2^{-10}$ m

32. (c) Given, $A : B : C = \frac{1}{5} : \frac{1}{6} : \frac{1}{10} = 6 : 5 : 3$

∴ Share of *A*

$= \frac{6}{6+5+3} \times 8400 = \frac{6}{14} \times 8400 = ₹3600$

33. (a) Given that,
Number of male employees (M) = 45
Number of female employees (F) = 15
Mean salary of male employee $(\bar{x}_M)$
= ₹5000
Total number of employees = (M + F)
= 45 + 15 = 60
Mean salary of employees $(\bar{x}_{MF})$ = ₹4800
Let mean salary of female employee is $\bar{x}_F$
By formula,

$$\bar{x}_{MF} = \frac{M\bar{x}_M + F\bar{x}_F}{(M+F)}$$

$$\Rightarrow 4800 = \frac{45 \times 5000 + 15 \times \bar{x}_F}{60}$$

$$\Rightarrow 4800 \times 60 - 45 \times 5000 = 15 \times \bar{x}_F$$

$$\therefore \bar{x}_F = 4800 \times 4 - 3 \times 5000$$

$= 300(16 \times 4 - 50) = 300 \times 14 = 4200.$

34. (d) Suppose number of passengers be x in the starting.
Number of passengers after 1st halt

$$= \left(x - \frac{x}{3}\right) + 120 = \frac{2x}{3} + 120$$

Number of passengers after 2nd halt

$$= \frac{1}{2}\left(\frac{2x}{3} + 120\right) + 100$$

According to question,
Number of passengers after 2nd halt

$$= \frac{1}{2}\left(\frac{2x}{3} + 120\right) + 100 = 240$$

$$\Rightarrow \frac{2x}{3} + 120 = (240 - 100) \times 2$$

$$\Rightarrow \frac{2x}{3} = 280 - 120$$

$$\frac{2x}{3} = 160$$

$$x = \frac{\overset{80}{\cancel{160}} \times 3}{\underset{1}{\cancel{2}}}$$

x = 240

35. (b) From figure,

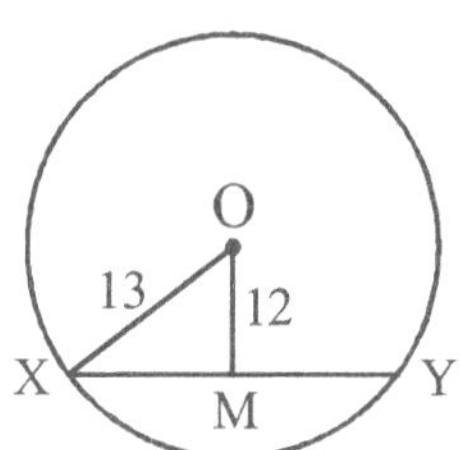

$XM = \sqrt{13^2 - 12^2}$

$= \sqrt{169 - 144} = 5$

∴ Length of the chord = 2 × XM
= 2 × 5 = 10 cm

36. (c) ∠ADC + ∠EDC = 180°
∠ADC + 120° = 180°
∠ADC = 60°
∠ABC = ∠ADC = 60°
(∠S in the same segment)

37. (b)

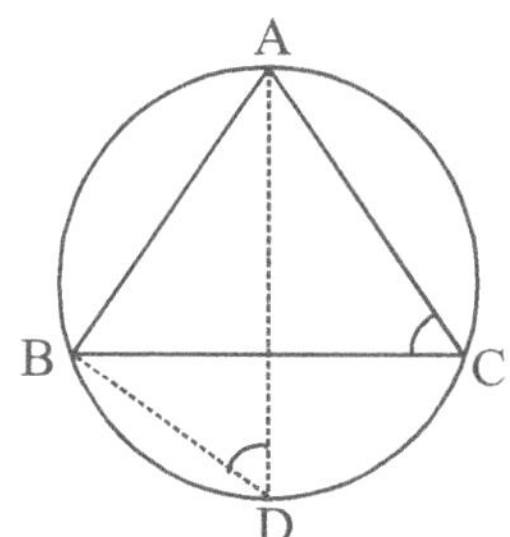

∠ADB = ∠ACB = 60°
(angles in the same segment are equal)

38. (b) $x + \sqrt{3}y - 6 = 0 \Rightarrow \sqrt{3}y = -x + 6 \Rightarrow$

$$y = \frac{-1}{\sqrt{3}}x + \frac{6}{3}$$

$$\therefore m = \tan\theta = \frac{-1}{\sqrt{3}} = -\tan 30°$$

$= \tan(180° - 30°) = \tan 150°$

∴ θ = 150°

39. (b) Let O = Centre of the balloon
OB = OC = Radii of the balloon

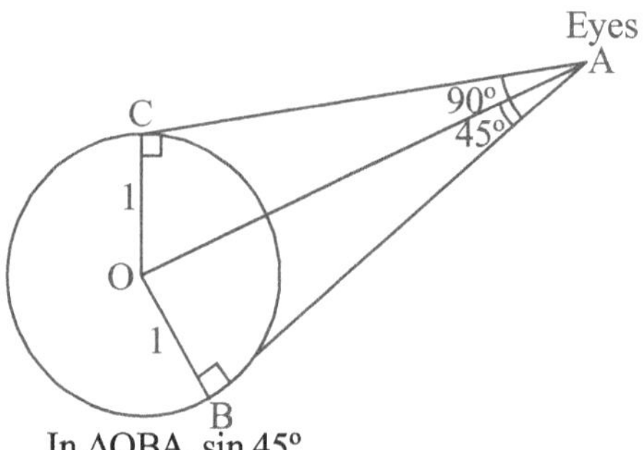

In ΔOBA, sin 45°

$$= \frac{OB}{OA} \Rightarrow \frac{1}{\sqrt{2}} = \frac{1}{OA} \Rightarrow OA = \sqrt{2}$$

40. (c) Let $\sqrt{\frac{x}{1-x}} = y$

$\therefore \quad y + \frac{1}{y} = \frac{13}{6} \Rightarrow (y^2+1)\,6 = 13y$

$\Rightarrow \; 6y^2 - 13y + 6 = 0 \Rightarrow 6y^2 - 9y - 4y + 6 = 0$

$\Rightarrow \; 3y(2y-3) - 2(2y-3) = 0$

$\Rightarrow \; (3y-2)(2y-3) = 0$

$\therefore \quad y = \frac{2}{3}$ and $\frac{3}{2}$

When, we put $y = \frac{2}{3} \Rightarrow \frac{x}{1-x} = \frac{4}{9}$

$\Rightarrow \; 9x = 4 - 4x \Rightarrow x = \frac{4}{13}$

When we put $y = \frac{3}{2}$

$\Rightarrow \; \frac{x}{1-x} = \frac{9}{4} \Rightarrow 4x = 9 - 9x \qquad \therefore \; x = \frac{9}{13}$

41. (a) $\frac{1}{1+p+q^{-1}} + \frac{1}{1+q+r^{-1}} + \frac{1}{1+r+p^{-1}}$

$$= \frac{1}{1+p+\frac{1}{q}} + \frac{1}{1+q+\frac{1}{r}} + \frac{1}{1+r+\frac{1}{p}}$$

$$= \frac{q}{1+pq+q} + \frac{r}{r+rq+1} + \frac{p}{p+rp+1}$$

$$= \frac{q}{1+pq+q} + \frac{r}{\frac{1}{pq}+\frac{1}{p}+1} + \frac{p}{p+\frac{1}{q}+1} \qquad (\because pqr = 1)$$

$$= \frac{q}{1+pq+q} + \frac{rpq}{1+q+pq} + \frac{pq}{pq+1+q}$$

$$= \frac{q+rpq+pq}{1+pq+q} \qquad (\because pqr = 1)$$

$$= \frac{q+1+pq}{1+pq+q} = 1$$

42. (b)

$$\begin{array}{r|l} & 9x^2 - 2 \\ 3x-1 & 27x^3 - 9x^2 - 6x - 5 \\ & \underline{\underset{-}{27x^3} \underset{+}{-9x^2}} \\ & -6x - 5 \\ & \underline{\underset{+}{-6x} \underset{-}{+2}} \\ & -7 \end{array}$$

43. (a) $(a+b+c)^2 - (a-b-c)^2$

$= (a+b+c+a-b-c)(a+b+c-a+b+c)$

$= 2a(2b+2c) = 4a(b+c)$

44. (b) Rest time = Number of rest × Time for each rest $= 4 \times 5 = 20$ minutes

Total time to cover 5 km

$= \left(\frac{5}{10} \times 60\right)$ minutes + 20 minutes = 50 minutes.

45. (d) Let BC = x m height of unfinished pillar and CD = h m = Raised height of pillar

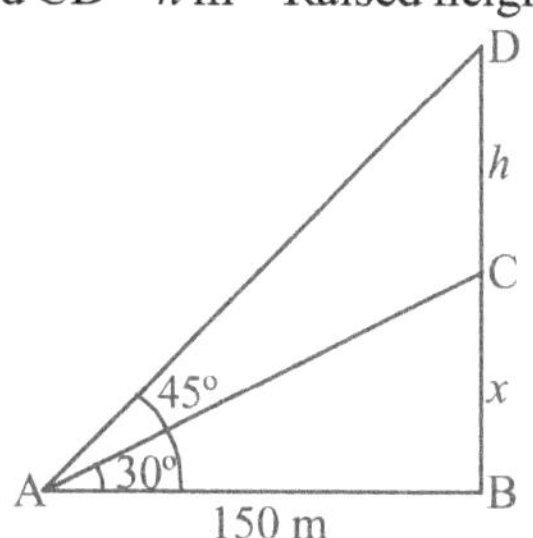

In ΔABC,

$\tan 30° = \frac{x}{150} \Rightarrow x = \frac{150}{\sqrt{3}}$

and in ΔABD,

$\tan 45° = \frac{h+x}{150} \Rightarrow 1 = \frac{h+x}{150}$

$\Rightarrow \quad 150 = h + \frac{150}{\sqrt{3}}$ [from Eq. (*i*)]

$\Rightarrow \quad \frac{150(\sqrt{3}-1)}{\sqrt{3}} = \Rightarrow$

$h = 150 \times \frac{(1.732-1)}{1.732}$

$= \frac{150 \times 0.732}{1.732} = 63.39 \approx 63.4$ m

46. (b) Required % increase

$= \frac{54}{418} \times 100 = 12.919 \approx 12.92\%$

47. (c) Required % $= \frac{510}{2854} \times 100 \approx 18\%$

48. (a) Since, area of circle = 4p cm² (given)

$\Rightarrow \quad \pi r^2 = 4\pi \Rightarrow r = 2$ cm

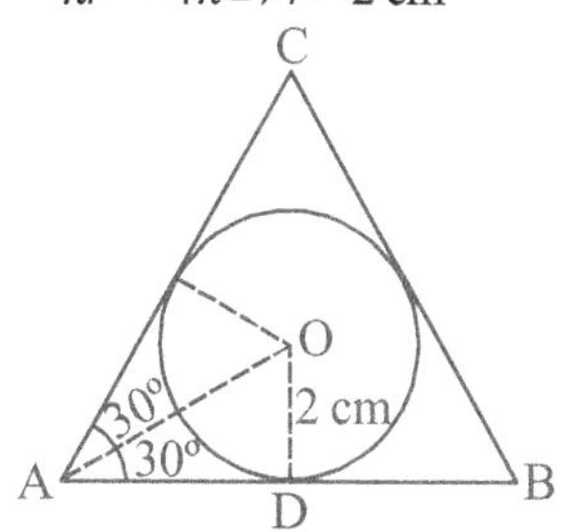

In ΔOAD, $\tan 30^\circ = \frac{OD}{AD} \Rightarrow AD = 2\sqrt{3}$ cm

Now, $AB = 2\,AD = 4\sqrt{3}$ cm

$\therefore$ Area of equilateral ΔABC

$= \frac{\sqrt{3}}{4}(AB)^2 = \frac{\sqrt{3}}{4}(4\sqrt{3})^2$

$= 12\sqrt{3}$ cm^2

49. (c) $x^4 - 1 = (x^2 - 1)(x^2 + 1) = (x - 1)(x + 1)(x^2 + 1)$ Now $x^4 - 2x^3 - 2x^2 - 2x - 3$
Putting x = -1 in this equation gives 0, so (x+1) is a factor, divide $x^4 - 2x^3 - 2x^2 - 2x - 3$ by (x+1) gives $x^3 - 3x^2 + x - 3$
Now put x = 3, gives 0, so another factor is (x–3), divide (x–3) gives $x^2 + 1$ which cannot be further divided
So $x^4 - 2x^3 - 2x^2 - 2x - 3 = (x^2 + 1)(x+1)(x-3)$
Now common factors in both expressions are $(x^2 + 1)(x+1)$ which is the HCF.

50. (a) Volume of cone, $C = \frac{1}{3}\pi R^2 H$

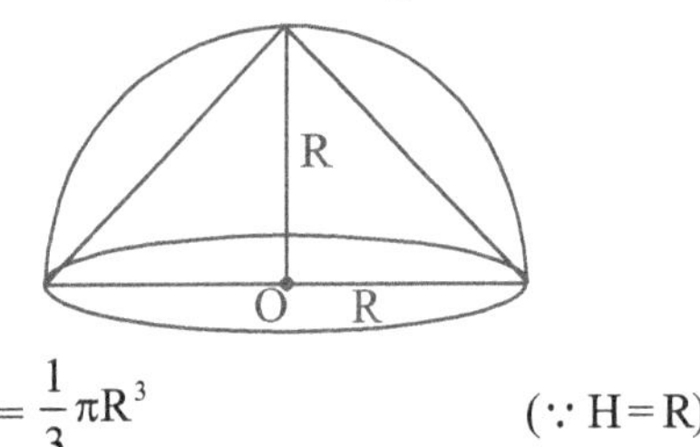

$= \frac{1}{3}\pi R^3$ $\quad (\because H = R)$

Volume of hemisphere, $H = \frac{2}{3}\pi R^3$

$\therefore \quad C : H = \frac{1}{3}\pi R^3 : \frac{2}{3}\pi R^3 = 1 : 2$

51. (b) 'With' is used for 'contentment'. All other options are not valid and do not have any sense.

52. (d) 'Disgrace to' is perfect as per Standard English Usage. 'for' can be used with disgrace as -
'His behaviour is a disgrace for all the love showered by society to his acts.' In this type of question it is very important to read and reread the sentence to get the true sense of the situation described in the statement.

53. (d) As are has been used in the first part of the sentence, the negating second part must have a compatible negative word which is obviously 'aren't. hence, option (d) as no improvement is required.

54. (a) A basic grammar rule requires not to follow 'to' after using told as it already implies said to. Rest everything is correct making option (a) the correct choice.

55. (b) I wanted to see whether they had actually read the notes.

56. (c) They made him treasurer because they considered him honest and efficient.

57. (b) Having finished the paper early he hed come out of the hall almost an hour before the bell rang.

58. (a)

59. (d) A talk on a religious or moral subject, especially one given during a church service and based on a passage from the Bible.

60. (c) ‘Palpable’ means ‘easily noticed’.

61. (c) Usurp means to seize prower or position of somebody else without right.

62. (d) 63. (b) 64. (c)

65. (a) ‘Outlandish’ means odd or strange.

66. (d) ‘Absolve’ means to state officially that someone is not guilty.

67. (c) 68. (d)

69. (c) In the gap 7, 'Aron had not signalled anyone' is the right option. Other options simply do not fit in here.

70. (b) 'Solo' means 'any activity that is performed alone without assistance' which Aron did. Other options 'supervised' means under observation or under the direction of a superintendent or overseer, team means form a team and shared means have in common; held or experienced in common.

71. (c) In the gap 7, the word 'trapped' is the right option while suppressed means kept from public knowledge by various means; captive means a person who is confined; especially a prisoner of war and entangled means deeply involved especially in something complicated.

72. (d) In the context of paragraph, the 'life-changing' may rightly be fit in here as it changed Aaron's life with the amputation of one of his arms. Other options are not relevant.

73. (b)	74. (d)	75. (d)	76. (b)	77. (c)
78. (b)	79. (a)	80. (b)	81. (c)	82. (d)
83. (d)	84. (a)	85. (d)	86. (c)	87. (a)
88. (d)	89. (d)	90. (c)	91. (a)	92. (c)
93. (d)	94. (d)	95. (b)	96. (b)	97. (d)
98. (a)	99. (a)	100. (b)		

PRACTICE SET- 6

GENERAL INTELLIGENCE & REASONING

DIRECTIONS (Qs. 1-3): *In questions below, select the related word/letter/number/figure from the given alternatives.*

1. King : Palace :: Eskimo : ?
(a) Caravan (b) Asylum
(c) Monastery (d) Igloo

2. AFKP : DINS :: WBGL : ?
(a) ORUX (b) OSWA
(c) OTYD (d) OQSU

3. 12 : 20 :: ?
(a) 15 : 37 (b) 16 : 64
(c) 27 : 48 (d) 30 : 42

DIRECTIONS (Qs. 4-5): *In questions below, find the odd number/letters/number pair form the given alternatives.*

4. (a) (47,49) (b) (5,7)
(c) (29,31) (d) (11,13)

5. (a) Marigold (b) Lotus
(c) Tulip (d) Rose

DIRECTIONS (Qs. 6 to 7): *Complete the given series.*

6. BDF, CFI, DHL, ?
(a) CJM (b) EIM
(c) EJO (d) EMI

7. 1, 3, 8, 19, 42, 89, ?
(a) 108 (b) 184
(c) 167 (d) 97

8. In a certain code DEPUTATION is written as ONTADEPUTI. How is DERIVATION written in that code ?
(a) ONVADERITI (b) ONDEVARITI
(c) ONVAEDIRTI (d) ONVADEIRIT

9. Arrange the following words as per order in the dictionary.
1. Forecast 2. Forget 3. Foreign 4. Forsook 5. Force
(a) 3, 5, 1, 2, 4 (b) 5, 1, 3, 2, 4
(c) 5, 1, 3, 4, 2 (d) 5, 1, 2, 3, 4

DIRECTION (Q.10): *In question which one set of letters/ numbers when sequentially placed at the gaps in the given series shall complete it?*

10. a_cdd__bcd_abc_dab_
(a) b a d d c (b) a b d d c
(c) b a d c d (d) b d a d c

11. Sohan ranks seventh from the top and twenty-sixth from the bottom in a class. How many students are there in the class ?
(a) 33 (b) 34
(c) 31 (d) 32

12. Keeping his back towards the rising sun, Reshma starts walking. After a few minutes, she turns left and keeps on walking. Then a little later she turns right and then left. In which direction is she going at the moment?
(a) East or South (b) South or West
(c) North or South (d) West or North

13. Seema's younger brother Sohan is older than Seeta. Sweta is younger than Deepti but elder than Seema. Who is the eldest ?
(a) Seeta (b) Deepti
(c) Seema (d) Sweta

14. In the given figure in a garden, square represent the area where jackfruit trees are grown, circle represent mango trees and triangle represent coconut trees. Which number represent the common area in which all types of trees are grown.

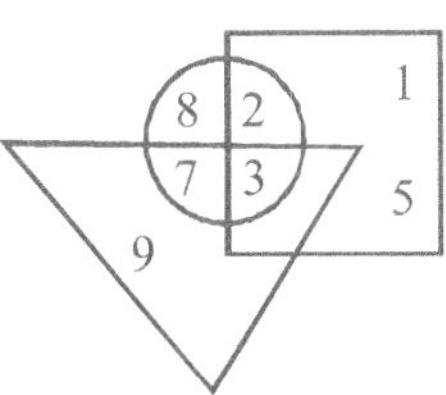

(a) 4 (b) 3
(c) 7 (d) 8

15. If a represents ÷, 'b' represents +, 'c' represents – and 'd' represents x then 24a 6d 4b 9c 8 = ?

(a) 6 (b) 17
(c) 20 (d) 19

16. Mani is double the age of Prabhu. Ramona is half the age of Prabhu. If Mani is sixty, find out the age of Ramona.

(a) 20 (b) 15
(c) 10 (d) 24

J = 1 K = 2 L = 5 M = 7

DIRECTIONS (Qs. 17-18): *In questions below, Select the missing number from the given responses.*

17.

	8				12				14	
6	54	7		8	51	4		9	?	5
	4				7				9	

(a) 53 (b) 71
(c) 76 (d) 68

18.

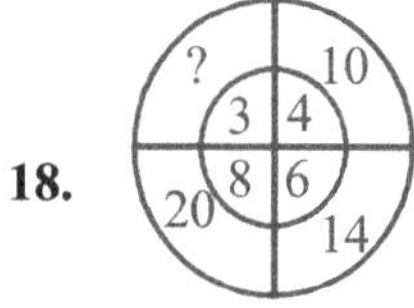

(a) 24 (b) 12
(c) 18 (d) 19

19. How many triangles are there in the following figure ?

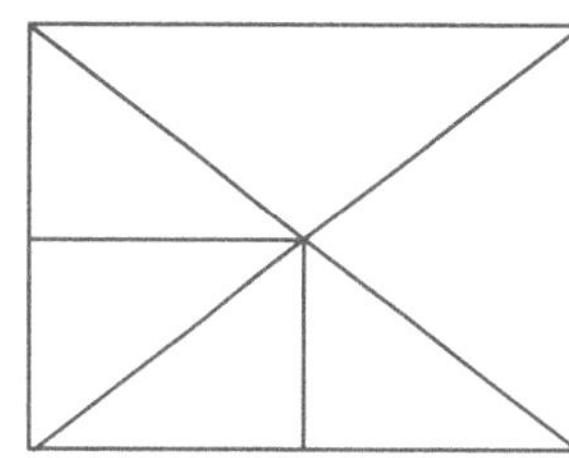

(a) 12 (b) 8
(c) 16 (d) 15

20. Four positions of a dice are given below. Find out the opposite suface of 6.

(a) 2 (b) 3
(c) 1 (d) 5

DIRECTION (Q. 21): *In question nos. 4 two statements are given followed by some conclusions. You have to consider the statements to be true even if they seems to be at variance from commonly known facts. You are to decide which of the given conclusion, if any, follow from the given statements.*

21. Statements :

1. All students are doctors.
2. No doctor is leader.

Conclusions :

I. All leaders are students.
II. Some doctors are students.

(a) Only conclusion I follows
(b) Only conclusion II follows
(c) Both conclusions I and II follows
(d) Neither conclusion I nor II follows

DIRECTIONS (Qs. 22-23): *In questions below, which anwser figure will complete the pattern in the question figure ?*

22. Question figure :

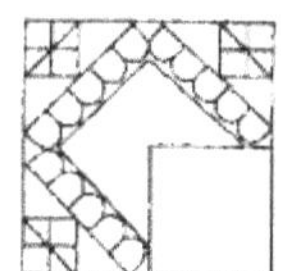

Answer figures :

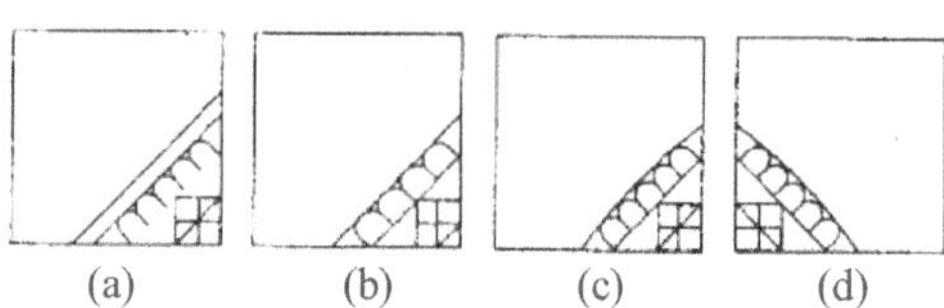

23. A piece of paper is folded and cut as shown below in the question figures. From the given answer figures, indicate how it will appear when opened.

Question figure :

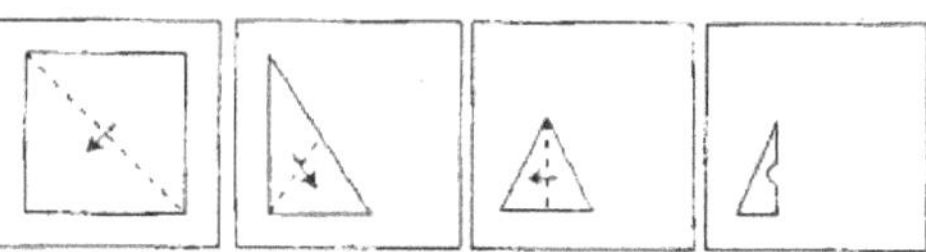

Anwser figures:

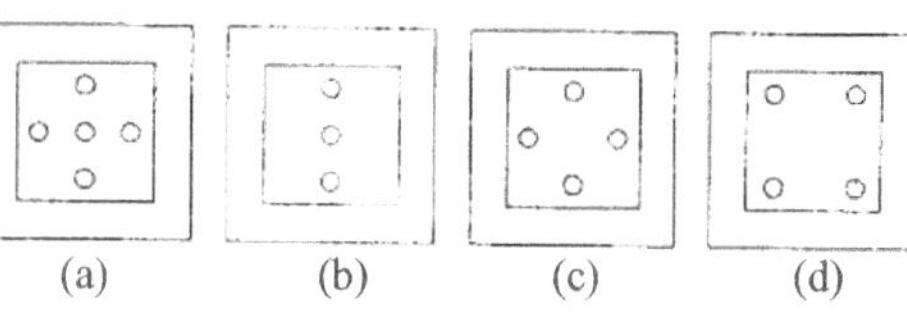

24. From the given answer figures, select the one in which the question figure is hidden/embedded.

Question figure :

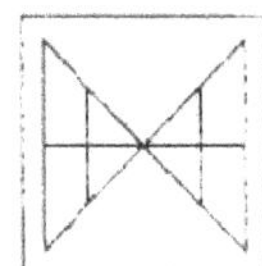

Answer figures:

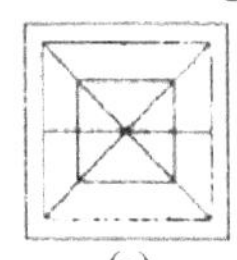
(a)

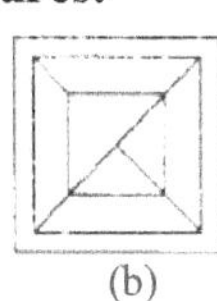
(b)

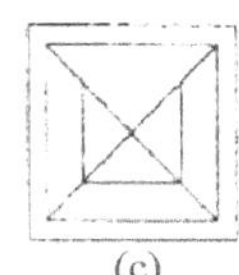
(c)

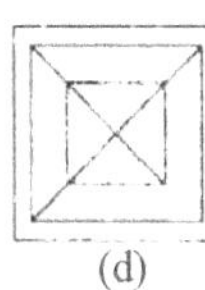
(d)

25. A word is represented by only one set of numbers as given in any one of the alternatives. The sets of numbers given in the alternatives are represented by two classes of alphabets as in two matrices given below. The columns and rows of Matrix -I are numbered from 0 to 4 and that of Matrix - II are numbered from 5 to 9. A letter from these matrices can be represented first by its row and next by its column, e.g., A can be represented by 01, 20, 42 etc. and H can be represented by 65, 57, 98 etc. Similarly, you have to identify the set for the word given in the question.

FAITH

Matrix-I

	0	1	2	3	4
0	F	A	N	O	I
1	I	O	F	A	N
2	A	N	O	I	F
3	O	F	I	N	A
4	N	I	A	F	O

Matrix-II

	5	6	7	8	9
5	S	E	H	B	T
6	H	S	E	T	B
7	B	T	S	E	H
8	E	H	T	B	S
9	T	S	E	H	B

(a) 24, 31, 10, 59, 57 (b) 12, 20, 40, 68, 65
(c) 31, 34, 23, 76, 79 (d) 43, 42, 41, 78, 89

QUANTITATIVE APTITUDE

26. The product of two successive numbers is 9506. Which is the smaller of the two numbers?
(a) 96 (b) 97 (c) 98 (d) 99

27. What is the square root of $9 + 2\sqrt{14}$?
(a) $1+2\sqrt{2}$ (b) $\sqrt{3}+\sqrt{6}$
(c) $\sqrt{2}+\sqrt{7}$ (d) $\sqrt{2}+\sqrt{5}$

28. There are two taps *A* and *B* to fill up a water tank. The tank can be filled in 40 min, if both taps are on. The same tank can be filled in 60 min, if tap *A* alone is on. How much time will tap *B* alone take, to fill up the same tank?
(a) 64 min (b) 80 min
(c) 96 min (d) 120 min

29. In how many different ways can the letters of the word DESIGN be arranged so that the vowels are at the two ends?
(a) 48 (b) 72 (c) 36 (d) 24

30. Distance between point P and Q is 480 km. A train starts from point P at 6:00 AM with 60 km/hr towards Q. Another train starts from point Q towards P at 7:00 AM with 80 km/kr. At what time the trains will meet?
(a) 9:40 AM (b) 10:30 AM
(c) 10:00 AM (d) 11:00 AM

31. Naresh purchased a TV set for ₹11,250 after getting discount of 10% on the labelled price. He spent ₹150 on transport and ₹800 on installation. At what price should it be sold so that the profit earned would be 15% if no discount was offered?
(a) ₹12,937.50 (b) ₹14,030
(c) ₹13,450 (d) ₹15,467.50

32. If $P:Q=\frac{3}{5}:\frac{5}{7}$ and $Q:R=\frac{3}{4}:\frac{2}{5}$, then what is $P:Q:R$ equal to?
(a) $\frac{3}{5}:\frac{5}{7}:\frac{2}{5}$ (b) $\frac{9}{20}:\frac{15}{28}:\frac{2}{7}$
(c) $\frac{3}{5}:\frac{3}{4}:\frac{2}{5}$ (d) $\frac{3}{5}:\frac{5}{7}:\frac{3}{4}$

33. Arun invested a sum of money at a certain rate of simple interest for a period of four years. Had he invested the same sum at the same rate for a period of six years, the total interest earned by him would have been fifty per cent more than the earlier interest amount. What was the rate of interest per cent per annum?
(a) 4
(b) 8
(c) 5
(d) Cannot be determined

34. Two-thirds of three-fourths of one-fifth of a number is 15. What is 30 per cent of that number?
(a) 45 (b) 60
(c) 75 (d) 30

35. The sum of the circumference of a circle and the perimeter of a square is equal to 272 cm. The diameter of the circle is 56 cm. What is the sum of the areas of the circle and the square?
(a) 2464 sq cm (b) 2644 sq cm
(c) 3040 sq cm
(d) Cannot be determined

36.
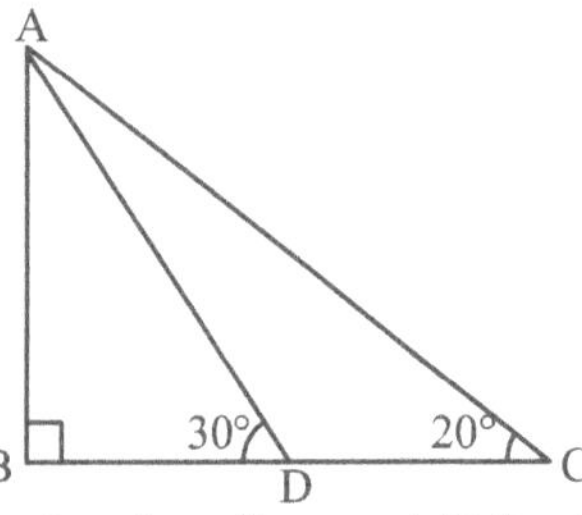

In the given figure, $\angle ABD = 90°$, $\angle BDA = 30°$ and $\angle BCA = 20°$. What is $\angle CAD$?
(a) 10° (b) 20°
(c) 30° (d) 15°

37. On a journey across Bombay, a tourist bus averages 10 km/h for 20% of the distance, 30 km/h for 60% of it and 20 km/h for the remainder. The average speed for the whole journey was
(a) 10 km/h (b) 30 km/h
(c) 5 km/h (d) 20 km/h

38. The diameter of two circles are 18 cm and 8 cm. The distance between their centres is 13 cm. What is the number of common tangents?
(a) 1 (b) 2
(c) 3 (d) None of these

39. A man can do a piece of work in 10 days but with the assistance of his son, the work is done in 8 days. In how many days, his son alone can do the same piece of work?
(a) 15 days (b) 22 days
(c) 30 days (d) 40 days

40. If $(3.7)^x = (0.037)^y = 10000$, then what is the value of $\frac{1}{x} - \frac{1}{y}$?
(a) 1 (b) 2
(c) 1/2 (d) 1/4

41. If $3^x + 27(3^{-x}) = 12$, then what is the value of x?
(a) 4 (b) 3
(c) 1 or 2 (d) 0 or 1

42. How many kg of salt at 42 P per kg must a man mix with 25 kg of salf at 24 P per kg so that he may, on selling the mixture at 40 P per kg gain 25% on the outlay?
(a) 15 (b) 20
(c) 25 (d) 30

43. If A : B = 3 : 4, B : C = 8 : 10 nad C : D = 15 : 17 Then find A : B : C : D.
(a) 9 : 12 : 13 : 11 (b) 4 : 5 : 6 : 7
(c) 9 : 12 : 15 : 17 (d) None of these

44. The difference between the simple interest and the compound interest compounded annually at the rate of 12% per annum on Rs 5000 for two years will be :
(a) ₹ 47.50 (b) ₹ 63
(c) ₹ 45 (d) ₹ 72

DIRECTIONS (Qs. 45-47): *Study the following Pie-chart carefully and answer the questions given below:*

A survey conducted on 5800 villagers staying in various villages and having various favourite fruits.

Favourite Fruits

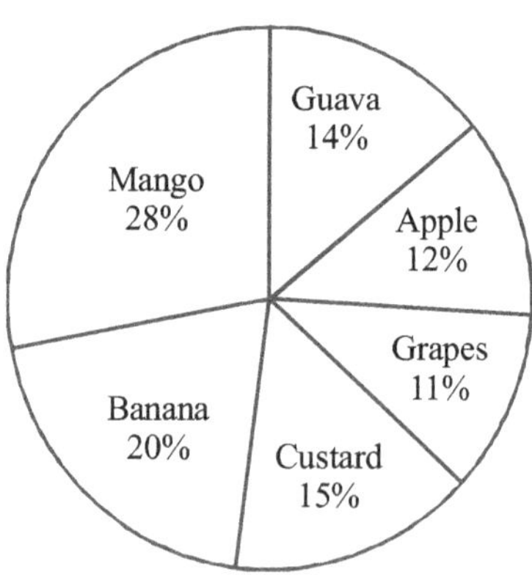

People staying in various villages

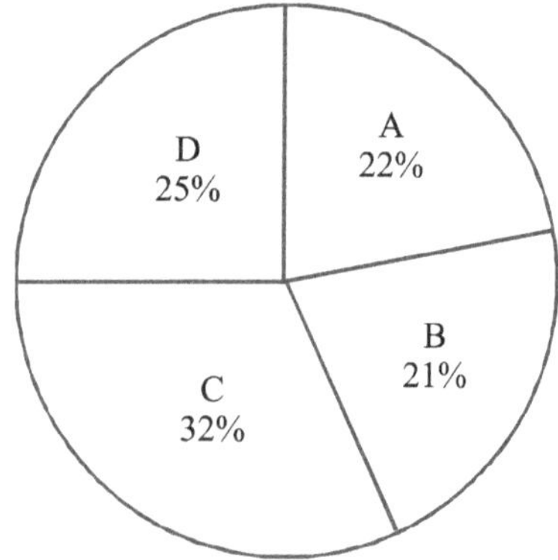

45. Mango is the favourite fruit of 50% of the people from village C. People having their favourite fruit as mango from village C form approximately what per cent of the people having their favorite fruit as mango from all the villages together?
(a) 48 (b) 53
(c) 61 (d) 57

46. 20% of the people from village D have banana as their favourite fruit and 12% of the people from the same village have guava as their favourte fruit. How many people from that village like other fruits?
(a) 764 (b) 896
(c) 874 (d) 986

47. How many people in all have custard as their favourite fruit?
(a) 850 (b) 864 (c) 870 (d) 812

48. A hollow cylindrical iron pipe of length 1.4 m has base radius 2.5 cm and thickness of the metal is 1 cm. What is the volume of the iron used in the pipe?
(a) 2640 cu cm (b) 2604 cu cm
(c) 2460 cu cm (d) None of these

49. A solid metallic cube of edge 4 cm is melted and recast into solid cubes of edge 1 cm. If x is the surface area of the melted cube and y is the total surface area of all the cubes recast, then what is $x : y$?
(a) 2 : 1 (b) 1 : 2
(c) 1 : 4 (d) 4 : 1

50. The angle of elevation of the top of a tower 30 *m* high from the foot of another tower in the same plane is 60° and the angle of elevation of the top of the second tower from the foot of the first tower is 30°. The distance between the two towers in *m* times the height of the shorter tower. What is m equal to?

(a) $\sqrt{2}$ (b) $\sqrt{3}$ (c) $\frac{1}{2}$ (d) $\frac{1}{3}$

ENGLISH LANGUAGE

DIRECTIONS (Qs. 51 - 52): *Pick up the most effective word from the given words to fill in the blanks to make the sentence meaningfully complete.*

51. The human mind seems to have built-in ________against original thought.
(a) prejudices (b) ideas
(c) interests (d) safeguards

52. The statue _________ a global symbol of freedom
(a) stands against (b) stands to
(c) stands for (d) stands as

DIRECTIONS (Qs. 53-54): *In questions given below out of four alternatives choose the one which can be substituted for the given word/sentence.*

53. Study of the evolution of man as an animal
(a) Archaeology (b) Anthropology
(c) Chronology (d) Ethnology

54. A person who speaks many languages
(a) Linguist (b) Monolingual
(c) Polyglot (d) Bilingual

DIRECTIONS (Qs. 55-56): *Sentence/ a part of the sentence is underlined. Below are given alternatives to the underlined part at (A), (B), (C) which may improve the sentence. Choose the correct alternative. In case no improvement is needed your answer is: (D).*

55. There is no universally agreed name for the events of this period.
(a) universal agreed
(b) No improvement
(c) universally agree
(d) universally agreeing

56. A number of revolts occured in areas not down under British rule and against native rulers, often as a result of local internal politics.
(a) in British rule
(b) under British rule
(c) No improvement
(d) in under British rule

DIRECTIONS (Qs. 57-58): *Find out which part of a sentence has an error :*

57. It was he who (a) / came running in the house (b) / with the news about the earthquake. (c) / No Error. (d)

58. Her mother does not approve of (a) / her to go to the party (b) / without dressing formally. (c) / No Error. (d)

DIRECTIONS (Qs. 59-60): *Out of the four alternatives, choose the one which best expresses the meaning of the given word.*

59. BREVITY
(a) Confused (b) Calmness
(c) Conciseness (d) Heaviness

60. IMMACULATE
(a) Spotless (b) Obscene
(c) Insane (d) Weak

DIRECTIONS (Qs. 61-62): *Choose the word opposite in meaning to the given word.*

61. QUASH
(a) Cancel (b) Revoke
(b) Persist (d) Permit

62. REMONSTRATE
(a) Protest (b) Argue
(c) Commend (d) Disagree

DIRECTIONS (Qs. 63-65): *Choose the alternative which best expresses the meaning of the Idiom/Phrase given in the questions below.*

63. Beat a hasty retreat -
(a) Beat someone harshly
(b) To pack things quickly
(c) To make a hasty withdrawal
(d) To make an exhaustive search

64. Easy come, easy go -
(a) To earn money without effort and giving away all of it
(b) A piece of work that is very easy to do
(c) A person who keeps his cool in difficult situations
(d) Readily won and readily lost

65. A pig in a poke -
(a) A never ending problem
(b) Something acquired without inspection which may therefore be worthless
(c) Someone who is quarrelsome
(d) Someone who interferes in others personal matters

DIRECTIONS (Qs. 66-69): *Select the most appropriate word from the options against each number :*

I peered at the river through a gap in the roots of the strangler fig. The thick branches of the tree__66__ me without really protecting me. I noticed the gentlest of ripples in the water and then something __67__ began to emerge from its depths. An enormous head upon a slender neck rose about the surface. I looked into the beast's cold, reptilian eyes. I could sense no mind or soul behind them. I had to refrain from letting out a frightened __68__! The time for retreating into the depths of the forest had arrived and I knew that it was __69__.

66. (a) either sooner rather than later
(b) either now or never
(c) neither now or never
(d) neither sooner nor later

67. (a) magnificent yet terrifying
(b) frightening yet scary
(c) wonderful yet grand
(d) amazing yet astonishing

68. (a) "Phew!" (b) "Aah!"
(c) "Aha!" (d) "Ouch!"

69. (a) were hiding (b) hiding
(c) hidden (d) was hiding

DIRECTIONS (Qs. 70-71): *In the following questions, group of four words are given in each group, one word is incorrectly spelt. Find the incorrectly spelt word.*

70. (a) Enthusiast (b) Pronounciation
(c) Vassal (d) Marginalise

71. (a) Population (b) Memorandum
(c) Associate (d) Comarades

DIRECTION (Q. 72): *In each of the following questions, a sentence has been given in Direct/ Indirect speech. Out of the four alternatives suggested select the one which best expresses the same sentence in Indirect/ Direct speech.*

72. She said to him, "Why don't you go today?"
(a) She said to him that why he don't go today.
(b) She asked him if he was going that day.
(c) She asked him why he did not go today.
(d) She asked him why he did not go that day.

DIRECTIONS (Qs. 73-75): *In the following questions, the 1st and Last part of sentences of the passage are numbered 1 & 6 and the rest of the passage is split into four parts and named P, Q, R and S. These four parts are not given in their proper order. Read the sentence and find out which of the four combinations is correct. Then find the correct answer.*

73. 1.These positive effects vary from genetic changes that
P. to other related infections,
Q. make us more resistant to the diseases responsible
R. for epidemics and
S. which have effects on human that are
6. hard to pin down and quantify.
(a) RPQS (b) QRPS
(c) SQPR (d) PRSQ

74. 1. After the entire generation of parents and teachers
P. the level of depression
Q. children's self-esteem and indicator of good mental health,

R. has worked hard to improved its
S. in young people has skyrocketed.
6. It is how we feel about ourselves,
(a) PQRS (b) QSRP
(c) RQSP (d) SPRQ

75. 1. The Bermuda Triangle is an area
P. of many unexplained disappearances,
Q. the three points of the triangle being Miami,
R. famous for being the supposed site
S. of the Atlantic Ocean off the coast of Florida and
6. Bermuda, and San Juan in Puerto Rico,
(a) PQRS (b) SRPQ
(c) QSRP (d) RPQS

GENERAL AWARENESS

76. The humidity of air measured in percentage is called
(a) absolute humidity
(b) specific humidity
(c) relative humidity
(d) all of these

77. Which one of the following was the original name of Tansen, the famous musician in the court of Akbar?
(a) Mahananda Pande
(b) Lal Kalwant
(c) Baz Bahadur
(d) Ramtanu Pande

78. When the productive capacity of the economic systems of a state is inadequate to create sufficient number of jobs, it is called
(a) seasonal unemployment
(b) structural unemployment
(c) disguised unemployment
(d) cyclical unemployment

79. Who drafted the Constitution of Muslim League, 'The Green Book'?
(a) Rahamat Ali
(b) Muhammad Iqbal
(c) Muhammad Ali Jinnah
(d) Maulana Muhammad Ali Jauhar

80. Bluetooth technology allows
(a) wireless communications between equipments
(b) signal transmission on mobile phones only
(c) landline to mobile phone communication
(d) satellite television communication

81. As which one of the following, does carbon occur in its purest form in nature?
(a) Carbon black (b) Graphite
(c) Diamond (d) Coal

82. Whose philosophy is called the Advaita?
(a) Ramanujacharya (b) Shankaracharya
(c) Nagarjuna (d) Vasumitra

83. Special Drawing Rights [SDRs] relate to
(a) the World Bank
(b) the Reserve Bank of India
(c) the World Trade Organisation
(d) the International Monetary Fund

84. The income elasticity of demand for inferior goods is
(a) less than one (b) less than zero
(c) equal to one (d) greater than one

85. In which one of the following Indian States is the game of polo said to have originated?
(a) West Bengal (b) Meghalaya
(c) Manipur (d) Sikkim

86. Which one of the following diseases is caused by virus?
(a) Tuberculosis (b) Typhoid
(c) Influenza (d) Diphtheria

87. Movement of cell against concentration gradient is called
(a) osmosis (b) active transport
(c) diffusion (d) passive transport

88. Plants that grow in saline water are called
(a) halophytes (b) hydrophytes
(c) mesophytes (d) thallophytes

89. The concept of Concurrent List in Indian Constitution is borrowed from the Constitution of
(a) U.S.A. (b) Japan
(c) Canada (d) Australia

90. The Himalayan mountain range is an example of
(a) Fold mountain
(b) Volcanic mountain
(c) Residual mountain
(d) Block mountain

91. The depletion of Ozone layer is mainly due to
(a) Chlorofluorocarbons
(b) Volcanic eruptions
(c) Aviation fuels
(d) Radioactive rays

92. Suspended colloidal particles in the water can be removed by the process of :
(a) Filtration (b) Adsorption
(c) Absorption (d) Coagulation

93. The second highest Gallantry award is
(a) Mahavir Chakra (b) Vir Chakra
(c) Arjuna Award (d) Ashok Chakra

94. The highest peace time gallantry award is
(a) Ashok Chakra (b) Param Vir Chakra
(c) Kirti Chakra (d) Vir Chakra

95. Which of the following is a pair names of the same game?
(a) Soccer - Football (b) Golf - Polo
(c) Billiards - Carrom (d) Volleyball – Squash

96. Which zone of a candle flame is the hottest ?
(a) Dark innermost zone
(b) Outermost zone
(c) Middle luminous zone
(d) Central zone

97. The scientists of which space agency have found superflares flares from the Young Red Dwarf Stars imperiling planets?
(a) ISRO (b) JAXA
(c) NASA (d) Roscosmos

98. Who has won the Wildlife Photographer Of The Year 2018?
(a) Thomas D Mangelsen
(b) Michael Nichols
(c) Marsel van Oosten
(d) Pal Hermansen

99. Which Indian photographer has won the 2018 Young Wildlife Photographer of the Year (Asia) Award for 'Pipe Owls'?
(a) Rajesh Bedi (b) Sunjoy Monga
(c) A K Raju (d) Arshdeep Singh

100. Which Indian-American personality has been honoured with US Presidential award for Combating Human Trafficking?
(a) Minal Patel Davis (a) Neil Jain
(c) Vivek R Sinha (d) Jagdeep Rajput

Hints & Explanations

1. (d) A palace is the official home of a King. Similarly,
An igloo is a small round house of an Eskimo.

2. (c) $A \xrightarrow{+5} F \xrightarrow{+5} K \xrightarrow{+5} P$

$D \xrightarrow{+5} I \xrightarrow{+5} N \xrightarrow{+5} S$

$W \xrightarrow{+5} B \xrightarrow{+5} G \xrightarrow{+5} L$

$O \xrightarrow{+5} T \xrightarrow{+5} Y \xrightarrow{+5} D$

3. (d) 12 : 20 :: $\boxed{30}$: $\boxed{42}$
(3×4) (4×5) (5×6) (6×7)

4. (a) All others except (a) are prime numbers.

5. (b) Lotus grows in the water but rest grow on the land.

6. (c)
$B \xrightarrow{+2} D \xrightarrow{+2} F,\ C \xrightarrow{+3} F \xrightarrow{+3} I,\ D \xrightarrow{+4} H \xrightarrow{+4} L,$
$E \xrightarrow{+5} J \xrightarrow{+5} O$

7. (b) Each of the numbers is doubled and 1, 2, 3, 4, 5, 6 is added in turn, so $89 \times 2 + 6 = 184$.

8. (a)
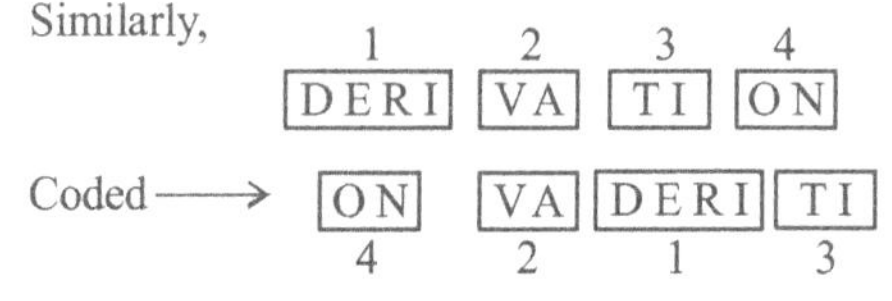

Similarly,

1	2	3	4
DERI	VA	TI	ON

Coded → ON VA DERI TI
4 2 1 3

9. (b)
5 1 3 2 4
Force → Forecast → Foreign → Forget → Forsook

10. (a) The sequence is : abcd d abcd d abcd d abc.

11. (d) Clearly, number of students in the class $= (6+1+25) = 32$

12. (b)
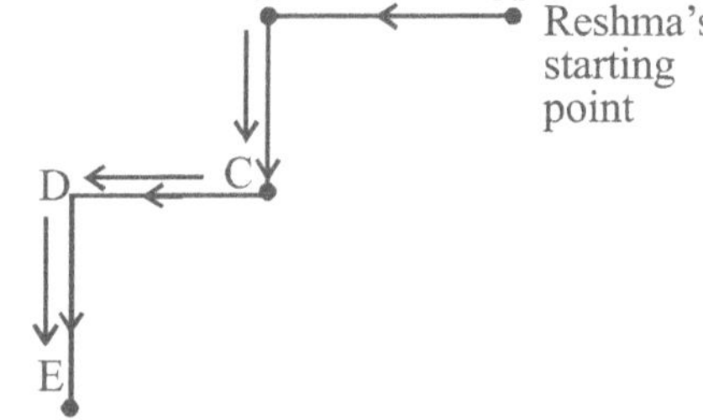

Now, Reshma is going to south direction

13. (b) Seema > Sohan > Seeta ...(i)
Deepti > Sweta > Seema ...(ii)
Combining (i) and (ii) we get
Deepti > Sweta > Seema > Sohan > Seeta

14. (b) 3 represents the area common to all types.

15. (b) $24 \div 6 \times 4 + 9 - 8$
$4 \times 4 + 9 - 8$
$16 + 9 - 8$
$25 - 8 = 17$

16. (b) Mani's Age = 60 years
Prabhu's Age = 60/2 = 30 years
Romana's Age = 30/2 = 15 years

17. (d) $14 + 9 = 23$
$9 \times 5 = 45$
$23 + 45 = 68$

18. (d) $3 + 4 + 3 = 10$
$4 + 6 + 4 = 14$
$8 + 6 + 6 = 20$
$8 + 3 + 8 = 19$

19. (a) These are twelve triangles in the above figure – ABE, AFE, DFE, DGE, GCE, CBE, ABC, DBC, DAB, ADC, AED and CED

20. (c) According to the dice I and III

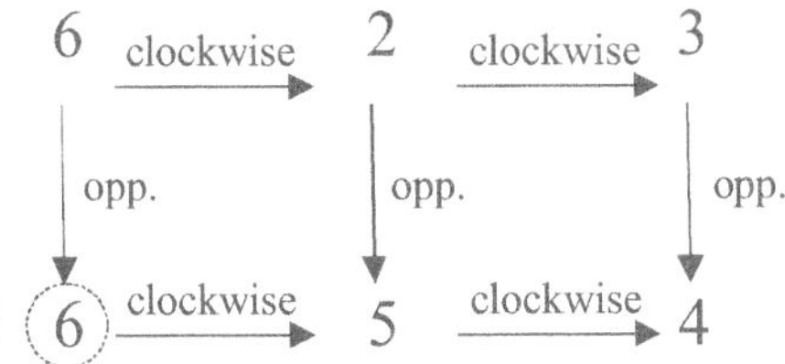

21. (b)

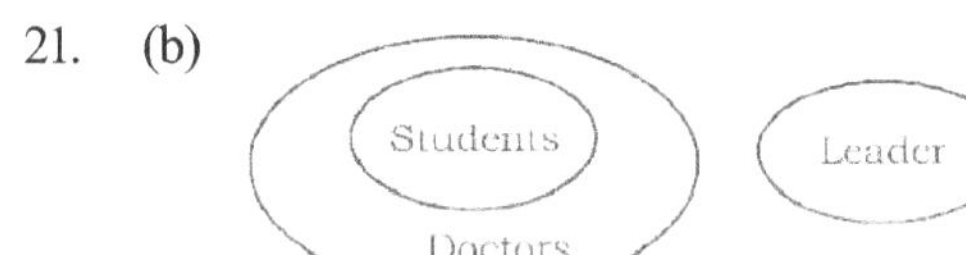

Conclusion- I. ×
II. ✓

22. (c) 23. (c)

24. (a)

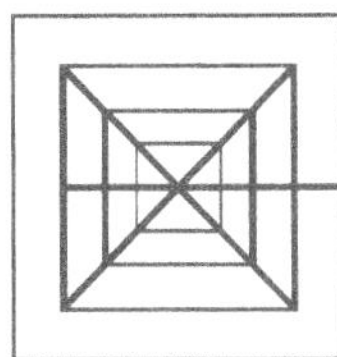

25. (c) F A I T H
↓ ↓ ↓ ↓ ↓
31 34 23 76 79

26. (b) From the given alternatives,
$97 \times 98 = 9506$
∴ Smaller number = 97

27. (c) $9 + 2\sqrt{14} = \left(\sqrt{7}\right)^2 + \left(\sqrt{2}\right)^2 + 2\sqrt{7} \times \sqrt{2}$

$= \left(\sqrt{7} + \sqrt{2}\right)^2$

$\therefore \quad \sqrt{9 + 2\sqrt{14}} = \left(\sqrt{7} + \sqrt{2}\right)$

28. (d) Work done by tap B in 1 min

$= \frac{1}{40} - \frac{1}{60} = \frac{3-2}{120} = \frac{1}{120}$

Total time taken by the tap B to fill the tank is 120 min.

29. (a) Required no. of ways
$= {}^2P_2 \times {}^4P_4 = 48$

30. (c) When 2nd train starts i.e. at 7 AM (1 hr after 6 AM), distance covered by first train is 60 km (i.e. in 1 hr).
Now 2nd train also starts and distance between them is now (480-60) = 420 km
Both coming in opposite direction, so relative speed = (60+80) = 140 km/hr
So time = 7:00 AM + (420/140) = 7:00 AM +3 hrs = 10:00 AM

31. (d) Cost price of TV when discount is not offered

$= 11250 \times \frac{100}{90} =$ ₹12500

Total cost of TV after transport and installation
= 12500 + 800 + 150 = ₹13450
To earn 15% profit, he must sell at

$13450 \times \frac{115}{100} =$ ₹ 15467.50

32. (b) Given, $P : Q = \frac{3}{5} : \frac{5}{7}$ ...(i)

$Q : R = \frac{3}{4} : \frac{2}{5}$ ...(ii)

From Eq. (*i*),

$P : Q = \frac{3}{5} \times \frac{3}{4} : \frac{5}{7} \times \frac{3}{4}$

$$= \frac{9}{20} : \frac{15}{28} \quad ...(iii)$$

From Eq. (*ii*),

$$Q:R = \frac{3}{4}\times\frac{5}{7} : \frac{2}{5}\times\frac{5}{7}$$

$$= \frac{15}{28} : \frac{2}{7} \quad ...(iv)$$

From equations (*iii*) and (*iv*),

$$P:Q:R = \frac{9}{20} : \frac{15}{28} : \frac{2}{7}$$

33. (d)

34. (a) $\frac{2}{3}\times\frac{3}{4}\times\frac{1}{5}\times a = 15; a = \text{Number}$

$\Rightarrow a = 150$

Then 30% of $a = \frac{30}{100}\times 150 = 45$

35. (c) Circumference of the circle

$= \pi \times$ diameter

$= \frac{22}{7}\times 56 = 176$ cm

∴ Perimeter of the square

$= (272 - 176 =) 96$ cm

∴ Side of the square

$= \left(\frac{96}{4}\right) = 24$ cm

∴ Area of the square

$= (24 \times 24 =) 576$ sq cm

∴ Area of the circle $= \pi r^2$

$= \frac{22}{7}\times 28 \times 28 = 2464$ sq cm.

∴ Required sum

$= (576 + 2464)$ sq cm $= 3040$ sq cm

36. (a) In ΔADC,

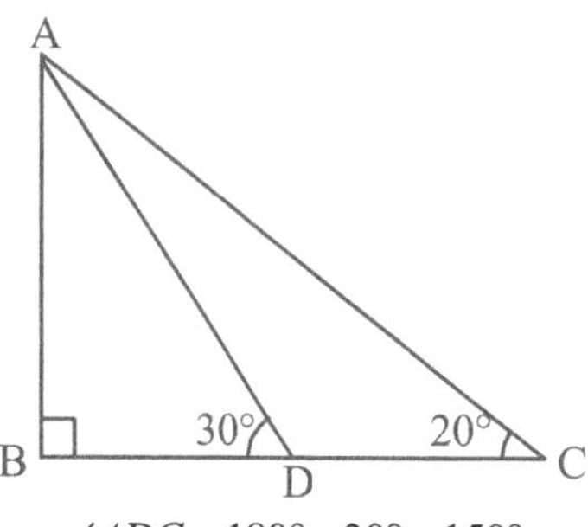

$\angle ADC = 180° - 30° = 150°$

$\therefore \angle DAC = 180° - (150° + 20°) = 10°$

37. (d) Let the average speed be x km/h.
and Total distance = y km. Then,

$$\frac{0.2}{10}y + \frac{0.6}{30}y + \frac{0.2}{20}y = \frac{y}{x}$$

$$\Rightarrow x = \frac{1}{0.05} = 20\text{km/h}$$

38. (c) Here, $r_1 = 9$ cm and $r_2 = 4$ cm

$r_1 + r_2 = 9 + 4 = 13$ cm

and $r_1 - r_2 = 9 - 4 = 5$cm

Also, $d = 13$ cm

Here, $d = r_1 + r_2$

$= 13$ cm

Hence, two circles touch each other externally, so there are three common tangents.

39. (d) (Man + Son)'s one day's work $= \frac{1}{8}$

Man's one day's work $= \frac{1}{10}$

$\Rightarrow$ Son's one day's work $= \frac{1}{8} - \frac{1}{10} = \frac{1}{40}$

∴ Son can do it in 40 days.

40. (c) Given, $(3.7)^x = (0.037)^y = 10000$

$\Rightarrow (3.7)^x = 10^4$ and $(0.037)^y = 10^4$

$\Rightarrow 37 = 10^{\frac{4}{x}+1}$ and $37 = 10^{\frac{4}{y}+3}$

$\Rightarrow 10^{\frac{4}{x}+1} = 10^{\frac{4}{y}+3} \Rightarrow \frac{4}{x} + 1 = \frac{4}{y} + 3$

$\therefore \frac{4}{x} - \frac{4}{y} = 3 - 1 \Rightarrow \frac{1}{x} - \frac{1}{y} = \frac{1}{2}$

41. (c) Given, $3^x + 27(3^{-x}) = 12$

Let $3^x = y$

$\therefore y + \frac{27}{y} = 12$

$\Rightarrow y^2 - 12y + 27 = 0$

$\Rightarrow y^2 - 9y - 3y + 27 = 0$

$\Rightarrow (y-3)(y-9) = 0 \Rightarrow y = 3, 9$

when $y = 3$; when $y = 9$

$\Rightarrow 3^x = 3$ $3^x = 9$

$\therefore x = 1$ $x = 2$

$x = 1, 2$ are value of x.

42. (b) Cost price of mixture $= 40 \times \frac{100}{125} P = 32P$ per kg

By the rule of fraction

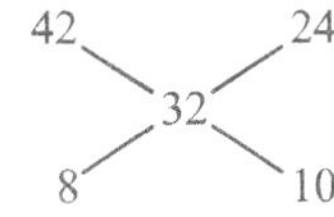

Ratio = 4 : 5

Thus, for every 5 kg of salt at 24 P, 4 kg of salt at 42P is used.

$\therefore$ the required no. of kg $= 25 \times \frac{4}{5} = 20.$

43. (c) A : B = 3 : 4

B : C = 8 : 10

C : D = 15 : 17

A : B : C : D = 3 × 8 × 15 : 4 × 8 × 15 : 4 × 10 × 15 : 4 × 10 × 17

= 9 : 12 : 15 : 17

44. (d) Required difference =

$$\left[5000\left(1+\frac{12}{100}\right)^2 - 5000\right] - \frac{5000 \times 12 \times 2}{100}$$

$$= 5000\left(\frac{28}{25} \times \frac{28}{25} - 1\right) - 1200$$

$$= 5000\left(\frac{784 - 625}{625}\right) - 1200 = ₹72$$

45. (d) No of persons from village C

= 32% of 5800 = 1856

From village C 50% of 1856 = 928 persons favourite fruit is mango.

28% of 5800 = 1624 people's favourite fruit is mango

$\therefore$ Required % $= \frac{928}{1624} \times 100 \approx 57\%$

46. (d) People in village D = 25% of 5800 = 1450

$\therefore$ Required no. of people

= {100 – (20 + 12)}% of 1450

= 68% of 1450 = 986

47. (c) Required no. = 15% of 5800 = 870

48. (a) $\therefore$ Volume of pipe, $V = \pi\left(r_1^2 - r_2^2\right) \times h$

$$= \frac{22}{7}[(3.5)^2 - (2.5)^2] \times 140$$

$$= \frac{22}{7}(12.25 - 6.25) \times 140$$

$= 22 \times 6 \times 20 = 2640$ cu cm

49. (c) Volume of solid cube $= (4)^3 = 64$ cm^3

Volume of recast cube $= (1)^3 = 1$ cm^3

$\therefore$ Total surface area of cube : Total surface area of recast cube $= x : y$

$\Rightarrow x : y = 6(4)^2 : 6(1)^2 \times 64 = 1 : 4$

50. (b) Let the height of shorter tower be h then distance between two tower = hm.

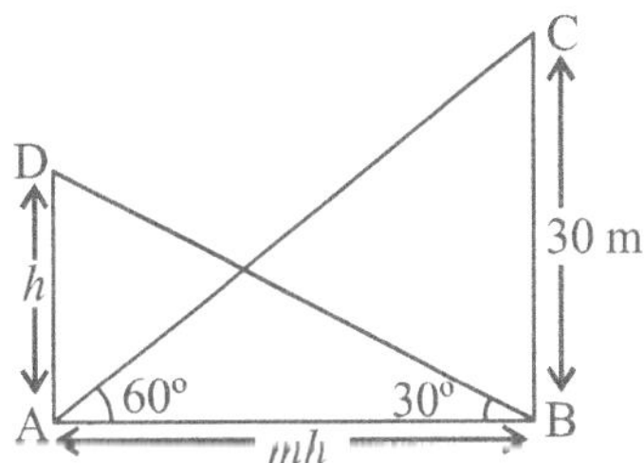

In ΔABD, $\tan 30^\circ = \frac{h}{mh} \Rightarrow \frac{1}{\sqrt{3}} = \frac{1}{m}$

$\therefore \quad m = \sqrt{3}$

51. (a) The word 'prejudice' will fill in the blank because here it means something or opinion which is not based on reason or experience and hence it seems to get conflicted with original thoughts.

52. (d) The phrase 'stands as' will fill in the blank because it means to signify.

53. (b) 54. (c) 55. (b) 56. (b) 57. (b)

58. (b) 59. (c) 60. (a)

61. (d) 62. (c)

63. (c) 64. (d) 65. (b)

66. (b) When you say 'either now or never', it means that you must do something immediately because you will not get another opportunity. Other options are simply out of context.

67. (a) When two pairs of words are connected with 'yet', they should usually be in contrast; despite anything to the contrary (usually following a concession); e.g. He was a stern yet fair master. Other options are just not relevant.

68. (a) In gap 92 the interjection 'phew!' rightly fits as it is used to express relief, fatigue, surprise, or disgust which is also the case here. Other options are out of context.

69. (a) Here 'were hiding' is the right form of the verb. Other options do not fit in here.

70. (b) 71. (d) 72. (d) 73. (b) 74. (c)

75. (d)

76. (c) The amount of water vapour in the air at any given time is usually less than that required to saturate the air. The relative humidity is the percent of saturation humidity, generally calculated in relation to saturated vapour density.

$$Relative\ Humidity = \frac{actual\ vapor\ density}{saturation\ vapor\ density} \times 100\%$$

77. (d) Tansen, who was one of the nine jewels or navaratnas in the court of Emperor Akbar, was born in a Hindu family at Behat near Gwalior in the Madhya Pradesh state. Father of Tansen was Makarand Pande, who named him Ramtanu Pandey.

78. (d) Cyclical unemployment is unemployment that results when the overall demand for goods and services in an economy cannot support full employment. It occurs during periods of slow economic growth or during periods of economic contraction.

79. (c) Muhammad Ali Jinnah drafted the constitution of Muslim league 'The green Book'.

80. (a) Bluetooth technology allows wireless communications between equipments.

81. (c) Diamond occurs in its purest form of carbon black in nature.

82. (b) Shankaracharya philosophy is called Advaita. The Advaita Vedanta focuses on the basic concepts as Brahman, atman, vidya (knowledge), avidya (ignorance), maya, karma and moksha.

83. (d) Special Drawing Rights (SDRs) are an international type of monetary reserve currency, created by the International Monetary Fund (IMF) in 1969, which operate as a supplement to the existing reserves of member countries.

84. (b) Inferior goods have a negative (less than 0) income elasticity of demand meaning that demand falls as income rises.

85. (c) The origins of the game in Manipur are traced to early precursors of Sagol Kangjei. This was one of three forms of hockey in Manipur, the other ones being field hockey (called Khong Kangjei) and wrestling-hockey (called Mukna Kangjei). In Manipur, polo is traditionally played with seven players to a side.

86. (c) Influenza is caused by virus and all other three diseases are bacterial, Influenza, generally called flu, is an infectious disease caused by RNA viruses of family Orthomyxoviridae.

87. (b) 88. (a)

89. (d) The concept of Concurrent List in Indian Constitution is borrowed from the Constitution of Australia. The Concurrent List or List-III is a list of 52 items(though the last item is numbered 47) given in Part XI of the Constitution of India, concerned with relations between the Union and States. This part is divided between legislative and administrative powers. The legislative section is divided into three lists: Union List, State List and Concurrent List.

90. (a) The Himalayan Mountain Range is an example of fold mountain.They are known as fold mountains because the mountains extend for 2500 km in length in a series of parallel ridges or folds and consist of three folds namely Himadri, Himachal, Shiwalik.

91. (a) The depletion of Ozone layer is mainly due to chlorofluorocarbons. A chlorofluorocarbon is an organic compound that contains only carbon, chlorine, and fluorine, produced as a volatile derivative of methane, ethane, and propane. They are also commonly known by the DuPont brand name Freon.

92. (d)

93. (a) 94. (a) 95. (a)

96. (c) Middle luminous zone of a candle flame is the hottest.

97. (c) 98. (c) 99. (d) 100. (a)

PRACTICE SET- 7

GENERAL INTELLIGENCE & REASONING

DIRECTIONS (Qs. 1-2) : *In questions, select the related word/letters/numbers from the given alternatives.*

1. PETAL : FLOWER
(a) salt : pepper (b) tire : bicycle
(c) base : ball (d) sandals : shoes

2. 8 : 28 :: 27 : ?
(a) 28 (b) 8
(c) 64 (d) 65

DIRECTIONS (Qs. 3-4) : *In questions, find the odd word/letters/numbers from the given alternatives.*

3. (a) FIK (b) DGI
(c) MPR (d) KND

4. (a) Google (b) Firefox
(c) Internet Explorer (d) Chrome

DIRECTIONS (Qs. 5-6) : *Complete the given series.*

5. LXF, MTJ, NPN, OLR, ?
(a) PHV (b) PIU
(c) PKX (d) PJW

6. 5, 16, 51, 158, ... ?
(a) 1452 (b) 483
(c) 481 (d) 1454

7. Which one set of letters when sequentially placed at the gaps in the given letter series shall complete it ?
a_bbc_aab_cca_bbcc
(a) bacb (b) acba
(c) caba (d) abba

8. In the following question, a group of letters is given which are numbered 1, 2, 3, 4, 5 and 6. Below are given four alternatives containing combinations of these numbers. Select that combination of numbers so that letters arranged accordingly, form a meaningful word.
C E L S M U
1 2 3 4 5 6
(a) 4, 6, 3, 5, 2, 1 (b) 5, 6, 4, 1, 3, 2
(c) 4, 6, 5, 2, 3, 1 (d) 5, 2, 3, 1, 6, 4

9. If in a code language, COULD is written as BNTKC and MARGIN is written as LZQFHM, how will MOULDING be written in that code ?
(a) CHMFINTK (b) LNKTCHMF
(c) LNTKCHMF (d) NITKHCMF

10. If FRIEND is coded as HUMJTK, how is CANDLE written in that code ?
(a) EDRIRL (b) DCQHQK
(c) ESJFME (d) FYOBOC

11. From the given alternatives select the word which cannot be formed using the letters of the given word :
INFLATIONARY
(a) FLAIR (b) FAULTY
(c) NATIONAL (d) RATION

12. If Neena says, "Anita's father Raman is the only son of my father-in-law Mahipal" then how is Bindu, who is the sister of Anita, related to Mahipal?
(a) Niece (b) Daughter
(c) Wife (d) Grand daughter

13. A cyclist goes 30 km to North and then turning East he goes 40 km. Again he turns to his right and goes 20 km. After this, he turns to his right and goes 40 km. How far is he from his starting point ?
(a) 25 km (b) 40 km
(c) 6 km (d) 10 km

14. If the positions of the first and the sixth digits of the group of digits 5904627813 are interchanged, similarly, the positions of the second and the seventh are interchanged, and so on, which of the following will be the fourth from the right end after the rearrangement?
(a) 4 (b) 9
(c) 1 (d) 0

15. Arrange the words given below in a meaningful order.
1. Protect 2. Pressure
3. Relief 4. Rain
5. Flood
(a) 2, 4, 3, 1, 5 (b) 2, 5, 4, 1, 3
(c) 2, 4, 5, 1, 3 (d) 3, 2, 4, 5, 1

16. A man said to lady, "Your mother's husband's sister is my aunt." How is the lady related to the man?
(a) Daughter (b) Grand daughter
(c) Mother (d) Sister

DIRECTION (Q. 17): *One statement is given followed by some conclusions. You have to consider the statements to be true even if they seems to be at variance from commonly known facts. You are to decide which of the given conclusion, if any, follow from the given statements.*

17. Statements :

Students are influenced more by their teachers.

Conclusions :

I. Students consider their teachers as their role models.

II. Much time of students is spent at school.

(a) Only conclusion I follows
(b) Only conclusion II follows
(c) Both conclusions I and II follows
(d) Neither conclusion I nor II follows

18. How many rectangles are there in the question figure ?

Question figure :

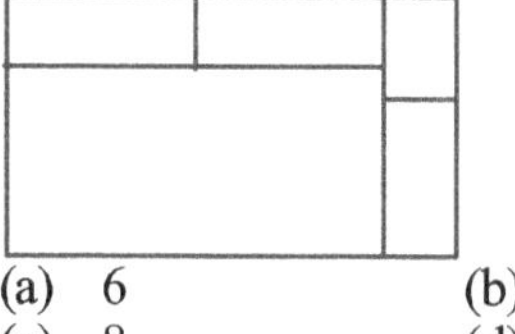

(a) 6 (b) 7
(c) 8 (d) 9

19. Find out the two signs to be interchanged for making following equation correct.

$5 + 3 \times 8 - 12 \div 4 = 3$

(a) + and – (b) – and ÷
(c) + and × (d) + and ÷

DIRECTIONS (Qs. 20-21) : *In questions below, select the missing number from the given responses.*

20.

7	9	8
2	4	3
5	7	6
16	32	?

(a) 17 (b) 23
(c) 47 (d) 73

21.

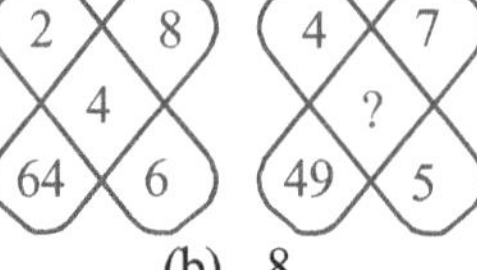

(a) 1 (b) 8
(c) 6 (d) 16

22. A piece of paper is folded and cut as shown below in the question figures. From the given answer figures, indicate how it will appear when opened.

Question figures :

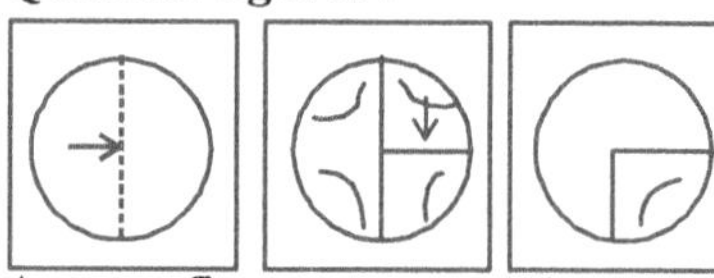

Answer figures :

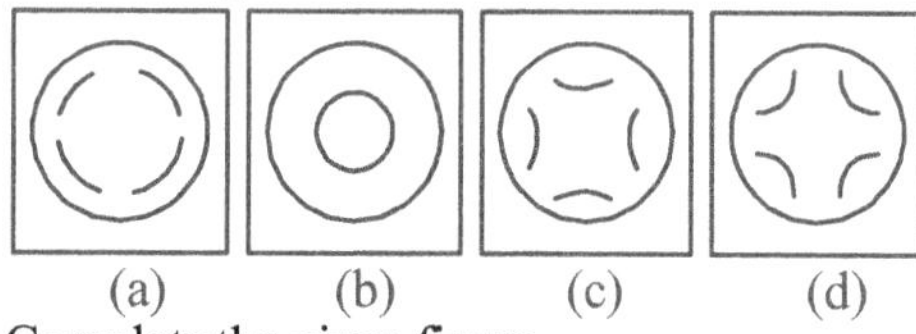

23. Complete the given figure.

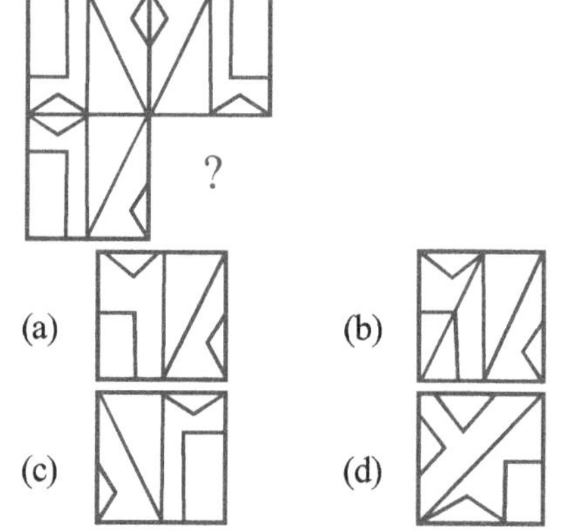

DIRECTION (Q. 24): *In the following question, choose the correct mirror-image of the Fig. (X) from amongst the four alternatives (a), (b), (c) and (d) given along with it.*

24.

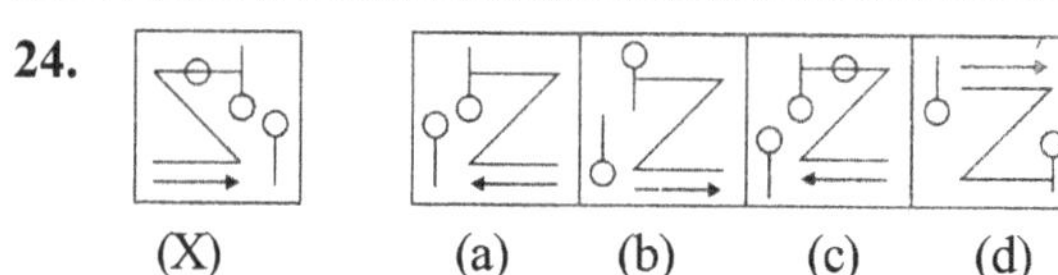

25. Select from the alternative, the box that can be formed by folding the sheet shown in figure (X) :

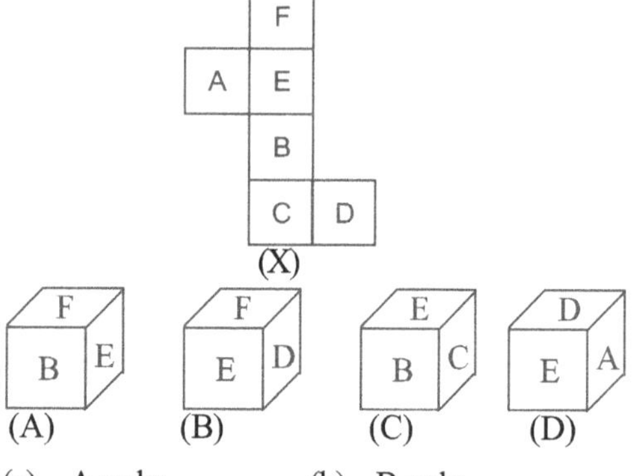

(a) A only (b) B only
(c) A and C only (d) A, B, C and D

QUANTITATIVE APTITUDE

26. How many numbers, between 1 and 300 are divisible by 3 and 5 together?
(a) 16 (b) 18
(c) 20 (d) 100

27. The value of

$$3 \div \left[(8-5) \div \left\{(4-2) + \left(2 + \frac{8}{13}\right)\right\}\right] \text{ is}$$

(a) $\frac{15}{17}$ (b) $\frac{13}{17}$
(c) $\frac{15}{19}$ (d) $\frac{13}{19}$

28. Kamya purchased an item for ₹46,000 and sold it at a loss of 12 per cent. With that amount she purchased another item and sold it at a gain of 12 per cent. What was her overall gain/loss?
(a) Loss of ₹662.40 (b) Profit of ₹662.40
(c) Loss of ₹642.80 (d) Profit of ₹642.80

29. The call rate of a SIM of company A is one paisa for every three seconds. Another SIM of company B charges 45 paise per minute. A man talked for 591 seconds from the SIM of company A and 780 seconds from the SIM of company B. What would be the total amount he spent?
(a) ₹7.80 (b) ₹7.40
(c) ₹7.46 (d) ₹7.82

30. An amount of money is to be divided among P, Q and R in the ratio of 3 : 5 : 7 respectively. If the amount received by R is ₹ 4,000 more than the amount received by O, what will be the total amount received by P and Q together?
(a) ₹ 8,000
(b) ₹ 12,000
(c) ₹ 16,000
(d) Cannot be determined

31. A 180-metre long train crosses another 270-metre long train running in the opposite direction in 10.8 seconds. If the speed of the first train is 60 kmph, what is the speed of the second train in kmph?
(a) 80
(b) 90
(c) 150
(d) Cannot be determined

32. In what time will ₹300000 amount to ₹746496 at 20% compound interest?
(a) 3 yrs (b) 4 yrs
(c) 5 yrs (d) 6 yrs

33. Two person Ravi and Shyam can do a work in 60 days and 40 days respectively. They began the work together but Ravi left after some time and Shyam finished the remaining work in 10 days. After how many days did Ravi leave?
(a) 8 days (b) 12 days
(c) 15 days (d) 18 days

34. What is the number whose 20% is 30% of 40?
(a) 90 (b) 80
(c) 60 (d) 50

35. The largest and the second largest angles of a triangle are in the ratio of 4 : 3. The smallest angle is half the largest angle. What is the difference between the smallest and the largest angles of the triangle?
(a) 30° (b) 60°
(c) 40° (d) 20°

36. Rahim and his uncle differ in their ages by 30 years. After 7 years, if the sum of their ages is 66, what will be the age of the uncle ?
(a) 39 (b) 41
(c) 51 (d) 49

37. If the cost price is 96% of the selling price, then what is the profit percent?
(a) 4.5% (b) 4.2%
(c) 4% (d) 3.8%

38. If $\frac{3}{x+y} + \frac{2}{x-y} = 2$ and $\frac{9}{x+y} - \frac{4}{x-y} = 1$,

then what is the value of $\frac{x}{y}$?

(a) $\frac{3}{2}$ (b) 5
(c) $\frac{2}{3}$ (d) $\frac{1}{5}$

39. The mean of 100 values is 45. If 15 is added to each of the first forty values and 5 is subtracted from each of the remaining sixty values, the new mean becomes
(a) 45 (b) 48
(c) 51 (d) 55

40. The sum of the square of a number and the square of the reciprocal of the number, is thrice the difference of the square of the number and the square of the reciprocal of the number. What is the number?
(a) 1 (b) $(2)^{1/4}$
(c) $(3)^{1/3}$ (d) $(4)^{1/4}$

41. If for two real constasnts a and b, the expression $ax^3 + 3x^2 - 8x + b$ is exactly divisible by $(x+2)$ and $(x-2)$, then
(a) $a = a, b = 12$ (b) $a = 12, b = 2$
(c) $a = 2, b = -12$ (d) $a = -2, b = 12$

42. Which one of the following is correct?

(a) $-\frac{7}{10} < -\frac{2}{3} < -\frac{5}{8}$ (b) $-\frac{5}{8} < -\frac{2}{3} < -\frac{7}{10}$

(c) $-\frac{5}{8} < -\frac{7}{10} < -\frac{2}{3}$ (d) $-\frac{7}{10} < -\frac{5}{8} < -\frac{2}{3}$

43. The number of two digit numbers which are divisible by 3 is

(a) 33 (b) 31
(c) 30 (d) 29

44. A horse is tethered to one corner of a rectangular grassy field 40 m by 24 m with a rope 14 m long. Over how much area of the field can it graze?

(a) 154 cm^2 (b) 308 m^2
(c) 150 m^2 (d) None of these

45. In a 800 m race around a stadium having the circumference of 200 m, the top runner meets the last runner on the 5th minute of the race. If the top runner runs at twice the speed of the last runner, what is the time taken by the top runner to finish the race ?

(a) 20 min (b) 15 min
(c) 10 min (d) 5 min

DIRECTIONS (Qs. 46-48): *Study the following table carefully and answer the questions given below.*

Percentage distribution of students in various disciplines in five different colleges

Discipline → Colleges ↓	Arts	Commerce	Science	Total number of students
A	25	35	40	17500
B	15	45	40	25000
C	15	30	55	35300
D	28	48	24	23000
E	29	30	41	32400

46. What is the average number of students from the discipline of Commerce from all the colleges together?

(a) 9745 (b) 9735
(c) 9720 (d) 9750

47. Which college has the least number of students from the discipline of Science?

(a) A (b) C
(c) E (d) D

48. What is the difference between the total number of students from the discipline of Arts from all the colleges together and the total number of students from the discipline of Science from all the colleges together?

(a) 22874 (b) 23863
(c) 22963 (d) 25963

49. If the number of square centimetres on the surface area of a sphere is three times the number of cubic centimetres in its volume, then what is its diameter?

(a) 1 cm (b) 2 cm
(c) 3 cm (d) 6 cm

50. For a plot of land of 100 m × 80 m, the length to be raised by spreading the earth from stack of a rectangular base 10 m × 8 m and vertical section being a trapezium of height 2 m. The top of the stack is 8 m × 5 m. How many centimeters can the level raised?

(a) 3 cm (b) 2.5 m
(c) 2 cm (d) 1.5 cm

ENGLISH LANGUAGE

DIRECTIONS (Qs. 51-52) : *Choose the one which can be substituted for the given words/ sentences*

51. An accomplished fact :

(a) fore (b) fait accompli
(c) ipso facto (d) ex post facto

52. One who does not care for art and literature :

(a) Bigot (b) Bohemian
(c) Philistine (d) Pacifist

DIRECTIONS (Qs. 53-55): *Choose the alternative which best expresses the meaning of the Idiom/Phrase*

53. Pyrrhic victory -

(a) A victory with great losses
(b) A victory by cheating
(c) A victory only in one's imagination
(d) To win at the last moment

54. Pull wires-

(a) to coerce someone into doing something
(b) To influence or control shrewdly
(c) To decide to break up with somebody
(d) To win hearts

55. Volte-face

(a) A sudden change of belief or plan to the opposite of what it was before
(b) An ugly face
(c) A difficult situation that can not be improved
(d) leave somebody awestruck

DIRECTIONS (Qs. 56-57): *In the following questions, groups of four words are given. In each group, one word is correctly spelt. Find the correctly spelt word.*

56. (a) mendatary (b) circulatary
(c) temporary (d) regulatary

57. (a) convinience (b) initative
(c) concessional (d) exaggerate

DIRECTIONS (Qs. 58-59): *Some part of the sentences have errors and some are correct. Find out which part of a sentence has an error and choose the answer according.*

58. The students were required to seriously study for examination.
(a) No error
(b) For examination
(c) The students were
(d) Required to seriously study

59. The little students that were in the class were sitting idle.
(a) Were sitting idle (b) No error
(c) Were in the class (d) The little students that

DIRECTIONS (Qs. 60-61): *In Question nos. 64 to 66, sentences given with blanks to be filled in with an appropriate word(s). Four alternatives are suggested for each question. Choose the correct alternative out of the four.*

60. Uncapped players _____ a lot of attention from the teams.
(a) recommended (b) showed
(c) reviewed (d) commanded

61. We expect to begin understanding what is _____ our candidates to take this giant leap for humankind.
(a) motivating (b) captivating
(c) suggesting (d) granting

DIRECTIONS (Qs. 62-63): *In Question nos. 67 to 69, a sentence/ a part of the sentence is underlined. Below are given alternatives to the underlined part at (a), (b), (c) which may improve the sentence. Choose the correct alternative. In case no improvement is needed your answer is (d).*

62. Let's have a party some time at the next week.
(a) sometime at next week
(b) sometime in the next week
(c) sometimes next week
(d) No Improvement

63. These days, it is difficult to make both ends meet.
(a) to have both ends meet
(b) to make all ends meet
(c) to make the ends meet
(d) No Improvement

DIRECTIONS (Qs. 64-65): *In Question nos. 70 to 71 out of the four alternatives, choose the one which best expresses the meaning of the given word.*

64. Discomfiture
(a) Calmness (b) Building
(c) Unease (d) Success

65. Sycophancy
(a) Abuse (b) Praying
(c) Criticism (d) Flattery

DIRECTIONS (Qs. 66-67): *Choose the word opposite in meaning to the given word.*

66. Eschew
(a) Reduce (b) Invite
(c) Use (d) Embrace

67. Iniquity
(a) Fairness (b) Dishonesty
(c) Peace (d) Apostasy

DIRECTIONS (Qs. 68-69): *In cach these questions a disarranged sentence is given in which words or phrases are letterd A, B, C and D. You are arrange to form meaningful sentence.*

68. A: in different regions of that federation
B: that was Yugoslavia
C: although the dismemberment of the federation
D: is seem more as the result of an ethnic conflict the fundamental came has been the very large difference in the quality of life

Which of the sequences present the most logical sentence?
(a) ABDC (b) DBCA
(c) BDCA (d) ABCD

69. A: but there is same merit in it
B: as distinct from consumption in sofar as it focuses attention on development expenses
C: bifurcation of plan and non-plan funds
D: in the budget is artificial

Which of the sequences present the most logical sentence?
(a) ABCD (b) CBDA
(c) CDAB (d) DACB

DIRECTIONS (Qs. 70-74): *Complete the passage by choosing the most suitable word/phrase from each list to tit the corresponding gap.*

Passage

In England, Gandhiji at first __70__ his time entirely to his studies. He tried to __71__ fashionable gentlemen in every way. He __72__ by what was new and foreign. He __73__ a lot of money on buying smart English Clothes. After three months he suddenly realised his mistake and __74__ to devote all his time to serious study.

70. (a) gave (b) were not given
(c) not given (d) did not give

71. (a) copy (b) copied
(c) to have copied (d) being copied

72. (a) had attracted (b) is attracted
(c) was attracted (d) attracts

73. (a) has wasted (b) wasted
(c) was wasting (d) wastes

74. (a) began (b) begin
(c) to begin (d) had begun

DIRECTION (Q. 75): *In the following questions, a sentence has been given in Direct/Indirect speech. Out of the four alternative suggested select the one which best expresses the same sentence in Indirect/ Direct speech.*

75. He said, "it used to be a lovely, quiet street."
(a) He said that it used to be a lovely, quiet street.
(b) He pointed out that it had used to be a lovely, quiet street.
(c) He said that there used to be a lovely, quiet street.
(d) He inquired whether there was a lovely, quiet street.

GENERAL AWARENESS

76. The Four Varnas are described in which Mandal of Rigveda?
(a) First Mandal (b) Third Mandal
(c) Tenth Mandal (d) Ninth Mandal

77. The Chief of State Election Commission is appointed by –
(a) The President
(b) The Governor
(c) The committee of elected members of State Legislative Assembly
(d) Election Commission of India

78. 'Defence Expenditure' forms part of which of the component of Union Budget?
(a) Plan Revenue Expenditure
(b) Non-Plan Revenue Expenditure
(c) Plan Capital Expenditure
(d) None of these

79. Any session of State Legislature is prorogated by –
(a) Presiding officer of the house
(b) The Chief Minister of the State
(c) The Governor
(d) None of the above

80. Where "Hathigumpha" inscription of Kharwel is located?
(a) Uttar Pradesh (b) Bihar
(c) Bengal (d) Odisha

81. The book 'The man who Divided India' was written by —
(a) Maulana Abul Kalam Azad
(b) Dr. Rajendra Prasad
(c) Rafiq Zakaria

82. Name the Viceroy who was killed in Andaman & Nicobar Island?
(a) Lord Mayo (b) Lord Elgin
(c) Lord Hastings (d) Lord Dalhousie

83. When did India become a member of the International Monetary Fund?
(a) 1952 (b) 1950
(c) 1947 (d) 1945

84. Which one is not micro nutrient?
(a) Iron (b) Zinc
(c) Sulphur (d) Manganese

85. An air bubble inside water behave as an:
(a) bifocal lens/ (b) convergent lens/
(c) divergent lens/ (d) cylindrical lens

86. Which of the following memories is an optical memory?
(a) Floppy Disk (b) Bubble Memories
(c) CD-ROM (d) Core Memories

87. Which among the following blood protein regulates the amount of water in plasma?
(a) Globulin (b) Albumin
(c) Fibrin (d) Fibulin

88. Hiuen Tsang visited the Pallava kingdom during the reign of?
(a) Narasimhavarman I
(b) Mahendravarman I
(c) Paramesvarvarman II
(d) Nandivarman II

89. When Alexander invaded india, who were the rulers of Magadha ?
(a) Haryankas (b) Shishunagas
(c) Nandas (d) Maurya

90. Bhakta Tukaram was a contemporary of which Mughal emperor?
(a) Babar (b) Akbar
(c) Jahangir (d) Aurangzeb

91. Who abolished the Dual Government of Bengal?
(a) Cornwallis (b) Robert Clive
(c) Warren Hastings (d) John Macfersson

92. In 1930, Mahatma Gandhi started Civil Disobedience Movement from:
(a) Sevagram (b) Dandi
(c) Sabarmati (d) Wardha

93. The waterfall 'Victoria' is associated with the river
(a) Amazon (b) Missouri
(c) St. Lawrence (d) Zambezi

94. The electric charge is stored in a device called
(a) Inductor (b) Capacitor
(c) Resister (d) Transformer

95. The folk dance 'Chhau' belongs to
(a) Odisha (b) Uttarakhand
(c) Jharkhand (d) Assam

96. Fertilization occurs normally in the
(a) Cervix (b) Vagina
(c) Fallopian tube (d) Uterus

97. Which of the following has become the first and only government corporation in India to launch a chat-enabled help-desk service program 'Ask Disha'
(a) India Post (b) SEBI
(c) IRDA (d) IRCTC

98. Which Indian social entrepreneur has been conferred with the IOC Sports and Active Society Development Grant award for 2018?
(a) Hanumappa Sudarshan
(b) Harish Hande
(c) Suheil Tandon
(d) Ajaita Shah

99. BSNL has recently signed pact with which technological giant to leverage Industry 4.0 for manufacturing excellence?
(a) Microsoft (b) Samsung
(c) Nokia (d) Lava

100. The famous Shahi litchi of which state has recently got the Geographical Indication (GI) tag?
(a) Bihar (b) Uttar Pradesh
(c) West Bengal (d) Assam

Hints & Explanations

1. (b) A petal is a part of a flower; a tire is a part of a bicycle.
2. (d) First number = 8 and the sum of the digits of the second number is 2 + 8 = 10.
Thus, the difference of the first number and the sum of the digits of second number is 10 - 8 = 2.
Similarly, the sum of the digits of third number is 2 + 7 = 9.
Hence, the sum of digits of fourth number should be 2 more than 9 i.e. 11 and 6 + 5 = 11
Hence, (d) 65 is the correct option.
3. (d) First letter move 3 step forward and second letter move 2 step forward.
4. (a) Google is a search engine while others are internet browsers.
5. (a) Ist Letter:
$L \xrightarrow{+1} M \xrightarrow{+1} N \xrightarrow{+1} O \xrightarrow{+1} \boxed{P}$
2nd Letter :
$X \xrightarrow{-4} T \xrightarrow{-4} P \xrightarrow{-4} L \xrightarrow{-4} \boxed{H}$
3rd Letter :
$F \xrightarrow{+4} J \xrightarrow{+4} N \xrightarrow{+4} R \xrightarrow{+4} \boxed{V}$
6. (c) $16 = 5 \times 3 + 1$, $51 = 16 \times 3 + 3$, $158 = 51 \times 3 + 5$
$\therefore$ Next term $= 158 \times 3 + 7 = 481$
7. (b) The pattern is, aabbcc/aabbcc/aabbcc. The pattern aabbcc is repeated.
8. (b) MUSCLE
9. (c) Each letter in the word is moved one step backward to obtain the corresponding letter of the code.
10. (a) The first, second, third, fourth, fifth and sixth letters of th word are respectively moved two, three, four, five, six and seven steps forward to obtain the corresponding letters of the code.
11. (b) There is no 'U' in the word INFLATIONARY.
12. (d)

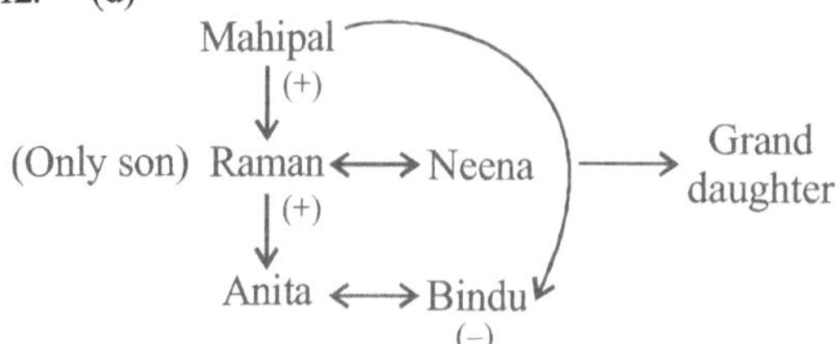

Hence, Bindu is the grand daughter of Mahipal.

13. (d)

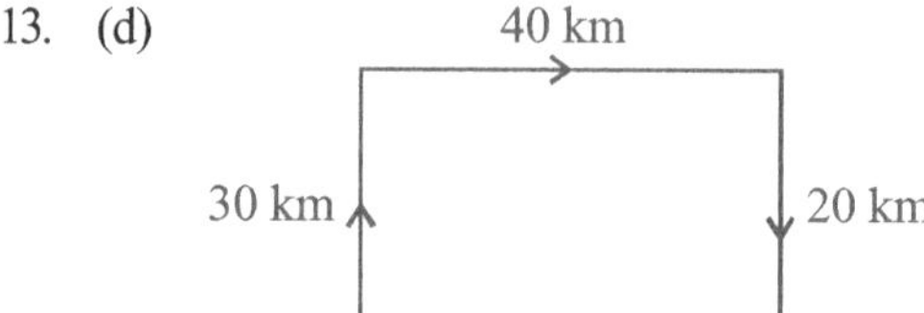

14. (b) In the original group of digits '7' is fourth from the right, which is interchanged with '9'. The new series is 2781359046. 9 will be 4th from the night end.
15. (c) The correct order is:

Pressure	Rain	Flood	Protect	Relief
2	4	5	1	3

16. (d) Lady's mother's husband → Lady's father
Lady's father's sister → Lady's Aunt.
So, Lady's aunt is man's aunt and therefore lady is man's sister.
17. (a)
18. (d)

A B E G C D F H K I J

□ABCD, □BEDF, □ EGFH, □ FHIJ, □AECF, □ EGJI, □ CFIK, □AGJK, □AEIK

19. (d) On interchanging – and ÷,
We get the equation as
$5 + 3 \times 8 \div 12 - 4 = 3$
or $5 + 3 \times 2/3 - 4 = 3$
or $3 = 3$, which is true
20. (b) $7 + 2^2 + 5 = 16$
$9 + 4^2 + 7 = 32$
$8 + 3^2 + 6 = \textcircled{23}$
21. (c) $3 + 9 - 5 = 7$
$2 + 8 - 6 = 4$
$4 + 7 - 5 = \textcircled{6}$
22. (d)
23. (c)

24. (c)

25. (b) When the sheet in fig. (X) is folded to form a cube, then 'F' appears opposite 'C' and 'A' appears opposite 'D'. Therefore, the cube in fig. (A) which shows 'F' adjacent to 'B', the cube in fig.(C) which shows 'E' adjacent to 'C' and the cube in fig. (D) which shows 'A' adjacent to 'D' cannot be formed.

26. (c) LCM of 3 and 5 = 15
Number divisible by 15 are 15, 30, 45 .....300.
Let total numbers are n
$300 = 15 + (n-1) \times 15$
$300 = 15 + 15n - 15$
$\Rightarrow n = 20$

27. (b) $3 \div \left[(8-5) \div \left\{(4-2) \div \left(2 + \frac{8}{13}\right)\right\}\right]$

$\Rightarrow 3 \div \left[(3) \div \left(2 \div \frac{34}{13}\right)\right]$

$\Rightarrow 3 \div \left[(3) \div \left(2 \times \frac{13}{34}\right)\right]$

$\Rightarrow 3 \div \left[\frac{3 \times 34}{13 \times 2}\right]$

$\Rightarrow \frac{3 \times 13 \times 2}{3 \times 34} = \frac{13}{17}$

28. (a) First S.P. $= \frac{46000 \times 88}{100} =$ ₹ 40480

Second S.P. $= \frac{40480 \times 112}{100} =$ ₹ 45337.6

∴ Loss = ₹(46000 – 45337.6) = ₹ 662.4

29. (d) Total amount spent

$= \left(\frac{591}{3} + \frac{45}{60} \times 780\right)$ paise

= (197 + 585) paise
= 782 paise = ₹ 7.82

30. (c) Amount received by R = ₹ 7x
Amount received by Q = ₹ 5x
So difference = 7x – 5x
7x – 5x = 4000
∴ x = 2000
Amount received by
P = 2000 × 3 = ₹ 6000
Q = 2000 × 5 = ₹ 10,000
Total amount = 6,000 × 10,000 = 16,000

31. (b) Relative speed of two trains

$= \frac{180 + 270}{10.8} \frac{m}{s} = \frac{4500}{108} \frac{m}{s}$

$= \frac{4500}{108} \times \frac{18}{5} \frac{km}{h} = 150$ km/hr

Speed of second train = 150 – 60 = 90 km/h.

32. (c) $300000\left[1 + \frac{20}{100}\right]^t = 746496$

$\therefore \left[\frac{6}{5}\right]^t = \frac{746496}{300000} = \frac{7776}{3135} = \left(\frac{6}{5}\right)^5$

t = 5

33. (d) Shyam alone worked for 10 days. So work done by him $= \frac{10}{40} = \frac{1}{4}$

∴ (Ravi + Shyam) have done

$1 - \frac{1}{4} = \frac{3}{4}$ of the work.

(Ravi + Shyam) do $\frac{3}{4}$ of the work in

$24 \times \frac{3}{4} = 18$ days

34. (c) Let the number be x
According to question 20% of x = 30% of 40

$\Rightarrow \frac{x \times 20}{100} = \frac{40 \times 30}{100}$

$\Rightarrow x = \frac{40 \times 30}{20} = 60$

35. (c) The smallest angle of the triangle is half of the largest angle.
∴ Ratio of the three angle = 4 : 3 : 2
∴ $4x + 3x + 2x = 180°$
∴ $9x = 180°$
∴ $x = 20°$
∴ required difference = $4x - 2x$
$= 2x = 2 \times 20° = 40°$

36. (b) Let uncle's present age = x
Rahim's present age = y
$y - x = 30$ ...(i)
After 7 year
$(x + 7) + (y + 7) = 66$
$x + y + 14 = 66$
$x + y = 52$ ...(ii)
combining (i) and (ii) we get
$(x + y = 52) + (x - y = 30)$
$2x = 82$
$x = 41$
Uncle's age is 41

37. (b) Let S.P. = Rs 100. Then, C.P. = Rs 96; Profit = Rs 4.
∴ Profit %
$= \left(\frac{4}{96} \times 100\right)\% = \frac{25}{6}\% = 4.17\%. \approx 4.2\%$

38. (b) Given,

$$\frac{3}{x+y}+\frac{2}{x-y}=2 \quad \text{...(i)}$$

and $$\frac{9}{x+y}-\frac{4}{x-y}=1 \quad \text{...(ii)}$$

Let $\frac{1}{x+y}=a$ and $\frac{1}{x-y}=b$

$\therefore$ $3a+2b=2$ ...(iii)

$9a-4b=1$ ...(iv)

On multiplying equation (iii) by 2 and addition of equation (iv) and new one, then we get

$$\begin{array}{l} 6a+4b=4 \\ 9a-4b=1 \\ \hline 15a \quad =5 \end{array}$$

$\Rightarrow$ $a=\frac{5}{15}=\frac{1}{3}$

$\therefore$ $\frac{1}{x+y}=\frac{1}{3}$

$\Rightarrow$ $x+y=3$ ...(v)

On putting the value of (a) in equation (iii), we get

$3\times\frac{1}{3}+2b=2$

$\Rightarrow$ $2b=2-1=1$

$\Rightarrow$ $b=\frac{1}{2}\Rightarrow\frac{1}{x-y}=\frac{1}{2}$

$\Rightarrow$ $x-y=2$ ...(vi)

$$\therefore \begin{array}{l} x+y=3 \\ x-y=2 \\ \hline 2x \quad =5 \end{array}$$

$\Rightarrow$ $x=\frac{5}{2}$

From equation (v),

$y=3-\frac{5}{2}=\frac{1}{2}$

$\therefore$ $\frac{x}{y}=\frac{\frac{5}{2}}{\frac{1}{2}}=5$

39. (b) Given that, mean of 100 values is 45

$\therefore$ Sum of 100 values, i.e. $\sum_{i=1}^{100} x=45\times 100$

$=4500$

According to condition,

$$\sum_{i=1}^{40}(x_i+15)+\sum_{i=41}^{100}(x_i-5)$$

$$=\sum_{i=1}^{40}x_i+15\times 40+\sum_{i=41}^{100}x_i-5\times 60$$

$$=\left(\sum_{i=1}^{40}x_i+\sum_{i=41}^{100}x_i\right)+600-300$$

$$=\sum_{i=1}^{100}x_i+300$$

$=4500+300=4800$ [from equation (i)]

$\therefore$ New mean $=\frac{4800}{100}=48$

40. (b) Let number be x, then its reciprocal be $\frac{1}{x}$.

According to question,

$$x^2+\frac{1}{x^2}=3\left(x^2-\frac{1}{x^2}\right)$$

$\therefore$ $x^2+\frac{1}{x^2}=3x^2-\frac{3}{x^2} \Rightarrow 2x^2=\frac{4}{x^2}$

$\Rightarrow$ $x^4=2 \Rightarrow x=(2)^{1/4}$

41. (c) $P(x)=ax^3+3x^2-8x+b$

$\therefore$ $P(-2)=-8a+12+16+b=0$

$\Rightarrow$ $-8a+b+28=0$ ...(i)

$\Rightarrow$ $P(2)=8a+12-16+b=2$

$\Rightarrow$ $8a+b-4=0$ ...(ii)

By equation (i) + (ii)

$2b+24 = 0$

$\Rightarrow$ $b=-\frac{24}{2}=-12$

From equation (i),

$-8a-12+28=0$

$\Rightarrow$ $-8a=-16 \Rightarrow a=2$

42. (a) By option (a),

$\frac{-7}{10} < \frac{-2}{3} < \frac{-5}{8}$

Here LCM of (3, 8, 10) = 120

$\frac{-7}{10} \times 120 < \frac{-2}{3} \times 120 < \frac{-5}{8} \times 120$

$-84 < -80 < -75$

So this is correct.

43. (c) Two digit numbers which are divisible by 3 are 12, 15, 18,..., 99;

So, 99 = 12+ (n – 1) × 3.

n = 30

44. (a)

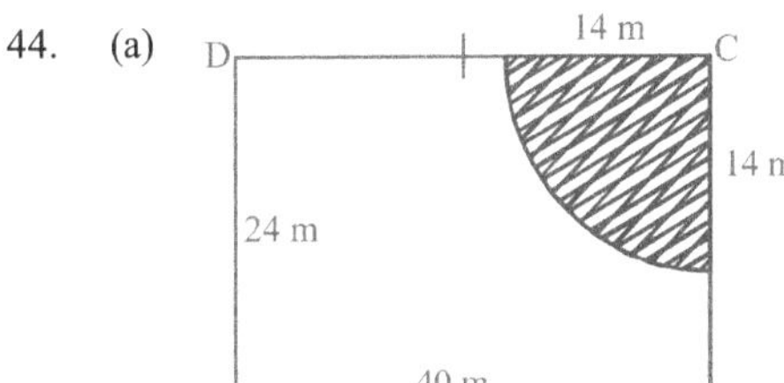

Area of the shaded portion

$= \frac{1}{4} \times \pi(14)^2 = 154 \text{ m}^2$

45. (c) After 5 minutes (before meeting), the top runner covers 2 rounds i.e., 400 m and the last runner covers 1 round i.e., 200 m.

∴ Top runner covers 800 m race in 10 minutes.

46. (a) Required average number of students

$= \frac{1}{5 \times 100}$ [35 × 17500 + 45 × 25000 + 30 × 35300 + 48 × 23000 + 30 × 32400]

$= \frac{1}{5}$ [6125 + 11250 + 10590 + 11040 + 9720]

$= \frac{1}{5} \times 48725 = 9745$

47. (d) D = 5520

48. (d) To calculate faster, instead of finding all the students of Arts and Science stream first and then subtracting, let's assume that in each college Science students are more and keep substracting the number of Arts students from the number of Science students collegewise.

Difference = (40% of 17500 – 25% of 17500) + (40% of 25000 – 15% of 25000) + (55% of 35300 – 15% of 35300) + (24% of 23000 – 28% of 23000) + (41% of 32400 – 29% of 32400)

= (15 × 175) + (25 × 250) + (40 × 353) + (–4 × 230) + (12 × 324)

= 2625 + 6250 + 14120 – 920 + 3888

= 25963

49. (b) According to question

Surface area of sphere = 3 (Volume of sphere)

$\Rightarrow \quad 4\pi r^2 = 3 \times \frac{4}{3}\pi r^3 \Rightarrow r = 1$

∴ Diameter = 2r = 2 cm

50. (d) The stack is in the form having vertical cross section of trapezium.

∴ Volume of Earth in the stack = Area of cross section of trapezium × Height

$\therefore \text{ Volume} = \frac{1}{2} \times (10 + 5) \times 2 \times 8$

$= 15 \times 8 \text{ m}^2$

According to the question,

Volume of Earth to be spread = (Area of field) × Level raised

$\therefore \quad \text{Level raised} = \frac{15 \times 8}{100 \times 80} = \frac{15}{1000} \text{m}$

= 1.5 cm

51. (b) 52. (a) 53. (a) 54. (b)

55. (a) 56. (c) 57. (d)

58. (d) Use 'study seriously'. 'To' should not be separated from its verb by inserting any adverb between the two. The split infinitive is grammatically wrong.

For Example - I advised him to carefully carry the bag. Say 'to carry carefully'.

59. (d) Use 'few' in place of 'little'. 'Little' is used for uncountable nouns, while 'few' is used for countable nouns. Using 'the' before 'few' gives the sense of 'some but all'.

For Ex: -

(i) He lost the few friends he had. (not many friends, but all of them)

(ii) I have little money to buy a house. (hardly any money)

60. (d) 61. (a) 62. (b) 63. (d)

64. (c) 65. (d) 66. (d) 67. (a)

68. (d) The passage speaks of the federation of Yugoslavia A, B that has come apart C due to ethnic conflict D in its different regions.

69. (c) The division of plan and non-plan funds into two parts C is artificial D. Yet there is some merit in it. A as distinct from consumption B because it draws our attention to development expenses D.

70. (d) 71. (a) 72. (c) 73. (b) 74. (a)

75. (a)
76. (c) The four classes were mentioned in Purush Sukta in 10th mandal of Rigveda.
77. (b) According to the Article 243 K (1), the chief of the State Election Commission is appointed by the Governor.
78. (b) Non- plan expenditure is largely the revenue expenditure of the government, although it also includes capital expenditure. It covers all expenditure not included in the Plan Expenditure. Non-Plan Expenditure constitutes the biggest proportion of the government's total expenditure. The biggest items of Non-Plan Expenditure are interest payments and debt servicing, defence expenditure and subsidies. For defence services, both revenue and capital expenditure are incurred.
79. (c) Any session of the state legislation is prorogated by the Governor.
80. (d) Hathigumpha inscription was built by Kharvel in Odisha, near Bhuvneshwar.
81. (c) "The Man who Divided India" was written by Rafiq Zakaria.
82. (a) Mayo came in India in 1869. He founded Mayo College in Ajmer. He was killed by an Afghan in 1872.
83. (d) India joined the IMF on December 27, 1945, as one of the IMF's original members. India accepted the obligations of Article VIII of the IMF Articles of Agreement on current account convertibility on August 20, 1994.
84. (c)
85. (c) The air bubble will behave as a diverging lens due to its bulging curvature.
86. (c) 87. (b)
88. (a)
89. (c) When Alexander invaded India, Nandas were the rulers of Magadha.
90. (c) Best answer is c as Tukaram (1608–1650) was a Marathi Bhakti poet and a devotee of Lord Krishna. Time period of Jahangir was 1605-1627.
91. (c)
92. (c) On 12 March, 1930, Gandhi started his civil disobedience movement by starting Dandi March from Sabarmati Ashram in Gujarat and reached Dandi on 6 April 1930 and broke the salt law.
93. (d) Victoria waterfalls is associated with the river Zambezi which is situated in Africa.
94. (b) Capacitor is a device which stors electric charge.

95. (c) 96. (c) 97. (d)
98. (c) 99. (c) 100. (a)

PRACTICE SET- 8

GENERAL INTELLIGENCE & REASONING

DIRECTIONS (Qs. 1-3): *In the questions, select the related word/ letters/numbers from the given alternatives.*

1. ACE : FHJ : : OQS : ?
   (a) PRT (b) RTU
   (c) TVX (d) UWY
2. Saint : Meditation : : Scientist : ?
   (a) Research (b) Knowledge
   (c) Spiritual (d) Rational
3. 7 : 56 :: 9 : ?
   (a) 63 (b) 81
   (c) 90 (d) 99

DIRECTIONS (Qs. 4–5): *In the following question, find the odd word/number from the given alternative.*

4. (a) Lord Dalhousie (b) Lord Mountbatten
   (c) Lord Linlithgow (d) Lord Tennyson
5. (a) 226 (b) 290
   (c) 360 (d) 170

DIRECTIONS (Qs. 6–7): *In the following question a series is given, with me term missing. Choose the correct alternative from the given ones that will complete the series.*

6. AYBZC, DWEXF, GUHVI, JSKTL, (?), POQPR
   (a) MQDRN (b) QMONR
   (c) MQNRO (d) NQMOR
7. 8, 15, 28, 53, ...?
   (a) 98 (b) 106
   (c) 100 (d) 102
8. In a certain code language NATIONALISM is written as OINTANMSAIL. How is DEPARTMENTS written in that code?
   (a) RADEPTSTMNE (b) RADPETSTMNE
   (c) RADPESTMTNE (d) RADPETSTNME
9. If 'green' is called 'white', 'white' is called 'yellow , 'yellow' is called 'red', 'red' is called 'orange', then which of the following represents the colour of sunflower?
   (a) red (b) yellow
   (c) brown (d) indigo
10. A man said to a woman, "Your mother's husband's sister is my aunt." How is the woman related to the man ?
    (a) Granddaughter (b) Daughter
    (c) Sister (d) Aunt
11. Rasik walks 20 m North. Then, he turns right and walks 30 m. Then he turns right and walks 35 m. Then he turns left and walks 15 m. Then he again turns left and walks 15 m. In which direction and how many metres away is he from his original position?
    (a) 15 metres West (b) 30 metres East
    (c) 30 metres West (d) 45 metres East
12. In a row of boys Akash is fifth from the left and Nikhil is eleventh from the right. If Akash is twenty-fifth from the right then how many boys are there between Akash and Nikhil?
    (a) 14 (b) 13
    (c) 15 (d) 12
13. P, Q, R and S are four men. P is the oldest but not the poorest. R is the richest but not the oldest. Q is older than S but not than P or R. P is richer than Q but not than S. The four men can be ordered (descending) in respect of age and richness, respectively, as
    (a) PQRS, RPSQ (b) PRQS, RSPQ
    (c) PRQS, RSQP (d) PRSQ, RSPQ

DIRECTION (Q. 14): *Arrange the following in a logical order:*

14. 1. Birth 2. Death
    3. Funeral 4. Marriage
    5. Education
    (a) 1, 3, 4, 5, 2 (b) 1, 5, 4, 2, 3
    (c) 2, 3, 4, 5, 1 (d) 4, 5, 3, 1, 2
15. Choose the diagram which represent the relationship among the following :- Capsules, Antibiotics, Injection.

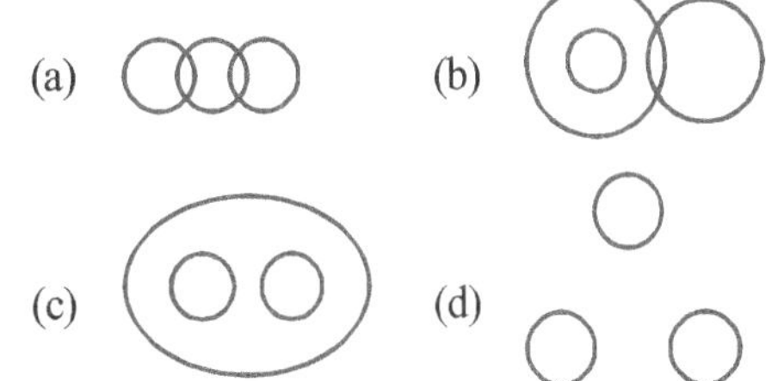

DIRECTION (Q. 16): *In the question belows are given two statements followed by two conclusions. You have to take the given statements to be true even if they seem to be at variance with commonly known facts. Read all the conclusions and then decide which of the given statements disregarding commonly know facts. Given Answer.*

Give answer (a) If only conclusion I follows.
Give answer (b) if only conclusion II follows.
Give answer (c) if either I or II follows.
Give answer (d) if neither I nor II follows.

16. Statements:
All leaders are good team workers.
All good team workers are good orators.
Conclusions:
I. Some good team workers are leaders.
II. All good orators are leaders.

17. If '–' stands for division, '+' for multiplication '÷' for subtraction and '×' for addition. Which one of the following equation is correct?
(a) $6 \div 20 \times 12 + 7 - 1 = 70$
(b) $6 + 20 - 20 \div 7 \times 1 = 62$
(c) $6 - 20 \div 12 \times 7 + 1 = 57$
(d) $6 + 20 - 20 \div 7 - 1 = 38$

DIRECTIONS (Qs.18–19): *In the following questions, select the missing number from the given response.*

18.

2	7	9
7	3	4
9	8	?
126	168	216

(a) 8 (b) 3
(c) 6 (d) 36

19.

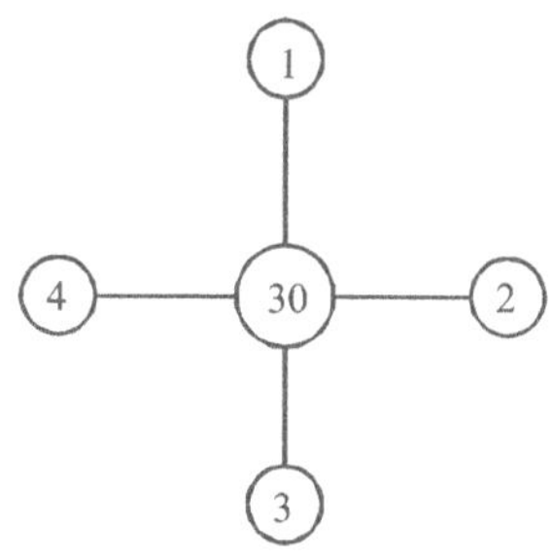

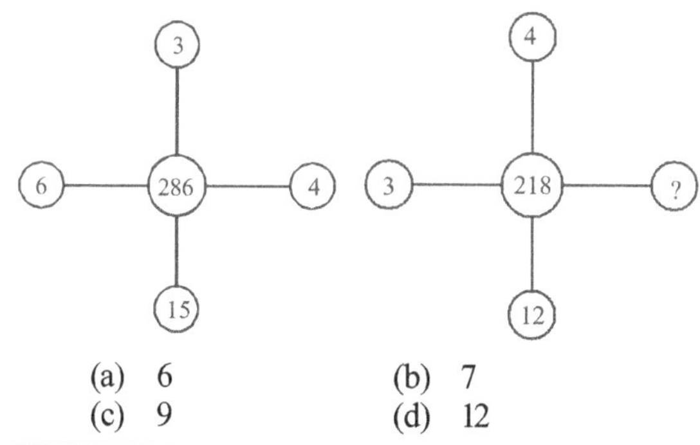

(a) 6 (b) 7
(c) 9 (d) 12

DIRECTION (Q. 20): *Choose the box that is similar to the box formed from the given sheet of paper (X).*

20.

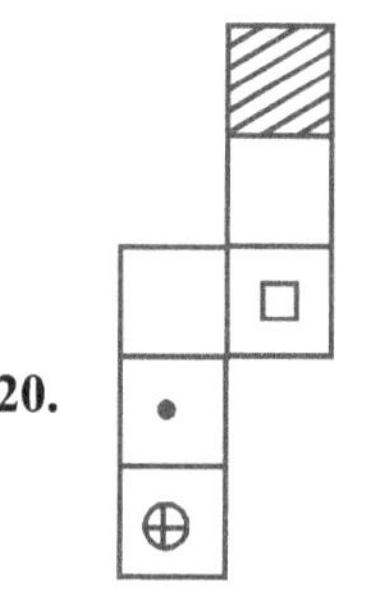

(X)

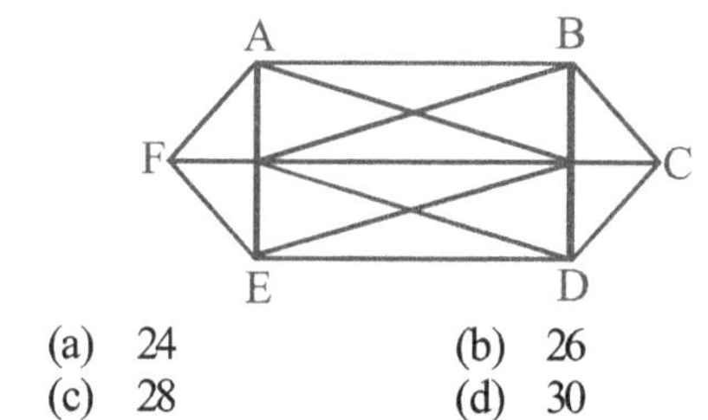

(a) 1 only (b) 2 and 3 only
(c) 1 and 3 only (d) 1, 2 and 4 only

21. How many triangles are there in the figure ABCDEF?

A B F C E D

(a) 24 (b) 26
(c) 28 (d) 30

DIRECTION (Q. 22): *From the given answer figures, select the one which is hidden/embedded in the question figure.*

22. 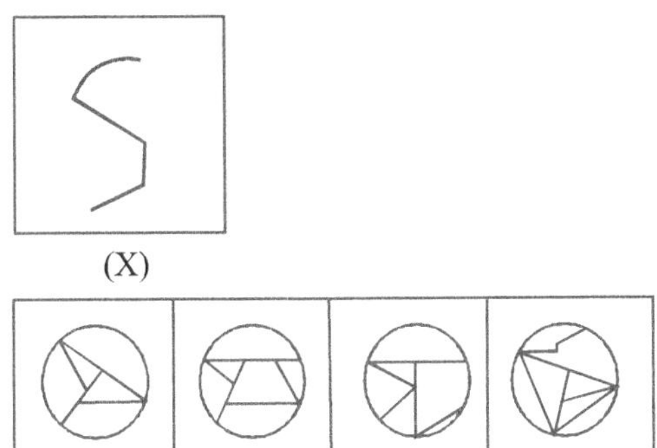

(a) (b) (c) (d)

DIRECTION (Q. 23) : *In the question a set of three figures A, B and C showing a sequence of folding of a piece of paper. Fig. (C) shows the manner in which the folded paper has been cut. These three figures are followed by four answer figures from which you have to choose a figure which would most closely resemble the unfolded form of fig. (C).*

23. 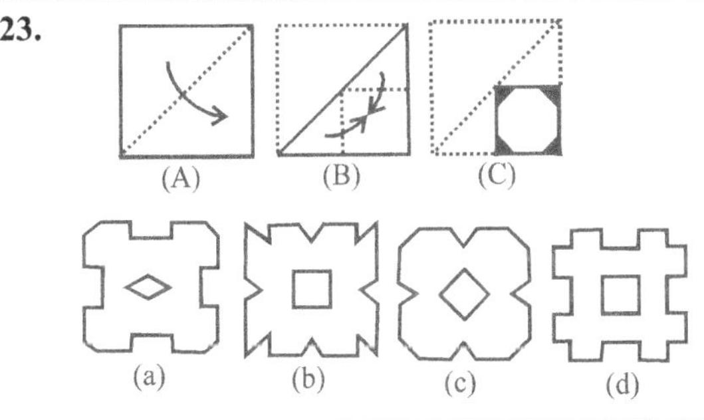

DIRECTION (Q.24): *In the following question, which answer figure will complete the pattern in the question figure?*

24. 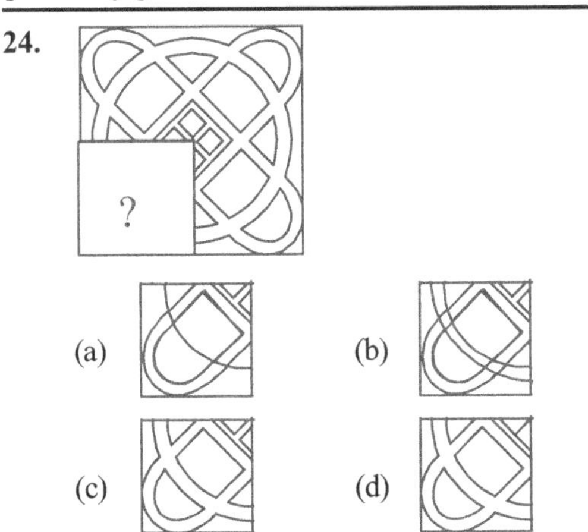

25. From the given alternative words, select the word which cannot be formed using the letters of the given word :

TRIVANDRUM

(a) RAIN (b) DRUM
(c) TRAIN (d) DRUK

QUANTITATIVE APTITUDE

26. A number being successively divided by 3, 5 and 8 leaves 1,2 and 4 as remainders respectively. What are the remainders if the order of divisors be reversed?
(a) 3, 3, 1 (b) 3, 1, 3
(c) 1, 3, 3 (d) None of these

27. Find the unit digit in the product $(2467)^{153} \times (341)^{72}$.
(a) 6 (b) 7
(c) 8 (d) 9

28. A shopkeeper bought 30 kg of wheat at the rate of ₹45 per kg. He sold forty per cent of the total quantity at the rate of ₹ 50 per kg. Approximately, at what price per kg should he sell the remaining quantity to make 25 percent overall profit?
(a) ₹ 54 (b) ₹ 52
(c) ₹ 50 (d) ₹ 60

29. 4 goats or 6 sheeps can graze a field in 50 days. 2 goats and 9 sheeps can graze the field in
(a) 100 days (b) 75 days
(c) 50 days (d) 25 days

30. If two numbers are respectively 20% and 50% of a third number, what is the percentage of the first number to the second ?
(a) 10 (b) 20
(c) 30 (d) 40

31. If the manufacturer gains 10%, the wholesale dealer 15% and the retailer 25%, then find the cost of production of a table, the retail price of which is ₹ 1265?
(a) ₹ 800 (b) ₹ 1000
(c) ₹ 900 (d) ₹ 600

32. Out of a certain sum, $\frac{1}{3}$rd is invested at 3%, $\frac{1}{6}$th at 6% and the rest at 8%. If the simple interest for 2 years from all these investments amounts to ₹ 600, find the original sum.
(a) ₹ 4000 (b) ₹ 5000
(c) ₹ 6000 (d) ₹ 7000

33. If the difference between S.I and C.I for 2 years on a sum of money lent at 5% is ₹ 6, then the sum B.
(a) ₹ 2200 (b) ₹ 2400
(c) ₹ 2600 (d) ₹ 2000

34. A contractor undertakes to built a walls in 50 days. He employs 50 peoples for the same. However after 25 days he finds that only 40% of the work is

complete. How many more man need to be employed to complete the work in time?

(a) 25 (b) 30

(c) 35 (d) 20

35. R and S start walking each other at 10 AM at the speeds of 3 km/h and 4 km/h respectively. They were initially 17.5 km apart. At what time do they meet?

(a) 2 : 30 PM (b) 11 : 30 AM

(c) 1 : 30 PM (d) 12 : 30 PM

36. Find the co-ordinates of the point which divides the line segment joining the points (4, –1) and (–2, 4) internally in the ratio 3 : 5

(a) $\left(\frac{6}{4}, \frac{7}{2}\right)$ (b) $\left(\frac{4}{7}, \frac{8}{7}\right)$

(c) $\left(\frac{7}{4}, \frac{7}{8}\right)$ (d) $\left(\frac{7}{12}, \frac{8}{4}\right)$

37. Present age of Sudha and Neeta are in the ratio of 6 : 7 respectively. Five years ago their ages were in the ratio of 5 : 6 respectively. What is Sudha's present age?

(a) 30 years (b) 35 years

(c) 40 years (d) Cannot be determined

38. A triangle and a parallelogram are constructed on the same base such that their areas are equal. If the altitude of the parallelogram is 100 m, then the altitude of the triangle is :

(a) 100 m (b) 200 m

(c) $100\sqrt{2}$ m (d) $10\sqrt{2}$ m

39. In a 800 m race around a stadium having the circumference of 200 m, the top runner meets the last runner on the 5th minute of the race. If the top runner runs at twice the speed of the last runner, what is the time taken by the top runner to finish the race ?

(a) 20 min (b) 15 min

(c) 10 min (d) 5 min

40. The equation of a line passing through the points A (– 1, 1) and B (2, – 4) is

(a) $3x + 5y + 2 = 0$ (b) $5x + 3y + 2 = 0$

(c) $2x + 3y + 5 = 0$ (d) None of these

41. X and Y can do job in 25 days and 30 days respectively. They work together for 5 days and then X leaves. Y will finish the rest of the work in how many days?

(a) 18 days (b) 19 days

(c) 20 days (d) 21 days

42. A dishonest dealer professes to sell his goods at cost price, but he uses a weight of 960 g for the kg weight. Find his gain per cent.

(a) 4% (b) $4\frac{1}{6}\%$

(c) 96% (d) 40%

43. If $x = 2 + \sqrt{3}$, then $x^2 + \frac{1}{x^2}$ is equal to

(a) 10 (b) 12

(c) –12 (d) 14

44. If $a^2 + b^2 + c^2 = 2a - 2b - 2$, then the value of $3a - 2b + c$ is

(a) 0 (b) 3

(c) 5 (d) 2

45. The least value of $3^x + 3^{-x}$ is :

(a) 2 (b) 1

(c) 0 (d) $\frac{2}{3}$

DIRECTIONS (Qs. 46-48) : *Study the following pie-chart carefully and answer the questions given below.*

Cost estimated by a family in renovation of their house

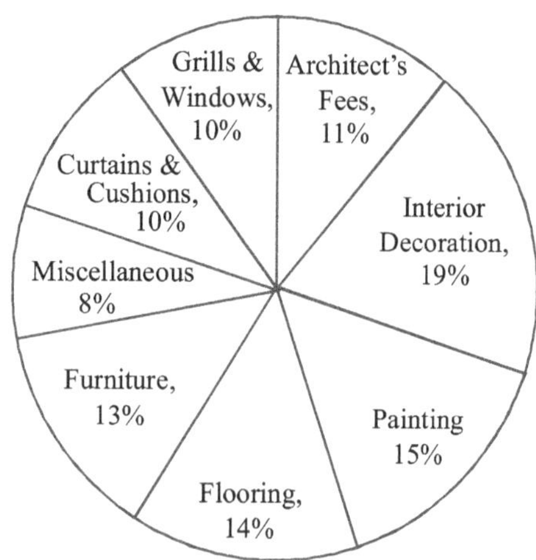

Total estimated cost is ₹1,20,000

46. What is the difference in the amount estimated by the family on interior decoration and that on architect's fees?

(a) ₹10,000 (b) ₹9,500

(c) ₹7,200 (d) ₹9,600

47. During the process of renovation, the family actually incurred miscellaneous expenditure of ₹10,200. The miscellaneous expenditure incurred by the family is what percentage of the total estimated cost?

(a) 9.5% (b) 9%

(c) 8.5% (d) 10.5%

48. Other than getting the discount of 12% on the estimated cost of furniture and the actual miscellaneous expenditure being ₹10,200 instead of the estimated one, the family's estimated cost is correct. What is the total amount spend by the family in renovating its house?
(a) ₹1,16,728 (b) ₹1,15,926
(c) ₹1,19,500 (d) ₹1,18,728

49. The length of a rectangular plot is thrice its breadth. If the area of the rectangular plot is 7803 sq. metre, what is the breadth of the rectangular plot?
(a) 51 metres (b) 153 metres
(c) 104 metres (d) 88 metres

50. A cylindrical tube open at both ends is made of metal. The internal diameter of the tube is 6 cm and length of the tube is 10 cm. If the thickness of the metal used is 1 cm, then the outer curved surface area of the tube is
(a) 140π sq cm (b) 146.5π sq cm
(c) 70π sq cm (d) None of these

ENGLISH LANGUAGE

DIRECTIONS (Qs. 51-52): *In the following questions, groups of four words are given. In each group, one word is correctly spelt. Find the correctly spelt word.*

51. (a) coimmission (b) comision
(c) commission (d) commision

52. (a) jewelery (b) jewellry
(c) jwellry (d) jewellery

DIRECTIONS (Qs. 53-55): *Four alternatives are given for the Idiom/Phrase given. Choose the alternative which best expresses the meaning of the Idiom/Phrase.*

53. A fool's paradise means –
(a) a foolish idea
(b) an imaginary idea
(c) an unexpected gain
(d) false hopes for a foolish person

54. Will o' the wisp –
(a) Anything which eludes or deceives
(b) To act in a foolish way
(c) To act in a childish way
(d) To have desires unbaked by efforts

55. To fly off the handle –
(a) To take off
(b) To be indifferent
(c) To dislocate
(d) To lose one's temper

DIRECTIONS (Qs. 56-57): *Out of the four alternatives, choose the one which can be substituted for the given words/sentences.*

56. That which comes and goes –
(a) transgressing (b) fitful
(c) vegetating (d) spontaneous

57. In a confused manner –
(a) nitty-gritty (b) pell-mell
(c) blurry (d) organised

DIRECTIONS (Qs. 58-59): *Out of the four alternatives, choose the one which best expresses the meaning of the given word.*

58. OVERWROUGHT
(a) Cool (b) Exhausted
(c) Quiet (d) Excited

59. INDUBITABLE
(a) Disputable (b) Certain
(c) Doubtful (d) Equivocal

DIRECTIONS (Qs. 60-61): *Choose the word* ***opposite*** *in meaning to the given word.*

60. COGNISANCE
(a) Idiom (b) Ignorance
(c) Abeyance (d) Anecdote

61. ANALYSIS
(a) Dialysis (b) Electrolysis
(c) Synthesis (d) Parenthesis

DIRECTIONS (Qs. 62-63): *Sentences given with blanks are to be filled in with an appropriate word. Four alternatives are suggested for each question.*

62. On the other hand, there is absolutely no time to _____ .
(a) get (b) create
(c) gain (d) lose

63. The graphics are brilliant and the game _____ up 5GB of space after storage.
(a) need (b) sways
(c) kills (d) takes

DIRECTIONS (Qs. 64-65): *To create logical scenario the following sentences need to be arranged in correct order. Choose the most logical order of the sentences from amongst the four given choices so as to form a logical scenario.*

64. A: One day, a 17-year old shepherd boy came to visit his brothers and asked, Why don't you stand up and fight the giant?"
B: We all know the story of David and Goliath,

in which there was a giant who was bullying and harassing the children in the village.

C: But David said, No, he is not too big to hit; he is too big to miss."

D: The brothers were terrified and they replied, Don't you see he is too big to hit ?"

Which of the sequences present the most logical scenario?

(a) BADC (b) ACDB
(c) BACD (d) BDCA

65. A: Michael Hofman, a poet and translator, accepts this sorry fact without approval.

B: But thanklessness and impossibility do not daunt him. Hofman feels passionately about his work and this is clear from his writings.

C: He acknowledges too-infact, he returns to the point often-the best translators of poetry always fail at some level.

D: In terms of the gap between worth and rewards, translators come somewhere near nurses and street cleaners.

Which of the sequences present the most logical scenario?

(a) DABC (b) DACB
(c) ADBC (d) CDAB

DIRECTIONS (Qs. 66-69): *Complete the passage by choosing the most suitable word/phrase from each list to fit the corresponding gap.*

India is said to be one of the most **66** and **67** countries in the world and our constitution is a **68** to this very fact. In many countries, democratic governments in the course of conducting a major review of their national constitutions **69** to curtail, if not abolish, the death penalty.

66. (a) orthodox (b) rigid
(c) liberal (d) flamboyant

67. (a) tolerable (b) tolerant
(c) rigid (d) secluded

68. (a) testimony (b) evidence
(c) declaration (d) witness

69. (a) powerful (b) engaging
(c) open (d) systematic

DIRECTIONS (Qs. 70-71) : *In each of the following questions, a sentence two been given in Direct/ Indirect speech, out of the four alternatives suggested select the one which best expresses the same sentence in Indirect/Direct speech.*

70. "Please don't go away", she said.
(a) She said to please her and not go away.
(b) She told me not to go away.
(c) She begged that I not go away.
(d) She begged me not to go away.

71. He said to me, "What time do the offices close?"
(a) He wanted to know what time the offices close.
(b) He asked me what time did the offices close.
(c) He asked me what time the offices close .
(d) He asked me what time the offices did close.

DIRECTIONS (Qs. 72-73): *In the following questions, some of the sentences have errors and some have none. Find out which part of a sentence has an error. The number of that part is the answer. If there is no error, your answer is (d) i.e. No error*

72. Knowledge of (a) / at least two languages (b) / are required to pass the examination (c)/ No error. (d)

73. The members of the Opposition Party in the Parliament
(a) / shout upon the minister (b) / if he makes a wrong statement (c)/No error (d)

DIRECTIONS (Qs. 74-75): *In the following questions, a part of sentence is printed in bold. Alternatives to the bold part, which may improve the sentence, are given at (a), (b), and (c). Choose the appropriate alternative. In case no improvement is needed, mark (d) as your answer.*

74. She has slept for eight hours last night.
(a) slept (b) had slept
(c) has been sleeping (d) No improvement

75. I have seen the film and she also have.
(a) has also (b) has too
(c) too has (d) No improvement

GENERAL AWARENESS

76. Which of the following is not evident at Mohenjodaro?
(a) Pasupati seal
(b) Great granary and great bath
(c) Multi-pillared assembly hall
(d) Evidence of double burials

77. When did Delhi first become capital of a kingdom?
(a) At the time of Tomar dynasty
(b) Tughlaq dynasty

(c) Lodhi dynasty
(d) None of these

78. Total schedules in Indian Constitution are:
(a) 22 (b) 10
(c) 16 (d) 12

79. Who was the President of the Constituent Assembly?
(a) Rajendra Prasad (b) B. R. Ambedkar
(c) K. M. Munshi (d) G. V. Mavlankar

80. By Which name/names is our country mentioned in the constitution?
(a) India and Bharat
(b) India and Hindustan
(c) Bharat Only
(d) India, Bharat and Hindustan

81. Which one of the following is a vector quantity?
(a) Momentum (b) Pressure
(c) Energy (d) Work

82. Acid rain is caused by the pollution of environment by
(a) carbon dioxide and nitrogen
(b) carbon monoxide and carbon dioxide
(c) ozone and carbon dioxide
(d) nitrous oxide and sulphur dioxide

83. Which one of the following hormones contains iodine?
(a) Thyroxine (b) Testosterone
(c) Insulin (d) Adrenaline

84. The major component of honey is
(a) glucose (b) sucrose
(c) maltose (d) fructose

85. In eye donation, which one of the following parts of donor's eye is utilized?
(a) Iris (b) Lens
(c) Cornea (d) Retina

86. Most highly intelligent mammals are
(a) whales (b) dolphins
(c) elephants (d) kangaroos

87. The last ruler of the Mughal dynasty was
(a) Babur
(b) Bahadurshah Zafar
(c) Akbar
(d) None of the above

88. The last month of the Saka year is
(a) Phalguna (b) Chaitra
(c) Asadha (d) Pausa

89. The first General Elections in India took place in
(a) 1948 (b) 1950
(c) 1952 (d) 1954

90. Richter scale is used for measuring
(a) density of liquid
(b) intensity of earthquakes
(c) velocity of wind
(d) humidity of air

91. Rangaswamy Cup is associated with
(a) archery (b) cricket
(c) football (d) hockey

92. Who developed Yahoo?
(a) Dennis Ritchie & Ken Thompson
(b) David Filo & Jerry Yang
(c) Vint Cerf & Robert Kahn
(d) Steve Case & Jeff Bezos

93. Under whose leadership was the all India Muslim League set up?
(a) Mohammed Ali Jinnah
(b) Sayyid Ahmed Khan
(c) Aga Khan
(d) All of the above

94. A device or system not directly connected to the CPU is
(a) On-line (b) Keyboard
(c) Memory (d) Off-line

95. Paper currency first started in India in
(a) 1861 (b) 1542
(c) 1601 (d) 1880

96. Lala Lajpat Rai is also known as
(a) Sher-e-Punjab
(b) Punjab Kesari
(c) Both (a) and (b)
(d) None of the above

97. The 5th edition of the Women of India Organic Festival will be held in which city?
(a) Guwahati (b) New Delhi
(c) Pune (d) Agartala

98. Which cricket statistican has authored the book "Indian Sports: Conversations and Reflections"?
(a) Sanjay Manjrekar (b) Jatin Sapru
(c) Sushil Doshi (d) Vijayan Bala

99. Who is leading the Indian delegation at the 8th European Congress on SMEs?
(a) Alka Arora (b) Sushma Swaraj
(c) Bhaskar Kalra (d) Giriraj Singh

100. Which of the following Indian research organisations has developed an affordable Water Disinfection System "OneerTM"?
(a) BARC (b) ISRO
(c) CSIR (d) DRDO

Hints & Explanations

1. (c) TVX : Each letter of the first group is moved five steps forward to obtain the corresponding letter of the second group.
2. (a) A saint practices meditation. While, a scientist does research.
3. (c) The relationship is x : x (x + 1)
4. (d) All except Lord Tennyson were either the Governor-General or the Viceroy of India.
5. (c) After a close look you will get that except 360 each number is one more than square of a natural number, i.e., $226 = 15^2 + 1$; $290 = 17^2 + 1$; $170 = 13^2 + 1$.
6. (c) The Pattern is–

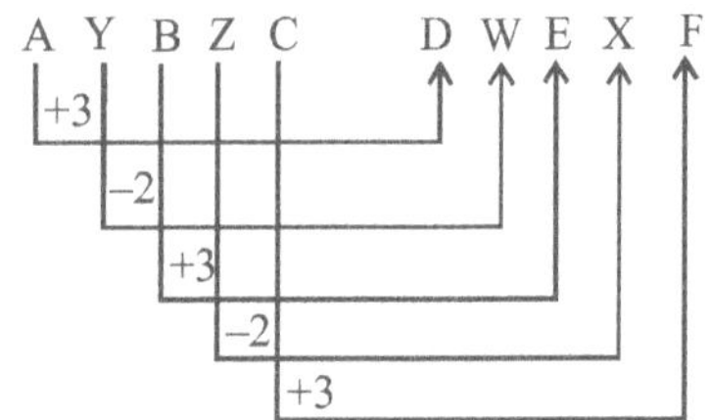

Therefore,

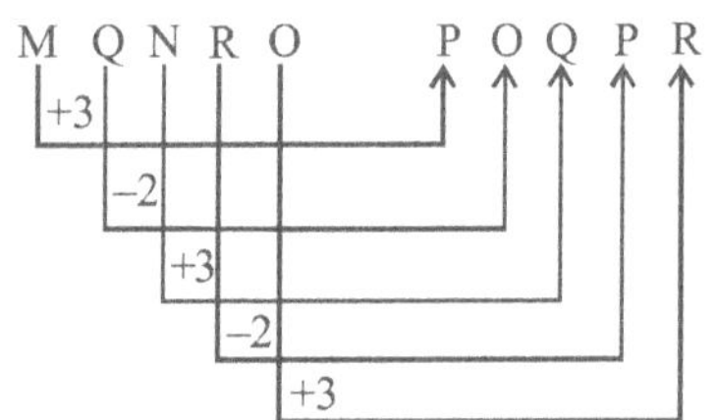

7. (d) $8 \times 2 - 1 = 15$, $15 \times 2 - 2 = 28$, $28 \times 2 - 3 = 53$, $53 \times 2 - 4 = 102$
8. (b)

unchanged

N A T I O N A L I S M

Reverse order

O I T A N N M S I L A

O I N T A N M S A I L

Similarly,

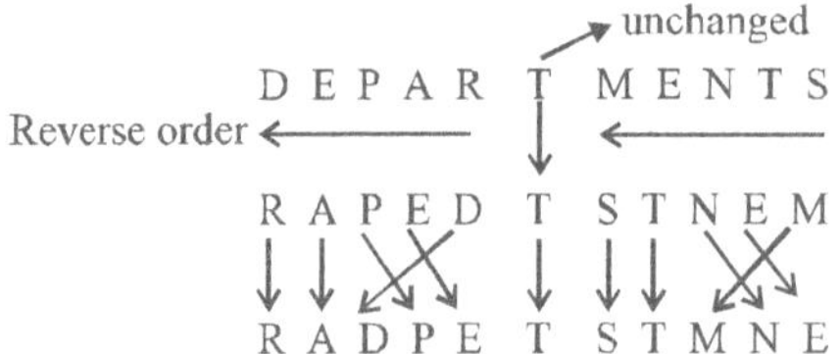

9. (a) The colour of sunflower is yellow and yellow is called 'red'. Hence sunflower is red.
10. (c) Woman's Mother's husband

↓

Woman's father

Woman's father's sister ⟶ Woman's Aunt.

Since, woman's aunt is man's aunt

∴ Woman is sister of man.

11. (d) The movements of Rasik from A to F are as shown in figure.

Since CD = AB + EF, so F lies in line with A.

Rasik's distance from original position A = AF = (AG + GF) = (BC + DE) = (30 + 15) m = 45m.

Also, F lies to the east of A.

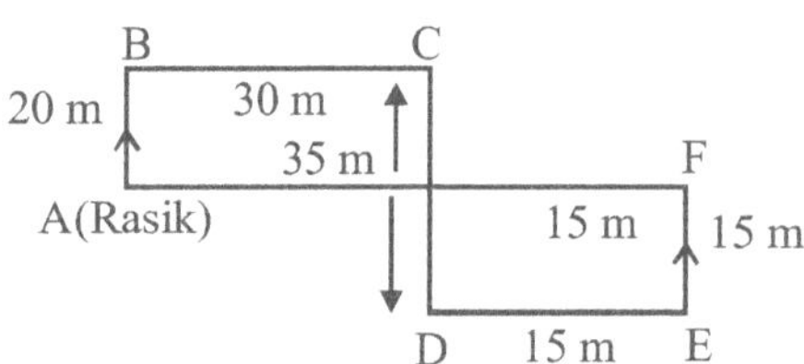

12. (b) There are (25 – 11 – 1) = 13 boys between Akash and Nikhil.
13. (b) Q > S, P > Q, R > Q

Age: As, Q > S, P > Q, R > Q

Also, P is the oldest.

∴ P > R > Q > S

Richness : As, P > Q, S > P

Also R is he richest.

∴ R > S > P > Q

14. (b) Clearly, the given words when arranged in the order of various events as they occur in man's life, term the sequence: Birth – Education – Marriage – Death – Funeral. So the correct order becomes 1 5 4 2 3
15. (c) Capsules are different from injection but both are uses as antibiotics.
16. (a) Conclusions I: True

Conclusions II: False

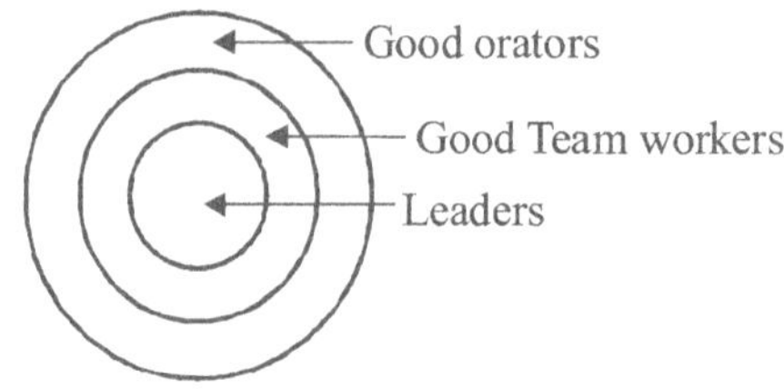

17. (a)

$- \Rightarrow \div, + \Rightarrow \times$
$\div \Rightarrow -, \times \Rightarrow +$

Option (a) : $6 \div 20 \times 12 + 7 - 1 = 70$
L.H.S. $= 6 - 20 + 12 \times 7 \div 1$
$= 6 - 20 + 84$
$= 90 - 20 = 70$ R. H.S.

18. (c) $2 \times 7 \times 9 = 126$
$7 \times 3 \times 8 = 168$
$9 \times 4 \times x = 216$
$\Rightarrow \quad x = 6$

19. (b) $4^2 + 1^2 + 2^2 + 3^2 = 30$
$6^2 + 3^2 + 4^2 + 15 = 286$
$3^2 + 4^2 + x + 12^2 = 218$
$169 + x = 218$
$x = 218 - 169 = \sqrt{49} = 7$

20. (c) When the sheet shown in fig. (X) is folded to form a cube, then the face with shading lies opposite to the free bearing a square, the face bearing a dot lies opposite to a blank face and the face bearing a circle (with a '+' sign inside it) lies opposite to another blank face. The cubes in figures (2) and (4) have the shaded face adjacent to the face bearing a square. Therefore, the cubes in these two figures cannot be formed. Hence, only cubes in figures (1) and (3) can be formed.

21. (c)

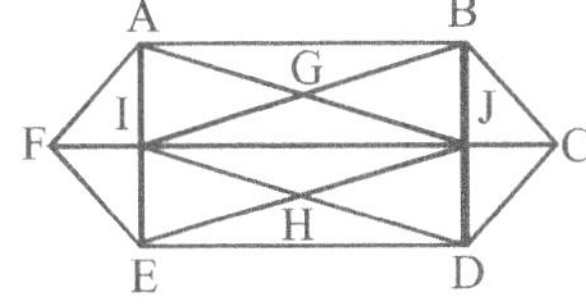

The triangles are:
ΔFAE; ΔFAI; ΔFIE; ΔCBD;
ΔCBJ; ΔCJD; ΔAIJ; ΔBJI;
ΔBJA; ΔAIB; ΔIED; ΔJDE;
ΔJDI; ΔIEJ; ΔGAB; ΔGAI;
ΔGJI; ΔGJB; ΔHJI; ΔHDE;
ΔHEI; ΔHJD; ΔAJF; ΔEFJ;
ΔBCI; ΔCDI; ΔIBD; ΔJEA.

22. (b)

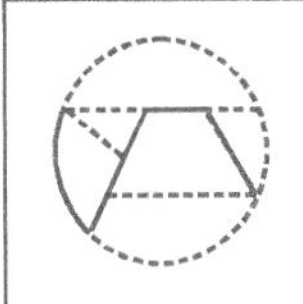

23. (c) Unfolded step I

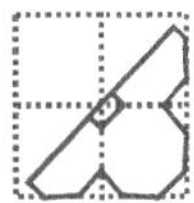

step II

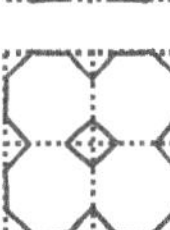

24. (c)

25. (d) DRUK cannot be formed using TRIVANDRUM as it does not contain letter 'K'.

26. (a) Complete remainder $= d_1d_2r_3 + d_1r_2 + r_1$
$= 3 \times 5 \times 4 + 3 \times 2 + 1 = 67$
Divided 67 by 8, 5 and 3, the remainders are 3, 3, 1.

27. (b) Clearly, unit's digit in the given product = unit's digit in $7^{153} \times 1^{72}$.
Now, 7^4 gives unit digit 1.
$\therefore$ 7^{153} gives unit digit $(1 \times 7) = 7$.
Also 1^{72} gives unit digit 1.
Hence, unit's digit in the product $= (7 \times 1) = 7$.

28. (d) CP of wheat $= 30 \times 45 =$ ₹1350
40% of 30 kg = 12 kg
SP of 12 kg $= 12 \times 50 =$ ₹600
For 25% profit, total SP of all the wheat is

$$1350 \times \frac{125}{100} = 1350 \times \frac{5}{4} = ₹\frac{6750}{4} = ₹\,1687.5$$

Remaining wheat $(30 - 12) = 18$ kg.
Rate of remaining wheat

$$= \frac{1087.5}{18} \approx ₹60$$

29. (d) Given that

1 Goats $= \frac{3}{2}$ sheeps.

Now, 2 goats + 9 sheeps

$= 2 \times \frac{3}{2}$ sheeps + 9 sheeps

= 12 sheeps

Here $M_1D_1 = M_2D_2$

$\Rightarrow \quad 6 \times 50 = 12 \times d_2$

$d_2 = 25$ days

30. (d) Let the third number be 100. Then, the first and second numbers will be 20 and 50, respectively.

Required % $= \frac{20}{50} \times 100 = 40\%$

31. (a) Let the cost of production of the table be ₹ x. Then, 125% of 115% of 110% of x = 1265

$\Rightarrow \frac{125}{100} \times \frac{115}{100} \times \frac{110}{100} \times x = 1265$

$\Rightarrow \frac{253}{160} x = 1265 \Rightarrow x = \left(\frac{1265 \times 160}{253}\right) =$ ₹ 800

32. (b) Rest part $= 1 - \left(\frac{1}{3} + \frac{1}{6}\right) = \frac{1}{2}$

Rate % per annum on total sum

$= \left(\frac{1}{3} \times 3\right) + \left(\frac{1}{6} \times 6\right) + \left(\frac{1}{2} \times 8\right) = 6\%$

$\therefore P = \frac{600 \times 100}{6 \times 2} =$ ₹5,000

33. (b) Difference $= \frac{PR^2}{10000}$

$\Rightarrow \quad 6 = \frac{P \times 5 \times 5}{10000}$

$\Rightarrow \quad 6 \times 400 =$ ₹2400.

34. (a) 50 men complete 0.4 work in 25 days. Applying the work rule,

$m_1 \times d_1 \times w_2 = m_2 \times d_2 \times w_1$

we have,

$50 \times 25 \times 0.6 = m_2 \times 25 \times 0.4$

or $m_2 = \frac{50 \times 25 \times 0.6}{25 \times 0.4} = 75$ men

Number of additional men required $= (75 - 50) = 25$

35. (d) Let after t hours they meet then,

$3t + 4t = 17.5 \Rightarrow t = 2.5$

$\therefore$ Time = 10 am + 2.5 h = 12 : 30pm

36. (c) Here $x_1 = 4,\ x_2 = -2,\ y_1 = -1,\ y_2 = 4$ and $m_1 = 3$ and $m_2 = 5$

$\therefore x = \frac{m_1x_2 + m_2x_1}{m_1 + m_2} = \frac{3(-2) + 5(4)}{3+5} = \frac{7}{4}$

and

$y = \frac{m_1y_2 + m_2y_1}{m_1 + m_2} = \frac{3(4) + 5(-1)}{3+5} = \frac{7}{8}$

$\therefore$ The required point is $\left(\frac{7}{4}, \frac{7}{8}\right)$

37. (a) Let Sudha's and Neeta's present ages be 6x and 7x years respectively.

According to the question.

$\frac{6x-5}{7x-5} = \frac{5}{6}$

$\Rightarrow 36x - 30 = 35x - 25$

$\Rightarrow x = 5$

$\therefore$ Sudha's present age $= 6 \times 5 = 30$ years

38. (b) Let the common base be x m.

Now, area of the triangle = area of the parallelogram

$\frac{1}{2} \times x \times$ Altitude of the triangle $= x \times 100$

Altitude of the triangle = 200 m

39. (c) After 5 minutes (before meeting), the top runner covers 2 rounds i.e., 400 m and the last runner covers 1 round i.e., 200 m.

$\therefore$ Top runner covers 800 m race in 10 minutes.

40. (b) The equation of the line is

$\frac{(y - y_1)}{(x - x_1)} = \frac{(y_2 - y_1)}{(x_2 - x_1)}$

i.e., $\frac{(y-1)}{(x+1)} = \frac{-4-1}{2+1} \Rightarrow \frac{y-1}{x+1} = \frac{-5}{3}$

$\Rightarrow 3y - 3 = -5x - 5 \Rightarrow 5x + 3y + 2 = 0$

41. (b) X's one day's work $= \frac{1}{25}$th part of whole work.

Y's one day's work $= \frac{1}{30}$th part of whole work.

Their one day's work $= \frac{1}{25} + \frac{1}{30} = \frac{1}{150}$th part of whole work.

Now, work is done in 5 days

$= \frac{11}{150} \times 5 = \frac{11}{30}$th of whole work

$\therefore$ Remaining work $= 1-\frac{11}{30}=\frac{19}{30}$th of whole work

Now, $\frac{1}{30}$th work is done by Y in one day.

$\therefore$ $\frac{19}{30}$th work is done by Y in

$\frac{1}{1/30}\times\frac{19}{30}=19$ days

42. (b) Error = 1 kg – 960 g
$= 1000\text{ g} - 960\text{ g} = 40\text{ g}.$

$\therefore$ Gain % $=\frac{40}{1000-40}\times 100$

$=\frac{40}{960}\times 100 = 4\frac{1}{6}\%$

43. (d) $x = 2+\sqrt{3}$

$\frac{1}{x}=\frac{1}{2+\sqrt{3}}\times\frac{2-\sqrt{3}}{2-\sqrt{3}}=2-\sqrt{3}$

$x^2+\frac{1}{x^2}=\left(x+\frac{1}{x}\right)^2-2$

$=\left(2+\sqrt{3}+2-\sqrt{3}\right)^2-2$

$=16-2=14$

44. (c) $a^2+b^2+c^2=2a-2b-2$
$(a^2-2a+1)+(b^2+2b+1)+c^2=0$
$(a-1)^2+(b+1)^2+c^2=0$
This equation is possible if
$a-1=0, b+1=0$ and $c=0$
$a=1, b=-1, c=0$
$3a-2b+c=3\times 1-2\times(-1)+0$
$=3+2=5$

45. (a) Working with the options, for x = 0, the least value of

$f(x)=3^x+3^{-x}=2$

Alternate :

Let $A = 3^x$ and $\frac{1}{A}=3^{-x}$

$\Rightarrow$ Both are positive.

Now, A.M. of A and $\frac{1}{A}$ is greater than or equal to their G.M.

i.e. $\frac{A+\frac{1}{A}}{2}\geq\sqrt{A.\frac{1}{A}}$

or $A+\frac{1}{A}\geq 2$

or $3^x+3^{-x}\geq 2.$

46. (d) Required difference

$=\left(\frac{19-11}{100}\right)\times 120000=9600$

47. (c) Required percentage

$=\frac{10200}{120000}\times 100=8.5\%$

48. (d) Estimated cost of furniture and miscellaneous expenditures

$=\left(\frac{13+8}{100}\right)\times 120000=25200$

Actual cost of furniture

$=\frac{88}{100}\times\frac{13}{100}\times 120000=13728$

Actual cost of furniture and miscellaneous expenditure
$=13728+10200=23928$
Total expenditure of the family
$=120000-25200+23928=118728$

49. (a) Let the breadth of the rectangular plot be x metre.
$\therefore$ Length $= 3x$ metre
According to the question,
$3x\times x=7803$

$\Rightarrow x^2=\frac{7803}{3}=2601$

$\therefore x=\sqrt{2601}=51$ metre

50. (d) Internal diameter of the tube = 6 cm

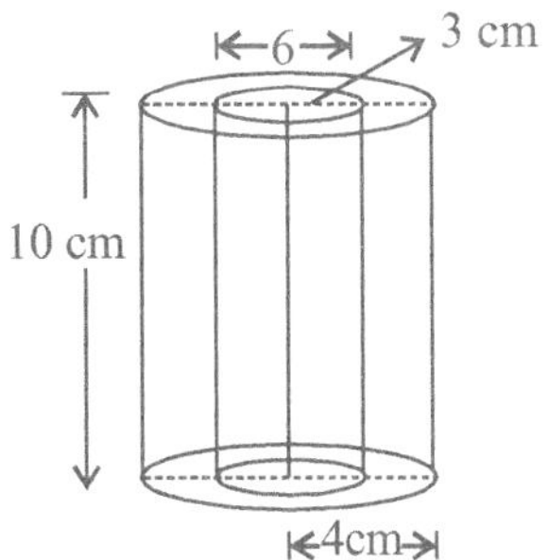

∴ Internal radius (r) = 3 cm
Height of the tube (h) = 10 cm
Thickness of the metal = 1 cm

∴ Outer radius (R) = Thickness of the metal + Internal radius = 1 + 3 = 4 cm

∴ Outer curved surface area

$= 2\pi rh + \pi R^2 + \pi(R^2 - r^2)$

$= 2\pi(3)(10) + \pi(4)^2 + \pi(16-9)$

$= 60\pi + 16\pi + 7\pi = 83\pi$ sq cm

51. (c) 52. (d) 53 (d) 54. (a) 55. (d)
56. (b) 57. (b) 58. (b) 59. (b) 60. (b)
61. (c) 62. (d) 63. (d)

64. (a) B is the opening line, as it introduces the narrative. This will be followed by A, which furthers the narrative. D is the reply to question asked in A and C has the rebuttal to the answer given in D, So the sequences is BADC.

65. (b) D is the opening sentence followed by A, which introduces the second subject. Then will be B, which has the pronoun subject 'he' referring to the noun subject in A. Since A ends with a negative verb – fails, the following sentence can be positive only if preceeded by the conjunction but, so B will followed C.

66. (c) Liberal is the appropriate answer. Liberal means having political or social views favouring reform and progress. Orthodox denotes adhering to what is commonly accepted. Rigid means incapable of or resistant to bending while flamboyant means elaborately or excessively ornamented.

67. (b)

68. (a) Testimony denotes something that serves as evidence. Her efforts are a testimony to her devotion. Evidence, declaration, witness are not to the purpose.

69. (c) Open is the right word which can fill in. Other options powerful, engaging, systematic are just out of context.

70. (d) 71. (b) 72. (c) 73. (b) 74. (a)
75. (c) 76. (d) 77. (a) 78. (d) 79. (a)

80. (a) Our country is mentioned in the constitution by the name of India and Bharat.

81. (a) Scalars are quantities that have magnitude only; they are independent of direction. Vectors have both magnitude and direction. Momentum is the product of the mass and velocity of an object (p = mv). Momentum is a vector quantity, since it has a direction as well as a magnitude. The rest of quantities in option pressure, work and energy have magnitude but not direction.

82. (a) Fuel value can be expressed in terms of calorific value of fuel. The calorific value of a fuel is the amount of heat produced by burning 1 kg of fuel. Hydrogen has the highest calorific value of (141,790 KJ/kg) thus have highest fuel value. Calorific value of charcoal, natural gas and gasoline are (29,600; 43,000; 47,300 kJ/kg) respectively. Natural gas majorly consists of methane.

83. (a) Thyroxine hormone and tri-iodothyronine hormone are secreted by thyroid follicular cells of thyroid gland. The major component of thyroxine hormone is iodine. Deficiency of iodine causes goitre in human.

84. (d) The major component of honey is fructose. Composition of honey in (percentage)

Fructose – 38.2 Sucrose – 1.5
Glucose – 31 Minerals – 0.5
Water – 17.1
Maltose – 7.2
Carbohydrate – 4.2

85. (c) Generally blindness is caused by the dryness and hardness of cornea. Cornea is a clear layer which helps passing of light. It is an outer layer and can be transfer from one person to another.

86. (b) 87. (b) 88. (a) 89. (c) 90. (b)
91. (d) 92. (b) 93. (c) 94. (d) 95. (a)
96. (c) 97. (b) 98. (d) 99. (a) 100. (c)

PRACTICE SET- 9

GENERAL INTELLIGENCE & REASONING

1. 'Hygrometer' is related to 'Humidity' in the same way as 'Sphygmomanometer' is related to
(a) Pressure (b) Blood Pressure
(c) Precipitation (d) Heart Beat

2. HEATER : KBDQHO : : COOLER : ?
(a) ALRHV (b) FLRIHO
(c) FLIRHO (d) FRLIHO

3. 12 : 30 : : 20:?
(a) 25 (b) 32 (c) 35 (d) 42

DIRECTIONS (Qs. 4 – 5) : *Find the odd word/letters/ number pair from the given alternatives.*

4. (a) Microbe (b) Microflim
(c) Microphone (d) Microscope

5. (a) BDGK (b) JLOS
(c) HJMQ (d) MORU

DIRECTIONS (Qs. 6 – 7) : *Complete the given series.*

6. YEB, WFD, UHG, SKI, (?)
(a) QOL (b) TOL (c) QGL (d) QNL

7. 2 12 36 80 150 ?
(a) 194 (b) 210 (c) 252 (d) 258

8. In a certain code language OUTCOME is written as OQWWEQOE. How is REFRACT written in that code?
(a) RTGITCET (b) RTGTICET
(c) RTGITECT (d) RTGICTET

9. If A = 1, PAT = 37 then TAP = ?
(a) 73 (b) 37 (c) 36 (d) 38

10. Introducing Rajesh, Neha said, "His brother's father is the only son of my grand father". How Neha is related to Rajesh?
(a) Sister (b) Daughter
(c) Mother (d) Niece

11. Ruchi's house is to the right of Vani's house at a distance of 20 metres in the same row facing North. Shabana's house is in the North- East direction of Vani's house at a distance of 25 metres. Determine that Ruchi's house is in which direction with respect of Shabana's house?
(a) North-East (b) East
(c) South (d) West

12. If the positions of the first and the fifth digits of the number 83721569 are interchanged, similarly, the positions of the second and the sixth digits are interchanged, and so on, which of the following will be the third from the right end after the rearrangement?
(a) 6 (b) 3 (c) 2 (d) 7

13. Some boys are sitting in a line. Mahendra is on 17th place from left and Surendra is on 18th place from right. There are 8 boys in between them. How many boys are there in the line?
(a) 43 (b) 42 (c) 41 (d) 44

DIRECTIONS (Qs. 14 – 15): *In the following questions find the missing number*

14.

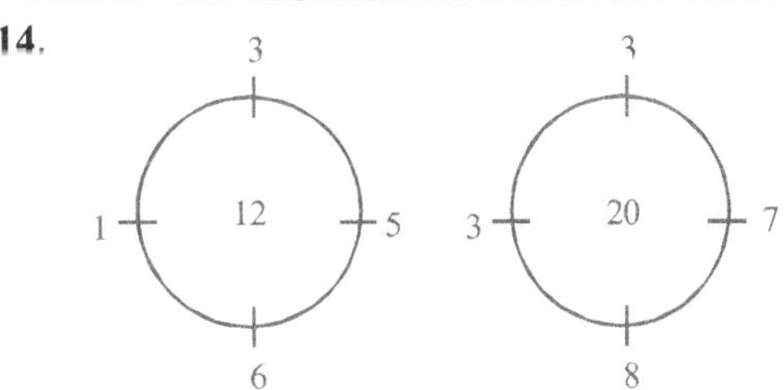

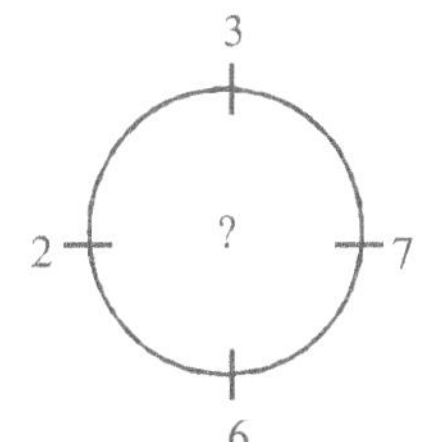

(a) 10 (b) 15 (c) 20 (d) 25

15.

21	24	36
11	14	12
3	?	4
77	112	108

(a) 2 (b) 4 (c) 3 (d) 5

DIRECTION (Q. 16): *Arrange the following in a logical order:*

16. 1. Millenium 2. Diamond Jubilee
3. Silver Jubilee 4. Centenary
5. Golden Jubilee
(a) 2, 3, 5, 4, 1 (b) 2, 5, 3, 1, 4
(c) 3, 5, 2, 4, 1 (d) 2, 3, 5, 1, 4

DIRECTION (Q. 17) : *In the following questions, a group of letters is given which are numbered 1, 2, 3, 4, 5 and 6. Below a re given four alternatives containing combinations of these numbers. Select that combination of numbers so that letters arranged accordingly form a meaningful word.*

17. INLASG
123456
(a) 6, 1, 3, 5, 4, 2 (b) 5, 1, 6, 2, 4, 3
(c) 3, 4, 6, 1, 2, 5 (d) 2, 4, 3, 6, 1, 5

18. In the following venn diagram identify the letter which denotes players who are also doctors but not artist.

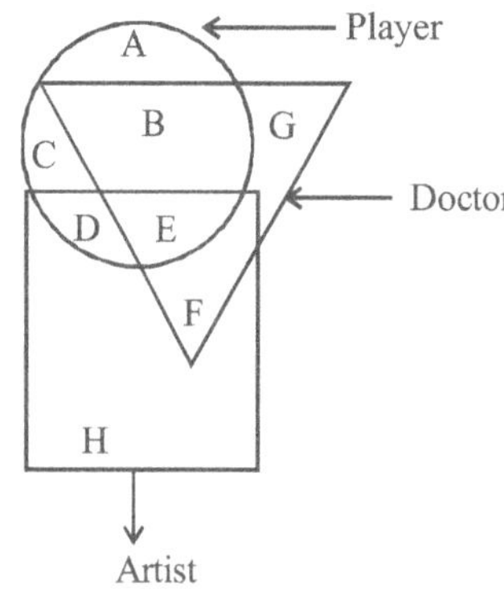

(a) B+E (b) E
(c) B (d) A

DIRECTION (Q. 19) : *In question the belows is given two statements followed by two conclusions. You have to take the given statements to be true even if they seem to be at variance with commonly known facts. Read all the conclusions and then decide which of the given statements disregarding commonly know facts. Given Answer.*

Give answer (a) If only conclusion I follows.
Give answer (b) if only conclusion II follows.
Give answer (c) if either I or II follows.
Give answer (d) if neither I nor II follows.

19. Statements:
All terrorists are human.
All humans are bad.

Conclusions:
I. All terrorists are bad.
II. No human can be a terrorist.

20. Which one of the following is correct?
6 * 4 * 9 * 15
(a) ×, =, – (b) ×, –, =
(c) =, ×, – (d) –, ×, =

21. If '–' stands for '+', '+' stands for '×', '×' stands for '–' then which one of the following is not correct?
(a) $22+7-3\times 9=148$
(b) $33\times 5-10+20=228$
(c) $7+28-3\times 52=127$
(d) $44-9+6\times 11=87$

22. The four different positions of a dice are given below: Find the number on the face opposite the face showing 6?

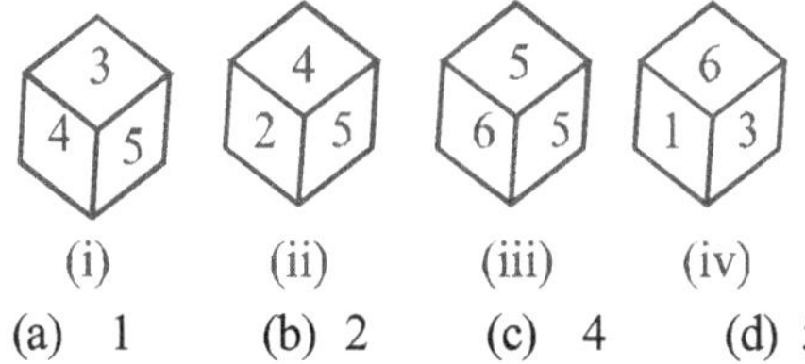

(a) 1 (b) 2 (c) 4 (d) 5

DIRECTION (Q. 23): *Which answer figure will complete the pattern in the question figure ?*

23.

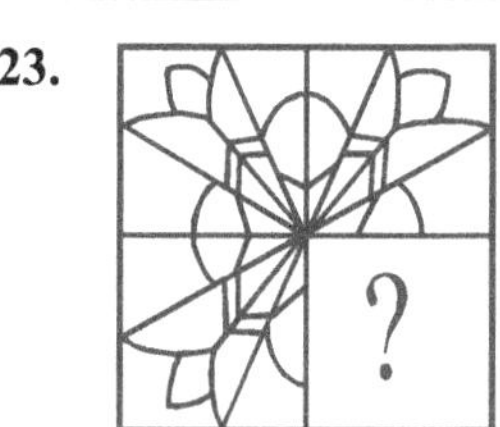

(a) 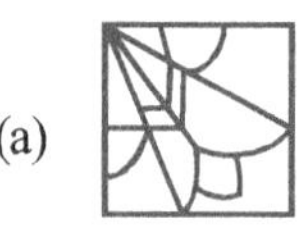 (b) 

(c) 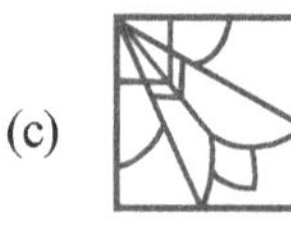 (d) 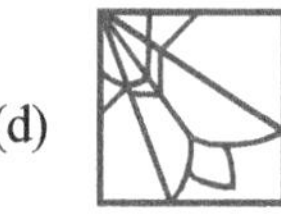

24. How many triangles are there in the given figure?

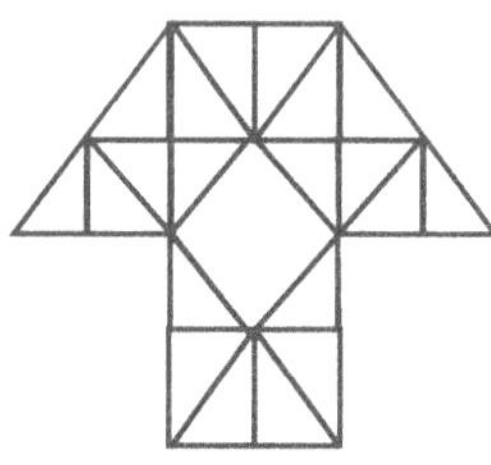

(a) 29 (b) 38 (c) 40 (d) 35

DIRECTION (Q. 25) : *In the following question a set of three figures A, B and C showing a sequence of folding of a piece of paper. Fig. (C) shows the manner in which the folded paper has been cut. These three figures are followed by four answer figures from which you have to choose a figure which would most closely resemble the unfolded form of fig. (C).*

25.

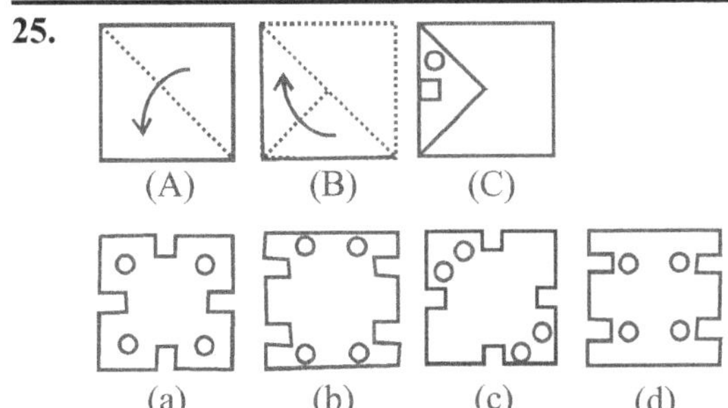

QUANTITATIVE APTITUDE

26. If $3\frac{4}{5}$ is subtracted from $6\frac{3}{5}$ and difference is multiplied by 355 then what will be the final number?
(a) 1004 (b) 884 (c) 774 (d) 994

27. How many times must 79 be subtracted from 5×10^4 so as to obtain 43759?
(a) 77 (b) 78 (c) 79 (d) 80

28. In a class of 65 students and 4 teachers, each student got sweets that are 20% of the total number of students and each teacher got sweets that are 40% of the total number of students. How many sweets were there?
(a) 845 (b) 897 (c) 949 (d) 104

29. An order was placed for supply of carpet of breadth 3 metres, the length of carpet was 1.44 times of breadth. Subsequently the breadth and length were increased by 25 and 40 per cent respectively. At the rate of ₹45 per square metre, what would be the increase in the cost of the carpet?
(a) ₹1020.6 (b) ₹398.8
(c) ₹437.4 (d) ₹583.2

30. In a mixture of milk and water the proportion of water by weight was 75% if in the 60 gms mixture 15 gms water was added, what would be the percentage of water in the new mixture?
(a) 75% (b) 80% (c) 90% (d) 100%

31. The sum of five numbers is 290. The average of the first two numbers is 48.5 and the average of last two numbers is 53.5. What is the third number?
(a) 72 (b) 84 (c) 96 (d) 86

32. The average weight of a class of 15 boys and 10 girls is 38.4 kg. If the average weight of the boys is 40 kg, then what is the average weight of the girls?
(a) 36.5 kg (b) 35 kg
(c) 36 kg (d) 34.6 kg

33. The angle of elevation of a cloud from a point 200 m above a lake is 30° and the angle of depression of its reflection in the lake is 60°. The height of the cloud is
(a) 200m (b) 300m (c) 400m (d) 600m

34. A and B can finish a work in 10 days while B and C can do it in 18 days. A started the work, worked for 5 days, then B worked for 10 days and the remaining work was finished by C in 15 days. In how many days could C alone have finished the whole work?
(a) 30 days (b) 15 days
(c) 45 days (d) 24 days

35. ABCD is a cyclic quadrilateral in which BC || AD, $\angle ADC = 110°$ and $\angle BAC = 50°$ find $\angle DAC$
(a) 60° (b) 45° (c) 90° (d) 120°

36. In a triangle ABC, the internal bisector of the angle A meets BC at D. If AB = 4, AC = 3 and $\angle A = 60°$, then the length of AD is
(a) $2\sqrt{3}$ (b) $\frac{12\sqrt{3}}{7}$ (c) $15\sqrt{\frac{3}{8}}$ (d) $6\sqrt{\frac{3}{7}}$

37. Some amount out of ₹7000 was lent at 6% per annum and the remaining at 4% per annum. If the total simple interest from both the fractions in 5 yrs was ₹1600, find the sum lent at 6 % per annum.
(a) 2000 (b) 16000
(c) 5400 (d) 3200

38. A is 30% more efficient than B. How much time will they, working together, take to complete a job which A along could have done in 23 days?
(a) 11 days (b) 13 days
(c) $20\frac{3}{17}$ days (d) None of these

39. ABCD is a square, F is the mid-point of AB and E is a point on BC such that BE is one-third of BsC. If area of $\Delta FBE = 108$ m^2, then the length of AC is :
(a) 63m (b) $36\sqrt{2}$ m
(c) $63\sqrt{2}$ m (d) $72\sqrt{2}$ m

40. If $a^2 = b + c, b^2 = c + a, c^2 = a + b$, then the value of
$$\frac{1}{1+a} + \frac{1}{b+1} + \frac{1}{1+c}$$
(a) abc (b) $a^2 b^2 c^2$
(c) 1 (d) 0

41. If $x+\frac{1}{y}=1$ and $y+\frac{1}{z}=1$, what is the value of xyz?
(a) 1 (b) – 1
(c) 0 (d) $\frac{1}{2}$

42. If p = 999, then the value of
$\sqrt[3]{p(p^2+3p+3)+1}$ is
(a) 1000 (b) 999
(c) 998 (d) 1002

43. By selling 33 metres of cloth, a man gains the sale price of 11 metres. The gain % is
(a) 50% (b) 25%
(c) $33\frac{1}{3}\%$ (d) 20%

44. The income of A is 150% of the income of B and the income of C is 120% of the income of A. If the total income of A, B and C together is ₹ 86000, what is C's income ?
(a) ₹30000 (b) ₹32000
(c) ₹20000 (d) ₹36000

45. A man walks half of the journey at 4 km/h by cycle does one third of journey at 12 km/h and rides the remainder journey in a horse cart at 9 km/h, thus completing the whole journey in 6 hours and 12 minutes. The length of the journey is
(a) 36 km (b) $\frac{1332}{67}$ km
(c) 40 km (d) 28 km

DIRECTIONS (Qs. 46-48): *Study the following graph carefully to answer these questions.*

Quantity of various items sold and price per kg.

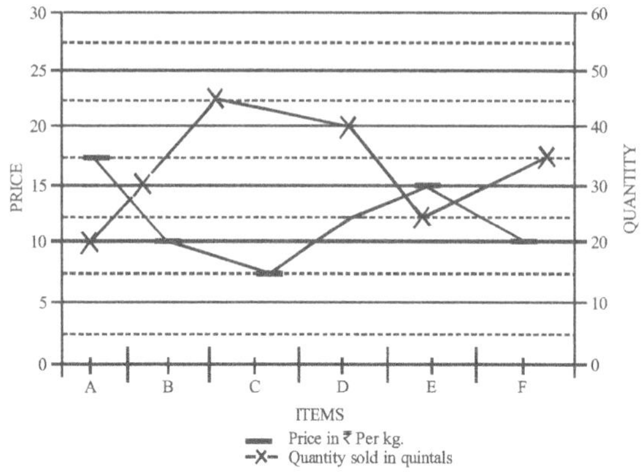

46. If the quantity sold of item D increased by 50% and the price reduced by 10%, what was the total value of the quantity sold for Item D?
(a) ₹675 (b) ₹6750
(c) ₹67550 (d) ₹67500

47. **Approximately**, what is the average price per kg of items A, B and C ?
(a) ₹9.50 (b) ₹8
(c) ₹7.50 (d) ₹11.6

48. What is the ratio between the total values of quantity sold for items E and F respectively?
(a) 15 : 14 (b) 3 : 2
(c) 5 : 7 (d) 7 : 5

49. From the top of a cliff 200 m high, the angles of depression of the top and bottom of a tower are observed to be 30° and 45°, respectively. What is the height of the tower?
(a) 400 m (b) $400\sqrt{3}$ m
(c) $400/\sqrt{3}$ m (d) None of these

50. For a plot of land of 100 m × 80 m, the length to be raised by spreading the earth from stack of a rectangular base 10 m × 8 m and vertical section being a trapezium of height 2 m. The top of the stack is 8 m × 5 m. How many centimeters can the level raised?
(a) 3 cm (b) 2.5 m
(c) 2 cm (d) 1.5 cm

ENGLISH LANGUAGE

DIRECTIONS (Qs. 51 to 53): *Four alternative are given for the Idiom/Phrase underlined in the sentence. Choose the alternative which best expresses the meaning of the Idiom/Phrase.*

51. Sachin prefers to have few friends who are as true as steel rather than have fifty acquaintances who refuse to recognize him when he needs them most.
(a) who are loyal
(b) who always speak the truth
(c) who are always with him
(d) who are influential

52. I am waiting for the old man to kick the bucket so that I can get his money.
(a) to kill (b) to die
(c) to absolve (d) to conclude

53. For your safety and the safety of others, always pay attention to the traffic signals.
(a) overlook (b) take head of
(c) glance at (d) repair

DIRECTIONS (Qs. 54 to 55): *A sentence/ a part of the sentence is underlined. Below are given alternatives to the underlined part at (a), (b), (c) which may improve the sentence. Choose the correct alternative. In case no improvement is needed your answer is (d).*

54. He parked his vehicle under the shade of a tree.
(a) on (b) in
(c) beneath (d) No improvement

55. God has bestowed man unusual gifts.
(a) bestowed with man
(b) bestowed for man
(c) bestowed on man
(d) No improvement

DIRECTIONS (Qs. 56 to 57) : *Out of the four alternatives, choose the one which can be substituted for the given words/sentences.*

56. A style full of words –
(a) verbose (b) pedantic
(c) rhetorical (d) abundant

57. To issue a thunderous verbal attack –
(a) languish (b) fulminate
(c) animate (d) invigorate

DIRECTIONS (Qs. 58 to 59): *Four words are given in each question, out of which only one word is correctly spelt. Find the correctly spelt word from the given option.*

58. (a) Momentary (b) Momentery
(c) Mommentary (d) Momenntery

59. (a) Misschievous (b) Mischievous
(c) Mischivious (d) Misschivious

DIRECTIONS (Qs. 60-64) : *In the following passages, some of the words have been left out. First read the passage over and try to understand what it is about. Then, fill in the blanks with the help of the alternatives given.*

PASSAGE

The Solar System has been a complicated wonder for the astronomers. This is a **60** to which we may never have the exact answer. Man has wondered **61** the age of the Earth **62** ancient times. There were all kinds of **63** that seemed to have the **64**.

60. (a) problem (b) question
(c) matter (d) query

61. (a) around (b) out
(c) about (d) on

62. (a) since (b) during
(c) around (d) from

63. (a) ideas (b) opinions
(c) stories (d) matters

64. (a) solution (b) novel
(c) book (d) answer

DIRECTIONS (Qs. 65 to 66): *Some part of the sentences have errors and some are correct. Find out which part of a sentence has an error and mark the correct option accordingly*

65. I agree to Mr. Saxena.
(a) Mr Saxena (b) No error
(c) agree to (d) I

66. The plump lady eats three times a day.
(a) No error (b) three times a day
(c) lady eats (d) The plump

DIRECTIONS (Qs. 67 to 68): *Sentences given with blanks to be filled in with an appropriate word. Four alternatives are suggested for each question. Choose the correct alternative out of the four.*

67. I realized that my pocket _____ picked.
(a) had been (b) was
(c) is (d) has been

68. No sooner did he go in _____ he came out.
(a) then (b) when
(c) and (d) than

DIRECTIONS (Qs. 69 to 70): *Out of the four alternatives, choose the one which best expresses the meaning of the given word.*

69. Lascivious
(a) Treacherous (b) Erotic
(c) Lustful (d) Vicious

70. Persuasions
(a) Personalities (b) Tastes
(c) Qualifications (d) Convictions

DIRECTIONS (Qs. 71 to 72): *Choose the option opposite in meaning to the given word.*

71. Timorous
(a) Trembling (b) Cowardly
(c) Bright (d) Bold

72. Briskly
(a) Sluggishly (b) Inadvertently
(c) Oddly (d) Secretly

DIRECTION (Q. 73): *In each of the following questions, a sentence has been given in Direct/ Indirect Speech. Out of the four alternatives suggested select the one which best expresses the same sentence in Indirect/Direct Speech.*

73. The teacher punished the boys who had not done their home work.
(a) The boys who had not done their homework had been punished by their teacher.
(b) The boys were punished by their teacher who had not done their homework.
(c) The boys who had not done their homework were punished by the teacher.
(d) The boys who had not done their homework were being punished by the teacher.

DIRECTIONS (Qs. 74-75): *In the following questions, the 1st and the last sentences of the passage are numbered 1 and 6. The rest of the passage is split into four parts and named P, Q, R and S. These four parts are not given in their proper order. Read the sentence and find out which of the four combinations is correct. Then find the correct answer.*

74. 1. Most of the people acquire
P. which makes them hesitant
Q. their ancestral culture and
R. to accept new ideas and theories of
S. tradition without questioning them,
6. the changing world.
(a) SPRQ (b) QRSP
(c) QSPR (d) PQRS

75. 1. Local industries often
P. protest the high salaries
Q. that this will unreasonably raise
R. arguing vehemently
S. offered by multinational firms
6. all wages to an excessive leave
(a) RQPS (b) PSRQ
(c) SRQP (d) PRSQ

GENERAL AWARENESS

76. Jiatrang Movement started in
(a) Nagaland (b) Tripura
(c) Manipur (d) Mizoram

77. Which term is not used in the preamble of the Indian constitution ?
(a) Republic (b) Integrity
(c) Federal (d) Socialist

78. The Prime Minister of India is the head of the
(a) State Government
(b) Central Government
(c) Both the State and Central Government
(d) None of them

79. How many types of writs can be issued by the supreme court?
(a) 2 (b) 3
(c) 5 (d) 6

80. Which zone of a candle flame is the hottest ?
(a) Dark innermost zone
(b) Outermost zone
(c) Middle luminous zone
(d) Central zone

81. Which one of the following is used to remove Astigmatism for a human eye?
(a) Concave lens (b) Convex lens
(c) Cylindrical lens (d) Prismatic lens

82. Which one of the following is a mixed fertilizer?
(a) Urea
(b) CAN
(c) Ammonium sulphate
(d) NPK

83. The most reactive among the halogens is
(a) Fluorine (b) Chlorine
(c) Bromine (d) Iodine

84. Which one of the following is present in chlorophyll which gives a green colour to plant leaves?
(a) Calcium (b) Magnesium
(c) Iron (d) Manganese

85. In human beings, the opening of the stomach into the small intestine is called
(a) caecum (b) ileum
(c) oeaophagus (d) pylorus

86. 'India of our Dreams' is a book written by
(a) Dr. S. Radhakrishnan
(b) Dr. C. Subramanian
(c) M.V. Kamath
(d) Dr. Rajendra Prasad

87. With which game is 'Bully' associated ?
(a) Cricket (b) Football
(c) Golf (d) Hockey

88. Indian Standard Time relates to
(a) 75.5° E longitude
(b) 82.5° E longitude
(c) 90.5° E longitude
(d) 0° longitude

89. US embassy launched a scholarship program for women of which country ?
(a) Myanmar (b) Afghanistan
(b) Sri Lanka (d) Bangladesh

90. Which language was patronised by the the rules of Delhi Sultanate?
(a) Hindi (b) Arabic
(c) Persian (d) Turkish

91. The earnings of the kings in the Medieval age were mostly derived from
(a) Offerings made at the temples
(b) Land revenue
(c) Trade
(d) Industrial production

92. 'Mansabdars' in Mughal period were
(a) Landlords and Zamindars
(b) Officials of the state
(c) Those who had to give revenue
(d) Revenue collectors

93. Which Indian States are known for their bandhani work?
(a) Rajasthan and Maharashtra
(b) Gujarat and Rajasthan
(c) Tamil Nadu and Karnataka
(d) Haryana and Gujarat

94. What type of mirror is used by motorists to see the road behind them ?
(a) Convex (b) Concave
(c) Plane (d) Concavo-convex

95. Who was the first Indian to win an individual medal in olympics ?
(a) Milkha Singh (b) P T Usha
(c) Karnam Mallshwari (d) KD Jadhav

96. First Governor General of India, after independence was
(a) C. Rajagopalachari
(b) Jawaharlal Nehru
(c) Lord Mountbatten
(d) Rajendra Prasad

97. Which of the following states is set to become the India's first smoke-free State?
(a) Karnataka
(b) Kerala
(c) Tamil Nadu
(d) Andhra Pradesh

98. Who has been named for 2018 Hridaynath Award for lifetime achievement?
(a) Javed Akhtar
(b) Amitabh Bachchan
(c) Mohammed Zahur Khayyam Hashmi
(d) Hariprasad Chaurasia

99. On which date, the 2018 World Trauma Day (WTD) is observed recently?
(a) October 15
(b) October 19
(c) October 16
(d) October 17

100. What is the theme of the 12th Asia-Europe Meeting (ASEM-2018)?
(a) Working Together for a Sustainable and Secure Future
(b) Global Partners for Global Challenges
(c) 20 years of ASEM: Partnership for Future
(d) Biodiversity and Cultural Heritage

Hints & Explanations

1. (b) First is an instrument to measure the second.

2. (b)

H	E	A	T	E	R
+3 ↓	−3 ↓	+3 ↓	−3 ↓	+3 ↓	−3 ↓
K	B	D	Q	H	O

Similarly,

C	O	O	L	E	R
+3 ↓	−3 ↓	+3 ↓	−3 ↓	+3 ↓	−3 ↓
F	L	R	I	H	O

3. (d) $12 = 3^2 + 3$, $30 = 5^2 + 5$: $20 = 4^2 + 4$: $? = 6^2 + 6$

4. (a) Microbe is living organism others are scientific apparatus.

5. (d)

6. (a) 1st letter moves –2 steps each time.
2nd letter moves +1, +2, +3, +4 steps respectively.
3rd letter moves +2, +3, steps alternatively.

7. (c) $1^3 + 1^2 = 2, 2^3 + 2^2 = 12, 3^3 + 3^2 = 36$ and so on $\therefore 6^3 + 6^2 = 252$

8. (a)

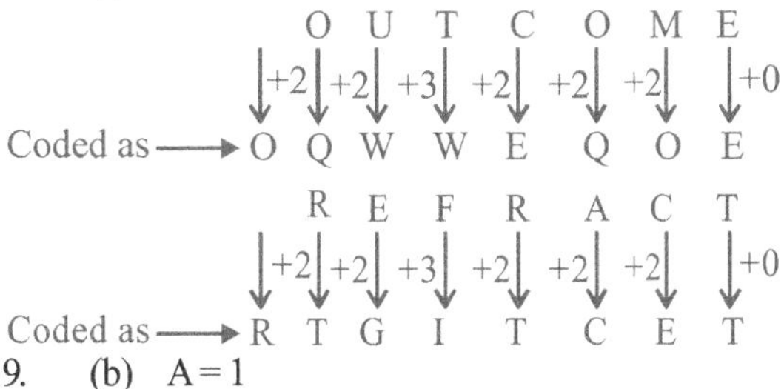

9. (b) A = 1

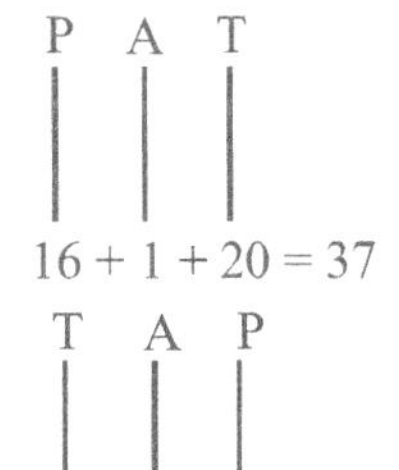

10. (a) Father of Rajesh's brother is the father of Rajesh. Rajesh's father is the only son of Neha's grandfather. Hence, Rajesh's father is Neha's father. So, Neha is the sister of Rajesh.

11. (c)

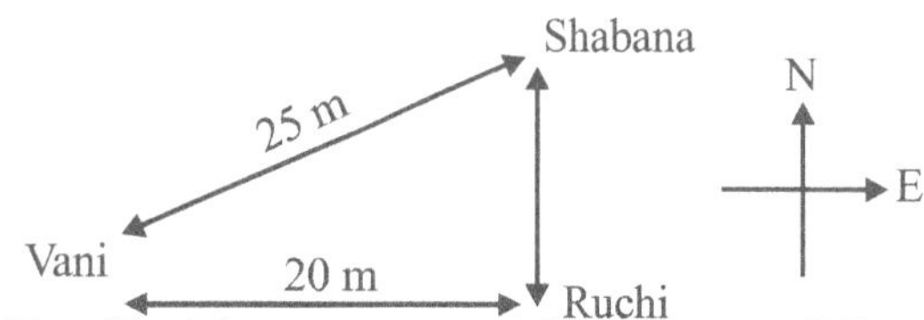

12. (b) New arrangement of numbers is as follows: 15698372
Hence, third number from right end is 3.

13. (a) Total boys

$$= \left[\begin{array}{c} \text{Mahendra's} \\ \text{place} \\ \text{from left} \end{array} + \begin{array}{c} \text{Surendra's} \\ \text{place} \\ \text{from right} \end{array} \right] + \left[\begin{array}{c} \text{Boys between} \\ \text{them} \end{array} \right]$$

$= [17 + 18] + 8 = 43$

14. (b) $(5-1) \times (6-3) = 12$
$(7-3) \times (8-3) = 20$
$(7-2) \times (6-3) = 15$

15. (c) As, $3 \times 7 = 21, 11 \times 7 = 77$
$4 \times 9 = 36,\ 12 \times 9 = 108$
Therefore, $14 \times 8 = 112$
$? \times 8 = 24$
$\boxed{? = 3}$

16. (c) Silver jublee - 25 yr.
Golden jublee - 50 yr.
Diamond jublee - 75 yr.
Centenary - 100 yr
Millennium - 1000 yr.

17. (b) SIGNAL

18. (c) Area common to ◯ and △.

19. (a) Conclusions:
I. (True)
II. (True)
Hence, option (a) is the correct answer.

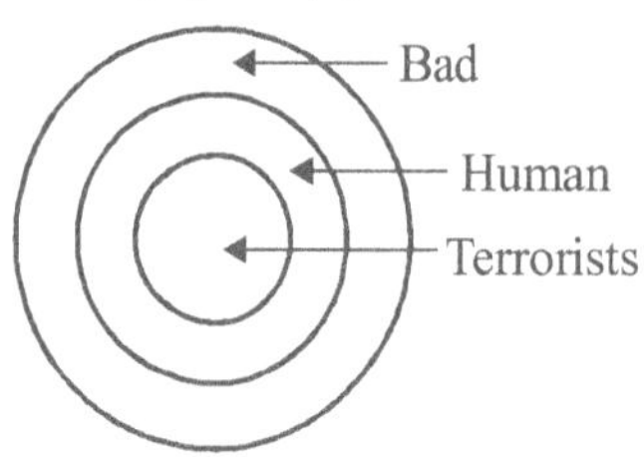

20. (b) $6 \times 4 - 9 = 15$

21. (c) By options –
(a) $22 \times 7 + 3 - 9 = 148$
$154 + 3 - 9$
$157 - 9 = 148$ (correct)
(b) $33 - 5 + 10 \times 20 = 228$
$33 - 5 + 200$
$200 + 33 - 5$
$233 - 5 = 228$ (correct)
(c) $7 \times 28 + 3 - 52 = 127$
$196 + 3 - 52$
$199 - 52 = 147$ (incorrect)
(d) $44 + 9 \times 6 - 11 = 87$
$44 + 54 - 11$
$98 - 11 = 87$ (correct)

22. (c) From figures (i), (ii) and (iii), we conclude that 3, 4, 2 and 6 lie adjacent to 5. Therefore, 1 must lie opposite 5.
From figures (i), (iii) and (iv), we conclude that 4, 5, 6 and 1 lie adjacent to 3. Therefore, 2 must lie opposite 3. Now, we have 1 opposite 5 and 2 opposite 3. Hence, 4 must lie opposite 6.

23. (b)

24. (c)

The simplest triangles are:
ΔPNO; ΔPNM; ΔMPQ;
ΔMQR; ΔAQP; ΔAQR;
ΔBRA; ΔBRC; ΔSRC;
ΔSCD; ΔSGR; ΔSGD;
ΔDFG; ΔDFE; ΔTLM;
ΔTJK; ΔTLK; ΔTIH;
The triangles composed of two components are:

ΔPON; ΔPMA; ΔAPR;
ΔRAM; ΔRAC; ΔRGC;
ΔDGC; ΔDGE; ΔMPR;
ΔGRD; ΔDGE; ΔTMK;
ΔTKI; ΔTIG
The triangles composed of four components are:
ΔAMO; ΔAMC; ΔCAG;
ΔCGE; ΔMKI; ΔGIK;
Other triangles are :ΔSPI; ΔDQK
Total number of triangles
$18+14+6+2=40$

25. (c)
26. (d) Required number
$=\left(6\frac{3}{5}-3\frac{4}{5}\right)\times 355=\left(\frac{33}{5}-\frac{19}{5}\right)\times 355$
$=\frac{14}{5}\times 355=994$
27. (c) Let x be the number of times, then
$79x+43759=50,000$
$\Rightarrow x=(50000-43759)\div 79=\frac{6241}{79}=79$
28. (c) Total number of sweets
$=65\times 65\times\frac{20}{100}+4\times 65\times\frac{40}{100}$
$=845+104=949$
29. (c) Initial area of the carpet
$=3\times(3\times 1.44)$ sq. metre
$=12.96$ sq. metre
After corresponding changes in dimensions, Area of the carpet
$=\left(3\times\frac{125}{100}\right)\times\left(3\times 1.44\times\frac{140}{100}\right)$
$=22.68$ sq. metre
∴ Increase in area
$=(22.68-12.96)$ sq. metre $=9.72$ sq. metre
∴ Increase in the cost
$=$ ₹ $(9.72\times 45)=$ ₹ 437.4
30. (b) In 60 gm. of mixture,
Quantity of water $=60\times\frac{75}{100}=45$ gm
Quantity of milk $=15$ gm
After mixing 15 gm of more water, Quantity of water in new mixture
$=45+15=60$ gm
∴ Quantity of water in 75 gm of mixture $=60$ gm
∴ 100 gm of mixture will contain
$=\frac{60}{75}\times 100=80\%$ of water
31. (d) Third number
$=290-2\times 48.5-2\times 53.5$
$=290-97-107=86$
32. (c) Let average weight of girls $=x$
Total weight of the boys $=40\text{ kg}\times 15$
$=600$ kg.
Average weight
$=\frac{\text{Total weight of girls + Total weight of boys}}{\text{No. of boys + No. of girls}}$
$\Rightarrow\ 38.4=\frac{600+10\times x}{15+10}$
$\Rightarrow\ 38.4=\frac{600+10x}{25}$
$\Rightarrow\ 38.4\times 25=600+10x$
$\therefore\ x=36$ kg
33. (c)

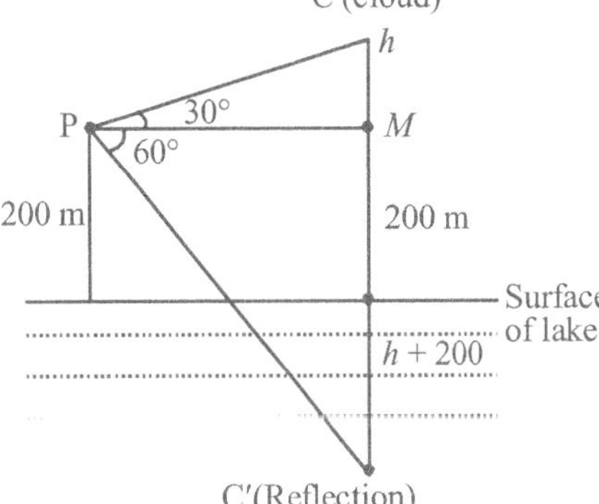

$\tan 30°=\frac{h}{PM}\Rightarrow PM=\sqrt{3}h$
$\tan 60°=\frac{h+400}{PM}\Rightarrow PM=\frac{h+400}{\sqrt{3}}$
$\sqrt{3}h=\frac{h+400}{\sqrt{3}}=3h-h=400$
$\Rightarrow\ 2h=400$
⇒ So, height of the cloud $=200+200$
$=400$m
34. (c) Let C completes the work in x days.
Work done by (A + B) in 1 day $=\frac{1}{10}$
Work done by (B + C) in 1 day $=\frac{1}{18}$
A's 5 days' work + B's 10 days' work + C's 15 days' work = 1
or (A + B)'s 5 days' work + (B + C)'s 5 days' work + C's 10 days' work = 1
or $\frac{5}{10}+\frac{5}{18}+\frac{10}{x}=1$ or $x=45$ days

35. (a) $\angle ABC + \angle ADC = 180°$ (sum of opposites angles of cyclic quadrilateral is 180°)

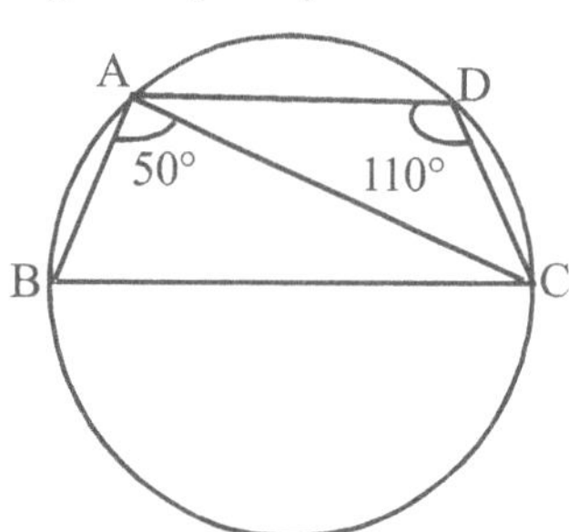

$\Rightarrow \angle ABC + 110° = 180°$

(ABCD is a cyclic quadrilateral)

$\Rightarrow \angle ABC = 180 - 110 \Rightarrow \angle ABC = 70°$

($\because AD \parallel BC$)

$\therefore$ $\angle ABC + \angle BAD = 180°$ (Sum of the interior angles on the same side of transversal is 180°)

$70° + \angle BAD = 180°$

$\Rightarrow \angle BAD = 180° - 70° = 110°$

$\Rightarrow \angle BAC + \angle DAC = 110°$

$\Rightarrow 50° + \angle DAC = 110°$

$\Rightarrow \angle DAC = 110° - 50° = 60°$

36. (b)

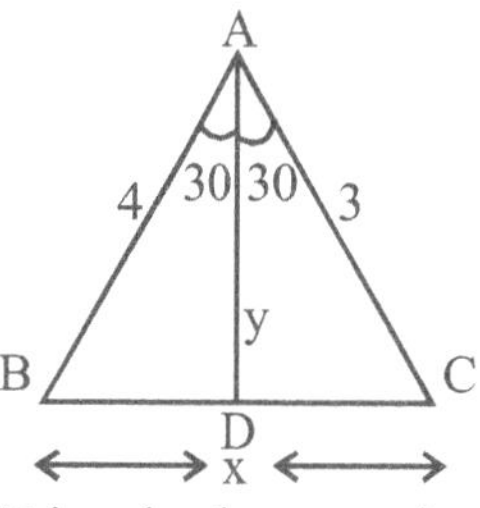

Using the theorem of angle of bisector,

$$\frac{BD}{DC} = \frac{AB}{AC} = \frac{4}{3}$$

$$\Rightarrow BD = \frac{4}{7}x \ \ \& DC = \frac{3}{7}x$$

In ΔABD, by sine rule, $\frac{\sin 30}{4/7x} = \frac{\sin B}{y}$ ...(i)

In ΔABC, by sine rule; $\frac{\sin 60}{x} = \frac{\sin B}{3}$

or $\frac{\sqrt{3}}{2x} = \frac{\sin 30.y}{4/7x \times 3}$

[putting the value of sin B from (i)]

$$\Rightarrow y = \frac{\sqrt{3}}{2x} \times \frac{4}{7} x \times 3 \times \frac{2}{1} = \frac{12\sqrt{3}}{7}$$

37. (a) Suppose ₹ x was lent at 6 % per annum.

Thus, $\frac{x \times 6 \times 5}{100} + \frac{(7000 - x) \times 4 \times 5}{100} = 1600$

or, $\frac{3x}{10} + \frac{7000 - x}{5} = 1600$

or, $\frac{3x + 14,000 - 2x}{10} = 16000$

$\therefore x = 16000 - 14000 =$ ₹2000

38. (b) Ratio of times taken by A and B = 100 : 130 = 10 : 13.

Suppose B takes x days to do the work.

Then, 10 : 13 : : 23 : x

$$\Rightarrow x = \left(\frac{23 \times 13}{10}\right) \Rightarrow x = \frac{299}{10}.$$

A's 1 day's work = $\frac{1}{23}$; B's 1 days work

$= \frac{10}{299}$.

(A + B)'s 1 day's work

$$= \left(\frac{1}{23} + \frac{10}{299}\right) = \frac{23}{299} = \frac{1}{13}.$$

$\therefore$ A and B together can complete the job in 13 days.

39. (b) Let the side of the square be x, then

$BE = \frac{x}{3}$ and $BF = \frac{x}{2}$

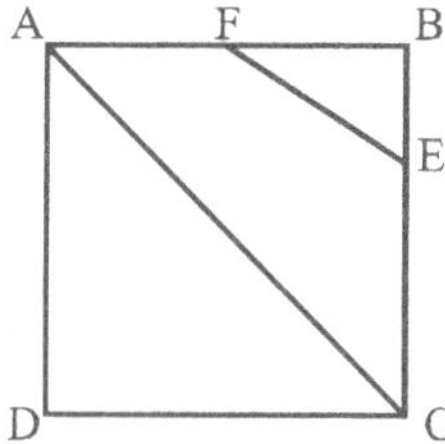

Area of $\Delta FEB = \frac{1}{2} \times \frac{x}{3} \times \frac{x}{2} = \frac{x^2}{12}$

Now, $\frac{x^2}{12} = 108$

$\Rightarrow$ $x^2 = 108 \times 12 = 1296$

In ΔADC, we have

$AC^2 = AD^2 + DC^2$

$= x^2 + x^2 = 2x^2 = 2 \times 1296 = 2592$

or $AC = \sqrt{2592} = 36\sqrt{2}$

40. (c) $\frac{1}{1+a} + \frac{1}{1+b} + \frac{1}{1+c}$ ...(i)

Given that,

$a^2 = b + c$

$a + a^2 = a + b + c$

$a(a+1) = a + b + c$

$$a + 1 = \frac{a+b+c}{a}$$

$$\frac{1}{a+1} = \frac{a}{a+b+c}$$

Similarly,

$$\frac{1}{b+1} = \frac{b}{a+b+c}$$

$$\frac{1}{c+1} = \frac{c}{a+b+c}$$

Put in eq. (i)

$$\therefore \frac{a}{a+b+c} + \frac{b}{a+b+c} + \frac{c}{a+b+c}$$

$$= \frac{a+b+c}{a+b+c} = 1$$

41. (b) Given that, $x + \frac{1}{y} = 1$

$\Rightarrow \quad xy + 1 = y \quad$ ...(i)

and $\quad y + \frac{1}{z} = 1$

$\Rightarrow \quad 1 - \frac{1}{z} - y$

$\Rightarrow \quad \frac{z-1}{z} = y \quad$ ...(ii)

From eq. (ii),

$$y = \frac{z-1}{z}$$

Comparing eqn. (i) with (ii)

$$xy + 1 = \frac{z-1}{z}$$

$\Rightarrow \quad xyz + z = z - 1$

$\Rightarrow \quad xyz = -1$

42. (a) p = 999 (Given)

Expression $\Rightarrow \sqrt[3]{p^3 + 3p^2 + 3p + 1}$

$\Rightarrow \sqrt[3]{(p+1)^3}$

$\Rightarrow p + 1 = 999 + 1 = 1000$

43. (a) Gain = S.P. of 33 metres – C.P. of 33 metres

= S.P. of 11 metres

⇒ S.P. of 22 metres = C.P. of 33 metres

$$\therefore \% \text{ gain} = \frac{\text{gain}}{\text{C.P. of metres}} \times 100$$

$$= \frac{\text{S.P. of 11 metres}}{\text{C.P. of 33 metres}} \times 100$$

$$= \frac{\text{S.P. of 11 metres}}{\text{S.P. of 22 metres}} \times 100 = \frac{11}{22} \times 100 = 50\%$$

44. (d) Suppose Income of B = ₹ x

$$\text{Income of A} = \frac{150}{100} \times x = ₹\ \frac{3x}{2}$$

$$\text{Income of C} = \frac{120}{100} \times \frac{3x}{2}$$

$$\frac{6}{5} \times \frac{3x}{2} = \frac{9x}{5}$$

$$\therefore \quad x + \frac{3x}{2} + \frac{9x}{5} = 86000$$

$$\frac{10x + 15x + 18x}{10} = 86000$$

43x = 860000

x = 20000

So, income of C = $\frac{9}{5} \times 20000$ = ₹ 36000

45. (a) Let the length of the journey = x km.

∴ Journey rides by horse cart

$$= x\left(1 - \frac{1}{2} - \frac{1}{3}\right) = \frac{1}{6}x \text{ km.}$$

Then, total time taken to complete journey

$$= \frac{31}{5} \text{hr}$$

$$\Rightarrow t_1 + t_2 + t_3 = \frac{31}{5}$$

$$\Rightarrow \frac{x}{2} \times \frac{1}{4} + \frac{x}{3} \times \frac{1}{12} + \frac{x}{6 \times 9} = \frac{31}{5}$$

$$\Rightarrow x = \frac{31}{5} \times \frac{216}{37} = 36.2\text{km} \approx 36\text{km}$$

46. (d) New quantity of item D

$$= 40 \times \frac{150}{100} = 60 \text{ quintal}$$

New price/kg of item D

= 90% of ₹ 12.5

$$= 12.5 \times \frac{90}{100} = ₹\ 11.25/\text{kg}$$

∴ Total price

= ₹ (60 × 100 × 11.25) = ₹ 67500

47. (d) Required average price/kg

$$= ₹\left(\frac{17.5 + 10 + 7.5}{3}\right) = ₹\ \frac{35}{3} = ₹\ 11.67$$

48. (a) Required ratio
$= 15 \times 25 : 10 \times 35 = 3 \times 5 : 2 \times 7 = 15 : 14$

49. (d)

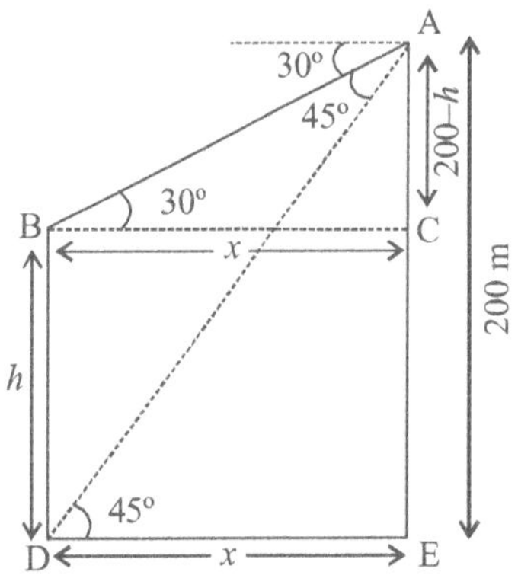

In ΔACB, $\tan 30^\circ = \frac{200-h}{x} = \frac{1}{\sqrt{3}}$

$= \frac{500-h}{x}$

$\Rightarrow \quad x = (200-h)\sqrt{3}$ ...(i)

In ΔADE,

$\tan 45^\circ = \frac{200}{x}$

$\Rightarrow \quad 1 = \frac{200}{x} \Rightarrow x = 200$ m

From Eq. (*i*)

$200 = (200-h)\sqrt{3}$

$\Rightarrow \quad h = 200\left(\frac{\sqrt{3}-1}{\sqrt{3}}\right)$ m

50. (d) The stack is in the form having vertical cross section of trapezium.
$\therefore$ Volume of Earth in the stack = Area of cross section of trapezium × Height

$\therefore$ Volume $= \frac{1}{2} \times (10+5) \times 2 \times 8 = 15 \times 8\ m^2$

According to the question,
Volume of Earth to be spread = (Area of field) × Level raised

$\therefore$ Level raised $= \frac{15 \times 8}{100 \times 80} = \frac{15}{1000}$ m = 1.5 cm

51. (a) 52. (b) 53. (b) 54. (b) 55. (c)
56. (a) 57. (b) 58. (a) 59. (b) 60. (b)
61. (c) 62. (d) 63. (b) 64. (d)
65. (c) Replace 'to' with 'with'. 'Agree to' is used for agreement to a plan or proposal, while 'Agree with' is used for agreement with a person.
66. (a) No error. The sentence is correct.
67. (a) 68. (d) 69. (c) 70. (d) 71. (d)
72. (a) 73. (c) 74. (c) 75. (b)
76. (c) Jatindra Nath Das (27 October 1904 - 13 September 1929), also known as Jatin Das, was an Indian freedom fighter and revolutionary. He died in Lahore jail after a continuous hunger strike for 63 days demanding equality for Indian prisoners and undertrials.
77. (d) 'Federal' term is not used in the preamble of the Indian constitution.
78. (b) The Prime Minister of India is the head of the Central Government.
79. (c) There are 5 types of writs can be issued by the Supreme Court
80. (d)
81. (c) In Astigmatism, eye cannot see objects in two orthogonal directions clearly simultaneously. This abnormality is removed by using cylindrical lens.
82. (d) Fertilizers are those compounds which provide essential primary nutrients (nitrogen, phosphorus and potassium) required for healthy growth of plants and crops. Nitrogeneous fertilizer provide nitrogen, phosphatic fertilizer provide phosphorus whereas potassh fertilizer provide potassium to soil.
NPK fertilizers are mixed fertilizers. They provide all three essential nutrients (nitrogen, phosphorus and potassium). NPK fertilizers contains nitrogen, phosphorus and potassium in different proportion depending upon the requirement of soil.
83. (a) Fluorine is the most reactive among all halogens. However the reactivity deceases from F_2 to I_2 (from top to bottom of group) may be attributed to
(1) Low dissociation enthalpies
(2) High electron affinities
84. (b) Chlorophyll is a tetrapyrole ring system that chelate the magnesium ion. The tetrapyrole ring system that chelates this magnesium shows a conjugated double bond. This bond provide the light absorption feature to chlorophyll and gives it green colour.
85. (d) The stomach is divided into two parts fundic and pyloric region. The pyloric region opens into small intestine through pyloric valve of pylorus.
86. (c) 87. (d) 88. (b) 89. (b) 90. (c)
91. (b) 92. (a) 93. (b) 94. (a) 95. (d)
96. (c) 97. (b) 98. (c) 99. (d) 100. (b)

PRACTICE SET- 10

GENERAL INTELLIGENCE & REASONING

DIRECTIONS (Qs. 1 to 3) : *In each of the following questions, there are two words / set of letters / numbers to the left of the sign :: which are connected in some way. The same relationship obtains between the third words / set of letters / numbers and one of the four alternatives under it. Find the correct alternative in each question.*

1. Foresight : Anticipation :: Insomnia : ?
   (a) Treatment (b) Disease
   (c) Sleeplessness (d) Unrest
2. PAPER : SCTGW : : MOTHER : ?
   (a) ORVLGW (b) PQVIGT
   (c) PQXJJT (d) PQXKJV
3. 182 : ? : : 210 : 380
   (a) 342 (b) 272
   (c) 240 (d) 156

DIRECTIONS (Qs. 4 to 6) : *Find the odd word/letters/ number pair from the given alternatives.*

4. (a) Anxiety (b) Worry
   (c) Inhibition (d) Curiosity
5. (a) PROQN (b) DECEG
   (c) GIFHE (d) KMJLI
6. (a) 117 – 143 (b) 142 – 156
   (c) 64 – 78 (d) 103 – 169

DIRECTIONS (Qs. 7 to 9) : *Complete the given series.*

7. ABD, DGK, HMS, MTB, SBL, ?
   (a) ZAB (b) XKW
   (c) ZKU (d) ZKW
8. 165, 195, 255, 285, 345, ?
   (a) 375 (b) 390
   (c) 420 (d) 435
9. 24, 60, 120, 210, ?
   (a) 300 (b) 336
   (c) 420 (d) 525
10. In a code, CORNER is written as GSVRIV. How can CENTRAL be written in that code?
    (a) DFOUSBM (b) GIRXVEP
    (c) GJRYVEP (d) GNFJKER
11. If LOVE is coded as 27 then how is COME coded as:-
    (a) 38 (b) 18
    (c) 28 (d) 8
12. A is B's sister. C is B's mother. D is C's father. E is D's mother. Then, how is A related to D?
    (a) Grandmother (b) Grandfather
    (c) Daughter (d) Granddaughter
13. M is to the East of D, F is to the South of D and K is to the West of F. M is in which direction with respect to K?
    (a) South-West (b) North-West
    (c) North-East (d) South-East
14. Ketan takes casual leave only on first working day of every month. The office has weekly offs on Saturday and Sunday. In a month of 30 days, the first working day happened to be Tuesday. What will be the day for his next casual leave?
    (a) Wednesday (b) Thursday
    (c) Friday (d) Monday
15. In a row of boys facing the North, A is sixteenth from the left end and C is sixteenth from the right end. B, who is fourth to the right of A, is fifth to the left of C in the row. How many boys are there in the row ?
    (a) 39 (b) 40
    (c) 41 (d) 42
16. Malay Pratap is on 13th position from the starting and on 17th position from the end in his class. He is on 8th position from the starting and on 13th position from the end among the students who passed. How many students failed?
    (a) 7
    (b) 8
    (c) 9
    (d) Cannot be determined

DIRECTIONS (Qs. 17 – 18): *In the following questions find the missing number*

17.

5	9	15
16	29	?
49	89	147

(a) 45 (b) 48
(c) 51 (d) 54

18.

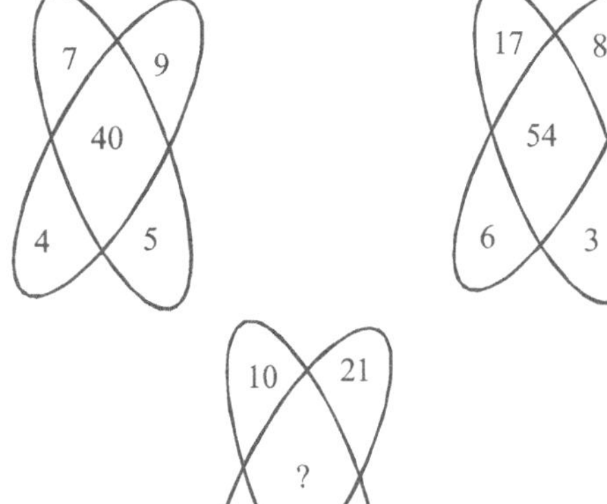

(a) 60 (b) 62
(c) 64 (d) 66

19. Which one of the given responses would be a meaningful order of the following ?

1. apartment 2. town
3. street 4. building
5. complex

(a) 1, 5, 4, 3, 2 (b) 4, 5, 3, 2, 1
(c) 2, 1, 3, 4, 5 (d) 1, 4, 5, 3, 2

DIRECTION (Q. 20) : *In question below are given two statements followed by two conclusions. You have to take the given statements to be true even if they seem to be at variance with commonly known facts. Read all the conclusions and then decide which of the given statements disregarding commonly know facts. Given Answer.*

Give answer (a) If only conclusion I follows.
Give answer (b) if only conclusion II follows.
Give answer (c) if either I or II follows.
Give answer (d) if neither I nor II follows.

20. Statements:

Some books are pens.
No pen is pencil.

Conclusions:

I. Some books are pencils.
II. No book is pencil.

21. If '–' stand for addition, '+' stands for subtraction, '÷' stands for multiplication and '×' stands for division, then which one of the following equations is correct?

(a) $25 \times 5 \div 20 - 27 + 7 = 120$
(b) $25 + 5 \times 20 - 27 \div 7 = 128$
(c) $25 + 5 - 20 + 27 \times 7 = 95$
(d) $25 - 5 + 20 \times 27 \div 7 = 100$

22. How many triangles are there ?

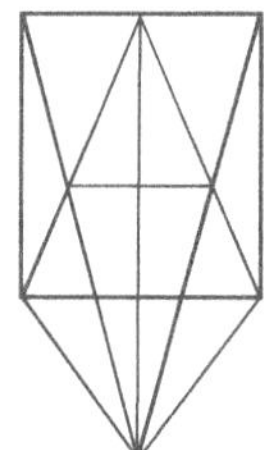

(a) 20 (b) 21
(c) 26 (d) 28

DIRECTION (Q. 23) : *In the following question, you are given a figure (X) followed by four alternative figures (a), (b), (c) and (d) such that fig. (X) is embeded in one of them. Trace out the alternative figure which contains fig. (X) as its part.*

23.

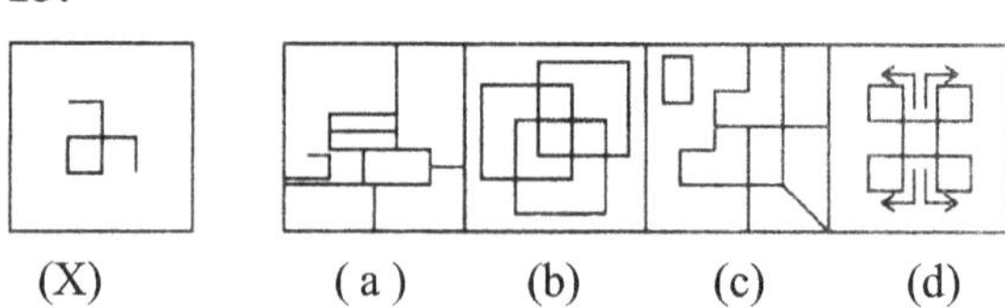

(X) (a) (b) (c) (d)

DIRECTION (Qs. 24) : *In each of the following questions, choose the correct* ***water image*** *of the figure (X) from amongst the four alternatives (a), (b), (c), (d) given alongwith it.*

24. absence

?

(a) ɐpƨɘᑌcɘ
(b) ɐqƨɘncɘ
(c) ɐpƨəncə
(d) ɐpsɘncɘ

25. There are two dots placed in the question figure. Find out the answer figure which has the possibility of placing the dots satisfying the same condition as in the question figure.

Questions Figure

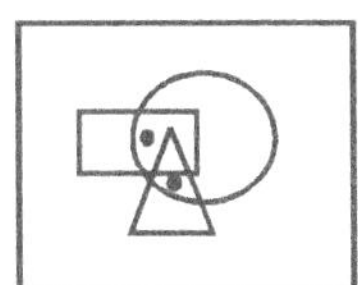

Answer Figure

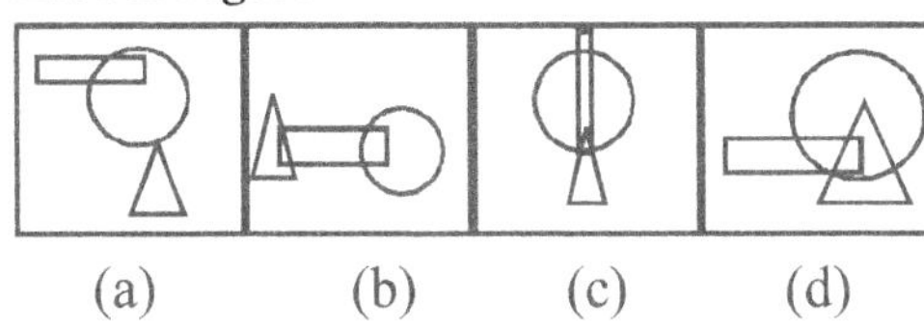

(a) (b) (c) (d)

QUANTITATIVE APTITUDE

26. A certain number is divided by 385 by division by factors. The quotient is 102, the first remainder is 4, the second is 6 and the third is 10. Find the number.
(a) 39654 (b) 32754
(c) 38554 (d) None of these

27. Two different numbers when divided by the same divisor, left remainder 11 and 21 respectively, and when their sum was divided by the same divisor, remainder was 4. What is the divisor?
(a) 36 (b) 28
(c) 14 (d) 9

28. A shopkeeper fixes the marked price of an item 20% above the cost price. He allows his customers a discount and makes a profit of 8%. Find the rate of discount.
(a) 8% (b) 9%
(c) 10% (d) 11%

29. Mr. Thomas invested an amount of ₹ 13,900 divided in two different schemes A and B at the simple interest rate of 14% p.a. and 11% p.a. respectively. If the total amount of simple interest earned in 2 years be ₹ 3508, what was the amount invested in Scheme B?
(a) ₹ 6400 (b) ₹ 6500
(c) ₹ 7200 (d) ₹ 7500

30. The difference between C. I. (Compound Interest) and S.I. (Simple Interest) on a sum of ₹ 4,000 for 2 years at 5% p.a. payable yearly is
(a) ₹ 20 (b) ₹ 10
(c) ₹ 50 (d) ₹ 60

31. A, B and C are partners. A receives 9/10 of the profit and B and C share the remaining profit equally. A's income is increased by ₹ 270 when the profit rises from 12 to 15%. Find the capital invested by B and C each
(a) ₹ 5000 (b) ₹ 1000
(c) ₹ 500 (d) ₹ 1500

32. A machine P can print one lakh books in 8 hours, machine Q can print the same number of books in 10 hours while machine R can print them in 12 hours. All the machines are started at 9 a.m. while machine P is closed at 11 a.m. and the remaining two machines complete the work. Approximately at what time will the work be finished?
(a) 11:30 am (b) 12 noon
(c) 12:30 pm (d) 1 pm

33. A man walks half of the journey at 4 km/h by cycle does one third of journey at 12 km/h and rides the remainder journey in a horse cart at 9 km/h, thus completing the whole journey in 6 hours and 12 minutes. The length of the journey is
(a) 36 km (b) 39 km
(c) 40 km (d) 28 km

34. If $x^2 + y^2 + 2x + 1 = 0$, then the value of $x^{31} + y^{35}$ is
(a) -1 (b) 0
(c) 1 (d) 2

35. If $2^x = 3^y = 6^{-z}$ then $\left(\frac{1}{x}+\frac{1}{y}+\frac{1}{z}\right)$, is equal to
(a) 0 (b) 1
(c) $\frac{3}{2}$ (d) $-\frac{1}{2}$

36. If $m + \frac{1}{m-2} = 4$ then, what is value of

$$(m-2)^2 + \frac{1}{(m-2)^2} = ?$$

(a) -2 (b) 0
(c) 2 (d) 4

37. If a man walks to his office at 5/4 of his usual rate, he reaches office 30 minutes early than usual. What is his usual time to reach office.
(a) 2 hr (b) $2\frac{1}{2}$ hr
(c) 1 hr 50 min (d) 2 hr 15 min

38. If the slope of a line passing through the points A (2, 5) and B (x, 3) is 2, then x is equal to

(a) 1 (b) 2

(c) – 1 (d) – 2

39. Two parallel chords of a circle of diameter 20 cm are 12 cm and 16 cm long. If the chords are in the same side of the centre, then the distance between them is

(a) 28 cm (b) 2 cm

(c) 4 cm (d) 8 cm

40. Average age of 36 children of the class is 15 years. 12 more children joined whose average age is 16 years. What is the average age of all the 48 children together?

(a) 15.25 years (b) 15.5 years

(c) 15.3 years (d) 15.4 years

41. A and B can finish a work in 10 days while B and C can do it in 18 days. A started the work, worked for 5 days, then B worked for 10 days and the remaining work was finished by C in 15 days. In how many days could C alone have finished the whole work ?

(a) 30 days (b) 15 days

(c) 45 days (d) 24 days

42. If the coordinates of the points A, B, C be (4, 4), (3, – 2) and (3, – 16) respectively, then the area of the triangle ABC is:

(a) 27 (b) 15

(c) 18 (d) 7

43. In how many minimum number of complete years, the interest on ₹212.50 P at 3% per annum will be in exact number of rupees?

(a) 6 (b) 8

(c) 9 (d) 7

44. If the cost price is 96% of the selling price, then what is the profit percent?

(a) 4.5% (b) 4.2%

(c) 4% (d) 3.8%

45. The average of four consecutive odd numbers is 36. What is the smallest of these numbers ?

(a) 31 (b) 35

(c) 43 (d) None of these

DIRECTIONS (Qs. 46-48): *Study the following graph carefully to answer the questions that follow:*

Number of Students Enrolled in Three Different Disciplines in Five Different Colleges

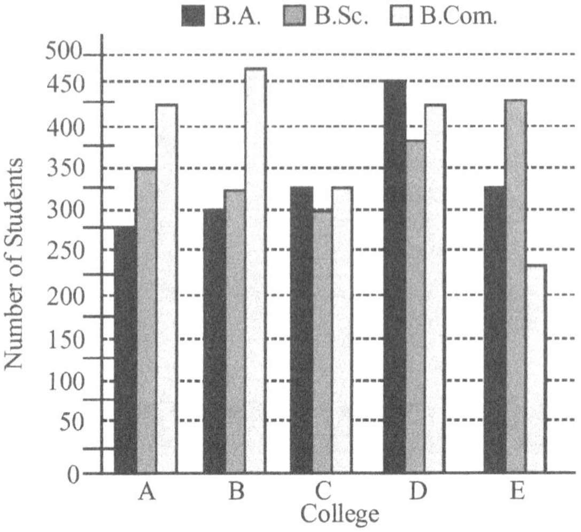

B.A. B.Sc. B.Com.

Number of Students

College

46. What is the total number of students studying B.Sc in all Colleges together?

(a) 1825 (b) 1975

(c) 1650 (d) 1775

47. What is the respective ratio of total number of students studying B.Sc. in the colleges C and E together to those studying B.A. in the Colleges A and B together?

(a) 24 : 23 (b) 25 : 27

(c) 29 : 23 (d) 29 : 27

48. What is the respective ratio of total number of students studying B.Sc., B.A. and B.Com. in all the Colleges together?

(a) 71 : 67 : 75 (b) 67 : 71 : 75

(c) 71 : 68 : 75 (d) 75 : 71 : 68

49. A cylindrical bucket of height 36 cm and radius 21 cm is filled with sand. The bucket is emptied on the ground and a conical heap of sand is formed, the height of the heap being 12 cm. The radius of the heap at the base is:

(a) 63 cm (b) 53 cm

(c) 56 cm (d) 66 cm

50. A conical vessel, whose internal radius is 12 cm and height 50 cm, is full of liquid. The contents are emptied into a cylindrical vessel with internal radius 10 cm. Find the height to which the liquid rises in the cylindrical vessel.

(a) 18 cm (b) 22 cm

(c) 24 cm (d) None of these

ENGLISH LANGUAGE

DIRECTIONS (Qs. 51 to 53): *Four alternative are given for the Idiom/Phrase bold in the sentence. Choose the alternative which best expresses the meaning of the Idiom/Phrase and mark it in the Answer Sheet.*

51. I trusted him but he **played me false**.
(a) played with me
(b) took it lightly
(c) treated me improperly
(d) deceived me

52. He **did me a good turn** by recommending me for the post of vice-principal.
(a) paid debts
(b) did an act of kindness
(c) improved my prospects
(d) became suddenly good

53. Please **look into** the matter personally as it is very important.
(a) see secretly (b) examine
(c) overlook (d) take care of

DIRECTIONS (Qs. 54 to 55) : *A sentence/ a part of the sentence is bold. Below are given alternatives to the bold part at (a), (b), (c) which may improve the sentence. Choose the correct alternative. In case no improvement is needed your answer is (d).*

54. **No person except** Ravi came forward to help me in the matter of my difficulties.
(a) Not a person except
(b) No person excepting
(c) No other person except
(d) No improvement

55. What are you looking **upon** in the dark ?
(a) over (b) after
(c) for (d) No improvement

DIRECTIONS (Qs. 56 to 57) : *Out of the four alternatives, choose the one which can be substituted for the given words/ sentences.*

56. A person claiming to be superior in culture and intellect to others –
(a) highbrow (b) aristocrat
(c) criminal (d) elite

57. Release of a prisoner from jail on certain terms and conditions –
(a) parole (b) parley
(c) pardon (d) acquit

DIRECTIONS (Qs. 58 to 59): *Four words are given in each question, out of which only one word is correctly spelt. Find the correctly spelt word from the given options.*

58. (a) gragerious (b) gregarious
(c) gregerious (d) gragarious

59. (a) extemporneous (b) extemporaneous
(c) extemporinious (d) extemporeneous

DIRECTIONS (Qs.60-64) : *In the following passages, some of the words have been left out. First read the passage over and try to understand what it is about. Then, fill in the blanks with the help of the alternatives given.*

PASSAGE

Once upon a time, two friends were **60** through the desert. During some point of the **61** they had an argument, and one friend slapped the other one in the face. The one who got slapped was **62**, but without saying anything, he wrote in the sand, "Today my best friend slapped me in the face." They kept on walking **63** they found an oasis, where they **64** to take a bath.

60. (a) crawling (b) speaking
(c) swimming (d) walking

61. (a) journey (b) sand
(c) running (d) border

62. (a) dead (b) captured
(c) presentable (d) hurt

63. (a) as (b) until
(c) from (d) with

64. (a) decided (b) fell
(c) made (d) want

DIRECTIONS (Qs. 65 to 66): *Some part of the sentences have errors and some are correct. Find out which part of a sentence has an error and mark the answer accordingly*

65. It took him (a)/ time to realize (b)/ that he offended the stranger. (c) / No error (d)

66. Even if you are a film star, (a)/ I would not care (b)/ for you. (c)/ No error (d)

DIRECTIONS (Qs. 67 to 68): *Sentences given with blanks are to be filled in with an appropriate word. Four alternatives are suggested for each question. Choose the correct alternative out of the four.*

67. _____ you wake me up so early on a Sunday ?
(a) Could (b) Dare
(c) Must (d) Will

68. A foreign language or mathematics may call for three or more hours per class, at least until you have mastered the _____.
(a) topic (b) subject
(c) language (d) fundamentals

DIRECTIONS (Qs. 69 to 70): *Choose the option opposite in meaning to the given word.*

69. ASCETICISM
(a) Comfort (b) Luxury
(c) Anti-Semitism (d) Humility

70. ENDURING
(a) Fleeting (b) Painful
(c) Permanent (d) Long lasting

DIRECTIONS (Qs. 71 to 72): *Choose the one which best expresses the meaning of the given word.*

71. LOUSY
(a) Unbearable (b) Unpleasant
(c) Awful (d) Stinking

72. PREDOMINANTLY
(a) Emphatically (b) Forcefully
(c) Mostly (d) Profoundly

DIRECTION (Q. 73) : *In each of the following questions, a sentence has seen given in Direct/ Indirect speech. Out of the form alternatives suggested, select the one which best expresses the same sentence in Indirect/Direct speech.*

73. The employer said to the workman, "I cannot pay you higher wages."
(a) The employer told the workman that he could not be paid higher wages.
(b) The employer forbade the workman that he could not pay him higher wages.
(c) The employer forbade the workman to pay higher wages.
(d) The employer warned the workman that he cannot pay him higher wages.

DIRECTIONS (Qs. 74-75) : *In the following questions, the 1st and the last sentences of the passage are numbered 1 and 6. The rest of the passage is split into four parts and named P, Q, R and S. These four parts are not given in their proper order. Read the sentence and find out which of the four combinations is correct. Then find the correct answer.*

74. 1. The multi sourcing of
P. financial mess with
Q. coins led to a
R. using their own mix of
S. different mints
6. metals and alloys.
(a) QPSR (b) PSRQ
(c) RPQS (d) SQRP

75. 1. It may seem odd
P. one should one read
Q. but people read for such a
R. to have to insist that
S. because one liked it
6. variety of reasons.
(a) QPSR (b) RSPQ
(c) SPRQ (d) RPSQ

GENERAL AWARENESS

76. In context of Mauryan period 'Gudhapurushas' referred to –
(a) Detectives
(b) Blacksmith
(c) Army commander
(d) Chariot rider

77. Who among the following led the agitation against the Partition of Bengal (1905)? (1905)
(a) Surendranath Banerjee
(b) C.R. Das
(c) Ashutosh Mukharjee
(d) Rabindra Nath Tagore

78. Graphite is used in nuclear reactors for –
(a) reducing the speed of fast neutrons
(b) cooling the reactor
(c) absorbing neutrons
(d) None of the above

79. How many members are nominated by the governor in the Legislative Council of the State?
(a) 1/3rd of the total membership
(b) 1/6th of the total membership
(c) 1/12th of the total membership
(d) 12 members

80. Which of the following is not an antibiotics?
(a) Penicilin (b) Ampicilin
(c) Streptomycin (d) Aspirin

81. Ginger is an example of–
(a) Modified Node
(b) Modified Root
(c) Modified Stem
(d) Tap Root

82. If the length of a simple pendulum is halved then its period of oscillation is –
(a) doubled
(b) halved
(c) increased by a factor $\sqrt{2}$
(d) decreased by a factor $\sqrt{2}$

83. Kalinga Prize is given in which of the following fields ?
(a) Arts (b) Medicine
(c) Creative writing (d) Science

84. Which state Government launched Kalinga Sikha Sathi Yojana (KSSY)?
(a) Madhya Pradesh (b) Maharashtra
(c) Odisha (d) Kerala

85. Which is the oldest paramilitary force in the country?
(a) Border Security Force (BSF)
(b) Assam Rifles
(c) Indo-Tibetan Border Police (ITBP)
(d) Coast Guard

86. Which of the following act as a channel of transmission of blood to the heart in the human body?
(a) Arteries (b) Muscle fibres
(c) Nerves (d) Veins

87. When is the World's Diabetes Day?
(a) 14th November (b) 11th December
(c) 15th October (d) 1st July

88. When the batsman, in cricket, is out without scoring a single run, is called
(a) drive (b) duck
(c) flight (d) googly

89. What is the S.I. unit of temperature?
(a) Kelvin (b) Celsius
(c) Centigrade (d) Fahrenheit

90. When did India enter into space age by launching the satellite 'Aryabhatta'?
(a) 1966 (b) 1932
(c) 1975 (d) 1990

91. Vitamin B12 is most useful for combating
(a) Anemia (b) Goitre
(c) night blindness (d) Rickets

92. The term of office of a Judge of the International Court of Justice is
(a) five years (b) six years
(c) nine years (d) ten years

93. Control Unit of a digital computer is often called the
(a) Nerve center (b) Clock
(c) ICS (d) All of these

94. How many banks were nationalized in 1969?
(a) 16 (b) 14
(c) 15 (d) 20

95. The world famous 'Khajuraho' sculptures are located in
(a) Gujarat (b) Madhya Pradesh
(c) Orissa (d) Maharashtra

96. Ozone hole refers to
(a) hole in ozone layer
(b) decrease in the thickness of ozone layer in troposphere
(c) decrease in thickness of ozone layer in stratosphere
(d) increase in the thickness of ozone layer in troposphere

97. Who has won the 2018 Man Booker Prize for Fiction?
(a) Anna Burns (b) Val McDermid
(c) Leo Robson (d) Leanne Shapton

98. Who has become the India's first silver-medallist in archery at the 2018 Youth Olympic Games?
(a) Swapana Kumar
(b) Jeremy Lalrinnunga
(c) Akash Malik
(d) Tababi Devi

99. What is the India's rank in the WEF's Global Competitiveness Index (GCI) for 2018?
(a) 45th (b) 77th
(c) 58th (d) 69th

100. Which of the following G7 countries has officially legalized recreational use of marijuana?
(a) France (b) Germany
(c) United States (d) Canada

Hints & Explanations

1. (c) The words in each pair are synonyms.

2. (c)

P	A	P	E	R
+3 ↓	+2 ↓	+4 ↓	+2 ↓	+5 ↓
S	C	T	G	W

Similarly,

M	O	T	H	E	R
+3 ↓	+2 ↓	+4 ↓	+2 ↓	+5 ↓	+2 ↓
P	Q	X	J	J	T

3. (a) $210 = (15)^2 - 15$ $15 + 5 = 20$

$380 = (20)^2 - 20$

$182 = (14)^2 - 14$

$(19)^2 - 19 = 342$ $14 + 5$

4. (d)

5. (b) Pattern is–

$P \xrightarrow{+2} R \xrightarrow{-3} O \xrightarrow{+2} Q \xrightarrow{-3} N$

So that, DECEG is out.

6. (a) Only 117-143 is divisible by 13. Therefore, it is odd one out.

7. (d)

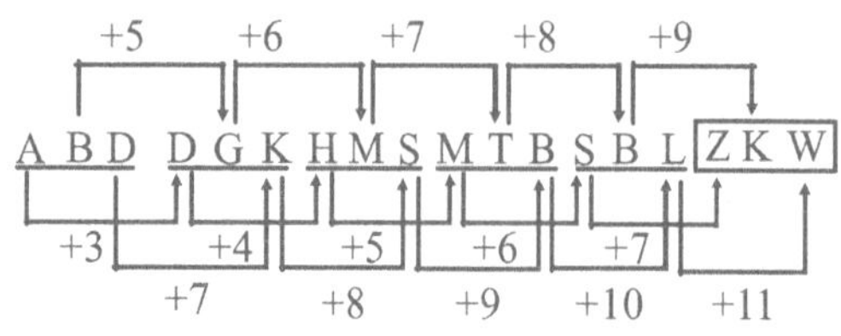

8. (d) Each number is 15 multiplied by a prime number i.e. $15 \times 11, 15 \times 13, 15 \times 17, 15 \times 19, 15 \times 23, \ldots$

So, missing term $= 15 \times 29 = 435$.

9. (b) 24 60 120 210 [336]

+36 +60 +90 +126

+24 +30 +36

+6 +6

10. (b)

	C	O	R	N	E	R
	+4 ↓	+4 ↓	+4 ↓	+4 ↓	+4 ↓	+4 ↓
Coded as:	G	S	V	R	I	V

Similarly,

C	E	N	T	R	A	L
+4 ↓	+4 ↓	+4 ↓	+4 ↓	+4 ↓	+4 ↓	+4 ↓
G	I	R	X	V	E	P

11. (b) L O V E

$12 + 15 + 22 + 5 = 54$

$\frac{54}{2} = 27$

Similarly,

C O M E

$3 + 15 + 13 + 5 = 36$

$\frac{36}{2} = 18$

12. (d) A is the sister of B and B is the son/daughter of C. So, A is the daughter of C.

Also, D is the father of C.

Thus, A is the granddaughter of D.

13. (c)

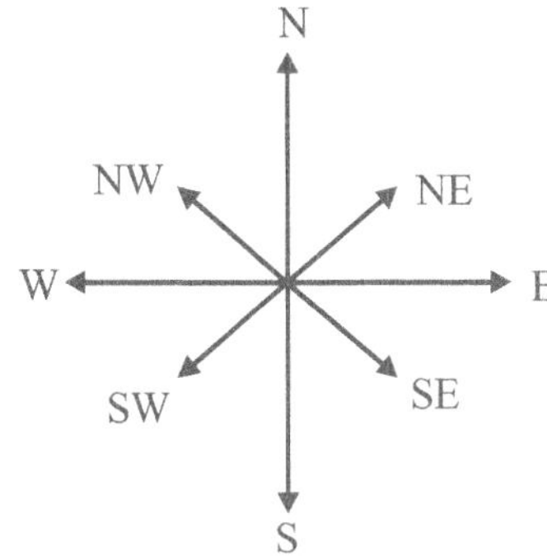

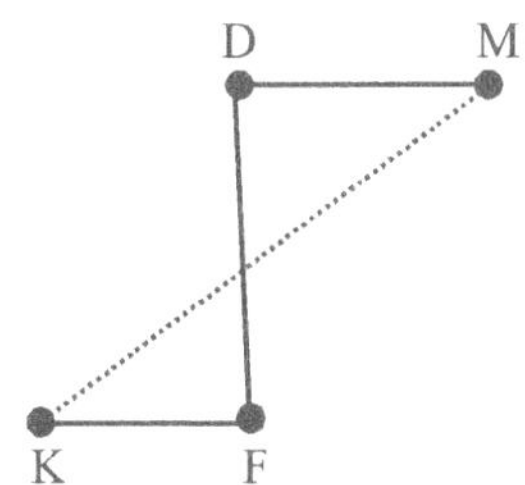

M is to the North-East of K.

14. (b) If the first working day happened to be Tuesday then 8th, 15th, 22nd and 29th of the month will be Tuesday. Hence, the last day of the month will be Wednesday (since, number of days in the month is 30). Thus, the next casual leave will be on Thursday.

15. (b)

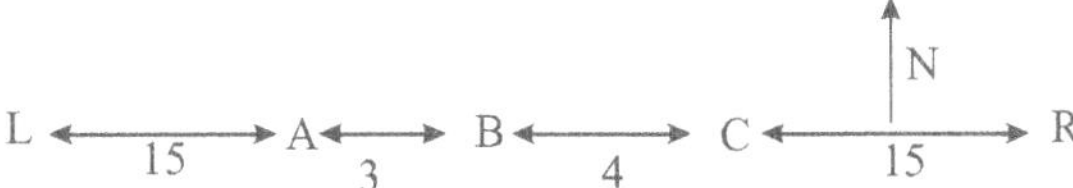

Clearly, according to the given conditions, there are 15 boys to the left of A, as well as to the right of C. Also, B lies between A and C such that there are 3 boys between A and B and 4 boys between B and C. So, number of boys in the row $= (15 + 1 + 3 + 1 + 4 + 1 + 15) = 40$.

16. (c) Total students

= [Malay's place from starting + Malay's place from end] −1

$= [13 + 17] - 1 = 29$

Number of passed students

= [Malay's place from starting + Malay's place from end] −1

$= [8 + 13] - 1 = 20$

$\therefore$ Number of failed students $= 29 - 20 = 9$

17. (b) $5 \times 3 + 1 = 16; 9 \times 3 + 2 = 29;$

$16 \times 3 + 1 = 49; 29 \times 3 + 2 = 89;$

$15 \times 3 + 3 = 48; 48 \times 3 + 3 = 147.$

18. (b) $(7 + 9 + 5 + 4) \times 2 - 10 = 40$

$(17 + 8 + 3 + 6) \times 2 - 14 = 54$

$(10 + 21 + 6 + 3) \times 2 - 18 = 62$

19. (d)

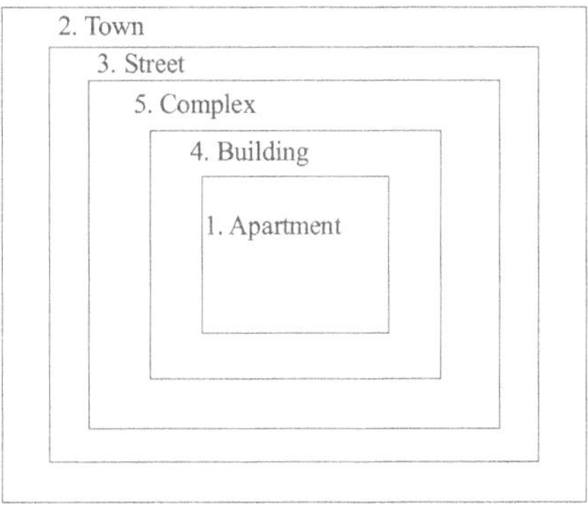

20. (c)

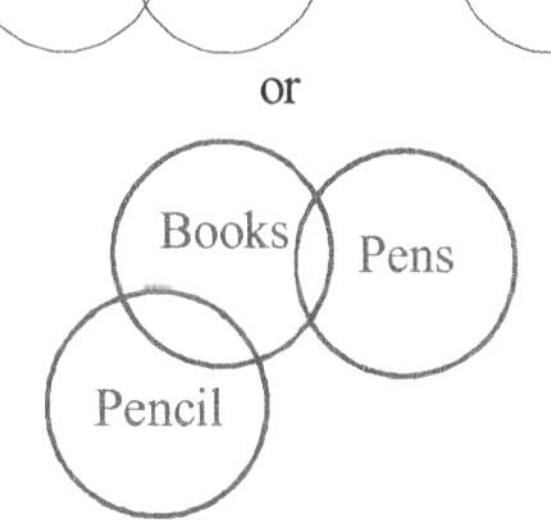

Conclusions:

I. False

II. False

Hence, either I, II follows

21. (a) Solve by options, we can check all the options one by one.

$25 \div 5 \times 20 + 27 - 7 \Rightarrow 5 \times 20 + 27 - 7$

$\Rightarrow 100 + 27 - 7$

$120 = 120$

22. (d)

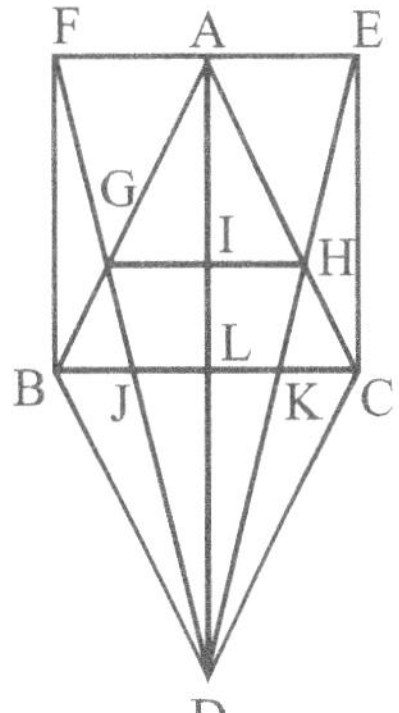

ΔFDE, ΔACD, ΔABD,
ΔFBD, ΔABC, ΔBCD,
ΔBKD, ΔBLD, ΔBJD,
ΔJCD, ΔJKD, ΔLDJ, ΔLCD,
ΔLKD, ΔHDC, ΔKDC, ΔEDC,
ΔHKC, ΔEKC, ΔAEC, ΔEHC,
ΔAEH, ΔAGH, ΔAIH, ΔAGI.
ΔAFB, ΔAGF, ΔFBG.
∴ Total 28 triangles.

23. (b)

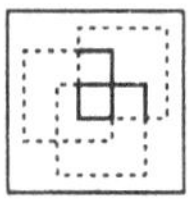

24. (a) The water image of 'a' is 'ɐ', 'b' is 'p', 'S' is 'Ƨ', 'e' is 'ɘ', 'n' is 'u', 'c' is 'c' and 'e' is 'ɘ'.

25. (b) 1 dot in rect and circle. One dot in train n circle, so only 4th figure can have these 2 dots

26. (a) Let the number be z. Now 385 = 5 × 7 × 11

5	z	Remainders
7	y	4
11	x	6
	102	10

x = 11 × 102 + 10 = 1132
y = 7x + 6 = 7 × 1132 + 6 = 7930
z = 5y + 4 = 5 × 7930 + 4 = 39654

27. (b) Divisor = [Sum of remainders]
– [Remainder when sum is divided]
= 11 + 21 – 4 = 28

28. (c) Let C.P. = ₹ 100. Then M.P. = ₹ 120 and S.P. = ₹ 108

$$\% \text{ discount } = \left(\frac{12}{120}\times 100\right)\% = 10\%$$

29. (a) Let the sum invested in Scheme A be ₹ x and that in Scheme B be ₹ (13900 – x). Then,

$$\left(\frac{x\times 14\times 2}{100}\right)+\left[\frac{(13900-x)\times 11\times 2}{100}\right]=3508$$

⇒ 28x – 22x = 350800 – (13900 × 22)
⇒ 6x = 45000
⇒ x = 7500.
So, sum invested in Scheme B = ₹ (13900 – 7500) = ₹ 6400.

30. (b) Required difference $= \frac{PR^2}{(100)^2}$

$\Rightarrow \frac{4000\times 5\times 5}{100\times 100}$ = ₹10

31. (c) Let the profit = x

Profit of $A = \frac{9x}{10}$, Remaining profit $= \frac{x}{10}$

Profit of $B = \frac{x}{20}$

Profit of $C = \frac{x}{20}$

Ratio of profit $= \frac{9}{10} : \frac{1}{20} : \frac{1}{20}$
$= 18 : 1 : 1$

A's income is increased by ₹ 270 . When profit rises 3%

Investment of $A = \frac{270}{3}\times 100 =$ ₹9000.

If investment of A, B and C = 18x, x and x
18x = 9000
x = 500
B's investment = ₹ 500.
C's investment = ₹ 500.

32. (d) (P + Q + R)'s 1 hour's work $= \left(\frac{1}{8}+\frac{1}{10}+\frac{1}{12}\right)=\frac{37}{120}$.

Work done by P, Q and R in 2 hours = $\left(\frac{37}{120}\times 2\right)=\frac{37}{60}$.

Remaining work $= \left(1-\frac{37}{60}\right)=\frac{23}{60}$.

(Q + R)'s 1 hour's work

$= \left(\frac{1}{10}+\frac{1}{12}\right)=\frac{11}{60}$.

Now, $\frac{11}{60}$ work is done by Q and R in 1 hour.

So, $\frac{23}{60}$ work will be done by Q and R in

$\left(\frac{60}{11}\times\frac{23}{60}\right)=\frac{23}{11}$ hours ≈ 2 hours.

So, the work will be finished approximately 2 hours after 11 a.m., i.e., around 1 p.m.

33. (a) Let the length of the journey = x km.

∴ Journey rides by horse cart

$= x\left(1-\frac{1}{2}-\frac{1}{3}\right) = \frac{1}{6}x$ km.

Then, total time taken to complete journey

$= \frac{31}{5}$ hr

$\Rightarrow t_1 + t_2 + t_3 = \frac{31}{5}$

$\Rightarrow \frac{x}{2}\times\frac{1}{4}+\frac{x}{3}\times\frac{1}{12}+\frac{x}{6\times 9} = \frac{31}{5}$

$\Rightarrow x = \frac{31}{5}\times\frac{216}{37} = 36.2\text{km} \approx 36\text{km}$

34. (a) $x^2+y^2+2x+1=0$

$\Rightarrow \quad x^2+2x+1+y^2=0$

$\Rightarrow \quad (x+1)^2+y^2=0$

$\Rightarrow \quad x+1=0 \Rightarrow -1$ and $y=0$

$\therefore \quad x^{31}+y^{35}=-1$

35. (a) $2^x = 3^y = 6^{-z} = k$

$\Rightarrow 2 = k^{\frac{1}{x}}; 3 = k^{\frac{1}{y}}; 6 = k^{-\frac{1}{z}}$

$\because 2\times 3 = 6$

$\Rightarrow k^{\frac{1}{x}} \times k^{\frac{1}{y}} = k^{-\frac{1}{z}} \Rightarrow k^{\frac{1}{x}+\frac{1}{y}} = k^{-\frac{1}{z}}$

$\Rightarrow \frac{1}{x}+\frac{1}{y} = -\frac{1}{z} \Rightarrow \frac{1}{x}+\frac{1}{y}+\frac{1}{z} = 0$

36. (c) $m+\frac{1}{m-2} = 4$

$m^2-6m+9=0$

$(m-3)(m-3)=0$

$m=3$

$m-2=1$

Now $(m-2)^2+\frac{1}{(m-2)^2}$

$= 1^2+\frac{1}{1^2} = 2$

37. (b) usual time $\times\left(\frac{4}{5}-1\right) = \frac{-30}{60}$

$\Rightarrow$ usual time $= \frac{1}{2}\times 5 = 2\frac{1}{2}$ hr

38. (a) $\frac{(3-5)}{x-2} = 2 \Rightarrow 2x-4 = -2 \Rightarrow 2x = 2 \Rightarrow x = 1$

39. (b)

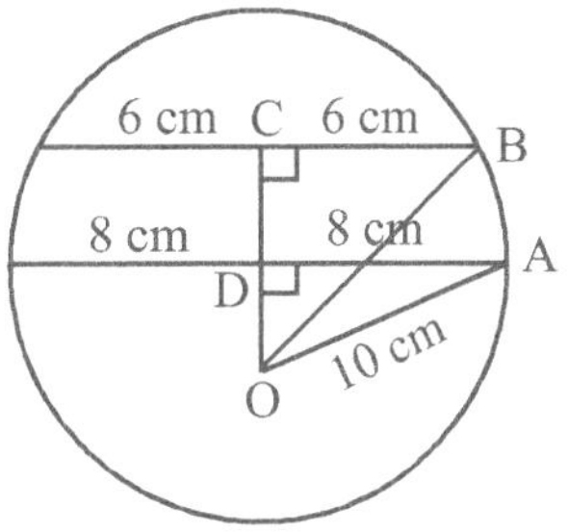

In ΔADO,

$OD = \sqrt{(AO)^2 - AD^2}$

$= \sqrt{100\text{cm}^2 - 64\text{cm}^2} = 6$ cm

In ΔBCO,

$OC - \sqrt{OB^2 - CB^2}$

$= \sqrt{100\text{cm}^2 - 36\text{cm}^2} = 8$ cm

Distance between chords = OC – OD = 2cm

40. (a) Required average age

$= \left(\frac{15\times 36+12\times 16}{36+12}\right)$ years

$= \left(\frac{540+192}{48}\right)$ years $= \left(\frac{732}{48}\right)$ years $=$ 15.25 years.

41. (c) Let C completes the work in x days.

Work done by (A + B) in 1 day $= \frac{1}{10}$

Work done by (B + C) in 1 day $= \frac{1}{18}$

A's 5 days' work + B's 10 days' work + C's 15 days' work = 1

or (A + B)'s 5 days' work + (B + C)'s 5 days' work + C's 10 days' work = 1

or $\frac{5}{10}+\frac{5}{18}+\frac{10}{x} = 1$ or $x = 45$ days

42. (d) $\frac{1}{2}[4-(2+16)+3(-16-4)+3(4+2)]$

$= \frac{1}{2}[56-60+18]=7$

43. (b) Interest for one year

$= ₹\ 212.50 \times \frac{3}{100} \times 1 = ₹\ \frac{51}{8}$

Thus in 8 years, the interest is ₹51.

44. (b) Let S.P. = ₹100. Then, C.P. = ₹96; Profit = ₹4.

∴ Profit %

$= \left(\frac{4}{96} \times 100\right)\% = \frac{25}{6}\% = 4.17\%. \approx 4.2\%$

45. (d) $x+x+2+x+4+x+6=4\times 36$

$\Rightarrow 4x+12=144 \Rightarrow 4x=144-12$

$\Rightarrow 4x=132 \Rightarrow x=\frac{132}{4}=33$

46. (d) Total number of students studying B.Sc. in all the colleges together

$=350+325+300+375+425$

$=1775$

47. (c) Total number of students studying B.Sc. in colleges C and E

$=300+425=725$

Total number of students studying B.A. in colleges A and B

$=275+300=575$

∴ Required ratio $=725:575$

$=29:23$

48. (a) Total number of students studying in different streams in all the colleges:

B.Sc. → 1775

B.A. → $275+300+325+450+325=1675$

B.Com. → $425+475+325+425+225=1875$

∴ Required ratio

$=1775:1675:1875$

$=71:67:75$

49. (a) Volume of the bucket = volume of the sand emptied

Volume of sand = $\pi(21)^2 \times 36$

Let r be the radius of the conical heap.

Then, $\frac{1}{3}\pi r^2 \times 12 = \pi(21)^2 \times 36$

or $r^2 = (21)^2 \times 9$ or $r = 21 \times 3 = 63$

50. (c) Volume of the liquid in the cylindrical vessel

= Volume of the conical vessel

$= \left(\frac{1}{3} \times \frac{22}{7} \times 12 \times 12 \times 50\right) cm^3$

$= \left(\frac{22 \times 4 \times 12 \times 50}{7}\right) cm^3.$

Let the height of the liquid in the vessel be h.

Then, $\frac{22}{7} \times 10 \times 10 \times h = \frac{22 \times 4 \times 12 \times 50}{7}$

or $h = \left(\frac{4 \times 12 \times 50}{10 \times 10}\right) = 24$ cm.

51.	(d)	52.	(b)	53.	(b)	54.	(c)	55.	(c)
56.	(a)	57.	(a)	58.	(b)	59.	(b)	60.	(d)
61.	(a)	62.	(d)	63.	(b)	64.	(a)	65.	(c)
66.	(a)	67.	(b)	68.	(d)	69.	(b)	70.	(a)
71.	(b)	72.	(c)	73.	(c)	74.	(a)	75.	(d)
76.	(a)	77.	(a)	78.	(a)	79.	(b)	80.	(d)
81.	(c)	82.	(d)	83.	(d)	84.	(c)	85.	(b)
86.	(d)	87.	(a)	88.	(b)	89.	(b)	90.	(c)
91.	(a)	92.	(c)	93.	(a)	94.	(b)	95.	(b)
96.	(c)	97.	(a)	98.	(c)	99.	(c)	100.	(d)

PRACTICE SET- 11

GENERAL INTELLIGENCE & REASONING

DIRECTIONS (Qs. 1-3): *In each of the following questions, select the related letters/word/number from the given alternatives.*

1. $\frac{M}{AC}:\frac{N}{AD}::\frac{O}{AE}:?$

(a) $\frac{P}{AF}$ (b) $\frac{Q}{AB}$

(c) $\frac{P}{AC}$ (d) $\frac{R}{AD}$

2. 6 : 11 : : 11 : ?

(a) 6 (b) 17

(c) 21 (d) 30

3. Patrol : Security : : Insurance : ?

(a) Money (b) Policy

(c) Savings (d) Risk

DIRECTIONS (Qs. 4-6): *In each of the following questions find the odd word/letters/number/ figure from the given responses.*

4. (a) Room (b) Chamber

(c) Veranda (d) Cabin

5. (a) 49 – 33 (b) 62 – 46

(c) 83 – 67 (d) 70 – 55

6. (a) JKOP (b) MNST

(c) CABD (d) OPWX

7. Arrange the following in the meaningful/logical order:

1. Exhaust 2. Night
3. Day 4. Sleep
5. Work

(a) 1, 3, 5, 2, 4 (b) 3, 5, 1, 4, 2

(c) 3, 5, 1, 2, 4 (d) 3, 5, 2, 1, 4

DIRECTIONS (Qs. 8-9): *In each of the following questions, a series is given with one term missing. Choose the correct alternative from the given ones that will complete the series.*

8. (?), PSVYB, EHKNQ, TWZCF, ILORU

(a) BEHKN (b) ADGJM

(c) SVYBE (d) ZCFIL

9. 975, 864, 753, 642, ?

(a) 431 (b) 314

(c) 531 (d) 532

10. M is the son of P. Q is the grand daughter of O who is the husband of P. How is M related to O?

(a) Son (b) Daughter

(c) Mother (d) Father

11. In a row of boys, Srinath is 7th from the left and Venkat is 12th from the right. If they interchange their positions, Srinath becomes 22nd from the left. How many boys are there in the row?

(a) 19 (b) 31

(c) 33 (d) 34

12. From the given alternative words, select the word which **cannot** be formed using the letters of the given word:

MISFORTUNE

(a) FORT (b) TURN

(c) SOFT (d) ROAM

13. If SPARK is coded as TQBSL, what will be the code for FLAME?

(a) GMBNF (b) GNBNF

(c) GMCND (d) GMBMF

14. If '–' stands for '÷' '+' stands for '×', '÷' for '–' and '×' for '+', which one of the following equations in correct?

(a) $30-6+5\times4\div2=27$

(b) $30+6-5\div4\times2=30$

(c) $30\times6\div5-4+2=32$

(d) $30\div6\times5+4-2=40$

15. If 841 = 3,633 = 5,425 = 7 then 217 – ?
(a) 6 (b) 7
(c) 8 (d) 9

16. Find the missing number from the given responses:

5	6	12
4	3	4
2	3	?
18	27	96

(a) 4 (b) 5
(c) 3 (d) 6

17. A child is looking for his father, he went 90 metres in the east before turning to his right. He went 20 metres before turning to his right again to look for his father at his uncle's place 30 metres from this point. His father was not there. From here he went 100 metres to his north before meeting his father in a street. How far did the son meet his father from the starting point ?
(a) 80m (b) 100m
(c) 260m (d) 140m

DIRECTION (Q. 18): *In the following question, two statements P and Q are given followed by four conclulions I, II, III and IV. You have to consider the two statements to be true even if they seem to be at variance from commonly known facts. You have to decide which of the given conclusions, if any, follow the given statements.*

18. Statements:
P. All men are women.
Q. All women are crazy.
Conclusions:
I. All men are crazy.
II. All the crazy are men.
III. Some of the crazy are men
IV. Some of the crazy are women
(a) None of the condusions follows
(b) All the conclusions follow
(c) Only I, III and IV follow
(d) Only II and III follow

19. How many triangles are there in the given figure?

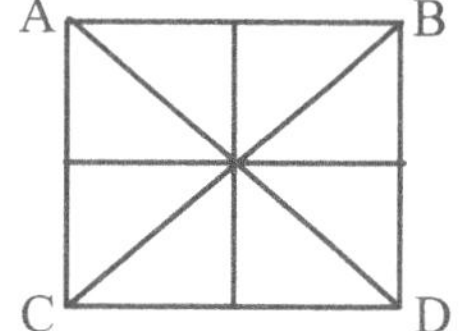

(a) 16 (b) 14
(c) 8 (d) 12

20. Which of the answer figure indicates the best relationship between milk, goat, cow, hen?

Answer figures:

(a)  (b) 

(c) (d)

DIRECTION (Q. 21): *In the following question which answer figure will complete the question figure?*

21. Question Figure :

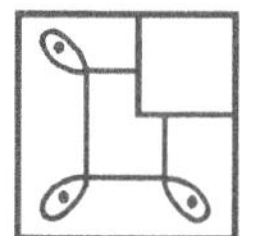

Answer Figures:

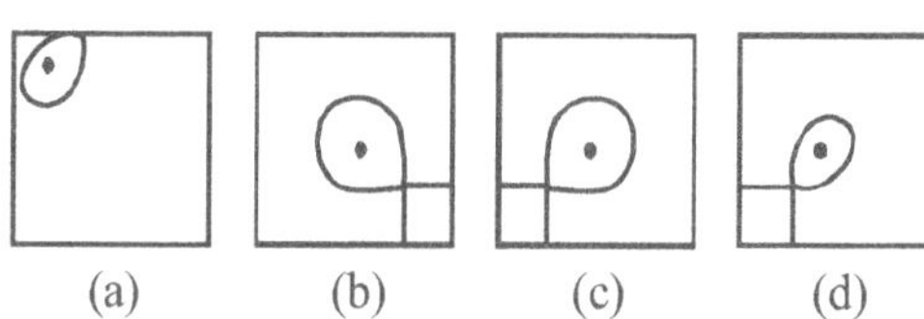

(a) (b) (c) (d)

22. From the answer figures, select the one in which the question figure is hidden/embedded.

Question Figure:

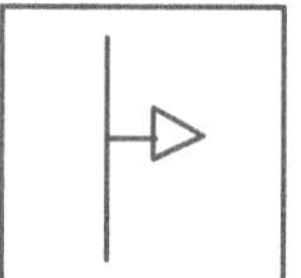

Answer Figures:

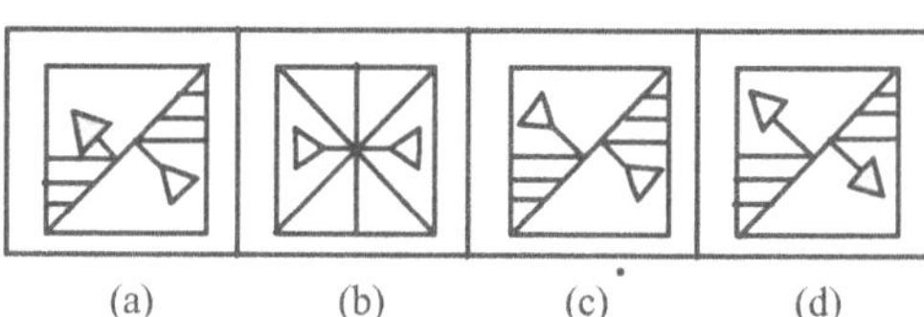

(a) (b) (c) (d)

23. A piece of paper is folded and cut as shown below in the question figures. From the given answer figures, indicate how it will appear when opened.

Question figures:

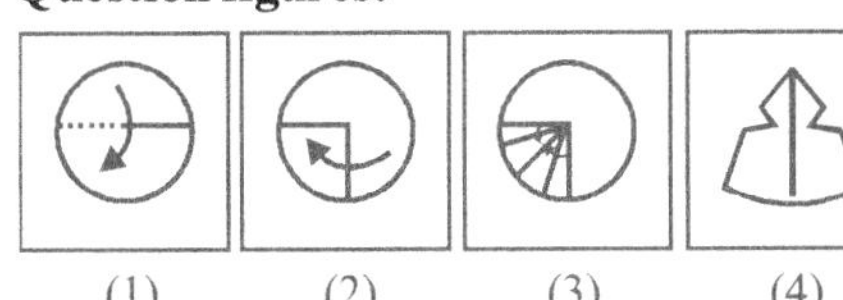

(1) (2) (3) (4)

Answer figures:

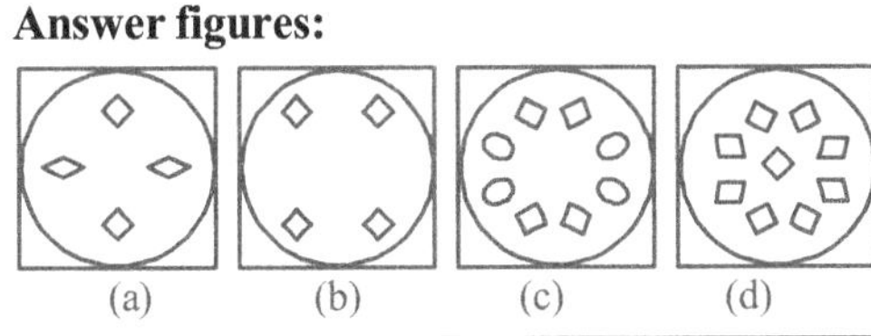

(a) (b) (c) (d)

DIRECTION (Q. 24): *If a mirror is placed on the line MN, then which of the answer figures is the correct image of the given question figure?*

24. Question Figure:

Answer Figures:

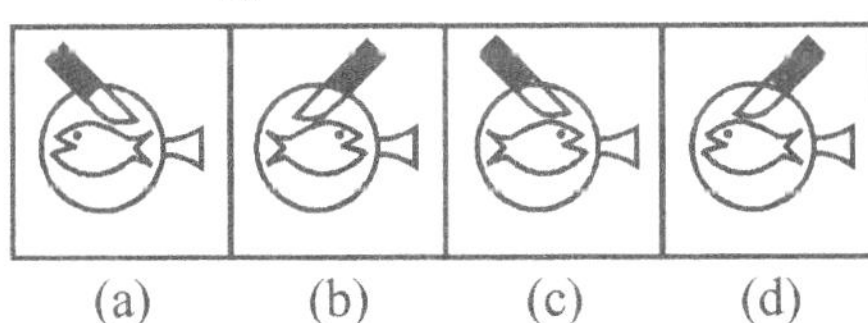

(a) (b) (c) (d)

25. A word is represented by only one set of numbers as given in any one of the alternatives. The sets of numbers given in the alternatives are represented by two classes of alphabets as in the matrix given below. The columns and rows of Matrix are numbered from 0 to 6. A letter from the matrix can be represented first by its row and next by its column, e.g.'A' can be represented by 42, 62, etc. and 'P' can be represented by 15, 43, etc. Similarly, you have to identify the set for the word 'CALM'.

Matrix

0	1	2	3	4	5	6
1	H	R	E	I	P	S
2	S	G	N	D	Z	I
3	B	U	F	T	K	L
4	V	A	P	C	Y	A
5	M	W	C	O	X	N
6	B	A	E	J	L	O

(a) 44, 62, 65, 51 (b) 53, 42, 65, 36
(c) 53, 54, 51, 31 (d) 44, 54, 65, 24

QUANTITATIVE APTITUDE

26. The H.C.F. and L.C.M. of two numebrs are 8 and 48 respectively. If one of the numbers is 24, then the other number is
(a) 48 (b) 36
(c) 24 (d) 16

27. The sum of the series
$(1+0.6+0.06+0.006+0.0006+....)$ is
(a) $1\frac{2}{3}$ (b) $1\frac{1}{3}$
(c) $2\frac{1}{3}$ (d) $2\frac{2}{3}$

28. The average of the first 100 positive integers is
(a) 100 (b) 51
(c) 50.5 (d) 49.5

29. If the ratio of cost price and selling price of an article be as 10 : 11, the percentage of profit is
(a) 8 (b) 10
(c) 11 (d) 15

30. Krishna purchased a number of articles at ₹10 for each and the same number for ₹ 14 each. He mixed them together and sold them for ₹13 each. Then his gain or loss percent is
(a) Loss $8\frac{1}{3}\%$ (b) Gain $8\frac{2}{3}\%$
(c) Loss $8\frac{2}{3}\%$ (d) Gain $8\frac{1}{3}\%$

31. Ram borrows a certain sum of money at 8% per annum simple interest and Rahim borrows ₹2,000 at 5% per annum simple interest. If the interest at the end of 3 years is equal, then the amount borrowed by Ram is
(a) ₹1,250 (b) ₹1,500
(c) ₹2,000 (d) ₹1,000

32. Buses start from a bus terminal with a speed of 20 km/hr at intervals of 10 minutes. What is the speed of a man coming from the opposite directiion towards the bus terminal if he meets the buses at intervals of 8 minutes?
(a) 3 km/hr (b) 4 km/hr
(c) 5 km/hr (d) 7 km/hr

33. If 5 men or 7 women can earn ₹ 5,250 per day, how much would 7 men and 13 women earn per day?
(a) ₹11,600 (b) ₹11,700
(c) ₹16,100 (d) ₹17,100

34. A drum of kerosene is $\frac{3}{4}$ full. When 30 litres of kerosene is drawn from it, it remains $\frac{7}{12}$ full. The capacity of the drum is
(a) 120 *l* (b) 135 *l*
(c) 150 *l* (d) 180 *l*

35. In a business partnership among A, B, C and D, the profit is shared as follows:

$$\frac{\text{A's share}}{\text{B's share}} = \frac{\text{B's share}}{\text{C's share}} = \frac{\text{C's share}}{\text{D's share}} = \frac{1}{3}$$

If the total profit is ₹ 4,00,000, the share of C is
(a) ₹1,12,500 (b) ₹1,37,500
(c) ₹90,000 (d) ₹2,70,000

36. ABCD is a quadrilateral in which diagonal BD = 64 cm, AL ⊥ BD and CM ⊥ BD, such that AL = 13.2 cm and CM = 16.8 cm. The area of the quadrilateral ABCD in square centimetres is
(a) 537.6 (b) 960.0
(c) 422.4 (d) 690.0

37. Two tangents are drawn from a point P to a circle at A and B. O is the centre of the circle. If ∠AOP = 60°, then ∠APB is
(a) 120° (b) 90°
(c) 60° (d) 30°

38. P is a point outside a circle and is 13 cm away from its centre. A secant drawn from the point P intersect the circle at points A and B in such a way that PA = 9 cm and AB = 7 cm. The radius of the circle is:
(a) 5.5 cm (b) 5 cm
(c) 4 cm (d) 4.5 cm

39. An equilateral triangle of side 6 cm has its corners cut off to form a regular hexagon. Area (in cm^2) of this regular hexagon will be
(a) $3\sqrt{3}$ (b) $3\sqrt{6}$
(c) $6\sqrt{3}$ (d) $\frac{5\sqrt{3}}{2}$

40. If (a – b) = 3, (b – c) = 5 and (c – a) = 1, then the value of $\frac{a^3 + b^3 + c^3 - 3abc}{a + b + c}$ is
(a) 17.5 (b) 20.5
(c) 10.5 (d) 15.5

41. If $x = 2+\sqrt{3}, y = 2-\sqrt{3}$, then the value of $\frac{x^2 + y^2}{x^3 + y^3}$ is
(a) $\frac{7}{38}$ (b) $\frac{7}{40}$
(c) $\frac{7}{19}$ (d) $\frac{7}{26}$

42. Minimum value of $x^2 + \frac{1}{x^2+1} - 3$ is
(a) –3 (b) –2
(c) 0 (d) –1

43. If $xy + yz + zx = 0$, then $\left(\frac{1}{x^2 - yz} + \frac{1}{y^2 - zx} + \frac{1}{z^2 - xy}\right)(x, y, z \neq 0)$ is equal to
(a) 0 (b) 3
(c) 1 (d) x + y + z

44. If $\sin\theta - \cos\theta = \frac{1}{2}$ the value of $\sin\theta + \cos\theta$ is:
(a) –2 (b) ±2
(c) $\frac{\sqrt{7}}{2}$ (d) 2

45. If $\cos A + \cos^2 A = 1$, then $\sin^2 A + \sin^4 A$ is equal to
(a) 1 (b) $\frac{1}{2}$
(c) 0 (d) –1

46. If x = cosecθ – sinθ and y = secθ – cosθ, then the value of $x^2y^2(x^2 + y^2 + 3)$ is
(a) 0 (b) 1
(c) 2 (d) 3

47. A ladder is resting against a wall at height of 10m. If the ladder is inclined with the ground at an angle of 30°, then the distance of the foot of the ladder from the wall is
(a) $10\sqrt{3}$ m (b) $20\sqrt{3}$ m
(c) $\frac{10}{\sqrt{3}}$ m (d) $\frac{20}{\sqrt{3}}$ m

DIRECTIONS (Qs. 48-50): *The pie chart, given here, represents the number of valid votes obtained by four students who contested election for school leadership. The total number of valid votes polled was 720.*

Observe the chart and answer the questions based on it.

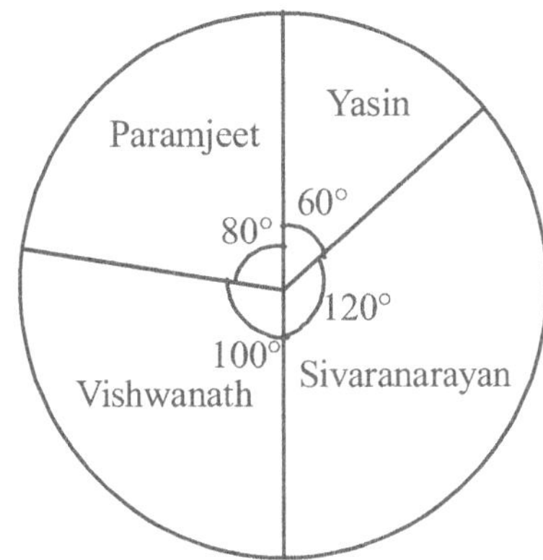

48. What was the minimum number of votes obtained by any candidate?
(a) 100 (b) 110
(c) 120 (d) 130

49. What was the winner....?
(a) Sivaraman (b) Paramjeet
(c) Yasin (d) Vishwanath

50. By how many votes did the winner defeat his nearest rival?
(a) 40 (b) 45
(c) 48 (d) 50

ENGLISH LANGUAGE

DIRECTIONS (Qs. 51-52): *In the following questions out of the four alternatives, choose the one which best expresses the meaning of the given word.*

51. Luxuriant
(a) Luxury loving (b) Lovely
(c) Rich (d) Abundant

52. Cantankerous
(a) Cancerous (b) Ferocious
(c) Quarrelsome (d) Fissiparous

DIRECTIONS (Qs. 53-54): *In the following questions choose the word opposite in meaning to the given word.*

53. Verity
(a) Sanctity (b) Reverence
(c) Falsehood (d) Rarity

54. Fervent
(a) Inexcilable (b) Enduring
(c) Dispassionate (d) Subdued

DIRECTIONS (Qs. 55-56): *Sentences are given with blanks to be filled in with an appropriate word(s). Four alternatives are suggested for each question. Choose the correct alternative out of the four.*

55. Like humans, zoo animals must have a dentist _____ their teeth.
(a) fill (b) filled
(c) filling (d) to be filled

56. It was very kind of you to do the washing-up, but you ______ it.
(a) didn't have to do (b) hadn't to do
(c) mightn't have done (d) mustn't have done

DIRECTIONS (Qs. 57-58): *In the following questions, some of the sentences have errors and some have none. Find out which part of a sentence has an error. The number of that part is your answer. Your answer is (d) i.e., No error.*

57. After knowing truth, (a)/ they took the right decision (b)/ in the matter. (c)/ No error (d)

58. He who has suffered most (a)/ for the cause, (b)/ let him speak. (c)/ No error (d)

DIRECTIONS (Qs. 59-60): *In the following questions, a part of the sentence is printed in* ***bold****. Below are given alternatives to the* ***bold*** *part at (a), (b) and (c) which may improve the sentence. Choose the correct alternative. In case no improvement is needed, your answer is (d).*

59. To get into the building I'll **disguise** as a reproter.
(a) disguise to be (b) disguise as one
(c) disguise myself (d) No improvement

60. He denied that he **had not forged** my signature
(a) would not forge (b) had forged
(c) did not forge (d) No improvement

DIRECTIONS (Qs. 61-62): *In the following questions, out of the four alternatives, choose the one which can be substituted for the given words/sentence.*

61. An underhand device resorted to in order to justify misconduct
(a) Subterfuge (b) Manoeurce
(c) Stratagem (d) Complicity

62. One who criticises popular beliefs which he thinks is mistaken or unwise
(a) Philistine (b) Iconoclast
(c) Imposter (d) Cannibal

DIRECTIONS (Qs. 63-64): *In the following questions, groups of four words are given. In each group, one word is correctly spelt. Find the correctly spelt word.*

63. (a) benidiction (b) besmerch
(c) beneficient (d) benevolence

64. (a) paraphamelia (b) parsimonious
(c) peccadilo (d) peadiatrics

DIRECTIONS (Qs. 65-67): *In the following questions, four alternatives are given for the idiom / phrase underlined in the sentence. Choose the alternative which best express the meaning of the idiom/phrase as your answer.*

65. His investments helped him make a killing in the stock market.
(a) lose money quickly
(b) plan a murder quickly
(c) murder someone quickly
(d) make money quickly

66. There is no gainsaying the fact that the country is in difficulties.
(a) ignoring (b) hiding
(c) forgetting (d) denying

67. For some people, writing verse is as duck takes to water.
(a) like taking the duck to water
(b) like bursting out suddenly
(c) like dropping the duck in the water
(d) like easily and naturally speaking

DIRECTIONS (Qs. 68-69): *In the following questions, the 1st and the last sentences/parts of the passage / sentence are numbered 1 and 6. The rest of the passage / sentence is split into four parts and named P, Q, R and S. These four parts are not given in their proper order. Read the passage/sentence and find out which of the four combinations is correct. Then find the correct answer.*

68. 1. When the Impressionists
P. they made them look like
Q. everyday and often putting
R people you would see
S. painted pictures of people
6. more emphasis on the scene.
(a) RQPS (b) SRQP
(c) PRQS (d) SPRQ

69. 1. Sherlock Holmes is the
P. who is in a state of grace
Q. is raised to the status
R. because in him scientific curiosity
S. exceptional individual
6. of a heroic passion.
(a) PRQS (b) SRQP
(c) SPRQ (d) RPSQ

DIRECTIONS (Qs. 70-74): *Read the passage carefully and choose the correct answer to each question out of four alternative and fill in the blanks.*

PASSAGE

Auctions are public 70 of goods, conducted by an 71 auctioneer. He encourages buyers to 72 higher prices and finally names the 73 bidder as the buyer of the goods. This is called 'knocking down' the goods, for when the bidding ends the auctioneer 74 a small hammer on a table in front of him.

70. (a) sale (b) marketing
(c) promotion (d) viewing

71. (a) authoritative (b) allowed
(c) authentic (d) approved

72. (a) bid (b) buy
(c) get (d) bargain

73. (a) smartest (b) highest
(c) biggest (d) strongest

74. (a) bangs (b) thrashes
(c) smashes (d) hits

DIRECTION (Q. 75): *In the following questions, a sentence has been given in Direct / Indirect. Out of the fouralternatives suggested, select the one which best expresses the same sentence in Indirect/Direct and mark.*

75. He said to me, "I grew these carrots myself."
(a) He told me that he had grown those carrots himself.
(b) He told me that he grew those carrots himself.

(c) He told me I grew these carrots myself.
(d) He told me that he grew these carrots himself.

GENERAL AWARENESS

76. Who was the founder of The Servants of India Society?
(a) G.K. Gokhale (b) M.G Ranade
(c) B.G Tilak (d) Bipin Chandra Pal

77. The term 'Caste' was derived from
(a) Portuguese (b) Dutch
(c) German (d) English

78. Judicial review in the Indian Constitution is based on:
(a) Rule of Law
(b) Due process of Law
(c) Procedure established by Law
(d) Precedents and Conventions

79. The proposal for the creation of new All-India Services can be considered only:
(a) if majority of State Legislatures make such demand
(b) if Lok Sabha passes a resolution by two-thirds majority
(c) if the Rajya Sabha passes a resolution by two-thirds majority
(d) None of the above

80. Formalised system of trading agreements with groups of countries is known as
(a) Trading blocks
(b) Trade ventures
(c) Trade partners
(d) Trade organisations

81. During periods of inflation, tax rates should
(a) increase (b) decrease
(c) remain constant (d) fluctuate

82. Brain drain has been caused by:
(a) failure to recognise talent in the originating country.
(b) the lure of high living standards
(c) lack of employment opportunities
(d) socio-economic instability

83. The messenger satellite launched by NASA is to study
(a) Mercury (b) Venus
(c) Satrun (d) Jupiter

84. A concave lens always forms an image which is?
(a) real and erect
(b) virtual and erect
(c) real and inverted
(d) virtual and inverted

85. Optical fibres are based on the phenomenon of
(a) Interference
(b) Dispersion
(c) Diffraction
(d) Total Internal Reflection

86. A vitamin requires cobalt for its activity. The vitamin is
(a) Vitamin B_{12} (b) Vitamin D
(c) Vitamin B_2 (d) Vitamin A

87. A form of condensation that reduces visibility and causes breathing problems is
(a) Dew (b) Frost
(c) Smog (d) Mist

88. One of the constituents of tear gas is
(a) Ethane (b) Ethanol
(c) Ether (d) Chloropicrin

89. In coriander, the useful parts are
(a) roots & leaves
(b) leaves & flowers
(c) leaves & dried fruits
(d) flowers & dried fruits

90. The disease that kills more people than lung cancer as a consequence of air pollution is:
(a) chronic bronchitis (b) asthma
(c) emphesema (d) heart attack

91. The stability of a pond ecosystem depends on
(a) micro-organisms and fishes
(b) micro-organisms and zoo planktons
(c) fishes and reptiles
(d) producers and consumers

92. Seismic sea waves which approach the coasts at greater force are known as
(a) Tides (b) Tsunami
(c) Current (d) Cyclone

93. A plant known only in cultivation having arisen under domestication is referred to as:
(a) Scion (b) Cultigen
(c) Cultivar (d) Clone

94. The total population divided by available arable land area is referred to as
(a) Population density
(b) Nutritional density
(c) Agricultural density
(d) Industrial density

95. The book titled 'The Indian War of Independence' was written by
(a) Krishna Verma (b) Madame Cama
(c) B.G Tilak (d) V.D. Savarkar

96. The Central Drug Research Institute of India is located at
(a) Madras (b) Lucknow
(c) Delhi (d) Bangalore

97. Which country has successfully tested world's largest unmanned transport drone "FH-98"?
(a) Germany (b) China
(c) Japan (d) Indonesia

98. Who has been elected as new Chairman of Association of Mutual Funds in India (AMFI)?
(a) M S Jha (b) Nimesh Shah
(c) Kailash Kulkarni (d) A Balasubramanian

99. Who has won the India's first medal in athletics at the Youth Olympic Games 2018?
(a) Simran (b) Lakshya Sen
(c) Suraj Panwar (d) Tababi Devi

100. 'Swastha Bharat Yatra' national campaign has been launched for which purpose?
(a) Safe Food (b) Healthy Drink
(c) Hygienic Locality (d) Secure Travelling

Hints & Explanations

1. (a) As,

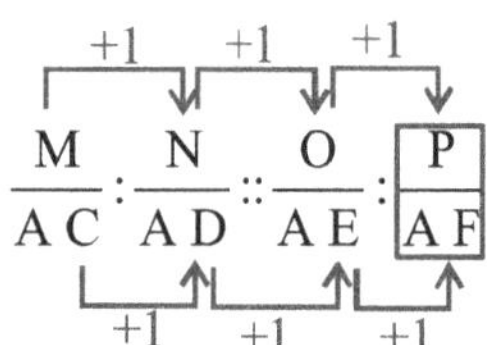

2. (c) As, $6 \times 2 - 1 = 11$
Similarly, $11 \times 2 - 1 = \boxed{21}$

3. (d) In order to ensure security, police or defence personnel patrol the area. Similarly, to cover risk, insurance is done.

4. (c) Except Veranda, all others are surrounded by four walls.

5. (d) $49 - 33 = 16, 62 - 46 = 16$
$83 - 67 = 16$ But, $70 - 55 = 15$

6. (b) Except MNST, all others are having a vowel.

7. (c) Meaningful order of the words:
3. Day → 5. Work → 1. Exhaust → 2. Night → 4. Sleep

8. (b) The pattern is as follows :

$P \xrightarrow{+3} S \xrightarrow{+3} V \xrightarrow{+3} Y \xrightarrow{+3} B$

$E \xrightarrow{+3} H \xrightarrow{+3} K \xrightarrow{+3} N \xrightarrow{+3} Q$

$T \xrightarrow{+3} W \xrightarrow{+3} Z \xrightarrow{+3} C \xrightarrow{+3} F$

$I \xrightarrow{+3} L \xrightarrow{+3} O \xrightarrow{+3} R \xrightarrow{+3} U$

Now, $P \xrightarrow{+4} T, E \xrightarrow{+4} I$

Therefore, the first letter of the first term should be

$E \xrightarrow{-4} A$

9. (c) 975 864 753 642 $\boxed{531}$
(−111, −111, −111, −111)

10. (a) O is the husband of P. M is the son of P. Therefore , M is the son of O.

11. (c)

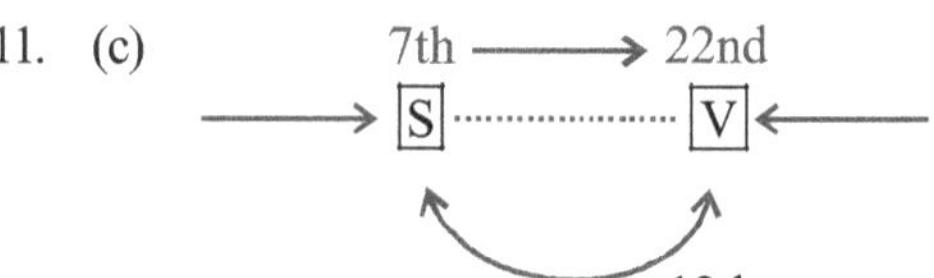

Total number of boys in the row
$= 22 + 12 - 1 = \boxed{33}$

12. (d) There is no 'A' letter in the given word.

13. (a)

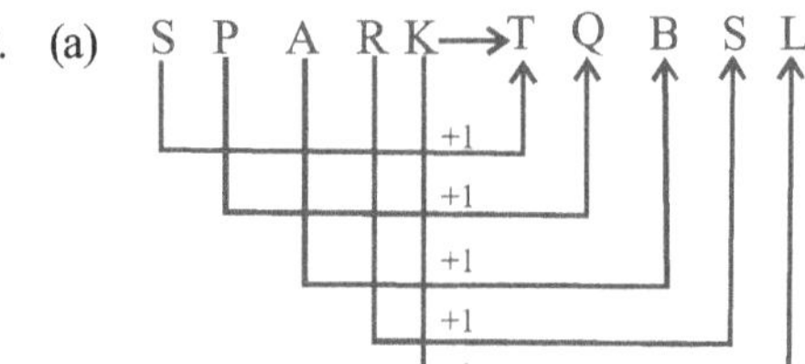

Similarly,

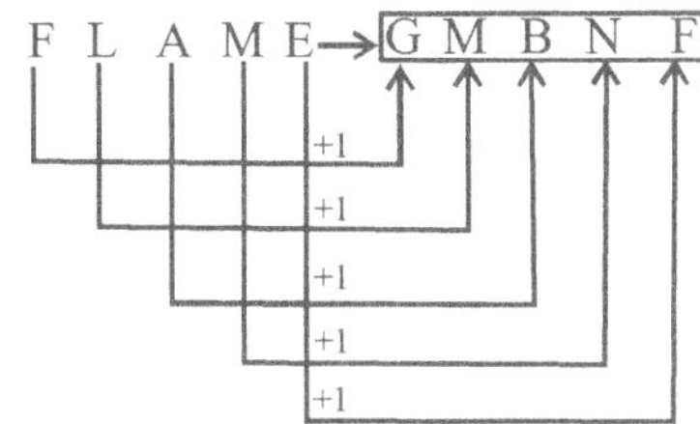

14. (a) $30-6+5\times4\div2=27$
$\Rightarrow 30\div6\times5+4-2=27$
$\Rightarrow 25+4-2=27$
$30+6-5\div4\times2=30$
$\Rightarrow 30\times6\div5-4+2=30$
$\Rightarrow 36-4+2\neq30$
$30\times6\div5-4+2=32$
$\Rightarrow 30+6-5\div4\times2\neq32$

15. (d) As, $\frac{8}{4}=2; 2+1=3$
$\frac{6}{3}=2; 2+3=5$
$\frac{4}{2}=2; 2+7=9$

16. (d) $5+4=9$ and $9\times2=18$
$6+3=9$ and $9\times3=27$
$12+4=16$ and ?
$=\frac{96}{16}=\boxed{6}$

17. (b)

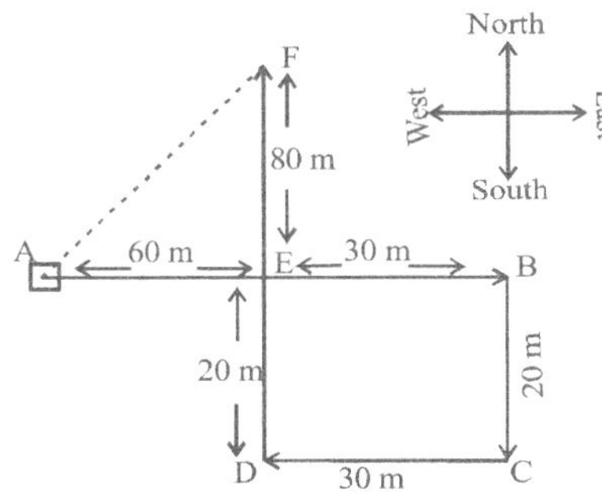

$\therefore$ Required distance = AF
$=\sqrt{(80)^2+(60)^2}$
$\sqrt{6400+3600}=\sqrt{10000}=\boxed{100m}$

18. (c)
19. (a)
20. (c)

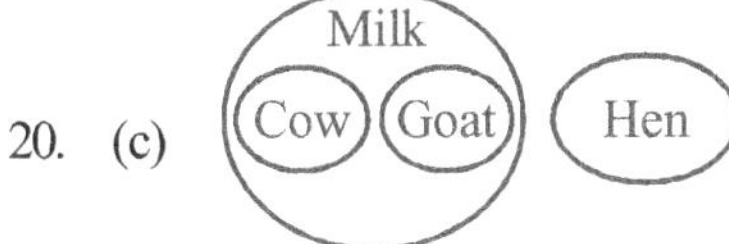

21. (d)

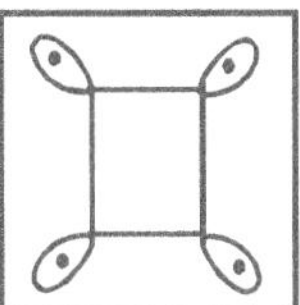

22. (d)
23. (c)
24. (c)
25. (a) By matching code
42, 62, 85, 51 Letters Resembles to CALM in the
MATRI X.
26. (d) $p\times q=HCF\times LCM$
$\therefore$ Second number $=\frac{8\times48}{24}=16$
27. (a) $1+0.6+0.06+0.006+0.0006+...=1.666...$
$=1.\bar{6}=1\frac{6}{9}=1\frac{2}{3}$
28. (c) $1+2+3+......+n=\frac{n(n+1)}{2}$
$\therefore$ Average of these numbers
$\therefore$ Average $=\frac{n+1}{2}$
$=\frac{100+1}{2}=50.5$
29. (b) Gain = 11x – 10x = ₹x
$\therefore p\%=\frac{p\times100}{p}\times100=\frac{x}{10x}\times100=10$
30. (a) Average cost of $=\frac{10+14}{2}=12$
QP = 13
$P\%=\frac{13-12}{12}\times100=8\frac{1}{3}$
31. (a) Let Ram borrowed ₹ P
$\frac{P\times8\times3}{100}=\frac{2000\times5\times3}{100}$
$P=\frac{2000\times5}{8}=$ ₹1,250
32. (c) Distance coverd in 10 minutes at 20 kmph = distance covered in 8 minutes at (20 + x) kmph
$\Rightarrow 20\times\frac{10}{60}=\frac{8}{60}(20+x)$

$\Rightarrow 200 = 160 + 8x$
$\Rightarrow 8x = 40$

$\Rightarrow x = \frac{40}{8} = 5$ kmph

33. (d) 5 men $\equiv$ 7 women

$\therefore$ 7 men $\equiv \frac{7}{5} \times 7 = \frac{49}{5}$ women

$\therefore$ 7 men + 13 women

$= \frac{49}{5} + 13 = \frac{114}{5}$ women

Now,

$\because$ 7 women $\equiv$ ₹5250

$\therefore \frac{114}{5}$ women

$\equiv \frac{5250}{7} \times \frac{114}{5} =$ ₹17100

34. (d) Let the capacity of the drum be x litres.

$\therefore \frac{3x}{4} - 30 = \frac{7x}{12}$

$\Rightarrow \frac{3x}{4} - \frac{7x}{12} = 30$

$\Rightarrow \frac{9x - 7x}{12} = 30$

$\Rightarrow \frac{x}{6} = 30 = x = 6 \times 30 = 180$ litres

35. (c) A : B = 1 : 3
B : C = 1 : 3 = 3 : 9
C : D = 1 : 3 = 9 : 27
$\therefore$ A : B : C : D = 1 : 3 : 9 : 27
Sum of ratios = 1 + 3 + 9 + 27 = 40
$\therefore$ C's share of profit

$= \frac{9}{40} \times 400000 =$ ₹90000

36. (b)

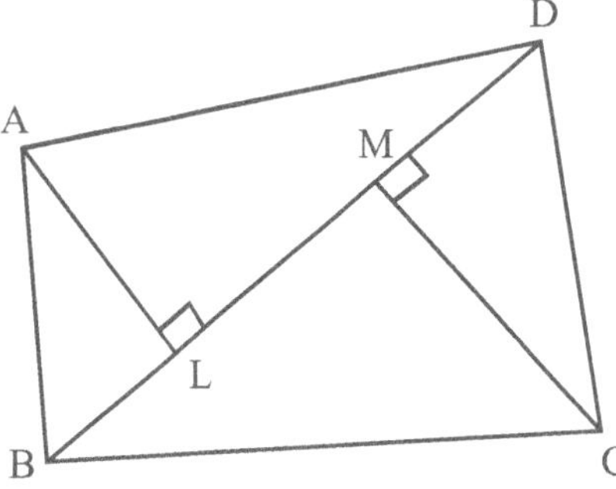

Given:
BD = 64 cm
AL = 13.2 cm
CM = 16.8 cm
So, Area (ABCD) = Area (ΔABD) + Area (ΔBCD)

$= \frac{1}{2} \times AL \times BD + \frac{1}{2} \times CM \times BD$

$= \frac{1}{2} \times BD \times (AL + CM) = \frac{64}{2}(13.2 + 16.8)$

$= 32 \times 30 = 960 \text{ cm}^2$

37. (c)

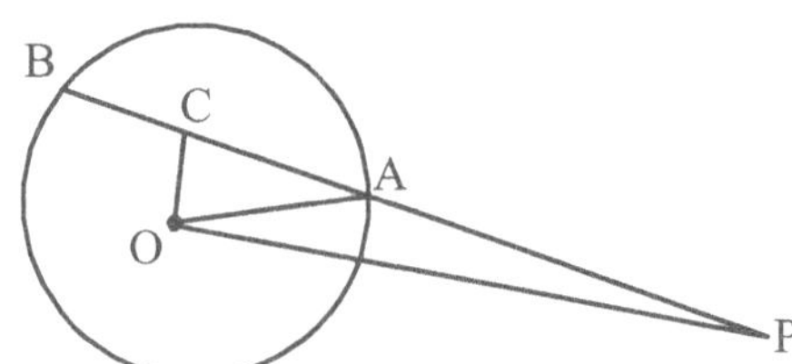

In right Δs OAP and OPB,
AP = PB, OA = OB
OP = OP
$\therefore \Delta OAP \cong \Delta OBP$
$\therefore \angle AOP = \angle POB$ and $\angle APO = \angle OPB$
From Δ AOP,
$\angle APO = 180° - 90° - 60° = 30°$
$\therefore \angle APB = 2 \times 30 = 60°$

38. (b)

OC $\perp$ AB
AC = BC = 3.5 cm OP = 13 cm
PC = 9 + 3.5 = 12.5 cm

$\therefore OC = \sqrt{OP^2 - PC^2}$

$= \sqrt{13^2 - 12^2} = \sqrt{12.75}$

$\therefore OA = \sqrt{OC^2 + CA^2} = \sqrt{12.75 + (3.5)^2}$

$= \sqrt{12.75 + 12.25} = \sqrt{25} = 5$ cm

39. (c)

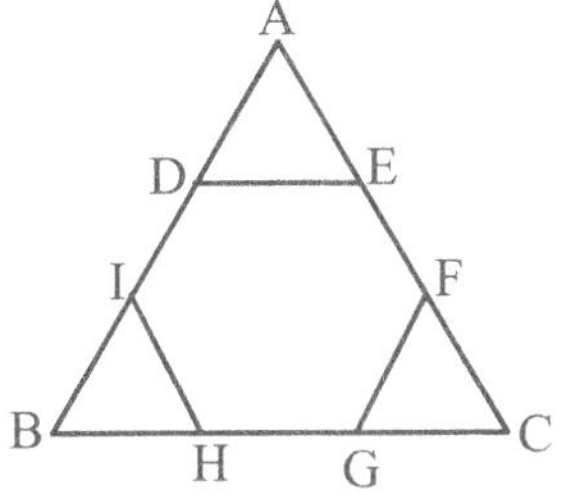

Side of the regular hexagon

$= \frac{1}{3} \times 6 = 2$ cm

$\therefore$ Area of the hexagon $= \frac{3\sqrt{3}}{2} a^2$

$= \frac{3\sqrt{3}}{2} \times 2 \times 2 = 6\sqrt{3}$ sq. cm.

40. (a) $a^3 + b^3 + c^3 - 3abc$
$= (a + b + 3)$

$= \frac{1}{2}(a+b+c)\left[(a-b)^2+(b-c)^2+(c-a)^2\right]$

$\therefore \frac{a^3+b^3+c^3-3abc}{a+b+c}$

$= \frac{1}{2}\left[(a-b)^2+(b-c)^2+(c-a)^2\right]$

$= \frac{1}{2}(9+25+1) = \frac{35}{2} = 17.5$

41. (d) $x = 2+\sqrt{3}, y = 2-\sqrt{3}$
$x + y = 4; xy = 4 - 3 = 1$

$\therefore \frac{x^2+y^2}{x^3+y^3} = \frac{(x+y)^2-2xy}{(x+y)^3-3xy(x+y)}$

$= \frac{16-2}{64-3\times 4} = \frac{14}{52} = \frac{7}{26}$

42. (b) $x^2 + \frac{1}{x^2+1} - 3$

is minimum when $x = 0$

$0 + \frac{1}{0+1} - 3 = -2$

43. (d)

44. (c) $\sin\theta - \cos\theta = \frac{1}{2}$

$\sin\theta + \cos\theta = x.$

On squaring and adding.

$2(\sin^2\theta + \cos^2\theta) = \frac{1}{4} + x^2$

$\Rightarrow x^2 = 2 - \frac{1}{4} = \frac{7}{4}$

$\Rightarrow x = \frac{\sqrt{7}}{2}$

45. (a) $\cos A = 1 - \cos^2 A = \sin^2 A$
$\therefore \sin^2 A + \sin^4 A = \sin^2 A + \cos^2 A = 1$

46. (b) $x^2y^2 (x^2 + y^2 + 3)$
$= (\text{cosec}\theta - \sin\theta)^2 (\sec\theta - \cos\theta)^2$
$\{(\text{cosec}\theta - \sin\theta)^2 + (\sec\theta - \cos\theta)^2 + 3\}$

$= \left(\frac{1}{\sin\theta} - \sin\theta\right)^2 \left(\frac{1}{\cos\theta} - \cos\theta\right)^2$

$\left\{\left(\frac{1}{\sin\theta} - \sin\theta\right)^2 \left(\frac{1}{\cos\theta} - \cos\theta\right)^2 + 3\right\}$

$= \left(\frac{1-\sin^2\theta}{\sin\theta}\right)^2 + \left(\frac{1-\cos^2\theta}{\cos\theta}\right)^2$

$\left\{\left(\frac{1-\sin^2\theta}{\sin\theta}\right)^2 + \left(\frac{1-\cos^2\theta}{\cos\theta}\right)^2 + 3\right\}$

$= \left(\frac{\cos^2\theta}{\sin\theta}\right)^2 \left(\frac{\sin^2\theta}{\cos\theta}\right)^2$

$= \left\{\left(\frac{\cos^2\theta}{\sin\theta}\right)^2 + \left(\frac{\sin^2\theta}{\cos\theta}\right)^2 + 3\right\}$

$= \cos^2\theta \times \sin^2\theta$

$\left(\frac{\cos^6\theta + \sin^6\theta + 3\cos^2\theta.\sin^2\theta}{\cos^2\theta.\sin^2\theta}\right)$

$= \cos^6\theta + \sin^6\theta + 3\cos^2\theta \sin^2\theta$

$= \left\{(\cos^2\theta)^3 + (\sin^2\theta)^3\right\} + 3\cos^2\theta.\sin^2\theta$

$= (\cos^2\theta + \sin^2\theta)^3 - 3\cos^2\theta.\sin^2\theta$
$(\cos^2\theta + \sin^2\theta) + 3\cos^2\theta.\sin^2\theta$
$= 1 - 3\cos^2\theta.\sin^2\theta + 3\cos^2\theta.\sin^2\theta = 1$

47. (a)

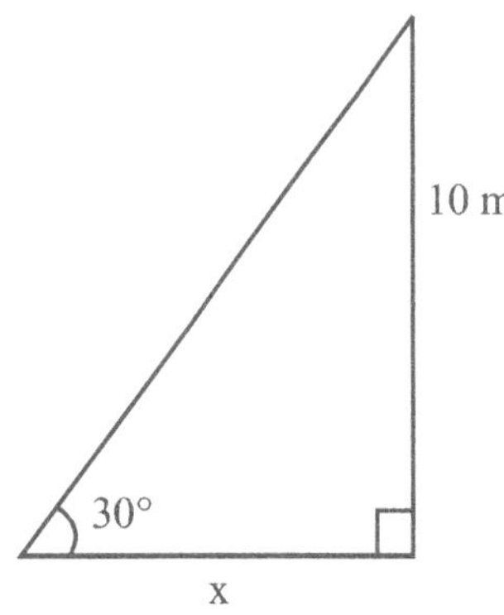

Let ‘x’ be the distance of foot of ladder

$\tan 30° = \frac{P}{B} = \frac{10}{x}$

$\Rightarrow \frac{1}{\sqrt{3}} = \frac{10}{x} \Rightarrow x = 10\sqrt{3}$ m

48. (c) Yasin got the minimum votes.

$\because 360° = 720$

$\therefore 60° = \frac{720}{360} \times 60 = 120$

49. (a) Sivaraman got the maximum votes. i.e.

$\frac{720}{360} \times 120 = 240$ votes

He was the winner.

50. (a) Angles of the difference of votes of the winner and the nearest rival = 120 – 100 = 20°

$\because 360° = 720$

$\therefore 20° = \frac{720}{360} \times 20 = 40$

51. (d) The word **Luxuriant (Adjective)** means: growing thickly and strongly; rich in something that is pleasant or beautiful; abundant.

52. (c) The word **Cantankerous (Adjective)** means : bad tempered and always complaining. Hence, the words **cantankerous** and quarrelsome are synonymous.

53. (c) The word **Verity (Noun)** means: a belief or principle about life that is accepted as true; truth.
Hence, the words **verity** and **falsehood** are antonymous.

54. (c) The word **Fervent (Adjective)** means: having or showing very strong and sincere feelings about something; ardent.
The word **Dispassionate (Adjective)** means: not influenced by emotion; impartial.
Hence, the words fervent and dispassionate are antonymous.

55. (c) Must have a dentist filling is the correct use of tense.

56. (d) Correct use of tense in the given context

57. (a) **After knowing the truth** will be correct usage.

58. (c) Replace **let him speak** by **should be allowed to speak.**

59. (c) disguise myself

60. (b) had forged

61. (c) Deceit used in order to achieve one is goal.

62. (b) A person who attacks or criticizes cherished beliefs or instructions.

63. (d) Correct spellings of other words are: benediction, besmirch and beneficent.

64. (b) Correct spellings of other words are: paraphernalia, peccadillo and paediatrics.

65. (d) Idiom **make a killing** means : to make a lot of money quickly.

66. (d) Idiom **Gainsay (verb)** means : to disagree; to deny.

67. (d) Idiom ‘as duck takes to water’ means: easily and smoothly.

68. (d) 69. (c) 70. (a) 71. (d) 72. (a)
73. (b) 74. (a)

75. (a) When the sentence is converted from direct speech to indirect speech, the pronoun 'I' is converted to 'he' and the simple past tense gets itself converted into past perfect tense.

76. (a) 77. (a) 78. (c) 79. (c) 80. (a)
81. (a) 82. (c) 83. (a) 84. (b) 85. (d)
86. (a) 87. (c) 88. (d) 89. (c) 90. (c)
91. (d) 92. (b) 93. (b) 94. (a) 95. (d)
96. (b) 97. (b) 98. (b) 99. (c) 100. (a)

PRACTICE SET- 12

GENERAL INTELLIGENCE & REASONING

DIRECTIONS (Qs. 1-2) : *In each of the following questions, select the related letters/word/number from the given alternatives.*

1. ABE : 8 : : KLO : ?
   (a) 37 (b) 39 (c) 38 (d) 36
2. Fox : Cunning : : Rabbit : ?
   (a) Courageous (b) Dangerous
   (c) Timid (d) Ferocious
3. Find out a set of numbers amongst the four sets of numbers given in the alternatives, which is the most similar to the numbers given in the question.
   Given : (6, 30, 90)
   (a) 6, 42, 86 (b) 7, 42, 218
   (c) 6, 24, 70 (d) 8, 48, 192

DIRECTIONS (Qs. 4-6) : *In each of the following questions find the odd word/letters/number/ figure from the given responses.*

4. (a) Mouth Organ (b) Electric Guitar
   (c) Keyboard (d) Sonata
5. (a) CAFD (b) TSWV
   (c) IGLJ (d) OMRP
6. (a) 162 (b) 405
   (c) 567 (d) 644
7. Which one of the given responses would be a meaningful order of the following words ?
   A. Family B. Community
   C. Member D. Locality
   E. Country
   (a) C, A, D, B, E (b) C, A, B, D, E
   (c) C, A, B, E, D (d) C, A, D, E, B

DIRECTIONS (Qs. 8-9) : *In Question, a series is given, with one/two term missing. Choose the correct alternative from the given ones that will complete the series.*

8. BMRG, DLTF, FKVE, HJXD, __ ? __
   (a) JIZC (b) JZIB
   (c) GIFB (d) MOLC
9. 7, 9, 13, 21, 37, ?
   (a) 58 (b) 63
   (c) 69 (d) 72
10. X and Y are brothers. R is the father of Y. S is the brother of T and maternal uncle of X. What is T to R?
    (a) Mother (b) Wife
    (c) Sister (d) Brother
11. The average age of 25 suboridinates in an office is 30 years. If the age of Manager is added, the average increases to 31 years. What is the age of the Manager?
    (a) 26 (b) 36
    (c) 46 (d) 56
12. From the given alternative words, select the word which can be formed using the letters of the given word:
    STRANGULATION
    (a) TRIANGLE (b) GARLAND
    (c) ROASTING (d) TRAUMA
13. In a certain code SISTER is written as RHRSDQ. How is UNCLE written in that code ?
    (a) TMBKD (b) TBMKD
    (c) TVBOD (d) TMKBD
14. If L denotes ×
    M denotes ÷ ; P denotes + ; Q denotes –
    then 16 P 24 M 8 Q 6 M 2 L 3 = ?
    (a) 10 (b) 9
    (c) 12 (d) 11

15. Some equations have been solved on the basis of a certain system. Find the correct answer for the unsolved equation on that basis. If 9 * 7 = 32, 13 * 7 = 120, 17 * 9 = 208, then 19 * 11 = ?
(a) 150 (b) 180
(c) 210 (d) 240

DIRECTION (Q. 16): *Select the missing number from the given responses :*

16.

7	3	2
4	9	6
2	1	5
69	91	?

(a) 58 (b) 51
(c) 65 (d) 64

17. K is a place which is located 2 km away in the north-west direction from the capital P, R is another place that is located 2 km away in the south-west direction from K. M is another place and that is located 2 km away in north-west direction from R. T is yet another place that is located 2 km away in the south-west direction from M. In which direction is T located in relation to P?
(a) South-west (b) North-west
(c) West (d) North

18. Two statements are given followed by four conclusions, I, II, III and IV. You have to consider the statements to be true, even if they seem to be at variance from commonly known facts. You are to decide which of the given conclusions can definitely be drawn from the given statements. Indicate your answer.

Statements :
(A) No cow is a chair
(B) All chairs are tables.

Conclusions :
I. Some tables are chairs.
II. Some tables are cows
III. Some chairs are cows
IV. No table is a cow
(a) Either II or III follow
(b) Either II or IV follow
(c) Only I and either II or IV follow.
(d) All conclusions follow

19. How many triangles are there in the figure ABCDEF?

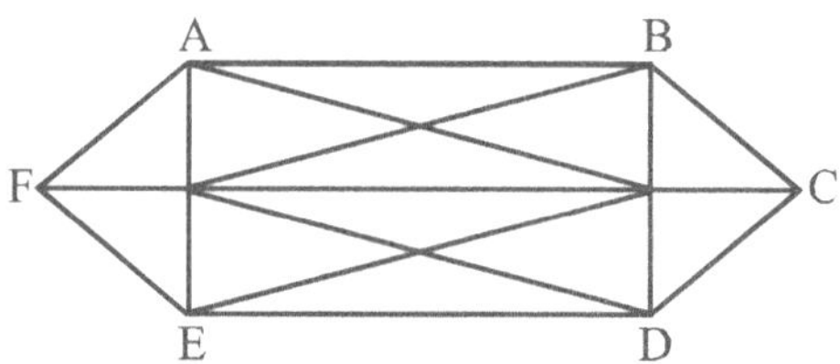

(a) 24 (b) 26
(c) 28 (d) 30

20. Identify the figure which best represents the relationship among Tree, Plant, and House.

Answer figures :

(a) 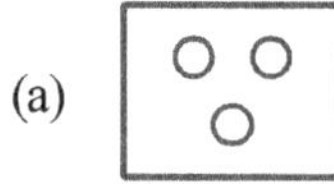 (b) 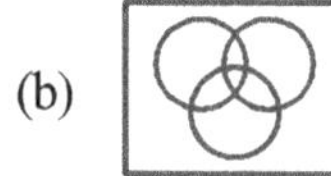

(c)  (d) 

DIRECTION (Q. 21) : *Which answer figure completes the pattern given in the question figure?*

21. **Question Figure :**

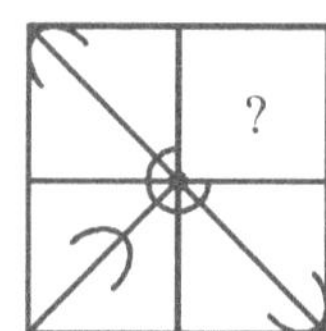

Answer Figures :

(a) 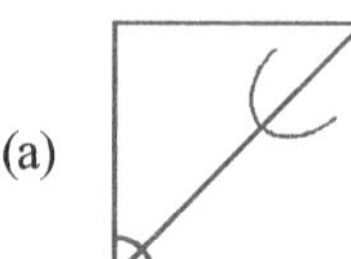 (b) 

(c)  (d) 

22. From the given answer figures, select the one in which the question figure is hidden/embedded

Question Figure

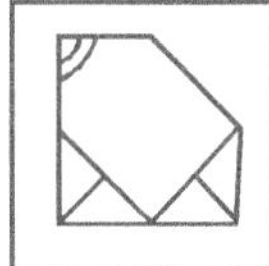

Answer Figures

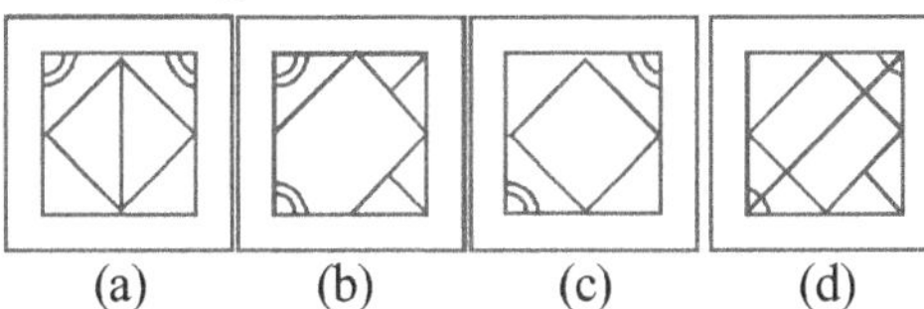

(a) (b) (c) (d)

23. A square sheet of paper has been folded and punched as shown below in the question figures. You have to figure out from amongst the four answer figures, how it will appear when opened?

Question Figures :

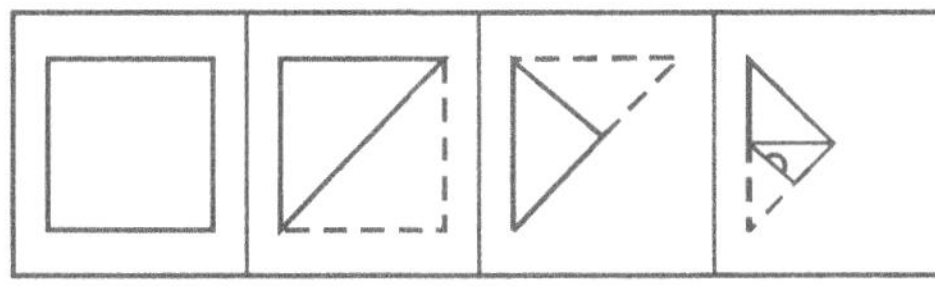

Answer Figures :

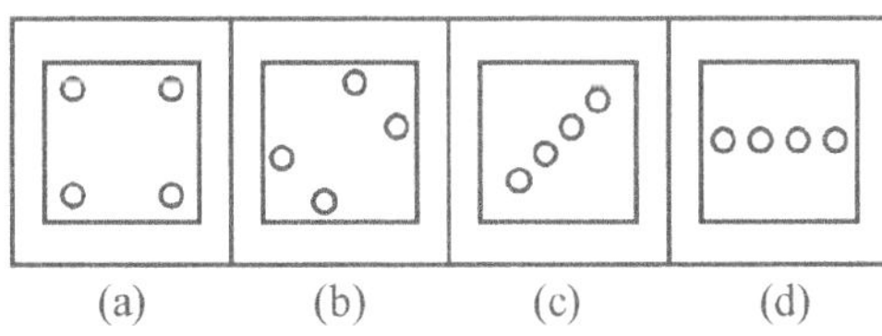

(a) (b) (c) (d)

DIRECTION (Q. 24) : *If a mirror is placed on the line MN, then which of the answer figures is the right image of the given figure ?*

24. Question Figure :

Answer Figures :

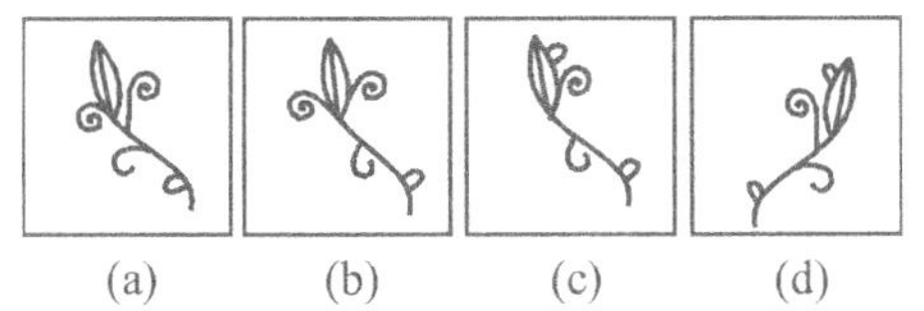

(a) (b) (c) (d)

25. A word is represented by only one set of numbers as given in any one of the alternatives. The sets of numbers given in the alternatives are represented by two classes of alphabets as in two matrices given below. Two columns and rows of Matrix I are numbered-from 0 to 4 and that of Matrix II are numbered from 5 to 9. A letter from these matrices can be represented first by its row and next by its column, e.g., 'B' can be represented by 67, 75 etc. Similarly, you have to identify the set for the word 'CARD'.

MATRIX I

	0	1	2	3	4
0	A	B	C	D	E
1	D	C	B	A	E
2	B	A	D	C	E
3	D	B	C	A	E
4	C	D	A	E	B

MATRIX II

	5	6	7	8	9
5	P	Q	R	S	T
6	Q	S	P	R	T
7	P	T	R	S	Q
8	Q	S	P	R	T
9	T	P	S	Q	R

(a) 32, 00, 56, 10 (b) 40, 21, 68, 44
(c) 11, 33, 57, 22 (d) 02, 42, 77, 20

QUANTITATIVE APTITUDE

26. The ninth term of the sequence 0, 3, 8, 15, 24, 35, ... is

(a) 63 (b) 70
(c) 80 (d) 99

27. $\sqrt{\dfrac{0.009 \times 0.036 \times 0.016 \times 0.08}{0.002 \times 0.0008 \times 0.0002}}$ is equal to

(a) 34 (b) 36
(c) 38 (d) 39

28. In a family, the average age of a father and a mother is 35 years. The average age of the father, mother and their only son is 27 years. What is the age of the son ?

(a) 12 years (b) 11 years
(c) 10.5 years (d) 10 years

29. A manufacturer marked an article at ₹50 and sold it allowing 20% discount. If his profit was 25% then the cost price of the article was

(a) ₹40 (b) ₹35
(c) ₹32 (d) ₹30

30. The population of a town is 15000. If the number of males increases by 8% and that of females by 10%, then the population would increase to 16300. Find the number of females in the town.

(a) 4000 (b) 6000
(c) 3000 (d) 5000

31. A sum amounts double in 8 years by simple interest. Then the rate of simple interest p.a. is
(a) 10% (b) 12.5%
(c) 15% (d) 20%

32. By walking at $\frac{3}{4}$ of his usual speed, a man reaches his office 20 minutes later than his usual time. The usual time taken by him to reach his office is
(a) 75 minutes (b) 60 minutes
(c) 40 minutes (d) 30 minutes

33. If A and B together can complete a piece of work in 15 days and B alone in 20 days, in how many days can A alone complete the work ?
(a) 60 (b) 45
(c) 40 (d) 30

34. If ₹1000 is divided between A and B in the ratio 3 : 2, then A will receive
(a) ₹400 (b) ₹500
(c) ₹600 (d) ₹800

35. Equal amounts of water were poured into two empty jars of different capacities, which made one jar $\frac{1}{4}$ full and the other jar $\frac{1}{3}$ full. If the water in the jar with lesser capacity is then poured into the jar with greater capacity, then the part of the Larger jar filled with water is
(a) $\frac{1}{2}$ (b) $\frac{7}{12}$
(c) $\frac{1}{4}$ (d) $\frac{1}{3}$

36. In ΔABC, $\angle B = 60°$, $\angle C = 40°$. If AD bisects $\angle BAC$ and $AE \perp BC$, then $\angle EAD$ is
(a) 40° (b) 80°
(c) 10° (d) 20°

37. If each intetior angle is double of each exterior angle of a regular polygon with n sides, then the value of n is
(a) 8 (b) 10
(c) 5 (d) 6

38. The perimeters of two similar triangle ΔABC and ΔPQR are 36 cm and 24 cm respectively. If PQ = 10 cm, then AB is:
(a) 25 cm (b) 10 cm
(c) 15 cm (d) 20 cm

39. The length (in metres) of the longest rod that can be put in a room of dimensions 10 m × 10 m × 5 m is
(a) $15\sqrt{3}$ (b) 15
(c) $10\sqrt{2}$ (d) $5\sqrt{3}$

40. If $(5x^2 - 3y^2) : xy = 11 : 2$, then the postive value of x/y is:
(a) 7/2 (b) 5/2
(c) 3/2 (d) 5/3

41. If $a^2 + b^2 + c^2 = 2(a - b - c) - 3$ then the value of $2a - 3b + 4c$ is
(a) 3 (b) 1
(c) 2 (d) 4

42. If $a + b = 5$, $a^2 + b^2 = 13$, the value of $a - b$ (where $a > b$) is
(a) 2 (b) −1
(c) 1 (d) −2

43. If $x = a - b, y = b - c, z = c - a$, then the numerical value of the algebraic expression $x^3 + y^3 + z^3 - 3xyz$ will be
(a) $a + b + c$ (b) 0
(c) $4(a + b + c)$ (d) $3abc$

44. tan 7° tan 23° tan 60° tan 67° tan 83° is equal to
(a) $\frac{1}{\sqrt{3}}$ (b) 1
(c) 0 (d) $\sqrt{3}$

45. If cot A + cosec A = 3 and A is an acute angle, then the value of cos A is:
(a) $\frac{4}{5}$ (b) 1
(c) $\frac{1}{2}$ (d) $\frac{3}{4}$

46. If $0 \le \theta \le \frac{\pi}{2}$, $2y\cos\theta = x\sin\theta$ and $2x\sec\theta - y\,\text{cosec}\theta = 3$, then the value of $x^2 + 4y^2$ is
(a) 1 (b) 2
(c) 3 (d) 4

47. The angle of elevation of a tower from a distance 100m from its foot is 30°. Height of the tower is :
(a) $100\sqrt{3}$m (b) $\frac{100}{\sqrt{3}}$m
(c) $50\sqrt{3}$m (d) $\frac{200}{\sqrt{3}}$m

DIRECTIONS (Qs. 48-50): *The pie chart, given here, shows the amount of money spent on various sports by a school administration in a particular year.*

Observe the pie chart and answer the questions based on this graph.

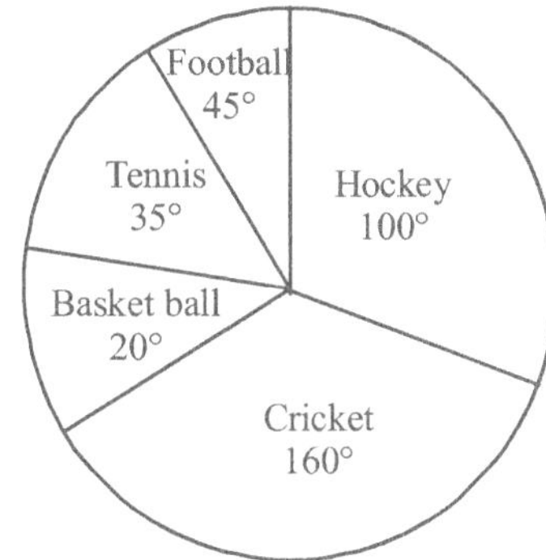

48. If the money spent on football was ₹ 9,000 how much more money was spent on hockey than on football ?
(a) ₹11,000 (b) ₹11,500
(c) ₹12,000 (d) ₹12,500

49. If the money spent on football was ₹ 9,000, what amount was spent on Cricket ?
(a) ₹31,000 (b) ₹31,500
(c) ₹32,000 (d) ₹32,500

50. If the money spent on football is ₹ 9,000, then what was the total amount spent on all sports ?
(a) ₹73,000 (b) ₹72,800
(c) ₹72,500 (d) ₹72,000

ENGLISH LANGUAGE

DIRECTIONS (Qs. 51-52): *In the following questions out of the four alternatives, choose the one which best expresses the meaning of the given word.*

51. Derision
(a) Humiliation (b) Embarrassment
(c) Ridicule (d) Condemnation

52. Trite
(a) Commonplace (b) Clever
(c) Brief (d) Impudent

DIRECTIONS (Qs. 53-54) : *In the following questions choose the word opposite in meaning to the given word.*

53. Florid
(a) Weak (b) Pale
(c) Monotonous (d) Ugly

54. Meandering
(a) Sliding (b) Slopping
(c) Strained (d) Straight

DIRECTIONS (Qs. 55-56) : *In the following questions sentences are given with blanks to be filled in with an appropriate word(s). Four alternatives are suggested for each question. Choose the correct alternative out of the four.*

55. ________ wins this civil war there will be little rejoicing at the victory.
(a) Whichever (b) Whoever
(c) Whatever (d) Wherever

56. As he got older his belief in these principles did not ________.
(a) wither (b) shake
(c) waver (d) dither

DIRECTIONS (Qs. 57-58) : *Some of the sentences have errors and some have none. Find out which part of a sentence has an error. The number of that part is your answer. If there is no error, your answer is (d).*

57. Judge in him (a)/ prevailed upon the father (b)/ and he sentenced his son to death. (c)/ No error (d).

58. One major reason (a)/ for the popularity of television is (b)/ that most people like to stay at home. (c)/ No error (d).

DIRECTIONS (Qs. 59-60): *In the following questions, a sentence or* **Bold** *part thereof is given which may need improvement. Alternatives as given at (a), (b) and (c) below, which may be a better option. In case no improvement is needed, your answer is (d).*

59. We generally select **one of the most intelligent student of the school** for this award.
(a) one of the most intelligent students of the school
(b) one of the intelligent most students of the school
(c) one of the intelligent most student of the school
(d) No improvement

60. My friend lives in a nearby street **whose name** I have forgotten.
(a) the name of which (b) which name
(c) of which name (d) No improvement

DIRECTIONS (Qs. 61–62): *In the following questions, out of the four alternatives, choose the one which can be substituted for the given words/ sentence.*

61. One who hides away on a ship to obtain a free passage
(a) Compositor (b) Stoker
(c) Stowaway (d) Shipwright

62. An unexpected piece of good fortune
(a) windfall (b) philanthropy
(c) benevolence (d) turnstile

DIRECTIONS (Qs. 63-64): *In the following questions, groups of four words are given. In each group, one word is correctly spelt. Find the correctly spelt word.*

63. (a) agnostik (b) accomplice
(c) advercity (d) acrimonous

64. (a) collaborate (b) comemorate
(c) colate (d) choclate

DIRECTIONS (Qs. 65 - 67) : *Four alternatives are given for the Idiom/phrase underlined in the sentence. Choose the alternative which best expresses the meaning of the Idiom/phrase and mark it in the Answer-Sheet.*

65. There is no point in discussing the new project with him as he always **pours cold water** on any ideas.
(a) puts off (b) dislikes
(c) disapproves of (d) postpones

66. Regadless of what her parents said, she wanted to **let her hair down** that night.
(a) really enjoy (b) wash her hair
(c) comb her hair (d) work till late

67. She didn't realize that the clever salesman was **taking her for a ride.**
(a) trying to trick her
(b) taking her in a car
(c) pulling her a long
(d) forcing her to go with him

DIRECTION (Q. 68): *In the following questions, a sentence has been given in Direct / Indirect. Out of the fouralternatives suggested, select the one which best expresses the same sentence in Indirect/Direct and mark.*

68. Mrs. Shankar said, "I know what it is to be depressed.
(a) Mrs. Shankar is depressed she said.
(b) Mrs. Shankar said that she was knowing what it was to be depressed.
(c) Mrs. Shankar said that she knew what it was to be depressed.
(d) Mrs. Shankar knows what it is to be depressed.

DIRECTONS (Qs. 69-70): *In the following questions, the first and the last part of sentence are numbered 1 and 6. The rest of the sentence is split into four parts and named P, Q, R and S. These four parts are not given in their proper order. Read the sentence and find out which of the four combinations is correct. Then find the correct answer.*

69. 1. The watchman
P. and found two thieves
Q. woke up when
R. with black masks
S. he heard the dog barking
6. trying to get in
(a) QSRP (b) PQRS
(c) QSPR (d) SPQR

70. 1. The student
P. touched the
Q. arrived and
R. their teacher
S. feet of
6. with reverence
(a) RQSP (b) QPSR
(c) QPRS (d) QRSP

DIRECTIONS (Qs. 71-75): *In the following passage, some of the words have been left out. Read the passage carefully and choose the correct answer to each question out of the four alternatives and fill in the blanks.*

One fine morning, a 71 man knocked at the doors of the home for the aged run by nuns. He told the nun in charge that as he was 72 to Delhi, he wanted to leave his servant-maid to the 73 of the nuns. He assured the nun of sending some money every month 74 she was an orphan. The nun 75 her saying that she had got an excellen master.

71. (a) gentle (b) bad
(c) nice (d) good

72. (a) moved (b) shifted
(c) changed (d) transferred

73. (a) care (b) home
(c) custody (d) protection

74. (a) because (b) and
(c) though (d) if

75. (a) loved (b) praised
(c) consoled (d) condoled

GENERAL AWARENESS

76. Mahatma Gandhi was profoundly influenced by the writings of
(a) Bernard Shaw (b) Karl Marx
(c) Lenin (d) Leo Tolstoy

77. Name the Maratha Saint who was a contemporary of Shivaji.
(a) Saint Eknath (b) Saint Tukaram
(c) Saint Dhyaneshwar (d) Namdev

78. The term 'Greater India' denotes
(a) Political unity (b) Cultural unity
(c) Religious unity (d) Social unity

79. The Drafting of the Constitution was completed on:
(a) 26th January, 1950
(b) 26th December, 1949
(c) 26th November, 1949
(d) 30th November, 1949

80. The authority to specify which castes shall be deemed to be scheduled castes rests with the:
(a) Commissioner for Scheduled Castes and Tribes
(b) Prime Minister
(c) President
(d) Governor

81. Depression formed due to deflating action of winds are called
(a) Playas (b) Yardang
(c) Ventifacts (d) Sand dunes

82. Which is the biggest tax paying sector in India ?
(a) Agriculture sector (b) Industrial sector
(c) Transport sector (d) Banking sector

83. The study of population is known as.
(a) Demography (b) Climatology
(c) Petrology (d) Hydrology

84. Which of the following countries has recently become the third largest market for Twitter ?
(a) China (b) India
(c) Brazil (d) Indonesia

85. The modulus of rigidity is the ration of
(a) longitudinal stress to longitudinal strain
(b) Volume stress to volume strain
(c) shearing stress to shearing strain
(d) tensile stress to tensile strain

86. 'Mirage' is an example of
(a) refraction of light only
(b) total internal reflection of light only
(c) refraction and total internal reflection of light
(d) dispersion of light only

87. An stomic clock is based on transitions in
(a) Sodium (b) Caesium
(c) Magnesium (d) Aluminium

88. The element which is used for vulcanizing rubber
(a) Sulphur (b) Bromine
(c) Silicon (d) Phosphorus

89. Plasma membrane in eukaryotic celle is made up of
(a) Phospholipid (b) Lipoprotein
(c) Phospholpo-protein (d) Phospho-protein

90. Which plant is called Herbal Indian Doctor?
(a) Amla (b) Mango
(c) Neem (d) Tulsi

91. 'Eutrophication' is associated with
(a) Nitrates and Phosphates
(b) Sewage
(c) Silt load
(d) Vegetation

92. The land of maximum biodiversity is
(a) Tropical (b) Temperate
(c) Monsoonal (d) Equatorial

93. Bark of this tree is used as a condiment–
(a) Cinnamon (b) Clove
(c) Neem (d) Palm

94. The iron and steel plant in Bihar is at:
(a) Visakhapatnam (b) Bokaro
(c) Burnpur (d) Vijay Nagar

95. The latest official language of the U.N. is
(a) Russian (b) Arabic
(c) Chinese (d) Spanish

96. Who was not a politician ?
(a) H.N. Bahuguna (b) I.K. Gujral
(c) S.L. Bahuguna (d) J.Jayalalitha

97. Who will lead the Indian delegation at the 12th Asia Europe Meeting (ASEM) summit 2018?
(a) Sushma Swaraj (b) Ram Nath Kovind
(c) Narendra Modi (d) Venkaiah Naidu

98. The festival of Fulpati has recently celebrated in which neighboring country of India?
(a) Myanmar (b) Nepal
(c) Sri Lanka (d) Bhutan

99. Which Indian armed force has launched an innovative mobile health App 'MedWatch'?
(a) Indian Air Force (b) Indian Navy
(c) Indian Army (d) Indian Coast Guard

100. Which of the following cities is the venue of the India International Silk Fair (IISF-2018)?
(a) Guwahati (b) Pune
(c) New Delhi (d) Lucknow

Hints & Explanations

1. (c) As, $A + B + E \Rightarrow 1 + 2 + 5 = 8$
Similarly,
$K + L + O \Rightarrow 11 + 12 + 15 = \boxed{38}$

2. (c) Here, animal-behaviour relationship has been shown. Fox is characterised by its cunningness. Similarly, rabbit is considered as timid.

3. (d) $6 \times 5 = 30, 30 \times 3 = 90$
$8 \times 6 = 48, 48 \times 4 = 192$

4. (d) Except Sonata, all others are instruments. Sonata is a piece of music composed for one instrument or two.

5. (b) TSWV does not have any vowel

C A F D (C → D: +1; A → C: −2; D → F: −2), I G L J (I → J: +1; G → I: −2; J → L: −2)

and O M R P (O → P: +1; M → O: −2; P → R: −2) but, T S W V (T → V: +2; S → T: −1; V → W: −1)

So, TSWV is odd one out.

6. (d) As, $162 \Rightarrow 16 \div 2 = 8$
$405 \Rightarrow 40 \div 5 = 8$,
and $567 \Rightarrow 56 \div 7 = 8$,
but, $644 \Rightarrow 64 \div 4 = 16$

7. (b) Meaningful order of the words
C. Member → A. Family → B. Community → D. Locality → E. Country

8. (a) The pattern is as follows :

$B \xrightarrow{+2} D \xrightarrow{+2} F \xrightarrow{+2} H \xrightarrow{+2}$ J
$M \xrightarrow{-1} L \xrightarrow{-1} K \xrightarrow{-1} J \xrightarrow{-1}$ I
$R \xrightarrow{+2} T \xrightarrow{+2} V \xrightarrow{+2} X \xrightarrow{+2}$ Z
$G \xrightarrow{-1} F \xrightarrow{-1} E \xrightarrow{-1} D \xrightarrow{-1}$ C

So, JIZC will complete the series.

9. (c) The pattern is as follows :

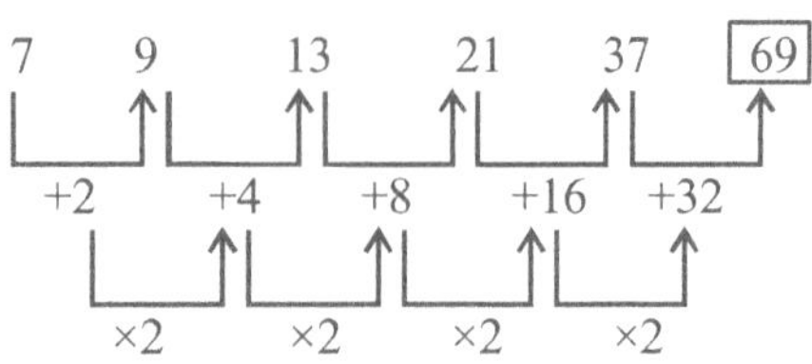

10. (b) R is father of X and Y.
S is maternal uncle of X and Y Considering the given options, it may be assumed that T is wife of R.

11. (d) Age of Manager = New Average Age + (No. of Subordinates × Change in Average)
$= 31 + (25 \times 1) = 56$ years

12. (c) [STRA] N [G] ULA T [ION]

13. (a) As,

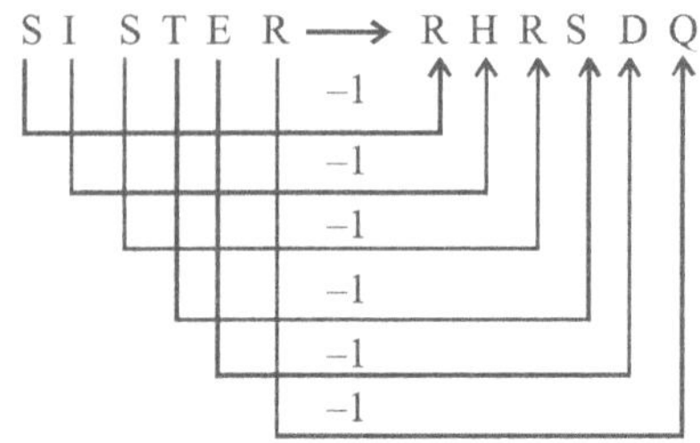

Similarly,

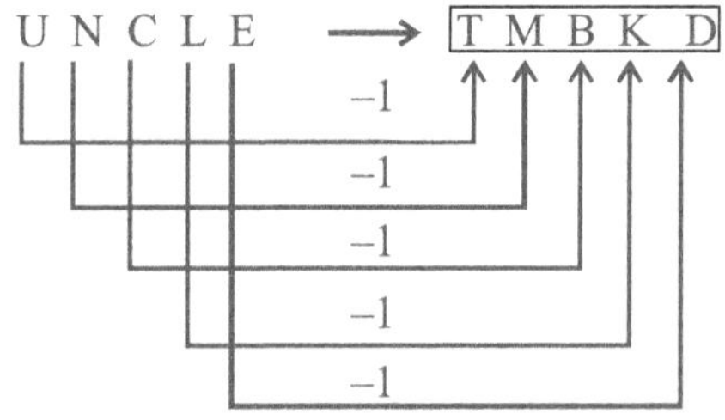

14. (a)

15. (d) $9 + 7 = 16$; $9 - 7 = 2$
$16 \times 2 = 32$
$13 + 7 = 20$; $13 - 7 = 6$
$20 \times 6 = 120$
$17 + 9 = 26$; $17 - 9 = 8$
$26 \times 8 = 208$
$19 + 11 = 30$; $19 - 11 = 8$
$30 \times 8 = \boxed{240}$

16. (c) Column wise
First Column,
$(7)^2+(4)^2+(2)^2=49+16+4=69$
Second Column,
$(3)^2+(9)^2+(1)^2=9+81+1=91$
Similarly, In third column,
$(2)^2+(6)^2+(5)^2=4+36+25=\boxed{65}$

17. (c)

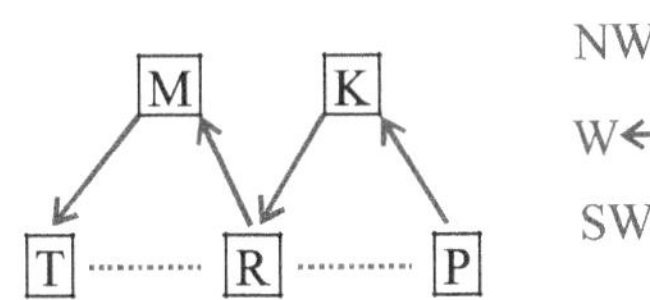

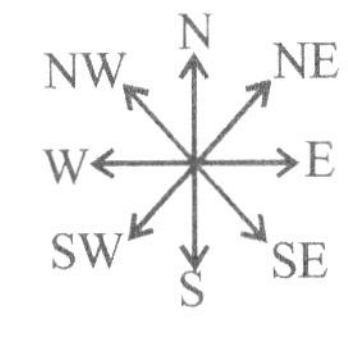

It is clear that T is located to the West of P.

18. (c)

19. (c) There are 28 triangles are formed in given figure.

20. (c) 21. (a) 22. (b) 23. (c) 24. (b)

25. (c)

26. (c) $0+3=3$
$3+5=8$
$8+7=15$
$15+9=24$
$24+11=35$
$35+13=48$
$48+15=63$
$63+17=\boxed{80}$

27. (b) Expression

$$=\sqrt{\frac{0.009\times0.036\times0.016\times0.08}{0.002\times0.0008\times0.0002}}$$

$$=\sqrt{\frac{9\times32\times16\times8}{2\times8\times2}}=3\times2\times3\times2=36$$

28. (b) Father + mother
$=2\times35=70$ years
Father + mother + son
$=27\times3=81$ years
$\therefore$ Son's age $=81-70=11$ years

29. (c) Marked price = ₹50
S.P. after discount = 80% of 50 = ₹40
If the CP of article be ₹x, then

$$\frac{125\times x}{100}=40$$

$$\Rightarrow x=\frac{40\times100}{125}=₹32$$

30. (d) If the number of females be x, then, number of males = 15000 – x

$$\therefore x\times\frac{10}{100}+(15000-x)\times\frac{8}{100}$$
$=16300-15000$
$\Rightarrow 10x+120000-8x$
$=1300\times100$
$\Rightarrow 2x=130000-120000$
$=10000$
$\Rightarrow x=5000$

31. (b) Let P be the principle amount and R be rate of interest.

$$2P=P+\frac{P\times R\times8}{100}$$

$$R=\frac{100}{8}=12.5\%$$

32. (b) $\frac{4}{3}$ of usual time = Usual time + 20 minutes

$\therefore \frac{1}{3}$rd of usual time
$=20$ minutes
$\therefore$ Usual time $=20\times3$
$=60$ minutes

33. (a) (A + B)'s 1 day's work $=\frac{1}{15}$

B's 1 day's work $=\frac{1}{20}$

$\therefore$ A's 1 day's work $=\frac{1}{15}-\frac{1}{20}=\frac{4-3}{60}=\frac{1}{60}$

34. (c) A's share

$$=₹\left(\frac{3}{5}\times1000\right)=₹600$$

35. (a) Amounts of water in two jars are equal; the jar with the greater capacity is $\frac{1}{4}$ full, and the Jar with lesser capacity is $\frac{1}{3}$ full.

$\therefore$ When the water in smaller jar is poured into the larger Jar, the addition of an equal amount of water will double the amount in the larger jar, which will then be $2\times\frac{1}{4}=\frac{1}{2}$ full.

36. (c)

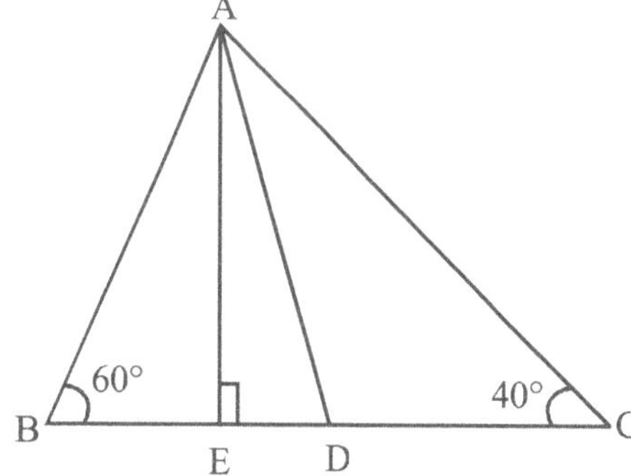

In ΔABC,
$\angle A+\angle B+\angle C=180°$
$\angle A+60°+40°=180°$
$\angle A=180°-60°-40°=80°$
AD bisects $\angle BAC$
$\therefore \angle A=\angle BAD+\angle DAC$
$\angle BAD=\angle DAC=40°$
Now, In ΔABE
$\angle B+\angle E+\angle BAE=180°$
$60°+90°+\angle BAE=180°$
$\angle BAE=30°$
$\therefore \angle EAD=\angle BAD-\angle BAE=40°-30°=10°$

37. (d) Let exterior $\angle$be $=x$
interior $\angle$be $=2x$
$x+2x=180$
$3x=180$
$x=60°$

$$\frac{360°}{60°}=6$$

38. (c) $\frac{AB}{PQ}=\frac{BC}{QR}=\frac{CA}{RP}=\frac{AB+BC+CA}{PQ+QR+RP}$

$\Rightarrow \frac{AB}{PQ}=\frac{36}{24}$

$\Rightarrow \frac{AB}{10}=\frac{36}{24}$

$\Rightarrow AB=\frac{36\times10}{24}=15$ cm

39. (b) Length of the longest rod
$\sqrt{a^2+b^2+c^2}$
$=\sqrt{10^2+10^2+5^2}$
$=\sqrt{225}=15$ metre

40. (c) $\frac{5x^2-3y^2}{2y}=\frac{11}{2}$
$10x^2-6y^2=11xy$
$10x^2-11xy-6y^2=0$
$10x^2-15xy+4xy-6y^2=0$
$5x(2x-3y)+2y(2x-3y)=0$
$(5x+2y)(2x-3y)$
$5x\neq 2y, 2x=3y$

$\frac{x}{y}=\frac{3}{2}$

41. (b) $a^2+b^2+c^2=2(a-b-c)-3$
$\Rightarrow a^2+b^2+c^2=2a+2b+2c+3=0$
$\Rightarrow a^2-2a+1+b^2+2b+1+c^2+2c+1=0$
$\Rightarrow (a-1)^2+(b+1)^2+(c+1)^2=0$
[If $x^2+y^2+z^2=0\Rightarrow x=0; y=0; z=0$]
$\therefore a-1=0\Rightarrow a=1$
$b+1=0\Rightarrow b=-1$
$c+1=0\Rightarrow c=-1$
$\therefore 2a-3b+4c=2+3-4=1$

42. (c) $a+b=5$
Squaring on both sides
$(a+b)^2=(5)^2$
$a^2+b^2+2ab=25$
$13+2ab=25$
$2ab=25-13=12$ ...(1)
Again, $a^2+b^2=13$
Subtracting $(-2ab)$ from both sides
$a^2+b^2-2ab=13-2ab$
$(a-b)^2=13-12$ from equation (1)
$(a-b)^2=1$
TRICK$\Rightarrow a=3$
$b=2\ (a>b)$
$a-b=1$

43. (b) $x+y+z=a-b+b-c+c-a=0$
$\therefore x^3+y^3+z^3-3xyz=0$

44. (d) tan 7° tan23° tan 60° tan 67° tan 83°
$\Rightarrow$ tan (90° – 83°) tan (90° – 67°) tan 60° tan 67° tan 83°
$\Rightarrow$ cot 83° cot 67° tan 60° tan 67° tan 83°
[$\because$ tan (90° – θ) = cotθ]

$$\Rightarrow \frac{1}{\tan 83^\circ} \times \frac{1}{\tan 67^\circ} \times \tan 60^\circ \times \tan 67^\circ \times \tan 83^\circ$$

$\Rightarrow \tan 60^\circ = \sqrt{3}$

45. (a) $\cot A + \operatorname{cosec} A = 3$
$\operatorname{cosec}^2 A - \cot^2 A = 1$
$(\operatorname{cosec} A - \cot A)(\operatorname{cosec} A + \cot A) = 1$

$\operatorname{cosec} A - \cot A = \frac{1}{3}$

$\operatorname{cosec} A + \cot A = 3$
By Adding

$2\operatorname{cosec} A = 3 + \frac{1}{3} = \frac{10}{3}$

$\operatorname{cosec} A \ \frac{\cancel{10}\,5}{\cancel{6}\,3} = \frac{H}{P}$

$B = \sqrt{5^2 - 3^2} = 4$

$\cos A = \frac{4}{5}$

46. (d) $2y \cos\theta = x \sin\theta$
$\Rightarrow x \sec\theta = 2y \operatorname{cosec}\theta$
$\therefore 2x \sec\theta \quad y \operatorname{cosec}\theta - 3$
$\Rightarrow 4y \operatorname{cosec}\theta - y \operatorname{cosec}\theta = 3$
$\Rightarrow 3y \operatorname{cosec}\theta = 3$
$\Rightarrow y \operatorname{cosec}\theta = 1$
$\Rightarrow y = \sin\theta$
$\therefore x \sec\theta = 2y \operatorname{cosec}\theta$
$= 2\sin\theta.\operatorname{cosec}\theta = 2$
$\Rightarrow x = 2\cos\theta$
$\therefore x^2 + 4y^2 = 4\cos^2\theta + 4\sin^2\theta = 4$

47. (b)

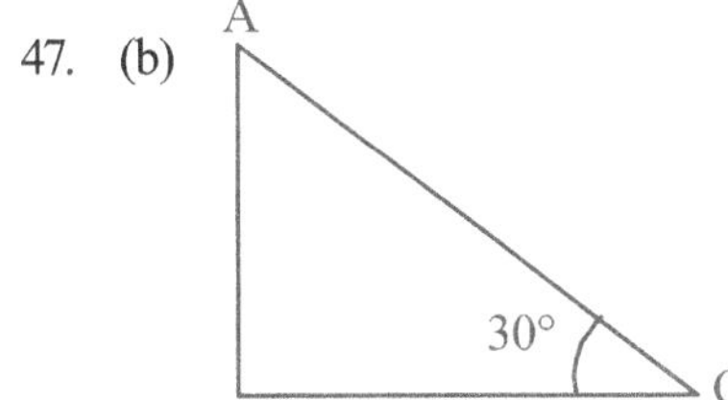

AB = h metre
$\angle ACB = 30^\circ$;
BC = 100 metre

$\therefore \tan 30^\circ = \frac{AB}{BC}$

$\Rightarrow \frac{1}{\sqrt{3}} = \frac{h}{100}$

$\Rightarrow h = \frac{100}{\sqrt{3}}$ metre

48. (a) $\because 45^\circ \equiv$ ₹ 9000

$\therefore 55^\circ \equiv \frac{9000}{45^\circ} \times 55^\circ =$ ₹11000

49. (c) $\because 45^\circ \equiv$ ₹ 9000

$\therefore 160^\circ \equiv \frac{9000}{45^\circ} \times 160^\circ =$ ₹ 32000

50. (d) $\because 45^\circ \equiv$ ₹ 9000

$\therefore 360^\circ \equiv \frac{9000}{45} \times 360^\circ =$ ₹ 72000

51. (c) The word **Derision (Noun)** means : rodicule; mockery; a strong feeling that somebody/ something is ridiculous and not worth considering seriously.

52. (a) The word **Trite (Adjective)** means : dull and boring because it has been expressed so many times before; not original; banal; very ordinary and containing nothing that is interesting or important.
Hence, the words trite and committee are synonymous.

53. (b) The word **Florid (Adjective)** means : rosy; gaudy; ornated; red; having too much decoration or detail.
The word **Pale (Adjective)** means : light in colour; not strong or bright; having skin that is almost white because of illness.

54. (d) The word **Meandering (Adjective)** means : not straight ; curved ; a course that does not follow a straight path.
Hence, the words **meandering** and **straight** are antonymous.

55. (b) Whoever wins is the correct use

56. (a) The word **wither** means : to become less or weaker.

57. (a) Sometimes Common Nouns are used as Abstract Nouns as they express qualities. In this situation, we use 'the' before them. Hence. **The Judge in him** should be used.

58. (c) Here, replace **that most people like to stay at home by most of the people** like to stay at home.

59. (a) implies only one from many
60. (a) the name of which I have
61 (c) A stowaway is a person who secretly boards a ship to travel free.
62. (a) Windfall refers to get a large amount unexpectedly.
63. (b) accomplice (agnostic; adversity; acrimonious).
64. (a) Correct spellings of other words are : commemorate, collate and chocolate.
65. (c) Idiom **pour/throw cold water on something** means : to give reasons for not being in favour of something; to criticize something
66. (a) Idiom **let your hair down** means : to relax and enjoy your-self especially in a lively way.
67. (a) Idiom **take somebody for a ride** means : to cheat or trick somebody.
68. (c) The pronoun 'I' of the sentence is converted to 'she' and the direct speech which is in present tense gets converted into past tense.

69. (c)	70. (b)	71. (a)	72. (d)	73. (c)
74. (a)	75. (c)	76. (d)	77. (b)	78. (b)
79. (c)	80. (a)	81. (b)	82. (b)	83. (a)
84. (c)	85. (b)	86. (c)	87. (b)	88. (a)
89. (a)	90. (a)	91. (a)	92. (a)	93. (a)
94. (b)	95. (b)	96. (c)	97. (d)	98. (b)
99. (a)	100. (c)			

PRACTICE SET- 13

GENERAL INTELLIGENCE & REASONING

DIRECTIONS (Qs. 1-3) : *In each of the following questions, select the related letters/word/numbers from the given alternatives.*

1. PNLJ : IGEC : : VTRP : ?
(a) OMKI (b) RSTU
(c) QSRC (d) RPOM

2. ? : 63 : : 08 : 26
(a) 12 (b) 9
(c) 18 (d) 15

3. Symphony : Composer : : Painter : ?
(a) Fresco (b) Colours
(c) Art (d) Leonardo

DIRECTIONS (Qs. 4-6) : *In questions, find the odd number/ letters/ word/ number pair from the given alternatives.*

4. (a) Mar (b) Remedy
(c) Maim (d) Mutilate

5. (a) (125, 27) (b) (64, 216)
(c) (216, 02) (d) (343, 01)

6. (a) EFH (b) OPQ
(c) BCE (d) IJL

7. Arrange the following words according to dictionary order:
1. Banquet 2. Bangle
3. Bandage 4. Bantam
5. Bank
(a) 3, 2, 4, 5, 1 (b) 3, 5, 2, 1, 4
(c) 3, 2, 1, 5, 4 (d) 3, 2, 5, 1, 4

DIRECTIONS (Qs. 8-9) : *In each of the following questions, a series is given with one term missing. Choose the correct alternative from the given ones that will complete the series.*

8. EJO, FKP, GLQ, HMR, ?
(a) ABC (b) DEF
(c) MNO (d) INS

9. 61, 52, 63, 94, 46, ___?___.
(a) 19 (b) 18
(c) 17 (d) None

10. C is the mother of A and B. If D is the husband of B, what is C to D ?
(a) Mother-in-law (b) Sister
(c) Mother (d) Aunt

11. Sita is elder than Swapna. Lavanya is elder than Swapna but younger than Sita. Suvarna is younger than both Hari and Swapna, Swapna is elder than Hari. Who is the youngest ?
(a) Sita (b) Lavanya
(c) Suvarna (d) Hari

12. From the given alternative words, select the word which cannot be formed using the letters of the given word:
DISINTEGRATION
(a) INTERROGATE (b) SIGNATURE
(c) INTERN (d) SINGER

13. If A = 1, ACE = 9, then ART = ?
(a) 29 (b) 38
(c) 10 (d) 39

14. If '+' means '÷', '×' means '+', '–' means '×' and '÷' means '–', then which of the following equations is correct?
(a) $36 + 6 - 3 \times 2 = 20$ (b) $36 \times 6 + 3 - 2 < 20$
(c) $36 \times 6 + 3 \times 2 > 20$ (d) $36 + 6 \times 3 + 2 = 20$

15. If 73 + 46 = 42 and 95 + 87 = 57, then 62 + 80 = ?
(a) 32 (b) 48
(c) 64 (d) 36

DIRECTION (Q. 16): *Select the missing number from the given responses.*

16.

3	4	6
5	7	3
1	2	7
35	69	?

(a) 90 (b) 94
(c) 80 (d) 75

17. Raghu starts from his house in his car and travels 8 km towards the North, then 6 km towards East then 10 m towards his right, 4 km towards his left, 10 km towards North and finally 4 km towards his right. In which Directions is he now with reference to the starting point?

(a) South (b) North East
(c) South East (d) North

DIRECTION (Q. 18) : *Two statements are given followed by two conclusions I and II. You have to consider the statements to be true even if they seem to be at variance from commonly known facts. You have to decide which of the given conclusions, if any, follow from the given statements.*

18. Statements:

(1) All books are novels.
(2) Some novels are poems.

Conclusions:

(I) Some books are poems.
(II) Some poems are novels.

(a) Only conclusion (II) follows
(b) Neither conclusion (I) nor (II) follows
(c) Both conclusions (I) and (II) follow
(d) Only conclusion (I) follows

19. Find the number of triangles in the given figure ?

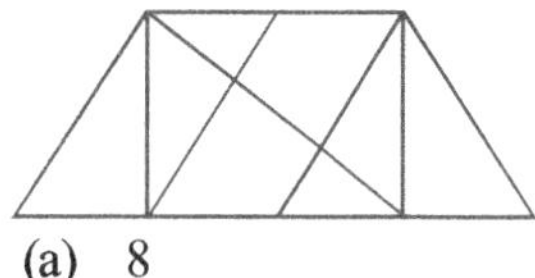

(a) 8 (b) 10
(c) 12 (d) 14

20. Which one of the following diagrams best depicts the relationship among Mammals, Cows and Crows?

(a)  (b) 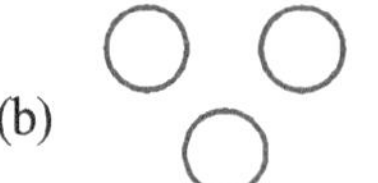

(c)  (d) 

DIRECTION (Q. 21): *In the question, which answer figure will complete the question figure ?*

21. Question Figure :

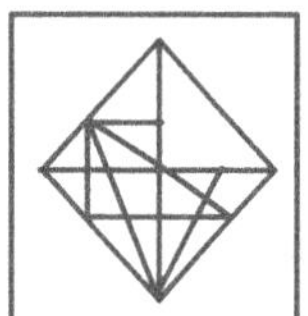

Answer Figures :

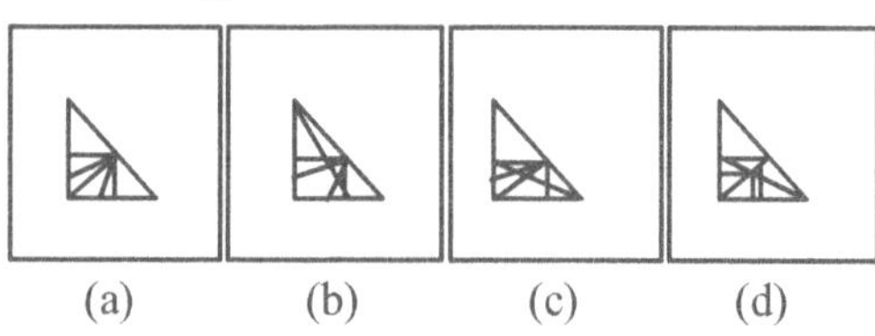

(a) (b) (c) (d)

22. From the given answer figures, select the one in which the question figure is hidden/embedded.

Question Figure :

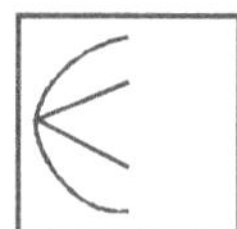

Answer Figures :

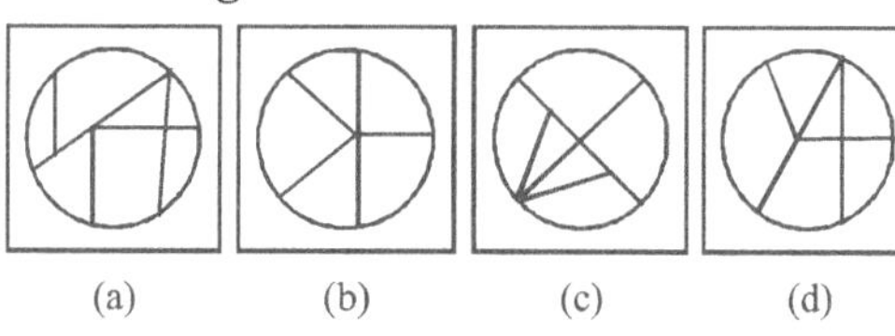

(a) (b) (c) (d)

DIRECTION (Q.23) : *In the following question, a piece of paper is folded and cut as shown below in the question figures. From the given answer figures, indicate how It will appear when opened?*

23. Question Figures:

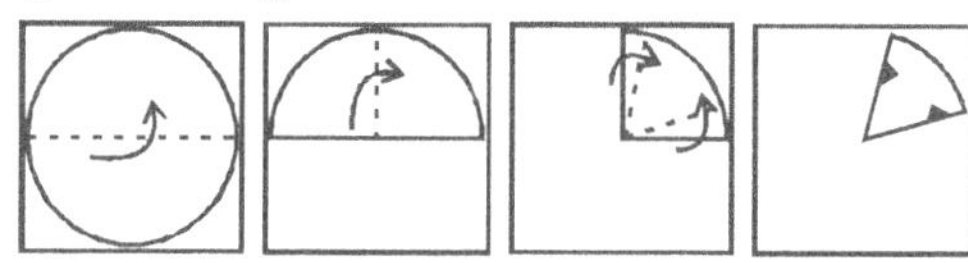

Answer Figures:

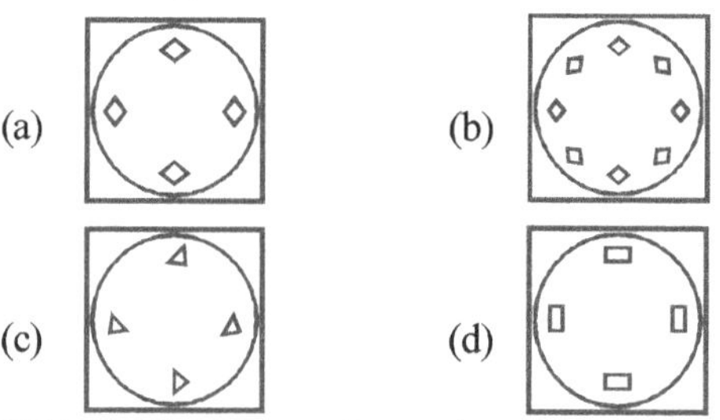

24. Which of the answer figures is exactly the mirror image of the given pattern of numbers when the mirror is held at MN?

Question Figure :

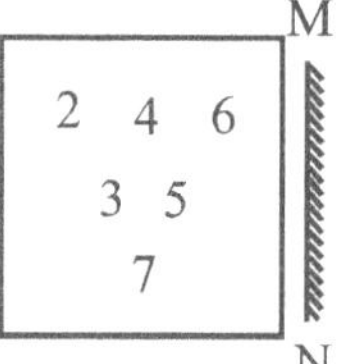

Answer Figures :

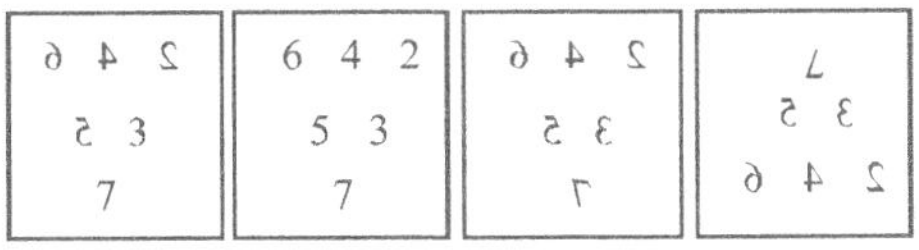

(a)	(b)	(c)	(d)
6 4 2 (mirrored) / 5 3 / 7	6 4 2 / 5 3 / 7	6 4 2 (mirrored) / 5 3 (mirrored) / 7 (inverted)	7 (inverted) / 5 3 (mirrored) / 6 4 2 (mirrored)

DIRECTION (Q. 25) : *A word is represented by only one set of numbers as given in any one of the alternatives. The sets of numbers given in the alternatives are represented by two classes of alphabets as in two matrices given below. The columns and rows of Matrix I are numbered from 0 to 4 and that of Matrix II are numbered from 5 to 9. A letter from these matrices can be represented first by its row and next by its column e.g., 'E' can be represented by 01, 13 etc., and 'L' can be represented by 56, 77 etc. Similarly, you have to identify the set for the word given in each question.*

25. **Matrix I** **Matrix II**

	0	1	2	3	4
0	Z	M	G	R	C
1	J	L	D	B	G
2	M	B	C	M	H
3	R	L	N	G	I
4	B	D	M	R	J

	5	6	7	8	9
5	X	K	T	E	S
6	Q	A	U	X	P
7	U	V	O	W	E
8	T	Y	A	F	U
9	O	O	E	V	A

LANE

(a) 11, 66, 33, 96 (b) 31, 87, 32, 97
(c) 31, 66, 33, 97 (d) 11, 67, 32, 97

QUANTITATIVE APTITUDE

26. If 'n' be any natural number, then by which largest number $(n^3 - n)$ is always divisible ?
(a) 3 (b) 6
(c) 12 (d) 18

27. $1.\overline{27}$ in the form $\frac{p}{q}$ is equal to

(a) $\frac{127}{100}$ (b) $\frac{73}{100}$

(c) $\frac{14}{11}$ (d) $\frac{11}{14}$

28. The mean of 19 observation is 24. If the mean of the first 10 observations is 17 and that of the last 10 observations is 24, find the 10th observation.
(a) 65 (b) 37
(c) –46 (d) 53

29. Successive discounts of 10%, 20% and 30% is equivalent to a single discount of
(a) 60% (b) 49.6%
(c) 40.5% (d) 36%

30. 72% of the students of a certain class took Biology and 44% took Mathematics. If each student took Biology or Mathematics and 40 took both, the total number of students in the class was
(a) 200 (b) 230
(c) 250 (d) 320

31. In certain years a sum of money is doubled itself at $6\frac{1}{4}$ % simple interest per annum, then the required time will be

(a) $12\frac{1}{2}$ years (b) 8 years

(c) $10\frac{2}{3}$ years (d) 16 years

32. Walking at 5 km/hr a student reaches his school from his house 15 minutes early and walking at 3 km/hr he is late by 9 minutes. What is the distance between his school and his house?
(a) 5 km (b) 8 km
(c) 3 km (d) 2 km

33. 'x' number of men can finish a piece of work in 30 days. If there were 6 men more, the work could be finished in 10 days less. The original number of men is
(a) 6 (b) 10
(c) 12 (d) 15

34. The ratio of weekly incomes of A and B is 9 : 7 and the ratio of their expenditures is 4 : 3. If each saves ₹ 200 per week, then the sum of their weekly incomes is
(a) ₹ 3,200 (b) ₹ 4,200
(c) ₹ 4,800 (d) ₹ 5,600

35. A invests ₹ 64,000 in a business. After few months B joined him with ₹ 48,000. At the end of year, the total profit was divided between them in the ratio 2 : 1. After how many months did B join ?
(a) 7 (b) 8
(c) 4 (d) 6

36. The length of the two sides forming the right angle of a right-angled triangle are 6 cm and 8 cm. The length of its circum-radius is :
(a) 5 cm (b) 7 cm
(c) 6 cm (d) 10 cm

37. By decreasing 15° of each angle of a triangle, the ratios of their angles are 2 : 3 : 5. The radian measure of greatest angle is:

(a) $11\pi/24$ (b) $\pi/12$
(c) $\pi/24$ (d) $5\pi/24$

38. Two circles with radii 5 cm and 8 cm touch each other externally at a point A. If a straight line through the point A cuts the circles at points P and Q respectively, then AP : AQ is

(a) 8:5 (b) 5:8
(c) 3:4 (d) 4:5

39. A river 3 m deep and 40 m wide is flowing at the rate of 2 km per hour. How much water (in litres) will fall into the sea in a minute?

(a) 4,00,000 (b) 40,00,000
(c) 40,000 (d) 4,000

40. If $a+\frac{1}{a+2}=0$, then the value of $(a+2)^3+\frac{1}{(a+2)^3}$ is:

(a) 2 (b) 6
(c) 4 (d) 3

41. If $x=\sqrt{a}+\frac{1}{\sqrt{a}}$, $y=\sqrt{a}-\frac{1}{\sqrt{a}}$, then the value of $x^4+y^4-2x^2y^2$ is

(a) 16 (b) 20
(c) 10 (d) 5

42. If the difference of two numbers is 3 and the difference of their squares is 39; then the larger number is :

(a) 9 (b) 12
(c) 13 (d) 8

43. If $a+b+c=9$ (where a, b, c are real numbers), then the minimum value of $a^2+b^2+c^2$ is

(a) 81 (b) 100
(c) 9 (d) 27

44. If $4x=\sec\theta$ and $\frac{4}{x}=\tan\theta$ then $8\left(x^2-\frac{1}{x^2}\right)$ is

(a) $\frac{1}{16}$ (b) $\frac{1}{8}$
(c) $\frac{1}{2}$ (d) $\frac{1}{4}$

45. If $(a^2-b^2)\sin\theta+2ab\cos\theta=a^2+b^2$, then the value of $\tan\theta$ is

(a) $\frac{1}{2ab}\left(a^2+b^2\right)$ (b) $\frac{1}{2}\left(a^2-b^2\right)$
(c) $\frac{1}{2ab}\left(a^2-b^2\right)$ (d) $\frac{1}{2}\left(a^2+b^2\right)$

46. $\frac{\sin\theta-\cos\theta+1}{\sin\theta+\cos\theta-1}\left(\text{where } \theta\neq\frac{\pi}{2}\right)$ is equal to

(a) $\frac{1+\sin\theta}{\cos\theta}$ (b) $\frac{1-\sin\theta}{\cos\theta}$
(c) $\frac{1-\cos\theta}{\sin\theta}$ (d) $\frac{1+\cos\theta}{\sin\theta}$

47. A kite is flying at a height of 50 metre. If the length of string is 100 metre then the inclination of string to the horizontal ground in degree measure is

(a) 90 (b) 60
(c) 45 (d) 30

DIRECTIONS (Qs. 48-50): *Population of five adjacent areas of a town, in the year of 2010, are represented in the following Pie-chart. the ratio of the numbers of males to that of females in these areas are stated in the table below. The total of the population in all the five areas is 72 lakh. Study the Pie-chart and the table and then answer the questions.*

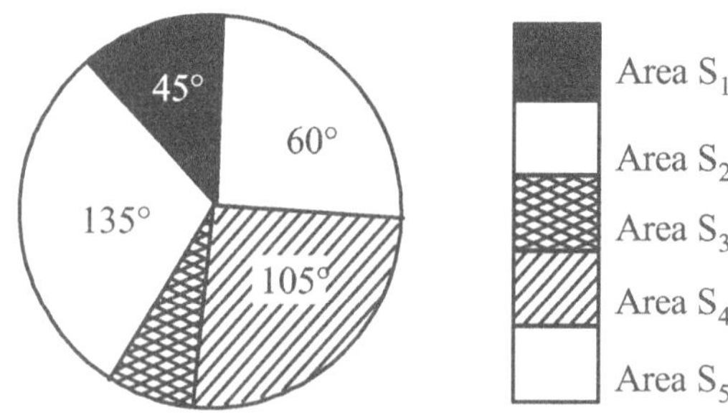

Ratio of numbers of males (M) to females (F)

Areas	S_1	S_2	S_3	S_4	S_5
Ratio M : F	3:2	4:1	7:3	2:3	13:7

48. 12 lakh is the population of the area

(a) S_1 (b) S_3
(c) S_5 (d) S_4

49. The number of males in the areas S_1 and S_4 together is
(a) 13.8 lakh (b) 8.2 lakh
(c) 16.2 lakh (d) 15.8 lakh

50. The ratio of number of females in the area S_2 to that in the area S_5 is
(a) 7 : 9 (b) 36 : 13
(c) 9 : 7 (d) 13 : 36

ENGLISH LANGUAGE

DIRECTIONS (Qs. 51-55): *Fill in the blanks choosing the word that is most appropriate in the context of the passage.*

Smile, they say, and soon there will be miles and miles of smiles. If we keep **(51)** ourselves and do not mix with others, we shall soon be left alone to ponder **(52)** the misfortunes of life. Nobody likes to come across a **(53)** and self-centered person. People **(54)** gregarious and outgoing souls who are prepared to share their joys and sorrows with them. Their joys double and sorrows **(55)** if they have the capacity to laugh away their problems and miseries.

51. (a) by (b) to
(c) with (d) into

52. (a) over (b) on
(c) at (d) upon

53. (a) sad (b) serious
(c) glum (d) selfish

54. (a) avoid (b) love
(c) hate (d) dislike

55. (a) disappear (b) vanish
(c) increase (d) fade out

DIRECTIONS (Qs. 56-57) : *Out of the four alternatives, choose the one which best expresses the meaning of the given word as your answer.*

56. Hyperbole
(a) Expansion (b) Imitation
(c) Decoration (d) Exaggeration

57. Eulogy
(a) Apology (b) Address
(c) Speech (d) Praise

DIRECTIONS (Qs. 58-59) : *Choose the word opposite in meaning to the given word as your answer.*

58. Zenith
(a) Climax (b) Crisis
(c) Acme (d) Nadir

59. Orderly
(a) Semitic (b) Colic
(c) Democratic (d) Chaotic

DIRECTIONS (Qs. 60-62) : *Sentences are given with blanks to be filled in with an appropriate word(s). Four alternatives are suggested for each question. Choose the correct alternative out of the four:*

60. Rajesh's car wasn't __________ Ramesh's, so we were too exhausted by the time we reached home.
(a) such comfortable
(b) as comfortable as
(c) comfortable enough
(d) so comfortable that

61. I don't suppose that Pramod will be elected __________ how hard he struggles as he is not completely supported by the committee.
(a) although (b) seeing as
(c) no matter (d) however

62. Can you please __________ my web site just before I publish it ?
(a) find out (b) go through
(c) set out (d) look up

DIRECTIONS (Qs. 63-64): *Some parts of the sentences have errors and some are correct. Find out which part of a sentence has an error corresponding to the appropriate letter (a, b, c). If a sentence is free from error, (d) in the Answer Sheet.*

63. If I would have realised (a) / what a bad shape our library is in (b) / I would have done something, (c) to arrest the deterioration. / No error (d)

64. He has been (a) / enhanced in position (b) / as a result of his diligence and integrity. (c) / No error (d)

DIRECTION (Q. 65): *Rearrange the parts of the sentence in correct order.*

65. (P) which one is closest in meaning
(Q) read the four sentences in your text book and decide
(R) to the statement you have heard
(S) when you hear a statement.
(a) SRPQ (b) SQPR
(c) SPQR (d) QPSR

DIRECTIONS (Qs.66-67) : *A sentence/a part of the sentence is underlined. Below are given alternatives to the underlined part at (a), (b), (c) which may improve the sentence. Choose the correct alternative. In case no improvement is needed your answer is (d). Mark your answer in the Answer Sheet.*

66. Why should <u>you be despaired of your success of your undertaking</u>?
(a) you despair of the success of your undertaking
(b) you despair of success of undertaking
(c) you be despaired of the success of your undertaking
(d) No improvement.

67. As Rees was <u>going to town in the High Street a savage dog attacked him and bit him</u>.
(a) going to town a savage dog attacked him and bit him in the High Street
(b) in the High Street a savage dog attacked him and bit him in the town
(c) going to town in the High Street a savage dog bit him and attacked him
(d) No improvement

DIRECTION (Q. 68): *In a question, a sentence has been given in Direct/Indirect form. Out of the four alternatives suggested, select the one which best expresses the same sentence in Indirect/Direct form.*

68. Socrates said, "Virtue is its own reward.".
(a) Socrates said that virtue had its own rewards.
(b) Socrates says that virtue is its own reward.
(c) Socrates said that virtue is its own reward.
(d) Socrates said that virtue was its own reward.

DIRECTION (Q. 69): *In a question, a sentence has been given in Active / Passive voice. Out of the four alternatives suggested, select the one which best expresses the same sentence in Passive/ Active voice..*

69. Circumstances will oblige me to go.
(a) I will oblige the circumstances and go.
(b) I shall be obliged to go by the circumstances.
(c) Under the circumstances, I should go.
(d) I would be obliged by the circumstances to go.

DIRECTIONS (Qs. 70–71): *Out of the four alternatives, choose the one which can be substituted for the given words/sentence.*

70. A political leader appealing to popular desires and prejudices
(a) dictator (b) tyrant
(c) popularist (d) demagogue

71. Enclosed in a small closed space.
(a) closophobia (b) clusterophobia
(c) claustrophobia (d) liftophobia

DIRECTION (Q. 72) : *There are four different words out of which one is correctly spelt. Find the correctly spelt word.*

72. (a) effervesent (b) efervescent
(c) effervescent (d) efferescent

DIRECTIONS (Qs. 73-75) : *In the following questions, four alternatives are given for the Idiom/ Phrase printed in* ***bold*** *in the sentence. Choose the alternative which best expresses the meaning of the Idiom/ Phrase.*

73. For this act of indifference he will be **taken to task** by the authority.
(a) he will get an offical reprimand from the authority.
(b) he will be rewarded by the authority.
(c) he will tender his resignation to the authority.
(d) he will be entrusted with an official job.

74. You need to **have something up your sleeve** if the present plan does not work.
(a) have some honest means
(b) have some hidden sources of money
(c) have a secret pocket in the sleeve
(d) have an alternative plan

75. Despite his initial arrogance he had to **eat humble pie**.
(a) he had to yield under pressure
(b) he maintained composure
(c) he failed to protest eventually
(d) he accepted the food oflfered

GENERAL AWARENESS

76. The call of "Back to the Vedas" was given by:
(a) Swami Vivekananda
(b) Swami Dayanand Saraswati
(c) Aurobindo Ghosh
(d) Raja Ram Mohan Roy

77. Who was the founder of the Aligarh Movement ?
(a) Syed Amir Ali
(b) Maulvi Chiragh Ali
(c) Sir Syed Ahmed Khan
(d) Abdul Halim Sharar

78. Despotism is possible in a
(a) One party state
(b) Two party state
(c) Multi party state
(d) Two and multi party state

79. In India, the Residuary Powers are vested with
(a) Union Government
(b) State Government
(c) Both the Union Government and the State Government
(d) Local Government

80. The Fundamental Rights can be suspended by the
(a) Governor
(b) President
(c) Law Minister
(d) Prime Minister

81. National Income is the
(a) Net National Product at market price
(b) Net National Product at factor cost
(c) Net Domestic Product at market price
(d) Net Domestic Product at factor cost

82. Economic planning is an essential feature of
(a) Socialist economy
(b) Capitalist economy
(c) Mixed economy
(d) Dual economy

83. Which one of the following is not a qualitative credit control measure of the RBI?
(a) Fixing margin requirements
(b) Variable interest rates
(c) Open market operations
(d) Credit rationing

84. Communication satellites are used to :
(a) transmit communication signal only
(b) receive communication signal only
(c) receive and redirect communication signal
(d) provide information of natural resources only

85. The material used in the manufacture of lead pencil is
(a) Graphite (b) Lead
(c) Carbon (d) Mica

86. The red, orange and yellow colours of leaves are due to:
(a) Carotenoids (b) Aldehydes
(c) Tannins (d) Lignins

87. Which of the following could be used as fuel in propellant or rockets?
(a) Liquid Hydrogen + Liquid Nitrogen
(b) Liquid Oxygen + Liquid Argon
(c) Liquid Nitrogen + Liquid Oxygen
(d) Liquid Hydrogen + Liquid Oxygen

88. Drying oils contain a fairly large proportion of:
(a) Unsaturaled fatty acids
(b) Fats
(c) Proteins
(d) Saturated fatty acids

89. Steel is more elasitc than rubber because it :
(a) is harder than rubber
(b) requires larger deforming force
(c) is never deformed
(d) is deformed very easily

90. The longest bone in the human body is:
(a) Ulna (b) Humerus
(c) Femur (d) Tibia

91. The sweet taste of fruits is due to
(a) Lactose (b) Fructose
(c) Maltose (d) Ribose

92. Green glands are associated with
(a) Reproduction (b) Excretion
(c) Respiration (d) Digestion

93. Hypothensmia occurs due to loss of excessive heat from body due to sudden low body temperature in :
(a) Snakes (b) Frogs
(c) Human beings (d) Lizards

94. Who coined the word 'Geography'?
(a) Ptolemy
(b) Eratosthenese
(c) Hacataus
(d) Herodatus

95. The HYV programme in India is also called as
(a) Traditional Agriculture
(b) New Agricultural Strategy
(c) White Revolution
(d) Blue Revolution

96. Which country has a high density of population?
(a) India (b) Canada
(c) Sweden (d) Greenland

97. The angle between the magnetic meridian and the geographical meridian at a place is
(a) Declination (b) Latitude
(c) Azimuth (d) Dip

98. Which of the following books has been written by Kishwar Desai?
(a) The Red Devil
(b) Witness the Night
(c) Tonight This Savage Rite
(d) Earth and Ashes

99. Who among the following is set to become the first female umpire to officiate in a men's one-day international match?
(a) Sarah Thomas
(b) Kathhy Cross
(c) Doris Turner
(d) Claire Polosak

100. Which of the following country topped the medal tally at the International Shooting Sport Federation (ISSF) World Cup?
(a) India
(b) China
(c) Japan
(d) Singapore

Hints & Explanations

1. (a) As,

+2
P N L J
+2 +2

:

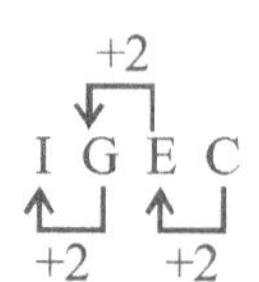

Similarly,

+2
V T R P
+2 +2

:

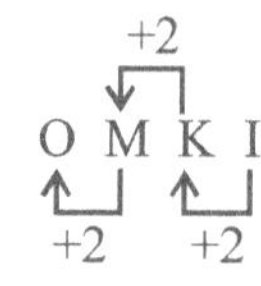

2. (d) $4^2 - 1 = 15$
$4^3 - 1 = 63$
$3^2 - 1 = 8$
$3^3 - 1 = 26$

3. (a) Fresco is an art of painting that is done on freshly spread moist lime plaster.

4. (b) Except remedy, all other terms denote loss of something.

5. (c) Except in (216, 02), in all others both the numbers are perfect cubes.

6. (b) E F H (+1, +2) O P Q (+1, +1)
B C E (+1, +2) I J L (+1, +2)

7. (d) According to dictionary, order is : Bandage, Bangle, Bank, Banquet, Bantam.

8. (d)

9. (b) Reversing number is giving a square number
16, 25, 36, 49, 64, <u>81</u> and 18

10. (a)
C(–)
Mother (A → C)
mother-in-law (D → C)
A B ⟺ D
(–) (+)

11. (c) Sita > Swapna ...(i)
S Sw
S > Lavanya > Sw ...(ii)
L
Hari, Sw > Suvarna ...(iii)
H Su
Sw > H ...(iv)
From all the statements :
S > L > Sw > H > Su

12. (a) SIGNATURE cannot be formed as reference word does not have 'U' alphabet.

13. (d) $A=1, \quad A+C+E=1+3+5=9$
$A+R+T=1+18+20=39$

14. (a) By checking options
$36 \div 6 \times 3+2=6 \times 3+2 \Rightarrow 20=20$

15. (d) As, $73+46=42$
$7-3=4, 4+6=10$
Add $4+10=14$
$14 \times 3=42$
Similarly, $6-2=4,\ 8+0=8$
$4+8=12$
$12 \times 3=36$

16. (b) **First Column**
$(3)^2+(5)^2+(1)^2$
$\Rightarrow 9+25+1=35$
Second Column
$(4)^2+(7)^2+(2)^2$
$\Rightarrow 16+49+4=69$
Third column
$(6)^2+(3)^2+(7)^2$
$\Rightarrow 36+9+49=\boxed{94}$

17. (b)

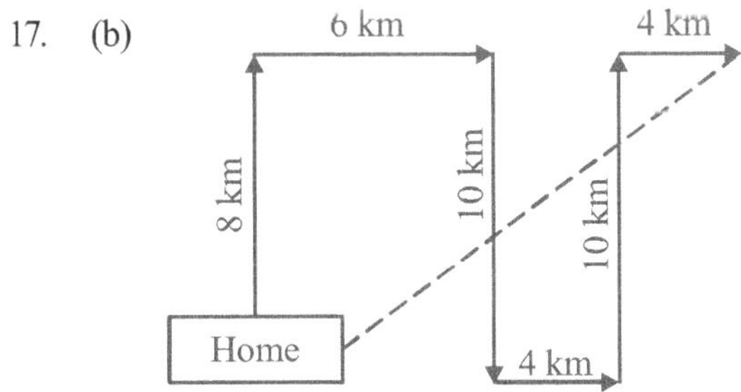

18. (a) 19. (d) 20. (c) 21. (c)
22. (c) 23. (b) 24. (c)

25. (b) L A N E
↓ ↓ ↓ ↓
31 87 32 97

26. (b) $n^3-n=(n^2-1)$
$\Rightarrow n(n+1)(n-1)$
For $n=2, n^3-n=6$
$2^3-2=6$
i.e. n^3-n is always divisible by 6.

27. (c) $1.\overline{27}=1\frac{27}{99}=1\frac{3}{11}=\frac{14}{11}$

28. (c) 10th observation
$=24 \times 10+17 \times 10-19 \times 24$
$=240+170-456=-46$

29. (b) Single equivalent discount for successive discounts of 10% and 20%.
$$=\left(10+20-\frac{20 \times 100}{100}\right)\%=28\%$$
Single equivalent discount for 28% and 30%
$$=\left(28+30-\frac{28 \times 30}{100}\right)\%=49.6\%$$

30. (c) Let the total number of students in the class be x.

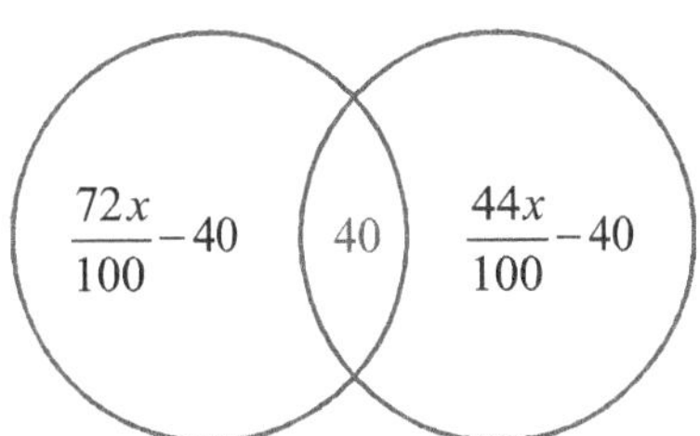

$$\because \frac{72x}{100}-40+40+\frac{44x}{100}-40=x$$
$$\Rightarrow \frac{72x}{100}x+\frac{44x}{100}-x=40$$
$$\Rightarrow \frac{16x}{100}=40 \Rightarrow x=\frac{40 \times 100}{16}$$
$\Rightarrow x=250$

31. (d) Let x be the principal amount
'y' be the time to double the money.
Then interest will also be 'x'.
$$\therefore \quad x=\frac{x \times 25 \times y}{4 \times 100}$$
$400=25y$

32. (c) Let the required distance be x km.
$$\therefore \frac{x}{3}-\frac{x}{5}=\frac{24}{60}$$
$$\Rightarrow \frac{5x-3x}{15}=\frac{2}{5} \Rightarrow \frac{2x}{3}=2$$
$\Rightarrow 2x=2 \times 3 \Rightarrow x=3\text{ km}$

33. (c) $m_1d_1 = m_2d_2$
$x(30) = (x+6)20$
$\Rightarrow 2x + 12 = 3x$
$\Rightarrow 3x - 2x = 12$
$\Rightarrow x = 12$ men

34. (a) Let monthly income of A and B be 9x and 7x
Expenditure = Income – Saving
ATQ

$$\frac{9x-200}{7x-200} = \frac{4}{3}$$

$27x - 6.00 = 28x - 800$
$x = 200$
Sum $= 200 \times 16 = 3200$

35. (c) Suppose, B Joined after x month
Then B's money was invested for $(12 - x)$ months
∴ According to question

$$\frac{64000 \times 12}{48000 \times (12-x)} = \frac{2}{1}$$

$$\frac{16}{12-x} = \frac{2}{1} \Rightarrow 16 = 24 - 2x$$

$2x = 24 - 16 = x = 4$
Hence, B joined after 4 months

36. (a) In a right angled Δ, the length of circumradius is half the length of hypotenuse.
∴ $H^2 = 6^2 + 8^2$
$H^2 = 36 + 64 \Rightarrow 100$
$H = 10$ cm
Circumradius = 5 cm

37. (a) $2x + 3x + 5x = 180° - 45° = 135°$
$\Rightarrow 10x = 135°$

$$\Rightarrow x = \frac{135}{10} = \frac{27}{2}$$

∴ Largest angle

$$= 5x + 15° = \left(5 \times \frac{27}{2}\right)° + 15°$$

$$= \frac{135+30}{2} = \frac{165°}{2}$$

∵ $180° = \pi$ radian

$$\therefore \frac{165°}{2} = \frac{\pi}{180} \times \frac{165}{2} = \frac{11\pi}{24} \text{ radian}$$

38. (b)

39. (b) Volume of water flowed in an hour
$= 2000 \times 40 \times 3\,m^3$
$= 240000\,m^3$
∴ Volume of water flowed in 1 minute.

$$= \frac{240000}{60} = 4000\,m^3$$

$= 4000000$ litre

40. (a) $$a + \frac{1}{a+2} = 0$$

$$\Rightarrow a + 2 + \frac{1}{a+2} = 2$$

On cubing,

$$\left[(a+2) + \frac{1}{a+2}\right]^3 = 8$$

$$\Rightarrow (a+2)^3 + \frac{1}{(a+2)^3} + 3(a+2) \times \frac{1}{(a+2)}\left(a + 2 + \frac{1}{a+2}\right) = 8$$

$$\Rightarrow (a+2)^3 + \frac{1}{(a+2)^3} + 3 \times 2 = 8$$

$$\Rightarrow (a+2)^3 + \frac{1}{(a+2)^3} = 8 - 6 = 2$$

41. (a) $x^4 + y^4 - 2x^2y^2$
$\Rightarrow (x^2 - y^2)^2 \Rightarrow [(x+y)(x-y)]^2$

$$\Rightarrow \left[\left(\sqrt{a} + \frac{1}{\sqrt{a}} + \sqrt{a} - \frac{1}{\sqrt{a}}\right)\left(\sqrt{a} + \frac{1}{\sqrt{a}} - \sqrt{a} + \frac{1}{\sqrt{a}}\right)\right]^2$$

$$\Rightarrow \left(2\sqrt{a} \times \frac{2}{\sqrt{a}}\right)^2 \Rightarrow 16$$

42. (d) Let the numbers are x, y.
$x - y = 3$ ...(1)
$x^2 - y^2 = 39$
$\Rightarrow (x-y)(x+y) = 39$

$\Rightarrow\ x+y=13$ ...(2)

Adding eqn (1) and (2)

$x+y+x-y=16$

$\Rightarrow\ x=8$

$\therefore\ y=3$

Hence, 8 is the larger number.

43. (d) $a^2+b^2+c^2=(a+b+c)^2-2(ab+bc+ca)$

$$= 9^2-2(ab+bc+ca)$$

$a^2+b^2+c^2$ will be minimum if ab + bc + ca is maximum.

$ab+bc+ca$ is maximum when $a=3, b=3$, and $c=3$.

$[\because\ a+b+c=9]$

$\therefore$ minimum value of $a^2+b^2+c^2$

$=81-2(3\times3+3\times3+3\times3)$

$=81-54=27$

44. (c) $4x=\sec\theta$

$$\Rightarrow x=\frac{\sec\theta}{4}$$

Again, $\frac{4}{x}-\tan\theta \Rightarrow \frac{1}{x}-\frac{\tan\theta}{4}$

$$\therefore 8\left(x^2-\frac{1}{x^2}\right)$$

$$=8\left(\frac{\sec^2\theta}{16}-\frac{\tan^2\theta}{16}\right)$$

$$=\frac{8}{16}\left(\sec^2\theta-\tan^2\theta\right)=\frac{1}{2}$$

45. (c) $(a^2-b^2)\sin\theta+2ab\cos\theta=a^2+b^2$

$$\frac{a^2-b^2}{a^2+b^2}\sin\theta+\frac{2ab}{a^2+b^2}\cos\theta=1$$

$$\sin\theta=\frac{a^2-b^2}{a^2+b^2}\qquad \cos\theta=\frac{2ab}{a^2+b^2}$$

$\{\sin^2\theta+\cos^2\theta=1\}$

$$\tan\theta=\frac{\sin\theta}{\cos\theta}=\frac{a^2-b^2}{2ab}$$

46. (a) $\frac{\sin\theta-\cos\theta+1}{\sin\theta+\cos\theta-1}$

Dividing Numerator and Denominator by $\cos\theta$

$$\Rightarrow \frac{\frac{\sin\theta}{\cos\theta}-\frac{\cos\theta}{\cos\theta}+\frac{1}{\cos\theta}}{\frac{\sin\theta}{\cos\theta}+\frac{\cos\theta}{\cos\theta}-\frac{1}{\cos\theta}} \Rightarrow \frac{\tan\theta-1+\sec\theta}{\tan\theta+1-\sec\theta}$$

$$\Rightarrow \frac{(\tan\theta+\sec\theta)-(\sec^2\theta-\tan^2\theta)}{\tan\theta-\sec\theta+1}$$

$$\Rightarrow \frac{(\tan\theta+\sec\theta)[1-\sec\theta+\tan\theta]}{\tan\theta-\sec\theta+1}$$

$$\Rightarrow \tan\theta+\sec\theta$$

$$\Rightarrow \frac{\sin\theta}{\cos\theta}+\frac{1}{\cos\theta} \Rightarrow \frac{1+\sin\theta}{\cos\theta}$$

47. (d)

100 m

50 m

θ

$$\sin\theta=\frac{50\text{m}}{100\text{ m}}=\frac{1}{2}$$

$\theta=30°$

48. (c) $\because$ 72 lakhs $\equiv$ 360°

$\therefore$ 12 lakhs $\equiv \frac{360}{72}\times12$

$60°=S_5$

49. (a) Population of region S_1

$$=\frac{45}{360}\times72=9\text{ lakhs}$$

Males $=\frac{3}{5}\times9=5.4$ lakhs

Population of region S_4

$$=\frac{105}{360}\times72=21\text{ laksh}$$

Males $=\frac{2}{5}\times21=8.4$ lakhs

Sum = 5.4 + 8.4 = 13.8 lakhs

50. (c) Population of region S_2

$= \frac{135}{360} \times 72 = 27$ lakhs

Females $= \frac{1}{5} \times 27 = 5.4$ lakhs

Population of region S_5

$= \frac{60}{360} \times 72 = 12$ lakhs

Females $= \frac{7}{20} \times 12 = 4.2$ lakhs

$\therefore$ Required ratio = 5.4 : 4.2 = 9:7

51. (b) Preposition 'to' is correct.

52. (a) Ponder over - is correct expression.
Ponder: to consider something deeply and thoroughly; meditate (often followed by over or upon).

53. (c) Glum- looking or feeling dejected; morose.

54. (b) Love is correct word.

55. (b) Vanish fits in the context of the sentence correctly.

56. (d)	57. (d)	58. (d)	59. (d)	60. (b)
61. (c)	62. (b)	63. (a)	64. (b)	65. (b)
66. (a)	67. (d)	68. (c)	69. (b)	70. (d)
71. (c)	72. (c)	73. (a)	74. (d)	75. (a)
76. (b)	77. (c)	78. (a)	79. (a)	80. (b)
81. (b)	82. (a)	83. (c)	84. (c)	85. (a)
86. (a)	87. (d)	88. (a)	89. (b)	90. (c)
91. (b)	92. (b)	93. (c)	94. (b)	95. (b)
96. (a)	97. (a)	98. (b)	99. (d)	100. (a)

PRACTICE SET- 14

GENERAL INTELLIGENCE & REASONING

DIRECTIONS (Qs. 1-3): *Select the related letter/ word/ number from the given alternatives.*

1. TEKCAR : RACKET : : TCEJBO : ?
   (a) TCEOBJ (b) OBJECT
   (c) CEJBOT (d) REJECT
2. 64 : ? : : 72 : 53
   (a) 44 (b) 54
   (c) 52 (d) 70
3. Elephant : Tusk : : Parrot : ?
   (a) Quill (b) Feather
   (c) Beak (d) Spine

DIRECTIONS (Qs. 4-6) : *In questions, find the odd number/ letters/ word/ number pair from the given alternatives.*

4. (a) Socrates (b) Beethoven
   (c) Mozart (d) Bach
5. (a) 5270 – 2936 (b) 186 – 69
   (c) 168 – 570 (d) 1001 – 100
6. (a) DH (b) FJ
   (c) HK (d) PR
7. Arrange the given words in a meaningful order:
   1. INFANT 2. ADOLESCENT
   3. CHILD 4. OLD
   5. ADULT
   (a) 3, 1, 2, 4, 5 (b) 1, 3, 2, 5, 4
   (c) 3, 2, 4, 5, 1 (d) 5, 4, 3, 2, 1

DIRECTIONS (Qs. 8-9) : *In a given series, with one term missing. Choose the correct alternative from the given ones that will complete the series.*

8. AKU, FPZ, ?, PZJ, UEO, ZJT
   (a) JUE (b) KVE
   (c) KUE (d) JVE
9. 5, 11, 24, 51, 106, ___?___.
   (a) 115 (b) 122
   (c) 217 (d) 221
10. Seema's younger brother Sohan is older than Seeta. Sweta is younger than Deepti but elder than Seema. Who is the eldest ?
    (a) Seeta (b) Deepti
    (c) Seema (d) Sweta
11. The average age of father and his son is 22 years. The ratio of their ages is 10 : 1 respectively. What is the age of the son ?
    (a) 24 (b) 4
    (c) 40 (d) 14
12. From the given alternatives select the word which ***cannot*** be formed using the letters of tne given word.
    SIGNATURE
    (a) SIGHT (b) GAIN
    (c) NATURE (d) GATE
13. If 'JUNE' is written as 'PQRS' an 'AUGUST' is written as 'WQFQMN'. How can 'GUEST' be written in this same coding language?
    (a) FPSMN (b) FQSMN
    (c) FQSNM (d) FQTMN
14. If × stands for addition, < for subtraction, + stands for division, > stands for multiplication, – stands for equation, ÷ stands for greater than, and = stands for less than, state which of the following is true ?
    (a) $3 \times 2 < 4 \div 16 > 2 + 4$
    (b) $5 > 8 + 4 = 10 < 4 \times 8$
    (c) $3 \times 4 > 2 - 9 + 3 < 3$
    (d) $5 \times 3 = 3 \times 8 + 4 < 1$
15. If 64 + 53 = 4, 86 + 42 = 4, then
    83 + 72 = ?
    (a) 12 (b) 10
    (c) 15 (d) 18

DIRECTIONS (Qs. 16) : *Select the missing number from the given responses.*

16. 16 49 64

25 36 81

9 13 ?

(a) 21 (b) 22

(c) 17 (d) 14

17. Satish start from A and walks 2 km east upto B and turns southwards and walks 1 km upto C. At C he turns to east and walks 2 km upto D. He then turns northwards and walks 4 km to E. How far is he from his starting point ?

(a) 5 km (b) 6 km

(c) 3 km (d) 4 km

DIRECTION (Q. 18) : *Two statements are given followed by two conclusions I and II. You have to consider the statements to be true even if they seem to be at variance from commonly known facts. You have to decide which of the given conclusions, if any, follow from the given statements.*

18. **Statements:**

All voters are adults. No children are voters.

Conclusions:

(I) No adults are voters.

(II) No voters are children.

(a) Only conclusion (II) follows

(b) Both conclusions (I) and (II) follow

(c) Neither conclusion (I) nor (II) follows

(d) Only conclusion (I) follows

19. Count the number of triangles in the given figure

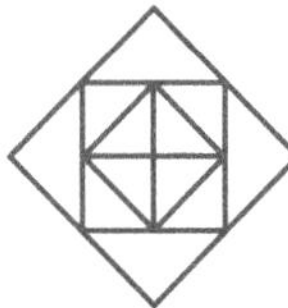

(a) 9 (b) 8

(c) 12 (d) 16

20. Which of the following Figure best represents the relationship amongst the Human being, Girl, Boy?

(a)  (b) 

(c)  (d) 

DIRECTION (Q. 21) : *In question, which answer figure will complete the pattern in the question figure?*

21. **Question figure**

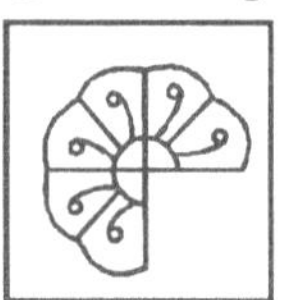

Answer figures

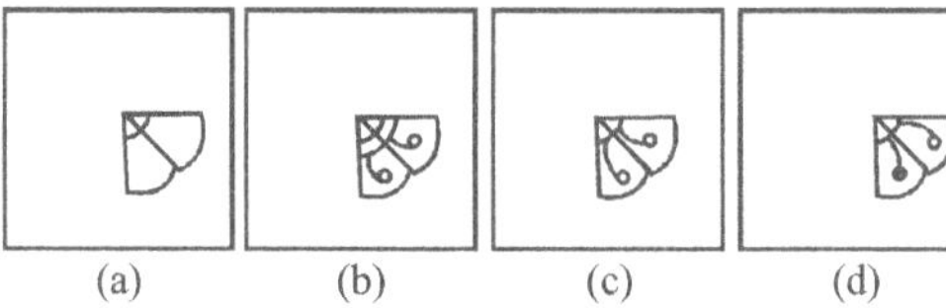

(a) (b) (c) (d)

22. Which one of the answer figures is hidden in the following question figure?

Question Figure :

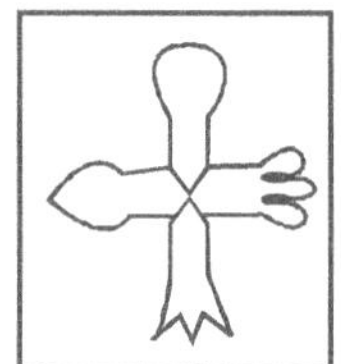

Answer Figures.

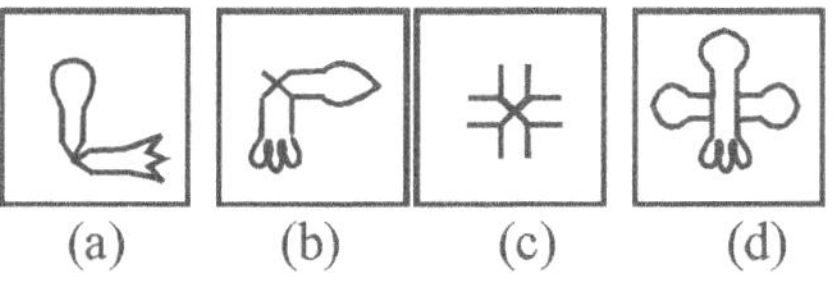

(a) (b) (c) (d)

DIRECTION (Q. 23) : *In the following questions, a piece of paper is folded and cut as shown below in the question figures. From the given answer figures, indicate how It will appear when opened?*

23. **Question Figures:**

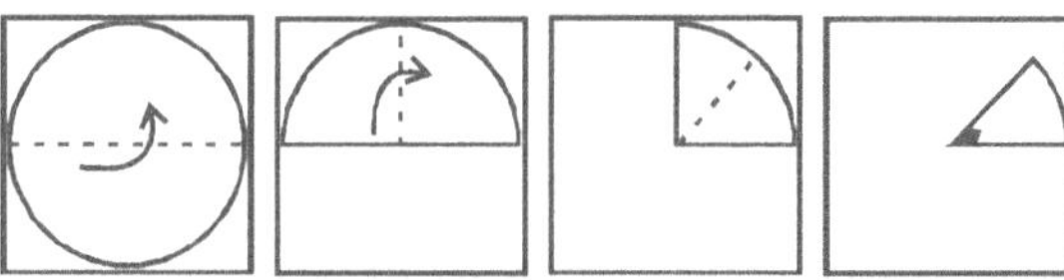

Answer Figures:

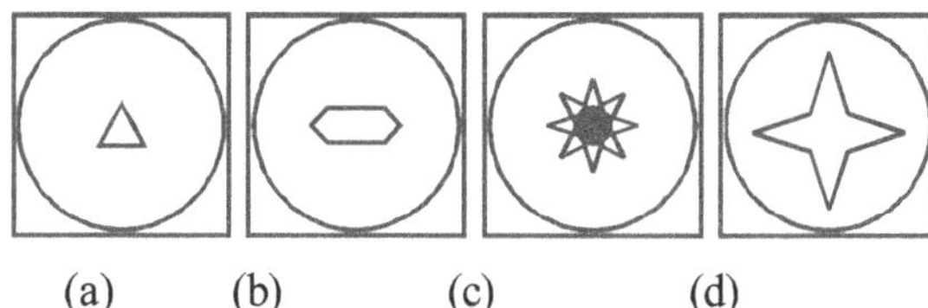

(a) (b) (c) (d)

24. Choose the right water-image of the question figure from the given answer figures.

Question Figure :

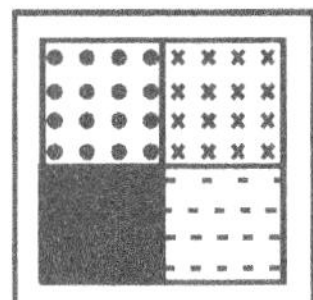

Answer Figures :

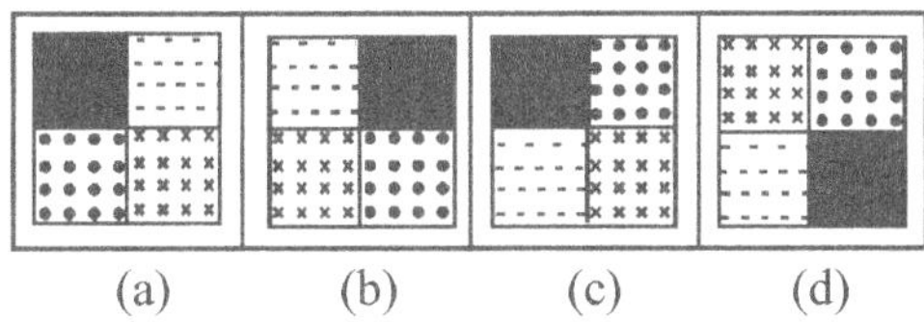

(a) (b) (c) (d)

DIRECTION (Q. 25) : *A word is represented by only one set of numbers as given in any one of the alternatives. The sets of numbers given in the alternatives are represented by two classes of alphabets as in two matrices given below. The columns and rows of Matrix I are numbered from 0 to 4 and that of Matrix II are numbered from 5 to 9. A letter from these matrices can be represented first by its row and next by its column e.g., 'E' can be represented by 01, 13 etc., and 'L' can be represented by 56, 77 etc. Similarly, you have to identify the set for the word given in each question.*

25. **Matrix I**

	0	1	2	3	4
0	A	E	M	N	P
1	N	P	A	E	M
2	E	M	N	P	A
3	P	A	E	M	N
4	M	N	P	A	E

Matrix II

	5	6	7	8	9
5	I	L	R	S	T
6	R	S	T	I	L
7	T	I	L	R	S
8	L	R	S	T	I
9	S	T	I	L	R

AIRS
(a) 12, 76, 99, 78 (b) 43, 55, 86, 95
(c) 00, 68, 78, 88 (d) 24, 69, 56, 78

QUANTITATIVE APTITUDE

26. The H.C.F. and L.C.M. of two numebrs are 8 and 48 respectively. If one of the numbers is 24, then the other number is
(a) 48 (b) 36
(c) 24 (d) 16

27. The value of $\dfrac{2\frac{1}{3}-1\frac{2}{11}}{3+\cfrac{1}{3+\cfrac{1}{3+\frac{1}{3}}}}$ is
(a) $\frac{38}{109}$ (b) $\frac{109}{38}$
(c) 1 (d) $\frac{116}{109}$

28. The average age of a jury of 5 is 40. If a member aged 35 resigns and a man aged 25 becomes a member, then the average age of the new jury is
(a) 30 (b) 38
(c) 40 (d) 42

29. The price of an article was first increased by 10% and then again by 20%. If the last increased price be ₹ 33, the original price was
(a) ₹ 30 (b) ₹ 27.50
(c) ₹ 26.50 (d) ₹ 25

30. If the price of sugar is raised by 25%, find by how much percent a householder must reduce his consumption of sugar so as not to increase his expenditure?
(a) 10 (b) 20
(c) 18 (d) 25

31. A certain sum will amount to ₹12,100 in 2 years at 10% per annum of compound interest, interest being compounded annually. The sum is:
(a) ₹12000 (b) ₹6000
(c) ₹8000 (d) ₹10000

32. A thief is noticed by a policeman from a distance of 200 m. The thief starts running and the policeman chases him. The thief and the policeman run at the rate of 10 km and 11 km per hour respectively. The distance (in metres) between them after 6 minutes is
(a) 190 (b) 200
(c) 100 (d) 150

33. A work can be completed by P and Q in 12 days, Q and R in 15 days, R and P in 20 days. In how many days P alone can finish the work?
(a) 10 (b) 20
(c) 30 (d) 60

34. Among three numbers, the first is twice the second and thrice the third. If the average of the three numbers is 49.5, then the difference between the first and the third number is
(a) 54 (b) 28
(c) 39.5 (d) 41.5

35. Three numbers are in the ratio 1 : 2 : 3. By adding 5 to each of them, the new numbers are in the ratio 2 : 3 : 4. The numbers are :
(a) 5, 10, 15 (b) 10, 20, 30
(c) 15, 30, 45 (d) 1, 2, 3

36. The length of radius of a circumcircle of a triangle having sides 3 cm, 4 cm and 5 cm is:
(a) 2 cm (b) 2.5 cm
(c) 3 cm (d) 1.5 cm

37. O is the circum centre of the triangle ABC with circumradius 13 cm. Let BC = 24 cm and OD is perpendicular to BC. Then the length of OD is:
(a) 7 cm (b) 3 cm
(c) 4 cm (d) 5 cm

38. If I is the In-centre of DABC and ÐA = 60°, then the value of ÐBIC is
(a) 100° (b) 120°
(c) 150° (d) 110°

39. A bicycle wheel makes 5000 revolutions in moving 11 km. Then the radius of the wheel (in cm) is (Take $\pi = \frac{22}{7}$)
(a) 70 (b) 35
(c) 17.5 (d) 140

40. If $a^2 + \frac{1}{a^2} = 98(a > 0)$, then the value of $a^3 + \frac{1}{a^3}$ will be
(a) 535 (b) 1030
(c) 790 (d) 970

41. If $5a + \frac{1}{3a} = 5$, then the value of $9a^2 + \frac{1}{25a^2}$ is
(a) $\frac{51}{5}$ (b) $\frac{29}{5}$
(c) $\frac{52}{5}$ (d) $\frac{39}{5}$

42. If $x = \sqrt{3} + \sqrt{2}$, then the value of $x^3 - \frac{1}{x^3}$ is :
(a) $14\sqrt{2}$ (b) $14\sqrt{3}$
(c) $22\sqrt{2}$ (d) $10\sqrt{2}$

43. A man buys 3 cows and 18 goats in ₹ 47,200. Instead if he would have bought 8 cows and 3 goats, he had to pay ₹ 53,000 mroe. Cost of one cow is :
(a) ₹ 10,000 (b) ₹ 11,000
(c) ₹ 12,000 (d) ₹ 13,000

44. If $2 - \cos^2 \theta = 3 \sin \theta \cos \theta$, $\sin \theta \neq \cos \theta$ then $\tan \theta$ is
(a) $\frac{1}{2}$ (b) 0
(c) $\frac{2}{3}$ (d) $\frac{1}{3}$

45. If α is a positive acute angle and $2\sin\alpha + 15\cos^2\alpha = 7$, then the value of $\cot\alpha$ is:
(a) 3/4 (b) 4/3
(c) $\frac{\sqrt{5}}{2}$ (d) $\frac{2}{\sqrt{5}}$

46. The angles of elevation of the top of a tower standing on a horizontal plane from two points on a line passing through the foot of the tower at a distance 9 ft and 16 ft respectively are complementary angles. Then the height of the tower is
(a) 9 ft (b) 12 ft
(c) 16 ft (d) 144 ft

47. If $2 (\cos^2 \theta - \sin^2 \theta) = 1$ (θ is a positive acute angle), then cot is equal to
(a) $\sqrt{3}$ (b) $-\sqrt{3}$
(c) $\frac{1}{\sqrt{3}}$ (d) 1

DIRECTIONS (Qs. 48-50) : *The following pie-chart represents the profits earned by a certain company in seven consecutive years. Study the pie-chart carefully and answer the question.*

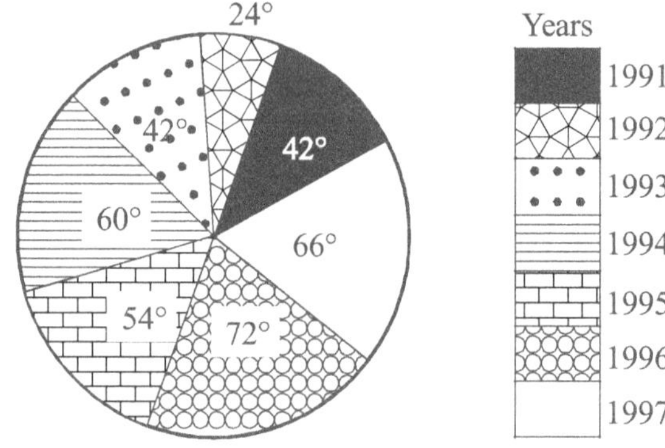

48. If the expenditure in the year 1993 was 30% more than the expenditure in the year 1991, then the income in the year 1993 exceeds the income in the year 1991 by 30% of
(a) the income in the year 1991
(b) the expenditure in the year 1993
(c) the income in the year 1993
(d) the expenditure in the year 1991

49. If x% of the total of profits earned in all the given years is same as the profit earned in the year 1994, then x is
(a) $16\frac{2}{3}$ (b) $33\frac{1}{3}$
(c) $12\frac{1}{2}$ (d) $11\frac{2}{3}$

50. The ratios of expenditures and incomes in the years 1992, 1994 and 1996 are given to be 6 : 5 : 8 and 2 : 3 : 4 respectively. The ratio of the income in the year 1996 to the total expenditure in the years 1992 and 1994 is
(a) 40 : 11 (b) 10 : 7
(c) 20 : 11 (d) 20 : 13

ENGLISH LANGUAGE

DIRECTIONS (Qs. 51-55): *In the following passage, some of the words have been left out. First read the passage over and try to understand what it is about. Then fill in the blanks with the help of the alternatives given. Mark your answer.*

Since you have never had to **(51)** me for anything, perhaps you wouldn't be **(52)** sticking **(53)** me now that I have run **(54)** debt, and **(55)** these people that it is in no way a Reflection on my character.

51. (a) Appreciate (b) Reproach
(c) Assert (d) Pester
52. (a) Averse to (b) Deprived of
(c) Indifferent to (d) Desirous of
53. (a) At (b) On
(c) For (d) To
54. (a) In (b) Into
(c) With (d) On
55. (a) Alluding (b) Making
(c) Convincing (d) Informing

DIRECTIONS (Qs. 56-57) : *In questions, out of the four alternatives, choose the one which best expresses the meaning of the given word and mark it in the Answer sheet.*

56. Annexure
(a) Retirement (b) Commencement
(c) Attachment (d) Development
57. Bequeath
(a) Give (b) Disclose
(c) Scold (d) Surround

DIRECTIONS (Qs. 58-59) : *In these questions choose the word opposite in meaning to the given word and mark it.*

58. Dormant
(a) Active (b) Inactive
(c) Dorsal (d) Domestic
59. Tranquility
(a) Disturbance (b) Quiet
(c) Serenity (d) Peace

DIRECTIONS (Qs. 60-62) : *Sentences are given with blanks to be filled with an appropriate word(s).*

60. He was assured by his friends ________ every type of help in an emergency.
(a) about (b) by
(c) of (d) with
61. Our monthly expenditure ________ by five hundred rupees when we decided to buy milk from the milkman.
(a) grew up (b) shot up
(c) got up (d) lifted up
62. ________ to people looked well enough, but when one looked more closely one saw that their faces were filled with despair.
(a) At first sight
(b) At first looking
(c) At first observation
(d) On first sight

DIRECTIONS (Qs. 63-64) : *In questions below, some parts of the sentences have errors and some are correct. Find out which part of a sentence has an error. If a sentence is free from error, mark blacken the oval corresponding to (d) as your Answer.*

63. In 1906 a earthquake (a) destroyed much (b)

of San Francisco. (c) No error. (d)

64. The college library is (a) not only equipped with (b) very good books but also with the latest journals. (c) No error. (d)

DIRECTION (Q. 65): *Rearrange the parts of the sentence in correct order.*

65. (P) expect others
(Q) those who cannot treat
(R) should not
(S) others well
(a) QSRP (b) QPRS
(c) RPQS (d) SRPQ

DIRECTIONS (Qs. 66-67) : *In these questions choose the word opposite in meaning to the given word and mark it.*

66. The second pigeon flew just as the first pigeon had flown.
(a) one had done
(b) one had flown away
(c) had done
(d) No improvement

67. The old man has acquired experience through age.
(a) developed experience
(b) experienced
(c) got experience
(d) No improvement

DIRECTION (Q. 68): *In a question, a sentence has been given in Direct/Indirect form. Out of the four alternatives suggested, select the one which best expresses the same sentence in Indirect/Direct form.*

68. He said to the interviewer, "Could you please repeat the question?"
(a) He requested the interviewer if he could please repeat the question
(b) He requested the interviewer to please repeat the question.
(c) He requested the interviewer to repeat the question.
(d) He requested the interviewer if he could repeat the question.

DIRECTION (Q. 69): *In a question, a sentence has been given in Active / Passive voice. Out of the four alternatives suggested, select the one which best expresses the same sentence in Passive/ Active voice.*

69. We waste much time on trifles.
(a) Much time was wasted on trifles.
(b) Much time will be wasted on trifles.
(c) Much time is wasted by us on trifles.
(d) Much time is wasted on trifles.

DIRECTIONS (Qs. 70-71): *Out of the four alternatives, choose the one which can be substituted for the given words/sentences.*

70. The group, especially in the arts, regarded as being the most experimental
(a) avant-garde (b) iconoclast
(c) revolutionary (d) nerd

71. One who helps people by giving them money or other aid
(a) benefactor (b) beneficiary
(c) tycoon (d) patriot

DIRECTION (Q. 72) : *In the question, four words are given in each question, out of which only one word is correctly spelt. Find the correctly spelt word.*

72. (a) Questionnaire (b) Questionnair
(c) Questionaire (d) Questionnare

DIRECTIONS (Qs. 73-75) : *In the following questions, four alternatives are given for the idiom / phrase underlined in the sentence. Choose the alternative which best expresses the meaning of the idiom / phrase and mark it in the Answer Sheet.*

73. The manager hesitated to assign the job to the newcomer as he was wet behind the ears.
(a) stupid and slow-witted
(b) young and inexperienced
(c) drenched-in the rain .
(d) unpunctual and lethargic

74. Mrs. Roy keeps an open house on Saturday evening parties— you'll find all kinds of people there.

(a) keeps the doors of the house open
(b) keeps the gates open for a few persons
(c) welcomes all members
(d) welcomes a select group of people

75. We cannot depend on him for this assignment as it needs careful handling and he is like a bull in a china shop.
(a) a felicitous person
(b) a clumsy person
(c) a tactful person
(d) a no-nonsense person

GENERAL AWARENESS

76. Simon Commission was boycotted by the nationalist leaders of India because:
(a) they felt that it was only an eyewash
(b) all the members of the Commission were English
(c) the members of the Commission were biased against India
(d) it did not meet the demands of the Indians

77. 'Prince of Pilgrims' was the name attributed to
(a) Plutarch (b) Hiuen Tsang
(c) Fa-Hien (d) I-Tsing

78. Marx belonged to
(a) Germany (b) Holland
(c) France (d) Britain

79. The National Commission for Minorities was constituted in the year
(a) 1990 (b) 1992
(c) 1980 (d) 1989

80. The main reason for the growth of communalism in India is
(a) Educational and economic backwardness of minority groups
(b) Political consciousness
(c) Social inequalities
(d) Imposing ban on communal organisations

81. Which among the following agencies released the report, Economic Outlook for 2009–10 ?
(a) Planning Commission
(b) PM's Economic Advisory Council
(c) Finance Commission
(d) Reserve Bank of India

82. The Rashtriya Barh Ayog (RBA) is related with
(a) Droughts and Floods
(b) Poverty Alleviation
(c) Floods
(d) Disaster Management

83. The 13th Five Year Plan will be operative for the period.
(a) 2010-2015 (b) 2011-2016
(c) 2012-2017 (d) 2013-2018

84. Which of the following is an impact printe ?
(a) Daisy wheel printer
(b) Ink jet printer
(c) Bubble jet printer
(d) Laser printer

85. Angle of friction and angle of repose are
(a) equal to each other
(b) not equal to each other
(c) proportional to each other
(d) None of the above

86. We receive sunlight on earth surface. What type of light beams are these?
(a) Random (b) Parallel
(c) Converging (d) Diverging

87. The addition of gypsum to portland cement helps in:
(a) increasing the strength of cement
(b) rapid setting of cement
(c) preventing rapid setting of cement
(d) reduction in the cost of cement

88. 'Dry ice' is the condensed form of
(a) sulphur tri-oxide
(b) carbon dioxide
(c) highly cooled water
(d) oxygen

89. Stains of rust on clothes can be removed by :
(a) H_2O_2 (b) Oxalic acid
(c) Petrol (d) Alcohol

90. White lung disease is prevalent among the workers of:
(a) Paper industry (b) Cement industry
(c) Cotton industry (d) Pesticide industry

91. The infective stage of Malaria is:
(a) Gametocyte (b) Ring stage
(c) Sporozoite (d) Merozoite

92. During respiration, the gases enter into the blood and leave the same by the process of
(a) Active transport
(b) Diffusion
(c) Diffusion and active transport
(d) Osmosis

93. The process of photosynthesis involves conversion of
(a) chemical energy into radiant energy
(b) chemical energy into mechanical energy
(c) solar energy into chemical energy
(d) mechanical energy into solar energy

94. Which of the following is called the 'ecological hot spot of India'?
(a) Western Ghats
(b) Eastern Ghats
(c) Western Himalayas
(d) Eastern Himalayas

95. Railway coaches are manufactured at
(a) Jamshedpur (b) Chittaranjan
(c) Perambur (d) Varanasi

96. The iron and steel plant in Chhattisgarh is at
(a) Burnpur (b) Salem
(c) Bhilai (d) Bokaro

97. An irrigation project is categorized as a major project if it covers a cultivable command area of
(a) less than 2,000 hectares
(b) 2,000 to 10,000 hectares
(c) above 10,000 hectares
(d) All the above

98. Which of the following folk/tribal dances is associated with Karnataka?
(a) Yakshagana (b) Veedhi
(c) Jatra (d) Jhora

99. Who among the following won the 2019 Badminton Asia Championships, in men's singles category?
(a) Lin Dan
(b) Kento Momota
(c) Chen Long
(d) Sameer Verma

100. The world's first-ever malaria vaccine was launched in a pilot project in-
(a) Botswana (b) Mozambique
(c) Burundi (d) Malawi

Hints & Explanations

1. (b) The letters have been written in reverse order.
TEKCAR ⇒ RACKET
Similarly,
TCEJBO ⇒ OBJECT

2. (b) $7+2=9$; $5+3=8$
$9-8=1$
$6+4=10$; $5+4=9$
$10-9=1$

3. (c)

4. (a) Socrates was a Greek philosopher. Ludwing Van Beethoven was a German Composer and Musician. Bach was also a German Composer. WA Mozart was a Austrian Compose.

5. (b) $1+8+6=15$ and $6+9=15$

6. (c)

D	H	F	J	H	K	P	R
↓	↓	↓	↓	↓	↓	↓	↓
4	8	6	10	8	11	16	18

Pair of odd and even number

7. (b)

8. (c)

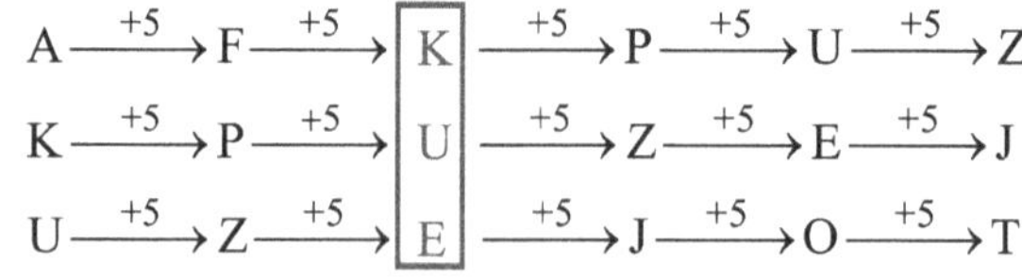

9. (c) $5\times2+1=11$
$11\times2+2=24$
$24\times2+3=51$
$51\times2+4=106$
$106\times2+5=\boxed{217}$

10. (b) Seema > Sohan > Seeta ...(i)
Deepti > Sweta > Seema ...(ii)
Combining (i) and (ii) we get
Deepti > Sweta > Seema > Sohan > Seeta

11. (b) Suppose the age of son is x years
Therefore, age of father = 10x years
According to question

$$\frac{10x+x}{2}=22$$

$\Rightarrow 11x=44 \therefore x=\frac{44}{11}=4$ years

Age of father $=10\times 4=40$ years

12. (a) There in no 'H' in the word SIGNATURE

13. (b) J U N E

↓ ↓ ↓ ↓

P Q R S

A U G U S T

↓ ↓ ↓ ↓ ↓ ↓

W Q F Q M N

Therefore,

G U E S T

↓ ↓ ↓ ↓ ↓

F Q S M N

14. (b) Option (b)

$5>8+4=10<4\times 8$

$\Rightarrow 5\times 8\div 4<10-4+8$

$\Rightarrow 5\times 2<18-4\Rightarrow 10<14$

15. (b) $\left.\begin{matrix}6-4=2\\5-3=2\end{matrix}\right]$ Addition $=4$

$\left.\begin{matrix}8-6=2\\4-2=2\end{matrix}\right]$ Addition $=4$

Similarly, $\left.\begin{matrix}8-3=5\\7-2=5\end{matrix}\right]$ Addition $=10$

16. (c) **First Column**

$\sqrt{16}+\sqrt{25}$

$\Rightarrow 4+5=9$

Second Column

$\sqrt{49}+\sqrt{36}$

$\Rightarrow 7+6=13$

Third column

$\sqrt{64}+\sqrt{81}\Rightarrow 8+9=\boxed{17}$

17. (a)

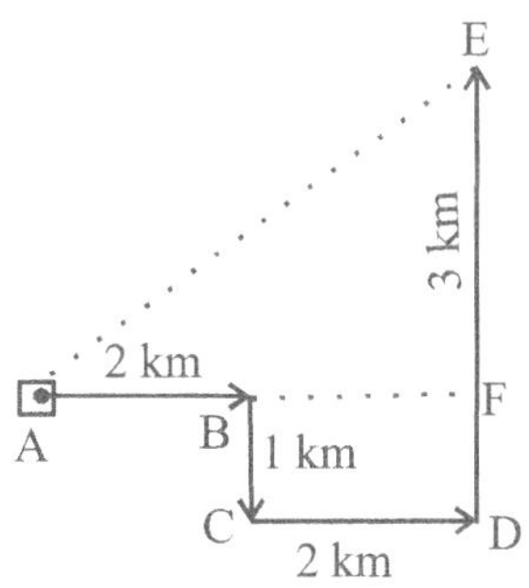

$\therefore$ Required distance AE,

$$=\sqrt{(AF)^2+(EF)^2}$$

$$=\sqrt{(4)^2+(3)^2}=\sqrt{16+9}=\sqrt{25}=\boxed{5\text{ km}}$$

18. (a) 19. (d) 20. (a) 21. (c) 22. (c)

23. (c) 24. (a) 25. (b)

26. (d) $p\times q=\text{HCF}\times\text{LCM}$

$\therefore$ Second number $=\frac{8\times 48}{24}=16$

27. (a) Expression

$$=\frac{\frac{7}{3}-\frac{13}{11}}{3+\frac{1}{3+\frac{1}{\frac{9+1}{3}}}}=\frac{\frac{77-39}{33}}{3+\frac{1}{3+\frac{3}{10}}}$$

$$=\frac{\frac{38}{33}}{3+\frac{1}{\frac{30+3}{10}}}=\frac{\frac{38}{33}}{3+\frac{10}{33}}$$

$$=\frac{\frac{38}{33}}{\frac{99+10}{33}}=\frac{38}{33}\times\frac{33}{109}=\frac{38}{109}$$

28. (b) Required average

$$=\frac{40\times 5-35+25}{5}=\frac{190}{5}=38\text{ years}$$

29. (d) Net increase percentage

$$=\left(10+20+\frac{20\times 10}{100}\right)\%=32\%$$

$$\therefore x\times\frac{132}{100}=33$$

$$\Rightarrow x=\frac{33\times 100}{132}=₹\,25$$

30. (b) Percentage decrease $=\frac{25}{125}\times 100=20$

31. (d) Final rate of interest for two pens

$$=x+y+\frac{xy}{100}$$

$$=10+10+\frac{10\times 10}{100}=21\%$$

Let principal be P.

$$\Rightarrow P \times \frac{121}{100} = 12100$$

$$P = 100 \times 100 = ₹\,10000$$

32. (c) Relative speed = 11 – 10 = 1 kmph
Distance covered in 6 minutes

$$= \frac{1000}{60} \times 6\text{metre} = 100 \text{ metre}$$

∴ Remaining distance
= 200 – 100 = 100 metre

33. (c) $(P+Q)$'s 1 day's work $= \frac{1}{12}$ ...(i)

$(Q+R)$'s 1 day's work $= \frac{1}{15}$ ...(ii)

$(R+P)$'s 1 day's work $= \frac{1}{120}$ ...(iii)

Adding all three equations, 2 (P + Q + R)'s 1 day's work

$$= \frac{1}{12} + \frac{1}{15} + \frac{1}{20} = \frac{5+4+3}{60} = \frac{12}{60} = \frac{1}{5}$$

∴ $(P+Q+R)$'s 1 day's work $= \frac{1}{10}$ ...(iv)

∴ P's 1 day's work
= Equation (iv) – equation (ii)

$$= \frac{1}{10} - \frac{1}{15} = \frac{3-2}{30} = \frac{1}{30}$$

∴ P alone will complete the work in 30 days,

34. (a) Let the second number be x.
∴ First number = 2x

∴ Third number $= \frac{2x}{3}$

$$\therefore 2x + x + \frac{2x}{3} = 49.5 \times 3$$

$$\Rightarrow 6x + 3x + 2x = 49.5 \times 9 = 445.5$$

$$\Rightarrow 11x = 445.5 \Rightarrow x = \frac{4455}{11} = 4.05$$

∴ Required difference

$$= 2x - \frac{2x}{3} = \frac{4x}{3}$$

$$= \frac{4 \times 40.5}{3} = 54$$

35. (a) Number = x, 2x and 3x

$$\therefore \frac{x+5}{2x+5} = \frac{2}{3}$$

$\Rightarrow 4x+10$
$\Rightarrow 3x+15$
$\Rightarrow x=5$
⇒ Number = 5, 10 and 15,

36. (b) Circumradius of a triangle

$$= \frac{abc}{\sqrt{(a+b+c)(a+b-c)(b+c-a)(a+c-b)}}$$

$$= \frac{3\times4\times5}{\sqrt{(3+4+5)(3+4-5)(4+5-3)(3+5-4)}}$$

$$= \frac{60}{\sqrt{12\times2\times6\times4}} = 2.5 \text{ cm}$$

37. (d)

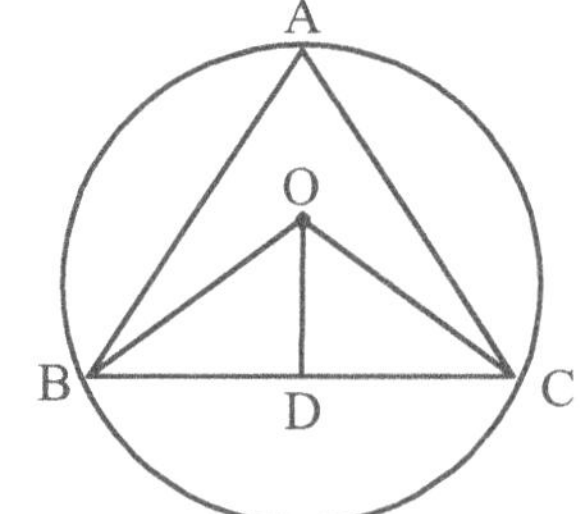

$$BD = \frac{BC}{2} = 12 \text{ cm}$$

OB = 13 cm
From Δ OBD,

$$= OD = \sqrt{OB^2 - BD^2}$$

$$= \sqrt{13^2 - 12^2} = \sqrt{169-144}$$

$$= \sqrt{25} = 5 \text{ cm}$$

38. (b) $\angle BIC = 90° +$
$= 90° + 30° = 120°$

39. (b) Distance covered by wheel in one revolution
= Circumference of wheel

$$= \frac{11000}{5000} = \frac{11}{5} \text{ m}$$

$$= \frac{11}{5} \times 100 \text{ cm} = 220 \text{ cm}$$

$\therefore 2\pi r = 220$

$\Rightarrow 2 \times \frac{22}{7} \times r = 220$

$\Rightarrow r = \frac{220 \times 7}{2 \times 22} = 35$ cm

40. (d) $a^2 + \frac{1}{a^2} = 98$

$\Rightarrow \left(a + \frac{1}{a}\right)^2 - 2 = 98$

$\Rightarrow \left(a + \frac{1}{a}\right)^2 = 100$

$\Rightarrow a + \frac{1}{a} = 10$

On cubing both sides,

$\left(a + \frac{1}{a}\right)^3 = 1000$

$\Rightarrow a^3 + \frac{1}{a^3} + 3\left(a + \frac{1}{a}\right) = 1000$

$\Rightarrow a^3 + \frac{1}{a^3} = 1000 - 30 = 970$

41. (d) $5a + \frac{1}{3a} = 5$

Multiply by $\frac{3}{5}$ on both sides

$\frac{3}{5}\left(5a + \frac{1}{3a}\right) = 5 \times \frac{3}{5}$

$3a + \frac{1}{5a} = 3$

Squaring on both sides

$9a^2 + \frac{1}{25a^2} + 2 \times 3a \times \frac{1}{5a} = 9$

$\Rightarrow 9a^2 + \frac{1}{25a^2} = 9 - \frac{6}{5} = \frac{39}{5}$

42. (c) $x = \sqrt{3} + \sqrt{2}$

$\frac{1}{x} = \frac{1}{\sqrt{3}+\sqrt{2}} \times \frac{\sqrt{3}-\sqrt{2}}{\sqrt{3}-\sqrt{2}} = \frac{\sqrt{3}-\sqrt{2}}{3-2} = \sqrt{3}-\sqrt{2}$

N o w ,

$x^3 - \frac{1}{x^3} = \left(\sqrt{3}+\sqrt{2}\right)^3 - \left(\sqrt{3}-\sqrt{2}\right)^3$

$= (a+b)^3 - (a-b)^3$ [Let $\sqrt{3} = a$ and $\sqrt{2} = b$]

$= a^3 + b^3 + 3a^2b + 3b^2 - (a^3 - b^3 - 3a^2b + 3b^2a)$

$= a^3 + b^3 + 3a^2b + 3b^2 - a^3 + b^3 + 3a^2b - 3b^2a$

$= 2b^3 + 6a^2b = 2\left(\sqrt{2}\right)^3 + 6\left(\sqrt{3}\right)^2\left(\sqrt{2}\right)$

$= 4\sqrt{2} + 18\sqrt{2} = 22\sqrt{2}$

43. (c) C.P of 1 cow = ₹ x

C.P of a goat = ₹ y

$3x + 8y = 47200$ ...(i)

$\Rightarrow 8x + 3y = 100200$ ...(ii)

By equation (i) × 3 – (ii) × 8, $9x + 24y - 64x - 24y$

$= 141600 - 801600$

$\Rightarrow 55x = 660000$

$x = \frac{660000}{55} =$ ₹12000

44. (a) $2 - \cos^2\theta = 3\sin\theta.\cos\theta$

Dividing by $\cos^2\theta$

$\frac{2}{\cos^2\theta} - 1 = \frac{3\sin\theta.\cos\theta}{\cos^2\theta}$

$\Rightarrow 2\sec^2\theta - 1 = 3\tan\theta$

$\Rightarrow 2(1 + \tan^2\theta) - 1 = 3\tan\theta$

$\Rightarrow 2\tan^2\theta + 2 - 1 = 3\tan\theta$

$\Rightarrow 2\tan^2\theta - 3\tan\theta + 1 = 0$

$\Rightarrow 2\tan^2\theta - 2\tan\theta - \tan\theta + 1 = 0$

$\Rightarrow 2\tan\theta(\tan\theta - 1) - 1(\tan\theta - 1) = 0$

$\Rightarrow (2\tan\theta - 1)(\theta - 1) = 0$

$\Rightarrow \tan\theta = \frac{1}{2}$ or 1

45. (a) $2\sin\alpha + 15\cos^2\alpha = 7$

$\Rightarrow 2\sin\alpha + 15(1 - \sin^2\alpha) = 7$

$\Rightarrow 2\sin\alpha + 15 - 15\sin^2\alpha = 7$

$\Rightarrow 15\sin^2\alpha - 2\sin^2\alpha - 8 = 0$

$\Rightarrow 15\sin^2\alpha - 12\sin\alpha + 10\sin\alpha - 8 = 0$

$\Rightarrow 3\sin\alpha(5\sin\alpha - 4) + 2(5\sin\alpha - 4) = 0$

$\Rightarrow (3\sin\alpha + 2)(5\sin\alpha - 4) = 0$

$\Rightarrow 5\sin\alpha - 4 = 0$

$\Rightarrow 5\sin\alpha = \frac{4}{5}$

$\therefore \operatorname{cosec}\alpha = \frac{5}{4}$

$\cot\alpha = \sqrt{\operatorname{cosec}^2\alpha - 1}$

$= \sqrt{\frac{25}{16} - 1} = \sqrt{\frac{9}{16}} = \frac{3}{4}$

46. (b) In ΔABC

$\tan\alpha = \frac{h}{9}$ ...(1)

In ΔABD

$\tan\beta = \frac{h}{16}$

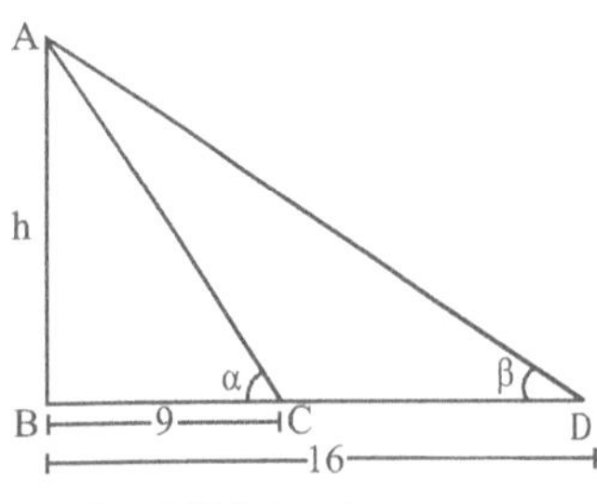

$\alpha + \beta = 90°$ (given)

$\beta = 90 - \alpha$

since $\tan\beta = \frac{h}{16}$

$\tan(90 - \alpha) = \frac{h}{16} \Rightarrow \cot\alpha = \frac{h}{16}$ or $\tan\alpha = \frac{16}{h}$ ...(2)

From eqn. (1) and (2)

$\frac{h}{9} = \frac{16}{h} \Rightarrow h^2 = 16 \times 9 \Rightarrow h = 12$ feet.

47. (a) $2\cos 2\theta = 1$

$\cos 2\theta = \frac{1}{2}$

$\theta = 30°$

$\cot 30° = \sqrt{3}$

48. (d)

49. (a) $x\%$ of $100.01 = 16.67\%$

$\Rightarrow x = 16\frac{2}{3}\%$

50. (c)

51. (b) Reproach- express to (someone) one's disapproval of or disappointment in their actions.

52. (a) Averse to- having a strong dislike of or opposition to something.

53. (d) Preposition 'to' is correct.

54. (b) Preposition 'into' is correct.

55. (c) Convincing- is correct choice.

56.	(c)	57.	(a)	58.	(a)	59.	(a)	60.	(c)
61.	(a)	62.	(a)	63.	(a)	64.	(d)	65.	(a)
66.	(a)	67.	(c)	68.	(d)	69.	(c)	70.	(a)
71.	(a)	72.	(a)	73.	(b)	74.	(c)	75.	(b)
76.	(b)	77.	(b)	78.	(a)	79.	(b)	80.	(a)
81.	(b)	82.	(c)	83.	(c)	84.	(a)	85.	(a)
86.	(a)	87.	(c)	88.	(b)	89.	(b)	90.	(d)
91.	(c)	92.	(b)	93.	(c)	94.	(a)	95.	(c)
96.	(c)	97.	(c)	98.	(a)	99.	(b)	100.	(d)

PRACTICE SET- 15

GENERAL INTELLIGENCE & REASONING

DIRECTIONS (Qs. 1-2): *Select the related letter/ word/ number from the given alternatives.*

1. JIHK : PONQ : : WVUX : ?
(a) KNML (b) RSTU
(c) HIGJ (d) MLKN

2. Eagle : Swoops : : Duck : ?
(a) waddles (b) floats
(c) swims (d) flits

3. Among the four sets, find out the set, which is like the given set.
Given set : (12, 72, 216)
(a) (4, 24, 48) (b) (7, 42, 252)
(c) (11, 60, 30) (d) (5, 30, 90)

DIRECTIONS (Qs. 4-6): *In questions, find the odd number/letter/number pair from the given alternatives.*

4. (a) Arunachal Pradesh
(b) Jammu and Kashmir
(c) Haryana
(d) Himachal Pradesh

5. (a) 400 (b) 484
(c) 625 (d) 729

6. (a) GALLOP (b) SINK
(c) ALBINO (d) CRAB

7. Arrange the following words in their ascending order, as in a dictionary:
1. Pick 2. Pith
3. Pile 4. Perk
5. Pour
(a) 4, 1, 2, 3, 5 (b) 4, 1, 3, 2, 5
(c) 4, 3, 2, 1, 5 (d) 5, 4, 3, 2, 1

DIRECTIONS (Qs. 8-9) : *Select the missing number from the given responses.*

8. ELFA, GLHA, ILJA, _?_ MLNA
(a) OLPA (b) KLMA
(c) LLMA (d) KLLA

9. 1944, 108, ?, 6, 3
(a) 16 (b) 18
(c) 11 (d) 12

10. A man showed a boy next to him and said - "He is the son of my wife's sister-in-law, but I am the only child of my parents." How is my son related to him?
(a) Brother (b) Uncle
(c) Nephew (d) Cousin

11. Five coaches P, L, R, M, O are in a row. R is to the right of M and left of P. L is to the right of P and left of O. Which coach is in the middle?
(a) P (b) L
(c) R (d) O

12. From the given alternatives select the word which can be formed using the letters of the given word.
DICTIONARY
(a) BINARY (b) DAIRY
(c) NATION (d) ADDITION

13. If MOBILE is written as ZAMSUM, how TUMOR can be written in that code?
(a) BRAIN (b) HGYAD
(c) GGXYA (d) IHZBE

14. If '+' stands for 'multiplication', '<' stands for 'division', '÷' stands for 'subtraction', '–' stands for 'addition' and '×' stands for 'greater than', identify which expression is correct.
(a) $20 - 4 \div 4 + 8 < 2 \times 26$
(b) $20 \times 8 + 15 < 5 \div 9 - 8$
(c) $20 < 2 + 10 \div 4 - 6 \times 100$
(d) $20 < 5 + 25 \div 10 - 2 \times 96$

DIRECTION (Q. 15) : *In the following question, some equations are solved on the basis of a certain system. On the same basis, find out the correct answer for the unsolved equation.*

15. If 235 = 38 and 452 = 45, then 345 =?
(a) 49 (b) 66
(c) 72 (d) 50

DIRECTION (Q. 16) : *In question below, select the missing number from the given responses*

16.

7	9	8
2	4	3
5	7	6
16	32	?

(a) 17 (b) 23
(c) 47 (d) 73

17. Ram and Sham start walking in opposite directions. Ram covers 6 kms and Sham 8 kms. Then Ram turns right and walks 8 kms and Sham turns left and walks 6 kms. How far each is from the starting point?

(a) 11 kms (b) 8 kms
(c) 9 kms (d) 10 kms

DIRECTION (Q. 18) : *In the following question, one statement is given followed by two conclusions I and II. You have to consider the statements to be true even if they seem to be at variance from commonly known facts. You have to decide which of the given conclusions, if any follow from the given statements.*

18. **Statement :** Songs always have singers to sing them. **Conclusions:**

I. Singers make a song.
II. There is no un-sung song.

(a) Only conclusion II follows
(b) Both conclusions I and II follow
(c) Neither conclusion I nor II follows
(d) Only conclusion I follows

19. Find the number of triangles in the given figure.

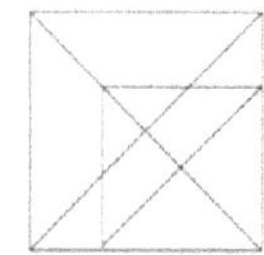

(a) 16 (b) 18
(c) 19 (d) 21

20. In the given figure, circles represent students studying three different subjects. How many students study all the three subjects?

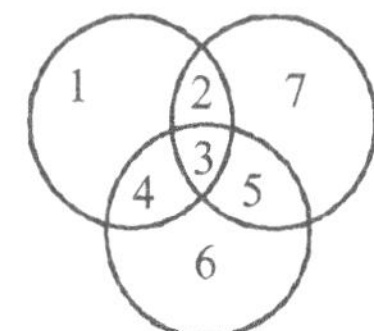

(a) 2 (b) 3
(c) 4 (d) 5

DIRECTION (Q. 21): *In question, which answer figure will complete the pattern in the question figure?*

21. Question figure :

Answer figures :

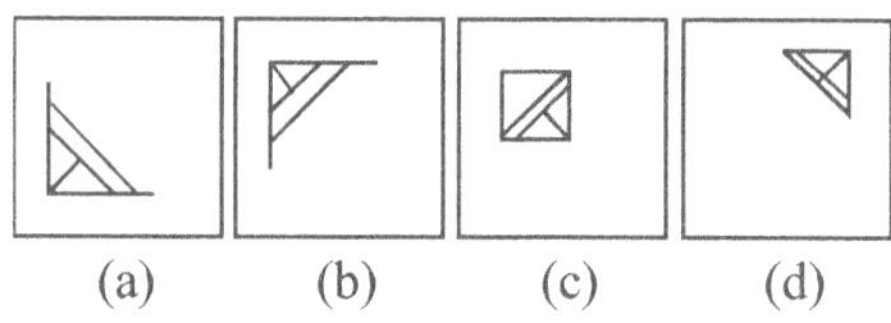

(a) (b) (c) (d)

22. From the given answer figures, select the one in which the question figure is hidden/ embedded.
Question Figure:

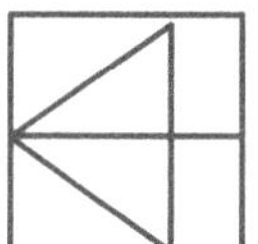

Answer Figures:

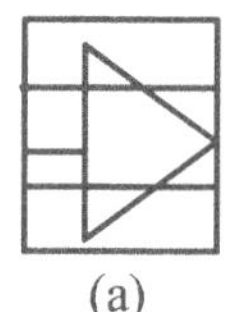
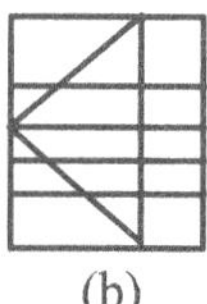
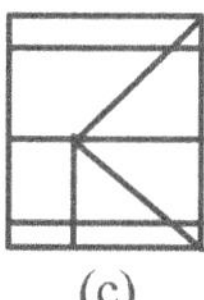
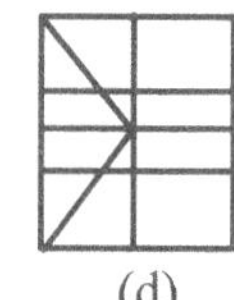

(a) (b) (c) (d)

23. A piece of paper is folded and cut/punched as shown below in the question figures. From the given answer figures, indicate how it will A appear when opened.
Question figures:

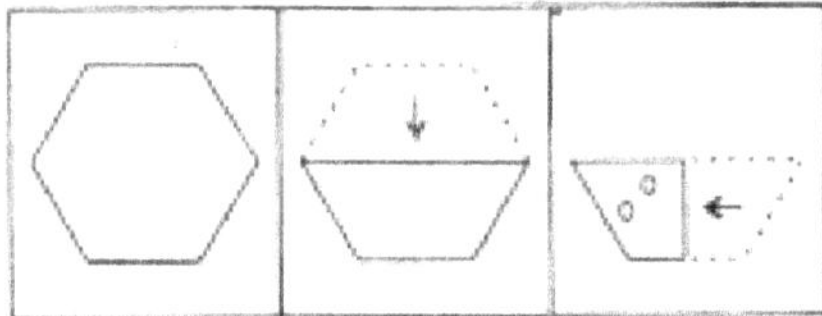

Answer figures:

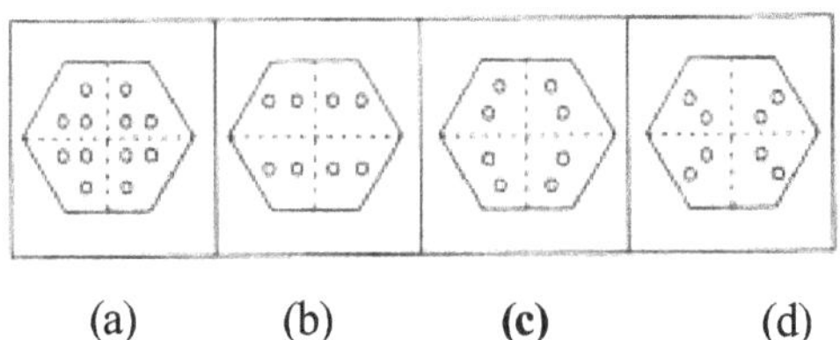

(a) (b) **(c)** (d)

24. Which of the answer figures is exactly the mirror image of the given figure when the mirror is held at MN?

Question Figure :

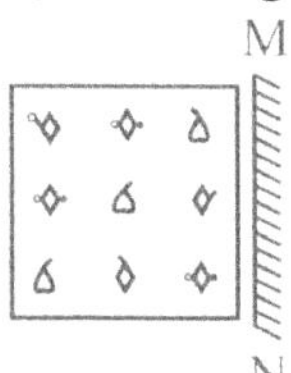

Answer Figures :

(a) (b) (c) (d)

25. A word is represented by only one set of numbers as given in any one of the alternatives. The sets of numbers given in the alternatives are represented by two classes of alphabets as in two matrices given below. The columns and rows of Matrix I are numbered from 0 to 4 and that of Matrix II are numbered from 5 to 9. A letter from these matrices can be represented first by its row and next by its column, e.g. 'A' can be represented by 03, 14 etc, and 'L' can be represented by 56, 65 etc. Similarly, you have to identify the set for the word 'BRIDE'.

MATRIX – I

	0	1	2	3	4
0	E	S	P	A	R
1	R	E	S	P	A
2	A	R	E	S	P
3	P	A	R	E	S
4	S	P	A	R	E

MATRIX–II

	5	6	7	8	9
5	B	U	I	L	D
6	U	I	L	D	B
7	I	L	D	B	U
8	L	D	B	U	I
9	D	B	U	I	L

(a) 96, 03, 75, 67, 22 (b) 55, 57, 21, 22, 86
(c) 96, 03, 75, 85, 22 (d) 55, 21, 57, 86, 22

QUANTITATIVE APTITUDE

26. The remainder when 3^{21} is divided by 5 is
(a) 1 (b) 2
(c) 3 (d) 4

27. The value of $\frac{3\sqrt{2}}{\sqrt{3}+\sqrt{6}} - \frac{4\sqrt{3}}{\sqrt{6}+\sqrt{2}} + \frac{\sqrt{6}}{\sqrt{3}+\sqrt{2}}$ is
(a) 4 (b) 0
(c) $\sqrt{2}$ (d) $3\sqrt{6}$

28. The average of 5 consecutive numbers is n. If the next two numbers are also included, the average of the 7 numbers will
(a) increase by 2 (b) increase by 1
(c) remain the same (d) increase by 1.4

29. A shopkeeper allows a discount of 10% to his customers and still gains. 20%. Find the marked price of the article which costs ₹ 450.
(a) ₹ 600 (b) ₹ 540
(c) ₹ 660 (d) ₹ 580

30. A team played 40 games in a season and won in 24 of them. What percent of games played did the team win ?
(a) 70% (b) 40%
(c) 60% (d) 35%

31. The simple interest on a certain sum of money at the rate of 5% per annum for 8 years is Rs. 840. Rate of interest for which the same amount of interest can be received on the same sum after 5 years is
(a) 7% (b) 8%
(c) 9% (d) 10%

32. A train overtakes two persons who are walking in the same direction in which the train is running, at the rate of 2 kmph and 4 kmph and passes them completely in 9 and 10 seconds respectively. The length of the train (in metres):
(a) 72 (b) 45
(c) 54 (d) 50

33. A is thrice as good a workman as B and is, therefore, able to finish a piece of work in 60 days less than B. The time (in days) in which they can do it working together is
(a) 22 (b) $22\frac{1}{2}$
(c) 23 (d) $23\frac{1}{4}$

34. If $x : y = 4 : 5$, then $(3x + y) : (5x + 3y) =$
(a) 3 : 5 (b) 5 : 3
(c) 17 : 35 (d) 35 : 17

35. ₹ 700 is divided among A, B, C in such a way that the ratio of the amount of A and B is 2 : 3 and that of B and C is 4 : 5. Find the amounts in ₹ each received, in the order A, B, C.
(a) 150, 250, 300 (b) 160, 240, 300
(c) 150, 250, 290 (d) 150, 240, 310

36. A, O, B are three points on a line segment and C is a point not lying on AOB. If $\angle AOC = 40°$ and OX, OY are the internal and external bisectors of $\angle AOC$ respectively, then $\angle BOY$ is
(a) 70° (b) 80°
(c) 72° (d) 68°

37. D and E are the mid-points of AB and AC of ΔABC; BC is produced to any point P; DE, DP and EP are joined. Then,
(a) $\Delta PED = \frac{1}{4}\Delta ABC$ (b) $\Delta PED = \Delta BEC$
(c) $\Delta ADE = \Delta BEC$ (d) $\Delta BDE = \Delta BEC$

38. The external bisectors of $\angle B$ and $\angle C$ of ΔABC meet at point P. If $\angle BAC = 80°$, then $\angle BPC$ is
(a) 50° (b) 40°
(c) 80° (d) 100°

39. The perimeter of a triangle is 40cm and its area is 60 cm^2. If the largest side measures 17cm, then the length (in cm) of the smallest side of the triangle is
(a) 4 (b) 6
(c) 8 (d) 15

40. If $x = 1 + \sqrt{2} + \sqrt{3}$, then the value of $(2x^4 - 8x^3 - 5x^2 + 26x - 28)$ is
(a) $6\sqrt{6}$ (b) 0
(c) $3\sqrt{6}$ (d) $2\sqrt{6}$

41. If $x = 3 + 2\sqrt{2}$, then the value of $\sqrt{x} - \frac{1}{\sqrt{x}}$ is
(a) $\pm 2\sqrt{2}$ (b) ± 2
(c) $\pm\sqrt{2}$ (d) $\pm\frac{1}{2}$

42. HOPEFUL : LUFEPOH :: ETHNICITY : ?
(a) ICINHTEYT (b) CINHTEYTI
(c) YTICINHTE (d) TICINHTEY

43. If $p - 2q = 4$, then the value of $p^3 - 8q^3 - 24pq - 64$ is :
(a) –1 (b) 2
(c) 0 (d) 3

44. If $\sin\theta + \cos\theta = \sqrt{2}\cos(90 - \theta)$, then $\cot\theta$ is
(a) $\sqrt{2}+1$ (b) 0
(c) $\sqrt{2}$ (d) $\sqrt{2}-1$

45. If x, y are positive acute angles, $x + y < 90°$ and $\sin(2x - 20°) = \cos(2y + 20°)$, then the value of $\sec(x + y)$ is
(a) $\sqrt{2}$ (b) $\frac{1}{\sqrt{2}}$
(c) 1 (d) 0

46. If $\sin^2\alpha = \cos^3\alpha$, then the value of $(\cot^6\alpha - \cot^2\alpha)$ is
(a) 1 (b) 0
(c) – 1 (d) 2

47. From the top of a light-house at a height 20 metres above sea-level, the angle of depression of a ship is 30°. The distance of the ship from the foot of the light-house is
(a) 20 m (b) $20\sqrt{3}$ m
(c) 30m (d) $30\sqrt{3}$ m

DIRECTIONS: (Qs. 48-50) : *The following table shows the productions of food-grains (in million tons) in a state for the period 1999 - 2000 to 2003 - 2004. Read the table and answer the questions.*

	Production (in million tons)			
Year	Wheat	Rice	Barley	Other cereals
1999-2000	680	270	250	450
2000-2001	800	420	440	300
2001-2002	680	350	320	460
2002-2003	720	400	380	500
2003-2004	820	560	410	690

48. In 2002 - 2003, the percentage increase in the production of barley as compared to the previous year was:
(a) 14.20 (b) 17.85
(c) 18.75 (d) 7.90

49. During the period 1999 - 2000 to 2003 - 2004, *x* per cent of the total production is production of wheat. The value of x is about:
(a) 12.6 (b) 37.4
(c) 37.8 (d) 20.2

50. In the year 2003 - 2004, the increase in production was maximum over the previous year for:
(a) Rice (b) Barley
(c) Other cereals (d) Wheat

ENGLISH LANGUAGE

DIRECTIONS (Qs. 51-55): *In the following passage, some of the words have been left out. First read the passage over and try to understand what it is about. Then fill in the blanks with the help of the alternatives given. Mark your answer.*

Human nature has an extraordinary power of **(51)** social and political institutions are Subject to the same laws of **(52)** to which all other things in the world are subject. If we have faith in the **(53)** of human nature, the healing power of time, the mutability of social and political institutions and above all the **(54)** of the people, the problems which divide us so fiercely today may appear to be purely **(55)** after some time.

51. (a) Resistance (b) Resilience (c) Patience (d) Toleration

52. (a) Gravitation (b) Mutation (c) Acceleration (d) Change

53. (a) Resilience (b) Patience (c) Perseverance (d) Toleration

54. (a) Generosity (b) Magnanimity (c) Goodwill (d) Sincerity

55. (a) Academic (b) Intellectual (c) Unproductive (d) Inane

DIRECTIONS (Qs. 56-57): *In the following questions, out of the four alternatives, choose the one which best expresses the meaning of the given word as your answer.*

56. Gaol
(a) Destination (b) Garden
(c) Jail (d) Bird

57. Pragmatic
(a) Intelligent (b) Wise
(c) Religious (d) Practical

DIRECTIONS (Qs. 58-59) : *Choose the word opposite in meaning to the given word.*

58. Gregarious
(a) Sociable (b) Societal
(c) Unsociable (d) Solitary

59. Pragmatic
(a) Indefinite (b) Vague
(c) Optimistic (d) Idealistic

DIRECTIONS (Qs. 60-62) : *Sentences are given with blanks to be filled in with an appropriate word(s). Four alternatives are suggested for each question. Choose the correct alternative out of the four.*

60. Raj was tired of Puja's ________ approach, so he asked her to make her final decision by that evening.
(a) silly-willy (b) dilly-dally
(c) wasting (d) dilly-nally

61. Ria is ________ at speaking languages. It is difficult to ________ only one puppy for animal shelter.
(a) adept, adapt (b) adapt, adapt
(c) adept, adopt (d) adapt, adopt

62. School days are considered to be the best years of your life. When my ________ year in school began. I began, to think of those past enjoyable days and of my future also.
(a) penultimate (b) absolute
(c) integral (d) termination

DIRECTIONS (Qs. 63-65) : *In Question, some parts of the sentences have errors and some are correct. Find out which part of a sentence has an error. If a sentence is free from errors mark in the answer sheet.*

63. Shakespeare has written (a) / many plays (b) / as well as some poetries (c) / No error (d)

64. Neither of the girls (a) / were willing to (b) / accept the proposal. (c) / No error (d)

DIRECTION (Q. 65): *Rearrange the parts of the sentence in correct order.*

65. (P) to get home early as I had promised
(Q) when I reached my office I phoned my mother
(R) that I wouldn't be able
(S) to tell her
(a) PQRS (b) RPQS
(c) QSRP (d) SQPR

DIRECTIONS (Qs. 66-67): *In Questions, a sentence/ a part of the sentence is underlined. Below are given alternatives to the underlined part which may improve the sentence. Choose the correct alternative. In case no improvement is needed choose "No Improvement". Mark your answer in the answer sheet.*

66. The others shook their heads and made vague noises of approval.

(a) nodded (b) No improvement
(c) turned around (d) hung

67. I took my mother some grapes when she was in hospital.
(a) I took some grapes for my mother
(b) No improvement
(c) I took for my mother some grapes
(d) I brought my mother some grapes

DIRECTION (Q. 68): *In a question, a sentence has been given in Direct/Indirect form. Out of the four alternatives suggested, select the one which best expresses the same sentence in Indirect/Direct form.*

68. He said, "it used to be a lovely, quiet street."
(a) He said that it used to be a lovely, quiet street.
(b) He pointed out that it had used to be a lovely, quiet street.
(c) He said that there used to be a lovely, quiet street.
(d) He inquired whether there was a lovely, quiet street.

DIRECTION (Q.69): *In a question, a sentence has been given in Active / Passive voice. Out of the four alternatives suggested, select the one which best expresses the same sentence in Passive/ Active voice.*

69. They have made him a king.
(a) A king has been made by them.
(b) He was made a king by them.
(c) They have been made kings by him.
(d) He has been made a king by them.

DIRECTIONS (Qs. 70-71): *In the following questions, out of the four alternatives, choose the one which can be substituted for the given words/ sentences.*

70. A story in which animals or objects speak and give wholesome moral lesson.
(a) Fable (b) Parable
(c) Allegory (d) Legend

71. Medical Study of skin and its diseases.
(a) Dermatology (b) Endocrinology
(c) Gynaecology (d) Orthopaedics

DIRECTION (Q. 72): *Four words are given in each question, out of which only one word is correctly spelt. Find the correctly spelt word and mark your answer in the Answer Sheet.*

72. (a) maintennance (b) manteinance
(c) maintenance (d) mentenance

DIRECTIONS (Qs. 73-75): *Four alternatives are given for the Idiom/Phrase underlined in the sentense. Choose the alternative which best expresses the meaning of the Idiom\Phrase and mark it in the Answer Sheet.*

73. With great difficulty, he was able to carve out a niche for himself.
(a) became a sculptor
(b) did the best he could do
(c) destroyed his career
(d) developed a specific position for himself

74. Where discipline is concerned I put my foot down.
(a) take a firm stand (b) take a light stand
(c) take a heavy stand (d) take a shaky stand

75. The convict claimed innocence and stood his ground in spite of the repeated accusations.
(a) knelt (b) surrendered
(c) kept standing (d) refused to yield

GENERAL AWARENESS

76. Who among the following British persons admitted the Revolt of 1857 as a national revolt?
(a) Lord Dalhousie (b) Lord Canning
(c) Lord Ellenborough (d) Disraeli

77. Where did Buddha deliver his first sermon?
(a) Sarnath (b) Rajagriha
(c) Kapilavastu . (d) Bodh-Gaya

78. Which one of the following is the guardian of Fundamental Rights?
(a) Legislature (b) Executive
(c) Political parties (d) Judiciary

79. In which of the following systems of government is bi–cameralism an essential feature?
(a) Federal system
(b) Unitary system
(c) parliamentary system
(d) Presidential system

80. A Retired Judge of a High Court is not permitted to practice as a lawyer in
(a) Supreme Court
(b) Any Court in India
(c) High Courts
(d) Except the High Court where he retired

81. India and U.S. have decided to finalise agreements related to which of the following?
(a) Trade and Investment
(b) Intellectual Property
(c) Traditional Knowledge
(d) All of the above

82. Low cost housing is an example for:
(a) Mixed wants (b) Social wants
(c) Private wants (d) Merit wants

83. The national income of a nation is the
(a) Government's annual revenue
(b) Sum total of factor incomes
(c) Surplus of public sector enterprises
(d) Exports minus imports

84. Who is the founder of "Facebook" which is currently the No. 1 social networking website in India?
(a) Orkut Buyukkokten
(b) Mark Zuckerberg
(c) Bill Gates
(d) Martin Cooper

85. If all bullets could not be removed from gun shot injury of a man, it may cause poisoning by
(a) Mercury (b) Lead
(c) Iron (d) Arsenic

86. Which colour/colours of light has the highest velocity through vacuum?
(a) Blue (b) Red
(c) Green (d) All of these

87. Iodoform is used as an:
(a) antipyretic (b) analgesic
(c) antiseptic (d) anaesthetic

88. What happens to the kinetic energy of gas molecules with rise of temperature?
(a) Remains same (b) Fluctuates
(c) Increases (d) Decreases

89. The percentage of nitrogen present in ammonium sulphate is :
(a) 18% (b) 21%
(c) 25% (d) 30.5%

90. An artificial ecosystem is represented by:
(a) pisciculture tank (b) agricultural land
(c) zoo (d) aquarium

91. Which of the following is meant for the ex-situ conservation of various species?
(a) Sperm bank (b) Blood bank
(c) Germplasm bank (d) Herbarium

92. Heart is devoid of
(a) Cardiac muscle (b) Involuntary muscle
(c) Voluntary muscle (d) Smooth muscle

93. Genomic (DNA) studies in camel have been completed recently by the scientists of
(a) South Africa (b) India
(c) China (d) Pakistan

94. The age of the Earth can be determined by
(a) Geological Time Scale
(b) Radio-Metric Dating
(c) Gravity method
(d) Fossilization method

95. A series of lines connecting places having a quake at the same time are called
(a) Homoseismal lines (b) Seismolines
(c) Coseismal lines (d) Isoseismal lines

96. The leading sesame producing country in the world is
(a) Mexico (b) U.S.A.
(c) China (d) India

97. The programme of 'Operation Flood' was concentrated on
(a) increasing irrigation facilities.
(b) flood control.
(c) increasing the milk production.
(d) increase the flood grains production.

98. The Headquarters of International Atomic Energy Agency is in
(a) Geneva (b) Paris
(c) Vienna (d) Washington

99. Asian Athletics Championships 2019 held at Doha in Qatar. It was the ________ edition of the Championships.
(a) 23rd (b) 26th
(c) 20th (d) 17th

100. Which country secured 1st position in Startup Ecosystem Ranking 2019 released by Startup Blink?
(a) United States (b) Canada
(c) United Kingdom (d) France

Hints & Explanations

1. (d) $J \xrightarrow{-1} I \xrightarrow{-1} H \xrightarrow{+3} K$

$P \xrightarrow{-1} O \xrightarrow{-1} N \xrightarrow{+3} Q$

$W \xrightarrow{-1} V \xrightarrow{-1} U \xrightarrow{+3} X$

$M \xrightarrow{-1} L \xrightarrow{-1} K \xrightarrow{+3} N$

2. (a) The movement of eagle is like swooping. Similarly, the movement of duck is called waddle.

3. (d) Given Set : 12, 72, 216 ($\times 6$, $\times 3$)

Similarly, 5, 30, 90 ($\times 6$, $\times 3$)

$\therefore$ Option (d) satisfy the condition.

4. (a) Jammu and Kashmir, Haryana and Himachal Pradesh are northern States of India. Arunachal Pradesh is estern-most States of India.

5. (d) Except the number 729, all others are perfect squares.

6. (c) The first and last are vowels.

7. (b) Perk > Pick > Pile > Pith > Pour

8. (d)

9. (b) $6 \times 3 = (18)$

$18 \times 6 = 108$

$108 \times 18 = 1944$

Hence, 18 is the missing number in the sequence.

10. (d)

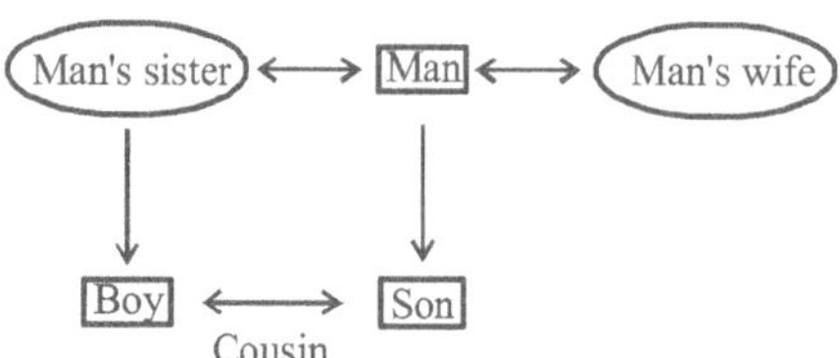

11. (a)

Left — M R P L O — Right

Hence, P coach is in the middle of the five coaches.

12. (b)

13. (c) As,

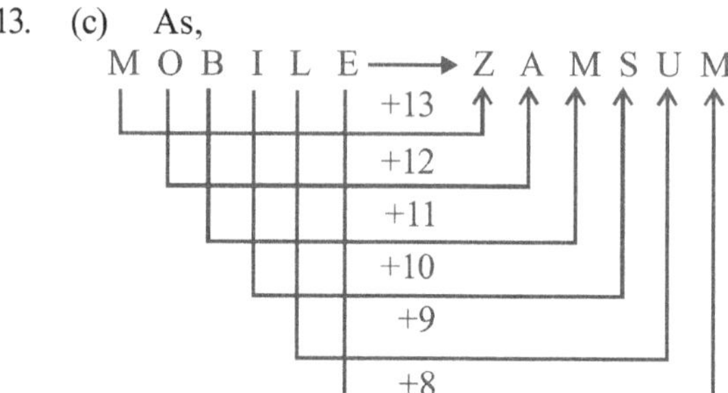

Similarly,

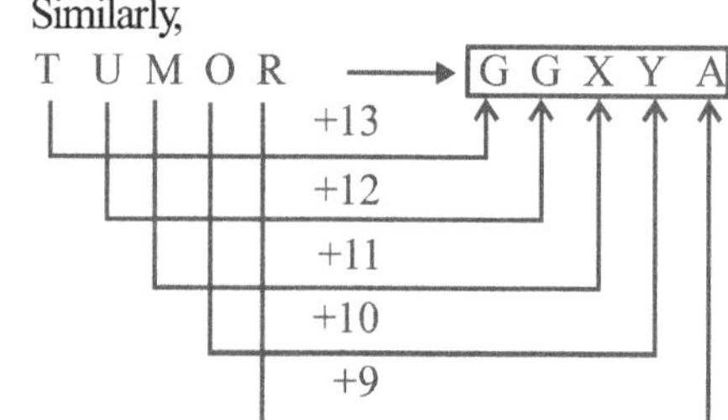

14. (c) Option (c)

$20 < 2 + 10 \div 4 - 6 \times 100$

$\Rightarrow 20 \div 2 \times 10 - 4 + 6 > 100$

$\Rightarrow 10 \times 10 - 4 + 6 > 100$

$\Rightarrow 100 - 4 + 6 > 100$

$\Rightarrow 106 - 4 > 100$

$\Rightarrow 102 > 100$

15. (d) $235 \Rightarrow (2)^2 + (3)^2 + (5)^2 = 38$

$452 \Rightarrow (4)^2 + (5)^2 + (2)^2 = 45$

$345 \Rightarrow (3)^2 + (4)^2 + (5)^2 = \boxed{50}$

16. (b) $7 + 2^2 + 5 = 16$

$9 + 4^2 + 7 = 32$

$8 + 3^2 + 6 = (23)$

17. (d)

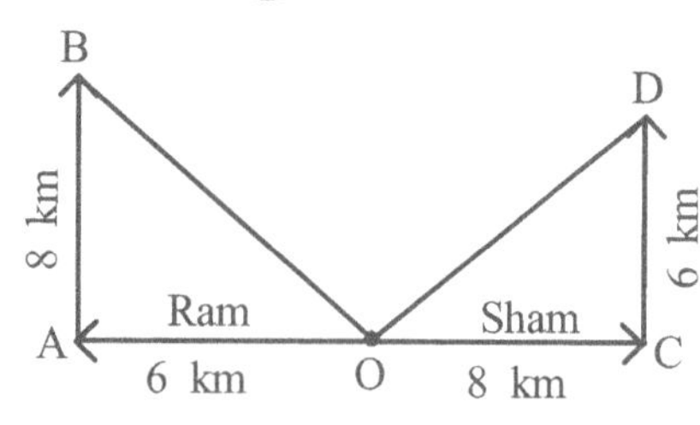

$OB = \sqrt{(AB)^2 + (AO)^2} = \sqrt{(8)^2 + (6)^2}$

$= \sqrt{64 + 36} = \sqrt{100} = 10km$

18. (d) Any written piece is recognised as song when it is sung by a singer. Therefore, only Conclusion 1 follows.

19. (d) Simple triangles are EFH, BIC, GHJ, GIJ, EKD and CKD i.e. 6 in number.

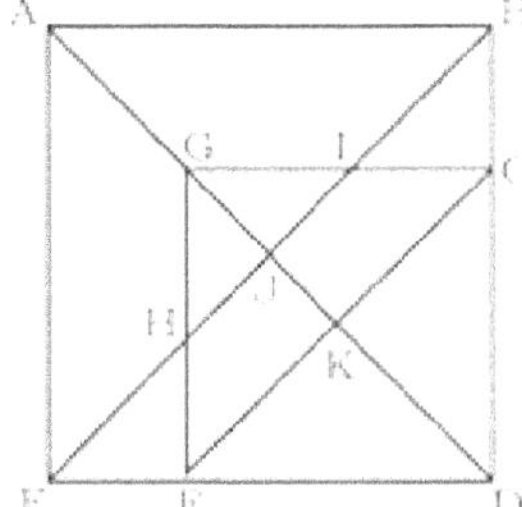

Triangles composed of two components are ABJ, AFJ, GCK, GEK, CED arid GHI i.e. 6 in number.
Triangles composed of three components are GCD, GED, DJB and DJF i.e. 4 in number.
Triangles composed of four components are ABF and GCE i.e. 2 in number.
Triangles composed of five components are ABD and AFD i.e. 2 in number.
There is only one triangle i.e. FBD composed of six components.
Therefore, Total number of triangles in the figure $= 6+6+4+2+2+1 = 21$.

20. (b) The number '3' is common to all the three circles.1

21. (b)

22. (b) 23. (d) 24. (b)

25. (d) If we read Matrix I & II carefully, alphabets in the word BRIDE can be found in this pattern.

B R I D E
55 21 57 86 22

26. (c) $3^1 = 3; 3^2 = 9; 3^3 = 27; 3^4 = 81; 3^4 = 243$
i.e. unit's digit is repeated after index 4.
Remainder after dividing 21 by 4 = 1
$\therefore$ Unit's digit in the expansion of $(3)^{21} = 3$
$\therefore$ Remainder after dividing by 5 = 3

27. (b) Expression

$$= \frac{3\sqrt{2}}{\sqrt{3}+\sqrt{6}} - \frac{4\sqrt{3}}{\sqrt{6}+\sqrt{2}} + \frac{\sqrt{6}}{\sqrt{3}+\sqrt{2}}$$

$$= \frac{3\sqrt{2}(\sqrt{6}-\sqrt{3})}{(\sqrt{6}+\sqrt{3})(\sqrt{6}-\sqrt{3})} - \frac{4\sqrt{3}(\sqrt{6}-\sqrt{2})}{(\sqrt{6}+\sqrt{2})(\sqrt{6}-\sqrt{2})} + \frac{\sqrt{6}}{(\sqrt{3}+\sqrt{2})} \times \frac{\sqrt{3}-\sqrt{2}}{\sqrt{3}-\sqrt{2}}$$

$$= \frac{3\sqrt{2}(\sqrt{6}-\sqrt{3})}{6-3} - \frac{4\sqrt{3}(\sqrt{6}-\sqrt{2})}{(6-2)} + \frac{\sqrt{6}(\sqrt{3}-\sqrt{2})}{3-2}$$

$$= \sqrt{2}(\sqrt{6}-\sqrt{3}) - \sqrt{3}(\sqrt{6}-\sqrt{2}) + \sqrt{6}(\sqrt{3}-\sqrt{2})$$

$$= \sqrt{12} - \sqrt{6} - \sqrt{18} + \sqrt{6} + \sqrt{18} - \sqrt{12} = 0$$

28. (b) Let the numbers be $n-2, n-1, n, n+1$ and $n+2$. Their average $= n$.

Next two consecutive numbers are $n + 3$ and $n + 4$.

Therefore the average of 7 consecutive numbers

$$= \frac{(n-2)+(n-1)+n+(n+1)+(n+2)+(n+3)+(n+4)}{7}$$

$$= \frac{5n+2n+7}{7} = n+1$$

29. (a) Let the marked price of the article be ₹ x.

$$\therefore x \times \frac{90}{100} = \frac{450 \times 120}{100}$$

$$\Rightarrow \frac{9x}{10} - 540$$

$$\Rightarrow x = \frac{540 \times 10}{9} = ₹600$$

30. (c) Required percentage $= \frac{24}{40} \times 100 = 60\%$

31. (b) When P = P, R = 5%, T = 8yr then SI = 840

$$\frac{PRT}{100} = 840$$

$$\frac{P \times 5 \times 8}{100} = 840$$

P = 2100

Case II: When P = 2100, R = ?, T = 5 SI = 840

$$P\% \ \frac{2100 \times 5 \times R}{100} = 840$$

R = 8%

32. (d) Let the length of train be x km and its speed by kmph.

$$\therefore \frac{x}{y-2}=\frac{9}{3600}=\frac{1}{400} \quad ...(i)$$

$$\frac{x}{y-4}=\frac{10}{3600}=\frac{1}{360} \quad ...(ii)$$

By dividing equation (i) by (ii),

$$\frac{y-4}{y-2}=\frac{360}{400}=\frac{9}{10}$$

$\Rightarrow 10y-40=9y-18$

$\Rightarrow y=40-18=22$

From equation (i),

$$\frac{x}{22-2}=\frac{1}{400}$$

$$\Rightarrow x=\frac{1}{20}\text{km}=\frac{1000}{20}=50 \text{ metre}$$

33. (b) If a completes the work in x days, B will do the same in 3x days.

$\therefore 3x-x=60$

$\Rightarrow 2x=60$

$\Rightarrow x=30$ and $3x=90$

$\therefore$ (A+B)'s day's work

$$=\frac{1}{30}+\frac{1}{90}=\frac{3+1}{90}=\frac{4}{90}=\frac{2}{45}$$

$\therefore$ A and B together will do the work in

$$\frac{45}{2}=22\frac{1}{2} \text{ days.}$$

34. (c) $\frac{x}{y}=\frac{4}{5}$

$$\therefore \frac{3x+y}{5x+3y}=\frac{3\left(\frac{x}{y}\right)+1}{5\left(\frac{x}{y}\right)+3}$$

$$=\frac{3\times\frac{4}{5}+1}{5\times\frac{4}{5}+3}=\frac{\frac{12+5}{5}}{7}=\frac{17}{35}$$

35. (b) $A:B=2:3=8:12$

$B:C=4:5=12:15$

$\therefore A:B:C=8:12:15$

Sum of ratio = 35

$$\therefore \text{A's share}=\frac{8}{35}\times 700=₹\,160$$

$$\text{B's share}=\frac{12}{35}\times 700=₹\,240$$

$$\text{C's share}=\frac{15}{35}\times 700=₹\,300$$

36. (a)

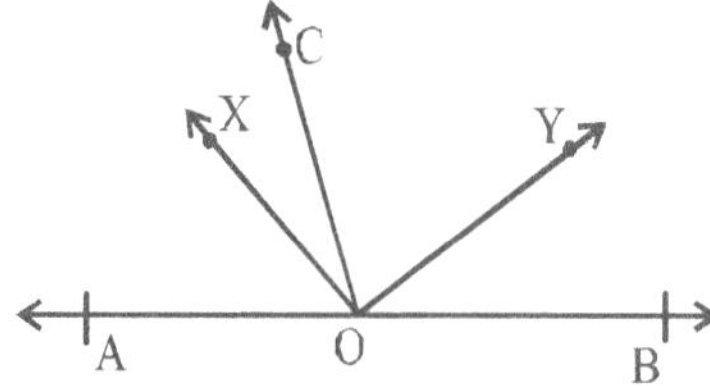

OX is the bisector of $\angle AOC$.

$\therefore \angle AOC=2\angle COX$

OY is the bisector of $\angle BOC$.

$\therefore \angle BOC=2\angle COY$

$\therefore \angle AOC+\angle BOC$

$=2\angle COY+2\angle COX=180°$

$\Rightarrow 2(\angle COX+\angle YOC)=180°$

$\Rightarrow \angle XOY=90°$

$\therefore \angle AOX+\angle XOY+\angle BOY=180°$

$\therefore \angle BOY=180°-90°-20°=70°$

37. (a)

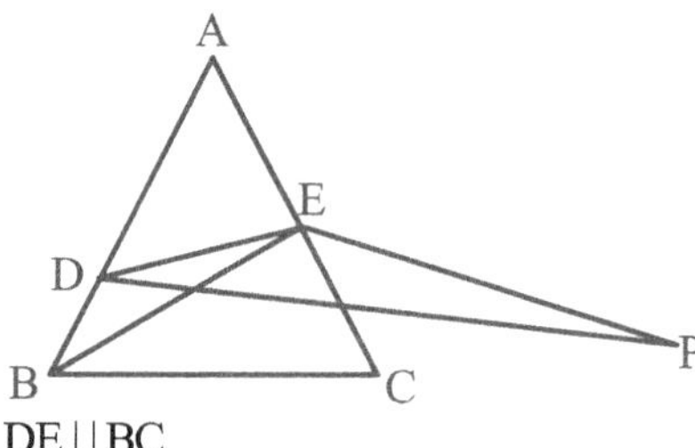

DE || BC

$$DE=\frac{1}{2}BC$$

$\therefore \Delta BDE=\Delta DEP$

$2\Delta BDE=\Delta BEC$

$\therefore \Delta ADE=\Delta BDE$

$\therefore \Delta ABC=4\Delta ADE$

$$\therefore PED=\frac{1}{4}\Delta ABC$$

38. (a) $\angle BPC=90°-\frac{A}{2}$

$=90°-40°=50°$

39. (c) Smallest side of the triangle = x cm (let)

$\therefore$ Second side of triangle

$=40-17-x=23-x$

$$\text{Semi-perimeter,} = s=\frac{40}{2}=20$$

$$\therefore \sqrt{s(s-a)(s-b)(s-c)}=60$$

$\Rightarrow \sqrt{20(20-17)(20-x)(20-23+x)} = 60$

$\Rightarrow (20-x)(x-3) = 60$

$\Rightarrow 20x - 60 - x^2 + 3x = 60$

$\Rightarrow x^2 - 23x + 120 = 0$

$\Rightarrow x^2 - 15x - 8x + 120 = 0$

$\Rightarrow x(x-15) - 8(x-15) = 0$

$\Rightarrow (x-8)(x-15) = 0$

$\Rightarrow x = 8 \text{ or } 15$

40. (a) $x - 1 = \sqrt{2} + \sqrt{3}$

On squaring,

$x^2 - 2x + 1 = 2 + 3 + 2\sqrt{6}$

$\Rightarrow x^2 - 2x - 4 = 2\sqrt{6}$

On squaring again,

$x^4 + 4x^2 + 16 - 4x^3 - 8x^2 + 16x = 24$

$\Rightarrow x^4 - 4x^3 - 4x^2 + 16x - 8 = 0$

$\Rightarrow 2x^4 - 8x^3 - 8x^2 + 32x - 16 = 0$

$\Rightarrow 2x^4 - 8x^3 - 5x^2 + 26x - 28 - 3x^2 + 6x + 12 = 0$

$\Rightarrow 2x^4 - 8x^3 - 5x^2 + 26x - 28$

$= 3x^2 - 6x - 12$

$= 3(x^2 - 2x - 4)$

$= 3 \times 2\sqrt{6} = 6\sqrt{6}$

41. (b) $x = 3 + 2\sqrt{2}$

$$\frac{1}{x} = \frac{1}{3+2\sqrt{2}} \times \frac{3-2\sqrt{2}}{3-2\sqrt{2}}$$

$$\frac{1}{x} = \frac{3-2\sqrt{2}}{9-8} = 3 - 2\sqrt{2}$$

$$\left(\sqrt{x} - \frac{1}{\sqrt{x}}\right)^2 = x + \frac{1}{x} - 2$$

$$\left(\sqrt{x} - \frac{1}{\sqrt{x}}\right)^2 = 3 + 2\sqrt{2} + 3 - 2\sqrt{2} - 2 = 4$$

$$\left(\sqrt{x} - \frac{1}{\sqrt{x}}\right) = \sqrt{4} = \pm 2$$

42. (c) Word has been written in reverse order.

	1	2	3	4	5	6	7
	H	O	P	E	F	U	L
coded as–	L	U	F	E	P	O	H
	7	6	5	4	3	2	1

Similarly,

1	2	3	4	5	6	7	8	9
E	T	H	N	I	C	I	T	Y
Y	T	I	C	I	N	H	T	E
9	8	7	6	5	4	3	2	1

43. (c) $p - 21 = 4$

cubing both sides,

$(p - 2q)^3 = 64$

$\Rightarrow p^3 - 8q^3 + 3p.\ 4q^2 - 3p^2.\ 2q = 64$

$\Rightarrow p^3 - 8q^3 + 12pq^2 - 6p^2q = 64$

$\Rightarrow p^3 - 8q^3 - 6pq(p - 2q) = 64$

$\Rightarrow p^3 - 8q^3 - 6pq \times 4 = 64$

$\Rightarrow p^3 - 8q^3 - 24pq - 64 = 0$

44. (d) $\sin\theta + \cos\theta = \sqrt{2}\cos(90 - \theta)$

$\sin\theta + \cos\theta = \sqrt{2}\sin\theta$

Divide eq. by $\sin\theta$

$1 + \cot\theta = \sqrt{2}$

$\cot\theta = \sqrt{2} - 1$

45. (a) $\sin(2x - 20°) = \cos(2y + 20°)$

$\Rightarrow \sin(2x - 20°)$

$= \sin(90° - 2y - 20°)$

$= \sin(70° - 2y)$

$\Rightarrow 2x - 20° = 70° - 2y$

$\Rightarrow 2(x + y) = 90°$

$\Rightarrow x + y = 45°$

$\therefore \sec(x + y) = \sec 45° = \sqrt{2}$

46. (a) If $\sin^2\alpha = \cos^3\alpha$

$\tan^2\alpha = \cos\alpha$ ...(1)

Now consider, $\cot^6\alpha - \cot^2\alpha$

$= \frac{1}{\tan^6\alpha} - \frac{1}{\tan^2\alpha}$ Since $\cot\alpha = \frac{1}{\tan\alpha}$

Substituting for $\tan^2\alpha$ with $\cos\alpha$ from (1) above equation will be

$$= \frac{1}{\cos^3\alpha} - \frac{1}{\cos\alpha} = \frac{1-\cos^2\alpha}{\cos^3\alpha} = \frac{\sin^2\alpha}{\cos^3\alpha} = \frac{\tan^2\alpha}{\cos\alpha} = 1$$

47. (b)

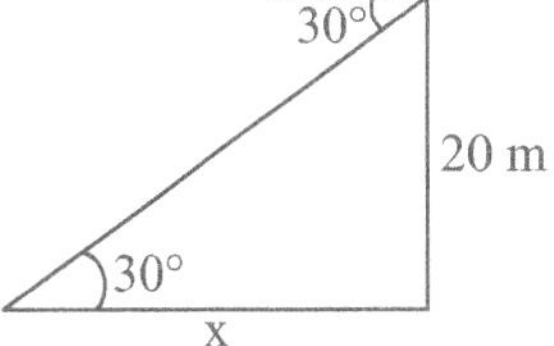

$\tan 30° = \frac{20}{x}$, $\frac{1}{\sqrt{3}} = \frac{20}{x}$

$x = 20\sqrt{3}$

48. (c) Percent increase $= \frac{380-320}{320} \times 100$

$= 18.75$

49. (b) Total production:

Wheat ⇒ 3700 million tonnes

Rice ⇒ 2000 million tonnes

Barley ⇒ 1800 million tonnes

Other cereals ⇒ 2400 million tonnes

50. (a) Percentage increase:

Rice $= \frac{160}{400} \times 100 = 40$

Cereals $= \frac{190}{500} \times 100 = 38$

51. (b) Resilience-the capacity to recover quickly from difficulties; toughness.
52. (b) Mutation- An alteration or change, as in nature, form, or quality.
53. (a) Resilience- is correct word.
54. (c) Goodwill- is correct word.
55. (a) Academic- is correct word.

56.	(c)	57.	(d)	58.	(c)	59.	(d)	60.	(b)
61.	(c)	62.	(a)	63.	(c)	64.	(b)	65.	(c)
66.	(a)	67.	(a)	68.	(a)	69.	(d)	70.	(a)
71.	(a)	72.	(c)	73.	(d)	74.	(a)	75.	(d)
76.	(d)	77.	(a)	78.	(d)	79.	(a)	80.	(d)
81.	(d)	82.	(d)	83.	(b)	84.	(b)	85.	(d)
86.	(d)	87.	(c)	88.	(c)	89.	(b)	90.	(d)
91.	(c)	92.	(c)	93.	(c)	94.	(b)	95.	(a)
96.	(d)	97.	(c)	98.	(c)	99.	(a)	100.	(a)

PRACTICE SET- 16

GENERAL INTELLIGENCE & REASONING

DIRECTIONS (Qs. 1-3): *Select the related letter/ word/ number from the given alternatives.*

1. BIMN : CKPR : : CURD : ?
(a) DWUH (b) WUHC
(c) UHDW (d) HUVN

2. 8 : 62 : : 9 : ?
(a) 64 (b) 79
(c) 18 (d) 81

3. Accommodation : Rent : : Journey : ?
(a) Fzreight (b) Octroi
(c) Fare (d) Expense

DIRECTIONS (Qs. 4-6): *In questions, find the odd number/letters/number pair from the given alternatives.*

4. (a) Fish (b) Frog
(c) Tortoise (d) Crab

5. (a) 1000 (b) 1725
(c) 2744 (d) 4096

6. (a) NLM (b) YXZ
(c) NMO (d) RQS

7. Arrange the following words as per order in the dictionary.
(i) Forge (ii) Forget
(iii) Forgo (iv) Forgive
(v) Format
(a) (v), (ii), (iv) , (iii), (i)
(b) (i), (iv), (iii), (ii), (v)
(c) (iii), (iv), (v), (ii), (i)
(d) (i), (ii), (iv), (iii), (v)

DIRECTIONS (Qs. 8-9) : *In each of the following questions, a series is given with one term missing. Choose the correct alternative from the given ones that will complete the series.*

8. KJL, ONP, SRT, ?
(a) WVX (b) VWX
(c) WXV (d) VUW

9. 95, 115, 145, 155, ?
(a) 215 (b) 175
(c) 185 (d) 165

10. Sunil is the son of Kesav. Simran, Kesav's sister, has a son Maruti and daughter Sita. Prem is the maternal uncle of Maruti. How is Sunil related to Maruti?
(a) Uncle (b) Brother
(c) Nephew (d) Cousin

11. Roshan is taller than Hardik who is shorter than Susheel. Niza is taller than Harry but shorter than Hardik. Susheel is shorter than Roshan. Who is the tallest ?
(a) Roshan (b) Susheel
(c) Hardik (d) Harry

DIRECTION (Q. 12): *In question, from the given alternatives select the word which cannot be formed using the letters of the given word.*

12. DISAPPOINTMENT
(a) POINTER (b) OINTMENT
(c) TENEMENT (d) POSITION

13. If DIVINE is coded as AFSFKB, then POWERFUL is coded as
(a) XLHOJVIM (b) MLTBOCRI
(c) MLWBOCRI (d) HLTBNCRI

14. If '–' stand for addition, '+' stands for subtraction, '÷' stands for multiplication and '×' stands for division, then which one of the following equations is correct?
(a) $25 \times 5 \div 20 - 27 + 7 = 120$
(b) $25 + 5 \times 20 - 27 \div 7 = 128$
(c) $25 + 5 - 20 + 27 \times 7 = 95$
(d) $25 - 5 + 20 \times 27 \div 7 = 100$

DIRECTION (Q. 15) : *In the following questions,. some equations are solved on the basis of a certain system. On the same basis, find out the correct answer for the unsolved equation.*

15. $2 \times 3 = 49, 5 \times 6 = 2536, 1 \times 9 = 181, 4 \times 7 = ?$
(a) 1628 (b) 1649
(c) 2549 (d) 1219

DIRECTION (Q. 16) : *In the following question, select the missing number from the given responses.*

16.

81	64	16
4	9	49
36	16	25
108	96	?

(a) 230 (b) 140
(c) 120 (d) 410

17. Sherly starting from a fixed point goes 15 m toward North and then after turning to his right he goes 15 m. Then he goes 10, 15 and 15 metres after turning to his left each time. How far is he from his starting point?
(a) 15 metres (d) 5 metres
(c) 10 metres (d) 20 metres

DIRECTION (Q. 18) : *In the following questions, one/two statements are given followed by two/ four conclusions I, II, III and IV. You have to consider the statements to be true even if they seem to be at variance from commonly known facts. You have to decide which of the given conclusions, if any follow from the given statements.*

18. Statements :
I. Some cats are dogs.
II. No dog is a toy.
Conclusions :
I. Some dogs are cats.
II. Some toys are cats.
III. Some cats are not toys.
IV. All toys are cats.
(a) Only Conclusions I and III follow
(b) Only Conclusions II and III follow
(c) Only Conclusions I and II follow
(d) Only Conclusion I follows

19. What is the number of triangles in the given figure?

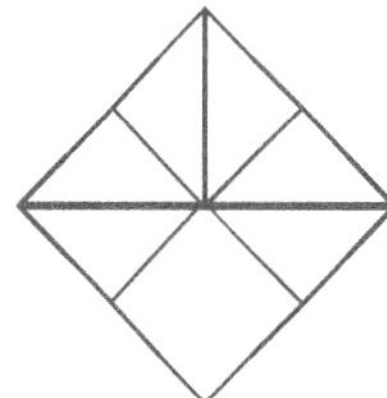

(a) 7 (b) 10
(c) 8 (d) More than 10

20. Identify the diagram that best represents the relationship among the classes given below : Liquids, Milk, River water

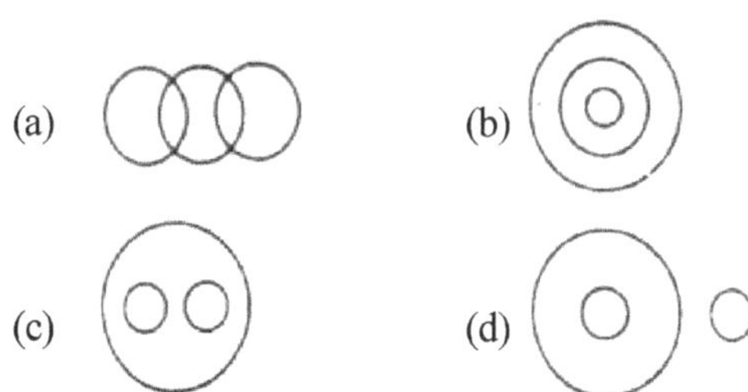

DIRECTION (Q. 21) : *In question, which answer figure will complete the pattern in the question figure?*

21. Question Figure:

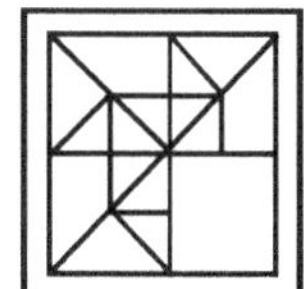

Answer Figures:

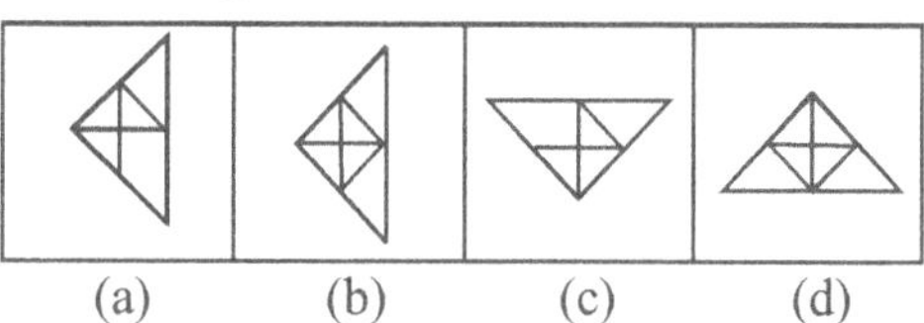

22. From the given answer figures, select the one in which the question figure is hidden/embedded.
Question Figure:

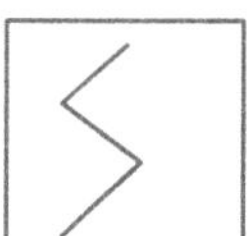

Answer Figures:

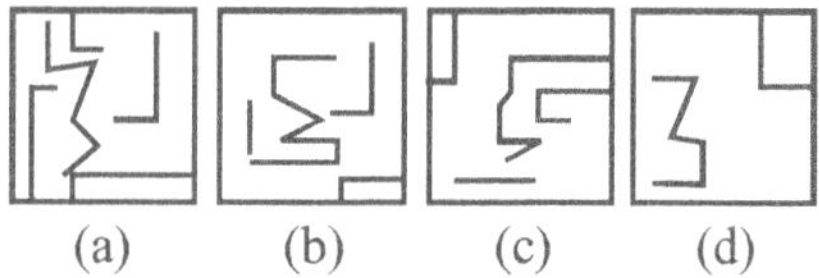

23. A square sheet of paper is folded and punched as shown below in question figures. Choose from amongst the following four answer figures, how will it appear when opened.
Question figure :

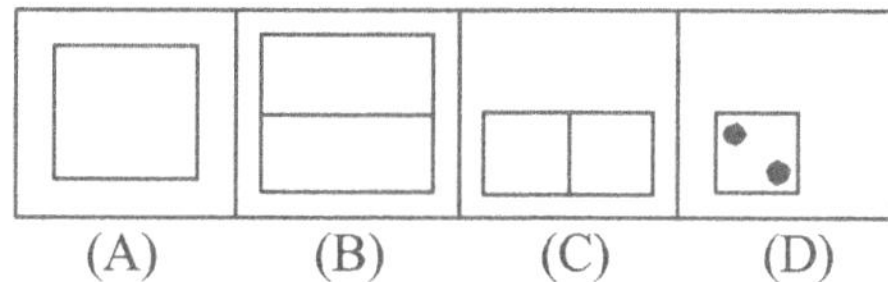

Answer figures :

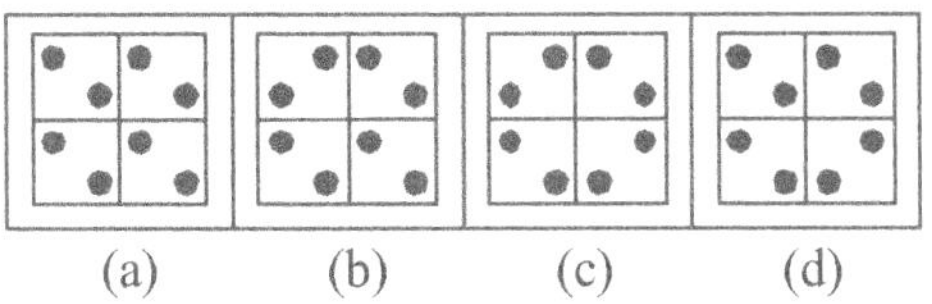

24. From the answer figures, find out the figure which is the exact mirror image of the question figure, when the mirror is placed on the line MN.

Question Figure :

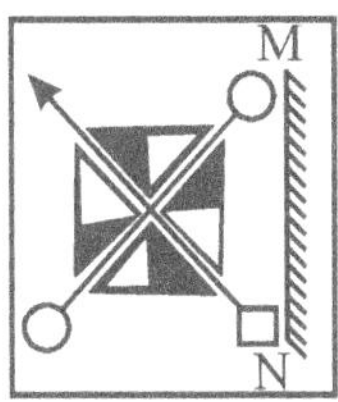

Answer Figures :

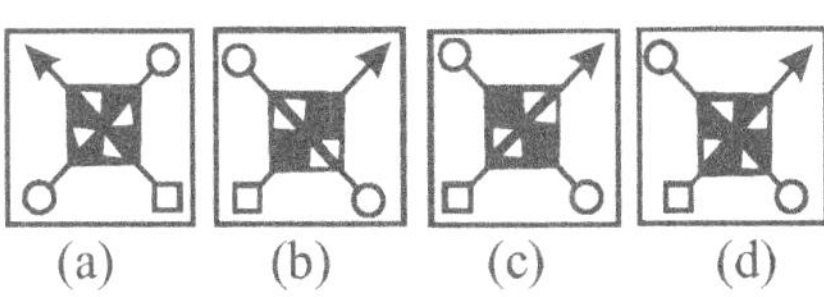

25. A word is represented by only one set of numbers as given in any one of the alternatives. The sets of numbers given in the alternatives are represented by two classes of alphabets as in two matrices given below. The columns and rows of Matrix-I are numbered from 0 to 4 and that of Matrix-II are numbered from 5 to 9. A letter from these matrices can be represented first by its row and next by its column, e.g, 'I' can be represented by 00, 14 etc , and 'N' can be represented by 59, 68 etc. Similarly, you have to identify the set for the word 'ROAD'.

Matrix I

	0	1	2	3	4
0	I	M	W	S	Q
1	M	W	S	Q	I
2	W	S	Q	I	M
3	S	Q	I	M	W
4	Q	I	M	W	S

Matrix II

	5	6	7	8	9
5	O	A	D	R	N
6	A	D	R	N	O
7	D	R	N	O	A
8	R	N	O	A	D
9	N	O	A	D	R

(a) 56, 67, 57, 96 (b) 67, 57, 96, 56
(c) 96, 67, 56, 57 (d) 67, 96, 56, 57

QUANTITATIVE APTITUDE

26. The last digit of $(1001)^{2008} + 1002$ is
(a) 0 (b) 3
(b) 4 (d) 6

27. $\sqrt{6+\sqrt{6+\sqrt{6+...}}} = ?$
(a) 2.3 (b) 3
(c) 6 (d) 6.3

28. A batsman in his 12th innings makes a score of 63 runs and there by increases his average scores by 2. What is his average after the 12th innings?
(a) 13 (b) 41
(c) 49 (d) 87

29. What single discount is equivalent to two successive discounts of 20% and 15%?
(a) 35% (b) 32%
(c) 34% (d) 30%

30. X sells two articles for ₹ 4,000 each with no loss and no gain in the interaction. If one was sold at a gain of 25% the other is sold at a loss of
(a) 25% (b) $18\frac{2}{9}\%$
(c) $16\frac{2}{3}\%$ (d) 20%

31. What would be the compound interest of ₹ 25000 for 2 yrs. at 5% per annum
(a) 2500 (b) 2562.5
(c) 2425.25 (d) 5512.5

32. With average speed of 40 km/hour, a train reaches its' destination in time. If it goes with an average speed of 35 km/hour, it is late by 15 minutes. The total journey is
(a) 30km (b) 40km
(c) 70km (d) 80km

33. Pipe A alone can fill a tank in 8 hours. Pipe B alone can fill it in 6 hours. If both the pipes are opened and after 2 hours pipe A is closed, then the other pipe will fill the tank in
(a) 6 hours (b) $3\frac{1}{2}$ hours
(c) 4 hours (d) $2\frac{1}{2}$ hours

34. The ratio of the quantities of an acid and water in a mixture is 1 : 3. If 5 litres of acid is further added to the mixture, the new ratio becomes 1 : 2. The quantity of new mixture in litres is

(a) 32 (b) 40
(c) 42 (d) 45

35. The ratio of monthly incomes of A, B is 6 : 5 and their monthly expenditures are in the ratio 4 : 3. If each of them saves ₹ 400 per month, find the sum of their monthly incomes.

(a) 2300 (b) 2400
(c) 2200 (d) 2500

36. In the following figure, O is the centre of the circle and XO is perpendicular to OY. If the area of the triangle XOy is 32, then the area of the circle is.

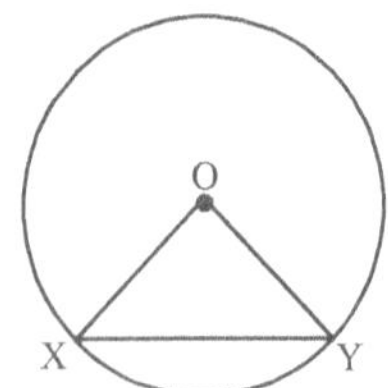

(a) 64π (b) 256π
(c) 16π (d) 32π

37. The length of the common chord of two circles of radii 15 cm and 20 cm whose centres are 25 cm apart is (in cm):

(a) 20 (b) 24
(c) 25 (d) 15

38. When a pendulum of length 50 cm oscillates, it produces an arc of 16 cm. The angle so formed in degree measure is (approx).

(a) 18°25′ (b) 18°35′
(c) 18°20′ (d) 18°08′

39. A copper wire is bent in the form of square with an area of 121 cm^2. It the same wire is bent in the form of a circle, the radius (in cum) of the circle is (Take $\pi = \frac{22}{7}$)

(a) 7 (b) 10
(c) 11 (d) 14

40. If the distance between two points (0,–5) and (x,0) is 13 unit, then x =

(a) 10 (b) ±10
(c) 12 (d) ±12

41. If $a+b+c=0$, the value of $\left(\frac{a^2}{bc}+\frac{b^2}{ca}+\frac{c^2}{ab}\right)$ is

(a) 2 (b) 3
(c) 4 (d) 5

42. If $a^2+b^2+c^2=2(a-b-c)-3$, then the value of $2a-3b+4c$ is

(a) 1 (b) 7
(c) 2 (d) 3

43. If $\frac{x}{x^2-2x+1}=\frac{1}{3}$, then the value of $x^3+\frac{1}{x^3}$ is:

(a) 27 (b) 81
(c) 110 (d) 125

44. If $x\sin^3\theta + y\cos^3\theta = \sin\theta\cos\theta$ and $x\sin\theta = y\cos\theta$, $\sin\theta \neq 0$, $\cos\theta \neq 0$, then x^2+y^2 is

(a) $\frac{1}{\sqrt{2}}$ (b) $\frac{1}{2}$
(c) 1 (d) $\sqrt{2}$

45. If $5\tan\theta = 4$, then the value of $\left(\frac{5\sin\theta-3\cos\theta}{5\sin\theta-3\cos\theta}\right)$ is

(a) $\frac{1}{7}$ (b) $\frac{2}{7}$
(c) $\frac{5}{7}$ (d) $\frac{2}{5}$

46. The simplified value of $(1+\tan\theta+\sec\theta)(1+\cot\theta-\text{cosec}\theta)$ is

(a) –2 (b) 2
(c) 1 (d) –1

47. A vertical pole and a vertical tower are standing on the same level ground. Height of the pole is 10 metres. Form the top of the pole is the angle of elevation of the top of the tower and angle of depression of the foot of the tower are 60° and 30° respectively. The height of the tower is

(a) 20m (b) 30m
(c) 40m (d) 50m

DIRECTIONS (Qs.48-50): *Production of three different flavours soft drinks X, Y and Z for a period of six years has been expressed in the following graph. Study the graph and answer the questions.*

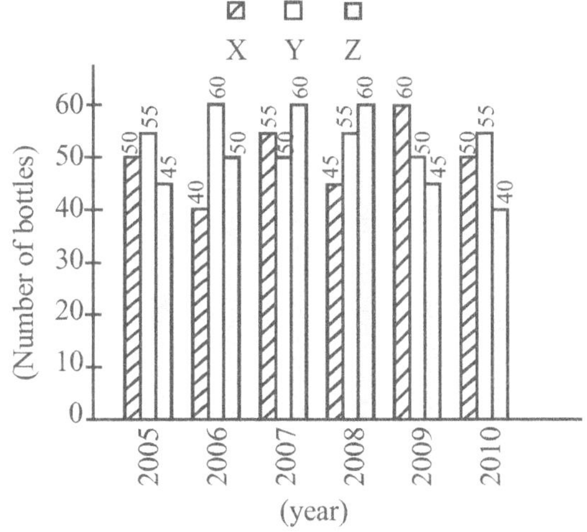

48. The approximate decline in the production of flavour Z in 2010 as compared to the production in 2008 is:
(a) 33% (b) 22.5%
(c) 42% (d) 25%

49. The average annual production was maximum in the given period for the flavour:
(a) Y only (b) Z only
(c) X and Z (d) X only

50. What percent of the total production of flavour X in 2005 and 2006 combined is the total production of flavour Z in 2007 and 2008 combined?
(a) 102.25 (b) 115.57
(c) 133.33 (d) 96.67

ENGLISH LANGUAGE

DIRECTIONS (Qs. 51-55): *In the following passages, some of the words have been left out. First read the passage over and try to understand what it is about. Then fill in the blanks with the help of the alternatives given. Mark your answer.*

Jawaharlal Nehru was probably the first important public leader to realise that if India were to **(51)** its problems, it would have to **(52)** the age of science. The Government of free India was one of the first in the world to set up a department of science and technology. The **(53)** the Government has attached to science is also clear **(54)** the fact that the portfolio of science and technology has always been **(55)** by the Prime Minister himself.

51. (a) Usher (b) Work
(c) Solve (d) Face

52. (a) Enter (b) Come
(c) Continue (d) Direct

53. (a) Depth (b) Weight
(c) Budget (d) Importance

54. (a) For (b) When
(c) Above (d) From

55. (a) Offered (b) Held
(c) Charged (d) Appointed

DIRECTIONS (Qs. 56-57): *In the following questions, out of the four alternatives, choose the one which best expresses the meaning of the given word as your answer.*

56. Notion
(a) Thought (b) Fact
(c) Truth (d) Hypothesis

57. Vivacious
(a) Poisonous (b) Energetic
(c) Tricky (d) Slow

DIRECTIONS (Qs. 58–59): *Choose the word opposite in meaning to the given word.*

58. Obtuse
(a) Sharp-witted (b) Transparent
(c) Timid (d) Blunt

59. Inadvertently
(a) Secretly (b) Accidentally
(c) Completely (d) Deliberately

DIRECTIONS (Qs. 60-62) : *In these questions sentences are given with blanks to be filled with an appropriate word(s). Four alternatives are suggested for each question. Choose the correct alternative out of the four.*

60. Many premier educational institutions come forward to have a _______ with flourshing industries.
(a) tie-down (b) tie-up
(c) tie-in (d) tie-on

61. They reached the railway station before the train _________ .

(a) had left (b) had been left
(c) left (d) was leaving

62. The Information and Communication Technology has _____ age and employes very highly paid technocrats.
(a) come of (b) come upon
(c) come out of (d) come through

DIRECTIONS (Qs. 63-64) : *In questions, some parts of the sentence have errors and some are correct. Find out which part of a sentence has an error. If a sentence is free from error, mark (d) in your Answer.*

63. The batsman completed (a) / his century (b) / on minimum number of balls. (c) / No error. (d)

64. The accident was fatal (a) / as the truck had a head-on collision (b) / against a van (c) / No error. (d)

DIRECTION (Q. 65): *Rearrange the parts of the sentence in correct order.*

65. (P) and did not know
(Q) at midnight he was nervous
(R) when he heard the hue and cry
(S) what to do
(a) PQRS (b) QSPR
(c) RQPS (d) SQPR

DIRECTIONS (Qs. 66-68) : *A sentence/a part of the sentence is underlined. Four alternatives are given to the underlined part which will improve the sentence. Choose the correct alternative. In case no improvement is needed, "No improvement" is the answer.*

66. They <u>have had a</u> real good time.
(a) have had a (b) have had really
(c) have had a really (d) No improvement

67. The sales boy told the <u>consumer</u> not to touch the products on display.
(a) buyer (b) shopper
(c) customer (d) No improvement

68. Please make it a point to send the letter <u>at</u> my address.
(a) on (b) to
(c) in (d) No improvement

DIRECTION (Q. 69): *In a question, a sentence has been given in Direct/Indirect form. Out of the four alternatives suggested, select the one which best expresses the same sentence in Indirect/Direct form.*

69. The new student asked the old one, "Do you know my name?"
(a) The new student asked the old one if he knew his name.
(b) The new student asked the old one that whether he knew his name.
(c) The new student asked the old one did he know his name
(d) The new student asked the old one if he knows his name

DIRECTON : (Qs. 70-71) : *Out of the four alternatives, choose the one which can be substituted for the given words/sentences.*

70. One who tends to patronize, rebuff or ignore people regarded as social inferiors and imitate, admire people regarded as social superiors
(a) Snob (b) Fob
(c) Dandy (d) Freak

71. A room where dead bodies are kept until burial
(a) Grave (b) Cemetery
(c) Mortuary (d) Pyre

DIRECTION (Q. 72) : *In the following question, four words are given. In each group, out of which only one word is correctly spelt. Find the correctly spelt word.*

72. (a) revolutionize (b) revoulutionize
(c) revvolutionize (d) revollutionize

DIRECTIONS (Qs. 73-74) : *In questions below, four alternatives are given for the Idiom/phrase underlined in the sentence. Choose the alternative which best expresses the meaning of the Idiom/ Phrase and mark it in the Answer Sheet.*

73. We must work with <u>all our might and main,</u> otherwise we cannot succeed.
(a) full force
(b) complete trust
(c) exceptional skill
(d) full unity

74. We had (had) better <u>batten down the hatches</u>. The weather is unpredictable.
   (a) stay in-door
   (b) prepare for a difficult situation
   (c) go somewhere safe
   (d) face the obstacles

DIRECTION (Q. 75): *In a question, a sentence has been given in Active / Passive voice. Out of the four alternatives suggested, select the one which best expresses the same sentence in Passive/ Active voice.*

75. Who taught you English?
   (a) By whom English was taught to you ?
   (b) By whom you were taught English ?
   (c) By whom was English taught to you ?
   (d) By whom are you taught English ?

GENERAL AWARENESS

76. Which of the following is called the 'shrimp capital of India'?
   (a) Mangalore (b) Nagapatnam
   (c) Kochi (d) Nellore
77. Name the Mughal Prince, who translated Bhagavat Gita into Persian ?
   (a) Dara Shukoh (b) Sulaiman Shukoh
   (c) Khusru (d) Murad
78. Sarkaria Commission was concerned with
   (a) Administrative Reforms
   (b) Electoral Reforms
   (c) Financial Reforms
   (d) Centre-State relations
79. Socialism succeeds in achieveing
   (a) higher standard of living of the people
   (b) equal distribution of income in the society
   (c) higher individual welfare in the society
   (d) maximum social welfare in the society
80. Which one of the following does not match?
   (a) Hindu Marriage Act : 1955
   (b) Medical Termination of Pregnancy Act : 1971
   (c) Domestic Violence on women Act : 1990
   (d) Cruelty against Women : 1995
81. The exchange of commodities between two countries is referred as
   (a) Balance of trade (b) Bilateral trade
   (c) Volume of trade (d) Multilateral trade
82. Consumption for the sake of enjoying social acknowledgement is called:
   (a) Rational consumption
   (b) Social consumption
   (c) Conspicuous consumption
   (d) Demonstration consumption
83. Externality theory is the basic theory of the following branch of Economics :
   (a) Macro Economics
   (b) Environomics
   (c) Fiscal Economics
   (d) International Economics
84. Identify the FIFO (First In First Out) structure among the following :
   (a) Stack (b) Queue
   (c) De-queue (d) Array
85. The time period of a pendulum when taken to the Moon would:
   (a) remain the same (b) decrease
   (c) become zero (d) increase
86. The ultimate source of energy in a hydroelectric power station is:
   (a) solar energy
   (b) the potential energy of water
   (c) the kinetic energy of water
   (d) the electro-chemical energy of water
87. The constituents of automobile exhaust that can cause cancer is are:
   (a) Oxides of nitrogen
   (b) Carbon monoxide
   (c) Polycyclic hydrocarbons
   (d) Lead
88. A reduction reaction involves
   (a) addition of oxygen
   (b) addition of nitrogen
   (c) addition of hydrogen
   (d) None of the above
89. Ethanol containing 5% water is known as :
   (a) Absolute alcohol (b) Dilute alcohol
   (c) Power alcohol (d) Rectified spirit
90. The world's only floating national park is situated in:
   (a) Manipur (b) Kuala Lumpur
   (c) Bilaspur (d) Dispur
91. An algae type ocean deposit is:
   (a) Neritic remains (b) Diatom Ooze
   (c) Pteropod Ooze (d) Pelagic deposits

92. Which of the following is a fungal disease?
(a) Leucoderma (b) Eczema
(c) Ringworm (d) Elephantiasis

93. Air quality depicting PM 2.5 is more hazardous to
(a) Archaeological Monuments
(b) National Parks
(c) Botanical Gardens
(d) Old Men and Women

94. How much of the Earth's land surface is desert?
(a) $1/10^{th}$ (b) $1/5^{th}$
(c) $1/3^{rd}$ (c) $1/6^{th}$

95. What would be the impact of global warming on mangrove forests?
(a) They will grow more luxurious
(b) Large areas of mangroves will be submerged
(c) Their role as carbon sinks will become more important
(d) Both (a) and (c) above

96. Which one of the following is not correctly matched?
(a) Darjeeling - West Bengal
(b) Mount Abu - Rajasthan
(c) Kodaikanal - Tamil Nadu
(d) Simla - Uttar Pradesh

97. According to Ferrel's law (Coriolis Force) winds change their direction
(a) Towards left in Northern hemisphere and towards right in Southern hemisphere.
(b) Towards right in Northern hemisphere and towards left in Southern hemisphere.
(c) Towards right in both the hemisphere.
(d) Towards left in both the hemisphere.

98. Ballots were first used in
(a) Australia (b) USA
(c) Ancient Greece (d) England

99. What is the theme of Earth Day 2019?
(a) Due to Human Activity
(b) Protect Our Species
(c) Plants and Wildlife Populations
(d) Focus on the Destruction Caused

100. India and _____ will conduct their largest ever naval exercise 'Varuna' in May 2019.
(a) USA (b) Germany
(c) UK (d) France

Hints & Explanations

1. (a) As,

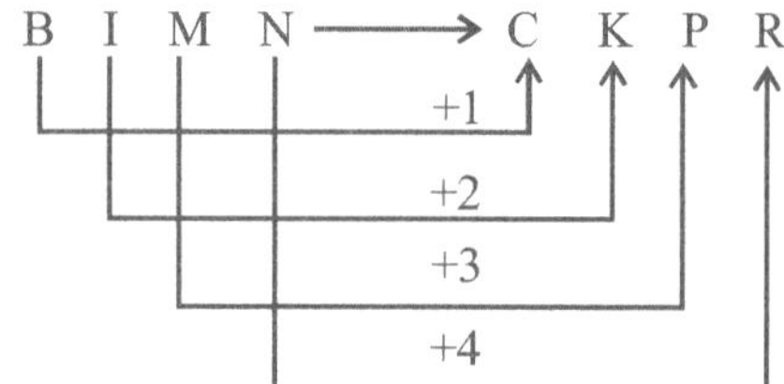

Similarly,

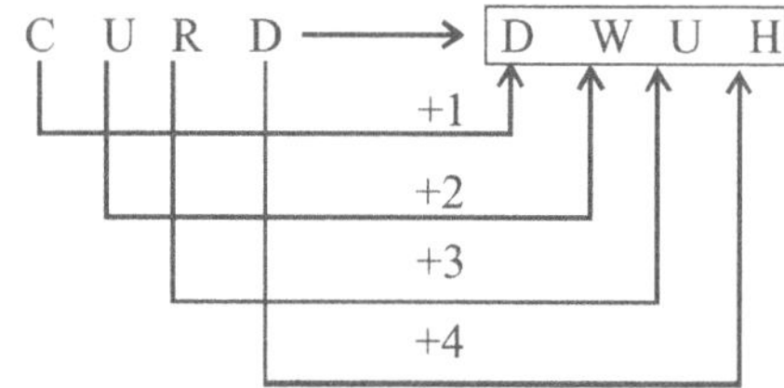

2. (b) $8^2 - 2 = 62$
$9^2 - 2 = 79$

3. (c) We pay rent for accommodation. Similarly, we pay fare for journey.

4. (b) Frog is an amphibian.

5. (b) Except the number 1725, all other numbers are completely divisible by 4. The number 1725 is completely divisible by 5.

$$\frac{1000}{4} = 250; \frac{2744}{4} = 686;$$

$$\frac{4096}{4} = 1024$$

$$\text{But, } \frac{1725}{5} = 345$$

6. (a)

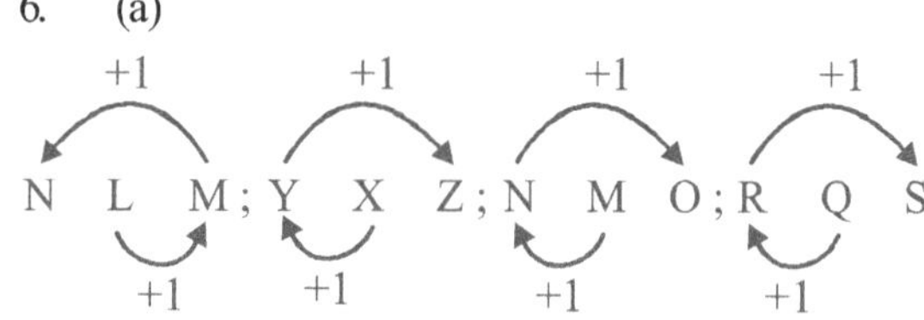

7. (d)

8. (a) $K \xrightarrow{+4} O \xrightarrow{+4} S \xrightarrow{+4} \boxed{W}$

$J \xrightarrow{+4} N \xrightarrow{+4} R \xrightarrow{+4} V$

$L \xrightarrow{+4} P \xrightarrow{+4} T \xrightarrow{+4} X$

9. (b) 95 115 145 155 $\boxed{175}$

+20 +30 +10 +20

−10 −10

10. (d) Prem ⟷ Kesav ⟷ Simran

Kesav → Sunil; Simran → Maruti, Sita

Hence, Sunil is the cousin of Maruti.

11. (a) Roshan, Susheel > Hardik
Hardik > Niza > Harry
Roshan > Susheel
Rohan > Susheel > Hardik > Niza > Harry
Therefore, Roshan is the tallest.

12. (a) There is no 'R' letter in the given word. Therefore, the word POINTER cannot be formed.

13. (b) As,

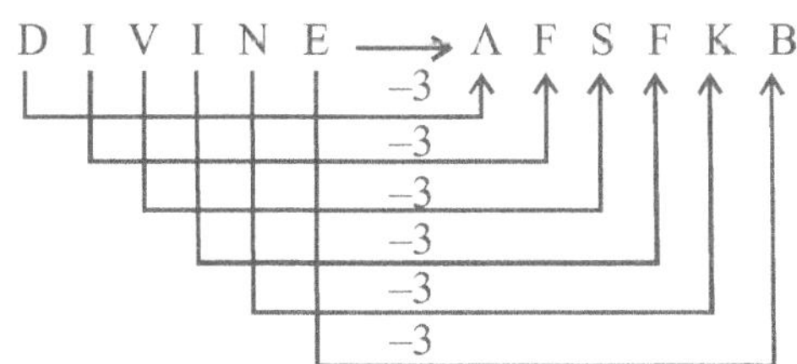

Similarly

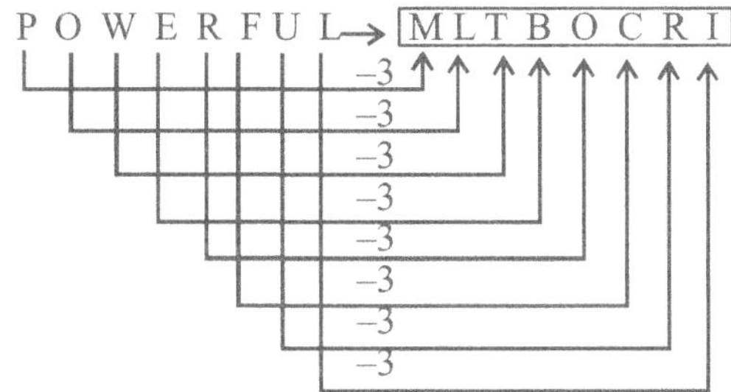

14. (a) Solve by options, we can check all the options one by one.
$25 \div 5 \times 20 + 27 - 7 \Rightarrow 5 \times 20 + 27 - 7 \Rightarrow 100 + 27 - 7$
$120 = 120$

15. (b)
2×3: $\times 2 \downarrow$ 4, $\times 3 \downarrow$ 9
5×6: $\times 5 \downarrow$ 25, $\times 6 \downarrow$ 36
1×9: $\times 1 \downarrow$ 1, $\times 9 \downarrow$ 81
4×7: $\times 1 \downarrow$ 16, $\times 7 \downarrow$ 49

16. (b) First Column
$\sqrt{81} \times \sqrt{4} \times \sqrt{36}$
$\Rightarrow 9 \times 2 \times 6 = 108$
Second Column
$\sqrt{64} \times \sqrt{9} \times \sqrt{16}$
$\Rightarrow 8 \times 3 \times 94$
Third column $\sqrt{16} \times \sqrt{49} \times \sqrt{25}$
$\Rightarrow 4 \times 7 \times 5 = \boxed{140}$

17. (c)

E 15 m D; 10m; B 15m C; 15m; 15m; A; North, South, East, West

$\therefore AF = AE - EF = 25 - 15 = 10$ metres

18. (a) 19. (b) 20. (c) 21. (c) 22. (a)
23. (c) 24. (d) 25. (d)
26. (b) Last digit of $(1001)^{2008} + 1002 = 1 + 2 = 3$
27. (b) $\sqrt{6 + \sqrt{6 + \sqrt{6.....}}} = x$
$6 = 3 \times 2$
By trick = 3 answe
28. (b) Let the average of batsman after 11th innings = A

$$\frac{\text{Total score made by batsman at the end of 11th innings}}{11} = A$$

$\therefore$ Total score after 11th innings = 11 A
Now,

$$\frac{\text{Total score after 11th innings} + \text{score made in 12th innings}}{12} = A + 2$$

$\Rightarrow 11A + 63 = (A + 2) \times 12$
$\Rightarrow 11A - 12A = 24 - 63$
$\Rightarrow A = 39$
12th innings average $= 39 + 2 = 41$

29. (b) Single equivalent discount

$$= \left(x + y - \frac{xy}{100}\right)\%$$

$$= \left(20 + 15 - \frac{20 \times 15}{100}\right)\% = 32\%$$

30. (d) SP of both articles is same. Profit on one is equal to loss on the other.
If loss per cent be x, then

$$25 - x - \frac{25x}{100} = 0$$

$$\Rightarrow 25 - x - \frac{x}{4} = 0 \Rightarrow 100 - 4x - x = 0$$

$\Rightarrow 5x = 100$
$\Rightarrow x = 20$

31. (b) $CI = P\left[1 + \frac{R}{100}\right]^t - P$

$$= 25000\left[1 + \frac{5}{100}\right]^2 - 25000$$

$$= 25000\left[\left(\frac{105}{100}\right)^2 - 1\right]$$

$$= 25000\left[\frac{11025 - 10000}{10000}\right]$$

$$5 \times \frac{1025}{2} = 2562.5$$

32. (c) If the total length of journey be x km, then

$$\frac{x}{35} - \frac{x}{40} = \frac{15}{60}$$

$$\Rightarrow \frac{8x - 7x}{280} = \frac{1}{4}$$

$$\Rightarrow \frac{x}{280} = \frac{1}{4}$$

$$\Rightarrow x = \frac{1}{4} \times 280 = 70 \text{ km}$$

33. (d) Part of the tank filled by both pipes in two hours

$$= 2\left(\frac{1}{8} + \frac{1}{6}\right) = 2\left(\frac{3+4}{24}\right) = \frac{7}{12}$$

Remaining part $= 1 - \frac{7}{12} = \frac{5}{12}$

Time taken by B in filling the remaining part

$$= \frac{5}{12} \times 6 = \frac{5}{2} = 2\frac{1}{2} \text{ hours}$$

34. (d) Let the quantity of acid in original mixture be x litre and that of water be 3x litre.

$$\therefore \frac{x + 5}{3x} = \frac{1}{2}$$

$\Rightarrow 2x + 10 = 3x \Rightarrow x = 10$
$\therefore$ Quantity of new mixture
$= 4x + 5 = 45$ litres

35. (c) Incomes of A and B
= ₹ 6x and 5x
Expenses of A and B
= ₹ 4y and 3y
$\therefore 6x - 4y = 400$ ...(i)
$5x - 3y = 400$ ...(ii)
By equation (i) $\times 3 -$ (ii) $\times 4$
$\Rightarrow 18x - 12y - 20x + 12y$
$= 1200 - 1600$
$\Rightarrow 2x = 400 \Rightarrow x = 200$
$\therefore$ Total income
$= 6x + 5x = 11x =$ ₹ 2200.

36. (a)

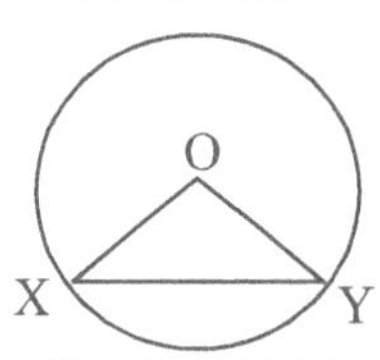

$\angle XOY = 90°; OX = OY =$ radices (r)
$\therefore \Delta XOY$ is a right angled triangle.

$$\therefore \frac{1}{2} \times (OX) \times (OY) = 32$$

$\Rightarrow r^2 = 2 \times 32 = 64$

$\therefore r = \sqrt{64} = 8$
$\therefore$ Area of circle $= \pi r^2$
$= 64\,\pi$ sq. units

37. (b)

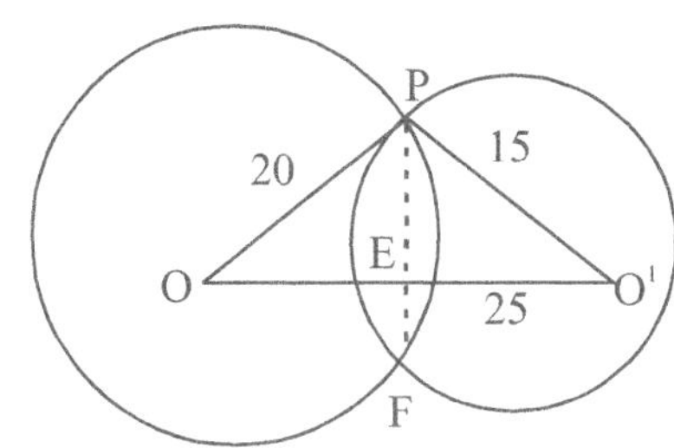

$\because$ 15 20 25

$\Rightarrow$ 3 : 4 : 5 and forming at Δ

or $\frac{1}{2}20\times15=\frac{1}{2}25\times x$

12=x

chord = 2 × 12 = 24 cm

38. (c) s = 16 cm

r = 50 cm

$\therefore \theta=\frac{s}{r}=\frac{16}{50}=\frac{8}{25}$ radian

$=\frac{8}{25}\times\frac{180}{\pi}$

$=\frac{8}{25}\times\frac{180}{22}\times7=\frac{1008}{55}\ =18\frac{18°}{55}$

$=18°\left(\frac{18}{55}\times60\right)\approx18°20$

39. (a) Side of square = $\sqrt{121}$ = 11 cm

$\therefore$ Length of wire = 4 × 11 = 44 cm

$\therefore 2\pi r=44$

$\Rightarrow 2\times\frac{22}{7}\times r=44$

$\Rightarrow v=\frac{44\times7}{2\times22}=7$ cm

40. (c) $\sqrt{(x-0)^2+(0+5)^2}=13$

$\Rightarrow x^2+25=169$

$\Rightarrow x^2=169-25=144$

$\therefore x=\sqrt{144}=12$

41. (b) If $a+b+c=0$

then $a^3+b^3+c^3=3abc$

Dividing both sides by abc

$\frac{a^3}{abc}+\frac{b^3}{abc}+\frac{c^3}{abc}=\frac{3abc}{abc}$

$\frac{a^2}{bc}+\frac{b^2}{ac}+\frac{c^2}{ab}=3$

42. (a) $a^2+b^2+c^2=2(a-b-c)-3$

$\Rightarrow a^2+b^2+c^2-2(a-b-c)+3=0$

$\Rightarrow a^2+b^2+c^2-2a+2b+2c+3=0$

$\Rightarrow (a^2+1-2a)+(b^2+1+2b)+(c^2+1+2c)=0$

$\Rightarrow (a-1)^2+(b+1)^2+(c+1)^2=0$

This is possible when $(a-1)^2=0, (b+1)^2=0$ and $(c+1)^2=0$.

$\Rightarrow a=1, b=-1, c=-1$

Thus, $2a-3b+4c=2(1)-3(-1)+4(-1)$

$=2+3-4=1$.

43. (c) $\frac{x}{x^2-2x+1}=\frac{1}{3}$

$\Rightarrow \frac{x^2-2x+1}{x}=3$

$\Rightarrow x-2+\frac{1}{x}=3$

$\Rightarrow x+\frac{1}{x}=5$

On cubing both sides

$x^3+\frac{1}{x^3}+3\left(x+\frac{1}{x}\right)=125$

$\Rightarrow x^3+\frac{1}{x^3}=125-3\times5=110$

44. (c) $x\sin^3\theta+y\cos^3\theta=\sin\theta.\cos\theta$

$\Rightarrow (x\sin\theta).\sin^2\theta+(y\cos\theta)$

$\cos^2\theta=\sin\theta.\cos\theta$

$\Rightarrow x\sin\theta.\sin^2\theta+x\sin\theta.\cos^2\theta$

$=\sin\theta.\cos\theta$

$\Rightarrow x\sin\theta(\sin^2\theta+\cos^2\theta)$

$=\sin\theta.\cos\theta$

$\Rightarrow x=\cos\theta$

$\therefore x\sin\theta=y\cos\theta$

$\Rightarrow \cos\theta.\sin\theta=y\cos\theta$

$\Rightarrow y=\sin\theta$

$\therefore x^2+y^2=\cos^2\theta+\sin^2\theta=1$

45. (a) $5\tan\theta=4$

$\Rightarrow \tan\theta=\frac{4}{5}$

$\therefore \frac{5\sin\theta-3\cos\theta}{5\sin\theta+3\cos\theta}=\frac{\frac{5\sin\theta-3\cos\theta}{\cos\theta}}{\frac{5\sin\theta+3\cos\theta}{\cos\theta}}$

$$= \frac{5\ \text{tin}\theta - 3}{5\ \tan + 3} = \frac{5 \times \frac{4}{5} - 3}{5 \times \frac{4}{5} + 3} = \frac{4-3}{4+3} = \frac{1}{7}$$

46. (b) $(1 + \tan\theta + \sec\theta)(1 + \cot\theta - \text{cosec}\,\theta)$

$$\Rightarrow \left(1 + \frac{\sin\theta}{\cos\theta} + \frac{1}{\cos\theta}\right)\left(1 + \frac{\cos\theta}{\sin\theta} - \frac{1}{\sin\theta}\right)$$

$$\Rightarrow \left(\frac{\sin\theta + \cos\theta + 1}{\cos\theta}\right)\left(\frac{\sin\theta + \cos\theta - 1}{\sin\theta}\right)$$

$$= \frac{(\sin\theta + \cos\theta)^2 - 1}{\sin\theta\cos\theta}$$

$$= \frac{\sin^2\theta + \cos^2\theta + 2\sin\theta\cos\theta - 1}{\sin\theta\cos\theta}$$

$$= \frac{2\sin\theta\cos\theta}{\sin\theta\cos\theta} = 2$$

47. (c)

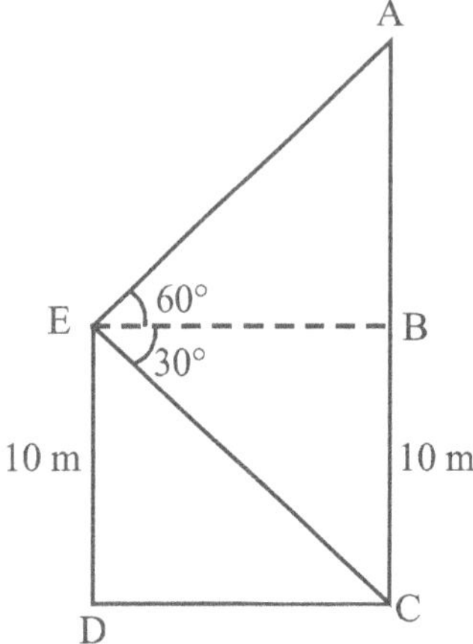

ED = BC = 10 m

In ΔABE, $\tan 60° = \frac{AB}{EB}$

$\sqrt{3} = \frac{AB}{EB} \Rightarrow AB = \sqrt{3}EB$

...(1)

In ΔEBC, $\tan 30° = \frac{BC}{EB}$

$\frac{1}{\sqrt{3}} = \frac{10}{EB} \Rightarrow EB = 10\sqrt{3}m$

Putting value of EB in (1)

$AB = \sqrt{3}(10\sqrt{3}) = 30m$

$AC = AB + BC = 40\ m$

48. (a) Percentage decrease

$$= \frac{60-40}{60} \times 100 = \frac{100}{3} = 33\frac{1}{3}\%$$

49. (a) Average annual production:

Flavour X $\Rightarrow \frac{1}{6} \times 300 = 50$ lakh bottles

Flavour Y $\Rightarrow \frac{1}{6} \times 325 = 54\frac{1}{6}$ lakh bottles

Flavour Z $\Rightarrow \frac{1}{6} \times 300 = 50$ lakh bottles

50. (c) Total production of flavour X in 2005 and 2006 = 90

Total production of flower Z in 2007 and 2008 = 120.

Required percentage $= \frac{120}{90} \times 100 = 133.3$

51. (c) Solve- fits in the context of the sentence correctly.
52. (a) Enter- fits in the context of the sentence correctly.
53. (d) Importance- fits in the context of the sentence correctly.
54. (d) From -fits in the context of the sentence correctly.
55. (b) Held- fits in the context of the sentence correctly.

56.	(a)	57.	(b)	58.	(a)	59.	(d)	60.	(b)
61.	(c)	62.	(a)	63.	(c)	64.	(c)	65.	(c)
66.	(b)	67.	(c)	68.	(b)	69.	(a)	70.	(a)
71.	(c)	72.	(a)	73.	(a)	74.	(b)	75.	(c)
76.	(d)	77.	(a)	78.	(d)	79.	(b)	80.	(c)
81.	(c)	82.	(c)	83.	(d)	84.	(a)	85.	(d)
86.	(b)	87.	(d)	88.	(c)	89.	(d)	90.	(a)
91.	(b)	92.	(c)	93.	(d)	94.	(b)	95.	(d)
96.	(d)	97.	(b)	98.	(a)	99.	(b)	100.	(d)

16. Select the missing number from the given alternatives:

7	9	8
8	9	?
4	9	6
60	90	70

(a) 9 (b) 8
(c) 7 (d) 6

17. Seema walks 30 m North. Then she turns right and walks 30 m then she turns right and walks 55 m. Then she turns left and walks 20 m. Then she again turns left and walks 25m. How many metres away is she from her Original position?
(a) 45 m (b) 50 m
(c) 66 m (d) 55 m

DIRECTION (Q. 18): *In question, two statements are given followed by two/four conclusions I and II. You have to consider the statements to be true even it they seem to be at variance from commonly known facts. You have to decide which of the given conclusions, if any, follow from the given statements.*

18. **Statements:**
I. All apples are bananas.
II. All bananas are sweet.
Conclusions:
I. Some apples are sweet.
II. Some bananas are apples.
(a) Conclusion I follows.
(b) Conclusion II follows.
(c) Either conclusion I or II follows.
(d) Both conclusions I and II follow.

19. Find the number of triangles in the given figure.

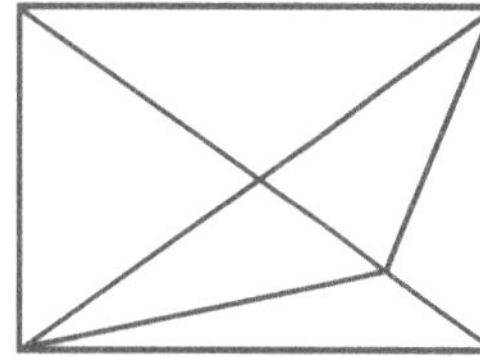

(a) 11 (b) 17
(c) 13 (d) 15

20. Find out the figure which best represents the relationship among Garden, Rose and Jasmine.

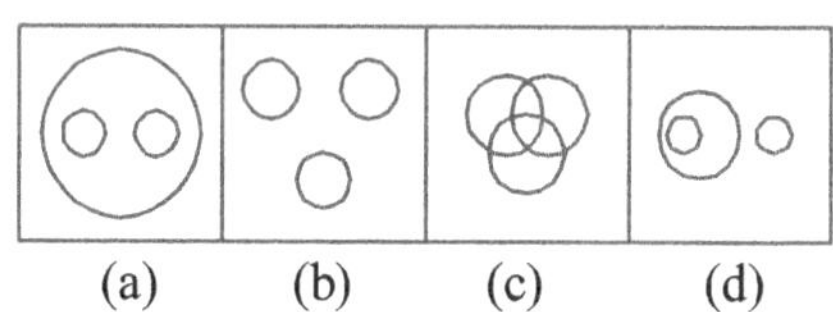

DIRECTION (Q. 21): *In question, which answer figure will complete the pattern in the question figure?*

21. **Question Figure:**

Answer Figures:

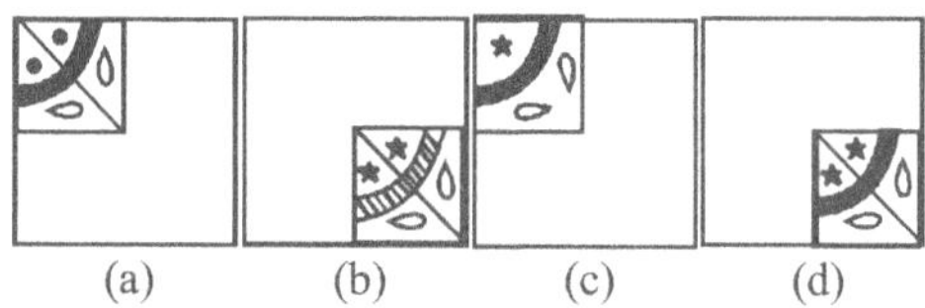

22. From the given answer figures, select the figure which is hidden/embedded in the question figure.
Question figure :

Answer figures :

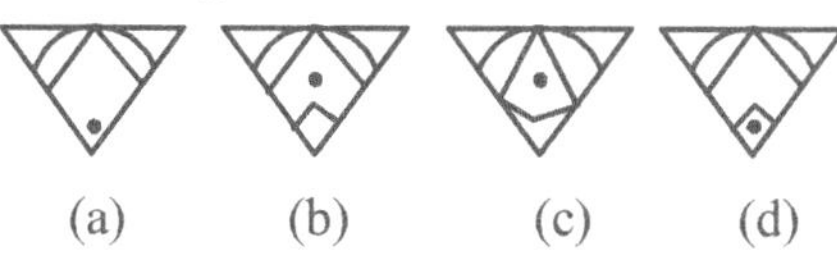

23. A sheet of paper when folded, punched and opened shows the question figure. Choose from the answer figures which punched hole pattern gives this figure.
Question figure (Open pattern) :

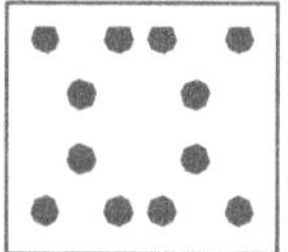

Answer figures (Punched hole patterns) :

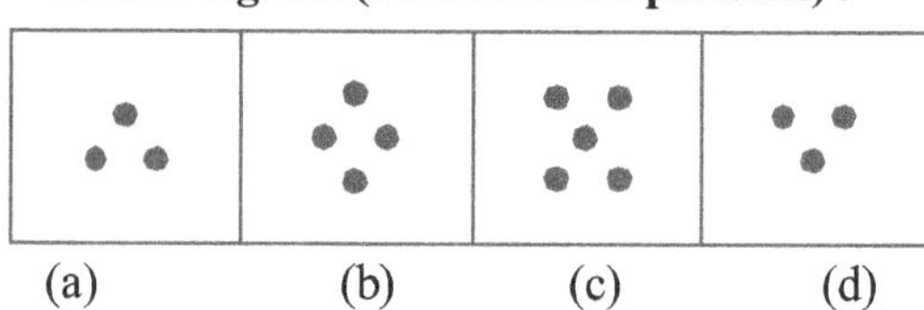

DIRECTION (Q. 24) : *A mirror is placed on line MN. Then which of the answer figures is the correct image of the given figure?*

24. Question Figure :

Answer Figures :

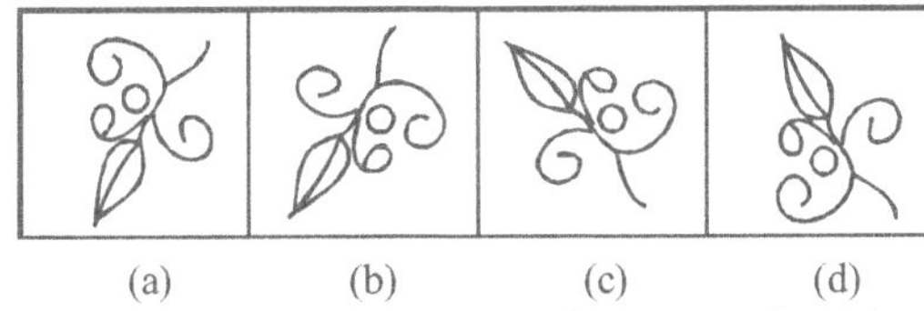

(a) (b) (c) (d)

25. A word is represented by only one set of numbers as given in any one of the alternatives. The sets of numbers given in the alternatiives are represented by two classes of alphabets as in two matrices given below. The columns and rows of Matrix I are numbered from 0 to 4 and that of Matrix II are numbered from 5 to 9. A letter from these matrices can be represented first by its row and next by its column, e.g.. 'A' can be represented by 01, 14 etc. and 'O' can be represented by 59, 67 etc. similarly, you have to identify the set for the word 'PEARL'.

Matrix – I

	0	1	2	3	4
0	P	A	G	R	Z
1	G	R	Z	P	A
2	Z	P	A	G	R
3	A	G	R	Z	P
4	R	Z	P	A	G

Matrix – II

	5	6	7	8	9
5	E	M	L	N	O
6	L	E	O	M	N
7	O	N	E	L	M
8	N	O	M	E	L
9	M	L	N	O	E

(a) 00, 55, 22, 11, 96 (b) 00, 66, 14, 32, 56
(c) 13, 77, 30, 14, 88 (d) 12, 88, 43, 32, 89

QUANTITATIVE APTITUDE

26. If $x * y = (x+3)^2 (y-1)$, then the value of $5 * 4$ is
(a) 192 (b) 182
(c) $\sqrt{2}$ (d) 356

27. The value of $3+\frac{1}{\sqrt{3}}+\frac{1}{3+\sqrt{3}}+\frac{1}{\sqrt{3}-3}$ is
(a) $3+\sqrt{3}$ (b) 3
(c) 1 (d) 0

28. The average of four consecutive even numbers is 9. Find the largest number.
(a) 12 (b) 6
(c) 8 (d) 10

29. If the selling price of 10 articles is equal to the cost price of 11 articles, then the gain percent is
(a) 10 (b) 11
(c) 15 (d) 25

30. If 125% of x is 100, then x is :
(a) 80 (b) 150
(c) 400 (d) 125

31. Alipta got some amount of money from her father. In how many years will the ratio of the money and the interest obtained from it be 10:3 at 6% simple interest per annum?
(a) 7 years (b) 3 years
(c) 5 years (d) 4 years

32. A ship is moving at a speed of 30 km/hr. To know the depth of the ocean beneath it, it sends a radiowave which travels at a speed 200 m/s. The ship receives the signal after it has moved 500 m. The depth of the ocean is
(a) 6km (b) 12km
(c) $\sqrt{6}$ m (d) 8km

33. If 12 men or 18 women can reap a field in 14 days, then working at the same rate, 8 men and 16 women can reap the same field in:
(a) 9 days (b) 5 days
(c) 7 days (d) 8 days

34. The ratio between two numbers is 2 : 3. If each number is increased by 4, the ratio between them becomes 5 : 7. The difference between the numbers is
(a) 8 (b) 6
(c) 4 (d) 2

35. A and B have together three times what B and C have, while A, B, C together have thirty rupees more than that of A. If B has 5 times that of C, then A has

(a) ₹60 (b) ₹65
(c) ₹75 (d) ₹45

36. The side BC of Δ ABC is produced to D. If $\angle ACD = 108°$ and $\angle B = \frac{1}{2}\angle A$ then $\angle A$ is

(a) 36° (b) 72°
(c) 108° (d) 59°

37. AB is a diameter of a circle with centre O. CD is a chord equal to the radius of the circle. AC and BD are produced to meet at P. Then the measure of $\angle APB$ is:

(a) 120° (b) 30°
(c) 60° (d) 90°

38. A rail road curve is to be laid out on a circle. What radius should be used if the track is to change direction by 25° in a distance of 40 metres?

(a) 91.64 metres (b) 90.46 metres
(c) 89.64 metres (d) 93.64 metres

39. The areas of three consecutive faces of a cuboid are 12 cm^2, 20 cm^2 and 15 cm^2, then the volume (in cm^3) of the cuboid is

(a) 3600 (b) 100
(c) 80 (d) 60

40. If 4x = 18y, then the value of $\left(\frac{x}{y}-1\right)$ is

(a) $\frac{1}{3}$ (b) $\frac{7}{2}$
(c) $\frac{2}{3}$ (d) $\frac{3}{2}$

41. If a, b, c are real and $a^3 + b^3 + c^3 = 3abc$ and $a+b+c \neq 0$, then the relation between a, b, c will be

(a) $a+b=c$ (b) $a+c=b$
(c) $a=b=c$ (d) $b+c=a$

42. Let $a = \sqrt{6}-\sqrt{5}, b = \sqrt{5}-2, c = 2-\sqrt{3}$.
Then point out the correct alternative among the four alternatives given below.

(a) $a<b<c$ (b) $b<a<c$
(c) $a<c<b$ (d) $b<c<a$

43. If $a^2 + b^2 + c^2 + 3 = (2(a-b-c)$, then the value of $2a - b + c$ is :

(a) 2 (b) 3
(c) 4 (d) 0

44. $\sec^4\theta - \sec^2\theta$ is equal to

(a) $\tan^2\theta - \tan^4\theta$ (b) $\tan^2\theta + \tan^4\theta$
(c) $\cos^4\theta - \cos^2\theta$ (d) $\cos^2\theta - \cos^4\theta$

45. The least value of $(4\sec^2\theta + 9\,\text{cosec}^2\theta)$ is

(a) 1 (b) 19
(c) 25 (d) 7

46. The value of tan 1° tan 2° tan 3° ... tan 89° is:

(a) 1 (b) 2
(c) undefined (d) 0

47. The length of the shadow of a vertical tower on level ground increases by 10 metres when the altitude of the sun changes from 45° to 30°. Then the height of the tower is

(a) $5(\sqrt{3}+1)$ metres
(b) $5(\sqrt{3}-1)$ metres
(c) $5\sqrt{3}$ metres
(d) $\frac{5}{\sqrt{3}}$ metres

DIRECTIONS (Qs. 48-50): *In the following pie-chart shows the number of students admitted in different faculties of a college. Study the chart and answer the question.*

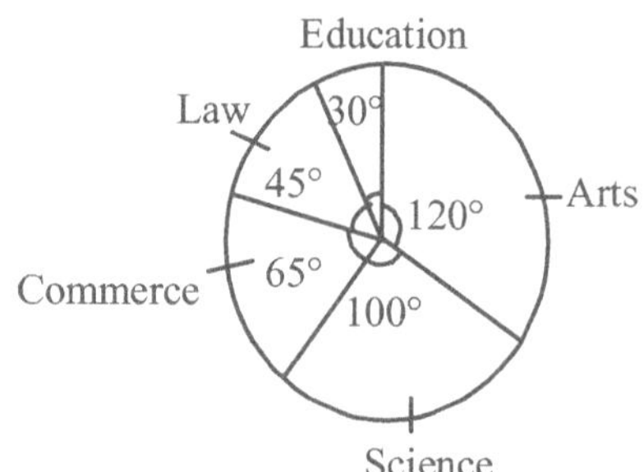

48. If 1000 students are admitted in science, what is the total number of students ?

(a) 360 (b) 180
(c) 1800 (d) 3600

49. If 1000 students are admitted in science, what is the ratio of students in science and arts ?
(a) 5 : 6 (b) 6 : 5
(c) 7 : 5 (d) 7 : 6

50. How many students are more in commerce than in law if 1000 students are in science ?
(a) 20 (b) 200
(c) 2000 (d) 500

ENGLISH LANGUAGE

DIRECTIONS (Qs. 51-55): *In the following passages, some of the words have been left out. First read the passage over and try to understand what it is about. Then fill in the blanks with the help of the alternatives given. Mark your answer.*

Within the **(51)** we are more friendly to each other than are many **(52)** of animals but in our attitude towards those outside the herd, in spite of all that has been done by moralists and **(53)** teachers, our emotions are as **(54)** as those of any animal, and our **(55)** enables us to give them a scope which is Denied to even the most savage beast.

51. (a) Society (b) Caste
(c) Herd (d) Institution

52. (a) Species (b) Kinds
(c) Types (d) Specimens

53. (a) College (b) School
(c) Religious (d) Social

54. (a) Uncontrolled (b) Hostile
(c) Wild (d) Ferocious

55. (a) Intellect (b) Intelligence
(c) Knowledge (d) Exuberance

DIRECTIONS (Qs. 56-57) : *In the following questions out of the four alternatives, choose the one which best expresses the meaning of the given word.*

56. Vociferous
(a) Violent (b) Loud
(c) Secret (d) True

57. Trivial
(a) Crucial (b) Significant
(c) Vital (d) Ordinary

DIRECTIONS (Qs. 58-59) : *In the following questions, choose the word opposite in meaning to the given word.*

58. Abusive
(a) Laudatory (b) Profuse
(c) Effusive (d) Noble

59. Amorphous
(a) Amoral (b) Definite
(c) Perfect (d) Irregular

DIRECTIONS (Qs. 60–62): *Sentences are given with blanks to be filled in with an appropriate and suitable word(s). Four alternatives are suggested for each question. Choose the correct alternative out of the four.*

60. Student-parking should be __________; students should not be charged to buy parking stickers.
(a) fined (b) free
(c) costly (d) cheap

61. If you have roses growing in your garden, you can make a lovely __________ of flowers at home.
(a) bouqutte (b) bucquete
(c) bouquete (d) bouquet

62. With the changing times, most of the students have become business-like they are __________ and want to take only those courses which they find rewarding.
(a) idealistic (b) pragmatic
(c) enthusiastic (d) partial

DIRECTIONS (Qs. 63-64) : *In questions below, some part of the sentences have errors and some are correct. Find out which part of a sentence has an error. If a sentance is free from error, mark (d) in your Answer Sheet.*

63. The team was / now in the field and / about to take their place. / No error
(a) (b) (c) (d)

64. The lions / kill the animals / and eat his meat. / No error
(a) (b) (c) (d)

DIRECTION (Q. 65): *Rearrange the parts of the sentence in correct order.*

65. (P) is generally the one who can
(Q) the man who can work very hard
(R) when he must work
(S) play most heartily when he has the chance of playing.
(a) QRPS (b) PSQR
(c) QRSP (d) SPQR

DIRECTIONS (Qs. 66-68) : *In questions, a part of the sentence is underlined. Below are given alternatives to the underlined part at (a), (b) and (c) which may improve the sentence. Choose the correct alternative. In case no improvement is needed, your answer is (d).*

66. Historians feel there is an earnest need for the review of history text books every five years and a revision of the same every ten years.
(a) imperative
(b) indispensable
(c) urgent
(d) No improvement

67. My car broke off on my way to the office.
(a) out
(b) in
(c) down
(d) No improvement

68. Freedom is a wonderful thing, for Jimmy was eager to experience it.
(a) though
(b) and
(c) but
(d) No improvement

DIRECTIONS (Qs. 69-70): *In questions below, out of the four alternatives, choose the one which can be substituted for the given words/sentences.*

69. A person who leaves his own country in order to go and live in another :
(a) emigrant (b) refugee
(c) immigrant (d) expatriate

70. That which cannot be avoided :
(a) inevitable (b) indifferent
(c) inestimable (d) infallible

DIRECTION (Q.71): *In a question, a sentence has been given in Direct/Indirect form. Out of the four alternatives suggested, select the one which best expresses the same sentence in Indirect/Direct form.*

71. I warned her that I could no longer tolerate her coming late.
(a) I said to her, "You can no longer tolerate my coming late."
(b) I said to her, "1 can no longer tolerate your coming late."
(c) I said to her, "He can no longer tolerate her coming late."
(d) I said to her, "I can no longer tolerate she coming late."

DIRECTION (Q. 72) : *In the following question, four words are given in each question, out of which only one word is correctly spelt. Find the correctly spelt word and mark your answer in the Answer Sheet.*

72. (a) Rejevanation (b) Rejuvenation
(c) Rejvenation (d) Rejuenation

DIRECTIONS (Qs. 73-74): *In questions, four alternatives are given for the Idiom/phrase underlined in the sentence. Choose the alternative which best expresses the meaning of the Idiom/Phrase and mark it in the Answer sheet.*

73. Instead of keeping his promise of helping me with office work, he just left me high and dry.
(a) left me feeling like a fool
(b) left me in a state of anger
(c) left me without a drop of water
(d) left me alone to do the work

74. Amit said to Rekha, "Don't make a mountain out of a molehill".
(a) attempt an impossible task
(b) start looking for molehills in mountains.
(c) create problems
(d) exaggerate a minor problem

DIRECTION (Q. 75): *In a question, a sentence has been given in Active / Passive voice. Out of the four alternatives suggested, select the one which best expresses the same sentence in Passive/ Active voice.*

75. One should keep one's promise.
(a) One's promise should be kept by us.
(b) One's promise has to be kept.
(c) A promise should be keeping
(d) A promise should be kept.

GENERAL AWARENESS

76. Mention the place where Buddha attained enlightenment
(a) Sarnath (b) Bodh Gaya
(c) Kapilavastu (d) Rajgriha

77. The surgery that was practised in ancient India is known from the works of which of the following scholars ?

(a) Atreya (b) Sushruta
(c) Charaka (d) Vagbhata

78. The speaker of the Lok-Sabha has to address his/her letter of resignation to
(a) Prime Minister of India
(b) President of India
(c) Deputy Speaker of Lok Sabha
(d) Minister of Parliamentary Affairs

79. The seat of Madhya Pradesh High Court is located at
(a) Gwalior (b) Indore
(c) Bhopal (d) Jabalpur

80. The vacancy of the office of the President must be filled within :
(a) 3 months (b) 6 months
(c) 12 months (d) 1 month

81. A want becomes a demand only when it is backed by the
(a) Ability to purchase
(b) Necessity to buy
(c) Desire to buy
(d) Utility of the product

82. Of the following economists, whom do you consider to be the Master of "Partial Analysis"?
(a) Leon Walras
(b) Alfred Marshall
(c) J. M. Keynes
(d) Lionel Robbins

83. Diamonds are priced higher than water because:
(a) consumers do not buy them at lower prices.
(b) they are sold by selected firms with monopolistic powers.
(c) their marginal utility to buyers is higher than that of water
(d) their total utility to buyers is higher than that of water

84. Which among the following standard protocols is the most widely used by the Internet?
(a) HTTP (b) TCP/IP
(c) SMTP (d) SLIP

85. The function of ball hearings in a wheel is:
(a) to increase friction
(b) to convert kinetic friction into rolling friction
(c) to convert static friction into kinetic friction
(d) just for convenience

86. The materials which are strongly attracted by magnet are called
(a) ferro-magnetic substances
(b) universal substances
(c) para-magnetic substances
(d) dia-magnetic substances

87. Which one of the following minerals is found in Monazite sand?
(a) Potassium (b) Uranium
(c) Thorium (d) Sodium

88. An antiknock for petrol is
(a) Sodium hydroxide (b) Ethanol
(c) Sodium benzoate (d) Lead tetraethyl

89. The density of water is 1 g/cc. This is strictly valid at
(a) 0°C (b) 4°C
(c) 25°C (d) 100°C

90. Who invented vaccination for 'Small Pox'?
(a) Sir Fredrick Grant Banting
(b) Sir Alexander Fleming
(c) Edward Jenner
(d) Louis Pasteur

91. Photosynthetic vesicle found in bacteria is called a:
(a) Mesosome (b) Chromatophore
(c) Genophore (d) Pneumatophore

92. Chickenpox is caused by
(a) DNA virus (b) Variola virus
(c) Streptococcus (d) Vibrio cholerae

93. Piped Natural Gas (PNG) is used for
(a) Mining (b) Welding
(c) Anaesthesia (d) Cooking

94. River Indus originates from:
(a) Hindukush range (b) Himalayan range
(c) Karakoram range (d) Kailash range

95. The brightest planet is
(a) Venus (b) Mercury
(c) Jupiter (d) Mars

96. The earth is at its maximum distance from the Sun on
(a) January 30th (b) December 22nd
(c) September 22nd (d) July 4th

97. Which one of the following atmospheric layers absorb ultraviolet rays of the sun?
(a) Troposphere (b) Stratosphere
(c) Ionosphere (d) Ozonosphere

98. Which of the following criteria is not used for the classification of human races?
(a) Nose (b) Hair
(c) Eyes (d) Ear

99. Which of the following country has announced that it will be hosting the G20 summit in November 2020?
(a) Israel (b) Japan
(c) India (d) Saudi Arabia

100. India's first exotic Bird Park 'Essel World Bird Park' was launched by Essel World Leisure Pvt. Ltd in______.
(a) Nagpur
(b) Pune
(c) New Delhi
(d) Mumbai

Hints & Explanations

1. (c) As,
H I L K
Similarly,

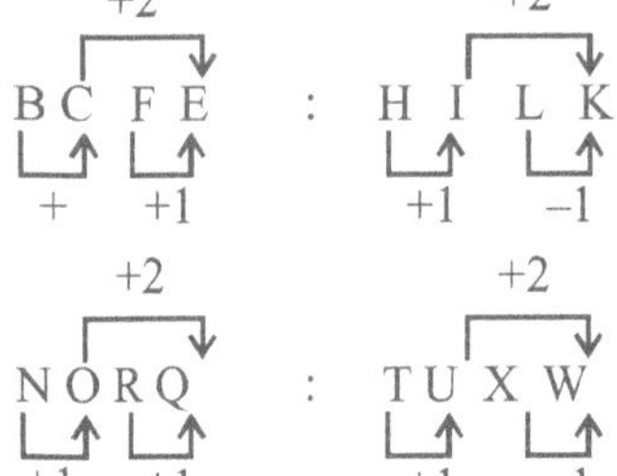

2. (a) $(1)^2 = 1\,;(3)^2 = 9 \Rightarrow 19$
Similarly, $(2)^2 = 4\,;(1)^2 = 1$
$\Rightarrow$ 41

3. (b) Fire causes smoke. Smoke comes out when something is burnt in fire. Similarly, cloud causes rain.

4. (d) Except Agenda, all other denotes a group of persons.

5. (c) Except the number pair 30 – 50, all other numbers pairs has ratio = $\frac{3}{4}$

6. (a) C J G, S Z W and P W T (+4, +3)

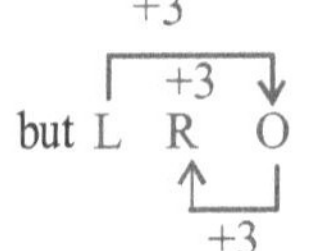

7. (a) The correct order is:
Objection > Objective > Obligation > Oblivion > Obscure

8. (a)

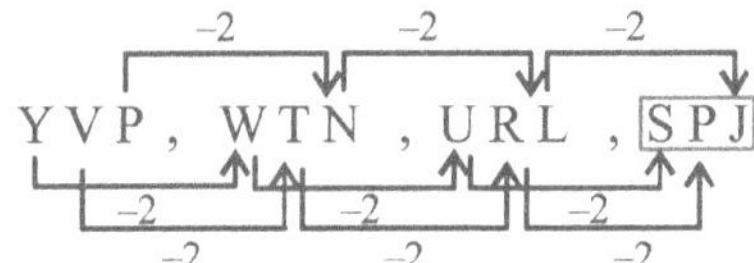

9. (c)

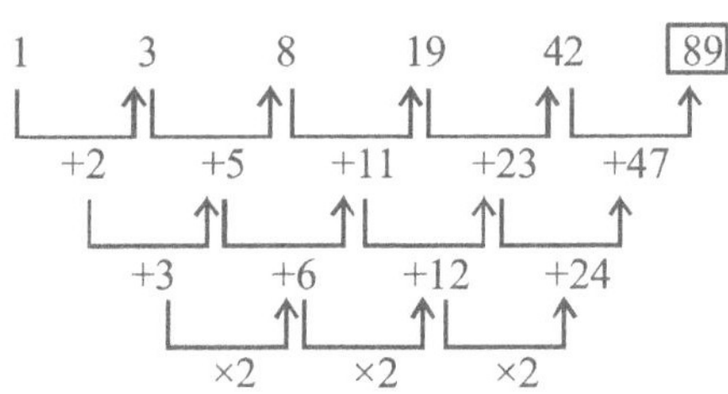

10. (a)

That man is son of Rita

11. (a) Son's age = 6 yrs.
Father's age = 30 yrs.
Let 'x' be the yr. after which father will be 4 times as old as his son.
According to question
$30 + x = 4(6 + x) = 30 + x = 24 + 4x \Rightarrow 6 = 3x.$
x = 2.
Hence, require year is 2 yrs.

PRACTICE SET- 17

GENERAL INTELLIGENCE & REASONING

DIRECTIONS (Qs. 1-3): *Select the related letter/ word/ number from the given alternatives.*

1. BCFE : HILK : : NORQ : ?
(a) TXWU (b) TXUW
(c) TUXW (d) TUWX

2. 13 : 19 : : 21 : ?
(a) 41 (b) 81
(c) 141 (d) 14

3. Fire : Smoke : : ?
(a) Children : School (b) Cloud : Rain
(c) Moon : Sky (d) Shoe : Polish

DIRECTIONS (Qs. 4-6): *In questions, find the odd number/letters/number pair from the given alternatives.*

4. (a) Board (b) Commission
(c) Team (d) Agenda

5. (a) 12–16 (b) 60–80
(c) 30–50 (d) 36–48

6. (a) LRO (b) CJG
(c) SZW (d) PWT

7. Arrange the following words as per order in the dictionary.
1. Obscure 2. Objective
3. Objection 4. Obligation
5. Oblivion
(a) 3, 2, 4, 5, 1 (b) 3, 2, 5, 4, 1
(c) 3, 2, 5, 1, 4 (d) 5, 2, 1, 3, 4

DIRECTIONS (Qs. 8-9) : *In questions, a series is given, with one term missing. Choose the correct alternative from the given ones that will complete the series. ;*

8. YVP, WTN, URL, ?
(a) SPJ (b) TQLS
(c) VSP (d) SRJ

9. 1, 3, 8, 19, 42, _?
(a) 65 (b) 71
(c) 89 (d) 93

10. Showing a man on the stage , Rita said , " He is the brother of the daughter of the wife of my husband. How is the man on stage related to Rita ?
(a) Son (b) Husband
(c) Cousin (d) Nephew

11. A father is 5 times as old as his son. His son is 6 years old. After how many years, will the father be 4 times as old as his son?
(a) 2 years (b) 5 years
(c) 6 years (d) 4 years

DIRECTION (Q. 12): *In question, from the given alternatives select the word which cannot be formed using the letters of the given word.*

12. DECOMPOSITION
(a) COMPOSE (b) ECONOMIST
(c) POSITION (d) DOCTOR

13. If SMART is coded as UKCPV, then WONDER is coded as
(a) YMPPRT (b) YMPBGP
(c) YMPBFP (d) YMBPPG

14. If 'P'denotes' 'multiplied by', 'T' denotes 'subtracted from', 'M' denotes 'added to' and 'B' denotes 'divided by' then : what should be the correct response of 12P6M 15 T 16 B 4 ?
(a) 70 (b) 75
(c) 83 (d) 110

15. If $4 \times 2 \times 6 = 1626, 3 \times 7 \times 4 = 974$, then $5 \times 6 \times 8 = ?$
(a) 3658 (b) 2568
(c) 5664 (d) 6456

12. (d) There is no 'R' letter in the given word. Therefore, the word DOCTOR cannot be formed.

13. (b)

14. (c) 12 P 6 M 15 T 16 B 4 = ?

$\Rightarrow ? = 12 \times 6 + 15 - 16 \div 4$

$\Rightarrow ? = 72 + 15 - 4 = \boxed{83}$

15. (b) $4 \times 2 \times 6 = 1626 = (4^2)26 = 1626$

$3 \times 7 \times 4 = 974 \Rightarrow (3^2)74 = 974$

$\therefore 5 \times 6 \times 8 = (5^2)68 = 2568$

16. (b) Here $R_1 \times R_2 + R_3 \to R_4$

$::\quad 8 \times x + 6 = 70$

$8x = 64$

$x = \boxed{8}$

17. (b)

30 m, 30 m, 55 m, 25 m, 20 m, Starting Point

$\therefore$ Required distance = 30m + 20 m = 50 m

18. (d) 19. (d) 20. (a) 21. (d) 22. (d)

23. (a) 24. (d)

25. (a)

P	E	A	R	L
↓	↓	↓	↓	↓
00	55	22	11	96

26. (a) $x \star y = (x+3)^2 (y-1)$

$\therefore 5 \star 4 = (5+3)^2 (4-1)$

$= 64 \times 3 = 192$

27. (b) $3 + \frac{1}{\sqrt{3}} + \left(\frac{1}{3+\sqrt{3}} - \frac{1}{3-\sqrt{3}}\right)$

$= 3 + \frac{1}{\sqrt{3}} + \left(\frac{3-\sqrt{3}-3-\sqrt{3}}{(3+\sqrt{3})(3-\sqrt{3})}\right)$

$= 3 + \frac{1}{\sqrt{3}} + \frac{-2\sqrt{3}}{9-3}$

$= 3 + \frac{1}{\sqrt{3}} - \frac{\sqrt{3}}{3} = 3 + \frac{1}{\sqrt{3}} - \frac{1}{\sqrt{3}} = 3$

28. (a) Let the consecutive even numbers are 2n, – 2n + 2, 2n + 4 and 2n + 6

$\text{Average} = \frac{2n + 2n + 2 + 2n + 4 + 2n + 6}{4}$

$8n + 12 = 4 \times 9 \Rightarrow n = 3$

Hence, the numbers are 6, 8, 10 and 21.

Largest among them is 12.

29. (a) Let the C.P. of each article be ₹ 1.

$\therefore$ C.P. of articles = ₹ 10

and S.P. of 10 articles = ₹ 11

$\therefore \text{Profit percent} = \frac{11-10}{10} \times 100 = 10\%$

30. (a) $\frac{125}{100} \times x = 100$

$\Rightarrow x = \frac{100 \times 100}{125} = 80$

31. (c) Let principal = 10x

Interest = 3x

$\frac{PRT}{100} = SI$

$\frac{10x \times 6 \times T}{100} = 3x$

T = 5 years

32. (a) Speed of ship = 30kmph

$= \frac{30 \times 5}{18} \text{m/sec.} = \frac{25}{3} \text{m/sec.}$

Time taken in covering 500 metre

$= \frac{500 \times 3}{25} = 60 \text{ seconds}$

Speed of radio waves

$= \frac{200}{1000} \text{km/sec.} = \frac{1}{5} \text{km/sec.}$

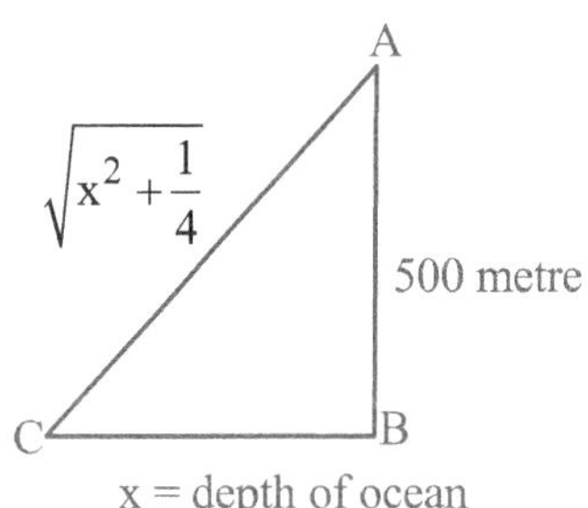

x = depth of ocean

$\therefore \frac{\sqrt{x^2 + \frac{1}{4}}}{\frac{1}{5}} + \frac{x}{\frac{1}{5}} = 60$

$$\Rightarrow \sqrt{x^2+\frac{1}{4}}+x=\frac{1}{5}\times 60=12$$

$$\therefore (12-x)^2=x^2+\frac{1}{4}$$

$$\Rightarrow 144+x^2-24x=x^2+\frac{1}{4}$$

$$\Rightarrow 24x=144-\frac{1}{4}=\frac{575}{4}$$

$$\Rightarrow x=\frac{575}{4\times 24}=6 \text{ km}$$

33. (a) $\because$ 12 men $\equiv$ 18 women
$\therefore$ 2 men $\equiv$ 3 women
$\therefore$ 8 men + 16 women = 28 women
$\therefore M_1D_1=M_2D_2$
$\Rightarrow 18\times 14=28\times D_2$

$$\Rightarrow D_2=\frac{18\times 14}{28}=9 \text{ days}$$

34. (a) Let the numbers be 2x and 3x.

$$\therefore \frac{2x+4}{3x+4}=\frac{5}{7}$$

$\therefore 15x+20=14x+28$
$\Rightarrow x=28-20=8$ (Required Difference)

35. (b) $A+B=3(B+C)$
$A+B+C=A+30$
$B=5C$
$\therefore A+B=3(B+C)$
$\Rightarrow A+5C=18C \Rightarrow A=13C$
$\therefore A+B+C=A+30$
$\Rightarrow A+5C+C=A+30$

$$\Rightarrow A+\frac{6A}{13}=A+30$$

$\Rightarrow 6A=30\times 13$
$\Rightarrow A=$ ₹ 65

36. (b)

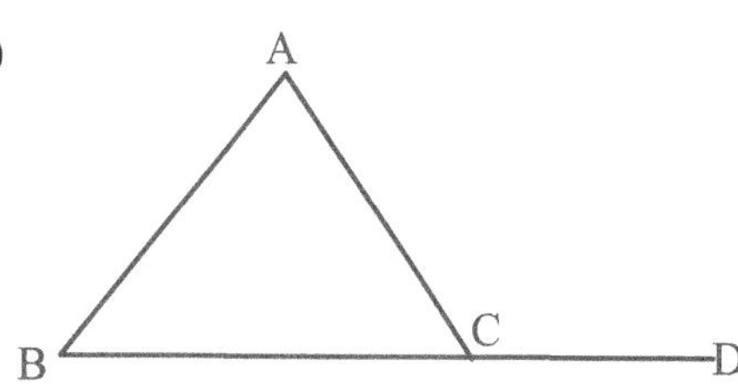

$\angle ACD=\angle ABC+\angle BAC$

$$\Rightarrow 108^\circ=\frac{\angle A}{2}+\angle A$$

$$\Rightarrow \frac{3\angle A}{2}=108^\circ$$

$$\Rightarrow \angle A=\frac{108\times 2}{3}=72^\circ$$

37. (c)

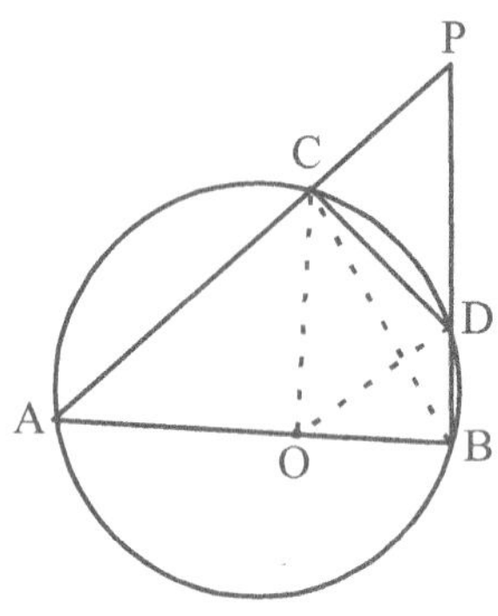

In Δ OCD,
$OC=OD=CD=r$
Δ OCD is an equilateral triangle,
$\angle COD=60^\circ$

$$\angle CBD=\frac{1}{2}\angle COD=30^\circ$$

$\angle ACB=90^\circ$
$\angle BCP=180^\circ-\angle ACB$
$=180^\circ-90^\circ=90^\circ$
In Δ BCP,
$\angle BCP=90^\circ, \angle CBP=\angle CBD$
$=30^\circ$
$\therefore \angle BCP+\angle CBP+\angle CPB=180^\circ$
$\Rightarrow 90^\circ+30^\circ+\angle CPB=180^\circ$
$\Rightarrow \angle CBP=60^\circ \Rightarrow \angle APB=60^\circ$

38. (a) $\theta=25^\circ=\frac{25\times\pi}{180}$ radians

$$=\frac{5\pi}{36} \text{ radians}$$

$$\theta=\frac{s}{r}$$

$$\Rightarrow r = \frac{s}{\theta} = \frac{40}{\frac{5\pi}{36}} = \frac{40 \times 36}{5\pi}$$

$$= \frac{40 \times 36 \times 7}{5 \times 22} \text{ metre} = 91.64 \text{ metre}$$

39. (d) If the length, breadth and height of the cuboid be x, y and z cm respectively, then
$xy = 12; yz = 20; zx = 15$
$\therefore x^2y^2z^2 = 12 \times 20 \times 15$
$= 3600 \text{ cm}^6$
$\therefore v = xyz = \sqrt{3600} = 60 \text{ cm}^3$

40. (b) $4x = 18y$
$$\Rightarrow \frac{x}{y} = \frac{18}{4} = \frac{9}{2}$$
$$\therefore \left(\frac{x}{4} - 1\right) = \frac{9}{2} - 1 = \frac{7}{2}$$

41. (c)

42. (a) $\sqrt{6} = 2.44, \sqrt{5} = 2.23, \sqrt{3} = 1.73$
$a = \sqrt{6} - \sqrt{5} = 0.21$
$b = \sqrt{5} - 2 = 0.23$
$c = 2 - \sqrt{3} = 0.27$

43. (a) $a^2 + b^2 + c^2 + 3$
$= 2a - 2b - 2c$
$\Rightarrow a^2 - 2a + 1 + b^2 + 2b + 1 + c^2 * + 2c + 1 = 0$
$\Rightarrow (a - 1)^2 + (b + 1)^2 + (c + 1)^2 = 0$
$\therefore a - 1 = 0 \Rightarrow a = 1$
$b + 1 = 0 \Rightarrow b = -1$
$c + 1 = 0 \Rightarrow c = -1$
$\therefore 2a - b + c = 2 + 1 - 1 = 2$

44. (b) $\sec^4\theta - \sec^2\theta$
$= \sec^2\theta(\sec^2\theta - 1)$
$= (1 + \tan^2\theta)(1 + \tan^2\theta - 1)$
$= \tan^2\theta + \tan^4\theta$

45. (c) $4\sec^2\theta + 9\text{cosec}^2\theta$
$= 4(1 + \tan^2\theta) + 9(1 + \cot^2\theta)$
$= 4 + 4\tan^2\theta + 9 + 9\cot^2\theta$
$= 4\tan^2\theta + 9\cot^2\theta + = 12 + 12 + 13$
$= (2\tan^2\theta - 3\text{Cot}^2\theta)^2 + 25$
$(2 + \tan^2\theta - 3\text{Cot}^2\theta) = 0$
the minimum value is 25.

46. (a) $\tan 1° \tan 2° \tan 3° \ldots \tan 89°$
$= \tan 1° \cot 2° \ldots \tan 45° \ldots \tan(90 - 2)\tan(90 - 1)$
$= \tan 1° \tan 2° \ldots 1 \ldots \cot 2° \cot 1°$
$= (\tan 1° \cot 1°)(\tan 2° \cot 2°) \ldots 1 = 1$

47. (a)

A
30°
45°
D
10 m
C
B

In $\Delta ABC, \tan 45° = \frac{AB}{BC}$

$1 = \frac{AB}{BC} \Rightarrow AB = BC$ ...(1)

In $\Delta ABD, \tan 30° = \frac{AB}{BD}$

$\frac{1}{\sqrt{3}} = \frac{AB}{BD}$

$BD = AB\sqrt{3}$

$DC + BC = AB\sqrt{3}$

$DC = AB\sqrt{3} - AB$ [from (i)]

$10 = AB(\sqrt{3} - 1)$

$AB = \frac{10}{\sqrt{3} - 1} \times \frac{\sqrt{3} + 1}{\sqrt{3} + 1} = 5(\sqrt{3} + 1)\text{m}$

48. (d) $\because 100° \equiv 1000$
$\therefore 360° \equiv \frac{1000}{100} \times 360 = 3600$

49. (a) Required ratio
$= 100 : 120 = 5 : 6$

50. (b) Difference between the angles of students of commerce and science
$\because 100° = 1000$
$\therefore 1° = 10$
$\therefore 20° = 200$

51. (c) Herd-(with reference to a group of people or animals) move in a group.

52. (a) Species- fits correctly in the context of the sentence of the paragraph.

53. (c) Religious- fits correctly in the context of the sentence of the paragraph.

54. (d) Ferocious- savagely fierce, cruel, or violent.

55. (b) Intelligence- fits correctly in the context of the sentence of the paragraph.

56.	(b)	57.	(d)	58.	(a)	59.	(b)	60.	(b)
61.	(d)	62.	(b)	63.	(a)	64.	(c)	65.	(a)
66.	(c)	67.	(c)	68.	(b)	69.	(a)	70.	(a)
71.	(b)	72.	(b)	73.	(d)	74.	(d)	75.	(d)
76.	(b)	77.	(b)	78.	(c)	79.	(d)	80.	(b)
81.	(d)	82.	(b)	83.	(c)	84.	(b)	85.	(b)
86.	(a)	87.	(c)	88.	(d)	89.	(b)	90.	(c)
91.	(b)	92.	(a)	93.	(d)	94.	(d)	95.	(a)
96.	(d)	97.	(d)	98.	(d)	99.	(d)	100.	(d)

www.ingramcontent.com/pod-product-compliance
Lightning Source LLC
Chambersburg PA
CBHW060112120726
48003CB00009B/2602

* 9 7 8 9 3 8 8 9 1 9 9 7 5 *